Inter-imperiality

LAURA DOYLE

Inter
imperiality

Vying Empires, Gendered Labor, and the
Literary Arts of Alliance

DUKE UNIVERSITY PRESS · DURHAM AND LONDON · 2020

Printed in the United States of America on acid-free paper ∞
Designed by Matthew Tauch
Typeset in ArnoPro by Westchester Publishing Services

Library of Congress Cataloging-in-Publication Data
Names: Doyle, Laura (Laura Anne), author.
Title: Inter-imperiality : Vying Empires, Gendered Labor, and the
Literary Arts of Alliance / Laura Doyle.
Description: Durham : Duke University Press, 2020. | Includes
bibliographical references and index.
Identifiers: LCCN 2020018207 (print)
LCCN 2020018208 (ebook)
ISBN 9781478010043 (hardcover)
ISBN 9781478011095 (paperback)
ISBN 9781478012610 (ebook)
Subjects: LCSH: Imperialism in literature. | Literature, Modern—21st
century—History and criticism. | Criticism. | Feminist theory. |
Critical theory. | Geopolitics.
Classification: LCC PN56.I465 D695 2020 (print) | LCC PN56.I465
(ebook) | DDC 809/.933582—dc23
LC record available at https://lccn.loc.gov/2020018207
LC ebook record available at https://lccn.loc.gov/2020018208

Cover art: Juan Gris (1887–1927), *Head of a Woman
(Portrait of the Artist's Mother)*, Paris, 1912. Oil on canvas,
21³/₁₆ × 18¼ in. (53.8 × 46.4 cm). The Leonard A. Lauder
Cubist Collection. The Metropolitan Museum of Art,
New York, NY, US. Image copyright © The Metropolitan
Museum of Art. Image source: Art Resource, NY

for Karen Klein

who set me off in the

very direction I needed to go

Contents

Acknowledgments   ix

THEORETICAL INTRODUCTION · Between States   1

PART I CO-CONSTITUTED WORLDS

CHAPTER ONE · Dialectics in the Longue Durée   35

CHAPTER TWO · Refusing Labor's (Re)production in   68
The Thousand and One Nights

PART II CONVERGENCE AND REVOLT

CHAPTER THREE · Remapping Orientalism among   95
Eurasian Empires

CHAPTER FOUR · Global Revolts and Gothic Interventions   121

CHAPTER FIVE · Infrastructure, Activism, and Literary Dialectics   156
in the Early Twentieth Century

PART III PERSISTING TEMPORALITIES

CHAPTER SIX · Rape, Revolution, and Queer Male Longing in   195
Carpentier's *The Kingdom of This World*

CHAPTER SEVEN · Inter-imperially Neocolonial: The Queer   227
Returns of Writing in Powell's *The Pagoda*

CONCLUSION · A River Between   251

Notes   255

Bibliography   331

Index   365

Acknowledgments

In writing an interdisciplinary book of this scope, I have learned from many generous colleagues across the disciplines, in many different ways. I am very pleased to acknowledge their generosity here. Yet the seeds for my habit of looking beyond disciplinary boundaries were actually laid long before I became a scholar, so I'll begin there.

The seeds were sown with this advice, given by my mother to all of her children: "If you have a question, ask." That permission to ask, I now see, bequeathed a way of life. My mother gave us this wisdom even before domestic violence drove her to divorce, and long before she was shunned by her Catholic community. She kept giving it after she returned to teaching in Chicago public schools and after she married an ex-Jesuit, a man who left the priesthood because he also asked questions—and a stepfather who encouraged my questions as he guided me toward college. They were both asking structural and justice questions, and the habit wore off on the children. Thank you, Mom, and thank you, Bill, for cultivating this commitment to asking questions, one that arose from need, but became a form of love.

And thank you, all of my family and my friends, for our communing together over questions, sometimes with vehemence, always in good spirit. This book also grows out of the years of friendship and dialogue we've shared.

Then there are the many scholars with whom I've been asking questions and from whom I've been learning for decades. Quite a few of them have read part or all of the book. Agreeing to read a colleague's work is time consuming and risky. What the writer most wants (beyond a bit of encouragement) is honesty—yet honest critique can be hard to give. I am lucky to have had many frank readers who combined critique and encouragement in a nourishing balance. For a book that has taken many years to write, the list of these readers is long, so first I simply list alphabetically. My heartfelt thanks to Joselyn Almeida-Beveridge, Sahar Amer, Carol Batker, Jerry Bentley, Elleke Boehmer, Nick Bromell, Antoinette Burton, Fred Cooper, Jane Degenhardt, Mary Lou Emery, Nergis Ertürk, Donette Francis, Maria Cristina Fumagalli, Regenia Gagnier, Simon Gikandi, Molly Greene, Isabel Hofmeyr, Revathi Krishnaswamy, Saumya Lal, Annette Damayanti Lienau, Johan Mathew, Asha Nadkarni, Mazen Naous, Zita Nunes, Peggy O'Brien, Mary Louise Pratt, Shu-mei Shih, Ann Stoler, Paul Young, and Hayrettin Yücesoy. Among these many intellectual friends, I wish to express special thanks to Mary Louise Pratt, Sahar Amer, Shu-mei Shih, Regenia Gagnier, Simon Gikandi, Asha Nadkarni, Jane Degenhardt, and Jerry Bentley for their early enthusiasm for the project and for their steady support along the way. Sadly, Jerry Bentley has passed away, but his impact and my gratitude remain. I also thank the many audiences at lectures and conferences who have asked generative questions and shared their knowledge. Finally I am deeply grateful to the external reviewers of the manuscript. Their sage advice substantially improved the book, and their encouragement kept me moving forward. I owe whatever merits this book has to the insights and generosity of these scholars and friends, while of course all errors are mine alone.

I am happy also to acknowledge the vital importance of the international research collaborative of the World Studies Interdisciplinary Project (WSIP) at the University of Massachusetts-Amherst. This book would be a much poorer thing without this community of scholars. My conception of it has been shaped at every turn by our vibrant dialogues and work-sharing, and by the collective commitment to dissolve those competitive, territorial impulses that often infect professional gatherings and hamper mutual learning. I particularly thank my colleague in the Economics Department at UMass-Amherst, Mwangi wa Gĩthĩnji, with whom I've codirected WSIP for nine years. It's hard to imagine a more generative, sustaining combination of intellectual work and friendship. Thank you, Mwangi.

I am grateful to many graduate students at UMass-Amherst, including, first of all, Saumya Lal, Kate Perillo, and Crystal Baines, who provided skilled research assistance as well as lively dialogue. Your keen minds have undoubtedly also sharpened my vision. My special thanks to Saumya Lal for reading the entire manuscript and sharing insights about its stakes (as well as catching errors in its style). I feel equally fortunate in my intellectual relationships with the many graduate students across several disciplines who have participated in WSIP and asked such good questions, especially those of you in the WSIP Ph.D. Workshop. I have learned from your projects, and in the final stages of writing this book, our conversations continually reminded me of the power and stakes of scholarly work.

I wish to express heartfelt thanks to Ken Wissoker, executive editor at Duke University Press. Thank you, Ken, for keeping faith in the book from beginning to end and for gracefully offering both advice and encouragement along the way. I am also very grateful to Lisl Hampton for shepherding the editorial process so carefully, efficiently, and flexibly, and to Matt Tauch for his expert design of the book. My thanks also to editorial assistant Joshua Tranen for keeping the early processes on track.

Several foundations generously supported the research for this project, including the American Council of Learned Societies, the Leverhulme Trust, and the Mellon Foundation. I am grateful for the extended time and concentration on the book that their support afforded me. I also thank Dean Julie Hayes and Dean Joel Martin for generous support from the College of Humanities and Arts at the University of Massachusetts-Amherst.

I wish to thank several journals for publishing earlier versions of this project. Parts of the introduction and chapter 1 appeared in *Interventions* (16.2), in *Globalizations* (11.5), and in PMLA (130.2). Parts of chapter 2 appeared in *Parergon* (35.2), and parts of chapter 4 appeared in *Nineteenth-Century Literature* (65.4).

Thank you to my soulmate, Nick, and to our children, Leon and Sam, our daughter-in-law, Claire, and our granddaughter, Celine. Your humor, playfulness, love, sanity, insight, patience, and good cooking have sustained me in every way.

This book is dedicated to Karen Klein, my dissertation director, who inspired my very first project and has remained a guiding spirit in every project since, all the way to this one. Thank you, Karen, for everything you taught me about feminism, for guiding me to Merleau-Ponty, and for modeling the joys of mingling mind, body, and soul.

Theoretical Introduction

Between States

Born into a world of mutual, uncertain, and unequal conditions of relation, humans survive through labors of care pressured by energies of coercion and domination. Our life on earth might be described not strictly as competitive engagement over scarce resources, as some thinkers have suggested, but rather as a microphysics of contingent survival and positioning that we enact with and against others at both intimate and macropolitical levels. This book aims to capture the degree to which relations span these interacting dimensions: of shifting attachments and coformations among persons and communities amid interacting geopolitical forces.[1] These multilateral dynamics continuously transform all participants, even as their patterns accrue slowly over time into material and ideological conditions that shape future interactions. Focusing on the geopolitical coordinates of what I call *inter-imperiality*, I develop a long-historical, dialectical theory of relationality and power that integrates feminist-intersectional, economic, materialist, literary, and geopolitical thought.[2] I will sometimes also refer to this dialectical model as horizontal: this framework considers a full 360-degree "horizon" of multiple simultaneous interactions shaping places and communities, which accumulate over time into determining pressures, kept alive in memory and in materiality.[3]

This conceptual model rests on the observation that, like persons, polities are co-constituted and thereafter coformed, despite all disavowals to the contrary. We might recall that a state's claim to sovereignty must be recognized by other states to exist or have force. Moreover, most empires, nations, kingdoms, and villages depend materially on trade, a relational activity. Even an embargo expresses a negative relation. Thus, neither persons nor polities have an original, a priori independence to revive or defend. No pure origin. Only fraught co-origination, requiring labor in every sense.

That both humans and polities originate within this condition of entangled coformation becomes clear when we recall, as so few philosophies do, that a person's physical survival depends from birth on another person who brings sustenance from the material world. G. W. F. Hegel's famous "lord and bondsman" arrive late on this scene. When Hegel positions the lord and bondsman's physical contest for control as the original intersubjective moment, much gets erased in one stroke.[4] For his life-or-death story of struggle over labor has no women in it. Yet without women's labors as well as men's, there is neither lord nor bondsman in the first place.

Alternatively, to include the demands of caretaking in these labor struggles is to begin to craft a sound philosophy of dialectical relationality grounded in historical conditions. Doing so requires that we track the coformations of gender and labor at the center of a long, wide history of interacting political economies, including those that precede or exceed forms of capitalism. To focus on the existential, historical condition of relationality in these terms is not, however, to posit an originary scene of innocent mother and child. Even when beautiful and generous, relationality is not simply benevolent; it is demanding on all sides. Relations are strenuously clothed and fed, so to speak. We could say that this condition rests on a foundational practice of nourishing, harboring, listening, and responding, yet these may be enacted amid stinging blows, or comforting embraces, or vacillating swerves between them. These dynamics are repeated among adults and among communities. We sometimes call them international relations.

Within this account of existential relationality, the meaning of sovereignty takes on a different cast, with implications for the use of this term by a range of current critical thinkers. Insofar as the notion of sovereignty assumes an originary condition of autonomy—even if only as what Giorgio Agamben calls "bare life"—it carries forward a certain romance, often a gendered one, with the idea that persons, states, and kin communities exist a priori, before messy dependencies and mixings.[5] There are strategic, sometimes urgent reasons for embracing a concept of sovereignty, as with similar uses of strategic essentialism, especially when these aim to foreground relational histories. Consider the Mohawk tribe's "refusal" of Canada's failure to "recognize" the Mohawk's long-standing sovereign claims to land and nationhood, as analyzed by Audra Simpson.[6] More than a claim to autonomy, the Mohawk stance in effect demands that Canada acknowledge historical relations: first, the Mohawk's historical relation to the land and, second, the state-to-state relation, expressed in treaties, between the Canadian nation and the Mohawk nation. The Mohawk refusal is, in other words, a refusal of Canada's disavowal of relationality (which Simpson describes as misrecognition).[7] Because it remains true that these pragmatic discourses of identity or sovereignty risk reinscribing the very politics they contest, this book's relational, existential analysis emphasizes the historical rather than the "time immemorial" claims underlying such demands, as does other recent work on sovereignty. Likewise, this book joins those decolonial-feminist models in which agency is understood not as an aspect of autonomy, nor as primarily individual or unidirectional, but rather as dialectical: always already arising interdependently.[8] Thus, as thinkers and activists retool notions of sovereignty, agency, and "radical" freedom, it's crucial to practice discernment about the vestigial individualist, masculinist, capitalist, or civilizationalist investments sometimes lurking in these notions.

When we think in terms of radical relationality rather than radical freedom, keeping in mind what Judith Butler calls precarity, we can more precisely name the crimes of states, capitalists, sovereigns, and persons. We can understand their violence as disavowals of this relationality, not just as crimes against certain communities or individual persons. We might then conclude, in an affirmation of Édouard Glissant's poetics of relationality, that this disavowal of relation constitutes bad faith, and we might consider *it* the fundamental violence.[9] In order to also acknowledge the historically gendered beginnings of both relationality and bad faith, this kind of decolonial theory likewise enfolds the insights of intersectional theory about the interlocking demands of racial, class, religious, and gender identities, installed at the very site of birth and caretaking. Carole Boyce Davies's term *critical relationality* aptly describes the combined postures of care and critique required for wise navigation in this field, an orientation further developed in recent studies of critique and care.[10]

To incorporate these insights is to move past the still-persisting binaries of self and other, past theories of *the* subject or *the* state or *the* empire. It is also to rethink existential freedom not as "freedom from" or "for" anything but as the difficult burden of acting within this not yet wholly determined terrain, of making ethical choices within a fraught interdependence. Finally, we might then speak not strictly in terms of respect for sovereignties or individuals but primarily of avowal and respect for conditions of relationality. The guiding ethical principle would be a refusal to do violence against that primal yet difficult envelopment, which Maurice Merleau-Ponty called "the flesh of the world."[11]

This book focuses on a key historical dimension of the dynamics of relationality: the millennia-spanning geopolitical fact of vying empires. Human struggles have unfolded in relation to the inorganic, organic, and human-animal worlds that sustain us, yet in ways that have often been pressured by interacting empires, whose violent legacies persist over centuries to electrify visions of peace, of reparation, and of revenge. Both political leaders and everyday folks thus occupy what I call the condition of inter-imperiality, a fraught position, lived all at once in the neighborhood, at the imperial court, on the road, in the body, and amid the invasive stream of political events and news. The *inter-* of *inter-imperiality* refers to multiply vectored relations among empires and among those who endure and maneuver among empires. I argue that it is not only the materialities of empires that have accrued over millennia but also the forms of relation through which communities have struggled amid empires.

Literature has exerted a structuring force in this existential-dialectical field in both oral and written forms, both instrumentalized by empires and turned against them. Its high stakes have made literature a site of contestation, as suggested by the long-standing practices of censorship and exile of authors. One of my primary aims in this book is to analyze this force in interdisciplinary terms so as to establish its importance for any well-rounded study of politics and history, as I argue more fully later in this introduction. For now it's sufficient to note that, while the imperial will to control certainly arises from a desire for profit, it is also driven, perhaps more profoundly, by a wish to manage and "conquer" the volatile terrain of existential relationality itself. This drive to control relations is epitomized in the instrumentalization of language and other representational arts. If we understand hegemony, as I do here, as a near monopoly of the power to name relations and "identities"—a wish to control the terms of relationality—we can better track how language, translation, and aesthetics serve as tools in an inter-imperial field of vying hegemonies. This is why language regimes and aesthetics must be part of any dialectical theory of geopolitical economy. This argument has implications for the reemergent field of "world literature," as I later describe, and although that field is not my central concern, I hope this book's analysis is useful for debates about its problematic nomenclature and politics.

In short, although other thinkers have sometimes used the term *inter-imperial* in passing, or in narrower ways, I develop the term *inter-imperiality* as a feminist-intersectional and political-philosophical concept for analysis of longue-durée politics as they have co-constituted world history and human memory.[12] In this introduction, I develop the dialectical grounds of the inter-imperial framework. I recast Hegel's account of labor in feminist-decolonial terms; I freshly position gendered, stratified systems as a primary structural pivot of macropolitical dynamics; and I specify literature's multivalent role in these dynamics. My particular combination of intersectional, interdisciplinary, and decolonial angles of analysis allows me to supply the backstories missing in much dialectical and critical theory.[13]

Some initial definition of terms may be useful at the outset. The book has a decolonial orientation in several senses. Most fundamentally it is fashioned as a project for "decolonizing the mind," in the senses initially developed by thinkers such as Ngũgĩ wa Thiong'o and Linda Tuhiwai Smith.[14] Here I expand on that sense of term from a feminist-intersectional angle, drawing on analyses such as Donette Francis's, which considers how, in the Caribbean, "state formation unfolds through the micropolitics of intimacy" and through "the macropolitics of revolutions."[15] This book is also decolonial in the sense developed by Latin American and other philosophers of indigeneity, who foreground the non-Eurocentric legacies of values and practices of ethical collectivity by which communities have sustained themselves beyond or against imperial colonization. In recent years some scholars have distinguished decolonial studies from postcolonial studies, arguing that postcolonial studies has mainly critiqued the modern/colonial Anglo-European world order, while decolonial studies has highlighted visions originating outside of that order, especially among indigenous peoples. Like my cohort in the World Studies Interdisciplinary Project, I aim to develop a long-historical interdisciplinary method that integrates the analyses and insights of both, for I agree with feminist theorists who have argued that these two projects are connected at the root and are best developed as complementary rather than opposed.[16]

That is, *Inter-imperiality* emphasizes that for more than two millennia a range of transhemispheric interactions has generated both the problems and the creative visions of the global world. Feminist, postcolonial, and decolonial studies have been inspired by the long collective legacy of these visions, and literature, though historically complicit, has also increasingly participated in both the critical and the creative dimensions of these struggles. I tend to use the term *decolonial* because it more clearly signals these dimensions and because it does so without assuming that there will be a time after colonialism. Akin to what Kuan-Hsing Chen calls "deimperialization," decoloniality here entails an ongoing resistance to conditions of inter-imperial positionality and an ongoing commitment to the possibilities and demands of geopolitical transformation.[17] Furthermore, as this book demonstrates, and as the history of women, of gendered others, and of many peoples attests, the decolonial project must reach back further than the rise of European hegemony, for unfortunately the gender, ethnic, colonial, and labor problems begin long before, in ways that forcefully shape the world today. At the same time, however, the resources for survival have likewise been cultivated, in ways that also forcefully shape the world today. Although I occasionally use the word *postcolonial*, especially regarding literary texts and in keeping with common usage, in most cases I favor *decolonial* as the term to capture this wide worldly project.

Finally, a word on my definition of *empire*. Here I understand an empire as an expansionist state that achieves sustained control over the labor, finances, administration, and material resources of a foreign territory through political, financial, and violent coercion. Furthermore, each empire's powers of control arise and develop in relation to other empires and polities. This last point is essential to my approach to empires. As will become clear, an empire's success or failure in controlling foreign territories—including its ability to suppress dissent—determines its ability to negotiate geopolitically with other powerful states.

An emphasis on inter-imperial dynamics most definitely does not imply that all empires have been the same or have engaged in precisely the same projects. When we speak of international relations we do not imply that all nations are the same; nor when we speak of interpersonal relations do we imply that all persons are the same. Accordingly, inter-imperial theory simply begins from the fact that different empires, of different sizes and means, centered in different yet linked geographical locations, form in dialectical relation: their differences and divergent histories as well as their linkages, alliances, and similarities shape their coformations. Furthermore, some states calling themselves empires express an aspiration more than a realized condition, and some empires have done much more damage and exerted more far-reaching power than others. Smaller empires, such as the Japanese or Ethiopian, certainly suffered from the coercions of larger empires and have had less leverage in the geopolitical field. Yet from the point of view of the populations they colonized (the Koreans, the Somalians), the Ethiopian and Japanese states merit the name *empire*. These two empires have also been pivotal in world events. The rise of the Japanese Empire in the early twentieth century clearly affected global dynamics, signaled by its wars with Russia and China and reaching through World Wars I and II. Meanwhile, European states have long recognized the geostrategic power of Christian Ethiopia; their failed efforts to align with or colonize it have shaped later inter-imperial alignments—for instance of Italy, whose unsuccessful attempts to win support from Russia for its invasions of Ethiopia led to Italy's defeat, weakening its position and feeding its turn toward fascism.

One last framing remark is in order. In my years of writing and discussing this book, I have encountered expressions of concern about any widening of the decolonial focus to earlier periods and non-European empires, for fear of taking pressure off Anglo-European responsibility for its destructive legacies. Some similarly worry about giving capitalistic exploitation a longer history, for essentially the same reason. These concerns are understandable in light of the continued aggressions and lasting harm inflicted by Anglo-Europeans and in the face of the Europhile pundits who continue to champion or distort those legacies—men such as Niall Ferguson, Samuel Huntington, and Robert Kaplan.[18] These men write within familiar, implicitly racialized narratives of modern versus backward states that misrepresent entire millennia and world regions. But these writers cannot be allowed to define the terms of the debate, nor to inhibit frank and full analyses. Nor should we allow ourselves to eclipse the longer gendered, raced, and labor histories that also still hold the world in their grip, impoverishing women, minorities, and laboring castes and classes.[19] The sedimented, multisided, and dialectically unfolding history must be told if the decolonial project is to avoid false claims and falsely limited parameters. To put it differently, the potential for transformation made possible by a wider perspective is too necessary and sustaining to ignore.

This book's intersectional, long-historical dialectical theory encompasses these wider parameters. More specifically, it clarifies several structural dimensions of power by tracking how state formations are gendered and intersectionally shaped *co*formations; how states' systems and economies have accrued together over time, violently installing inequalities while rationalizing them; and how communities who labor to resist, endure, or maneuver within the inter-imperial field of relations have likewise shaped world history at many levels, enabling cooperative survival. The next section lays the theoretical ground for this analysis.

Deepening Dialectics

Dialectical theory treats relation as a fundamental condition of life on earth. Both early Chinese Daoist philosophers and pre-Socratic Greek thinkers sought to name the interacting elements that constitute phenomena, physically and metaphysically.[20] European philosophers of dialectics, including G. W. F. Hegel, Karl Marx, and Maurice Merleau-Ponty, shared this effort while also focusing on the social dimensions of these co-constituting interactions. As is well known, Hegel formulated starkly racist descriptions of world history, yet in his early philosophy he articulated ideas that have since been retooled to undercut those racialized histories and teleologies, by thinkers from Karl Marx and Frantz Fanon to Mae Henderson and Audra Simpson.[21] Here I will add a gender critique to the critiques of his racism, while joining those who retool his analysis of the dialectics of labor. Given the resurgence of both Daoist and Confucian theories in recent international relations (IR) scholarship, it's valuable to mention that Hegel's descriptions resonate with the Daoist tradition, and it's likely that Hegel was at least indirectly influenced by Chinese philosophy. So we should not assume that these two lineages are separate, nor that they are identical.[22] Scholars of international relations such as L. H. M. Ling have productively proposed that Daoist dialectical philosophy offers a less combative notion of world politics, but it is not as radically different from Hegel's thought as Ling implies, which is less surprising in light of the influence of Chinese philosophy on German philosophy.[23] Indeed the general lack of awareness of the transhemispheric movements and the borrowing of ideas over the longue durée itself reflect geopolitics, as one state elides the contributions of the others even while absorbing and sublating those same contributions. In any case, Hegelian philosophy distinctly echoes the Daoist concepts of both interpenetration and coforming plurality, and this book's inter-imperial framework reworks these concepts. Along the way it sheds light on the political processes by which such Chinese and German notions have themselves arisen from interpenetration.

The Hegelian dialectics that influenced Marx have often been oversimplified, due in part to the redactions of Alexander Kojève.[24] Although both Hegel and Marx (and, later, Lenin) sometimes articulated a binary dialectics within phased teleological schemes of history, Hegel's and Marx's scrutiny of co-constituting elements importantly encompassed what Hegel called the "manifold self-differentiating expanse of life."[25] Marx of course cultivated the critical seed germinating in Hegel's dialectical exploration of the self-consciousness of the bondsman, which Hegel had traced to the laborer's active engagement in materiality and which Marx then analyzed as the laborer's alienated self-consciousness under capitalism. Yet before turning to this key element of labor, it's important to recall Hegel's theorization of the processes of coformation, sublation, and contingency, which are central to my analysis in this book.

In *The Phenomenology of Spirit*, Hegel developed a "volatile" relational philosophy, to borrow Elizabeth Grosz's term.[26] That is, he tracked the human grappling with other beings and objects in a physical field of energetic, coforming "forces" (a conception influenced by the work of G. W. Leibniz, himself influenced by Chinese philosophy). Although Hegel considers all such forces and interactions an aspect of a spiritually ordered universe, he treats them not as "objective" facts, nor as metaphysical certainties, but rather as phenomena experienced by a consciousness and as phenomena constituting the state of relations for that consciousness. This method is what makes his philosophy a phenomenology—that is, a descriptive project rather than an ontological, essentialist, or positivist one.

Within this field of transforming relations, Hegel's emphasis is not on the meeting of opposites, as Kojève and others have suggested, but on the co-constituting differences in the world's phenomena, as Jacques Derrida elaborated. For instance, when Hegel comments on the lived distinction between night and day, he does not define night and day as opposing poles but rather as differentiated, interpenetrating elements for perception. He points out that "day" is the "negative" that subtends the human statement "now it is night."[27] Day is not night's opposite but rather its condition of perception. Moreover, in this way, day is also preserved, to use Hegel's word, in the perception "now it is night." Thus, as Hegel puts it more generally, although the "matters" of the world's phenomena appear as "independent" entities, in their experienced unfolding they "are each where the other is; they mutually interpenetrate."[28] When he concludes that all matters "are absolutely porous or are sublated," he means that phenomena are co-constituted, in perception, by their differentiating relation to each other.[29] They are sublated in the sense that, as they emerge over time, each entity enfolds others and contains elements of those encountered forms. For Hegel, it is this ongoing co-constitution of "the matters" that composes their "unity" as phenomena for consciousness and thus creates their participation in the "universal" or Spirit as an all-embracing medium.[30] Clearly, then, for Hegel, dialectical movements do not center on a "synthesis" of thesis and antithesis. They entail the interpenetration of sublated elements whose differences from the newly dominant entity remain active—like enzymatic yeast—preparing future moments of unfolding.

Inter-imperial theory considers this volatile, other-sublating coformation as a first principle in its analysis of states and of the relations among humans as we are ensconced in or between states. The theory also takes a powerful cue from Hegel's analysis of "lordship and bondage," where he explains the lord's power over the laborer yet also reveals that his power is precarious because the interdependence remains in play. Susan Buck-Morss has valuably understood Hegel's description as an encoded, suppressed reflection on the Atlantic economy of slavery insofar as it registers the sense of vulnerability in the master class. I suggest here that there are related implications in his theory's occlusions of women.[31] To see this point, some parsing is required.

Hegel first of all emphasizes that each human encounter entails a pressure to adapt to or subsume the distinguishing "differences" of other actors. In any encounter, according to Hegel, when two persons encounter each other, each "find[s] itself as an other being" and each wishes to "supersede this otherness of itself."[32] The wish is not only to supersede the other being but specifically to supersede the othering effect of the onlooker's gaze, prompting a desire to overcome the threat of domination by that onlooking being, who perceives the first self as an object for its vision. Meanwhile, the same is happening for the other person. Both of them are simultaneously perceiving and perceived, both fearing and seeking domination. Hegel stresses the uncertainty and wish for control arising from these encounters, which issue in a "double movement" or interdependent exchange of practices between the actors. For, in this agonistic relation, one person borrows from and imitates the other, exactly and ironically in order to counter control by the other. In this double movement, as Hegel says, "Each does itself what it demands of the other, and therefore also does what it does only insofar as the other does the same."[33] Paradoxically, to manage the other's gaze and maintain independence, each acts more like the other. As I'll discuss later, this process underlies what Barbara Fuchs has identified as imperial and cultural mimesis.[34] To secure the stance of autonomy and independence in the face of this entanglement, the borrowing is disavowed: the other's powers and practices must be incorporated and sublated, and then that process of interdependent genesis must be denied. Here we can notice the origin-eluding contingency and precarity in this process, which lays the ground for a struggle.

And it will be a struggle over labor.

Hegel distills this dynamic of struggle by positing a primal scene in which two men literally battle with one another for domination. When one man has achieved enough physical control to threaten his rival with death, the other concedes defeat to save his life. It is at this point, Hegel posits, that the dominant man can claim control of the labors of the "bondsman." Coercive control of labor is here installed as the very fulcrum of relations. This fulcrum bears further pressure, as Hegel points out, because the dominant man harbors a cloaked awareness that he is actually dependent on that laboring man insofar as the bondsman performs the labor that sustains the life of the lord.[35] The lord therefore is "not certain of being-for-itself as the truth of himself."[36] His discomfiting awareness of being othered and being co-constituted with others cannot be wholly assuaged.

Meanwhile, the laboring man also develops a cloaked awareness, not only of the master's dependence on him but also of his own making and laboring powers. Hegel strikingly proposes that the bondsman develops a productive and empowering self-relation through his work with things in the material world. The laborer's work is first of all materially productive insofar as, in Hegel's words, his "work forms and shapes the thing."[37] Moreover, this relation to things produces a certain "consciousness" in the bondsman, shaped by knowledge of an existential truth: that, like night and day, dependence and independence interpenetrate. Through work, the laborer (always a man in Hegel's account) learns at once that "the object has independence" and that he can perceive its independence only by having a relation to it. In short, work yields a consciousness fruitfully steeped in relational in(ter)dependence.[38] As Hegel concludes, "It is in this way, therefore, that consciousness, qua worker, comes to see in the independent being [of the object] its own independence."[39] Although Hegel here emphasizes independence, he is meanwhile describing the relational genesis and co-constituted ground of independence. These are the passages that helped to inspire Marx's theory of work and his effort to name the alienation from meaningful work under capitalism (although the problem also exceeds capitalism, as we'll see). These passages also clarify how the fundamentally co-constituting, labor-intensive conditions of existence install a dynamic interdependency and in turn an ethical call at the heart of relations. Empire builders eschew that call when they exploit productive labor and simultaneously disavow their dependence on its world-shaping efforts.

Yet while Hegel foregrounds the lord and bondsman's struggles, he occludes another one—conveniently so, for the world of empires. One could almost imagine a shadow flitting across Hegel's page: the shadow of the laboring women on whom his own work and household depend, not to mention his very existence. Given these conditions, many men have implicitly apprehended that, in order to buttress fantasies of utter independence, they must simultaneously appropriate and denigrate women's powers—including the generative powers women have developed as laborers: the discerning powers of self-relation and the ready avowal of human relations to other creatures and things that also recognizes those others' independence. In order to be recognized as men, men are implicitly encouraged to disavow these powers and relational conditions and meanwhile redirect women's powers toward men's ends.[40]

Nancy Chodorow's analysis of what she calls "asymmetrical parenting" pinpoints the structural origins of this ingrained habit of simultaneously using and disavowing women's labor powers. As Chodorow explains in *The Reproduction of Mothering*, the social reproduction of gender division through asymmetrical parenting means that, although initially all children are intimate with the parent who sustains them and who has typically been a biological woman (though cultural differences create significant variation),[41] those children who are ascribed as "boys" must increasingly (and especially at puberty) define themselves as "not-her." They must understand themselves as not like the person to whom they owe their survival and to whom they are closely attached, physically and emotionally.[42] Children who are ascribed as girls, by contrast, are expected to be her, to reproduce her labors of care. Perforce, they must cultivate an emulative identification with the mother and with her role as a serving, loving laborer. Women are not allowed to disavow relationality and mimesis, in other words, whereas men who avow intimate and interdependent relationality are suspicious men. All men and particularly heteronormative men accrue psychic, social, and material advantages from this unequal labor arrangement, typically beginning with the benefits of the care bestowed on any household they occupy. No wonder political theorists from Aristotle forward considered control of the household as the first principle for control of the state.

Women's labors occupy a pivotal place not only in local and family relations but also in inter-imperial relations. As feminist scholars have noted, ruling classes regulate sexuality in ways that serve to reproduce race and class hierarchies, that is, to secure their group's power within kin lines and to ensure the reproduction of laboring classes especially in slavery and serfdom.[43] State eugenic projects are only the most obvious manifestation of this fundamental logic. One contribution of this book to that understanding is its positioning of the long-historical regulation of sexuality in relation to the large-scale cultural projects that in turn direct the infrastructural and institutional projects through which polities expand and compete.

Here we also begin to expose the gendered elisions of dialectical theory that have often limited its critical insights. As I'll discuss later in this introduction, important critical thinkers sometimes have erased the material and often gendered labors that enable human survival—even as they have spoken of the "care" and "being-with" required for existence (as in Martin Heidegger's and Jean-Luc Nancy's thought) or the fundamental condition of "natality" (as in Hannah Arendt's political philosophy). Invocations of natality, sociality, and bare life in recent world theory unwittingly repeat the problem, as I discuss below. To undo these erasures is also to reveal the structural function of identity categories and names—and, by extension, of the world-structuring function of languages—in political economy. Identities have determined the forms, distribution, and unequal recognition of labor, fixed in place by the terms *man* and *woman*, or *white* and *black*, or *lord* and *bondsman*. By extension identities determine who has a seat at the state diplomatic or treaty table, which further affects the dynamics of relation among competing states. Thus are these labor-sorting identities co-constituted within the field of competing states. Recognition of this structuring in turn sheds light on forms of resistance, explaining why gender and ethnic identity discourses have become critical points of leverage against states, often in a difficult balancing act that avoids essentialist beliefs in the categories. To consider "identity" as a superstructural distraction from material problems is therefore to repeat the disavowal, or at least to ignore the fact, as historical economists note, that identities and labor roles have long been linked, in a range of ways.[44] In the more problematic patterns, discourses of identity have regulated systems and reproduced states that conscript certain bodies into the constant, demanding labors of care and food cultivation while freeing other bodies from those labors.

Again here, then, labor is at the heart of the matter. As I detail in chapter 1, drawing on a rich body of historical evidence, control of labor has long been at the core of the coforming relations between merchants and empires in a world of vying empires, over millennia. All their projects have required laborers, including those who produce the laborers and the rulers, as well as those who carry the sellable goods or building and food supplies, grow the food to feed the workers, and build the schools, forts, and ports. Controlling labor, and controlling the racialized stratifications that distinguish rulers from laborers, requires control of women's sexuality. In turn, the ruling-class orientation of these projects has ensured the uneven distribution of access to material resources: to water, land, and animals, as well as to housing, ports, roads, and ships and to tools, schools, and systems. An intersectional analysis of these conditions clarifies the structural depth at which labor is a fulcrum of relations, which Hegel's account both highlights and distorts (as does Friedrich Engels in his admirable but unsuccessful attempt to link class and gender stratifications).[45] To focus on the horizon of vying empires and their coforming projects is thus to capture the fuller workings of the traffic in women and laboring men as an aspect of macropolitical economy.[46]

Yet the other side of this coin must also be named. Human interactions do not move solely along an agonistic set of circuits driven always by a will to control. Born with our strenuous births, activated geopolitically and microphysically, the taut ropes of contestation are also tightly tangled with acts of care and collaboration. It is essential not to dismiss the sustaining collaborations as unreal or demote them to secondary status as epiphenomenal. Humans wouldn't still be here if they were. The salient point, which directs this study as a whole, is that there is a fundamental, unstable, ever-unfolding relationality that subtends both opposition and cooperation. This field is in effect what Heidegger called "the open," into which we are "thrown" at birth together with others—but his choice of this term allows him, when needed, to evacuate a field of relations that is, in fact, thickly populated.[47] It is a field of dialectically coforming bodies that are also intersubjectively intertwined within the existential condition that Merleau-Ponty called "intercorporeality."[48] Within this existential field, there are stakes in all encounters, macro and micro, and there is a fundamental interdependency among players. Rarely a strict matter of win or lose, the result of any conflict is more frequently a redistribution of material and relational sustenance as well as of the power to name relations, all of which, however, remain unstable. Such a conception of existence digs below "realist" and "evolutionary" theories of world politics that take primal "rivalries" among "hominids" who forever seek "status" as the fundamental relation.[49] It also digs below critical theory's sometimes totalizing accounts of relations, for instance as *wholly* directed by capitalism. By heightening our consciousness of an uncontrollable and difficult yet fruitful existential relationality, this intersectional dialectical conception values the labors of sustenance. It honors the centuries of everyday care that have fed pleasure, laughter, endurance, resistance, and solidarity.

Perhaps the uncertain, plural-sided intercorporeality of relational dialectics with its attendant instabilities is what realist or neorealist political theorists perceive as anarchy in a world of conflict and competition.[50] If so, anarchy is standing in here for everyday difficulty and everyday love. To respond to this everyday difficulty becomes the everyday ethical challenge.

Although domination often shadows other kinds of relation in these engagements, and accordingly I often focus on them, the book's dialectical method keeps in view the coexistence of coercion and care, including through literature, which can enact its own labors of care.

Such is the existential, embodied depth of historical dialectics. Despite Hegel's frequent crystallization of these dynamics into an engagement between only two male actors, and despite his related "denials of coevalness," as Johannes Fabian put it, with non-European peoples, his descriptions hint that there is a proliferation of such engagements within the "manifold differentiating expanse" of the world, as when he adds that the lord and bondsman's struggle is "entangled in a variety of relationships."[51] The inter-imperial analysis unpacks this horizonal, historical, and volatile field of engagements.

Vectors of Inter-imperiality and Resistance

A historical tracking of these dialectics that begins "before European hegemony," to use Janet Abu-Lughod's phrase, crucially deepens our understanding of their persistent force in the present.[52] To study the co-constitution of sophisticated empires, economies, institutions, and cultures before 1500 and outside of western Europe not only further dislodges Eurocentric narratives of modernization, although it helpfully does that. It also firmly establishes the breadth and accruing force of coforming empires, and it reveals the dynamic range of multivectored contestations. Here I foreshadow some of these implications, developed at more length in chapter 1 and throughout.

The long perspective first of all brings into clearer view the multifaceted struggles of communities that, for centuries, have lived in the "shatterzones" of successive and converging colonizations, as in the Middle East, Indonesia, eastern Europe, the Andes, the Caribbean, and the Maghreb.[53] Such regions need to be understood and honored, I argue, not as peripheral territories but as strategic inter-imperial zones, again and again vied over for their resources (including laborers) and their geopolitical location—before, during, and since the height of European hegemony. Situated at strategic crossroads and along sea-lanes, parts of the Middle East and North Africa have, for instance, been repeatedly invaded by empires, reaching from Persianate Empires and the Macedonian Empire of Alexander the Great, through the Roman and the Byzantine Empires, to the Ottoman and European Empires. Each reorganization has left its sediments in material, linguistic, philosophical, and political forms, shaping future conflicts. Parts of Kashmir have likewise been repeatedly invaded, claimed, and shaped by competing states—from the Chinese and the Mughals to the British—which in turn has influenced the vying claims on the region by India and Pakistan today. Similarly the states of eastern Europe have for two millennia endured successive waves of invasion and occupation, reaching from the Celtic and Roman invasions to those of the Ottoman Empire, the Hapsburgs, and the Soviet Union. In the Atlantic world, the crisscrossing colonizations and revolutions of the Caribbean archipelago epitomize inter-imperial dialectics, as I discuss in chapters 6 and 7. These regions continue to suffer under inter-imperial jockeying for control of them, and this situation evokes deep, yet different resonances for each. As Sanja Bahun argues about eastern Europe, we understand the pivotal importance of such regions in the contemporary world only when we consider the sedimented layers of knowledge, intersectional configuration, and state practice that have constituted them and that are tapped within contemporary conflicts. Recently, scholars are valuably developing longue durée, inter-imperial analyses of diverse regions.[54]

This angle of vision particularly calls our attention to the linguistic and legal histories that continue to shape these regions, as discussed by literary scholars.[55] Each invading empire has installed its own discourses and its own codes for language, law, religion, property, education, marriage, and labor. They have renamed and reorganized relations, including relations with the material landscape. Such regions have developed not only as palimpsests of infrastructural accretion and economic extraction. They are vessels of layered collective memory, replete with cultural resources, sustaining values, and seasoned forms of wisdom as well as with memories of betrayal, vying identifications, and defensive attachments to gendered forms of civilizationalism, all of which may be reenergized by particular events in the contemporary field of inter-imperial pressures.

These long-accruing formations *are* the world. They compose the field of difficult relations in which we are called on to act. These are the kinds of world-shaping dynamics and determinations that an interdisciplinary, inter-imperial method can capture.

As hinted, these interlocking histories have also shaped the dynamics of resistance and revolt. Our sense of the field of power and the history of relations changes when we acknowledge this fact: that anti-imperial actors and many other persons have shrewdly managed a multilateral, multiscalar field of political relations, facing off against not merely one empire but a horizon of maneuvering empires. Consider Toussaint-Louverture negotiating with agents of the British Empire who offered to support the struggle in

Saint-Domingue against the French Empire. Or Roger Casement negotiating with agents of the German Empire to win Irish independence from the British Empire. Or Sharif Hussein ibn Ali, emir of Mecca and the leader of the Arab uprising against the Ottoman Empire during World War I, encouraged and abetted by the British Empire, although eventually betrayed by that empire in the Balfour Declaration.

In their struggles against one empire, all of these anticolonial and imperially entangled actors were ultimately betrayed by "other" empires, which were all along maneuvering for their own ends. Yet even when they did not immediately "win," these activists often gained ground for future maneuvers. Such was the case, for instance, during the pitched contest between Britain and India on the eve of Indian independence: for that decolonizing transformation took shape partly through risky affiliations between anti-British Indian nationalist leaders and Japanese politicians in the context of an expanding Japanese empire, which itself was operating under the pressure of continuing border skirmishes between Russian and Chinese expansionist states and amid the emergent polarization of communist versus capitalist states. Intersectional contestations also shaped these developments. In India, for instance, the writers and artists of the Progressive Writers' Association (WPA) raised discomfiting questions about long-historical norms of sexuality and gender as well as about hierarchies among Muslims, Hindus, and Dalit communities. Many magnets of affiliation and many inequalities thus operated simultaneously within these vectored imperial coordinates, pressuring the uncertain contingencies of action, as twentieth-century postcolonial state builders understood. In formulating a "third-world" politics of nonalliance and "positive neutrality" in relations with the other two "worlds," early postindependence thinkers such as Ghanian leader Kwame Nkrumah in effect articulated theory and strategy for managing interimperial positionality.[56]

In other words, as jockeying empires competed with each other they regularly encountered dissent and rebellion, which in turn affected their competition. We might recall that in Napoleon's communications with his brother Joseph (when Joseph took charge of newly conquered Italian territories), Napoleon advised him to make plans for quelling "insurrection" because, he noted, "insurrection is an event that constantly occurs in occupied countries."[57] Napoleon took it as a matter of course that there would be resistance to his claims to control; the resistance inherently shaped the practices and structures of empires, spiraling in this case into total war, as I discuss in chapter 4.

Although regional studies have sometimes taken account of contemporaneous, vying Anglo-European empires, such as in scholarship on the early Atlantic world or the so-called scramble for Africa, rarely have these multivectored dialectics been made central to postcolonial, decolonial, or intersectional theory. When we take stock of the full horizon of empires, both successive and contemporaneous, the landscape of power at once intensifies and opens into a wider, more complex galaxy of charged relations. Its nodes are several, yet they are not exactly decentralized. Rather, they are co-constituted. Guns, gold, and sugar as well as soldiers, laborers, and exchangeable women stream through their infrastructurally connected channels, as do fears, memories, desires, and inter-imperially oriented calculations. As I've suggested here and as later chapters address, these processes have been shaped by the press of layered historical sublations: sedimented languages, identities, inequalities, resources, and alliances, active in memory and influential in the practices of minoritized communities. The vocabularies of co-constitution, sublation, and disavowal thus serve throughout this book to name the dynamics of world politics and the costructuring of aesthetic culture and political economy.

These vocabularies also serve to capture the ways that material technologies and infrastructures themselves have become sites of dialectical contestation and sublation amid struggles over labor and resources. As I describe in chapter 5, during World War I both revolutionaries and imperial soldiers exploded railway tracks to impede their antagonists. Furthermore, in this era as in earlier periods, empires battled directly over infrastructure, as when in the 1904 Russo-Japanese War Japan invaded Manchuria in part to seize the port and railway infrastructures that Russia had built there. Those railway lines became "interpenetrating" Russian-Japanese entities whose coformation entailed appropriations and sublations of the other's powers. Meanwhile, for the inhabitants and workers, this interpenetration represented yet another coercive colonization, complete with new protocols and language demands. Such effects further ensured that these technologies would remain an object of contestation by this full range of actors and states.

When we revisit women's conditions in this context, we see more clearly that their struggles issue not merely from their positions "between men" and not merely from their positions between colonizing and colonized men, but also from their status as pawns in a whole terrain of men jockeying in and among empires, who tactically move, divide, and capture women on their chessboards, even at times in the service of anti-imperial revolution. Positioned thus, and often resisting or negotiating with this positioning, women have been cast as a dangerously uncertain element in the field of relations—an Achilles's heel in men's control of states. Indeed we might recall that some of the best-known stories of the world blame women for the downfall of the state or for the colonization of it. Cleopatra and Helen of Troy were blamed for ruining empires, while in some anticolonial narratives women are blamed for "letting in" the conquerors, as with the figure of La Malinche in Mexican tradition, or "the adulteress" blamed in Irish nationalist rhetoric for bringing "the Saxon robbers here" (as Joyce parodies in his portrait of "the Citizen" in *Ulysses*).[58]

The familiarity of such gendered narratives of macropolitics returns us to the structural importance of art and literature. For it indicates that inter-imperial legacies "occupy" the habitus over long-historical time, not only spatially, in segregated spaces and systems, but also psychically, in art, memory, and feeling. These more invisible occupations have been reinforced in the histories of literatures and languages—a pattern further ensured by the exclusion of women from education and multilingual knowledge. By the same dialectical token, however, literary and other artists have sometimes been provoked to cultivate their audience's critical imaginaries, so much so that, as the book's later chapters establish, culture makers have increasingly allied with dissenting sociopolitical movements in recent centuries. Authors have variously incorporated and contested these masculinist legends—and this, too, has constituted dialectical history.

Finally, in approaching dialectical history from this interdisciplinary longue-durée perspective, this book also makes visible a wider range of political imaginaries, preserved and channeled partly through the arts. In keeping with recent formulations of resilience or Afropessimism, attention to the sensibilities shaped by inter-imperial positionality can help to delink political narrative and theory from liberal or progressivist teleologies and heroic narratives of freedom battles. As Stephen Joyce argues, the Korean philosophical posture of *han*, often expressed in Korean literature, offers one such instance.[59] Han is epitomized in the proverb invoked by Chang-rae Lee in his novel *Native Speaker*, spoken by the protagonist's mother: "San konno san itta. Over the mountains there are mountains."[60] Stephen Joyce situates the attitude politically, in the context of the waves of colonization suffered by Koreans: he considers it an expression of "the hard-won wisdom of a people living beneath successive empires who understand that there is no promised land on the other side of the mountains."[61] That is, rather than preparing for liberation at the summit of a sociopolitical struggle, one must instead prepare for another uphill struggle. Difficult dialectics continue. For the Korean novelist Park Kyong-ni (박경리), the philosophy of han means "both sadness and hope at the same time" and it names "the core of life."[62] She considers literature itself as both "an act of Han and a representation of it."[63] In this light, Stephen Joyce calls for embrace of vocabularies that include these "affective structures of understanding" generated by "the emotions of endurance"—an endurance achieved, I would venture to add, through gendered labors.[64] As I sketch in the next section, understanding the long past of diverse political imaginaries and their conditions of imagining in literature is crucial to the twin projects of "decolonizing our minds" and acknowledging our fundamentally dialectical conditions of relation.[65]

Worlding Literature

As suggested above, literature like other arts has been a force in this history of relations. In the next section I outline the key dimensions of its power. Yet here, with my literary colleagues in mind, I situate my analysis in relation to current debates in postcolonial and world literature studies.

While postcolonial and world literature scholarship often incorporates history, and some of these studies encompass the longue durée of literary history, there is still a need for more attention to the wealth of recent economic and decolonial historiography on non-European empires. Strikingly, while literary scholars have otherwise built a veritable industry of new interpretations from Immanuel Wallerstein's world-systems theory, few have taken up Abu-Lughod's conversation-changing world-systems analysis of earlier periods in her 1989 book, *Before European Hegemony*. There she amasses evidence of the interlocking political economies of the tenth to fourteenth centuries shaped by Chinese, Islamicate, and other empires. Her irrefutable account offers a model for further analysis of early systems in other regions, and indeed it has inspired a wealth of critical historiography in the fields of anthropology, history, and sociology, though not always Marxist and decolonial in orientation. Meanwhile, this material has been widely ignored by critical theorists across disciplines, including literary and cultural studies, who continue to think within the Eurocentric coordinates of premodern and modern or feudal and capitalist.

Wider reading of these materials promises to enrich literary studies and clarify its proper place in theories and histories of geopolitical economy. It thus might also assuage the current worries over the demise of postcolonial studies and displacement of this field by an apolitical world literature studies. It would certainly help to undo two linked elisions in much literary theory: the eclipse of systemic political economies in what is commonly (and inaccurately) called "precolonial" or "premodern" history, and the persistent minoritization of feminist-intersectional analysis, which, when centered, quickly draws more attention to the problems of exploitation in those earlier histories and to the ways that erasure of these histories persists in both colonial and critical postcolonial thinking.

When we put the intersectional and the longue-durée histories back together, as I aim to do here, another world of understanding opens, yielding more sustainable world visions as well as more trenchant critique. For it enables us to plumb the depths at which literatures have structured and mediated the intersectional violence of empires for millennia, not merely since 1492. This book only scratches the surface of the revelations that follow from this deeper study, yet there are signs of a turn in the tide.[66]

This inter-imperial, intersectional perspective particularly promises to rectify the problems of depoliticization in the expanding subfield of world literature. As has been argued by many postcolonial critics, the very category of world literature sometimes operates simply as a new canon yet without clear grounds of definition beyond, for instance, the most widely translated texts. The subfield has thus spawned wide debate and critique in both articles and edited collections for its evacuation of politics, including the politics of translation, especially when it also cherry-picks from widely translated postcolonial texts for its "world" canon without attention to political and historical dimensions.[67]

Spurred by these problems in the field of world literature, literary scholars have begun to develop fresh methods for capturing the worldly reach of texts while simultaneously grounding them in specific politics, locales, languages, or histories. Shu-mei Shih has for example proposed that literary scholars might define their objects of study less in relation to "the world" as a whole and more specifically along "arcs of relation" created by events (such as the Vietnam War) and systems (such as the global plantation complex of bonded and enslaved labor), studying the ways that these generate a linked corpus of texts across regions and languages.[68] Other scholars have begun to incorporate longer-historical models and track literary intertextuality within regions, as advocated for instance by Karima Laachir, Sara Marzagora, and Francesca Orsini. They propose that critics might demote the centrality of nations and national languages and instead frame their analyses within "significant geographies," that is, regions where for centuries texts have accrued political intertextualities and overlapping cosmologies, as in Indonesia or the Maghreb.[69]

The framework I develop here shares the investments of these studies, especially with those calling for a long-historical, non-Eurocentric perspective. But as an intentionally interdisciplinary study, *Inter-imperiality* focuses as much on retheorizing geopolitical economy and the dialectics of history as it does on retheorizing literature's structural relation to these. This emphasis also entails extensive discussion of feminist-intersectional and decolonial-existential dimensions of world politics at a more structural level. I hope my formulations encourage more such analysis in studies of world literature as well as of world history and world politics, for in these fields, the feminist-intersectional dimensions are often as neglected as the long-historical or geopolitical dimensions. The few exceptions include, for example, the work of Revathi Krishnaswamy, which develops longue-durée, closely historicized frameworks that are also intersectionally attuned.[70] Krishnaswamy has drawn attention both to the gendered politics of older literary genres (such as the ancient tradition of framed tales and the gender-inflected voicing of bhakti lyrical poetry) and to ancient literary theory (as in ancient Tamil theories of landscape and literature), clarifying the ways that literature has for millennia critiqued and created social collectivities even as it has also evinced entanglement in the colonial, caste, and gendered politics of its own day. Increasingly, other studies take up similar intersectional work, especially on old narrative traditions, but there is still a need for fuller rethinking of the geopolitical economies in which these genres did their work.[71]

In the realm of debates on world literature, the existential orientation and concerns of my analysis have most in common with the work of Pheng Cheah, including both his first book, *Inhuman Conditions: On Cosmopolitanism and Human Rights*, and his more recent one, *What Is a World? On Postcolonial Literature as World Literature*.[72] In *What Is a World?* Cheah argues that literature is a structuring force in the world, as I do here, and he too theorizes its constitutive, ethical power. Yet, our paths diverge not only in our historical treatment of political economy but also, a bit more subtly, in our feminist-philosophical analyses of what Cheah refers to as the "*a priori* principle of sociality."[73] Taken together, our differences and our shared commitments further highlight the need for more intersectional, interdisciplinary theorization of world politics, economies, and literatures, so I pause here to parse our divergences.

In *Inhuman Conditions*, Cheah carefully analyzes the structural role of gendered work in world politics and economy, and he focuses on the problematic of instrumentality. That is, building on Kant, he argues that ethical problems begin when humans and states make other humans and states into instruments for their own ends, specifically for their own profit and power. In both *Inhuman Conditions* and *What Is a World?* Cheah identifies this problem with the workings of capitalism, often deeming capitalism omni-determining: "There is no solution to the instrumentalization of human relations since this is rooted in the very nature of economic development within global capitalism."[74] Yet at moments in this earlier work Cheah also slips into a significantly different formulation, as when he comments that instrumentality is "a form of technical production that cannot be regulated and transcended because it is the condition of possibility of humanity. It forms the concrete human being and all its capacities at the most material level."[75]

This fleetingly mentioned existential condition moves to the center of Cheah's next book, *What Is a World?*, especially in its emphasis on the "*a priori* principle of sociality." In this second monograph, Cheah also adjusts his totalizing account of capitalism; it becomes a less absolutely determining force. Although he follows world-systems and other materialist critics in placing capitalism at center as the hegemonic form of political economy that literature challenges, he rejects those world-systems approaches that reduce literature to a function of or a reflection on political economy. He argues that doing so underestimates "the ethico-political horizon [literature] can open up for the existing world."[76] He further posits that our condition of "being in time" allows this opening. Through engagement with philosophers from Hegel and Heidegger to Arendt and Derrida, he argues that temporality is the unfolding element—the "to-come"—through which "the other" continually arrives, bringing unpredictability yet also reaffirming "the immanent sociality of human life."[77] Insofar as narrative literature refuses closure it keeps open the conditions of possibility. I wholly agree, as will become clear, that reconfigurations of temporality are key to literature's political-phenomenological power and its decolonial work.

What's puzzling here, however, is the degree to which in *What Is a World?* Cheah consistently hovers near the gendered conditions of an "a priori sociality" (for instance noting that "we are not and cannot be solitary and solipsistic beings in the primary instance"), but in his several philosophical chapters he never addresses these conditions, despite his concern with political economy.[78] He does not pause over the typically female labors entailed in this "primary instance," nor at how those labors constitute and practice the principle of sociality. It's important to notice that Cheah is led into these elisions by the theorists he taps. The habituation to these canonical western theorists offers an object lesson about the necessity for scholars of all stripes to immerse themselves in (and cite) the long tradition of feminist-intersectional philosophy and critical theory, which has seeped into theory without acknowledgment and as a consequence has often therefore been imperfectly understood. Specifically here, the problem is that the "primary instance" of people-making and world-sustaining labor lurks as the inadmissible supplement in the philosophies of Hegel, Heidegger, Arendt, and Derrida, even as these thinkers seem to discuss it. If the fact of birth appears in these thinkers, it does so always in the passive voice and in the absence of reference to any birthing or laboring bodies.[79] We might well say that the fact of birth has always already been instrumentalized by these thinkers.

These habitual elisions in theory that follow from minimal understanding of and attention to the wide tradition of philosophical intersectional theory are further reinforced when theorists limit their account of history to the history of capitalism.[80] Sustained attention to the world's much older imperial and masculinist economies better explains why women have cultivated the kind of maternal traditions that Cheah later discusses and to some extent romanticizes. This sustained attention would furthermore reveal how literature's handling of temporality and narrative has served heteronormativity, hierarchy, and empire as often as it has challenged them.

Focusing on literature's powerful yet also sometimes complicit involvement in worlding, and noticing the labors that actualize the principle of sociality, *Inter-imperiality* differently frames literature's part in the history of struggle.

The Vectored Dialectics of Art

Ultimately, the inter-imperial method situates literature as deeply as possible in the politically nested and often vying worlds that produce it and with which it engages. Taking a cue from Ngũgĩ wa Thiong'o's concept of globalectics and incorporating fully intersectional postcolonial approaches, I ask: How do works of literature, however local, arise from and co-constitute the inter-imperially shaped field of relations?[81] How, and under what accruing and contemporary inter-imperial conditions, have literatures transformed their present? How have they crafted their engagements or occlusions, and with what immediate or long-term effects? These questions can be asked whether a work is oral or written, obscure or canonical, translated or untranslated, radical or conservative. Again, this analysis is less concerned with world literature as a canon or category than with the historical, existential, and political conditions under which literature exerts its worlding force.

A quick outline of the salient features of an inter-imperial analysis of literature may be helpful for scholars inside and outside literary studies. Most fundamentally, this analysis understands inter-imperial positionality as both a condition of aesthetic production and an object of literary representations. Second, as a result of its long-historical scope, this approach enables readers to discern how, over time, literatures become reservoirs of a sedimented political consciousness—what I will sometimes refer to, following Fredric Jameson, as an inter-imperial political unconscious.[82] I argue that communities and persons, including authors, have often acted within these sedimented legacies, whether consciously or unconsciously.

Third, this attention to inter-imperial positionality over the longue durée also reveals the precise ways that literary and other arts have arisen and dissented from the world's imperial economies. For, caught up as they often are in empires' efforts to control discourses of relationality, creative artists and intellectuals have navigated carefully. As Jean-Paul Sartre might put it, writers have made decisions about whether and how they will embark on the rocky seas of existential freedom by challenging the powers that be. Their fraught choices merit analysis not only in themselves but also insofar as they have had structural impact on political and literary histories. An inter-imperial analysis keeps an eye both on the direct involvement of writers in state building—for instance as court poets, historians, speech writers, or manuscript translators—and on their subversive interventions, whether spoken inside hallowed halls or inscribed in graffiti. It also acknowledges writers' impulses simply to imagine otherwise or to connect with others by describing the exquisitely reticulated planetary world we share.

Sometimes it is exactly because artists and writers are anchored in this wisdom that they are moved to expose bad-faith disavowals of entanglement, at times alluding to their own entanglement. This reflexivity composes a fourth important element of an inter-imperial analysis of literature. As Theodor Adorno argued, and as I emphasize throughout, artistic forms often self-reflexively hold up and reenact, in a "negative" dialectical engagement, the very processes and limit conditions that have produced them.[83] Authors have commented implicitly on their own compromises within a world of vying states and stratified economies, as in the case of Stephen Dedalus in Joyce's *Ulysses* lamenting his position as "the servant of two masters"—the British and the Roman Catholic Empires—while nonetheless teaching the same old narratives of imperial history to his students.[84] In this way, authors also dramatize their audiences' compromising entanglements. These audiences include critical intelligentsia such as ourselves, whose livelihoods depend on inter-imperially generated institutions and literatures. My reading of *The Thousand and One Nights* in chapter 2 reveals, for instance, how this text positions Shahrazad between Persianate and Islamicate empires and how it tracks her interventions in empires' politics from within the very imperial court and its legacies of learning: for, as we are told, she had "read the books of literature, philosophy, and medicine. She knew poetry by heart, had studied historical reports, and was acquainted with the sayings of men and the maxims of sages and kings."[85] Many subsequent authors have likewise rendered the in-between positions and charged global/local conjunctures that have shaped not only their characters and their writing labors but also their audiences. A dialectical inter-imperial method attends to these texts' implicit calling out of audiences through metacommentaries and subtexts. Most importantly, it honors these ethical struggles at the heart of art making.

In fact, close study of the genres and forms of literature in this light reveals how fully the writing of literature dramatizes the ethical problems rooted in relationality. Across languages and periods, in both oral tale-telling and stately theater, authors have registered the nuances of power-inflected relationality, including what Sara Suleri has called the "colonial intimacies" of relations.[86] Through cunningly crafted language, gesture, and structure, texts delineate the dynamics of power at many scales, mirroring the ways that macropolitics play out in bodily microphysics. Literature has also provided a means for subtle commentary by servants, minorities, and women whose critiques must operate undercover and from within the fraught labors and entanglements of the household. Texts often render these dynamic conditions more acutely than do historical documents, sociological data, or theory. For the "evidence" provided by literature is not a factual "representation" of history (indeed it typically strays from facts). It is rather a laying bare of the forms of our lives, sometimes a renaming of the very terms of our relationality. Scholars outside literary studies might more often attune their gaze to these restructuring techniques, instead of reading only for theme or historical fact.

Finally, as a sixth element of inter-imperial literary analysis, the above optics and practices open the way to new literary histories, non-Eurocentric and nonandrocentric. They allow us to consider, for instance, how the rise of vernacular literatures in late medieval Europe, often considered a singularly European innovation, instead reflects strategic language choices made under the intensely pressured inter-imperial conditions of the Mediterranean and the Crusades, as I discuss in chapter 1. Likewise, the millennia-long history of imperial library-building and translation projects requires us to rethink Europe's claims to have founded "enlightened" institutions and discourses. And again, the longer histories enable wider consideration of gender and sexuality in literary traditions, allowing us to make fuller sense of their queer and estranging elements.

This literary-historical rethinking not only further "provincializes" Europe. It also prompts retheorization of the temporalities, geopolitics, and dialectics of literary genres more broadly.[87] In turn, this literary-historical reconfiguration unveils the diverse histories and politics streaming into recent postcolonial texts. It brings into view the plural forms of address in postcolonial writing, as authors "write back" to multiple invaders or empires, create longer-historical time lines, and weave new intertextual relations with older literary forms—sometimes rekindling long-sublated elements or tropes. In effect, as my final chapters argue, this study resituates Wai Chee Dimock's notion of deep time within geopolitical and institutional histories, revealing that many authors of the last century have grappled with *deep inter-imperial time*.

Taken together, attention to these literary dimensions and practices explains literature's capacity to open up a perceiving space around "events" in which readers and listeners may, at least inwardly, gain distance and perhaps loosen attachments to the hegemonic terms of relationality. We might say that literature cultivates a certain mindfulness about the enactments and elisions of existential coformations. It allows us to notice the political stylizing and structuring of our collective being-in-the-world, including over long-historical time and as embodied in the arts all around us. In turn, we see more fully how each text and sign is a structuring event. Each interaction with a text or performance constitutes a historical moment like any other, operating simultaneously as a relational event and a reflection *on* such events, which incrementally also affects geopolitical events. Most broadly, the inter-imperial method establishes how fully the writing of literature is a dialectical engagement with the world's tumultuous history.

The Approach

Inter-imperiality unfolds these interdisciplinary and theoretical arguments within a historical arc. Led by the historical evidence, I eschew the periodizations of premodern and modern, or precolonial and colonial, that typically organize analyses of political economy and culture. Instead I begin

approximately a millennium earlier than the usual medieval/modern periodization, and I end in the late twentieth century. In part, this arc allows me
to capture what I propose is an intensifying set of processes over centuries.
It shows that, as empires adopt and retool each other's technologies and
state practices, they also become more interconnected and more homog-
enized, as well as more invasive. Troops, technocrats, and propaganda arrive more quickly, as states conscript, exploit, and indebt more aggressively.
Yet dissidents in their turn have increasingly appropriated the tools and
extended the reach of their political movements—tapping the powers of
solidarity and sustaining care. This activism forces empires to regroup and
realign, again and again. The historical organization of chapters allows me to
track these dialectics of intensifying struggle.

The chapters also develop through a rhythm of diastole and systole, a
widening and localizing that mirrors dialectical processes. My analyses
often expand to encompass far-reaching linkages and pressures and then
contract to register the regional conditions, adaptations, and locally positioned struggles, so as to capture their co-constituting relations. The systole-
diastole action directs my movements within each chapter and in some
cases my movements from one chapter to the next. At the same time, each
chapter puts back together the worlding forces that academic disciplinar-
ity has taken apart. Many studies of world problems assume that history,
state formation, and political economy can be understood separately from
aesthetics, culture, and identity. Rejecting this assumption, in every chapter
I combine historical analysis of inter-imperial economies with analysis of
languages and literatures, although in different proportions.

Thus in part I, "Co-constituted Worlds," the first chapter builds a wide
historical frame and enfolds discussion of literary formations, whereas the
second chapter narrows its focus to a literary-political case study, interweaving historical threads about specific state formations. That is, chapter 1,
"Dialectics in the Longue Durée," widens the view in order to capture the
dynamics through which empires have been radically co-constituted: accretively over centuries, competitively in any one era, and unstably through
their interacting attempts to quell dissent—and dissent there always is. This
first chapter also redescribes the ways that political and infrastructural formations in Afro-Eurasia and the Americas converged, provoking multivectored
riptides of transformation across the world. The approach taken here is neither comparative, circulatory, nor merely connective, but strongly dialectical, with emphasis on the unfolding of history through manifold dynamics
of domination, disavowal, destabilization, dissent, and alliance. This first

chapter then closes with analysis of literary and political formations in the Mediterranean world of roughly the eleventh through fifteenth centuries. Positioning Mediterranean language politics within the crucible of converging, contesting forces, this specific case also epitomizes inter-imperial dialectics.

Chapter 2, "Refusing Labor's (Re)production," then contracts to interpret the shape-shifting, oft-translated text of *The Thousand and One Nights*. Focusing on the frame story that has remained virtually the same since the earliest extant version, I argue that the frame shrewdly encodes the interlocking sexual, racial, and labor stakes of inter-imperial and literary dialectics. Formed at the root by Persianate and Islamicate empires, the text stages the full drama. It is set in motion by the catalyzing threat of transgressive female sexuality and women's alliances with laborers and slaves, and these bring forth the empires' weapons not only of bodily execution but also of translation and learning in the form of Shahrazad's vizier father, who attempts to prevent her act of solidarity through tales of control, including over language. But such tales "do not deter" Shahrazad, as she says, and she wields her own language instruments in opposition.[88] Nor, as later chapters show, have later artists and communities been deterred as they have faced off against the converging powers of empires.

The three chapters of part II, "Convergence and Revolt," focus respectively on three periods: the sixteenth through early eighteenth centuries, the later eighteenth through early nineteenth centuries, and the twentieth century. I track the inter-imperial coformations that in each period unfolded across hemispheres in escalating dynamics of state coercion and antistate resistance. These chapters do not conform to standard narratives organized around the "rise of Europe," although that is a strand of the story. Instead, they keep in view a global field of contestations, aiming to convey the interdependent nature and unpredictability of outcomes at each stage. Literature, as the chapters show, played a part at every turn. Chapter 3, "Remapping Orientalism among Eurasian Empires," begins by expanding the traditionally western European frame to encompass the shifting battles and alliances among the Mughal, Safavid, Ottoman, and Russian Empires in the sixteenth century, a portrait that "provincializes" England's early efforts to enter the inter-imperial field. The chapter emphasizes the pivotal importance of the Russian Empire, and it foregrounds the role of literary culture in these dynamics, specifically as enacted through the multilateral genesis of Orientalism. In closing, the chapter revisits the thoroughly inter-imperial conditions under which Antoine Galland—cultural attaché for the French Empire living in the Ottoman Empire—created an embellished "translation" of the tales of *The Thousand and One Nights*. This text and adaptations of it immediately catalyzed a profound transformation of Anglo-European literatures, feeding Orientalist imaginaries yet also eventually being retooled for anti-imperial and feminist critique. In other words, this metamorphizing text helped to drive the vectored transhemispheric coformations of inter-imperial dialectics.

These dialectics also led to ever more aggressive war and to ever bolder rebellions, as detailed in chapter 4. This chapter, "Global Revolts and Gothic Interventions," takes account of the multiple sites of rebellion that both pre-date and intersect with European revolutions, from China and Russia to Haiti and South America. While describing the distinctive inter-imperial positioning of each rebellion, I also pinpoint the shared catalysts of these events, including taxes, conscription, and deliberately destabilizing interventions among rival empires. Accordingly this chapter also tracks an emergent anticolonial or what I call an anticipatory "post/colonial" sensibility, building out from the work of recent scholars. In the second part of the chapter I uncover the extent to which Gothic literature of the period frames these events within the longue durée of violent empires. Here I take as a case study the 1820 Gothic novel *Melmoth the Wanderer*, written by the Anglo-Irish author Charles Maturin. Setting his novel in a rebellion-wracked Ireland, Maturin undertakes (in today's terms) an Adornian negative-dialectical engagement with history while also offering a Trotskyist critique of combined and uneven development. He also reflects on literature's long entanglement with these problems by structuring his novel as a Shahrazadian all-night storytelling session between alienated inheritors of empire, a Spaniard and a British man. Quickly translated into French and Russian, and influencing both Balzac and Dostoevsky, this novel struck an inter-imperial nerve in this age of revolutions. It embodies all of the dialectical motions of literature.

One century later, as I consider in "Infrastructure, Activism, and Literary Dialectics in the Early Twentieth Century," the final chapter of part II, the Gothic's dark visions spiraled into a worldwide reality of "total" inter-imperial war in the twentieth century, accompanied by ravenous extraction, crippling economic crisis, and eugenic programs for women and the "lower races." Yet this early twentieth-century period also saw the makers of literature and other arts step forward more assertively. The very travel, communications, and military technologies that served ever more deadly war and systems of domination also enabled wider solidarities, as reflected in the intertwining of literary and political movements. Under these conditions, the techno-infrastructures of trains, telegraph, and radio became key dialectical sites of contestation, both between empires and between insurgents and empires. Indeed, writers understood that print and radio were themselves technologies to be mobilized for a political reimagining of the world. At the same time, in this early twentieth-century period, there emerged a problematic mixture, including among activists, of anti-imperial critique and masculinist rhetoric. My commentary highlights the degree to which these competitive discourses reflect the long, wide imperial interpellation of communities and subjectivities, a pattern called out by feminists of the period. I argue that, when seen through a longue-durée, inter-imperial lens, salient features of twentieth-century literature come into clearer view, especially the connections between their infrastructural, intersectional concerns and their genre experiments. With its wide coverage of these developments, chapter 5 sets the stage for the book's final section, which follows twentieth-century fiction, especially in the Caribbean, as it carries us into the maelstrom of neocolonial inter-imperial tempests—and leaves us stunned but alive on shore, asking searching questions.

In this final section, "Persisting Temporalities," I first of all survey the ways that twentieth-century literary experiments with temporality undercut what critics have called "empire time."[89] While most studies focus on their engagement with contemporaneous imperial conditions, these chapters recover the degree to which authors also reconfigure long-historical empire time. They expose the accruing violence, and they render the hidden history of tenderness under duress. As their narratives loop or fragment, the texts repeatedly re-create the present as a moment of dialectical struggle situated at the meeting point of past and present, determinism and agency, and microintimacies and macropolitics. They make us feel the momentum of history's determinations and contradictions bearing down on their protagonists in the inter-imperial present.

After surveying an array of novelists I turn to two Caribbean novels, in chapters 6 and 7: Alejo Carpentier's *The Kingdom of This World* (1949) and Patricia Powell's *The Pagoda* (1998). Caribbean fiction epitomizes literature's grappling with the pressures of inter-imperiality. Like other writers situated in particularly intense inter-imperial battle zones, Caribbean thinkers and authors have had much to reveal about the ethics of acting in unfolding time. As is well known, over centuries the Caribbean archipelago became a crucial point of convergence and a leveraging fulcrum for jockeying European empires, especially given its role as matrix of the world's sugar economy. Yet for this reason, it simultaneously became a seedbed of determined resistance, anticolonial theory, and avant-garde literature.

The last two chapters unpack Carpentier's and Powell's pointed engagements with inter-imperiality, while also highlighting their different handling of the sexual violence and masculinist narratives central to inter-imperial destruction. Carpentier's much-discussed depiction of the Haitian Revolution in *The Kingdom of This World* focalizes mainly through the enslaved laborer Ti Noël, who is closely attuned not only to labor as the fulcrum of empires since at least the Roman Empire but also to gendered practices of power and sexuality. Yet Carpentier creates him as a highly ambiguous observer of and participant in sexual violence, one who has an equivocally queer attachment to men that flows through his commitment to revolution. Carpentier's equivocal representations of these intertwined energies illustrate how literature sometimes walks an uncertain line between exposure of and perpetuation of masculinist, imperial structures. Scholarship on the text itself repeats this problem, as reflected in the plethora of studies focused on Carpentier's treatment of revolution in the novel and near absence of studies that take notice of the novel's emphatic pattern of rape. Revolution is fetishized; rape is elided.

Powell's *Pagoda* by contrast places aesthetic, imperial, and sexual legacies at the heart of a layered history, in this case reaching from Chinese practices of daughter selling to nineteenth-century European "coolie" bonded labor and rape in Jamaica. Her tale exposes and unravels the gendered, economic order of things, as the narrative submerges us claustrophobically in the consciousness of a Chinese woman struggling to emerge from her life as an "indebted" concubine in Jamaica. Understanding Carpentier's and Powell's narrative repetitions, breaks, and layerings as divergent mirrorings of history's coercions, I argue that nonetheless both novels call out to readers (subtextually in Carpentier's case) to acknowledge the weight of overdetermined choices and habits that perpetuate terror and impoverishment.

At its heart, *Inter-imperiality* seeks to echo this relational call: the call to honor the struggles and the sustaining practices that often escape the frames of both history and dialectical theory. It aims to join the project of repairing and reintegrating the worlds that androcentric and imperial history have put asunder. However daunting, the effort seems worth it, for the better we understand how we got here together, the more we undo the denial of our radically relational condition.

PART I CO-CONSTITUTED WORLDS

Dialectics in the Longue Durée

Every successful assertion of domination simultaneously reveals an inability
to attain total hegemony. —**REVATHI KRISHNASWAMY**, *Effeminism*

Imperialist narratives of history rest on the denial of interdependence.
Culture makers have played key roles in this denial, since empires have
for millennia bestowed favor on the historians, authors, artists, and entertainers whose legend making elides not only that state's violence but also
its beholdenness to a world of others—to laborers, reproductive women,
and other empires. Be it Britain, the United States, or the Chinese Middle
Kingdom, an empire often constructs itself as the center of the world while
positioning other polities and regions as dependents, peripheries, or lesser
rivals.[1] Each empire understates its necessary dependence on trade relations
and alliances with others (including through marriage), and each down-
plays its reinstrumentalization of the infrastructures, knowledge, labor,
and local governance of the communities it has colonized. Likewise, the
legendary notion of *translatio imperii* implies that the triumphant empire
has wholly usurped the central place of a "prior" reigning empire. While an
empire often traces its lineage to one ancestral empire, as Europeans have

often done with ancient Rome, it typically assigns a narrative of decline or collapse to contemporaneous states.[2] Johannes Fabian's account of racist denials of coevalness and contemporaneity with other peoples can thus also describe empires' elisions of the contemporaneity of other empires.[3] These may include formidable rivals who are neither conquered, "backward," nor in decline but alive and well, and therefore requiring discursive denigration, as in the characterizations of the Ottoman Empire as the "sick man of Europe."[4] Art has both helped and hindered this erasure. In both cases, as this book emphasizes and as literary art displays, the denial of coeval interdependence evinces deeper wishes: to deny indebtedness to diverse pasts, to minimize the problems of the inter-imperial present, and to veil the indeterminacy of the future.

The broad success of European empires in the practice of disavowal has issued in Eurocentrism, epitomized in Europe's claim to have created the "modern world" that superseded a "Dark Ages." The continuing use of the words *premodern* and *modern* among diverse scholars in every discipline is a measure of this tactic's continuing success. As Kathleen Davis points out in *Periodization and Sovereignty*, in European historiography a periodizing divide between medieval and modern has become standard in studies of states and capitalism as well as culture and has been continued by thinkers as different as J. G. A. Pocock and Antonio Negri.[5] This binary between *medieval* and *modern* typically ramifies into corollary divisions between the contrasting epistemes of hierarchy and democracy, sacred and secular, or static and dynamic culture. These in turn have organized narratives of hemispheres, so that northern and western have been deemed dynamically modern, while southern and eastern have been cast as the medieval opposites, still attached to a shadowy past before the rise of systems, states, and regulated economies. Among other useful effects for Anglo-European self-fashioning, these periodizing divisions have obscured the African, Asian, Middle Eastern, and Mesoamerican sources of the globe's systems, institutions, economic mechanisms, and knowledge-building projects. They veil the fact of western Europe's late entry into systemically networked worlds: of sophisticated finance and markets; of transport, manufacture, and agricultural technologies; and of highly literate metropole culture. The systemic sophistication of earlier states and economies has been repressed in the mythical, imperializing narrative of northwestern Europe's creation of so-called modernity.[6]

This narrative dissolves before one's eyes, however, when one takes account of the most recent archival and archeological scholarship on pre-1500 periods in the Eastern and Southern Hemispheres, as I do in this chapter.

The evidence reveals not only the depth of cultural influence moving from south and east to north and west but also the global longevity and reach of the world-system structures that existed "before European hegemony," as Janet Abu-Lughod put it.[7] While this chapter partly undertakes an adjustment in chronologies and a remapping of influences, my main purpose is not to establish new periodization but to pinpoint some of the most important inter-imperial dynamics and interpositionalities that, over at least a millennium and at several scales, have forged systems and catalyzed human struggles.

The implication of this analysis is not that empires alone create historical conditions, always overriding local dynamics and histories. On the contrary, an inter-imperial analysis brings into view overlooked elements of the regional and local, as will become clear in this and subsequent chapters. Just as the workings of any single empire provide a context for understanding the microlevel histories of ordinary people, so, too, does analysis of multiple expansionist empires and of the groups engaged with them clarify the habits of communities and gendered groups within this geopolitical field. The long-historical framework makes clear that successive waves of imperial hegemonies persist within local sites in both practices and sedimented attachments (political, linguistic, economic, and social). As noted in the introduction, the emphasis on these inter-imperial dynamics does not imply that all empires have been the same or have engaged in precisely the same projects. Rather, inter-imperial theory simply begins from the fact that different empires, of different kinds, sizes, and means, form in dialectical relation. The character of their coformations arises, in fact, from their differences and divergent histories as well as their historical linkages and alliances. To understand any of them we must to some degree take account of all these elements among contemporaneous and successive empires.

To do so is to counteract those disavowals on which imperial hegemonies depend, as Edward Said suggested in *Culture and Imperialism*. Having noted that, in addition to the British and French, "the United States, Russia, . . . Japan and Turkey [*sic*], were also imperial powers for some or all of the nineteenth century," Said proceeds to identify two persistent elisions in these imperialists' naming of their historical situation: "the [fact of] the contending native and the fact of other empires."[8] Scholars have since highlighted the actions of the "contending native," but the determining force of "other empires" has received limited attention, which has also obscured what this surround of multiple empires means from the perspective of the colonized. Historian Anthony G. Hopkins has directly called for "a fundamental appraisal of world history to bring out the extent to which, in recent history, it has been shaped by the interactions of several empires," and he observes that "such an approach would capture both the differences between empires and their dynamism."[9] Seeing that dynamism, we are better able to locate both the labors of literary culture and the dialectics of dissent.

New historiographic studies fortunately make these analyses more feasible, and I draw on many of them.[10] But there is a need for more decolonial and interdisciplinary analysis of this historiography to loosen theory yet further from the grip of Eurocentrist models and to tease out the implications for contemporary geopolitics. This chapter undertakes this work, laying ground for all subsequent chapters. The chapter combines a wide scope with illustrative instances to capture the reverberating effects of distinctive regional engagements across increasingly interlocked fields of power.

As I lay out briefly in the chapter's first section, attention to the sophisticated state and economic formations of earlier periods in relation to their technological, intellectual, and cultural formations exposes the limits of the neutral vocabularies of exchange, connection, circulation, synergy, and efflorescence that are common in long-historical studies. I argue that we need more dialectical, political, and affective vocabularies in order to take the measure of world history more precisely and in turn to analyze its force in the present. The terminology of this book therefore pinpoints processes of contestation, coformation, maneuvering, and sublation as well as the actions of disavowal, betrayal, and struggle. This chapter traces historical dynamics in these terms and in the following order:

- the co-constitution and destabilizations of states, including as shaped by subordinated or border communities and by contestation or overthrow;
- the co-constituting interactions among empires and of empires with economic actors in pre-1500 periods, which reveal their joint involvement in labor-controlling, capital-accruing, and gendered state-building projects;
- the inter-imperial coproduction of infrastructures, technology, and intellectual-bureaucratic institutions, which become the imperially sedimented habitus; and
- the structuring and mediating work of literature and translation in this history, its mediations, innovations, and maneuvers, which have shaped subsequent cultural and geopolitical economies.

This recasting of the intertwined genesis of states, capitalism, and culture does not claim priority for one element over the other, nor is it centrally concerned with precise dates of origin for capitalism or with debates about the term *modernity*. Too often, these are caught up in the competitive or Eurocentric thinking that the book critiques, and too often, theorists of capitalism who reject earlier periodizations have read next to nothing about either earlier periods or regions outside of Europe. Rather the task of the chapter and this book is to develop a dialectical interpretation of the multiscalar, intersectional, and longue-durée histories that have issued in contemporary geopolitics and human struggles.

Reframing the Longue Durée: Beyond Connectivity

In *Before European Hegemony*, Janet Abu-Lughod established the presence of a formidable early world system in North Africa, the Middle East, and China, emerging in approximately 1000 CE and reaching its heyday between 1250 and 1350 CE. Her work has inspired a generation of scholars, some of whom similarly tap Immanuel Wallerstein's world-systems approach so as to study systems in other places and periods while also adjusting and updating Abu-Lughod's claims (and correcting her minimal attention to Africa).[11] These scholars find several indicators of world-system configurations among polities since at least the first millennium CE. They have shown that linked regions interacted through cores, peripheries, and systems of exploitative extraction, that they underwent transregional "pulsations" or synchronous periods of economic growth and decline, and that they were supported by capital accumulation and financial tools.[12] Philippe Beaujard concludes that in the first century CE "there emerged a Eurasian and African world-system in which different regions evolved in tandem," and Michael Smith likewise argues for a Mesoamerican world system centered in the Aztec metropole.[13] While some propose that a southeastern world-system economy was in formation by the fourth millennium BC, centralized in Mesopotamia and reaching from Egypt to western Asia, most scholars date the emergence of truly interlocking systems to the first millennium.[14]

Even when not focusing strictly on systems, many scholars now emphasize the long-historical formations of world regions, such as the coformations of different and successive Mesoamerican states and the mutually transforming contact of American and Afro-Eurasian states in the fifteenth century and after.[15] Their work remaps and reperiodizes system-building projects, emphasizing their "interactive emergence" over two thousand years.[16] David Christian considers modernization to be "the product of an economic and technological synergy that was generated over several millenniums," while historians of economy, culture, or technology sometimes speak of "shared efflorescences" across pre-1500 linked world systems.[17] These scholars argue that systemic developments "were not closed national events" but have instead been "multi-causal and contingent," involving a "path-dependent interweaving with circumstances" across hemispheres.[18]

This emphasis on contingency and interweaving needs qualification, however. Seen from a political angle, the "multicausal" turns out to be less contingent, more regulated, and more determining than it might appear. Vocabularies of synergy, connectivity, and circulation too often obscure the political energies that drive historical processes. For example, in his otherwise valuable research, Jerry Brotton refers to the "fluid transactions" in the sixteenth century when "Europe began to define itself by purchasing and emulating the . . . cultured sophistication of the cities, merchants, scholars, and empires of the Ottomans, the Persians, and the Egyptian Mamluks."[19] He places these transactions within "an expanding world where people exchanged ideas and things often regardless of political and religious ideology."[20] As I discuss in chapter 3 on the sixteenth and seventeenth centuries, such purchasing and emulating by Europeans was utterly entwined with state and religious projects, for traders were sometimes missionaries, and trading companies often required patents from rulers. Furthermore, given the depth of human attachments to culturally inculcated values and beliefs, it seems unlikely that such exchanges could easily sidestep these investments.

A geopolitical analysis shows that such exchanges were enabled by imperial systems while the humans involved in the exchanges maneuvered carefully between and across these systems, sometimes evading their control.[21] Without resurrecting a clash of civilizations model, it's possible to study how the relationships that enabled those "transactions" were channeled through religious and political value systems and enacted via state-built ports and roads. In his trilogy Sources of Social Power, for instance, Michael Mann develops a long-historical analysis of how states and especially empires have for millennia mobilized large-scale projects, serving as motors for interacting political economies, built environments, and cultural-ideological formations from ancient to contemporary periods—even as small communities often acted "interstitially."[22] In his work on the Arabian Seas in the fifteenth to eighteenth centuries, R. J. Barendse also emphasizes interaction, noting that the Mughal and Safavid Empires were not only "comparable but . . . causally linked in myriad ways. Not merely did they both participate in a common Indo-Persian culture, but their economies were intertwined, both through overland routes and through the Arabian seas."[23] Ferdinand Coronil likewise observes that Spain built its structures on those of Aztec and Incan empires, which had "subjected and integrated large regions and populations" and "provided persisting structures of rule."[24] Coronil also concludes that "capitalism and imperialism are coeval processes that mutually condition each other" and points out that capitalism's "origins lie not in one region but between regions in the processes that formed them," although he focuses only on post-1500 periods.[25]

It's important to be clear: this historiography's emphasis on earlier systems as formative for later systems does not exclude the fact of ruptures and significant systemic transformations. Indeed, part of Abu-Lughod's argument, seconded by later scholars, is that the eighth-century growth of Islamicate states caused a major shift in Afro-Eurasian systems, and she likewise proposes that the bubonic plague caused a widespread crash in the system, destroying key nodes of trade and encouraging the Ming dynasty to adopt a more isolationist posture. This crash in turn affected trade and political economies across hemispheres, giving fresh openings to nondominant states, including some in northwestern Europe. Both accretions and volatile transformations in an increasingly interconnected field of states and systems affected the emergence of patterned practices.[26] The terms *modernity*, *premodern*, and *modern* neither correlate accurately with the key transhemispheric shifts nor describe their nature with any precision. The same is true, as noted, with the terms *precolonial*, *colonial*, and *postcolonial*. I have not set out to find substitutes but only to highlight the pertinent data and the ongoing processes. In the next section, I focus on the vectored dialectical processes of anti-imperial and inter-imperial contestation that have created both ruptures and accretions, before analyzing the coformations of economies and states in the subsequent section.

Riptide Dialectics: Contestation and State Formation

Inter-imperial and anti-imperial maneuverings have a long history. Since ancient eras, multiple empires have vied for dominance and in the process have shaped each other while also provoking resistance that has further shaped them. Martin Wight's 1977 book, *Systems of States*, establishes these dynamics from ancient to contemporary periods, including, for instance, among states in the fourth century BC. Although Wight's Eurocentric orientation weakens his analysis, his discussion of ancient periods, by contrast, highlights exactly the multidimensional dynamics of intervention and dissent he later dismisses.[27] He notices, for example, that the revolt by the satrap of Lydia against the Persian Achaemenid Empire ultimately directed the outcome of the war between Sparta and Athens. For when Athens decided to support the rebellious satrap, the Persian emperor threw his economic and military support behind Sparta, the rival of Athens.[28] If, as Wight argues, "it was the combination of Persia and Sparta that defeated Athens," then this Lydian revolt determined the outcome of one of the most famous and consequential of wars in ancient history.[29]

Scholars are increasingly crafting multivectored models to capture these complexities. Commenting on both early American and Afro-Eurasian systems, Mann was among the first to observe that in ancient periods decentralized states or groups living at the edges of established empires eventually exploited the size and "institutional rigidity" of those empires, and then "emerge[d] interstitially," often establishing more flexible kinds of "power organizations."[30] T. J. Barfield has studied the formation of "shadow empires" along nomadic frontiers in pre-1500 centuries, including the striking case of the Chinese Song dynasty, overthrown by the clans of Mongol horsemen that the empire had originally hired as guards.[31] In short, these histories point to an ancient historical pattern in which states arise from bordering communities and contestations that serve as "catalysts of systemic change."[32] These interventions and transformations partly constitute what I'm calling inter-imperial dynamics.

While empires have often dominated the dynamics, conquered and minority communities within states (both elite and laboring) have also maneuvered in ways that affected state transformation, which reveals the centrality of dissent in this field of relations. On one side, empires have fomented minority dissent in other empires for their own geopolitical ends, often under the pretense of protecting or liberating those communities. That is, one of their key strategies has been to manipulate the discontent and aspirations of minority and disenfranchised communities in order to check, destabilize, or collapse their rivals, as was the case in Russia's sponsorship of client communities in the Polish and Swedish empires in the eighteenth century.[33] Likewise, in their eighteenth- and nineteenth-century Atlantic-world contests, the British, French, and Spanish Empires each fostered insurgency in the others' empires, including among Indian tribes, enslaved communities, and American and Caribbean political radicals. Later, US imperial and neocolonial policy in many parts of the world, notoriously in the cases of Cuba and the Philippines, similarly supported independence fighters' efforts to oust the reigning empire, yet afterward the United States jailed revolutionaries, dominated finance and trade, and reinforced the subordinate, racialized status of many laborers and women. As later chapters detail, this inter-imperial strategy is widespread and long lived—as is still apparent in the present.

At the same time, as these examples suggest, colonized or disenfranchised communities have in their turn manipulated these inter-imperial rivalries, courting and gaining support or weapons from one empire for their rebellions against "their own" empire. Haitian revolutionaries courted British support for their struggle against France, while in the same period the Irish garnered troops and arms from the French for their battles against the British. Such a strategy is always risky, yet it has sometimes worked, as in the struggle for Indian independence. Leaders of India's independence movements living in exile in Japan joined with Indian prisoners of war captured while serving the British in World War II. Together this coalition formed the Indian National Army and also extracted concessions from the British under the threat of alliance between these leaders and the Japanese imperial government—which had its own ambitions in South Asia, as the British understood.[34] In the nineteenth century, the Serbian community in the Ottoman Empire also played the powers against each other, with partial success. In this period, the Austrian-Hapsburg, French, and Russian Empires were working together to destabilize the Ottoman Empire while simultaneously competing against one another. Well aware of this situation, Serbian leaders sometimes exploited the contests among them, culling support for their independence struggles from whichever states they could. In return for Russian support they promised Russia the use of Serbian troops, and they simultaneously promised the French and the Austrian-Hapsburgs that an independent Serbian state formed with their support would stand as a buffer against Russian invasion.[35] The Serbian leaders played their inter-imperial cards well enough to win near independence in 1817, becoming a protectorate of Russia as agreed in negotiations between the Ottomans and Russians.

Such patterns have several implications for global political history. First, they establish that while colonized communities have suffered as pawns of competing empires they have also learned to leverage that interpositionality, sometimes successfully, to win a measure of independence and at times to mount a revolution and found a new state. In other words, practices of dissent have been strategically designed for maneuvering within an inter-imperial field, and governance in new states is also to some extent guided by this knowledge (as in postcolonial states' embrace of "third-world" neutrality).

By the same token, however, as postcolonial history also shows, the states that emerge from revolution are not phoenixes arising from the ashes. The old embers keep burning, and they are the embers of inter-imperial energies that may be rekindled by diverse conquered communities, often mingling with still-combustible elements of yet earlier state histories. These sublated elements and divisions can light fires within the state, sometimes sparking further revolutions. Because conquered or minoritized communities are directly affected by these subsisting resentments and attachments, they have sometimes played pivotal roles in revolutions. (Women have also been important, though not always by choice.) Two quite different cases—from early Islamicate empires and from the Russian Empire—can serve as examples of how coerced coformations also underlie destabilizations, with lasting effects for world history.

In the seventh century CE (first to second century AH), the Umayyad Caliphate warred with and ultimately conquered the vast neo-Persian Sassanian Empire. Thereafter, leading Sassanian families converted to Islam and became key players in the Umayyad state, much prized for their economic networks and wealth and their expertise in governance, including intellectual institution building.[36] Among these converted Persianate elites was the highly educated, powerful merchant family of the Barmakids.[37] Yet while serving the Umayyads, the Barmakids also formed alliances with the Abbasid family, which harbored designs on the caliphate. The Barmakids provided not only merchant inroads in trade for the Abbasids but also linked them to discontented Persianate communities in Khurasan, where resentment brewed against Umayyad Arabization programs and other forms of disempowerment. Most particularly these relations enabled the Abbasid connections with Abu Muslim, a man descended from a Persian slave woman, who became one of the most formidable military leaders of the revolution. Through this range of alliances, in 750 CE (132 AH), the Abbasids successfully overthrew the Umayyads, eventually transforming the state into a sophisticated hegemonic empire across a vast territory, until 1258 CE when it was defeated by the Mongols.[38]

In short, because the formation of the Umayyad state entailed the incorporation of diverse conquered Persianate communities, elite and nonelite, and of enslaved peoples who often themselves hailed from other regions, it created conditions for alliance and resistance, including between these communities and factions within the Muslim elite. These conditions were the lever for the Umayyad downfall and the Abbasid rise.

In this case, the transformations have had long-term dialectical effects for world history. Survivors among the overthrown Umayyads fled to North Africa and eventually southern Spain, where they formed a rival caliphate and took power over Mediterranean Catholic states. They did so largely by installing their specific forms of state formation, knowledge, technology, trade practice, and marriage practice, thus leading to further coformations. Among other pivotal matters, as I'll discuss later, the Umayyads' libraries and scholarly communities in these regions attracted European princes, scholars, and artists and ignited the rise of scholasticism, translation, and humanism in Europe, helping to generate the so-called Anglo-European Renaissance.

This turn of events also illustrates one way that gender has shaped the inter-imperial field of relations and in turn world politics, for the forced travels of enslaved women formed another important channel of this volatile history. One of the most important Umayyad survivors, Abd al-Rahman, chose to flee to North Africa apparently in part to return to the land of his Berber mother, Ra'ha, who had been brought to the Umayyad court as a concubine for the Umayyad prince Mu'awiya ibn Hisham.[39] In other words, in the absence of these gendered practices and this particular lineage, the African and European Mediterranean basin might not have become the center of learning and powerful statehood that it did. Such are the submerged channels by which women's lives have been part and parcel of dialectics: not only through their positions as reproducers and sexual commodities but also as carriers of lineage and diasporic community whose histories shape the choices of state actors. The influences of family, lineage, and gender can thus cut in many directions. Yet clearly, as empires expand or reconstitute themselves, they reproduce androcentric and hegemonic power and simultaneously provoke dissent or destabilization wherever they go.

The presence of diverse conquered communities and captive persons in imperial states has affected imperial formations and world dialectics in a range of other ways, determined partly by their forms of governance. While some empires have aggressively enforced the homogenization of language, laws, and religion, others have found it more effective to rule multiconfessional states, as in the case of the North African Fatimid Empire (909–1171 CE), which, after establishing its rule, won the support of minoritized Jews, Coptic Christians, and Maltese Christians by allowing them to practice their faiths. Later states also developed plural legal codes and "differentiated governance" for different conquered populations, gaining the cooperation of local communities, including elites, religious leaders, and merchants who could support trade and mediate between metropole and principality.[40] Yet even as this tolerance provided strength and stability, such arrangements contained their own disruptive potential.

The Russian Empire provides a case in point. Its "imperial social contract" intentionally enfolded the local customs of conquered and incorporated communities through a "series of regulations and decrees that asserted the particular rights and obligations of whole groups of people, defined by territory, confession, ethnicity, or even work."[41] According to Jane Burbank, such deals with local populations served as "a cheap way to keep the peace," even as the codes also took those communities seriously.[42] Village assemblies were by law required to include one local specialist in Islamic law and one in adat law, together with elders representing the rural communities of the region. Eventually, however, inter-imperial pressures from the nineteenth century to the early twentieth led to destabilizing changes in this Russian imperial formation, which played out as western European empires worked to foment unrest in Russia.

These changes reflected clashing dialectical energies that expressed several kinds of inter-imperial pressure. First, by the later nineteenth century, Russian rulers had begun to lump together all peoples of the peripheries as merely "barbarian," eroding the practice of co-opting elites or of honoring conquered communities with designated rights. Adeeb Khalid attributes this change to "imperial competition with other European powers" for whom "imperial rule over 'uncivilized' peoples was clearly a hallmark of civilization."[43] At the same time, this turn away from locally designated rights also reflected the pressure from Russian reformers inspired by nationalist and democratic movements, who urged the state to adopt "universal regulations."[44] These movements found expression in the provisional government of the 1917 Russian Revolution, which abolished the township courts and required that the members of the new township zemstvo have a secondary education. Although the zemstvo elections were democratic, many peasants saw them as "disenfranchisement" and chose not to participate.[45] These forms of dissent and the eventual state repression of them were among the processes that fed the violence of the Russian Revolution and the turn toward "management" of peasant communities in the Stalinist state. As here, the "modernizing" state often refuses to acknowledge the structural and affective depth, the community-shaping life of its people, moving that state toward repression and violence as its main instrument of rule.

As suggested by the cases of Abu Muslim as well as Abd al-Rahman and his mother Ra'ha, marriage practices and laws deserve a new wave of attention within these inter-imperial and diasporic histories. Several generations of scholars have analyzed "nationalisms and sexualities," and feminist empire studies have shed particular light on the relations of colonizing men with colonized women, tracing implications for state formation.[46] Until recently, however, much of this work focused only on western European empires and recent centuries. Fortunately in the past decade or so, feminist scholars have forged rich archival studies of specific periods, locations, and non-European empires. These include scholarship that finally treats female rulers as more than an oddity and also unearths the lesbian lives and circles in early Islam.[47] Particularly pertinent for this book are studies that trace how imperial legal codes have shaped women's situations and how women have leveraged and maneuvered in these systems, as in Leslie Pierce's important study, *Morality Tales: Law and Gender in the Ottoman Court of Aintab*. In light of the latter kind of non-Eurocentric feminist historiography, Indrani Chatterjee argues that attention to "long-lived imperial formations" and "the medieval record . . . hold the keys for furthering the debate within feminist scholarship." Chatterjee specifically calls for more research on "women and Islamic laws in Eurasian and African pasts," which would take account of how "already shared concepts from a composite [Islamic] legal-ethical universe" shaped women's lives across regions and empires. And more broadly, she suggests that this work may yield "a more expansive and capacious concept of selfhood" than exists within mainstream European thought, which "may in turn productively adjust our contemporary practices of scholarship."[48] In this book I hope to cultivate the possibilities that Chatterjee outlines.

Yet there is much work to do, not least because in global studies and in the historiography of empires, gender is still rarely studied as a structural element of state formation, much less of revolutionary transformation, as Antoinette Burton and Louise Yelin have pointed out.[49] Some of the recent work on conquered elites lays promising ground for future feminist studies, but often the feminist aspects remain underdeveloped. The recent collection *Cosmopolitanism and Empire* is typical. Some essays helpfully note that, since ancient periods, marriage has been a tactic for ameliorating and integrating conquered elites; yet most of the authors quickly skip past the pattern, commenting on it briefly from the perspective of the "architects and administrators of empire" who sought simultaneously "to overcome difference and to derive strength from diversity and multiplicity."[50] Although there is mention of "ethno-elite" groups and of "mixed marriages," both the structural role of these gendered elements and the implications for history and women's conditions, then and now, are only glancingly considered.[51]

Yaqing Qin's book *A Relational Theory of World Politics* exemplifies a more severe version of the problem—the problem of viewing history and gender relations from above and only through the androcentric eyes of the state. Despite its talk of relationality, the book quietly underwrites the state's coercive relations with both women and minority populations. Guided by a spurious principle of "relational management," Yaqing Qin notes that "In dynastic China, [the practice of] marrying daughters of the Han imperial family to rulers of minority nationalities was an important policy for pacifying such groups and maintaining good relations with them."[52] From whose point of view these relations are good? Yaqing Qin's cooptation of feminist relational vocabularies for statist, masculinist ends would be of less concern if it had not so easily seduced the well-known IR scholars who endorse the book, calling it "a landmark in the creation of a truly global discipline of IR" and a "path-breaking catalyst for moving the field of IR beyond its traditional Western-centric concepts."[53] The value of the book is that it exposes the instrumental importance of state control over women's marriage and bodies, both to "manage" minority dissent and to engineer stratifications in the state. Inadvertently, the glowing endorsements establish the need to reorient IR and political science scholarship. Taking literary history seriously as one source of other perspectives would be one step in the right direction, for as we will see in later chapters literature has often told the fuller relational and structural tale.

For now we can see that an inter-imperial framework informed by recent world historiography can tease out the less-studied intersecting forces of gender and political economy that affect co-constituted state building and transformation. In other words, this approach provides a fuller understanding of what Marx spelled out in searingly clear terms: that history is fundamentally shaped by dialectical power struggles.

Merchants, States, and Labor

A long-historical, inter-imperial analysis of relations between trade and states promises to unveil yet other aspects of these struggles. Certainly it exposes the extent to which state building, infrastructure building, and profit making through long-distance trade and labor arrangements have been co-produced by merchants and states, beginning before the rise of Europe and persisting today. It thereby clarifies the genesis of the neocolonial financial systems of the twentieth and twenty-first centuries, as I suggest here and develop in later chapters. Although jealousies, jockeying, and subterfuge were probably as endemic to state-merchant relations in earlier periods as they are now (as suggested by the Barmakid-Abbasid relation), even a rocky marriage, so to speak, can produce children and have long-term dialectical effects.

Here I specify the begrudging but mutual accommodations of states and merchants. First, as we've glimpsed, in some cases in earlier periods, merchants operated in tandem with states or within organized structures codified or decreed by empires (if not always strictly enforceable by them) and whose rules the merchants violated at their own risk. They were seldom autonomous agents whose "activity ignored the frontiers of empires," as Braudel once suggested.[54] The rules included codes for place of habitation and trade within the port city, length of stay, unloading procedures, bills of sale or lending, and tax or tribute for the imperial host. Yet merchants benefited from the fact that rulers put taxes to use not only in palace building but also (contrary to stereotypes) in infrastructure building, shipbuilding, animal training, and labor capturing, all of which served the goals of merchants while also serving the state's military campaigns and political ambitions. Beaujard remarks that, generally, "Capitalist networks could hardly do without the state because they require[d] a stable world to develop their operations and/or a military force to defend their access to vital resources."[55] In addition, state infrastructure building enabled merchant travel, and the capture and training of "beasts of burden" (humans, elephants, horses, and others) served their transport needs.

Merchant trade in turn provided benefits to empires, from the goods, travels, and transactions that could be taxed to the exotic merchandise that could be donned or displayed, projecting the empire's reach. Merchants also provided services to elites, such as tax collection or conversion of goods into money for state projects and trade.[56] Many states benefited from ties with merchant families, including the dynasties of the Song, the Mongol, and the Qing, as did the Abbasids in the case of the Barmakids. Despite its reputation for war, the Mongol dynasty "placed a high value on trade and diplomacy, and their states offered special protection to merchants and other travelers," with the result that the silk roads were strengthened and extended under the Mongols—bringing Marco Polo safely to the center of their empire. During their reign, furthermore, there was a wave of "hemispheric integration" reaching from sub-Saharan Africa to northern China.[57] Finally, insofar as merchant families sometimes acted as agents of the state, those states calibrated their relations with each other partly through such agents.

In this sense, even as merchant families developed relations with "their" particular state, they were connected to others and thus were inter-imperially positioned, profitably if also precariously (as we will see dramatized in *The Thousand and One Nights*).

Again, the Abbasid Empire particularly consolidated the linking of state and merchant practices, as Abu-Lughod showed and others have since confirmed. The Abbasids put in place "the legal and institutional prerequisites for financing and administering 'capitalist' production and exchange," including through the creation of banks and of instruments for mercantile credit and lending contracts.[58] Among these were the *suftaja* (similar to modern checks) and the *commenda* agreements later emulated by Italians. The latter was a form of investment capital contract securing promissory transfer of capital from one party to another for purchase of raw materials and production of goods, with profits to be shared by both parties. In addition, under the Abbasids, military men and others were paid in wages— another element often considered a later, distinctive feature of "modern" economy. This money circulation across the empire also positioned Baghdad as a financial center for a transhemispheric system.[59]

With these features in mind, scholars have suggested that the Abbasids together with the Barmakids (and, we might add, once-enslaved leaders) in effect mounted a "bourgeois revolution."[60] As I'll shortly discuss, this overthrow thereafter influenced other formations elsewhere. The evidence challenges the stereotypical picture of earlier states ruled by kings whose despotism or decadence inhibited capital accumulation and states' economic planning. It likewise seems to call for adjustment in the reigning assumption that Europeans forged the first systemic relation of states and capitalist production.[61] Yet whether these formations are called capitalist or bourgeois is less important for this study than the evidence that merchant-state relations have fostered empire building both within an empire and across the field of empires.

This co-constituted and competitive state building of course required many kinds of labor, including systematized regimes and reproductive and child-raising labor. Large-scale coordinated labor regimes served the mining of metals as well as the infrastructural projects of land clearing, irrigation, and road building undertaken by imperial states in Asia, the Middle East, Africa, and the Americas. The Incas, for instance, conscripted local villagers to serve as laborers in their road-building and other projects, while requiring them also to supply food for the emperor and his forces.[62] The "gravitational pull" that these prosperous states exerted on "intercommunicating zones" also brought populations to metropoles and trading nodes, ranging from conquered elites and small traders to captive laborers, refugees, exiles, and adventurers.[63] The millions of slaves captured in wars and sold in markets throughout Europe, Asia, and Africa performed a range of functions. These included hard labor on agricultural and construction projects, as in the case of the teams who performed the body-bruising work of scraping salt from the flood plains of the Euphrates in preparation for the planting of sugarcane under the Abbasids.[64] Whether by carrot or stick and from ancient periods to the present, the pursuit of wealth and power by competing states and merchants carried workers away from kin and communities who needed their labor, clustering them instead in strategic and labor-intensive imperial territories, at least in certain seasons. These relocations themselves generated further dialectical effects by carrying knowledge, languages, arts, and cultural practices across regions, seas, and continents.[65]

Countering standard assumptions, this evidence establishes that large-scale state projects and regimented labor practices that are often deemed European and "modern" actually have a much longer history. These, too, deserve critique from Marxist, postcolonial, indigenous, and intersectional scholars, and by the same token the typical narratives of these critical schools of thought need rethinking in this light. In eighth-century China, some seven thousand workers were relocated to serve in the mining and forging industries, producing a capacity equivalent to 70 percent of what the British produced in the early eighteenth century.[66] The laborers in these metal industries minted coins and forged agricultural tools and weaponry—including, by the thirteenth and fourteenth centuries, guns and cannons—for the empire's financial, military, and labor-sustenance programs. Our narratives about labor histories and migrations widen further when we consider that trade often involved staples as well as luxury goods, contrary to earlier historiographic assumptions. Agricultural products and raw materials in general "were part of trade networks from the very beginnings of the [Afro-Eurasian] system," including grains, oils, tar, wood, dairy products, and herbal medicines in all hemispheres.[67] This trade required many hundreds of porters, guards, sailors, cooks, and animal caretakers.

Women, too, traveled these circuits, affecting interstate relations and serving in a range of ways. Elite and nonelite Mongol women commonly traveled with Mongol troops, as Anne F. Broadbridge shows, operating regularly as organizers of the camps, while also sometimes serving as advisors and in some cases participating in battle.[68] Many captured and enslaved women meanwhile were carried to metropoles and peripheries, where they could be forced to do menial labor or displayed as symbols of prowess for elite men and rulers; they also served to nurse and reproduce communities in every sense, including the reproduction of identity hierarchies through marriage or concubinage.[69]

In the repeating, tragic side of dialectical history, these many kinds of system-supporting labor enabled the further control of laborers themselves. As the next sections detail, all these dynamics formed together with a human-built material world and with the institutions of governance and culture that determined their meanings.

Infrastructures: Coproduction, Accretion, and Sublation

The habitats and technologies of the built world have, after all, been among the primary stakes of inter-imperial conflicts and anti-imperial struggles—these and the laborers, scientists, engineers, artists, and managers who have designed and operated them. Over millennia, empires have not only built infrastructures but also conquered in order to seize control of the infrastructures built by others. The Incas did so in the fifteenth century with the roads and drainage systems of the Chimor Empire; the Japanese did so after the 1904–5 Russo-Japanese War that gave them control of the new railways built in Manchuria by Russians. As they have expanded, empires and their willing or coerced agents have installed infrastructures across ever larger distances, managing relations with faster, more cost-effective modes of transport and communication.[70] Rulers have required infrastructural control to conquer, and they have been lured to conquer by the promise of infrastructural control.

In their pursuit of monopoly over technological and engineering resources, empires have also precipitated diverse coformations by forcibly "resettling" peoples. The northern coast of what is now Peru had become the center of metallurgical craftsmanship in the American hemisphere during the height of the Moche civilization (100–400 CE). Yet when the Incas conquered the region and made the inland city of Cuzco their imperial center, they forcibly moved Moche peoples from the coast to Cuzco, redirecting their skills and technological knowledge. Moche artisans crafted exquisite ornamental and symbolic objects for elites, as well as copper tools such as needles and mass-produced goods for the less elite.[71] The Incas also resettled populations for other harsher physical forms of labor, such as cultivating cocoa and repairing roads, in the process creating laboring classes referred to in Quechua as *mitmaqkuna* (or *mitimaes*).[72] In Southeast Asia, wars served in part to enable the resettling of skilled laborers, as in the interkingdom conquering of Burma and Thailand in the eighteenth and nineteenth centuries (which also deserve study within the larger inter-imperial surround). These wars were motivated in part by the desire to capture skilled laborers—ranging from engineers, temple architects, and elephant veterinarians to silk weavers, instrument makers, and performers—who were then relocated and conscripted to work for the state.[73] While peoples encountered each other and transformed each other's cultures and skills, states incorporated and instrumentalized these.

Such sublations of peoples' past practices have issued in the dissemination and retooling of what have been called "resource portfolios" and "technological complexes" across hemispheres and centuries.[74] The history of agricultural and water management technologies provides an important case, especially insofar as it sheds fresh light on the longue-durée, cause-effect sequences that eventually shaped Anglo-European colonization of the Americas. This sequence ultimately involves the convergence of ancient Mesopotamian and pre-Columbian Mesoamerican agricultural technologies. One important early phase in Eurasia begins when ancient Asian and Mesopotamian states undertook "macro-level hydraulic engineering projects," including in the Mesopotamian case the creation of five major transverse canals that served to divert and connect rivers, promoting population growth and thereby increasing labor resources.[75] Later, as ancient Persian dynasties expanded, they supplemented these with filtration and irrigation systems, such as the qanat (gravity-flow tunnels used for irrigation of arid lands), which by the sixth century BCE reached across one thousand miles of the Iranian plateau, from Iraq to Afghanistan. The Persian Sassanid Empire updated these systems several centuries later, and in the seventh century, the Umayyad state inherited them when they conquered the Sassanids.[76] Abbasid caliphs further extended and refined them as they expanded their empire.[77] Although scholars have recently modified Andrew Watson's claim that it was above all the Abbasid renewal and diffusion of these systems that led to a wholesale "green revolution" in this region, the Abbasid restoration of standing systems nonetheless served as one basis for the increase in food production and populations, and the revival of large cities in the empire.[78] That is, the Abbasid Caliphate consolidated its imperial metropolitan power while increasing its agricultural output and labor force by building on the technological knowledge of a conquered Persian Empire (some of whose scientists worked for them), as well as on the partial ruins of much earlier empires. Such is the tale of infrastructural inter-imperiality.

The inter-imperial conquering that had first extended these water technologies also propelled them westward. As Burke traces, elements of "the hydraulic package assembled under Islam" were borrowed in Venice and then in the Low Countries, including in Dutch dykes and Rhineland dams.[79] In the Low Countries, adaptations of these technologies fostered the important medieval Flemish markets and textile trade, which some scholars have considered central to the rise of capitalism. At the same time, knowledge of water systems such as the qanat arrived in Andalusian Spain via the Umayyads, and this knowledge was then carried to the Americas. There, the Spanish also encountered the water engineering marvels created in the Andes over successive empires, including drainage and irrigation techniques for terraced farming in the steep Andean mountains.[80] Combining these technologies, while conscripting indigenous and African laborers and gaining an edge in the global economy by the mining of South American silver and gold, the states of Portugal and Spain managed to insert themselves into Afro-Eurasian economies. Their successes then drew envy and competition from other western European states, intensifying the infrastructural and expansionist projects of all imperial contenders. In a classic dialectical return, Anglo-European wealth and power eventually undercut the preeminence of those states of the Global East and South that had made the European emergence possible. And so it goes, as Kurt Vonnegut would say.

At every turn of course the interpenetrating dynamics of American and Afro-Eurasian inter-imperial world systems drove forward the engineering projects that have installed deeply unequal material conditions. In this light we can see that what Kenneth Pomeranz calls the "great divergence" of the later eighteenth century, when western Europe began to gain trans-hemispheric dominance, was also a great *convergence*—a politically propelled convergence of several systems.[81] European emulation of non-European systems fueled the dialectical motor, with both centralizing and destabilizing results, and ultimately with disastrous results for many laborers and for the earth itself. Today, it seems less important, as well as less accurate, to think about "modernity" as a period and more important to investigate the long-accruing micro- and macroprocesses of systemization as they have moved along pressured, multivectored political paths.[82]

This long perspective supplements the insights of Pierre Bourdieu about how the built environment of cities and infrastructures materializes stratifications and segregates bodies, further reinforced in cultural discourses and affecting physical routines and social aspirations. Because durable instruments and systems (plumbing, cities, walls, media technologies) are installed in one region or city neighborhood rather than another, built by some but benefiting others, these infrastructural systems also become long-historical forces, perpetuating material inequalities, including through the stratification of labor-linked identities. They perform what Michael Mann has so aptly called the "track-laying" work that directs future sociopolitical dynamics, inhibiting access to sustainable life for some groups while enabling it for other groups. In the latest, twenty-first-century wave of indigenous resistance to states, organizers are demanding recognition of exactly this long history, as noted in the introduction. At the same time, as archeologist Vernon Scarborough suggests, "the relationship between infrastructure and its ritualized sanctioning" in ancient states can clarify the imbrications of state and culture that persist today while also providing "resiliency lessons" for current environmental crises.[83]

These accretions and dynamics also explain the double systemic effects of homogenization and destabilization, potentially yielding insights about historical and economic cycles.[84] On the one hand, the enduring, accruing power of centralizing systems perpetuates the stratified field of relations, organized via ethnicity, gender, language, and religion and reinforced in discourses and knowledge institutions. Yet on the other hand, these cumulative, centralizing effects cut both ways, for widely adopted systems increase the possibility that "uncredentialed" actors will seize hold of the tools. Laborers have sometimes literally seized the oppressors' tools, as in mutinies on ships, or slave and peasant communities' use of agricultural tools as weapons against masters. And sometimes, as discussed above, revolutionaries have gotten hold of arms by playing one empire against another. Moreover, the dialectical effects of forced labor migrations remain unpredictable and potentially destabilizing for empires, as relocated laborers transform their arts, knowledge, and techniques under new conditions. These effects are well documented in the case of African arts and agriculture in the Americas, and likewise, for the originally captive populations from Burma, Laos, and Malaysia who thereafter shaped the musical and theater history of "Thai" culture from top to bottom.[85] Although their styles and skills were appropriated by elites, the "Thai" artists thereafter slyly intervened by creating satiric forms that commented on both the hybridity and the conquering backstory of their music. We might call these effects "the return of the sublated."

The record of these complex, interpenetrating movements of peoples and practices calls for adjustments in studies of world economy. This longer horizonal perspective can more fully establish what Braudel called the "different conjunctural rhythms affecting the economy, political life, demography and indeed collective attitudes" of societies, including "the different schools of art or literature."[86] Furthermore it reveals that the movement across frontiers would often have been experienced not as extraimperial but as inter-imperial.[87] As I discuss next, the longer view opens new angles for understanding how these conjunctural rhythms are co-constituted with cultural forms and institutions.

Institutions: Print, Translation, and Contestation

As I hope is by now clear, when we track the ways that anti- and inter-imperial actors engage with unequal infrastructural legacies, how they transform them despite uneven distribution, we give a proper place to the microphysics of dissenting bodies within the macrophysics of state formation and historical change. Arts, media, and intellectual institutions have been pivotal in these processes. Technologies and institutions of literacy, in particular, have been a key dialectical matrix of economy, empire, and culture over the last thousand years.

Paper matters in this story. It matters for economy. It matters for state building through literate bureaucracy. And it matters for the dialectics of decolonial transformation insofar as contestations have played out through print, including today's virtual forms of print culture. By the first millennium CE, a range of polities had of course developed nonpaper forms of record keeping that combined financial-numerical and cultural-aesthetic practices, through which they developed trade and science, projected their status, and exercised control. These included Egyptian papyrus, North American wampum, the Incas' knotted ropes for measuring, the Maya's extensive writing and mathematical inscriptions on fig tree bark scrolls, and European parchment and vellum. Yet paper's combined qualities of durability, transportability, and synthetic reproducibility quickly made it a favored technology. These features enabled the faster, cheaper creation of money and in turn the paying of wages; they consolidated the state control of contracts; and they also allowed more mechanized production of books and the translation projects that were instrumental to empire building. Paper was first manufactured in China in the first century CE, and its reproducibility was enhanced by printing techniques developed in the seventh century.

The production of the first paper money (in China, as far as we know) particularly strengthened the capitalist integuments of the system. Apparently contemporaries understood this, for soon there were champions and theorists of print money, for example the eleventh-century prime minister Wang Anshih (appointed in 1069 under the Song Dynasty of the Chinese Empire), who wrote shrewdly and approvingly of money's capacity to multiply its value as it changed hands through trade.[88] In a sense, paper created all kinds of easily circulated "promissory notes," so to speak, from edicts and *commenda* to illustrated maps and navigation plans, which secured loyalties, contracts, and infrastructural projects. All these paper forms fostered the state's expansion, yet it most importantly launched China's literacy-centered state building. Authorized by the symbolic pairing of ruler and sage, the state privileging of literacy also created a patronage economy for scholars, eventually generating a large-scale civil service corps with state-controlled examinations, as Mark Edward Lewis traces.[89] In short, paper enabled the wide interpellation of populations, the regulated institution building, and the "imagined community" of this expanding empire.

Given paper's state-building power, its manufacture provoked the interest of other expanding states and became a sought-after technology. Most immediately it drew the interest of the Abbasid Empire in the eighth century, which, as it expanded eastward, collided with the westward-expanding Chinese Tang dynasty. In this coadaptive encounter, Islamicate states eventually developed their own forms of paper-based state bureaucracy, cultivating a sophisticated culture of the book and thus increasing the reach of Dar al-Islam as an intellectual, religious, economic, and political force. Like Chinese dynasties, Islamicate states built elaborate religious and civil service bureaucracies; and they initiated a system of schools to teach literacy. That these were sometimes funded by rich merchants further exemplifies the entanglement of state, finance, and culture, as we will see more fully in chapter 2.[90] By the tenth century, the network of Islamicate states reached from Afghanistan to Africa and the Mediterranean, supported by paper, library building, and highly structured forms of literate institutions. Said Arjomand has argued that from the eleventh to the fourteenth centuries, Islamicate schools, known as madrasas, evolved into an "institutional mechanism for the social production of the state"—offering both an avenue for "social mobility" and an instrument for "the reproduction of a subordinate civil society."[91]

Like the engineered systems, these intellectual and institutional infrastructures were co-constituted by vying states, just as states were co-constituted through this appropriation of cultural capital. Empires deliberately borrowed or stole from their neighbors' and rivals' library collections, seeking strategic reasons to understand their science, religion, and arts.[92] To allied empires they sent delegations of scholars who brought and hoped for manuscripts as gifts, and to enemy empires they sent officers with orders to capture and preserve manuscript collections as valuable booty, for instance in Abbasid wars with the Byzantine Empire. Sometimes scholars themselves were "stolen" or forcibly assimilated, as in the case of conquered Sassanian Persian scholars who worked in the Abbasid House of Wisdom. In addition, the state employed teams of scholars who translated manuscripts in support of the state's infrastructural and colonizing projects, including texts in optics, astronomy, and physics as well as religion and literature. Thus the "translation of Persian, Greek, and Indian works into Arabic became a regular state activity" in the Abbasid Empire.[93] These translation projects built on well-established Persian imperial practices, intensely cultivated at the sixth-century Sassanian court of Husraw I (r. 531–79), to which the Abbasids were "a direct heir" through conquering.[94] Likewise, translation of Chinese Buddhist manuscripts served to build an island-wide hegemony for seventh-century Japanese kings.[95]

All these practices were eventually emulated by western Europeans. And they had some catching up to do. By the tenth century, when the largest libraries in Christendom contained a few thousand volumes, Islamicate empires had accrued vast collections. The numbers are worth noting: ten thousand volumes in the tenth-century Baghdad Abbasid library; four hundred thousand in the Andalusian Umayyad library of the caliph al-Hakam (r. 961–76); and half a million in the library of the African Fatimid caliphate of al-Amin.[96] It should be no surprise, therefore, if sixteenth-century Europeans felt "imperial envy," to use Gerald MacLean's witty phrase, toward these other states.[97] It is also no surprise, then, that in 1500 after the Spanish had taken Al-Andalus from Muslim rule, the Inquisitor Cardinal Francisco Giménez de Cisneros first ordered the confiscation of all Muslim-owned Arabic books—and then he sorted them: he had all Qur'āns and religious books publically burned and he ordered that all scientific, medical, and astronomical books in Arabic be preserved and carried to the library of the university he had created in Alacáled Henares.[98]

European efforts to emulate, purge, and compete all at once, as I discuss further in the final section, makes evident that what has been called the "social construction of knowledge" has entailed the charged inter-imperial co-construction of knowledge.

The cultivation of mathematical systems most clearly epitomizes the production of knowledge via coformed states, economies, and cultural institutions—and displays its far-reaching effects for globalizing processes. The dissemination of the decimal system for mathematical computation began with the publication of al-Khwarizmi's ninth-century book, *Calculation of the Hindu Numerals* (ca. 825 CE), in which he elaborated on the Hindu and Arabic numerical systems to describe computational methods using the zero and the notion of place value. His work depended on the inter-imperially generated availability of paper, and it reflected the inter-imperial history of state formation, for al-Khwarizmi was of Persian descent. Most important, translation of his publication into Hebrew and Latin enabled further tightening of inter-imperial systems, for this new computational practice became a transhemispheric mechanism for trade and state accounting, as the Geniza archive in Cairo demonstrates. (For the record, though score keeping is not the point, the Mayan Empire had already worked out the use of zero as a placeholder in the fourth century CE.)[99] Traveling along the circuits of empire and propelled by the imperial rivalries and interpenetrations outlined above, this mathematical innovation helped to create "a single market from Spain [and Africa] to India and China, with a single language of administration (Arabic) and a single monetary system (the trimetallic system of gold dinar, silver dirham, and copper fils)."[100] It thus facilitated the integration of European markets and eventually American markets into an increasingly global world system. Invested in by states, the translation of mathematical thinking thus became one of the continuities that fostered the spread of capitalist practices.

When print enters this picture (in its early forms, also from outside Europe), matters intensify yet again.[101] Most significantly, as print and translation practices spread, they become potent tools in the hands of dissenters who maneuver inter-imperially. This trend becomes very clear by the eighteenth-century era of revolutions, as I discuss in chapter 4, but it had begun to emerge earlier. Take the case of Martin Luther and the Protestant Revolution. Attention to the interactions of print and inter-imperiality in this instance fundamentally revises the Westphalian account of state-formation history, a key referent in most international relations textbooks, which credits Europeans with founding the "modern state" and its principles of sovereignty.[102] Scholars agree that print "played a fundamental role" in Martin Luther's rapid mobilization of the populace against the Roman Catholic Empire, as indicated in the fact that his tract challenging papal authority and corruption (*To the Christian Nobility of the German Nation*) sold four thousand copies in three weeks.[103] Furthermore, translation and print operated together as transforming instruments, as Luther apparently understood, for he eventually published a translation of the Bible in German vernacular, and his tracts were quickly translated into several languages, which enabled a trans-European transformation in popular attitudes toward the Roman Catholic Empire. (The Dutch and English similarly deployed print media to win their independence from the Catholic Empire.)[104]

Martin Luther, furthermore, combined the power of print with shrewd inter-imperial maneuvering, for he published his critiques of the Holy Roman Empire while the Ottoman army marched on Vienna. Knowing that the Roman Catholic Empire depended on Hapsburg military personnel for its campaigns against the Ottomans, Luther openly, in print, refused to endorse military support, since "the Roman Curia is more tyrannical than any Turk."[105] Although he was himself no friend of Muslims, Luther's tactic paved the way for a subsequent pattern of inter-imperial leveraging by Protestants. In fact, later Protestants sometimes gained material support from the Ottomans and more directly aligned with them for trade and diplomacy amid their battles against the Roman Catholic Hapsburg Empire. Such dynamics have led Sean Foley to argue that "Ottoman power drove important political change in Europe," and some analysts have argued that these Ottoman-European relations played a part in the emergence of capitalism.[106]

These coforming changes were intellectual and ideological as well. Protestant writers such as John Milton held up the Ottoman Empire as a proper religious state, insofar as it allowed for liberty of conscience and at the same time "enlarged [its] empire as much by the study of liberal culture as by the force of arms."[107] Indeed, ample evidence suggests that the traditions of the Ottoman Empire and other states inspired many of the "Enlightenment" values often considered to have originated in Europe, including notions of sovereignty, diplomatic practices, and the growth of a "public sphere" cultivated in coffeehouses.[108] Contrary to the Westphalian narrative of state formation and other Eurocentric assumptions, this history displays that the dialectical emergence of paper, translation, and print technologies— together with inter-imperial maneuvering—shaped the structural emergence of European states.

In sum, as we will see is also true in later periods, technologies and infrastructures are inter-imperially generated tools that then become pivotal in the dynamics of revolution and state formation. Cultural institutions and translation projects emerge in tandem with other circulating "tool kits" under these conditions. Such processes are not eccentric to "the formal limits of imperial state building," nor to processes of "modular modeling."[109] Rather, they are, and they deserve study as, part of the primary dialectical processes driving world politics. All communities that are entangled with such formations—whether they are serving, fleeing, or sabotaging empires—affect the "interactive emergence" of material and psychic conditions in a globalizing world. As the next and final section argues, literary and intellectual histories need resituating within these long-historical dynamics.

Linguistic Maneuvers: Literary, Vernacular, and Translated

I began this chapter by noting that the medieval/modern divide has "disappeared" a whole history of political-economic coproductions across hemispheres and periods. It is time to revisit that divide in the realm of literary history. I can only scratch the surface of this task, drawing from recent scholarship to indicate some possibilities for further inter-imperial analysis. I focus on the eleventh through fifteenth centuries to reframe the important changes unfolding in the Mediterranean, many of which catalyzed transformations in European thought and literature as well as in Islamicate states.

In Al-Andalus (encompassing parts of present day Portugal and southern Spain), this period has sometimes been celebrated as the era of Convivencia, a time when Jews, Christians, and Muslims lived together and shared knowledge harmoniously under Muslim rule. Although there is some truth in this account, recent scholarship has exposed its elision or romanticization of the conflicts, instead revisiting the power dynamics. The Mediterranean world did indeed host a "sea of languages" in this period, but their crosscurrents were neither transcendent of politics nor wholly determined by them.[110] Literary languages formed under churning inter-imperial conditions, fed by creative and contesting energies, all at once political, innovative, and unpredictable. Building on new work in medieval studies, I offer provisional, inter-imperial interpretations of these formations, highlighting how they counter standard Eurocentric narratives.[111]

Students of what westerners call the medieval period have long known that Anglo-European scholars learned about ancient Greek philosophy, particularly Aristotle, mainly through Arabic- and Hebrew-language philosophers and translators of the Global Southeast. They have also known that Al-Andalusian "radical Aristotelians" such as Averroes developed rationalist principles and scientific methods. Until the middle of the twentieth century, however, most of the scholarship stopped there, resistant to any claims that might decenter Europe as the origin of rational, modern, and world-changing knowledge. But intrepid scholars have since documented the degree to which European intellectual, literary, and scientific innovations were spurred by contact with the intellectual traditions of the Global South and East.[112]

The Europeans' interest was not merely neutral; it was propelled by competitive energies. As intellectual historian John Harvey remarks, "because of the realization that Christendom lagged behind Islam in the sciences as well as in medicine and natural history," important scholars of the so-called new science, such as Roger Bacon, led the way in the founding of chairs of Arabic at the universities of Latin Christendom, including in Rome, Oxford, Paris, Bologna, and Salamanca.[113] Bacon was among the most explicitly anti-Muslim, strongly oriented toward defense of divine papal authority and inherently shaped by competition over *translatio studii et imperii*. Others were less so. Scholar Daniel Morley deliberately traveled to Al-Andalusian Toledo to read the Arabic texts of the "wisest philosophers," and he returned to England, as he put it, "bringing a precious multitude of books."[114] Among scientists and natural philosophers, scholars who built on Arabic thought and scholarly translations also include Robert of Ketton, who completed the first English translation of the Qur'an, and Adelard of Bath, who translated Euclid's *Elements* from Arabic into Latin. Adelard's influential study, *Quaestiones naturales* (ca. 1120), borrows the Arabic categories of analysis that would thereafter become standard in Europe (e.g., human nature, astronomy, botany, and zoology). Dante's political writing likewise drew on Arabic-Islamicate vocabularies, beginning with such core Averronian concepts as secular justice and the notion that states should be the guardians of rationality and peace.[115]

Similarly in the world of literature, the political-cultural Islamicate presence in the Mediterranean powerfully affected Anglo-European formations. Like Giovanni Boccaccio, Geoffrey Chaucer adapted the Arabic genre of framed, linked travelers' tales, in his case for *The Canterbury Tales*. Chaucer undoubtedly understood the political horizons of such literary developments, for he, too, traveled to the Mediterranean, and not merely as a wandering poet but as a king's agent. On one occasion Chaucer was commissioned to negotiate peace settlements with southern French principalities, and on another he was sent to help establish an English port in Genoa. As more scholars study the several languages and interpenetrations of European and Arabic cultures in this period, Chaucer's late fourteenth-century writing is increasingly understood in this context.[116]

And yet his work was actually a late expression of this literary-political dialectical history. In the eleventh through the thirteenth centuries, a potent set of encounters and inter-imperially shaped coformations were already underway, affecting authors from the Languedoc troubadours to Dante, as a range of scholars has established.[117] Partly as a result of the world-system expansion documented by Abu-Lughod and discussed earlier in this chapter, Christian European authors in the Mediterranean world were becoming familiar with Arabic-language traditions of thought and literature. More particularly, in this era of the Crusades, European princes and nobles traveled east for battle, and some enjoyed long stays at Islamicate courts either as diplomats or politely hosted captives. Christian Europeans were thus exposed to Arabic Muslim arts, learning, and literature as well as to Islamicate statecraft. As we saw earlier in this chapter, European emulation of these states included the adoption of generous patronage of learning and the arts.

The case of troubadour poetry deserves first mention, for its vernacular love lyrics sung by traveling poets have been touted as the European invention of vernacular and demotic literature, for instance by Ezra Pound. More recently this poetry has been deemed the European origin of "modern" world literature by Pascale Casanova.[118] Yet the story changes when we learn that troubadour poetry—famously performed to music—arose in the court of William IX of Aquitaine directly after he resided in the Middle East for several months and after he visited Al-Andalus, places where he would likely have heard Arabic lyric poetry performed to musical accompaniment. Furthermore, on returning home, William IX accorded Arabic music, language, and styles of poetry a place of honor at his court in southern France, and poets of the region began performing lyrics in vernacular Languedoc, including at William IX's court. Although the complex origins of troubadour poetry remain unclear, these were certainly among the contexts in which they emerged. Walter Cohen's important and wide-ranging discussion of the political conditions under which vernaculars enter the mainstream might be combined with an inter-imperial analysis to explore the degree to which troubadour poetry arose from the same interpenetrations that shaped other literary innovations in these centuries.[119]

The turn to the vernacular also had a precedent in the Andalusian Arabic lyric forms, particularly the *muwashshahât*, which is characterized by a final stanza in vernacular Arabic rather than in classical Arabic, although again direct influence is difficult to establish.[120] According to Cynthia Robinson, certain other patterns in Andalusian Arabic love poetry—such as the mingling of sexual and political imagery—also began to appear in European poetry (including troubadour poetry) after Europeans were exposed to this practice in the Islamicate Mediterranean world. Her analysis reveals, moreover, that gender and sexuality operate at the matrix of literary formations as they do in political formations. For Robinson argues that this poetry allegorized the intertwined sexual and political relations of the court, particularly in this Al-Andalusian period referred to as the *taifa* (fragmentation), named for the breakdown of centralized Umayyad caliphal control.[121] As loyalties were increasingly to local princes or elites, she argues, the poetry's intimacy of address and garden setting, together with its themes of betrayal, register the shifting, unstable alliances among Christian, Muslim, and Jewish elites.

As with other transfers and translations across languages, literary innovations and language choices thus emerged within nested inter-imperial force fields, in subtler ways than can be heard within a "clash of civilizations" framework. Such formations deserve study, moreover, not only as an effect of interpenetrations or a tactic in local maneuvers but also as a strategy operating within the larger macropolitical world of vying empires—and thus affecting world history. In Europe, the thirteenth-century Christian and Majorcan scholar Ramon Llull not only translated Arabic texts such as Al-Ghazali's logic, he also had his many texts in Latin translated into vernaculars in order to disseminate them widely, and to win Muslim converts; he met with a number popes and monarchs across Europe to enlist their patronage for his projects.[122] Hayrettin Yücesoy's work on the Samanid state (once part of the Persian Empire) indicates other ways that language had been operating in these inter-imperial fields for centuries. After centuries of the hegemonic enforcement of Arabic across Abbasid territories, the rulers of the peripheral Samanid state chose, as the Abbasid Empire weakened, to resuscitate Persian as a language of state as well as literary production. This maneuver, Yücesoy argues, allowed elites not only to reclaim some of Persian culture's lost ground as a force in the region but also to win internal support from elites educated in Persian.[123] Partly as a result of such histories, arguments about the precedence or interpenetration of Persian and Arabic literary histories can still be controversial today.

The promotion of vernacular Italian by Frederick II in twelfth- and thirteenth-century Sicily epitomizes such inter-imperial language maneuvers, again with effects that continue to echo in today's political atmosphere. In these centuries, Mediterranean states and islands underwent volatile political transition as Norman Christians began to win back kingdoms that had been ruled by Islamic kings for three or more centuries. As Karla Mallette establishes, after Christian Norman kings conquered the Islamicate Emirate of Sicily (902–1061), the Normans retained the Muslim Sicilian governance and legal institutions for more than a century. They also employed Arabic artists and artisans for their ambitious architectural projects, including the reconstruction of mosques into churches—a visual emblem of dialectical interpenetration and coformation. These kings also continued the use of Arabic as well as Greek and Latin as languages of state, and they created a strategic linguistic interpenetration by encouraging the composition of Arabic poetry to praise their kingships.[124] Only with the ascendance of the ambitious Frederick II did these practices change significantly, as Mallette analyzes. At the turn into the thirteenth century, in tandem with his efforts to expand his power on the continent, he initiated less favorable conditions for Muslims on the island and began to demote the poetic status of Arabic.

Frederick II was not simply currying favor with the papacy, however; in fact he regularly challenged the power of the papacy within the Holy Roman Empire and was excommunicated several times. Rather, he was carving out elbow room where he could make his own claim to power. And he succeeded, eventually laying claim to the title of Holy Roman Emperor, which he held for several decades (1220–50). Like many an emperor before him, he instrumentalized language and literature to do so. Frederick knew Latin, Greek, and Arabic as well as Sicilian, Middle High German, and *langues d'oïl*. But instead of aligning his court with any of these, he promoted Italian Sicilian poetry, demoting the status of both Latin and Arabic. If we follow the logic of Yücesoy's analysis of the resuscitation of Persian in the Samanid state, we are led to speculate that, in doing so, Frederick offered local Sicilian Christian authors and elites new access to or precedence in the halls of power. With this one move, he could win local loyalty while also implicitly declaring to the papacy and other European states that he aimed to achieve a version of *translatio imperii* by promoting a new vernacular form of *translatio studii*.[125]

In other words, the volatile inter-imperial conditions of conquering and reconquering in the Mediterranean at this time—including Roman Catholic, Byzantine, and Islamicate states—may explain why these Mediterranean and southern European sites became crucibles for the literary experiments that Europeans later celebrated as native inventions. An inter-imperial account displaces not only the Eurocentrism of these claims but also the underlying logic of Anglo-European histories of "modern" states and literatures. In typical portraits, the brilliant ruler Frederick II garners credit as one of the first "modern" state builders, especially for his creation of a strong centralized bureaucracy and his active patronage of learning and the arts. This historiography overlooks the fact that many of the state institutions for which he is given credit were first put in place by Islamicate rulers, including support for and instrumentalization of the arts and learning. Frederick II is specifically credited with founding the Sicilian school of poetry, known for its use of a Romance language (Sicilian Italian) rather than Latin or Arabic. The poets are in turn enshrined as creators of an utterly new literary practice, since, famously, the Sicilian school gave rise to the sonnet form, fashioned by Petrarch and later adapted by English poets. As with troubadour poetry, Anglo-European critics have claimed that the sonnet went hand in hand with the "birth of the modern mind," expressing a newly "interiorized" and "modern" European subjectivity.[126] Yet the longer, wider, and intertwined history of states and literary form recasts this picture, and it productively raises a whole host of new questions about literature as a force in world politics.

The Eurocentric elision of these histories further illustrates the point with which this chapter began: imperialist narratives of the world rest on the denial of a interdependence. To reconstruct the fuller inter-imperial field of relations is to expose the layered collusions and contests within which communities have navigated and in turn to perceive the intertwining of culture with political economies. In particular, a reformulation of literary-political history in inter-imperial terms clarifies the fraught position of artists and scholars as they have navigated in these turbulent, contested waters. It allows us to see that they have created "world traditions" of thought and art under several sets of watchful imperial eyes. Partly under these pressures Arabic-language scholars promoted a distinction between spiritual and secular realms—and European Christians such as Adelard of Bath followed suit. The long record of exiled, censored, or captive intellectuals registers this pressure. Dante Alighieri's exile and the church's censorship of his work for centuries after his death was itself shaped by the inter-imperial turmoil of the Mediterranean world, a world in which rationalist Averronian ideas about the state and promotion of vernacular writing could signal dissent from the coercive practices of both Latinate and Arabic empires.

The case of the sixteenth-century Muslim scholar al-Hasan al-Wazzan (known to Europe as Leo Africanus) dramatizes another version of writers' inter-imperial importance and also precarity, in part due to their multilingual powers. Born in Granada and educated at the University of al-Qarawiyyin in Morocco, he afterward traveled throughout Africa, the Mediterranean, and the Middle East. In 1518, he was captured by Spanish corsairs and eventually brought to the papal court. Although "welcomed" and eventually given a pension by Pope Leo X in return for translating Arabic texts, al-Wazzan undoubtedly also faced the pressures and dangers of most of the intelligentsia. For translations were of course crucial during this period when the Ottoman Empire threatened further invasion and when Protestants sometimes aligned with the Ottomans to win concessions from the Holy Roman Empire. Eventually managing to depart, al-Wazzan then traveled back to North Africa, where he played a mediating role by writing transculturated histories of the Arab world in Latin. In comparing his translations for Pope Leo X and his later transculturated histories of the Arab world, Natalie Zemon Davis argues that through subtle cues in his signatures and prefaces al-Wazzan addressed different audiences in guardedly coded terms.[127] Al-Hasan al-Wazzan thus further illustrates the ways that authors write strategically from inter-imperial positions.

Of course not all wordsmiths or culture makers live at court or receive formal education and patronage. Artists live anywhere and everywhere, as minstrels, storytellers, painters, drummers, potters, and popular artists of all kinds, sometimes forced to labor on the ships and silk roads of empires. These arts, too, have shaped literature and aesthetics, in ways that are more difficult but not impossible to trace, as evident in recent studies that track the retooling of subaltern arts in cultures around the world.[128] Aesthetic forms have served mediating or dissenting functions at many scales over the longue durée, as I address in the next chapter on *The Thousand and One Nights*. It's important that these literary legacies be neither absorbed complacently into a naive version of world literature nor dismissed as inconsequential superstructures. Rather, these histories beckon critics to study the ways that literatures have continually reshaped the geopolitical economies that catalyzed their creation. In giving proper due to the inter-imperially pressured field of relations, we better grasp the interlocking formations of micropolitics and macropolitics, the complexities of alliance and resistance, and the structural co-constitution of political economy and culture.

Chapter two

Refusing Labor's (Re)production
in *The Thousand and One Nights*

Born amid the dynamics of inter-imperial history, literature also critiques them, holding them up for our notice. Spoken or written, literature has intervened not only by bearing witness to a history of entangled selves and states but also by dramatizing our inherent condition of mutually transforming relationality. It often entangles us in its dramas as participants and witnesses by structural design, while self-reflexively, quietly encoding the writers' own conditions of relation and production. Literature calls on audiences to acknowledge our involvement in these conditions.

Literary genres structured around situations of address, telling, and listening especially foreground this fraught relationality. Theater performances do so most obviously when they include a choral element or a soliloquy that reaches through the so-called fourth wall of the stage, incorporating the audience as participant in the conflict. Breaching the distinction between imagined and real, stage and viewer, this practice also impinges on the safety of the audience zone—where conflict presumably involves others, not ourselves. Other techniques and subgenres differently enfold these dynamics. In poetry, an "ekphrastic" poem, which addresses a work of art such as a painting of a patron or famous ruler, hails that patron into a relationship, and calls on the reader to witness that relation. For the author, this arrangement sometimes encodes the conditions of the poem's production, with purposely ambiguous political implications.

Among narrative forms, it is the "framed tale" that most artfully involves the audience in these stagings of pressured relationality. For it ensconces storyteller and listener in the text itself, mirroring the position of the text's audience. Among framed tales, *The Thousand and One Nights* is by far the most famous and the most widely translated, across states, centuries, and languages. For some scholars, this circulation makes it a preeminent world literature text. For this study, its status as world literature is less important than its worldly interventions, in both the politics of empires and the intersectional conditions of literature's production. When we overlook these elements we misconstrue the existential and political reasons for the text's wide appeal.

I study *The Nights* as a kind of urtext: both exquisite example and historical catalyst of inter-imperial maneuvering through aesthetic forms. Turning from the expansive reach of the last chapter, this chapter tightens its focus to this single text. From its early written versions, *The Nights* self-consciously performs literature's dialectical workings, and the text's Arabic-language compilers, I argue, shrewdly called on us to see it this way. For when we closely consider the relation between the tales and the frame, we find an implicit tale of two empires, Persian Sassanid and Arabic Islamicate, a history mediated by Shahrazad, the Persian vizier's daughter. She not only occupies a position between states but also allies herself with laborers and other women. (My discussion follows Husain Haddawy's translation of character names and place-names.)[1] In telling nightly tales to the emperor under threat of death, with her sister Dinarzad as witness, Shahrazad embodies the embattled positions and the ethical solidarities of those who inhabit a world of empires. Through her interwoven tales and tellers, Shahrazad calls on the emperor to witness the keen demands of relationality, which he implicitly recognizes when he is moved to end his woman killing.

Shahrazad's cunning action has rightly been appreciated by feminist readers as a tale of women's artistry and solidarity. Others have celebrated the tales' carnivalesque, multicultural spirit and magical elements, which seem to offer a parade of diverse peoples moving across borders, with chance encounters among wanderers, merchants, emperors, viziers, djinns, wives, doctors, and slaves—seeming thus to "ignore the frontiers of empires" and the boundaries of ethnicity and status.[2] Recently, historical studies have offered a corrective to the largely European emphasis on the fabulous elements, instead highlighting the tales' realistic details about such things as the contemporaneous merchant economy. Postcolonial scholars have in their turn traced the Orientalisms that shape the text's European afterlives in the wake of Antoine Galland's eighteenth-century translation of a version of the text shared with him by Hanna Diab, as I discuss in chapter 3. My discussion benefits from this diverse body of scholarship.[3]

Yet this chapter's inter-imperial analysis of *The Nights* calls readers back to the frame, which does much more than introduce Shahrazad as story-teller. In presenting a world of ruling brothers and mediating viziers, the frame allegorizes the ways that these men instrumentalize tale-telling, translation, and Aristotelian political theory to enforce the captive conditions of women and laborers, on whom their power depends.

The opening situation of two ruling brothers lays bare the logic of sexual and racial politics at the heart of political economies, as we will see: the logic whereby control of women enables the stratified labor formations and (re)production of states—and the logic in which loss of control over women threatens the state. This backstory also unveils the disavowals that underlie control, as women are blamed for the betrayals of and among competing men. In other legendary stories, as noted in the introduction, women are scorned for "letting in" the conqueror, as with Helen of Troy, La Malinche (the Nahua woman who, legend has it, aligned with Hernán Cortés in the conquest of Mexico), or in the Irish version (as parodied by James Joyce), "MacMurrough's wife," the "faithless" one who "first brought strangers to our shore here."[4] In *The Nights*, it is the royal wives who dance with slaves and servants who cause the destabilization of the state—allowing "entry" from below by laborers who are also racialized. The ruling brothers blame their wives' "infidelity" and "cunning" for the shah's decision to marry a virgin each night and execute her the next morning. Yet as *The Nights* dramatizes and many later texts explore, the problem of betrayal begins with men's competition and their engineering of stratified (re)production. That is, the problem begins with the a priori coercion of intimate relations, which provokes women's subterfuge.

In what follows I first highlight how both frame and tales are inter-imperially situated—shrewdly so—beginning with the earliest extant versions.[5] Emerging as it does from Farsi Persian and Arabic Islamic traditions, the text that is variously called *The Arabian Nights* and *The Thousand and One Nights* is co-constituted within a political field of relations, as the variation in titles already hints. (For this reason I will refer simply to *The Nights*.)[6] Most fundamentally, the Arabic-language version of *The Nights* borrows its frame story from the Persian text, *Hazâr afsâna* (*A Thousand Tales*), while also incorporating some of its stories and emulating the Persian genre of linked tales (which was itself perhaps influenced by the Indian collection *Panchatantra*).[7] Yet many tales are also distinctly Arab and Muslim, and the early extant version has an overall Islamicate cast.

In other words, this complex text has been shaped at its foundations by the convergence of the Arabic Islamicate and the Persian Sassanid Empires discussed in chapter 1. This history of inter-imperial relations adds urgency to the brothers' desire to suppress the transgressions of their wives and laborers. Yet their wife-killing solution provokes a standoff between the "learned" Shahrazad and her vizier-father, who attempts to dissuade her from marrying the shah by telling tales that urge obedience from women. The vizier's tales also feature translation as a tool of control over labor. But the failure of the vizier's effort yields the success of Shahrazad's—issuing in the long dialectical life of *The Thousand and One Nights*, translated and re-imagined throughout the accruing history of competing empires.

Framing Empires

The opening drama of *The Nights* is familiar. Night after night, Shahrazad tells tales to her husband, Shahrayar, the Sassanid Persian emperor, in order to defer his plan to execute her the next morning. Ever since Shahrayar discovered an earlier wife's infidelity, he has vowed to marry a new wife each day, take the wife's virginity that night, and have her executed the next morning, since he believes that women cannot be trusted to remain faithful beyond one night. When the text opens we learn that he has already married and executed the daughters of many princes and army officers and then moved down the social hierarchy until "it became King Shahrayar's custom to take every night the daughter of a merchant or commoner, spend the night with her, and have her put to death the next morning."[8] After many virgins have died, as the frame storyteller of *The Nights* records, "there arose a clamour among the fathers and mothers" of the realm (11). The state is in crisis. And the crisis is sexual.

Enter Shahrazad, a woman of the court, the daughter of the emperor's vizier. Despite her father's remonstrations, she insists on marrying the Emperor Shahrayar, and only by telling stories to him each night does she succeed in deferring his violence—until finally he agrees to spare her life and end the state killing. The people rejoice in their release from the emperor's violence toward its women, and the state's gender crisis abates. Such is the scenario passed down from the Persian text *Hazâr afsâna*, adopted in the Arabic-language text, eventually to become one of the most widely imitated frame stories in literature.

The Arabic-language retention of the Sassanid Persian frame is the first hint of the text's inter-imperial conditions of production. It places us explicitly in "the time of the Sassanid dynasty," a pre-Islamic Persian empire that, as mentioned, ruled territories from the Mediterranean to Central Asia from the third to the seventh centuries. Yet Shahrazad, our seventh-century Persian narrator, also relays tales set in eighth-century Baghdad, featuring, for instance, the eighth-century Islamic Abbasid caliph and emperor Harun al-Rashid. In other words, her stories include historical figures who were born after her own lifespan. The tales are thus embedded in an anachronistic structure, in which the stories of one empire are enveloped within the time frame of a prior conquered empire.[9] Implicitly, this framing structure positions the Persian Shahrazad between and across empires, both spatially and temporally.

At one level, this anachronism simply indicates the many ways that Arabic-language texts of *The Nights* draw on a trove of sources, including not only the Persian *Hazâr afsâna* but pre-Islamic subgenres of advice to kings, animal fables, and ill-fated lovers' tales. In this way it embodies the Islamic Arabic absorption of earlier literary and intellectual traditions that I discussed in chapter 1. Yet these observations do not fully explain why the Arabic texts so explicitly retain the Persian historical frame. As Muhsin al-Musawi demonstrates in detail, the Arabic manuscript versions of the text give it an Islamic character, from inclusion of the morning call to prayer and the weaving in of Islamic poetry and aphorisms, to the aspersions cast on the "Magians" (who suspiciously retained their Persian Zoroastrian religion within Islamic Empire), as well as the appearances of Harun al-Rashid.[10] Given this Muslim transformation of the text, why not change the Persian frame as well? Below I suggest some possible answers to this question, but here it is sufficient simply to note that when readers enter the text we encounter an inter-imperial force field.

The key political fact is that the Persian Sassanid Empire did not simply predate the Islamic states of the Umayyad and Abbasid caliphs and bequeath its literature: it was *conquered by* the Islamic Umayyads, whose state was later taken over by the Abbasids and eventually led by caliph Harun al-Rashid. Persian institutions were absorbed and retooled, including those managed by learned viziers and sometimes their daughters, as I'll discuss later. Thus *The Nights* displays how the Islamicate state that had come to occupy the Persianate state also retroactively occupied the imagined "interior" of the

Sassanid world. The point is not to claim that the text is therefore "really Persian" or "really Islamic," as critics have been tempted to do.[11] To choose one tradition or the other is to repeat the habit of inter-imperial rivalry. Instead we can consider this disjunctive frame-to-tale relation as an expression of its geopolitical conditions of production. When we recall that some members of the Umayyad and the subsequent Abbasid courts descended from originally Persian Sassanid families who had assimilated, including vizier families like Shahrazad's, we have further grounds for exploring how the text gestures toward this political palimpsest.

In the very first sentence of the framing prologue, the narration encourages us to be active listeners and follow its political hints. In a sly interjection it mentions that some things may "lie hidden" in the frame tale: "It is related—but God knows and sees best what lies hidden in the old accounts of bygone peoples and times—that long ago during the time of the Sassanid dynasty, in the peninsulas of India and Indochina, there lived two kings who were brothers" (3). (Although the name "Sassanian" has become more common, here I follow Haddawy's translation.) This immediate contrast between what "is related" and what might "lie hidden" in these "old accounts" invites us to consider the very status of this framing story, including its anachronistic historicism. Might this embedding of an eighth-century Islamicate world inside a seventh-century Persianate world encourage readers to recall the political relation between them?

It seems so, for the retention of the Sassanid frame seems to allow a number of political insinuations, although of course the meanings ultimately depend on the perspectives of the tale-tellers and the audiences. From an Arabic Islamic point of view, the hints of political disorder in the Persian Sassanid Empire (including sexual transgressions and state violence) might have served to justify the original Umayyad Islamic invasion of the Sassanid Empire. The attribution of state disarray or corruption might also reinforce the imputations of negative intrigue associated in the text with the Persian Magians and other religious traditions (perhaps offering a warning to any such believers inhabiting Islamicate states). The retention of the frame may thus serve simultaneously to affiliate the text with the legendary literary prestige of the Persian Sassanid Empire and to display the Islamic state's ascendancy over that formidable legacy.

On the other hand, if we imagine a Persian-aligned storyteller, perhaps this choice to retain the Persian Sassanid imperial frame for a tenth-century or fourteenth-century Arabic version of the tales expresses a covert wish to honor Persia. Or, more strongly, it might hint that the Persian

Sassanid Empire created the *framing* conditions—the very conditions of possibility—for the state-building accomplishments of Islamicate empires. And then there is the third possibility: that this textual yoking of the two empires conveys dissent from empires and inter-imperial coercions per se. For the text's structure quietly allows comparison between the flaws of Persian and Islamic rulers, between the shah of Persia and Harun al-Rashid of the Abbasid Empire, especially as displayed in relations to women, slaves, and viziers. The fact that Harun al-Rashid is a drunkard in some of the later tales (such as in "The Slave-Girl Anis al'Jalis") also suggests this possibility (307).

Moreover, several tales implicitly refer to the lingering friction between descendants of the two empires, including tales that dramatize women's mediating function. For instance, the linked fifty-page sequence of tales about the secret love affair of Nur al-Din Ali ibn-Bakkar and Shams al-Nahar mentions the "blame" that Persianate peoples might harbor toward Muslim rulers. We learn early on that Nur al-Din Ali ibn-Bakkar is "a descendant of the kings of Persia" (296), and he becomes an object of attraction for Shams al-Nahar, the "favorite" concubine of Harun al-Rashid (referred to here as "the Commander of the Faithful" [297]). Before the affair begins, Shams al-Nahar specifically asks about Ali ibn-Bakkar, "Is he Persian?" She seeks out a relationship with him partly to ensure that "he may not blame us and say that there are no generous people in Baghdad" (297).[12] The hint of "blame" directed toward an "us" clearly gestures toward the conflict, as contemporaries would have discerned, especially since, in the thirteenth and fourteenth centuries, Islamicate states were fragmenting while Persian tributary states were renewing their Persian literary-linguistic and political identities.[13] In short, together with the cluster of tales about female concubines (the last several in the Baghdad text), the Shams al-Nahar tale illustrates the ways that women mediate and maneuver between imperial legacies and jealousies—as the storyteller Shahrazad does at a meta-level in telling these tales.

Likewise several tales featuring viziers indicate their fraught mediating and potentially destabilizing in-between positions within a competitive inter-imperial field that encompasses not only Persianate and Islamicate states but also the Byzantine Empire, contemporary of both the Sassanid and Abbasid Empires. In the "Tale of King Yunan and the Sage Duban," when the vizier of the Persian king Yunan attempts to turn the king against the Byzantium sage Duban, he emphasizes that Duban has "come from Byzantium" and is an "enemy who has come to destroy your power and steal your wealth" (40). Yet meanwhile, as Mazen Naous points out, the hybridizing mixture of names in this tale undercuts these neat divisions: Duban, the name of the Byzantium sage in the tale, is also the name of a Persian village, and the Persian king's name is a Hebrew name though written in Arabic.[14]

The tales thus repeatedly undercut or complicate the divisions on which empires stand, positioning both women and "sages" as pivotal actors, sometimes ameliorating, sometimes dissenting. Here again we should pause to consider the question of who authored this originally oral tradition of tale-telling. The encoded hints about women's mediations may take on a more feminist cast in light of the scholarship proposing that women compiled the Sanskrit text of the *Panchatantra*, which influenced *The Nights*.[15] If a woman or women played a part in crafting *The Odyssey*, as Samuel Butler long ago suggested, then perhaps we should remain open to this possibility that women played a role in constructing *The Nights*.[16] Whoever the authors were, they seem to have had a sense of women's in-between position among empires and imperial legacies.

In short, the temporal anachronism of the frame-tale structure of *The Nights* has a political edge. It suggests that Islamicate-Persianate and other inter-imperial relations were on the minds of the storytellers. As I discuss next, the frame also establishes the trope of ruling brothers who face woman trouble, which repeats throughout the tales, hinting that gender relations were inherent to these inter-imperial preoccupations. Just as the combined Persianate frame and Islamicate core of *The Nights* registers the historical conflict between these states, so the opening story of the brothers, who respectively rule the core and the periphery of the Sassanid Empire, indicates that their rule requires control of women and laborers.

Precarity in the State: Brothers, Wives, Laborers

In *The Nights*, the backstory that leads to the emperor Shahrayar's discovery of his first wife's betrayal is laid out in the frame prologue as a tale of two states and two brothers within the Sassanid Empire. The brothers discover that, in their absence, their wives are sleeping with the servants and slaves of the court. This backstory gestures toward the class, race, and gender trouble in the state that is later echoed in several tales of brothers vying for power.[17]

In this light, I propose, we can supplement feminist readings of Shahrazad's inclusion of her younger sister as listener to her tale-telling, seeing more clearly how she sets up sisterhood as antidote to the competitive forms of brotherhood that control the geopolitical field. This reading also lays ground for the analysis in later chapters of anti-imperial writers who carry forward the trope of vying brothers. As we will see, in Charles Maturin's nineteenth-century Gothic novel *Melmoth the Wanderer*, competition among Jesuit "brothers" feeds acrimony among the brothers of wealthy families, which in turn destroys their sisters, all within an antagonistic surround of "Moorish," Protestant, and Catholic empires. A century later in James Joyce's *Ulysses*, Stephen Dedalus reflects ruefully not only on the "nightmare" of inter-imperial history but also on "the brother motive" spurring the violence of those nightmares, destroying both sisters and mothers. Not all anticolonial texts manage to avoid repeating the history of misogyny. Salman Rushdie's *Midnight's Children* exposes the violence spawned by Shiva and Saleem's battle for figurative control of India, yet his narrator casually scapegoats sisters and women in general and underplays their sister Jamila's position as a pawn of vying brothers and states. In counterpoint, women's postcolonial fiction often tells the prior tale of brothers' jealous dominance over sisters, for instance in *The God of Small Things*, Arundhati Roy's story of the destruction of Ammu, which her son and daughter struggle to heal.[18] All these authors allude to *The Nights*, confirming that they have discerned its political and intersectional subtexts.

The story of the "brother motive" opens *The Nights*. After recalling in its first sentence that "long ago, during the time of the Sassanid dynasty, . . . there lived two kings who were brothers," the text sketches the division and hierarchy of power between Shahrayar and his brother Shahzaman (3). The older, Shahrayar, is the emperor: "a towering knight and a daring champion" who "lived and ruled in India and Indochina" and whose "power reached the remotest corners of the land and its people" (an inflated geographical claim that is nonetheless retained in standard translations).[19] He gives "to his brother . . . the land of Samarkand to rule as king" (3). Neutral as this division of power is made to sound, cast as a gesture of generosity on Shahrayar's part, the history and discourse of ruling brothers tells otherwise. History is replete, of course, with wars of succession and jealous betrayals among brothers competing for the role of king or emperor: from the ancient battles between Eteocles and Polynices for Thebes to the Incan battles between Huáscar and Atahualpa in the sixteenth century. Within Persian history, the wars between the emperor Artaxerxes and his brother Cyrus the Younger for the Persian Achaemenid Empire (famously recounted by Xenophon since they also intersected with the Spartan Athenian Wars) would have been well known to the early audiences of *The Nights*, as would the rivalry between Peroz and Hormizd (457–59 CE) for the Persian Sassanid Empire.

Moreover, a political *discourse* of a kingly "brotherhood" has circulated since ancient periods, serving to endorse and euphemize relations both within and between states.[20] In *The Brotherhood of Kings: How International Relations Shaped the Ancient Near East*, Amanda Podany tracks this discourse of brothers as the language of what she calls international relations, although they are more properly called inter-imperial relations, given the expansionist wars. A quick look at one of her examples reveals the double labors of this discourse and sheds light on the "brotherly" frame of *The Nights*. As expressed in cuneiform tablets that preserve letters between kings of Mesopotamia, Babylonia, Syria, and Egypt (ca. 2300 to 1350 BCE), these "great powers" of the Near East increasingly cultivated a language of brotherhood for alliances or arranged marriages as they maneuvered to offset each other's encroachments. Thus does the ancient king of what is now Syria, Tushratta, write in the fourteenth century BCE to the king of Egypt, assuring him that if any "enemy of my brother . . . invade my brother's land, [then] my brother writes to me, and the Hurrian land, armor, arms . . . will be at his disposition"; and likewise he hopes that "if there be for me an enemy . . . I will write to my brother, and my brother will dispatch . . . [from] the land of Egypt, armor, arms."[21] Podany stresses "brotherly" alliances, yet her evidence also establishes the warring field of invasions and unreliable promises that these "brotherly" letters attempt to manage. Indeed this very letter from Tushratta turns out to have been written when the Egyptian king was distancing himself from Tushratta and in fact holding some of Tushratta's messengers in detention for unspecified crimes. The king of Egypt to whom he writes was meanwhile developing an alliance with Suppiluliuma, emperor of the newly powerful and expanding kingdom of Hatti (roughly in the region that is now Turkey). In order to seize and hold the throne without rivals, moreover, Suppiluliuma had already undertaken the assassination of all of his literal brothers, including the rightful successor to the kingship.[22] Thus, in these ancient periods, as in *The Nights*, the "diplomatic" story of brotherhood carries coded subtexts and ambivalent associations, laying ground for the motif of betrayal that, as I note in all chapters, continues to shape the world's dialectical history both factually and discursively.

The story of vying brothers also carries a particular resonance in Abbasid history, linked both to the decline of its imperial power and to sexual-cultural jealousies. For early listeners it would likely have called to mind the battle for succession among the sons of the Abbasid caliph Harun al-Rashid. Although there is debate about exactly what al-Rashid declared in the original 802 Mecca Protocol outlining the principles of his sons' succession, it is agreed that he designated his sons al-Amin and al-Ma'mun as successors to the caliphate in sequence, assigning al-Amin as the first inheritor of the caliphate and al-Ma'mun as governor-prince of Khurasan (later to become caliph at the death of al-Amin).[23] It is also agreed that the rivalry between al-Amin and al-Ma'mun created catastrophic civil war in the empire, which weakened its power and left Baghdad in ruins, as had been predicted by some contemporaries and was remembered by all subsequent generations. (In this context it's also noteworthy that, as Tayeb el-Hibri has shown, early Muslim chroniclers and commentators on the questions of caliphal succession invoked biblical stories of vying brothers, for instance the story of Jacob and Esau.)[24]

Readers might well hear an echo of the protocol in the opening lines of *The Nights*. The protocol decrees that "the Commander of the Faithful has given [al-Ma'mun] Khurasan and its marches and districts to rule over"; and as we saw, *The Nights* opens by reporting that Shahrayar "gave to his brother . . . the land of Samarkand to rule as king" (3). These words would also recall legacies of unrest because Samarkand was located in the western province of Khurasan and the western region of Khurasan was a strategic center of the Abbasid revolt against the Umayyad Caliphate. It was also the source of the Persianate elites in Abbasid Baghdad.[25] Finally, the gendered dimension of Arab/Persian inter-imperial history also lurks here in the different status of the mothers of these two sons, for Amin was famously the son of an Arab woman of the Abbasid clan while Mamun was the son of a Persian concubine. Might this tangled history be another reason to retain the Sassanid frame for the Islamicized tales? Certainly, the opening mention of ruling brothers would have conjured partisan sentiments and memories of war between brothers. This pattern is reinforced later in in the text's several vizier tales featuring vying brothers, for instance, in the "Tale of Two Viziers" (157) told by Harun al-Rashid's vizier Ja'far, as well as in "The Slave Girl and Nur al-Din" (345).

Yet in the frame it also becomes clear that there is one kind of crisis that can supersede the brothers' competition and secure their solidarity with each other: the threat of transgressive women. The structure of the backstory about faithless women lays out the entire political logic.

Just after Shahrayar and Shahzaman are introduced, we learn that Shahrayar invites his younger brother to travel the long distance to pay him a visit—an invitation that would have had the force of a summons. On the eve of Shahzaman's departure from his province in Samarkand, he finds his power flouted. Having gathered with his men outside the city, he seeks out his wife for one final farewell after she thinks him gone and he finds her "lying in the arms of one of the kitchen boys" (4). The latter point is particularly emphasized when Shahzaman expresses outrage that her consort is "some cook, some kitchen boy" (4). This disruption of both gender and labor hierarchies in the provincial periphery ultimately leads to revelations of similar trouble at the imperial center. For the visiting brother soon becomes the means for Shahrayar to discover a similar sexual treachery in his own imperial court.

The dynamics by which these revelations surface signal the unnamed power dynamics in the brothers' ostensibly amicable relations. Although eventually the brothers come together to manage the states' parallel sexual crises, the shadow of envy and rivalry hovers before they cooperate. After killing both his wife and the cook, Shahzaman travels to the emperor Shahrayar, depressed and quiet. Shahzaman forbears to tell the emperor why he is depressed, and Shahrayar forbears to ask him, though we are explicitly told that Shahrayar notices. Why? Perhaps more is involved than the humiliation of a cuckolded husband hiding his shame from his loving brother. For contemporaries, it might have been clear that if there is trouble in the realm of the younger brother—who holds his land as a gift from the emperor, while the emperor in turn depends on his younger brother to maintain stability and hierarchical power in that land—then there is trouble in the empire as a whole, potentially sparking friction between the brothers. This political subtext may explain why the younger brother suddenly becomes happy when he discovers the crisis in his older brother's imperial court; he is at much less risk of facing his brother's wrath since it will be more difficult for the emperor to denigrate him for the very trouble by which the emperor's control has also been challenged.

Indeed, the situation in the shah's palace is worse. His wife doesn't merely have sexual relations with one servant. She hosts a veritable orgy of feasting and pleasure in the emperor's garden "day and night" when he is away, always initiated by a subterfuge of cross-dressing, and she consorts with a man explicitly characterized as a "black slave" (7). Shahzaman witnesses one of these orgies after he has declined the emperor's invitation to go on a hunting expedition with him and instead stays in the palace, unbeknownst to the emperor's wife. Shahzaman gazes unseen from his window when the shah's wife enters the garden, followed, apparently, by "twenty slave-girls, ten white and ten black" (5).[26] Yet ten of these slave women turn out to be men dressed as women, who soon disrobe and "mount the ten girls." Meanwhile the Shah's wife calls out to "Mas'ud," a "black slave" who has been hiding in a garden tree, who promptly "topped the lady" and they all "carried on till noon" (5). This cross-dressing, gender-bending, race- and class-crossing orgy dramatizes the multiply transgressive implications of the wife's actions, including simply a dangerous embrace of sex for mere pleasure by a royal woman conscripted to create proper heirs of the empire. The story might have had particularly strong resonance for some readers, given that a key leader of the Abbasid Revolution was the freed slave Abu Muslim.

After witnessing this scene, Shahzaman becomes "lighthearted and care-free" (6), reflecting, "Even though my brother is king and master of the whole world, he cannot protect what is his, his wife and his concubines, and suffers misfortune in his very home. . . . By God, my misfortune is lighter than that of my brother" (5). The Arabic word used for "home" here and elsewhere is *beit*, a word also associated with the state seat, thus suggesting the larger stakes of the situation, which both brothers quickly grasp.[27] On his return, the emperor Shahrayar notices his brother's improved mood and demands an explanation, but Shahzaman trembles, fearing to explain the truth, and indeed when he finally reveals it, Shahrayar is "furious and his blood boil[s]" (7). After Shahrayar hides out and witnesses for himself "the spectacle of his wife and the slave-girls," he exclaims: "Such doings are going on in my kingdom and in my very palace. . . . This is a great calamity in-deed!" (8). The discovery unsettles the emperor's sense of sovereign power and his commitment to the imperial state. "Greatly amazed at the deceit of women," Shahrayar concludes that "no one is safe in this world" (6, 8). He immediately proposes to his younger brother that they "leave our royal state and roam the world for the love of the Supreme Lord. If we should find one whose misfortune is greater than ours, we shall return. Otherwise, we shall continue to journey though the land, without the need for the trappings of royalty" (8).

In other words, Shahrayar proposes that they give up the state and aban-don the imperial project, which is in ruins, it is implied, without control of the wives, concubines, servants, and slaves. The origin of the wife-killing violence, then, lies in a disruption of control over racialized sexual and labor relations, with import for sovereign control over both core and periphery. Yet the effects are dialectical. Insofar as the emperor's wife killing triggers Shahrazad's intervention, creating the text of *The Nights*, his reaction yields further disruption: it not only prompts her political action, but it also gen-erates female and implicitly subaltern solidarity and a set of tales that, over centuries, have often (though not always) served to expose coercive rela-tions. Thus the murderous cooperation between the two Sassanid brothers representing imperial core and province triggers ongoing and unpredictable effects, importantly channeled, as I will later discuss at more length, through the very institutions and narrative forms cultivated to protect and advise emperors.

Yet before turning to that dimension, we must pause to notice one more lacuna that "lies hidden" here. The misfortune that turns the brothers back from their travels to the "royal trappings" of empire involves a kidnapped woman, captured on her wedding night by a "demon" and kept in a locked casket for years. The text handles the implications ambivalently, however, for as we will see it both registers and elides the prior political conditions that require the wives' perfidy. As told in the frame, when the brothers journey away from the metropole, they come to rest near the sea and suddenly out of the water rises a "black demon, carrying on his head a large glass chest with four steel locks" (8). On shore the demon unlocks the chest, lets out a woman, and promptly takes a nap. The woman espies Shahrayar and Shahzaman and calls them out from their hiding place. She insists against their pleadings that they each make love to her, threatening to wake the demon and have him kill them if they do not. She explains, "This filthy, monstrous cuckold has imprisoned me . . . and tried to keep me pure and chaste, not realizing that nothing can prevent or alter what is predestined and that when a woman desires something, no one can stop her" (9–10). With fear and trembling, the brothers each have sex with her. She then takes their rings and adds them to her collection of the rings of ninety-eight other men with whom she has done the same. Their experience leads the brothers to exclaim, "Great is woman's cunning" (10).

Strangely, in the text's recounting, this woman in effect becomes the rapist and traitor. Apparently the "one whose misfortune is greater than ours" is the demon rather than the woman, as implied when Shahrayar exclaims, "Look at this sorry plight. By God it is worse than ours. This is no less than a demon who has carried a woman away on her wedding night, imprisoned her in a glass chest, locked her up with four locks, and kept her in the middle of the sea, thinking that he could guard her from what God had foreordained" (10). Also striking, their remark echoes verse 28 in the Surah of Yusuf in the Qur'an, which translates roughly as "Surely it is the cunning of you women! Certainly mighty is your cunning!" This echo of a sacred Islamic text in the Persian frame appears at the moment when the men decide to re-embrace their imperial powers, a point to which I'll return. "Brother," continues Shahrayar, "let us go back to our kingdoms and our cities, never to marry a woman again" (10). This passage at once narrates and disavows the imprisonment of women as the original political condition, eliding the implication that the men are responsible for their own plight. On their return, Shahrayar simply announces his decision "to marry for one night only and kill the woman the next morning" (10). Thus "Shahrayar sat on his throne and ordered his vizier . . . to find him a wife" (10).

Perhaps this disavowed feminist political implication in the text is another of those things that "lies hidden in the old accounts of bygone peoples and times." That is, perhaps the invocation of the Qur'anic apostrophe to women's "mighty cunning" invites a double reading insofar as it is juxtaposed against this tale that reveals *why* God "foreordained" women's cunning. Perhaps the text's creators are themselves practicing a narrative cunning.

In any case, the brothers' actions indicate that, for them, the experience of being outmaneuvered by a woman is a lesson in political control—and the need for a more brutal exercise of control in the face of women's unwillingness to be utterly controlled. Certainly a punishing revenge of women follows, for when the brothers return home, the emperor carries out the execution not only of his wife but "every one of his slave-girls" (10). Having concluded that "there is not a single chaste woman anywhere on the entire face of the earth," he then sets forth on his wife killing so as "to *save himself* from the wickedness and cunning of women"—and to counter the threat to his empire (10, emphasis added). Thus, although initially "amazed" by a pitched battle "from below" as wives join with concubines, cooks, and racialized slaves, the brothers have ultimately reclaimed the prerogatives of sovereignty and violence to win that battle.

Implicitly, then, the framing structure not only positions the Persian empress Shahrazad *between* empires; it suggests that her interpositional effort to stop the shah's killing is provoked precisely by the raced and classed politics of sexual control, which affects all women and all who labor under coercive powers. It is from this position that she quietly embodies a dissenting existential-political situation, one that many communities, generations, and historical actors, perhaps especially reproductive women, have shared with her: the situation of living dangerously between power-wielding men and among multiple empires. Featuring a Persian wife who tells tales often centered on the troubles of sexuality, race, and labor, and who enfolds tales of the very empire that will conquer her husband's empire, the composite text of *The Nights* sends a "hidden" message: that imperially ordered and stratified sexuality lies at the heart of the reproduction, or destruction, of inter-imperial power.

In its counterstructure of two sisters, furthermore, the text challenges the pattern of fraternally forged sovereignty that gets resealed by the compact between Shahrayar and Shahzaman, two sexually threatened brothers. In the emperor's very chambers, the sisters Shahrazad and Dinarzad model an alternative relationality, founded on alliance and witnessing. In this way the text calls us to participate as additional witnesses to an open negotiation with the powers of sovereignty and to the cunning turns made possible by dialectical relationality.

Yet before the sisters can launch their plan, Shahrazad must challenge her father, the vizier, who faces not only the prospect of murdering her at the emperor's command but also the possibility of losing his own life for her treachery. Like the trope of ruling brothers, this positioning of the vizier offers a microcosm of, and a commentary on, the men's own inter-imperial vulnerabilities. At the same time, in centering this last sequence of the frame on a vizier and his daughter, the text reminds us that the imperial will to power operates not only in the pursuit of wealth (as Muhsin al-Musawi highlights), nor only through violent control of women and sexuality, but also via cultural institutions and specifically through the instrumentalization of translation for control of women and laborers.[28] In short, it offers a condensed allegory of the uses of "learned" culture in and between empires.

Viziers and Literature's Political Economy

The fact that Shahrazad is a vizier's daughter is key to the text's implicit exposure of the dialectics of art and political economy. The second half of the frame features the vizier's attempt to dissuade his learned daughter from risking her life in her marriage to Shahrayar through a two-part fable about power and language (15). Seldom discussed by scholars, these fables deserve more attention. For when we recall that such tales were part of a long-standing textual tradition of "mirrors for magistrates" in statecraft literature, we can see that Shahrazad's subsequent tale-telling provides a set of countertales. Her intervention testifies to the centrality of literate institutions and imaginative literary creation to geopolitical histories.

In Muslim political thought, furthermore, such tales often skillfully reworked the Aristotelian political model, which deemed the patriarchal household a subunit and microcosm of the state.[29] Such household-state models were later adopted by European theorists of state after they encountered the Arabic translation of Aristotle. Early Arabic and Persian audiences would have understood that the vizier's two-part tale about what he calls "good management" of the home and its laborers is also about state management. This fact should in turn alert *us* as readers to the "state" implications of Shahrazad's tale-telling—and her inclusion of her sister in the tale-telling situation—as an articulation of an alternative political philosophy. As we will see, in the face of her father's disciplinary tales, Shahrazad creates her own mirror for magistrates, rewriting the lessons of statecraft from within the center of the state, with potentially transformative effects.

It's worth noting that the household-state model also had Chinese corollaries in these centuries, since it confirms that men understood and deliberately practiced control over women for stratified state building. In *The Great Learning*, a Chinese statecraft book dating to the Song Dynasty (960–1279), the writers explain that "The ancients who wished to order well their states, . . . first regulated their families."[30] This thinking blended well with the more open Confucian advice regarding women and servants, as expressed in *The Analects*: "The Master said, 'In one's household, it is the women and the small men that are difficult to deal with. If you let them get too close, they become insolent. If you keep them at a distance, they feel badly done by.'"[31] In *The Nights*, the vizier's fables about household management become yet more explicit.

But to appreciate the vizier's maneuvers first of all requires discussion of the historical role of viziers in Islamicate societies. The vizier was a minister of state, and a grand vizier was a prime minister or highest advisor to the caliph, overseeing many departments and serving as the link between the sovereign and the people. Typically a man of wealth with extensive provincial landholdings, a vizier was usually also a learned man descended from a line of scholars within "vizier families" and sometimes was himself an accomplished scientist, philosopher, jurist, or poet. In many Islamicate states, vizier families, such as the Barmakids, were originally of Persian origin, and although their forebears might have long ago converted to Islam, the tincture of Persian kinship rather than Arab Bedouin or other lineages sometimes fostered suballegiances within and across states. This was the case, as we saw, in the Abbasid Empire, as it also was in the Il-Khanid Mongol state after the Mongol conquering of the Abbasids in the thirteenth century, as Said Amir Arjomand describes. Here, too, "Persian viziers . . . avoided depredation and destruction by peacefully accepting the Mongol suzerainty."[32]

In Islamicate states from the Abbasids to the Mamluks and Ottomans, viziers eventually came to operate as both patrons and administrators of culture, that is, of the libraries, madrasas (colleges), and teaching hospitals of the empire. Although these institutions emerged from within "the political economy of the patrician household," the members of these families increasingly moved into roles as high officials of state.[33] Particularly important for my purposes, the wealth of viziers and their families, drawn from provincial landholdings and trade, came to be funneled into the state through these cultural institutions.

Here is where the vizier becomes a meeting point for culture, state, and economy—indeed, an intentional agent of their coformation. Viziers regularly "endowed" one or more madrasas, funded with revenues from their estates and typically given as gifts or *waqf* (understood as a perpetual trust or endowment for the benefit of God or society). Although these gifts fell within the domain of sharia law (a source of authority separate from the state whose history is immensely complicated), in practice they affected both domains, especially since these domains sometimes overlapped in the person of the vizier (sometimes provoking contention). The viziers' practice of founding madrasas out of their landholdings and profits took hold by the tenth century, so they would likely have been in place by the time of the fourteenth-century transcription of the tales.

Arjomand proposes more specifically that "by the eleventh century the possibility of control of public education through the law of *waqf* suggested it as an instrument of public policy."[34] Amending George Makdisi's emphasis on the private ownership of the colleges, Arjomand points to Seljuq viziers such as Nazim al-Murk, who "institutionalized the systematic use of the law of *waqf* as a major instrument of public policy . . . in education and welfare."[35] Nazim al-Murk's correspondence also seems to confirm that he viewed his endowment practices as "public act[s]."[36] He described himself as "not acting as a private person" but rather as required by "the government policy and the dictates of justice."[37] In his correspondence with the sultan, Nazim al-Murk further explained that "he did not consider the enormous funds he devoted to training a corps of military slaves or creating a network of colleges throughout the empire his own personal property but, rather, the means of carrying out the duties of his office."[38] In effect public and private at once, the endowing of madrasas "throughout the empire" allowed viziers to shape the political or religious orientations of the colleges and teaching hospitals, and thereby further strengthen the mutual coformation of cultural production, state policies, and a revenue-yielding economy.

Ultimately, these educational infrastructures came to serve as "the institutional mechanism for the social reproduction of state," in Arjomand's assessment.[39] By the fourteenth century CE in Egypt (the century from which the standard Baghdad text dates), the madrasas provided students with stipends and residences and thus became "a major mechanism for social mobility," even as they also served to "secure the reproduction of a subordinate civil society."[40] This scenario suggests that what Michel Foucault deemed the "modern" and "disciplinary" society actually had earlier instantiations. The point is affirmed insofar as Nazim al-Murk combined his military and educational institution building by "training a corps of military slaves" and "creating a network of colleges throughout the empire."[41] Given that this institutional "network" would also have housed colonial translation projects, it would have served the empire's management of conquered populations as well.

Thus the vizier emerges as a matrix of economy, culture, and coforming states, including military corps—a hinge figure in the coformations of an inter-imperial political economy. When we also recall how many state viziers were executed (nearly all the great Seljuq and il-Kahnid viziers were executed),[42] we also understand the volatility of the system and the dangers of inter-imperial positionality even for the powerful. Economic motives may have encouraged these executions (since madrasa properties could be confiscated for the state after death, whereas other kinds of property could not), but Arjomand also points out that some viziers and scholars dissented or indeed became revolutionaries and may have suffered state persecution for these activities.[43]

Finally, and particularly important for the feminist dimensions of my discussion, the *women* of vizier families were often also learned. The text carefully establishes Shahrazad as one such woman, for we are told she had "read the books of literature, philosophy, and medicine. She knew poetry by heart, had studied historical reports, and was acquainted with the sayings of men and the maxims of sages and kings. . . . She had read and learned" (11). Historically these women also sometimes founded madrasas, even competing in their endowments with grand viziers, as in the Seljuq state—a point to keep in mind when considering Shahrazad's bold face-off with her father in the practice of statecraft wisdom tales.[44] In other words, historically, daughters at court could indeed assert their power to participate in or challenge state powers.

Translation, Betrayal, and Alliance

In this light, Shahrazad's tale-telling emerges as a strategic act of political retheorizing as well as a deferral tactic to stem the killing. In both form and content, her tale-telling undercuts the stratified, women-controlling household model of state that, we will now see, is embedded in her father's tales. In "The Tale of the Ox and the Donkey" and its sequel "The Merchant and His Wife," the vizier lays out the tools of control over women and laborers, which include language as well as violence (11–16).

To illustrate his advice to Shahrazad that "he who misbehaves, ends up in trouble," the vizier tells "The Tale of the Ox and the Donkey." It features "a wealthy merchant" who "owned many camels and herds of cattle and employed many men" and who "was taught the language of the beasts" (11–12). In the first part of the tale, the merchant's knowledge of the foreign tongues of "every kind of animal" enables his control over their labor; in the sequel, the merchant battles with his wife over her access to that translator's power. Interested in surplus profit, he combines his bilingual human-animal powers with practices of surveillance and beating so as to undercut the animals' impulse toward solidarity and thereby to divide and conquer their resistance to his enforced laboring. Because these tales have to my knowledge received no close reading along these lines, I will parse them carefully.

First, in "The Tale of the Ox and the Donkey," the merchant overhears an exchange in which the ox comments that the donkey lives an easier life than the ox: as the ox explains, while the donkey is well groomed and fed for his work of transporting goods, each and every day in the ox's case "they clamp on my neck something they call yoke and plow, push me all day under the whip to plow the field," and "they work me from nighttime to nighttime" (12). The donkey kindly advises the ox about how to improve his situation. He suggests that, first, the ox openly resist (by "butting and beating with your horns") and the next day pretend to fall ill: "If you do this," the donkey explains, "life will be better and kinder to you, and you will find relief" (12). The ox follows the donkey's advice and for a time gains better treatment.

But meanwhile, having overheard the ox's report about this improvement (drawing on his learning of the "language of the beasts"), the merchant orders his plowman instead to "place the yoke" on the donkey's neck and to "drive him with blows . . . until his sides were lacerated and his neck flayed" (13). By the end of the tale, the donkey concludes, "If I don't find a way to return the ox to his former situation, I will perish" (13). Combining his powers of translation with a practice of surveillance, the merchant landholder undercuts the animals' impulse toward solidarity and thus divides and conquers them to quell their resistance.

Offering this political allegory of the dangers of solidarity in a state that instrumentalizes translation and storytelling, the vizier tells Shahrazad directly: "You, my daughter, will likewise perish because of your miscalculation," advising, "Desist, sit quietly, and don't expose yourself to peril" (13). That is, he discourages Shahrazad from acting in solidarity with other women in her aim to make life "better and kinder" for them. Yet Shahrazad continues to "insist" that her father "must give me to [the emperor]," decreeing that "this is absolute and final" (11). The vizier replies with equal insistence, threatening, "If you don't desist, I will do to you what the merchant did to his wife" (11). He then tells the tale of "The Merchant and His Wife," with its own parrying dialogue of "insistence," ending with punishment of the wife.

This sequel story begins when the merchant overhears the donkey breaking solidarity and revising his advice to the ox. The donkey lies and tells the ox that he has overheard the merchant say he will have the ox slaughtered if he does not do his work. That is, the donkey becomes a "native informer" figure who betrays the ox. The merchant is so pleased at the success of his maneuver that he laughs out loud. Yet now another event of overhearing and surveillance occurs, for the merchant's wife hears him laughing for no apparent reason, and she "insists" that he tell her the cause. Hearing his story, she then demands that he teach her the language of the beasts. The husband explains that he cannot because he has been told—by some unidentified power—that he was taught this language "on the condition that if he revealed his secret he would die" (12). This decree by an undisclosed agent to keep this language knowledge secret under the threat of death suggests that the state powers of sovereignty hover in the background.

The wife is not concerned about these threats, however: when her husband tells her to "desist" in her curiosity, she counters (like Shahrazad), "I insist and will not desist . . . even if you have to die" (14). The husband initially gives in and is "about to interpret to her the language of the animals"—until he overhears the rooster laughing at him. The rooster remarks that "our master" ought to take his wife and "push her into a room, lock the door, and fall on her with the stick, beating her mercilessly until he breaks her arms and legs and she cries out 'I no longer want you to tell me or explain anything'" (15). Abashed, the merchant does exactly this, until "the wife emerged penitent, the husband learned good management, and everybody was happy" (15).

Although the vizier spells out the analogy between household management and state management, promising to "do to you what the merchant did to his wife," Shahrazad simply replies: "Such tales do not deter me. . . . I can tell you many such tales" (15). In the end of course she does exactly that. Within the very halls of power that hold power-accruing translation projects, her father has attempted to control her through tales about translation and violence as tools of state. Yet in these same halls, Shahrazad wields this political tale-telling tradition, first against her father and then against the emperor, ultimately illustrating other principles of "management." When she shares her plan with her sister, Dinarzad, she explains, "I will begin to tell a story, and it will cause the king to stop his practice, save myself, and deliver the people" (16). At the close of the prologue frame, although she *asks* the emperor permission to tell a story and he *grants* it, she then gives him a command: "Listen" (16). In the end, it is the shah who "desists." Furthermore, Shahrazad's nesting of tales, one inside the other, in her "thousand and one nights" of storytelling dramatizes a more complex world of relationality, especially as she mingles tales of poor and rich, Persian and Arab, merchants and caliphs, and of concubines, learned women, and trickster women. Likewise, her explicit demand that her sister be present for her nightly storytelling "insists" on a different kind of household "management," one that includes compassionate witnessing.

Rounding off all the inter-imperial, intersectional implications of the frame and pointing toward the co-constitution of sovereignty, merchant wealth, gender, and labor, Shahrazad begins her nightly tale-telling for the shah with the tale of "The Merchant and the Demon." Her story features a man, as she explains, who "had abundant wealth and investments and commitments in every country" as well as "many women and children and kept many servants and slaves" (17). In light of her father's tales, these are loaded words. Her emphasis on the reach of the merchant's "investments and commitments in every country" and her pairing of servants and slaves with women and children together stake out the full inter-imperial territory that is the target of her literary insurgency. Here, too, we should recall that when later she tells tales about Harun al-Rashid, the Abbasid caliph, he listens in disguise to the inhabitants of his metropole, rather like the merchant eavesdropping on his laboring beasts.

When we also keep in mind that this Abbasid tale is anachronistically told by a Persian Sassanid woman, we see how Shahrazad and her creators operated as cunning mediators of those geopolitical relations in which husbands and owners beat women and laborers "with a stick until they cry out, 'I no longer want you to tell me or explain anything.'" Implicitly *The Nights* invites storytellers and translators to brave such threats by seizing the powers of language from within the interstices of empires.

Precarious Economies of Art

In one sense, the frame of *The Nights* tells the whole tale of labor, race, and gender in the political economy of empires. The pitting of Shahrazad's tales against the vizier's tales furthermore pinpoints literary art as a pivotal, often institutionalized tool of contestations. Yet there is one more thing that still lies hidden: the text's Adornian, negative-dialectical motions, or in other words its meta-reflexivity about these politics of art. I close this chapter with discussion of the sequence "The Story of the Hunchback," which slyly dramatizes this dialectical reflexivity.

The hunchback is a musician and entertainer who performs at night on the streets. The story begins with his accidental death when he chokes on his food while entertaining a tailor and his wife who have heard him on the street and invited him back to their home for feasting and more performance (207). His seeming corpse (for he miraculously later awakens) becomes a sort of hot potato, passed along with great anxiety, especially once it is learned that the hunchback is one of the Chinese emperor's favorite entertainers at court. His body, with its marked physicality, is tossed out windows, stuffed into corners, moved from household to household, and eventually passed from tradesman to craftsman to tradesman across long distances.

Filling nearly one hundred pages in the Haddawy edition (206–95), this sequence of tales within tales follows the men's travels as they ply their wares and services through China, Baghdad, and Egypt—encompassing the very world system described by Janet Abu-Lughod and discussed in chapter 1. In the text's rendering, the network includes transactions among Christians, Jews, and Muslims, who provide services for kings and emperors (for instance the Christian character is a "king's broker" [210]). Thus the sequence registers the system in which, as noted in Shahrazad's first tale, merchants accumulated "abundant wealth and investments and commitments in every country," funding their "many women and children and . . . many servants and slaves" (17). The hunchback artist is himself both commodity and laboring entertainer in this network, exchanged by traveling tradesmen and brokers. In this chain of relations, no one wants to take responsibility for the hunchback's death—that is, for the death of the artist. Yet their rough handling of the artist also puts their lives at risk: eventually they are forced to appear together before the Chinese emperor who has learned of the hunchback's death and who demands that they tell their tales of encounter or lose their lives—an echo of Shahrazad's condition. The staged storytelling before an emperor implies that artists, tradesmen, and craftsmen are all to some degree situated within this inter-imperial system.

Moreover, the tale-within-tale sequence specifically renders both the geographic and historical reach of this world. While the final scenes place the men at the mercy of the Chinese emperor, their tales also refer to earlier times and other emperors. This layered temporality and interpositionality appears most clearly in the long sequence of "The Barber's Tale," which carries us into another anachronistic time warp. For the barber refers to his own time as the thirteenth century. He comments that he had originally told his tale to an Islamic caliph, but this scene is also implicitly told by Shahrazad during the reign of the Sassanid Empire (224–651 CE), before the seventh-century rise of Islamicate states. Thus, like the Shahrazadian frame, the barber's performance is inter-imperially entangled both temporally and spatially, addressed to a Chinese and an Islamic emperor in the thirteenth century and simultaneously told by Shahrazad to a pre-Islamic Persianate emperor in the seventh century. Last but not least, "The Barber's Tale" is a tale about greedy treachery among *brothers*, a sly comment on the battling relations among empires and on all scenes of tale-telling before a sovereign who wields the power of execution.

Thus the many tales spawned by "The Story of the Hunchback" reprise the situation of the artist occupied by Shahrazad, yet with ambiguous implications. These are perhaps purposely left obscure, given the dangers of naming and renarrating the past. On one hand, the text seems to indicate that ultimately the emperor exercises sovereign control over both merchants and artists—or in other words, over both economy and culture. Furthermore, here as in several other tales, the emperor "command[s] that the story of the barber and the hunchback be recorded," not just told orally (295).[45] The implication is that the writing down of retold tales reflects the accruing influence of emperors, who appropriate and regulate the powers of literary art through the instrument of writing. And economy also plays a part of course, since those who perform before emperors win rich rewards: at the end of the long sequence of Hunchback tales, the Chinese emperor "bestowed robes of honor" on all the men and, in the barber's case, "assigned him a regular allowance, and made him his companion" (295). In this way, the text of *The Nights* registers its imperial conditions of production, and it displays the need for metatextual shrewdness in the perilous worlds of powerful states.

Yet on the other hand, exactly by conveying this point, the text insinuates that something else lies hidden. For the men, together, *do* successfully save each other's lives by telling tales to the Chinese emperor, just as Shahrazad saves her own and many other women's. Their tale-telling, like hers, embodies a different "political theory" of relations, centered on alliance and witnessing. Their tangled, nested tale-telling dramatizes an inextricable relationality among all parties, expressed in an alternating dynamic of telling and listening, all of which stands at odds with sovereign control of the naming of relationality. The multiply framed tale-telling suggests that, even though they, too, are captives of empire, readers and listeners of all kinds may also undertake this (re)tooling of literary arts as a force in the field of power. The anachronistic layering of the tales implicitly also flaunts the ability of storytellers to conflate empires and thereby expose the inter-imperially shared practices of domination. Shahrazad and the hunchback (and, more profitably, the tradesmen) thus provide a "mirror for magistrates" in a double sense. Their performances claim some control over the dialectics of inter-imperial history even as they make clear that they are caught up in them.

To read *The Nights* in this way is finally to see how pointedly literature entangles its audiences in these dialectics. It reminds us that, in our very reading of texts, we, too, have been coformed in a world of empires. It recalls for us the long, deep past of our difficult present. Yet it simultaneously places us beside the witnessing sister Dinarzad, whose presence embodies an alternative political theory and a different understanding of history. Diverging from the serial, triumphant narrative of *translatio imperii*, *The Nights* captures the transtemporal, multivectored, and interpositional forces not only of violence but also of creation and care, which often "lie hidden" in the open. It offers a "lesson to those who would consider," as one storyteller puts it (150). Interpellating us as yet another ring of potential tellers, it beckons us to eschew habits of disavowal while embracing the demands of witnessing and critical, ethical relationality.

With its translation into Anglo-European languages in the eighteenth century, *The Nights* was pulled once more into the vortex of inter-imperial history, retooled by another set of states and emperors and made to serve the emergent hegemony of Orientalist ideology. The next chapter turns to the shifting inter-imperial conditions of the fifteenth to eighteenth centuries in order to trace later instantiations of world dialectics and to resituate the literary imaginaries that both appropriated and transformed Shahrazad's tales of gendered geopolitical economy.

PART II CONVERGENCE AND REVOLT

Chapter three

Remapping Orientalism among
Eurasian Empires

Concern over the *translatio imperii* was matched by an equally acute interest in the *translatio studii*. . . . The linkage of poetry and inter-state rivalry is persistent. —**BRIDGET ORR**, *Empire on the English Stage*

Western Europe owes its civilization to its translators. —**LOUISE G. KELLY**, *The True Interpreter: A History of Translation Theory and Practice in the West*

It is your knowledge, delegates, that knowledge you so lovingly cultivate, that knowledge of things oriental which is the bright star, radiating its brilliance to reach the farthest corners of the globe and bring these peoples out of their centuries-old darkness. —**KING UMBERTO I**, opening address to delegates of the XII International Congress of Orientalists (1899)

Imagine an all-night dialogue between Edward Said and Shahrazad. Envision them sharing tales and exchanging ideas about the arts of the state, the politics of translation, and the ways that gender and labor structure the begetting of wealth. Shahrazad would not be surprised to discover that her story had been taken up by later empires and their denizens. She would have understood the force of what became Orientalism, perhaps smiling wryly at the proliferating translations and the adaptations of her stories—and shaking her head at European distortions of those places from which they had stolen and borrowed so much. She might have seen parallels to the Abbasid-Sassanid relation. She certainly would have shared Said's lament that Orientalizing arts are "too often mistaken as merely decorative or 'superstructural'" instead of being understood as part of a "structure of . . . domination."[1] Yet she might also have encouraged Said to pay more attention to the multidirectional dynamics of Orientalist appropriations, as recent scholars have. She might have pointed to the earlier histories of state-sponsored academies and their translation projects. And she might have suggested that, like all hegemonies, Orientalism's effort to structure the terms of existential and political relation continues to provoke countermotions, played out in the same expressive realms it seeks to dominate.

This chapter follows these latter possibilities, widening the historical lens to analyze what Aamir Mufti calls the "global ensemble" of Orientalism.[2] My purpose is both historical and theoretical. Historically, this reframing of Orientalism offers a revised narrative of geopolitics in in the sixteenth through early eighteenth centuries that gives proper attention to the warring field of Eurasian empires, including the Russian, Chinese, Safavid, Mughal, and Ottoman Empires as well as the western European. Theoretically, it develops my argument that aesthetic and cultural projects stand at the center of inter-imperial competition, instrumentalization, and interpenetration, with effects for world politics. The chapter further clarifies how Orientalism, like other hegemonies, becomes a site of contestation over gendered histories and cultural identities exactly because these have determined subject positions in state and economy—that is, in the uneven field of co-constituted relationality. Although I do not focus in this chapter on the gendered aspects of Orientalism (well documented by others),[3] my discussion here lays ground for analysis of them in chapter 4, specifically as they have been encoded in Gothic literature.

In order to reset approaches to Orientalism, this chapter first of all traces the dynamics among the Russian, Chinese, Safavid, Mughal, and Ottoman Empires in the sixteenth and seventeenth centuries, establishing these as the theater of action that western European states strove to enter and that soon became the matrix of Orientalist contestations. I then track England's halting entry into this terrain, foregrounding the ways that in England as elsewhere diplomats, missionaries, and writers of all kinds grappled with the dangers and setbacks of their states' early efforts to gain ground in Eurasia. The expanding Russian Empire was pivotal in these dynamics, although it is rarely understood in these terms, especially in English-language studies.[4] Yet in this period English writers frequently turned their attention to Russia, whether as a potential partner or as an aggressor. Their descriptions of Russia seeded key terms for future political discourses—including *tyranny, freedom,* and *slavery*. These terms would eventually feed the Orientalist rhetoric by which England (and later the United States) positioned itself as the liberty-protecting empire.

In this light, the chapter also foregrounds Russian Orientalist projects, both because they were among the most ambitious and because they were initially the most geopolitically aggressive, pursued in tandem with Russian invasions of the Safavid Empire and its libraries. Russia's cultural projects are often cast as imitations of western European trends. But closer attention to their links to political and specifically inter-imperial history suggests another genesis, wherein this better-positioned Eurasian state knowingly played a central role in the instrumentalization of eastern learning and arts. Furthermore, as has sometimes been noted but not fully explored, it was under the specific threat of Russian expansion that scholars in Safavid and Mughal states began to develop "self-indigenizing" discourses, which shaped the emergence of Orientalist philology and ideology by the start of the eighteenth century.[5]

This is the inter-imperial and incipiently Orientalizing world that *The Nights* reentered in the early eighteenth century, as I argue in the final sections of the chapter. In particular this inter-imperial matrix set conditions for the translation of *The Thousand and One Nights* into French by Antoine Galland, which dramatically boosted the spread of western Orientalist projects, moving them beyond philological and information-gathering projects toward a hegemonic political imaginary, with reconstellating effects for global politics. Galland's French translation of *The Nights* arose from his diplomatic service in Constantinople in the 1670s, where he worked as translator and cultural attaché in support of the French Empire's effort to repair relations with the Ottoman Empire. His collaboration there with the Maronite Syrian Hanna Diab eventually issued in *Les mille et une nuits*, the effects of which rippled across Europe, soon translated into English and several European languages. As marveled at by critics then and now, the translations utterly transformed the Anglo-European political-historical imagination. They embodied yet another wave of those transhemispheric coadaptations and sublations that constituted Europe, following on those that had occurred in the eleventh to sixteenth centuries. In the centuries to come, a range of historical actors—from elites to working classes—

participated in this Orientalizing turn and rechanneled the powers of this text, as the final section of this chapter sketches. At every turn and among all parties, poetic and political power were interdependent, directing the micro- and macrodynamics of history.[6]

Eurasian Inter-imperial Contests

In the fifteenth through seventeenth centuries, the Chinese, Safavids, Mughals, Ottomans, and Russians increasingly engaged in war as well as trade, invading each other's territories, vying over inter-imperial zones, suppressing uprisings in annexed lands, and brokering treaties.[7] As western Europeans made missionary and merchant inroads into Eurasia and installed coastal factories, they thus encountered these several empires, which were already engaged with each other. The Russian Empire was a particularly important player, both because it had been expanding at the most rapid rate in this period and because, as a Christian rather than Muslim state, western Europeans sought it out as a potential ally, trading partner, and channel to eastern lands.

In 1547, Ivan IV had laid claim to the title of tsar (meaning "Caesar") and begun a series of conquests of the khanates of central Asia. By the time of his death in 1584, he had expanded Moscow's city-state into a multiethnic "Russian" Empire stretching 1.5 million square miles. Yet throughout the late sixteenth and seventeenth centuries, as Russia proceeded to expand its frontiers, so too did the Chinese, Mughals, Safavids, and Ottomans, leading to a range of multivectored contests. For instance, in the seventeenth century, the Russian and Chinese empires battled over the khan-dominated territories of Mongolia. Under the Qing dynasty, the Chinese had undertaken a series of expansionist campaigns, eventually incorporating Chinese Turkestan (Xinjiang), Outer Mongolia, and Tibet and forcing the khans to pay tribute. Early in Peter the Great's reign (1672–1725), Russians began to court the khans so as to profit from fur production in this interborder area (additionally motivated by the growth of the American fur market), until the Chinese and Russian empires came to a standoff.

When they finally came to terms in the 1689 Nerchinsk Treaty, the khans of Mongolia were themselves at the diplomatic table.[8] In this illustrative case of vectored inter-imperial maneuvering, the khans had leveraged their position to play one empire against the other. As historian Peter Perdue notes, while "the two giant empires dealt with each other as equals," this treaty "was not just a two-sided contract, but a global agreement," for "the Tungusic, Siberian, and Mongol tribes created the Nerchinsk settlement just as much as did the Russian, Polish, Manchu, Chinese, and Jesuit diplomats."[9] Perdue's mention of Polish and Jesuit diplomats reminds us of the several states jockeying within this field, although not yet including either England or France. Meanwhile, active trade and diplomatic relations between China and Russia continued throughout the next centuries—important to recall in light of the emphasis in western European historiography on China's closed nature. At the same time, the leveraging of the khanates bears out the arguments of recent scholars, discussed in chapter 1, about the roles that nonstate and border peoples have played in the geopolitical formation of states.[10]

In these same centuries, relations among the three Islamicate empires (Mughal, Ottoman, and Safavid) were also multivectored and were also affected by Russian expansion. From 1556 to 1605 under Akbar the Great, the Turkic Mughal Empire tripled its size, and by the end of the seventeenth century, under the emperors Jahangir and Aurangzeb, it covered most of the Indian subcontinent as well as Afghanistan. While at first the Mughal and Safavid states pursued amicable relations, these soured after the Safavid invasion of the city of Kandahar, a strategic trade crossroads in Afghanistan held by the Mughals. This development, in turn, temporarily shifted the relations between the Mughal and Ottoman Empires. Although these two empires had been largely hostile toward each other, and the Mughals had refused to recognize the Ottoman Caliphate, in the face of Safavid ambitions the Mughal emperor Jahangir attempted to form an alliance with the Ottomans, although it was not realized before his death.

Meanwhile the Persianate Safavid state found itself in an increasingly squeezed inter-imperial position, faced with Ottoman invasion and, later, Russian designs on its northern and western borders. At first the Ottoman threat led to occasional alliances between the Safavids and Russians against the Ottomans. Yet after initially lending support to the Safavids against the Ottoman Empire in exchange for parcels of land, Russia increasingly pressed for more land and influence in northern Safavid territories, ultimately leading to the Russo-Persian War of 1722–23 in which Russia won key northern lands. During Nader Shah's short but impressively expansionist reign (1736–47), Russia was forced to retreat and return most of its gains, but it renewed its aggressions in the early nineteenth century, leading to the Russo-Persian Wars of 1804–13 and 1826–28, with the result that the Safavid Qajar dynasty lost much of its northern territory to the Russians.

By the later eighteenth century, the Safavid economy was also being disrupted by the arrival of Portuguese, Dutch, and British traders in its southern territories (perhaps with encouragement from the Russians, who had played middleman for trade contacts between Safavid Persia and western European merchants). As I'll shortly discuss, in all these contests military invasions went hand in hand with cultural invasions, in keeping with the age-old practice, precipitating competition for Persian, Arabic, and other eastern traditions of learning and cultural capital. Here lay the seeds for the Orientalism that also encouraged camaraderie and self-Orientalization among the scholars of the Safavid and Mughal Empires who sought to protect these traditions. In the meantime, *western* Europeans' belated arrival in eastern states together with their simultaneous enrichment through colonization in the Atlantic world not only propelled their competitive drive toward expansion but also gave rise to Orientalizing discourses that were initially directed toward Russia as much as other eastern states. The writers and intelligentsia of these states were variously critiquing, mediating, and profiting from the shifting inter-imperial economy—and by the later seventeenth century feeding Occidental/Oriental political imaginaries.

England's economic, political, and discursive relations with Russia deserve special notice in part because Russia was and has remained a pivotal imperial player while, at the same time, English-language discourses have become widely hegemonic. By the seventeenth century England and other western European states had of course divided along Catholic-Protestant lines in the wake of the Reformation, itself partly enabled by inter-imperial leveraging between Protestant princes and the Ottoman Empire, as discussed in chapter 1. Tensions only increased as these states competed for trade footholds in both the Eastern and Western Hemispheres. On the eastern front, Russia offered a potential entry or leveraging point that was at once economic and geopolitical. As John Archer documents, England's Muscovy Company (chartered in 1555 by Queen Mary and supported by Queen Elizabeth I) eagerly sought connections with Russia:

> Protestant England turned toward orthodox Russia as a possible ally against the Catholic Church and Holy Roman Empire, and sought to consolidate its position in northern Europe by balancing Russian interests against the divergent interests of Holland, Poland, and Denmark. Russia also represented a series of commercial opportunities to English projectors. . . . If dynastic politics provided the machinery for contacts with Russia, English travel in the region was fueled by the need to trade

in staple goods like rugged kersey cloth as well as the twin dreams of northeast and southern passages to the riches of Asia.[11]

English guilds played their part in this effort to link up with Russia and other regions. They raised funds to sponsor the travel and the writing of men like Richard Hakluyt, and they penned texts. For instance, in 1568 textile merchants made their case, writing that "this trade [with Russia] will maynetene thirtie or fortie greate shippes, . . . vent the most of our coullarid clothes, and in shorte tyme if neade require all the Karsaayes maid within the realme, whereby her majesties subjects may be sette a worke."[12] The English successfully established rights to trade with Russia and other states in this period, but their standing fluctuated in competition with other European states. Thus, for instance, in 1588 Queen Elizabeth was more than once forced to dispatch a diplomat to Russia to "argu[e] the Muscovy Company's case against competition by the Dutch and rival English traders and forestall a Russian alliance with the Hapsburgs."[13]

English difficulties were exacerbated by instability at home, where Protestant-Catholic schisms ignited a series of violent regime changes from the later sixteenth to the early eighteenth centuries, with alternating government purges of Protestants and Catholics. These had also become entangled with colonization projects in Ireland and the Americas, all of which were linked to the seizing of lands at home and in Ireland through enclosure and the seizure of estates. The embrace of Protestantism by Henry VIII in 1534 had led immediately to widespread purges, beginning with the dismissal of Catholics in high government posts and the closing of monasteries, followed by the selling of those lands to the king's loyal associates.[14] These sudden changes provoked riots among commoners, whose land-based livelihoods were disrupted, and it led to executions of both commoners and nobility. When Catholic Queen Mary reversed the English Reformation in 1553, hundreds of Protestants, in their turn, were burned at the stake. The divisions continued under the Stuarts, contributing to civil war and eventually enabling Cromwell's intensified land theft and his positioning of Ireland as a laboratory for brutal colonial practices.[15]

During these cataclysms, including the Stuart crisis and the English Civil War of the 1640s, the English lost much of their edge in the Russian trade. The blundering attempts of the Stuart king Charles I to maneuver inter-imperially between the Catholic Spanish and the Protestant Dutch weakened his power and contributed to his overthrow and beheading—at which point the Russian tsar immediately expelled English merchants from all locations in Russia except one port city. Thereafter the Dutch gained a powerful advantage. While apparently England's lack of experience in diplomacy with non-European states also hampered its efforts, the English also struggled as latecomers, for example in North Africa where they could not gain ground in the Cairo textile markets against Italian and French traders.[16] Having failed to win trading concessions from the Ottomans, Elizabeth was forced to turn her sights toward the North African states that were not under Ottoman suzerainty, as Nabil Matar points out.[17]

England's case thus exemplifies the dynamics by which domestic affairs are utterly entangled with foreign affairs. Indeed it establishes that these dimensions are co-constituted within an inter-imperial field. It also illustrates, as I discuss next, the degree to which diverse texts have guided these coformations, ultimately generating key terms for Orientalist discourses.

"The Theater of the Whole World": Textual Mediations

Like many others, English authors took up their pens in this careening world of warring states and shifting economies. Missionary and travel texts as well as literary and historical works brooded on England's effort to gain a foothold in the imperial field of trade, wealth, and labor. Themselves navigating among these pressures, authors also inherently positioned their audiences within the wider global field. That is, they simultaneously interpellated domestic populations into the inter-imperial order of things, *and* they named the experience of anxiety, violence, and alienation arising from that order. Their writing clarifies the interweaving of literary and geopolitical economies and explains the tenor of these authors' consistent invocation of *translatio imperii* narratives.[18] Again I focus on English writing, in hopes that this analysis contributes to the scholarship on other literatures and arts in this field of empires.

English writing was produced by merchants, missionaries, and diplomats as well as scholars, poets, and playwrights who understood that their livelihoods increasingly depended on England's nascent relations with a range of states. Profits from England's emergent capitalist ventures abroad supported the worlds of theater and art, directly and indirectly. While patronage continued to ensure that artists served noble-class and state interests, artists such as Shakespeare also held stocks in foreign merchant companies.[19] Furthermore, as Jane Degenhardt points out, "unlike the medieval theater, the public theater was authorized not by the Church but primarily by the commerce of paying customers, and it was thus directly implicated in London's transforming global economy. Its very financial structure involved shareholders and outside investors."[20] Fully entangled, English authors performed important mediating work in this political economy by implicitly identifying the ethics, perils, and profit-serving promise of the state's and merchants' involvement in empire building.

These literate men combined literary and political discourses. Thus, after his 1588 diplomatic mission to Russia, Giles Fletcher came home to write about it in *Of the Russe Commonwealth*.[21] Similarly, Richard Chancellor, a diplomatic leader of the first sponsored voyage to Russia, was author of early descriptions of that empire. Chancellor's work was very likely known by the poet Philip Sydney, for Chancellor was raised alongside Philip in the household of the lord deputy of Ireland, Sir Henry Sydney. Philip Sydney himself became not only a celebrated poet (known today for such canonical texts as *Astophil and Stella* and *Arcadia*) but also a member of Parliament who authored a defense of his father's aggressive colonial policies in Ireland. Other connections between writers and the imperial economy include the English diplomat Anthony Jenkinson, who made four visits to Russia in the 1550s and 1560s, producing maps as well as influential narratives. He dedicated his impressive map of Russia and Tartary to Sir Henry Sydney (in 1562, when Philip was eight years old). Although Philip eventually concentrated his attention on Ireland, later canonical writers continued the tradition of writing about Russia, such as John Milton who in 1682 wrote *A Brief History of Muscovy*. Likewise, as Archer points out, to read Shakespeare's *Antony and Cleopatra* beside Sir Walter Raleigh's *History of the World* is to see that they both evince the Elizabethan concern about competition over Egypt's economy, which gets threaded through sexual and racial discourses.[22]

Missionary John Cartwright's book *The Preachers Travels* [sic] (1611) embodies many of the elements common to these authors. First, Cartwright takes up the historiographic trope of *translatio imperii* that many authors had imbibed from their classical studies (which drew on Arabic as well as Latin translations).[23] Narrating the past of Mesopotamia and North Africa as a train of successive empires, he strategically positions contemporary seventeenth-century states in these regions as weakened inheritors of ancient Babylonian, Ethiopian, and Egyptian Empires. His account begins with Babylon, explaining that "first she was subdued by the *Medes*, then by the *Persians*; after by the *Grecians*, then by the *Saracens*; then by the *Tartars*, after that by the *Persians* againe: and now by the *Turkes*."[24] His implication that the peoples of one state were repeatedly incorporated into a new conqueror's state formation actually provides a fitting image of the successive sedimentations embedded in inter-imperial histories, for it rightly depicts the past as a series of subjugating sublations. Tellingly, the state is figured as a woman repeatedly "subdued." This gendering is a rhetorical strategy, but it is also in one sense accurate for, as discussed in chapter 1, the conquering of a state does entail enslaving or marrying that state's women, so as to reorganize the reproduction of stratified ethnicities and classes and in turn the uneven distribution of resources. While implicitly spelling out the dialectical sublations of states and knowledges, Cartwright joins others who position the English as the next conquerors in the series.

Also typical are Cartwright's comments on the infrastructural and intellectual achievements of empires past and his notice of the political stakes of vernaculars in state formation. He praises ancient Babylon's "conduits [and] the rareness of her bathes" along with "the hugeness of her towers, the greatnesse of her Temples," and he echoes ancient debates about the genesis of learning, laws, and arts. Joining a long-standing classical debate about whether Ethiopia or Egypt modeled the best imperial practices, he cites the ancient historian Diodorus Siculus on the relation between learned and vernacular languages.[25] Diodorus favors Ethiopia because of its more democratic language practices: for in Ethiopia, "all the Men use[d] the same Figures and Characters of sacred Letters," whereas in Egypt the "sacred Letters [were] knowne only to their Priests."[26] It's no surprise that Cartwright and other English writers would take interest in the question of whether the language of state and religion is known to the "common people," for in England vernacular publication of both the Bible and political pamphlets had recently been pivotal in the success of the Reformation. As Cartwright penned his work, vernacular print newspapers and pamphlets were feeding the events that led to the English Revolution.

Clearly Cartwright is concerned with the present, for his concern leads him to stray from the grand narrative of succession and briefly acknowledge the glut of *contemporaneous* states and European merchants that are outstripping England in the race to establish empires. His move from a torch-passing imperial history to the present competition indicates how a *linear* narrative of triumphant powers can serve rhetorically to offset the threat of precarity in the current field of relations. Cartwright bemoans the fact that cities such as Cairo are no longer "place[s] of great trade and profit" because "the Portugalls, Englishmen, and Hollanders, have by their traffique into East-Indies, cut off almost all the trade of Marchandize into the gulfs of Arabia and Persia," and therefore "both Grand Cairo in Egypt and Bagdat in Assyria, are not now of that benefit, as they have beene, either to the merchant, or great Turke [*sic*]."[27] Cartwright introduces uncertainty about both the *translatio imperii* narrative and England's imperial aspirations by establishing that multiple competitors destabilize the hold of any one empire and that historical change involves trade and merchants as well as imperial states.

English poets and dramatists meanwhile reflected implicitly on England's imperial ambitions. Christopher Marlowe's play *Doctor Faustus* encapsulates this critical awareness, as Jane Degenhardt shows, and it also begins to establish the Faustian figure as a future channel for such literary reflections in centuries to come.[28] Writing shortly after the defeat of the Spanish Armada and gesturing toward his own authorial conditions, Marlowe positions Faustus within a volatile landscape of ambitions. In Degenhardt's words, *Doctor Faustus* serves as a "cautionary tale" about England's entry into the global inter-imperial field. Faustus dreams of possessing riches from both old and new worlds, including "orient pearl"; "gold" from "India"; "huge argosies" from Venice; and fruits arriving from "all corners of the new-found world." With a clear gesture toward England's inter-imperial envy of Spain, he specifically desires "the golden fleece" from America "that yearly stuffs old Philip's treasury."[29] To fulfill his dream, Dr. Faustus operates as a shrewd inter-imperial maneuverer within the contemporary field of Protestant-Catholic schisms and Ottoman-European relations—one who pays strategic visits to both Roman Catholic courts and those of the "Great Turks."

For this study, it is particularly telling that Marlowe creates Faustus as an inter-imperially maneuvering *scholar*, one who makes a pact with the devil to attain knowledge as well as power and wealth. The play hereby comments on the intertwining of culture and political economy. In Marlowe's portrait, Dr. Faustus is a learned man well versed in history who has studied at Wittenberg and who comes to identify himself with a long line of conquerors from Alexander the Great to Charles V. He is seduced by the vision of becoming a "great emperor of the world."[30] In portraying Faustus as both scholar and geopolitical maneuverer, Marlowe invites reflection on the long history of artists caught within or seduced by the inter-imperial field of power, including some of his own contemporaries. As has been amply studied, for instance, Shakespeare was among those who simultaneously held investments in joint-stock companies and created plays critiquing ambitious monarchs. Infamously in the case of *The Tempest*, his work both exposes and endorses colonial land theft, enslavement, and racism.[31] In this incipient period of English colonization, Marlowe stands out as a playwright who broods not only on the ways the state's internal politics are affected by its foreign ambitions but also on the entanglement of those ambitions with aesthetic and knowledge projects. Encoding this set of problems, the figure of Faustus later took strong root in Anglo-European Gothic literature, in some cases shown to provoke the energies of rebellion, as discussed in the next chapter.

One last discursive strand that emerged in this period also deserves mention, for it was eventually woven into the English Orientalist imagination: the discourse of freedom, slavery, and tyranny. These key terms eventually served to contrast England with other states in the field of power, and it has since continued to structure geopolitical imaginaries in both literature and politics, as I argued in *Freedom's Empire*.[32] Initially however this discourse targeted Russia, and it did so partly to register concern about a seeming trend toward tyranny among empire-seeking English kings and queens.

According to Archer, in the sixteenth and seventeenth centuries "the absolute power of tsar and the barbarity of his people became a constant refrain in English writing about Russia."[33] Writers particularly worried about the connection between expansion abroad and tyranny at home, although the risks of execution held them back from open dissent. In 1557, for instance, after his return from Russia, Jenkinson combines comment on the tsar's widespread conquering and implicitly links it to domestic tyranny: "This emperor is of great power, for he hath conquered much as well of the Livonians, Poles, Latvians, and Swedes, as also of the Tartars, and gentiles called Samoyeds, having thereby much enlarged his dominions. He keepeth his people in great subjection; all matters pass his judgment be they never so small."[34] In a dedicatory epistle to Queen Elizabeth in *Of the Russe Commonwealth*, Giles Fletcher shrewdly distinguishes England from Russia in these terms, exercising flattery while also implicitly recommending a different practice. Russia represents, he says, "a true and strange face of a *Tyrannical state* . . . (most unlike to your own)" for "you are a Prince of subjects, not of slaves, that are kept within dutie by love, not by feare."[35] Some writers denigrated the Russians themselves, by implicit contrast with the proudly "freeborn" English. In *The Theatre of the Whole World* (Latin 1570; English 1606), for instance, Abraham Ortelius decries the apparent fact that the Russian people are "rather delighted to live in servitude and slavery, than at large and in liberty."[36]

By the time of Peter Heylyn's *Cosmographie in Four Books* (1652–70), written in the years reaching from the Interregnum to the Restoration, the freedom/slavery discourse was being extended to both African and Asian states, with increasing contrasts among "peoples."[37] Heylyn develops the narrative by which such peoples, once so grand, now never defend "either their ancient reputation, or their native liberties but [suffer] themselves to be won, lost, fought for, and again recovered by their quarrelsome Masters."[38] Milton drew on Heylyn's account of Asian empires in *Paradise Lost*, where it influences his imagining of the "fortunate fall" into freedom, an inheritance which, he implies, the English best represent and which he urges them to practice. In the long run, both the Faustus figure and the Whig freedom narrative of English history served Orientalism by attributing greed and tyranny to eastern and southern states and claiming the banner of freedom-honoring, righteous empire for the English.[39]

Orientalisms across Empires

The emergence of Orientalism embodies all these dialectical processes. To uncover its multivectored unfolding is also to weaken its forceful hold on the present. Initially finding expression in the ceremonial performances of empires, these projective appropriations of eastern cultural traditions eventually took concrete root in scholastic and state projects. In these forms, as Said established, they generated a full-fledged Orientalism that affected both colonial policy and the wider cultural imagination of European peoples. Once again translation projects were central, serving as the institutionalized site where *translatio imperii* met *translatio studii*.

Ironically, as the Whig narrative took hold from the turn of the seventeenth century into the eighteenth century, English authors more openly endorsed England's colonizing ambitions. Accordingly, English literature was increasingly saturated with figures of tsars, shahs, queens, and emperors, transporting audiences to dazzling foreign courts and extravagant costumes in the Americas as well as in Afro-Eurasia, as Bridget Orr traces in *Empire on the English Stage, 1660–1714*. These "dramas of state" were staged in "heroic" plays performed for elites as well as in the popular theaters serving more diverse audiences: English people were entertained by scenes from Ottoman, Persian, African, Indian, and Chinese history as well as "Moorish" Spanish and South American history.[40] The play's plots announced their imperial preoccupations, while the costumes and sets participated materially in the process of *translatio imperii*—that is, of appropriation of the aesthetic symbols of other empires. These theatrical enactments of what Barbara Fuchs calls "imperial mimesis" often accompany or set the ideological stage for the military "theaters" of empire building.

In fact some writers directly linked performative modes and political ambition, recommending emulation of other empires. In his comments on King Charles II's new habit of donning "Persian garb," John Evelyn observed that a nation's adoption of foreign clothing has "(like [their adoption] of Language) ultimately prov'd a Fore-runner to the spreading of their Conquests there," eventually fostering their ability "to impose, and give laws to the habits of another (as the late *Tartars* in China)."[41] The essayist John Dennis makes a similar point in *The Epistle Dedicating His Advancement and Reformation of Modern Poetry to the Earl of Mulgrave* (1701). He points out that "Poeticall art" in France in the seventeenth century had been "very instrumental in . . . raising the esteem of their Nation to that degree, that it naturally prepar'd the Way for their Intrigues of State, and facilitated the Execution of their vast Designs."[42] Thus, as Orr puts it, "the concern over the *translatio imperii* was matched by an equally acute interest in the *translatio studii*."[43] Whether authors challenged, accommodated, or hedged their bets, "the linkage of poetry and inter-state rivalry [was] persistent."[44]

The artists and writers of the Spanish and Portuguese Empires, of course, had been staging and mediating such political-aesthetic dynamics since the sixteenth century, as Mary Louise Pratt long ago established in *Imperial Eyes* and as Fuchs developed further in *Mimesis and Empire*. As Fuchs emphasizes, during centuries when Spain still faced the threat of Ottoman invasion and Al-Andalusian Muslims continued to resist the Catholic Spanish in southern Spain, Spanish colonizers in South America strategically fashioned themselves in the "garb" of both Old World and New World empires.[45] Soon, the British were similarly "staging" their competitive relations to Spain in a triangulated relation to southern and eastern states. In English plays set in Spanish and Spanish-colonial metropoles, English authors champion Britain as the freedom-protecting empire while cultivating the "Black Legend" of Spain as an empire corrupted by "Moorish" Islamic and Roman Catholic influences.[46] In other words, the practices in this period that literary critic Stephen Greenblatt dubbed "self-fashioning" were not only imperial.[47] They were pointedly inter-imperial.

Such are the imitative, aesthetic, adaptive dynamics that compose longue-durée global dialectics. Accretively, such aesthetic processes were reconstituting the "inside" of England and Europe from the outside—in cultural, material, military, political, and economic dimensions. If we also recall that political and aesthetic ideas had been migrating into Europe for several centuries and continued to do so, as discussed in chapter 1, then we further grasp the workings of sublation and coformation. That is, Anglo-Europeans were continually using notions and practices borrowed from other states to engage with the increasingly proximate and intense demands of inter-imperial codependence. By the sixteenth and seventeenth centuries these past coadaptations were merging with new waves of influence. European political philosophy of this period was for instance directly influenced by Chinese political philosophy that correlated the structures of state with the spatial design of imperial gardens.[48] These aesthetic philosophies informed the political thought of the Earl of Shaftesbury, Joseph Addison, Alexander Pope, and Immanuel Kant—men who are often considered originators of "European" Enlightenment thought and culture. In *Abyssinia's Samuel Johnson*, Wendy Belcher similarly reveals that Samuel Johnson was profoundly influenced by the tenets of Abyssinian (that is, Ethiopian) aesthetics and philosophy after he translated *A Voyage to Abyssinia* by Jeronimo Lobo. Abdullah Al-Dabbagh argues in *Shakespeare, the Orient, and the Critics* that the philosophy of Sufism influenced Shakespeare's ethics and aesthetics. And of course, as Arjun Appadurai discusses in *The Social Life of Things*, idioms and ideas were all along migrating through "things" and commodities as well as through plays, poems, and everyday practices.[49]

Again, the point is that states and geopolitical economies have been *co-formed by* these material-aesthetic-intellectual dialectics, as have persons and communities. We miss their co-constitutive processes if we approach aesthetics as mere representation or superstructure. Focusing instead on their inextricability, we make fuller sense of the Eurasian matrix of the Orientalist turn.

Orientalisms in Translation: The Russian Vector

In his mid-twentieth-century magnum opus, *La renaissance orientale*, Raymond Schwab partly acknowledges the formative force of "Oriental" cultures for Europe's formation. In fact, he proposes that in eighteenth-century Europe the study of Asian languages and cultures, especially Sanskrit, initiated a "second" renaissance, equal in importance to the "first" or classical Renaissance of the fifteenth and sixteenth centuries (without noting however that the "first" Renaissance was itself sparked by Arabic and Hebrew scholarship). Celebrating this influence without any attention to its imperial thrust, Schwab argues that the "Romantic turn" in European culture and thought followed directly from the philological studies of European "Oriental scholars." When Said wrote his foreword to the 1984 English translation of Schwab's book, he critiqued the book's lack of political analysis, but he also credited Schwab with forging a method that would become useful for critical historiography, including of intellectual history, for instance by tracking the manuscripts loaned, borrowed, and procured by scholars and states.[50] Indeed, recent scholarship has done exactly this and has begun to clarify the processes by which geopolitics has been shaped by cultural projects as well as state usurpations.

Thus scholars have identified the multilingual Mughal intellectuals, such as Mirza I'tisam al-din, who schooled famous European Orientalists but were left shrouded and unnamed in Schwab's account.[51] These intellectuals translated Sanskrit, Turkish, and Arabic texts into Persian, wrote literary histories, and engaged in theoretical debates about literary and linguistic matters. As Mohamad Tavakoli-Targhi puts it, their research establishes that "'the Oriental Renaissance' in Europe, in reality depended on the intellectual achievements in Moghul India."[52] Mirza I'tisam al-din, for instance, traveled to England in the 1760s, when he was translating a Persian dictionary that had been compiled many decades earlier at the Mughal imperial court. In England, he helped William Jones learn Persian and shared his dictionary project with Jones.[53] Jones then drew on these materials for his "academic best-seller," *A Grammar of the Persian Language*—although without explicitly acknowledging I'tisam's fundamental role. Partly with such facts in mind, Amit Chaudhuri comments that "the Orient, in modernity, is not only a European invention but also an Oriental one."[54] Aamir Mufti further highlights the ways that eastern and western scholars began to reconceive their histories in Orientalist and self-indigenizing terms and thereby created the "global ensemble" of Orientalism.[55]

The inter-imperial dimensions of this ensemble become more visible when we recall both the earlier inter-imperial politics in which Persian Farsi played a role and the contemporaneous inter-imperial contests that pressured these scholarly activities, including the contests between the Russian and Safavid Empires. First, the inter-imperially conditioned intermixing of Arabic and Persian languages in the eighth and ninth centuries prepared the genesis of language studies that fed into Orientalism. After the conquering of Persianate states, as mentioned in chapter 1, the Umayyad Caliphate instituted Arabization programs across their lands, installing Arabic as the official language and displacing Persian. By the tenth century, however, as fractures arose in the Abbasid's control over its peripheries, the Samanid tributary state began to reestablish the Persian Farsi language as a favored literary language and increasingly as an official state language. As Hayrettin Yücesoy argues, the Samanids thus implicitly challenged the prestige of

Arabic, contributing to the erosion of Abbasid hegemony.[56] Furthermore, the poetic theories and literary histories of Persian that developed in the thirteenth century are referenced and reframed in the era of Mughal hegemony, as Sunil Sharma documents.[57]

Thus the renewal and preservation of Persian literary history in turn ensured the prestige of Persianate scholarship and literature within the Mughal court several centuries later. Sharma suggests that the embrace of a Persian-centered literary history by the Mughal court indicates "an anxiety on the part of the Mughals about their rightful place in the literary cosmos."[58] At the same time, strategically, the Mughal Empire's support of Persian-language projects of translation and authorship would have burnished their reputation among a range of populations in those regions, wooing support from the Persian-language elites. The strategic thinking of Mughal court scholars might also be reflected in their crafting of a generously *regional* literary history. For instance, Amin Razi's 1591 *Haft Eqlim* (*Seven Climes*) gives praise to regions and authors outside the classic Persian canon, although overall in his account Iran retains its privilege "as the traditional center of the world."[59]

Yet by the end of the seventeenth century, the very conditions of inter-imperiality that had fostered the preservation of a privileged Persian archive would make Safavid and Mughal libraries a target of inter-imperial appropriation, propelling the emergence of Orientalism. Among Safavid and Mughal scholars, the increasing threat of Russian invasions in particular created a sense of urgency about the completion of Persian-language projects, for these states faced possible looting and destruction as well as appropriation of these materials. Rastegar remarks briefly that the threat of Russian invasions propelled the state-supported translation and philological recovery activities of Iranian, Mughal, and Egyptian scholars, and Sunil Sharma similarly observes that "the preservation of the Persian past" (including literary histories) became more pressing "in the wake of the fall of the Safavids" to Russian and Ottoman aggression.[60] Yet these geopolitical pressures deserve fuller study for their bearing on the genesis of Orientalism.

Certainly Russia's intention to combine cultural invasion with military invasion is clear. Peter the Great ordered his troops to loot for Persian manuscripts during their wars with the Safavids, and he simultaneously made early efforts to found an Oriental faculty at Russian academies.[61] In this latter project he was equally concerned with China, as David Schimmelpenninck van der Oye details in *Russian Orientalism*. Peter the Great launched the first Russian ecclesiastical mission in Beijing (alumni of which would later become influential Sinologists). In 1700 he also directed his agents to find "two or three good and learned young monks who might learn Chinese and Mongolian"—since, as Schimmelpenninck van der Oye puts it, "the tsar's expansive commercial and political plans for Asia required officials competent in its languages."[62] By the late eighteenth century, Russia had expanded into the territories of the dismantled Safavid Empire as well as into Crimea and other regions, accompanied and proclaimed by Russia's spectacular Orientalist projects.

Russian Orientalism came to full fruition under Catherine the Great (1762–96), working hand in hand with her ambitious, expansionist military campaigns. She proved herself a master of the techniques by which aesthetics could be instrumentalized for inter-imperially directed displays of power, as evident in her expansion of the Chinese Pavilion in the gardens of Tsarskoye Selo, the tsars' country residence. This massive project included the creation of two artificial hills, a large pavilion, a theater, and a small village featuring Chinese-styled buildings. An elaborate mural along the pavilion's main hallway guided viewers through a procession of empires from past to present, culminating in a vast ceiling painting titled *Uniting Europe and Asia*, in which Russia stood at the center. Jennifer Milam interprets this project as part of the empress's cosmopolitanism, deeming Tsarskoye Selo the "most expansive example of the taste for chinoiserie in eighteenth-century Europe."[63] But in light of Russia's aggressive relations with Persian and Chinese states, it is clearly also much more than that.

Catherine the Great's deployment of Orientalist aesthetic projects as accompaniments of military invasion and instruments of geopolitical messaging is clearest in the epic spectacle she launched after her successful colonization of the Crimean Peninsula. Hosting a cadre of diplomats, poets, philosophers, and emperors on a seven-month, three-thousand-kilometer journey through her territories, she at once aligned herself with an inter-imperial set of cosmopolites and awed them with a flamboyant military display during one encampment. As described by a guest, the display began with a procession of many hundreds of her Cossack imperial guard, twelve hundred newly conscripted Crimean Tatar cavalry, and even a regiment of "Amazons" clad in "crimson skirts, neoclassical breastplates, green tunics, and white ostrich plumes"—aligning Catherine with both ancient Eurasian empires and powerful women (enacted however by not-so-powerful Greek women). After the procession, Catherine's Kalmyk horsemen—"resembling Chinese"—performed a mock battle for her eminent guests.[64] As Schimmelpenninck van der Oye points out, "These spectacular displays of exotic militaria were more than a theatrical caprice. By confidently placing her party under the protection of an assortment of nationalities who in centuries past had menaced Muscovy's southern frontier, Russia's tsarina was unambiguously demonstrating her dominion over Asian subjects."[65]

While the story of Catherine's chinoiserie and her intellectual projects is often told as her emulation of trends in western Europe, it is more accurate to say that, contemporaneously with western Europe, she and Peter the Great masterfully positioned Russia *at the center* of Orientalizing trends in the inter-imperial field. As implied by the palace painting *Uniting Europe and Asia*, they deemed Russia as the very matrix of these relations. Kirsten Jobst therefore argues that Orientalism in Russia was a project of "collective self-positioning of Russian elites between an essentialized East and an equally essentialized West" in the geopolitical "field of tension."[66] Especially when performed by a rapidly expanding empire with a strong strategic position in Eurasia, this *aesthetic* messaging would have been well understood by rival and adjacent states as a tactical practice. Catherine clearly understood, like the Englishman John Dennis, that "Poeticall art" could be "very instrumental in . . . raising the esteem of [a] Nation," "prepar[ing] the Way" for its "vast Designs" and "Intrigues of State."[67]

When we return to Mughal translation projects in this light, we see that the "self-indigenizing" discourses of Mughal scholars who preserved eastern languages arose partly as countermeasures. Although in the shifting terrain of the seventeenth and early eighteenth centuries no one state had yet achieved a new transhemispheric hegemony, the widening expansions of the Ottoman, Russian, and western European Empires increasingly loomed as a serious menace, in effect raising the value of "Oriental" cultural capital. In the co-constituting field of human relations dominated by empires, eastern scholars pursued interpositional maneuvers, resisting the threat of new hegemonies through their self-indigenizing translation and aesthetic projects. Yücesoy's and Chaudhuri's studies of scholarship as a "career" rightly highlight scholars' ongoing, active involvement in world dialectics. These projects constitute the precedents for today's scholarly entanglements and interventions.

To study inter-imperiality is thus to further concretize Mufti's point that "we cannot ignore the global relations of force" under which Orientalism emerged, nor ignore "the enormous role played by the institution of literature in the emergence of the hierarchies and identities that structure relations."[68] To fully appreciate how Orientalist arts came to permeate the field of human relations and how translation projects occupy the matrix of inter-imperial relations, we must return to the story of Shahrazad.

A Thousand and One Translations

The conditions of Antoine Galland's arrival in Constantinople in 1672 were certainly inter-imperial. A talented young French scholar of "Oriental languages," Galland traveled to Constantinople first as the secretary and translator for Monsieur de Nointel, the new French ambassador to the Ottoman Sublime Porte. At a tense moment in French-Ottoman relations (due to French support for Venice and Austria in the latter's territorial battles with the Ottomans), Nointel's charge was to ease the friction and reestablish good terms. King Louis XIV particularly hoped Nointel would reaffirm the 1604 Capitulations which had given France both special trade privileges and sponsorship rights for Christians in the Ottoman Empire. Galland's language gifts had won notice during his studies at the Enfants de langues program, set up under Louis XIV by chief minister Jean-Baptiste Colbert (which laid the foundation for what is now the School of Oriental Languages). As a student of Persian, Turkish, and Arabic as well as of Greek and Latin, Galland's role was to translate the correspondence between Nointel and his Ottoman and other associates.[69]

In other words, Galland was an heir to the imperial traditions in which translation and scholarship provided an axis of negotiations. Although judging by the journals he kept, Galland was as interested in the bookstalls and libraries of Constantinople as he was in the machinations of diplomats, it's important to keep in mind how much one set of conditions enabled the other. That is, the very presence of so many books from around the world in Constantinople manifests state power built on this coformation of states, trade, and knowledge. Galland's avid collecting of books, artifacts, and coins subsequently led Colbert to commission him during the 1670s to gather manuscripts and artwork for the Bibliothèque nationale de France (commissions made, notably, in conjunction with the French East India Company). Colbert also completed the Bibliothèque orientale (Oriental Library), the massive collection of material about Islamic culture begun by Barthélemy d'Herbelot de Molainville. Eventually Galland was appointed antiquary to the king and before his death he was honored with the title of chair of Arabic at the Collège de France. Intellectual history is clearly also geopolitical history.

In his manuscript-gathering expeditions, Galland began to find and translate eastern tale collections, such as the Arabic *Kalila wa Dimna*, the Indian *Fables of Bidpaï*, and eventually the *Voyages of Sinbad*. The success of these publications encouraged his pursuit of other tales. Having heard tell of a larger corpus of stories, Galland continued to correspond with Syrian and other contacts to try to find the "whole." In Constantinople he eventually met Hanna Diab, a Syrian Maronite from Aleppo who, as Galland records in his journal, recited many tales by heart, and eventually acquainted Galland with the fourteenth-century Syrian, Arabic-language manuscript of *Alf layla wa layla—The Thousand and One Nights*. It seems that Diab may have written out some tales for Galland, but we are unlikely ever to know the exact nature of their authorial transactions. Such are the untold microevents of dialectically formed histories. Certainly both men joined the millennial ranks of scholar-translators who have shaped and been shaped by those inter-imperial conditions of production that interweave art, cultural hegemony, and political economy.

Published as *Les mille et une nuits* in twelve volumes (1704–17), Galland's highly stylized French "translation" of *Alf layla wa layla* utterly transformed Anglo-European literatures. It was quickly retranslated and bowdlerized into many European languages, including English (1706), German (1712), Italian (1722), Dutch (1732), Russian (1763), and Polish (1768). Even while its metamorphoses sometimes eluded imperialist control, it quickly became *the* fetishized jewel in the contesting crowns of Orientalizing states. It was also translated into Persian in the early nineteenth century and eventually back into Arabic versions, sparking debates among eastern scholars about the text's literary history and its literary value, for instance in a special issue of the journal *Al-Hilal*.[70] Aware of the European embrace of the text despite its lowly status in Arabic literary categories, these scholarly dialogues became one more site at which literature mediated geopolitics. As reified fetish object and shape-shifting, trickster text, *The Nights'* catalyzing effects confirm both Mufti's point about literature's role in "the hierarchies and identities that structure relations" and Said's reflections on the arts as much more than "superstructural."[71]

Literature's political meanings are often shrouded in a dance of veils, and they are in turn frequently mistaken or romanticized by audiences, which does not however diminish its effects. *The Nights'* transmigrations profoundly affected the imaginations of a range of European writers and diplomats, among whom it was often turned into a dreamy, romanticized lens through which the beneficiaries of northwestern empires could see the world. In Russia, *The Nights* was "probably the most popular source about the Islamic world among Russian readers"; it inspired Alexander Pushkin's *Ruslan and Ludmilla* (1820), for instance, the book that made his reputation as a poet and fed into his poetry about the Caucasus.[72] The French diplomat

Louis-Philippe, comte de Ségur, traveling as one of Catherine the Great's guests on the journey through newly conquered lands of Crimea, confessed that the geographies and peoples "appear[ed] to me rather like a page from the *Arabian Nights*."[73] In France, Victor Hugo conjured the text's heady influence in his preface to *Les Orientales* (1829), where he comments that Oriental literatures had "imprint[ed] themselves" on many of his "dreams and thoughts," suffusing his writing with elements that were "Hebraic, Turkish, Greek, Persian, Arab, even Spanish, because Spain is still the Orient; Spain is half African, Africa is half Asiatic."[74] The elisions of Hugo's dreamy visions simultaneously reveal what Wendy Belcher calls the "discursive possessions" affected by the circulation of "foreign" texts.[75] That is, such texts take deep hold in the culture even as artists and thinkers distort, misread, or debase the source text. In this range of ways, *The Nights* was being taken up and radically reworked in the eighteenth century as it had been in earlier centuries, made to mediate the current, more fully global wave of inter-imperial contests. In the remainder of this section I establish its constitutive force by tracking its impact on English-language literature, including as recorded by contemporaries.

As soon as the first volume of Galland's *Les mille et une nuits* arrived in England in 1706, translations of it proliferated, starting what became a long career of English printings and adaptations, as documented by Muhsin Jassim Ali. By 1713 there were four English editions; by 1793 there were eighteen editions; by 1833 there were thirty-six editions. Between 1723 and 1726, the *London News* serialized *The Nights* in 445 installments, while eventually other widely read magazines published their own series, including *Bellamy's General Magazine*, the *Lady's Magazine*, and the *Novelist's Magazine*.[76] The range of English authors who imitated or adapted *The Nights* reaches from such canonical figures as Joseph Addison, Samuel Johnson, and Eliza Heywood, to nearly all Gothic and historical novelists, including Charles Dickens, George Eliot, and George Meredith, as well as authors from Britain's periphery such as Charles Maturin, as we will see in the next chapter.

Translations of this text in turn sparked an interest in other Arabic genres, including among English poets and English scholars of Arabic. Again the supposedly indigenous modernity of English Romantic literature turns out to have been partly shaped and inspired by Arabic forms of poetry, albeit distorted in translation. In particular, as Peter Caracciolo documents, the book *Specimens of Arabic Poetry* (1796) published by J. Dacre Carlyle, a Cambridge professor of Arabic, spurred the work of Robert Southey (who in *Thalaba* [1801] refers explicitly to Carlyle's materials) as well as that of

Wordsworth and Coleridge, who had studied under Dacre.[77] Most striking is the similarity between Carlyle's claims for the democratic nature of Arabic poetry and Wordsworth's call, in the famous preface to the *Lyrical Ballads*, for a poetry written in "a language really used by men."[78] Carlyle had highlighted the ways that, in contrast to the highly stylized language of European pastoral poets, the Arab poet "described only the scenes which were before his eyes," echoing "the language of [their] herds-men" and interweaving "the genuine language used by them, by himself and by his readers."[79] A few years later, in his preface to the 1802 edition, Wordsworth writes that his "experiment" in the poems was to avoid "the gaudiness and inane phraseology" of much contemporary poetry and instead to use "a language really used by men," while choosing "incidents and situations from . . . the humble and rustic life."[80]

The impact of Arabic forms on fiction was also widely noted by contemporary writers, prompting new literary histories. In *Arthur; or, The Northern Enchantments* (1789), Richard Hole speculated about an Arabic origin for fiction that joined streams with the Greek, and James Beatie suggested that "romance and fiction originated in Arabia."[81] In 1834, one critic offered the observation that the novel, which he called "that modern . . . species" of composition, was "probably of oriental origin."[82] In discussions of *The Nights* in particular, many writers highlighted the magical and exotic elements, yet some also discerned the historical and social elements in Arabic traditions, even suggesting that its narrative tales might "represent the first appearance of the spirit of history in fiction," thus leading the "imagination itself [to turn] antiquarian."[83] Literary historian John Sismondi suggested that the similarity in "merchant" economies might have encouraged English interest in the tales, for "we recognize the style of a merchant people."[84] The historian Edward Gibbon compared *The Nights* to Homer and to epic more broadly, remarking on the tales' political acumen.[85]

By the later nineteenth century, critics implicitly began to notice the ways that English literature was, in effect, not strictly English. They were anticipating Ros Ballaster's recent claim in *Fabulous Orient* that the "realist occidental novel, like the western Enlightenment of which it was a part, was always already oriental."[86] The nineteenth-century critic Robert Chambers virtually named the processes of sublation in his remark that *The Nights* had so permeated English literature that its elements mingled with "similar things of our own which constitute the national literary inheritance."[87] An *Athenaeum* writer observed that imitations and adaptations of *The Nights* were so widespread that they "must form no uninteresting chapter in any comprehensive history of modern literature."[88] Without saying so, these men registered the fact that *The Nights* had set in motion a field of inter-penetrations and generic transformations, changing the symbolic economy.

In the twentieth century, critics implied that these sublations and "min-glings" had been so fully incorporated that they needed recalling—and then repossession for the English. Martha Pike Conant's book-length study, *The Oriental Tale in England in the Eighteenth Century* (1908), remains a rich scholarly source mostly untainted by Orientalist remarks. Yet her whimsical comment that "*The Arabian Nights* was the fairy godmother of the English novel" suggests that this literary history was itself being fashioned as an *English* bedtime tale.[89] In *The March of Literature* (1938–39), Ford Madox Ford more problematically recalls this wider literary past, in distinctly Orientalist terms. After exhorting the reader to "get into his head an image of a vast pa-norama of the eastern world across which shimmered two streams of liter-ary influence" (from the Nile and from China), he then claims ownership of those streams, explaining that they "discharged into the Mediterranean to form that civilization which is today our own."[90]

At the same time, as the next and final section emphasizes, literature's political work even in the case of Orientalism remained manifold and multi-vectored, with highly equivocal results for the dialectics of domination and dissent.

Retooled Orientalisms

In the long run, like other ideologies, Orientalist discourse became an am-bivalent tool in many hands. By the nineteenth century, after the initial ro-mance with "Oriental" styles and imagery among Anglo-European authors, and after these had been absorbed as un/conscious sublation, and after rebellions from Haiti to India challenged Anglo-European inter-imperial incursions, the denigrating work of the discourse took over, seeping into internal state formation.

Many populations were "Orientalized" in this discursive field. In nineteenth-century Britain, as Saree Makdisi has shown, Orientalist dis-course was deployed to interpellate and discipline underclass English popu-lations into English and Occidental whiteness.[91] That is, working-class and poor communities in Britain found themselves faced with discourses that compared them with "Orientals," casting them as lazy, unruly, and back-ward. They were told, in effect, that in order to identify as "white" they must discipline themselves according to the state's capitalist labor demands and racialized norms or be excluded from the state's wealth and benefits. All such biopolitics of course also sent gendered messages about reproduction, femininity, and masculinity.

The disciplinary and hierarchizing functions of Orientalism have similarly served other states and regions. Ussama Makdisi makes a comparable argument about "Ottoman Orientalisms," and Manuela Boatcă does so regarding eastern European Orientalisms.[92] Get in line with the gendered political economy or be "other" to the state. Orientalisms were reworked as an instrument of geopolitical biopolitics in the Americas as well, tapping incipient forms used earlier by the Spanish and Portuguese. Both internally and externally Latin Americans faced identity discourses that all at once Orientalized, medievalized, feminized them.[93] In discourses that messily merged notions of Al-Andalusian "Moors" with Africans and Latin Americans, and sometimes both of these with indigenous Americans, South America and its internal territories could be dismissed as backward regions caught in a medieval past. In other versions, Anglo-Europeans laid claim to South America by claiming that ancient Mediterranean and European peoples shared genealogies with Incan and Aztec peoples. Likewise in US ideologies from the eighteenth century to the present, writers have conveniently conflated "Oriental" and all non-northern European cultures, variously appropriating and denigrating the legacies of indigenous and diasporic peoples.[94]

At the same time and in counterpoint, Orientalism has been retooled from below, for instance in versions that Orientalized elites. On the popular British stage of the nineteenth century, for instance, British working-class writers and performers tapped into Orientalist tropes to critique the corrupt, oppressive ruling classes, as Bridget Orr argues.[95] Their performances implicitly mocked all imperial decadence, including the British, and positioned white working-class men and women as the honest working heroes amid all this corruption. In effect these were the underclass retorts to the state's Orientalizing interpellation effort, yet they often nonetheless pivoted on racist discourses and served "white" subject formations. Such are the instabilities of the dialectic. Indeed, in some cases, rather than assuming that underclass retoolings diminish racist formations, we might explore the ways that they can infuse racism with new life: for instance, by equating the working-class spirit of dissent against state corruption with a more righteous "whiteness." Anglo-Atlantic racism today, as displayed in the Brexit vote and in US politics, seems to have roots in these earlier class-linked racializing processes. Certainly what Orr calls "demotic Orientalism" thus reveals yet another dimension of the multivalent, inter-imperial positioning, increasingly racialized, undertaken through Orientalist aesthetics.[96] Opening yet another angle of this complexity, Teresa Ko has analyzed tactical uses of Orientalism among Asian diasporic communities in South America who queer or lay claim to the cachet of eastern inheritances so as to make a virtue of outsider status.[97]

We see a particularly complex version of this history in Irish identities, beginning with Ireland's old affiliations with eastern genealogies. As Joseph Lennon recounts in *Irish Orientalism*, equations between Irish and Asian peoples have roots in ancient texts and medieval monastic scholarship. Ancient Greek writers had dismissively grouped Irish and Asians as borderland barbarians; yet medieval monks gave dignity to this linkage by arguing that the Irish language preserved the roots of the original biblical language fragmented by the Fall of Babylon.[98] During the sixteenth and seventeenth centuries, Irish scholars pieced together links of "ancient Ireland to the Egyptians and Scythians as . . . an integral element in asserting Ireland's right to independent sovereignty."[99] When in the eighteenth century British philologists began to make their own claims on ancient "Aryan" and eastern inheritances and simultaneously invoked ancient Greeks as authorities on Irish barbarity, Irish-language linguists re-entered this competitive discourse, asserting their ancient kinship with the heritages of the Global South and East. Given its specific genealogical discourses and its political situation as a British colony in northern Europe, Irish Orientalism became a distinctive strategic practice. As Lennon suggests, it operated from "an inclusive both/and perspective . . . rhetorically taking advantage of both the Orientalist perspective of the colonizer and the nationalist convictions of the colonized," or in other words, a doubled embrace of civilizationalism and anti-imperialism, which has persisted into the twentieth and twenty-first centuries.[100]

Meanwhile, at the end of the eighteenth century the inter-imperial vectors and pressures that were partly channeled through Orientalism came to a head in this "era of revolutions," including in Ireland. Under these conditions, the tropes of *The Nights* were made to serve diverse mediations. As I argue in the next chapter, its hidden maneuvers were brilliantly suited to intervene in that era of widening inter-imperial terrors and global insurgencies.

Chapter four

Global Revolts and
Gothic Interventions

The association between the Oriental and the Gothic modes is too obvious to pass without mention. —**MUHSIN JASSAM ALI**, *Scheherazade in England*

[The Gothic is] the necessary offspring of the revolutionary upheaval which affected the whole of Europe. —**MARQUIS DE SADE**, "An Essay on Novels"

I cannot put my pen down. —**NAPOLEON BONAPARTE**, quoted in Andy Martin, *Napoleon the Novelist*

"Include in your calculations," Napoleon wrote in 1806 to his brother Joseph (deputized to govern the recently conquered Sicily), "the fact that within a fortnight, more or less, you will have an insurrection. It is an event that constantly occurs in occupied countries."[1] Napoleon's success may be traced in part to his readiness to plan for this insurrectionary effect. Yet in the long run, the "total war" he set in motion across hemispheres, with mass destruction of villages where resistance was suspected, radicalized many populations. This radicalism spread across continents, through print forms and the news from refugees and colonial troops, including a small number of black troops from Haiti taken prisoner during the Haitian Revolution who fought in Napoleon's army.[2] Following the American and French Revolutions as well as rebellions that exploded around the world from Ireland, the Caribbean, and South America to China and India, Napoleon's transhemispheric conquering joined a concatenation of events that sent world dialectics into a tailspin at the turn into the nineteenth century. This "age of revolution" was global, inter-imperial, and multi-scalar, with profound effects for political consciousness.[3] Literature played its catalytic part.

By the last third of the eighteenth century, older and newer states faced off in an increasing number of territories, while the leverage Europe had gained in conquering the Americas and controlling the Atlantic recalibrated the so-called balance of global power. As the borrowing of technologies continued, each empire refined and strengthened its systems of centralization and its extraction of material, monetary, and human resources. The wars and system building in turn required states to expand taxation, institute military conscription, and exert more direct pressure on laborers to produce food and goods. As I describe in the first sections of this chapter, these conditions provoked unexpected alliances between elites and laborers, issuing in both spontaneous mutinies and carefully planned insurgencies. Historian David Bell argues that ultimately "the Napoleonic empire was overwhelmed by forces that Napoleon himself had unleashed" in the form of "fierce, damaging revolts."[4] The fierce potency of these revolts was partly fed, I propose, by these unexpected alliances.

I further argue that, in tandem with armed revolt, there emerged an incipient yet collective anticolonial sensibility, which I will sometimes refer to as a post/colonial consciousness. The slash here between *post* and *colonial* represents the discrepancy between the future vision and the present condition, between the imagined overthrow and the lived condition of oppression. This split condition finds full expression in Gothic literature, foreshadowing the "nervous condition" of colonized peoples and anticolonial dissidents of the early twentieth century.[5] For in this period, as news traveled more quickly via print and migrants, laborers, and soldiers, literary forms were adapted and transformed to tell the longer story of global violence, affecting political consciousness in many places. Especially during and after both the French revolutionary Terror and the Haitian Revolution, texts began regularly to depict stark scenes of torture, corruption, and imprisonment, implicitly linking them to the energies of repression and rebellion, as Marquis de Sade observes in the epigraph above. This literature registers what Anthony Maingot calls a "terrified consciousness" among the colonizers as well as a radicalized or critical consciousness among the oppressed.[6] Distilling these conditions within gendered plots of betrayal, some Gothic novels conjure the possibility of overthrow of the imperial order—incorporating the hopes of the colonized, the fears of the colonizers, and the apprehensive uncertainty of all.

Feminist critics have read Gothic literature for its plots of rape, while postcolonial critics have linked such plots to colonialism's crimes and tracked its Orientalist troping of colonized peoples.[7] Still other critics have interpreted Gothic fiction in relation to world-system instabilities in this period.[8] I link all these dimensions to the Gothic's scenes of rebellion and its corollary expression of both imperial and anti-imperial consciousness. Some texts condemn rebellion, some transform rebellion into reform, and others provocatively align readers with the rebels, particularly the texts of Ireland and the Caribbean. Echoing the tales of betrayal and sexualized state crisis at the heart of *The Nights*, they also gesture toward the long, accruing past of empires. Finally, many such authors comment implicitly on their own conditions of production by featuring Faustian knowledge seekers who are mesmerized by or memorialized in "medieval" manuscripts.[9]

No Gothic novel in English exposes these "total" conditions of inter-imperial betrayal and violence more searingly than Charles Maturin's *Melmoth the Wanderer* (1820), as I explore in the second half of the chapter. Featuring the Faustian scholar Melmoth, the novel's exposé of inter-imperial power brilliantly reworks both the tale-telling structure and the inter-imperial dynamics of *The Nights*—while also incorporating what we would now call a Trotskyan critique that casts combined and uneven development as a symptom of imperialism, as we'll see. Influential in Ireland and lauded by Sir Walter Scott and Lord Byron, the text was soon translated into Russian and French, attracting writers who were citizens of Britain's most formidable imperial rivals.[10] Fyodor Dostoevsky acknowledged the novel as a key inspiration for his own writing, and Honoré de Balzac wrote a sequel affiliating Maturin's Faustian protagonist with French financiers.[11] The Romantic painter Eugène Delacroix, famous for his epic paintings of Napoleonic wars and Greek wars of independence, chose in 1831 to depict a torture scene from *Melmoth the Wanderer*. Thus Maturin's novel traveled influentially through the imperial circuits that had generated it. Here I place it most centrally within the connected histories of the Atlantic world, where French, Irish, and Haitian rebellions unfolded in dialectical relation to each other, as did Atlantic-world Gothic literatures.

To explain the attraction and geopolitical force of such Gothic creations, it's necessary to recall the inter-imperial conditions that provoked rebellion and dissent in this era.

War, Taxes, and Rebellion

The argument that fin-de-siècle revolutionary ideas and practices originated in the American and French Revolutions and then spread elsewhere contains some truth; but these two revolutions have often been overdrawn as the origin and cause, as recent scholarship has shown.[12] Even before these revolutions, the pattern of rebellion was evident in a range of regions, as I'll detail here. The increasingly harsh conditions created by war provoked cross-class and cross-racial efforts at rebellion, as peasants and laborers sometimes found allies in military men or colonial elites, or both. Meanwhile, as a strategic part of state policy, empires sometimes supported rebellion in rival states, while dissidents, in their own inter-imperial moves, sometimes evoked the past imperial grandeur of their conquered states so as to rally allies and soldiers. I detail these multivectored maneuvers before demonstrating how the practices of total war in the Napoleonic era and the conditions of bondage pushed matters to the breaking point and precipitated the spread of a post/colonial political consciousness.

During the eighteenth and nineteenth centuries, constant warring put heavy burdens on many populations. States first of all expanded impressment practices well beyond the long-standing traditions in which villages were expected to supply a certain number of conscripts on a regular calendar basis, and the trend eventually led to the institutionalization of conscription during the Napoleonic Wars. As the numbers of soldiers participating in single battles grew from approximately 100,000 in the early eighteenth century to 500,000 by the early nineteenth, village households also bore the increasing burden of quartering soldiers, while women faced sexual predations.[13] At the same time, states' overextended military budgets often meant that food rations for soldiers, sailors, and laborers were meager, wages were inadequate or went unpaid, and aggressive punishment for desertion or insubordination was common. Such were the conditions, for instance, that sparked the Nore and Spithead mutinies in the British Royal Navy in 1797 (reprised in Herman Melville's Gothic novella *Billy Budd*, a story of mutiny infused with queer, racialized betrayals and desires).[14]

While impressment and labor coercion mostly affected the common people, aggressive taxing affected many ranks of society, catalyzing alliances across class, ethnic, and military/civilian boundaries. Like impressment, exorbitant taxing by states had also been a common state practice; yet in the later eighteenth century these conditions became so widespread and crippling that many populations balked and began actively to protest.

The American Revolution against the British Empire is only one of the best known of such tax rebellions. Britain faced tax rebellion in India as well, where resistance was differently shaped by inter-imperial history. For instance after the Battle of Buxar, in which the British won the right to collect taxes in the Bengali region, the zamindars and other landholders of Bengal (originally established as a tax-collecting class in the Mughal Empire) now in their turn faced double tax burdens. Several leaders refused to pay British taxes, as in the case of Durjan Singh, a displaced zamindar who in 1799 organized the so-called Chuar Revolt, taking over several villages and targeting East India Company establishments. The British eventually suppressed this and other rebellions, but their sense of the threat is indicated by their immediate execution of scores of villagers and leaders.

An acute version of tax unrest arose in Russia, where taxes tripled under Peter the Great as he pursued expansionist wars amid the jockeying Safavid, Chinese, Ottoman, and European states, as discussed in chapter 3. By 1794 under Catherine the Great, 46 percent of the empire's budget was devoted to the military, prompting wider "tax farming."[15] This destructive coupling of war and taxes ignited Pugachev's Rebellion in 1773–75, the largest peasant rebellion in Russian history. It grew from an alliance between a discontented Yaik Cossack military lieutenant, Yemelyan Pugachev, and the sorely exploited serf and peasant classes. Unrest among the Cossacks stemmed not only from the increasing hardships of their military service but also from a sharp government hike in taxes on their fisheries, the basis of Yaik Cossacks' livelihood. Pugachev knew he would find allies not only among the Cossacks but also among peasants, for there had been dozens of peasant revolts in the 1760s (estimates range from 50 to 160 peasant uprisings between 1762 and 1772).[16] In these decades, Russian serfs not only faced impressment into the military along with other villagers, but they also faced increasingly desperate economic conditions, exacerbated by recent laws allowing them to be sold separately from land, including for labor in the Ural mines. Pugachev initially won followers by invoking Peter III (recently assassinated); his ranks swelled further as he promised to ease exploitative conditions for the poor, urging serfs to "hang the landlords." Because, as Yuri Bosin notes, the "ruling classes were not prepared for the fierce rise in peasant discontent that ignited Pugachev's Rebellion," Pugachev's forces won control of the large swath of territory between the Volga River and the Urals, before he was captured and many rebels were killed.[17]

Similarly, in South America, the Spanish Bourbon government's continual tax increases provoked resistance. Colonial elites were angered not only by tax hikes but also by reforms designed to squelch tax evasion, a reform that benefited merchants and coastal cities at the expense of the longer-standing, traditional governors in noncoastal lands. The new rules also had an inter-imperial dimension, for the revenues partly served to fund the Spanish Empire's covert support for the American revolutionaries fighting the British. This was galling to Spanish colonial governors because they had received scant support during their battles against the British in the six Anglo-Spanish wars since 1702. In other words, the Bourbon government was funding its destabilization of Britain's North American colonies by taxing South American colonies that it had earlier failed to arm adequately against the British. Here, it's worth recalling, as a sign of the geopolitical interconnectedness of this period, that Russia similarly loaned support to the American revolutionaries as part of its own inter-imperial maneuvering to thwart British ascendancy. Indeed, one could ask: without the subversive support of Russia, Spain, and France through arms supplies and a trade embargo against Britain, would the American Revolution have succeeded? In other words, was it an inter-imperially achieved revolution?

In any case, the simmering discontent in South America exploded into violent resistance in 1779, in regions of what are now Colombia and Venezuela. Again, the rebellions made strange bedfellows of elites and laboring and indigenous communities. Although earlier uprisings of indigenous groups in South America had been suppressed by the creole colonial classes, some of these very same creole elites now sought out indigenous and other laborers as allies (a variation of which would happen in Saint-Domingue/Haiti). The Creole leader Juan Francisco Berbeo gathered more than ten thousand troops through such a coalition, achieving significant victories outside Bogotá. In a classic betrayal, however, the Bourbon Spanish governors first signed a treaty with the rebels, then dismissed it and promptly executed rebel leaders.

Thus did global inter-imperial military contestations force new waves of taxing that led dialectically to local revolt, all the while sowing seeds for the independence movements of the early nineteenth century. Yet these revolts were not always strictly *anti*-imperial per se; their leaders sometimes invoked the glory of past empires to galvanize resistance against empires of the present. Such was the case in the Rebellion of Túpac Amaru II (1780–ca. 1782) in the regions of present-day Peru and Argentina, which was provoked by the Bourbon tax reforms. The rebel leader José Gabriel Condorcanqui, a well-established Mesoamerican leader with claims to Incan lineage, brought together a coalition of mestizo, indigenous, and creole supporters. His campaign was inspired by a prophecy that the Incas would return to power, and apparently in his vision the British supported the Incan re-ascendance (an idea Britain promoted, eager to destabilize its Spanish rival).[18] Condorcanqui took the Incan name Túpac Amaru II and succeeded briefly in overcoming the Spanish colonial army, until reinforcements were sent and Túpac's forces were defeated. Today the name of Túpac conjures strictly revolutionary associations, but his discourse and affiliations were inter-imperially entangled. This tapping of past imperial affiliations by anticolonial actors is one of many dialectical ironies that, as we will see again in chapter 5, continually complicate anticolonial struggles.

A combination of imperial and anti-imperial elements also infused the so-called White Lotus Rebellion in Qing China (1794–1805), provoked partly by the inroads of western states and partly by the internal perception of Qing complacency. It too began in part as a tax rebellion mounted by a coalition, in this case between poor peasants and religious groups that wished for the return of the previous Ming dynasty. The guerrilla tactics of the White Lotus Rebellion shook the foundations of the Qing dynasty, which managed to defeat the rebels only by reorganizing its forces into local militias—and killing as many as 100,000 rebels and villagers. Events like these dramatize the depth of imperial subjectivization as it accrues over time and in memory, repeatedly stirred into new aggression by the maelstrom of inter-imperial violence. Throughout the decades to come in China, memories of Qing violence persisted and mingled with nostalgia for Ming grandeur in ways that energized political discontent with the Qing well into the twentieth century.[19]

The 1804–5 Serbian Revolution provides the clearest case in which revolutionaries refurbished an earlier imperial identity, evoking the glory of empires past in order to maneuver among powerful empires in the present. In this period, the Austrian Hapsburg, French, and Russian Empires all sought influence in the Balkan regions of the Ottoman Empire. With one hand, these European empires signed agreements with the Ottomans that defined trade between them as well as relations between European empires and client Ottoman Christian populations; with the other hand, European empires promised support for the Serbian Christians struggling for more rights under the Ottomans. In 1804, tired of being played as pawns in the machinations of empires and, more internally, suffering under the violence between Janissaries and the sultans, the Christian Serbs forged a vision for throwing off the Ottoman "yoke," one that called for revival of the pre-Ottoman fourteenth-century medieval Serbian Empire in the form of an "Illyrian" state. Propelled by this idea, Serbian leaders culled support from whichever states they could, sometimes playing the Hapsburgs, French, and Russian Empires against one another. For instance, in return for Russian support for their rebellion, they promised Russia a supply of Serbian troops, and they simultaneously promised the French and the Austrian Hapsburgs that their Illyrian state would stand as a buffer against Russian invasion.[20]

Ultimately their fate would be decided not by this Illyrian vision but rather by the outcome of inter-imperial wars first between the Russian and Ottoman Empires, and then between the French and Russian Empires as the Ottomans aligned with Napoleon. Yet the Serbian leaders played their inter-imperial cards well enough to win near independence in 1817, becoming a protectorate of Russia as agreed in negotiations between the Ottomans and Russians.

Total War, Total Resistance

As all of these cases illustrate, throughout these fin-de-siècle decades, state coercion and antistate resistance unfolded in an escalating coforming dynamic. As the abolitionist Thomas Clarkson noted in 1792 about the Caribbean, the policies of colonizing states were regularly adjusted in light of the potential for insurgency; fear of uprisings shaped and reshaped trade, marriage, military, and immigration codes.[21] That is, states were and have often been structured by the fact of rebellion. State and local maneuvers coconstituted each other. As we saw above, the Qing dynasty had to reorganize its military structures at local levels to counter the covert, widespread resistance of the White Lotus Rebellion and root out its guerrilla-like insurgency. David Bell makes a similar point when he argues that the French revolutionary government's effort to quell counterinsurgencies against the revolution led to changes in state militia practices, which then also shaped the Napoleonic Wars, as Napoleon noted in his advice to his brother Joseph.

In France, the combination of war, taxes, underclass impoverishment, and cross-class alliance that exploded first in the French Revolution and then under Napoleon catalyzed a trans-European epidemic of total war, as states encouraged civilians and soldiers to battle without limit against other civilians and soldiers. Authors registered the cataclysmic effects, as when William Wordsworth remarked, "the war of the present time is a war of all against all." With an eye on Spain, he also registered the tottering of empires ("Another year! Another deadly blow! / Another mighty Empire overthrown!").[22] The younger poet Percy Bysshe Shelley mourned the horror of "millions to fight compell'd, to fight or die," describing the many who "in mangled heaps on War's red altar lie."[23]

To grasp the spread of brutal civilian-on-civilian violence, it helps to begin with the Terror (what used to be called the Reign of Terror). In the early 1790s, as the revolutionaries took full power, they sent "hell columns" of French soldiers into the Vendée region to suppress dissent among peasants and villagers fighting to defend their beliefs in Catholicism and monarchy and to take a stand against the control of the Parisian metropole. Records indicate that more than a quarter of the Vendée population was exterminated in 1793–94, approximately 220,000 to 250,000 people. Soldiers were deployed to pillage every hamlet in the region. They killed livestock and slaughtered inhabitants, then set fire to homes, forests, and stores of food. The soldiers also apparently practiced rape wherever they went. As the mayor of La Flocelière recorded in his eyewitness account, "They raped the women . . . thirty of them taking turns on just one," all while boasting that they would rape and then kill all the women in the village—"except the pretty one," who undoubtedly would rather have been dead.[24] After inflicting all manner of violation, the troops strapped the inhabitants of La Flocelière to barges and ferried them out into the Loire estuary. Then they sank the barges.

It's important to pause over not only the human slaughter but also the pervasive rape. Historians regularly tally the dead and wounded of wars. But very few have proffered estimates of the numbers of women raped.[25] This is understandable given the difficulty of gathering information. Yet this, too, is history. These, too—these thousands of rapes—have shaped dialectics. The long history of rape in war has undoubtedly included boys and men, but it has also undoubtedly been perpetrated far more often and more systematically on women. The rape of women and the silence about rape (in war and everyday life) have structural effects for communities, arising from the presence of the survivors: the alienated children born, the women with broken bodies and souls banished to backstreets, and the rageful men drinking in taverns who consider themselves emasculated because the invaders have raped "their" women. This legacy also belongs at the center of historiography. Literature has told us as much, allegorizing the ways that rape has shaped the history of states since ancient times, as reflected in *The Rape of Lucrece* (where rape catalyzes the founding of Rome) and in the frame tale of *The Thousand and One Nights* as discussed in chapter 2. In Gothic texts, as we will see, rape and rebellion intertwine—though the connection often remains, to borrow from *The Nights*, one of those "things that lie hidden."

While authorizing or countenancing daily brutal violence of these kinds, France and other European states also sent hundreds of thousands of young men to die on battlefields. For this side of the catastrophe, we do have numbers. Before the revolution, most European battles against other Europeans involved fewer than 100,000 combatants, but the numbers multiplied dramatically thereafter. In 1809 Europeans sent 300,000 troops to the Battle of Wagram, and in 1813 they sent 500,000 to the Battle of Leipzig. At the end of the Napoleonic Wars, France had suffered approximately 1 million war deaths, while Europe as a whole had lost at least 3.5 million people and perhaps as many as 6.5 million.[26] As always, furthermore, continental and colonial killing worked in tandem, just as continental and colonial economies did, with co-constituting escalation on all fronts, as I discuss further below. As wealth accumulated in metropoles, the competitive drive for wealth spread and the need for control of labor intensified—so much so that resistance broke out everywhere. Antiwar, antislavery, and socialist movements also spread, seeding an incipient post/colonial consciousness even as states and capitalists trumped up the drive toward war, border control, militarization, and taxation. Adding the pattern of rape to this picture, we might well pause to imagine the relational, dialectical reach of these events at all scales, from intimate to imperial.

On the continental fronts, the violence escalated in the face of Napoleon's seemingly unstoppable invasions, as resistance grew and as other states also resorted to total-war destruction and aggressive conscription. Deputized to lead the resistance in Portugal, British general William Carr Beresford "used Portuguese institutions to impose effective conscription, insisted that inhabitants evacuate and lay waste to any territory in danger of French occupation, and in general mobilize their entire country for war."[27] Everyone became a guerrilla fighter—in fact, the word *guerrilla* was coined in this era, adapted from the Spanish for "little war." Under these conditions of unbounded warfare, local peoples could sometimes hardly know who was their main enemy; yet ultimately, hatred for the French became the driving force. As Bell describes it, "From Portugal to the Tyrol to Russia, insurgents declared total war on France. . . . [T]hey pledged every adult male to the fight, insisted that the entire population contribute in any way possible, and called for the death of every French soldier polluting their soil."[28]

Facing widespread resistance, by 1812 Napoleon was driven to invade new lands mainly in order to seize new tax revenues and new conscripts.[29] Yet at each turn, the pressures on invaded populations ignited more rebellions, as in Bologna where a new tax on the milling of wheat catalyzed the uprising of thousands of peasants. Here as in other places, peasants armed with scythes and pitchforks converged on the city, where they attacked property and people.[30] Bell concludes that these guerrilla insurgencies marked a fundamental shift in geopolitics not only by widening the field of battle but also through "the place they came to occupy in the European imagination," which was permeated with memories of "the long, grinding, hate-filled struggles of 1806–1814."[31] In imaginations outside of Europe, the memory of long, grinding struggle was older, and the hate-mongering cultivated by colonizers could not but provoke deepening anger among those who were creating the wealth over which Europeans warred. As we will see in later sections of this chapter, early nineteenth-century Gothic novels dramatize both the uprisings and repression and the desperate emotions they provoked.

The Strains of Post/Coloniality

The inter-imperial conditions and the emergent anti-imperial consciousness that I theorize in this section were most potently embodied in the one case in this period in which insurgents decisively defeated imperial forces: the Haitian Revolution. Its effects were amplified for the British by the simultaneous and nearly successful 1798 rebellion in Ireland, as described below. Haitian revolutionaries pointedly managed the rivalries among European empires in order to garner arms, offset serial invasion, and sustain trade. Initially, they successfully courted British and Spanish support in their battles against France, in the form of food and medical supplies as well as military aid. And when the British in their turn strove to take control of the island, Toussaint Louverture courted American support, successfully leveraging that relationship to pressure British general Thomas Maitland to withdraw British troops from Haiti. With each new turn of events, inter-imperial greed and war provoked shifting alliances and betrayals, intensified by conditions of terror peculiar to slavery and the plantation colony. Nonetheless, the people of color on this Caribbean island achieved the expulsion of European colonists, sending shock waves through the world and its imperial systems of control.

Already in this period of rebellions, the comings and goings of people and goods had been keenly watched, not only in the Caribbean and Americas but also across the English Channel, the Irish Sea, the Indian Ocean, and the Mediterranean.[32] But the Haitian Revolution intensified these, propelled by the contagion of "white fear," for, as Robin Blackburn observes, "the consolidation of black power in Haiti had a terrible message for the slave order throughout the Americas."[33] The revolution furthermore forced a diaspora among colonial elites who carried that fear across the world to Australia, Canada, and of course to the slave-holding empire of the United States.[34] Plantation owners fleeing Haiti and emigrating to the United States found that their slaves were jailed on arrival, since they were felt to be a likely source of insurgency. Throughout the Caribbean and the United States officials became suspicious of all gatherings, including literary salons and theater performances among free Blacks, for they suspected, sometimes correctly, that the gatherings might be a cover for subversive networking.[35]

But there was also more to it than providing cover, for such gatherings also signaled the increasingly close coformations of activist politics and the arts in the nineteenth century. Literature was becoming a consciousness-raising platform that reached across long distances and encouraged new solidarities, as Ifeoma Nwankwo shows in *Black Cosmopolitanism* and Ellen Malenas Ledoux illustrates in *Social Reform in Gothic Writing*.[36] Amy Martin similarly tracks the ways that Gothic tropes streamed through anticolonial Irish newspapers such as the *Nation*, figuring imperial states as bloodthirsty vampires and expressing solidarity with rebellions in India and the Caribbean. In Martin's account, this discourse developed into a "Gothic Internationalism" that came to the fore in Irish journalism especially after the 1857 Indian Rebellion and the 1865 Morant Bay Rebellion in Jamaica. Ties between literary and political imagination also circulated in the incipient anti-imperial nationalism that Partha Chatterjee traces in nineteenth-century India.[37]

As we measure the potential force of these literary interventions we should keep in mind literature's ancient entanglement with states and education systems. On one hand, authors such as Thomas Carlyle penned racist apologias for British colonial policy, and many texts perpetuated the tropes of threatening "Moors" or subservient Blacks.[38] On the other hand, the centrality of literary culture among the elite also meant that these new gothic interventions had the power to echo disturbingly in their halls of state. While critiques of literature's complicity in the semiotics of power still stand, this period also shows authors exposing and retooling those codes, including African Atlantic authors who were deconstructing the hypocrisies of Africanist, Orientalist, and Saxonist discourses of freedom and slavery.[39] Literature was becoming a channel for an anticipatory, incipient post/colonial consciousness, even in texts that aimed to contain it.[40]

This proleptic post/coloniality of vision constitutes an anticipatory counterpart to the afterlives of coloniality. Commenting on these afterlives,

Nelson Maldonado-Torres distinguishes between the time-space of colonialism as institution and the time-space of coloniality as a state of being that extends beyond colonialism proper: "Colonialism denotes a political and economic relation in which the sovereignty of a nation or a people rests on the power of another nation, which makes such nation an empire. Coloniality, instead, refers to long-standing patterns of power that emerged as a result of colonialism, but that define culture, labor, intersubjective relations, and knowledge production well beyond the strict limits of colonial administrations. Thus, coloniality survives colonialism."[41] The struggle with the lived "coloniality of being" that reaches beyond colonialism proper may have its corollary and precursor in the affective and material milieu that drives resistance *under* colonialism. That is, the precarious sense of the postcolonial possibility on the horizon is itself a condition and form of consciousness, entailing the anticipatory posture and future-oriented actions required for the undoing of the colonial state. This post/colonial consciousness was also expressed elsewhere, as in the case of dissidents in Ireland. In his 1803 speech from the execution block, the condemned rebel leader Robert Emmet invoked such a future when, in addressing his executioners, he proclaimed that "by a revolution of power, we might change places."[42] By conjuring a revolutionary future, Emmet challenged the colonizer's assumption of control over the terms of relationality, facing off against their disavowals and fears of existential interdependence.[43]

As nineteenth-century Gothic literature makes manifest, this anticipatory post/colonial orientation finds potent expression across those realms that Maldonado-Torres identified as "culture, labor, intersubjective relations, and knowledge production."

The Gothic Novel and the Nightmare of History

Gothic novels dramatize this strained consciousness and its inter-imperial conditions in their violent scenes of cruelty and protest and in their long-historical narratives of succession, betrayal, and transformation. They render the political imagination as an interiorized, terrorized sensibility colonized by imperial institutions and affecting all forms of intimacy.[44] The underlying political-economic conditions are often rendered implicitly, allegorized through manuscripts found in medieval dungeons and through plots of stolen inheritance involving the violation of a woman. Tapping Orientalist imagery while often borrowing narrative structures from *The Nights,* this Gothic literature ambiguously displays the "nervous condition" of post/coloniality. In certain cases, Gothic texts also gesture toward forms of ethical relationality that counter empire's violent history.

This chapter later analyzes Maturin's *Melmoth the Wanderer* as one such text. A full study of its structure and voicing reveals the novel's incisive linking of moral-sexual crises and macroeconomic-political ones, all unfolded through a narrative situation that foregrounds existential relationality. Other texts laid important ground for Melmoth's epic work, and I begin with these so as to reveal the literary-political streams already feeding global imaginations.

Among British Gothic novels of this period, Matthew Gregory Lewis's novel *The Monk* (1796–97) is easily the most gruesome. It includes scenes of torture, rape, imprisonment, forced starvation, and devilish pacts. Shaped by a colonialist perspective, the devilishness enters this novel, predictably, in the form of a spider from the American colonies (a *cientipedro* "brought into Spain from [Cuba] in the vessel of Columbus").[45] This "serpent's" poisonous bite prompts the crimes of a power-hungry couple, the monk Ambrosio and his criminal consort Matilda. In pursuit of their dreams of power, they torture, murder, and, in Ambrosio's case, rape; within the institutional walls of monasteries and convents, abetted by colluding authorities. When their crimes are exposed, an infuriated crowd gathers, begins to riot, and burns an eminent convent to the ground. Ambrosio and Matilda are finally sent to jail, where they make a Faustian pact with the devil. Yet this devil who promises to help them escape promptly betrays them and throws them to their deaths from the cliffs of Sierra Morena in Spain. Discovering betrayal at each turn, all of it ambiguously associated with colonialism, the text conjures a total-war world with enemies everywhere and trust nowhere.

Although audiences were shocked, in retrospect the novel's horrors should come as no surprise—especially if we consider Lewis's biography during the period when he was writing it, which provides a clear reminder of many writers' entanglement in the imperial economy.[46] Lewis's father (also named Matthew Lewis) served as British deputy secretary of war during the younger Monk's childhood and the French revolutionary years. Planning for his son to become a diplomat, he sent him to live in Germany in his teens and learn German. When young "Monk" Lewis was a mere nineteen years old, his father arranged a British embassy post for him at The Hague. This was 1794, the second year of the Terror in the Vendée region, when the hell columns fanned out across the region in grids, under orders to make the entire region uninhabitable. It was also the year that Lewis conceived and drafted his novel. In 1795, while he was revising the novel, the Second Ma-roon War broke out in Jamaica, which required five thousand British troops and eight months to squelch. This, too, would have affected Lewis, for his family owned two slave plantations in Jamaica, as absentee landlords. Dur-ing these years, furthermore, Lewis's parents were estranged, and he was thrown into the impossible position of "umpire," as he put it, between his battling parents. Lewis records feeling coerced by his father, and scholars have suggested that part of the problem may have been that Lewis was gay or queer (as hinted in queer cross-dressing scenes in *The Monk*).[47] Lewis's case illustrates how interlocking personal and geopolitical conditions can issue in new literary formations.

Yet Lewis's was not the first Gothic novel. The subgenre had been launched more mildly in the decades before the French Revolution, with *The Castle of Otranto: A Gothic Story* (1764). Written on a whim by mem-ber of Parliament Horace Walpole, son of the powerful early eighteenth-century statesman Sir Robert Walpole, Walpole's text brings into play all the key elements that would become de rigueur in Gothic texts—including more elements than have typically been discussed by scholars.[48] My discus-sion of *The Castle of Otranto* here lays ground for my analysis of *Melmoth the Wanderer*, which transforms Walpole's seemingly harmless and sometimes comical treatment of sexual crisis and longue-durée inter-imperiality into an epic anti-imperial vision.

Walpole sets his story about state succession in the Mediterranean world during the era of the late Crusades, invoking the layered history of Islami-cate and Christian states. The murder and threatened rape of women by a "tyrant" in the story (Walpole's word) invokes this discourse linked to Ori-entalism and by association to *The Thousand and One Nights*, while his in-clusion of supernatural events and his framing of the story as a "translated tale" further taps into the popularity of Orientalist fiction. This choice of setting also immediately lays down what will become another Gothic pat-tern: a "medieval" Mediterranean locale, where political and sexual machi-nations play out in the underground vaults and hidden passages of church or state institutions. Indeed in his 1949 novel, *The Kingdom of This World*, Alejo Carpentier will invoke this eighteenth-century Gothic Mediterranean in his rendering of the Haitian Revolution, a point I will revisit in chapter 6. Finally, Walpole also installed the trope of the found and translated manu-script that would also become classically Gothic when in the preface to the first edition he falsely claimed to be the translator rather than the author (he later revealed his authorship). These are the reasons why critics consider

Otranto the first Gothic novel, and it is also why Muhsin Jassam Ali, in his seminal study *Scheherazade in England,* considers "the association between the Oriental and the Gothic modes" to be "obvious."[49]

Under the guise of editor, Walpole suggested that the manuscript was produced in 1529, though emphasizing that its events occurred in "the years between 1095, the era of the first crusade, and 1243, the date of the last," most probably during the time of the "the Arragonian kings in Naples." That is, he sets it in Naples just after the Norman conquest of Islamicate Sicily.[50] The Gothic's Mediterranean settings have been rightly understood by readers then and now as an implicit critique of Catholic empires, part of the British "black legend" about the horrors of Italian and Spanish Catholicism. Yet when we take a second look we also see that, from *Otranto* forward, these locales often encompass the inter-imperial past of Christian and Muslim states and allegorize these states' "underground" connections, as in the case of Sicily in the transition from Muslim to Christian rule. As discussed in chapter 1, at first the Norman Christian kings (Roger I and Roger II) maintained Sicilian Muslim bureaucratic institutions, employed Muslim artisans, and patronized Arabic-language poets who praised their kingships.[51] Yet soon after Frederick II ascended the throne (as the son of Roman Catholic Hohenstaufen emperor Henry VI), he began the process of demoting Arabic arts and making Muslims second-class citizens.

In this founding Gothic text, Walpole uses the names of actual figures of this Sicilian period, including Frederick, Isabella, Manfred, Alfonso, and Conrad. He implicitly references some of the tangled events, with hints to his contemporaries about inter-imperial dynamics in the eighteenth century. The historical thirteenth-century Manfred was an *illegitimate* son of Frederick II (note the gender politics), who controversially named his son the prince of Taranto, the very province containing Walpole's titular city of Otranto. Walpole's villainous usurping protagonist, King Manfred, shares a name with the thirteenth-century Prince Manfred, who did indeed attempt to usurp the rights of his half brother Conrad, king of Germany. Most important, the historical Manfred transgressively formed an inter-imperial alliance with Muslim "Saracens" in his effort to expand and maintain control of his state, for which he was threatened with papal excommunication. Walpole undertakes his own act of elision and sublation when he omits this last detail, although some of his readers would have known the history and linked the fictional Manfred with contemporary Christian-Muslim controversial alliances and antagonisms. Specifically, mention of Manfred's treachery and "Saracen alliances" would likely have brought to mind France, whose long-standing close relations with the Ottoman Empire had bred resentment in Europe, most recently regarding the 1739 Treaty of Belgrade, in which the French aligned with the Ottomans in Ottoman-Austrian battles.

Walpole centers *The Castle of Otranto* on the trope of a succession crisis—that is, a crisis in the reproduction and inheritance of state power. In his story, when the tyrant Manfred's only son dies, Manfred fears that a prophecy about his rule will come true: that his wrongly gotten kingly line will end with him. Suggestively, as we eventually learn, the rightful heir, Theodore, has been fighting in the Crusades, where he was taken captive by Islamic princes but from which he has now returned to take his rightful place. Theodore is quickly imprisoned by Manfred, the usurping king, who, we are repeatedly told, rules by "tyranny" (as described ten times in this short narrative).[52] In a desperate attempt to continue his line—that is, to reproduce the state in its current configuration—he imprisons and attempts to marry his dead son's fiancée, Isabella. Isabella's father's name is, suggestively, Frederic, recalling not only the medieval Sicilian king Frederick II but also the contemporary Frederick the Great of Prussia, who had recently entered the inter-imperial fray, aiming to gain an edge in the balance of power among the Russian, Austrian, British, Ottoman, and Safavid Empires. Walpole's Manfred fails in every way. For instance, in attempting to stab Theodore, Manfred mistakenly kills his own daughter, thus absolutely ensuring the end of his line. At the same time, the rightful heir, Theodore, successfully pursues his plan to overthrow Manfred, a plot of subterfuge that in later Gothic texts will take the form of outright riots and rebellions.

When, at the close of the text, Walpole has Manfred hope that "this bloody record [will] be a warning to future tyrants!," Walpole not only echoed the freedom-slavery discourse, but he also retooled the brotherly tale of *The Thousand and One Nights*, ensuring that its sublated imperial history would form an underlayer of the English Gothic.[53] This author who was also a member of Parliament simultaneously sent a message to Britain's rivals and allies in the contemporary inter-imperial field. His final warning was strangely prescient. He unwittingly gathered the medieval Mediterranean elements that would recombine to shape the character of a Corsican man named Napoleone di Buonaparte, a man who resented the French imperial control of his island, yet who would eventually become the "future tyrant" who would reconquer it under a revolutionary banner.

As a telling indication of how literary and political discourses together shape events, it's worth noting that Napoleon was himself an avid reader and fan of the Gothic style, as well as an aspiring writer who wrote his own

Gothic tales. It's quite possible that he read Walpole's very popular *The Castle of Otranto*. Walpole was also well known in France, maintaining friendships with French intellectuals such as the historian Abbé Raynal, whom Napoleon also came to know.[54] Certainly the Corsican Napoleon would have been attracted to Otranto's Mediterranean history, as we can also glean from Napoleon's text, *Corsican Novella*, which registers Corsican resentment of the French takeover of the island in 1768. Perhaps most pertinent, Napoleon's self-styled mission as a liberator of the conquered finds expression in his use of Gothic Orientalist tropes.[55] He claimed in dramatic terms that he was freeing the people from "tyranny," as when he announced that he had freed Mediterranean Europe from the "iron yoke" of "Austrian tyranny." Likewise, in rousing addresses to his troops, he invoked the language of the Gothic sublime, describing how the soldiers had "rushed like a torrent from the top of the Apennines" and "overthrown and scattered all that opposed your march," while "sowing on all sides terror, flight, and death."[56]

David Bell calls Napoleon "the world's first 'media general,'" for his skills as propagandist as well as his use of semaphore telegraphy for military coordination.[57] Gothic literature played a part in the success of this propaganda, for it had shaped the political imaginaries of both Napoleon and his audiences. Or to put it differently, Napoleon was himself one of the conduits through which the circulating energies of a violent inter-imperial sensibility shaped contemporary politics. This man who in his twenties had been unable "to put my pen down" would, by his thirties, be unable to put down his sword, with powerful effects for the world's subsequent history.

During and after the Napoleonic years, Gothic texts spoke back to this world-ravaging horror in diverse ways. They registered a highly anxious post/colonial consciousness in stories of domination, corruption, subterfuge, rape, and insurrection, even though many texts ultimately defended the gendered and imperial order of things. Their patterns became embedded in Anglophone fiction from Charlotte Brontë's *Jane Eyre* (where the imprisoned Caribbean wife Bertha burns the master's house to the ground) to those late nineteenth-century texts that Patrick Brantlinger called the "late imperial Gothic," which continued to display "white fear," as epitomized in Ryder Haggard's *She*.[58] Fears of racialized rebellion also found early expression in the white Anglo-American Gothic tradition, beginning with Charles Brockden Brown's *Wieland* and reaching through both Herman Melville's *Benito Cereno* and Edgar Allan Poe's Gothic tales such as "A Tale of the Ragged Mountains." All of these are clearly situated within the inter-imperial violence and uprisings of the era. At the same time, however,

African Atlantic writers retooled the Gothic subgenre so as to expose its real-historical underpinnings in slavery and colonialism, such as in the historical slave memoirs of Olaudah Equiano and Harriet Jacobs, the "conjure" tales of Charles Chesnutt, and much later in twentieth-century fiction, including writers such as Toni Morrison and Octavia Butler and encompassing contemporary horror and zombie films.[59]

In sum, Gothic literature, Orientalist ideology, and revolutionary action should be read as co-constitutive formations within an inter-imperial field, whether yielding texts that are anti-imperial or imperial, feminist, queer, or homophobic. Charles Maturin's *Melmoth the Wanderer* (1820) seals the case for this dialectical interpretation of the Gothic, as I argue in the rest of this chapter. While sometimes expressing anti-Irish prejudice and perpetuating Orientalist imagery, Maturin exposes both the structural logic of the inter-imperial order and the gendered betrayals of existential relationality inherent to this order. And, like *The Nights*, Maturin's entangled narrative form also gestures toward alternative world relations.[60] Readers from Fyodor Dostoevsky to Charles Baudelaire, and perhaps Alejo Carpentier, took note.

Maturin's Inter-imperial Gothic

When Baudelaire singled out Charles Maturin as one of the first truly "modern" writers, he remarked especially on the "diabolical laughter" of Maturin's Faustian protagonist Melmoth. Baudelaire understood this laughter as "the perpetual explosion of [Melmoth's] anger and his suffering" and "the necessary result of his double, contradictory nature."[61] Here I trace Melmoth's contradictory nature to his agonistic complicity in the raced and gendered inter-imperial economy depicted in the novel, a condition reminiscent of Maturin's own position as an impoverished Anglo-Irish cleric living restlessly on the post/colonial slash, so to speak.[62]

Set in Ireland shortly after a series of Irish rebellions from the late eighteenth to the early nineteenth centuries, to which it subtextually alludes, the novel's retold tales arise from crises of imperial inheritance, both personal and macropolitical. In the main storytelling frame, Alonzo Moncada, a young aristocratic Spaniard fleeing torture and captivity within the Spanish Empire, tells harrowing tales to a young Anglo-Irishman, John Melmoth, who is about to inherit his Anglo-Irish estate. Not coincidentally, Maturin creates this framing male-male tableau of *translatio imperii* in the historical period when Spain was dramatically weakened and its people terrorized by Napoleonic invasions, while Britain's power was growing in Spanish South American colonies as elsewhere. As my extended reading of the novel argues, Maturin's structural critique also extends to competitive male relations shaped by primogeniture and "noble" reproduction. In queering the relations between John and Alonzo, who wish for a different kind of brotherliness, the text implies that male-male relations must be transformed if the world's inhabitants, including women, are to throw off imperial domination of their bodies.

Irish revolutionary history of the period provides the most immediate context for Maturin's far-reaching critique, a history that importantly coincides with wider Atlantic-world political struggles. For instance, in the very years that Toussaint Louverture was maneuvering among multiple European powers, Irish insurgents were likewise planning an overthrow of the British, in their case with French support. Furthermore, earlier revolutionary events had prepared the ground for this effort, beginning with the American Revolution, during which many British colonial troops were relocated from Ireland to America, leaving Ireland less fully militarized. The French Revolution then presented the Irish with further opportunities, which they quickly pursued under the leadership of Wolfe Tone who colluded with the French to launch an invasion. In 1796, according to a plan coordinated with the French Republican admiralty, a fleet of fifteen thousand French troops set out to invade Ireland, with Tone as adjutant general in the French army. History seemed ready to swerve in a new direction. But storms prevented the fleet from landing, and the British swooped in to arrest Irish collaborators, executing several leaders of the United Irishmen and aggressively imposing martial law. Hereafter French interest in the Irish battlefront waned—undoubtedly partly due to events in Saint-Domingue. Meanwhile, for the British the sense of threat from several directions continued, as reflected in the fact that in 1797 the British government worried that Nore and Spithead mutineers were connected to Irish and French revolutionaries.

And indeed, the Irish rebels persisted. In the summer of 1798, the Irish launched another uprising, with more limited French support. During the two months of pitched battle, roughly three thousand British and Anglo-Irish Protestants were killed—a significant number, even if it is dwarfed by the toll for Irish Catholic rebels and citizens (estimates range from twelve thousand to twenty-seven thousand). Under these conditions, the Earl of Westmorland urged that the British act decisively to "root out the spirit [of rebellion]" in Ireland, but Lieutenant Colonel Robert Crauford expressed doubt, averring that "the people of Ireland are, and *will continue to be* ripe for general insurrection" because "it is not in the nature of things that men's minds should become less influenced in consequence of the chastisement inflicted on them."[63] Crauford was proven right in subsequent years, as was made especially evident in Robert Emmet's 1803 rebellion in Dublin, which involved attempted coordination with Michael Dyer's rebel networks in County Wicklow. This is terrain that Maturin knew well, counties that he traveled in these very years. And this is where he set his Faustian inter-imperial tale.

Although Emmet's insurrection, too, was defeated, culminating with his public execution, Emmet's speech from the execution dock expressed the growing audacity of the revolutionaries. First, Emmet reminded the presiding judges and executioner that the "barbarity" of English powers had pooled so much blood that "Your Lordship might swim in it."[64] He then articulated the emerging post/colonial consciousness of the period, telling his executioners that "by a revolution of power, we might change places."[65] He even hints, "with the confidence of intimate knowledge" (alluding here to secret Irish societies), that plans were already underway to ensure Ireland's "emancipation from the superhuman oppression under which she ha[s] too long . . . travelled."[66] From his politically charged, existential position on the dock, Emmet projects a post/colonial vision while doing his best to foster a "terrified consciousness" in his colonizers.

Maturin's novel alludes to these Irish rebellions both implicitly and explicitly, and it furthermore positions them inter-imperially by linking them to sixteenth-century Spanish riots against Inquisition leaders. To capture these interconnected long-historical struggles, Maturin creates a Chinese box structure of tales within tales, encompassing the lives of Irish, Spanish Catholic, and Jewish subalterns, with passing references to earlier southeastern empires. All the tales are relayed to young John Melmoth by the traumatized Spanish refugee Alonzo Moncada over the course of one long night inside the Anglo-Irish "Big House" that John is poised to inherit. In both this frame and the tales, many characters are visited by the Faustian figure of Melmoth the Wanderer, John's seventeenth-century English ancestor, who arrived in Ireland under Cromwell, later made a pact with the (colonial) devil during his travel in foreign lands, and now offers immortality and world knowledge to anyone who might agree to take his place as world wanderer. (For clarity, I will usually refer to the transhistorical older Melmoth as "the Wanderer," and I will refer to his young nineteenth-century descendant as John.)

Ultimately, the knowledge that the Wanderer gains through his long view of history is, I argue, an anguishing "Gothic" knowledge of the twin forces of systemic domination and intimate violation, in which he is complicit, as he has come to see. His struggle is recorded most dramatically in a long manuscript titled "Tale of the Indians," which Alonzo Moncada recounts to young John Melmoth and which occupies the center of the novel. The manuscript narrates the Wanderer's seduction of the innocent Immalee, a young girl who was shipwrecked during her Spanish father's trade voyage and has grown up as a single castaway on an island in the Indian Ocean. As he "educates" her about the "crimes and passions" of the world through his magical transhistorical telescope, the Wanderer cannot resist the attractions of her innocent goodness.[67] He continues to visit her even after she is reunited with her family in Spain, until eventually she conceives a child with him. Thrown into prison as an unwed mother, Immalee ultimately dies there along with her infant daughter. As I'll trace, this interpolated tale is Maturin's embedded allegory for the ruin of women as they are conscripted into the reproduction of empire's stratified, racialized economies.[68]

Most important for my reading, Maturin embeds this transhistorical tale of Immalee and the Wanderer in a translingual manuscript. That is, he self-reflexively registers the underlying importance of language and translation in this history: for the suppressed story of Immalee (like other "things that lie hidden," to borrow again from the frame of *The Nights*) has been encoded in *"the Spanish language* [yet] written in *the Greek characters"* (301; emphasis in original). Furthermore, our Spanish tale-teller Alonzo has, as he explains, been made to translate this document into Roman script by a man named Adonijah, an underground Jewish scholar in Catholic Spain. Adonijah has for many years kept the manuscript in a vault, and he promises to aid Alonzo's escape from the Spanish Inquisition if Alonzo undertakes this act of translation.

In other words, to escape the corrupt cruelties of the Spanish Catholic Empire and to counter his own entanglement, Alonzo Moncada must face the repressed multilingual, en*script*ed, gendered history of Spain—and of empires in general. His task is to "translate" that knowledge for other inheritors of empire, including his interlocutor, young John Melmoth. Maturin links the importance of writing to that of media technology more broadly when he puts the Wanderer in possession of a magical telescope: a deep-time, long-distance technology that enables his transhistorical and transhemispheric perspective on the world. Maturin's Gothic allegory of gender, empires, and world knowledge thus traces the interlingual genesis of an inter-imperial field founded on "systematized vice," as we will see Maturin makes clear.

As is evident in his novels and his sermons, the Anglo-Irish Maturin was ambivalent about rebellion against the imperial order of things, and his text participates in anti-Catholic, anti-Irish, and Orientalist prejudice.[69] Yet given his sharp critiques of the linked cruelties of religion and empire, it seems that Maturin was also laboring to make ethical and emotional sense of the blood of colonialism that was "so deep you could swim in it," as Emmet had put it. Furthermore, as I discuss at the end of the chapter, Maturin comments implicitly both on his own complicity and on the risks of making art that exposes imperial complicities and cruelties. Himself struggling with a post/colonial consciousness, he offers an unflinching anatomy of the global inter-imperial condition.

Marxist Melmoth, Imperially Framed

It's tempting to speculate that Karl Marx and Leon Trotsky drew inspiration from *Melmoth the Wanderer*. Marx certainly tapped Gothic imagery for his depictions of capitalism's vampiric feeding on the world's laborers and poor, as scholars have noted.[70] Yet *Melmoth the Wanderer* offers more than Gothic imagery. It develops structural critiques in accord with later Marxist critiques, for the Wanderer's "knowledge" centers on his understanding of uneven and combined development.

The Wanderer begins his analysis by exposing the depths of "systematized vice." The third-person narrator of the manuscript (who sometimes also refers to the Wanderer as "the stranger") remarks, "the stranger had incredible difficulty to make Immalee comprehend how there could be an unequal division of the means of existence" (336). When she asks, "Why should some have more than they can eat, and others nothing to eat?" he answers that humans have made "the most exquisite refinement on that art of torture": in his view, the "civilized" crowd into cities, "nominally for security and protection, but really for the sole purpose to which their existence is devoted—that of aggravating [the poor's] miseries by every ingenuity of refinement," and especially by "placing misery by the side of opulence" (336). As a result, "the wretch who dies for want" must feed merely "on the sound of the splendid equipages which shake his hovel as they pass" (336). The Wanderer furthermore specifies the institutional and propertied dimensions of this condition, commenting on the collusion of "law" with economy. Although law is supposedly a "security for . . . persons and their property," it is actually, the Wanderer points out, a system that "contrives to convert a difficulty into an impossibility, and punish a man for not doing what it has rendered impossible," so that for instance when a man is "unable to pay his debts, it deprives him of liberty and credit, to insure the inability still further"—a point that would have cut close to the bone of the underpaid, debt-ridden Maturin (340–41).

War receives the same sardonic treatment. The Wanderer characterizes it as the "pastime" of the rich who collect "the greatest number of human beings that can be bribed to the task, to cut the throats of a less, equal, or greater number of beings, bribed in the same manner for the same purpose" (338). When Immalee puzzles over the motives, the Wanderer not only links war and economy but also exposes state interpellation through aggrandizing masculine symbols and language:

> Some of them fight for ten inches of barren sand—some for the dominion of the salt wave . . . but all for pay and [escape from] poverty, and the love of action, and love of change, and the dread of home, . . . and the admiration of the showy dress in which they are to perish. The best of the jest is, they contrive not only to reconcile themselves to these cruel and wicked absurdities, but to dignify them with the most imposing names their perverted language supplies—the names of fame, of glory, of recording memory, and admiring posterity. (339)

Throughout this scourge, as always, Maturin keeps in view the effects for the domestic world of women and children, while also emphasizing the performative "theater" of power by which men are seduced: "Thus a wretch whom want, idleness, or intemperance, drives to this reckless and heart-withering business,—who leaves his wife and children to the mercy of strangers, or to famish, (terms nearly synonymous),—the moment he has assumed the blushing badge that privileges massacre, becomes, in the imagination of this intoxicated people, the defender of his country, entitled to her gratitude and to her praise" (339). The Wanderer next turns his telescope to the linked performances of religious and state power, which bend thousands to the coerced labor required for imperial pomp. The text indicts both European and non-European practices, but Maturin also uses some standard European Orientalist imagery. For instance he includes the oft-invoked and decried juggernaut procession in his description of an immense jewel- and gold-studded carriage "dragged forward by a thousand bodies" (325). Yet Maturin's language suggests a more structural critique by focusing on the ways that "the impulse was so unequal, that the whole edifice rocked and tottered, . . . and this singular union of instability and splendor, of trembling decadence and terrific glory, gave a faithful image of the meretricious exterior and the internal hollowness" (325–26). In light of this passage's description of the system's "singular union of instability and splendor" and of the "unequal" effort of labor under the meretricious "trembling decadence" of owners and rulers, one might well wonder whether Trotsky found inspiration in Maturin. The thought is reinforced when shortly hereafter the Wanderer turns his telescope to the European ships in foreign lands, indicting empires' extractive economies:

> There came on the European vessels full of the passions and crimes of another world—of its sateless cupidity, remorseless cruelty, its intelligence, all awake and ministrant in the cause of its evil passions, and its very refinement operating as a stimulant to more inventive indulgence, and more systematized vice. [Immalee and the Wanderer] saw them approach to traffic for "gold and silver, and the souls of men";—to grasp with breathless rapacity, the gems and precious produce of those luxuriant climates, and deny the inhabitants the rice that supported their inoffensive existence;—to discharge the load of their crimes, their lust and their avarice, and after ravaging the land, and plundering the natives, depart, leaving behind them famine, despair, and execration; and bearing with them back to Europe, blasted constitutions, inflamed passions, ulcerated hearts, and consciences that could not endure the extinction of a light in their sleeping apartment. (334)[71]

In these images of both the famished despair of the natives and the ulcerated hearts and consciences of the exploiters, which repeat throughout, Maturin's pithy critique of empires invokes the bodily, gendered, and psychic effects more starkly and directly than any other English-language Gothic novel. While the Wanderer concludes that we everywhere find "malignity, ambition, and the wish for mischief," Maturin makes sure to have him add "it is the system, not the individual, we must blame" (336).

In tracking the system, the Anglo-Irish author himself struggles to explain his own involvement and his own blasted constitution. He encodes his ambiguous position in relation to post/colonial consciousness by having the Wanderer attempt at one point to alert Immalee's father to the danger she's in—even though he is himself that danger. Maturin's self-reflexive encoding finds further expression in the novel's frame story and in its portrait of insurgency.

Maturin's novel opens with the familiar trope of a troubled inheritance story, but he sets his story on the blood-soaked soil of Irish rebellion. On the first page we meet young John Melmoth as he travels to his dying uncle's Anglo-Irish estate, to which John is heir. As he journeys by stagecoach through southern Ireland in this "succession" moment, John reflects on the irony of inheriting wealth from his "awful" miserly uncle whose "caprice and moroseness" had tortured both him and his parents and allowed them to struggle in poverty: a classic case of the "uneven" brotherly inheritance that also broods over *The Nights*. Yet John feels burdened by another pressure that apparently arises from the locale itself: "The beauty of the country through which he traveled (it was the county Wicklow) could not prevent [John's] mind from dwelling on many painful thoughts, some borrowed from the past, and more from the future" (9). With mention of County Wicklow, Maturin would have evoked "painful thoughts" for his readers, for as mentioned, Wicklow and other southern counties were key sites of insurgency and raids dating from the 1798 uprising, and reaching forward to the time of the 1803 rebellion led by Emmet.

In other words, as John rides through Wicklow toward his Anglo-Irish inheritance, his uncle's home in Wicklow in 1816, he also travels through recent Irish history. John's journey parallels Maturin's own, for shortly after the 1798 rebellion (when he was a divinity student at Trinity College) Maturin took this very journey on his way to Galway for his first clerical position. The allusion to Wicklow seems designed to prompt discomfort in Anglo-Irish and English readers who might well feel worried still about whether there would be a "revolution of power."[72] The description of John's mental turmoil disconcertingly conflates John's "dependency" with that of the struggling Irish.[73] Recalling "his own dependent state," John is assailed by memories that "fell like blows fast and heavy on his mind" (9). Although he "rouse[s] himself to repel them," he fails in this effort. The third-person narrator comments, "when the mind is thus active in calling over invaders, no wonder the conquest is soon completed" (9–10). Spoken in County Wicklow and written by an Anglo-Irish author, these are fighting words. Read allegorically, they imply that the ever-fighting colonized Irish are now asking for it, caught in the self-destructive mindset of the colonized.

Yet read within the larger Atlantic history and interpreted within a dialectical perspective, the next phases of Maturin's portrait emerge as a study of Hegelian lord/bondsman alterity. The fears that plagued the colonizing class and the destabilizing gazes of the colonized feed John's anxious sense of limited control over the household and over the narrative of his own relation to it. Arriving at his uncle's Anglo-Irish "Big House," he encounters an Irish community that is poor and hungry but also threatening, as suggested by the "barefooted boy" who opens the corroded gate and then by the "furious barking of a mastiff, who threatened at every bound to break his chain" and whose "yell and growl," Maturin adds, "savoured as much of hunger as of rage" (12). Inside, John enters a circle of neighbors and female servants, seated in the kitchen around a well-stoked turf fire (in a scene also laced with references to *The Nights* [16]). As the uncle lies upstairs on his deathbed, the servants are feasting on the household's stores of food and liquor, all of which would appall the miserly uncle who has hoarded supplies and let the house fall into decrepitude rather than spend money. A partial countercolonization is underway in the Big House.

John soon finds himself suffering another kind of "dependency," for he is beholden to the servants not only for his food and board but also, we soon learn, for the details of his own family history. Curious about his ancestor Melmoth "the Wanderer," John must seek out the Irish servant Biddy Brannigan. This "withered Sybil" gazes at him with a "mingled look of servility and command" as he struggles to translate what he calls her "irishcisms [sic]" (12, 27, 25). Biddy's post/colonial consciousness is further implied in the history she tells, for, as John soon learns from her, the story of the Melmoth family encapsulates the history of the colonization of the isles.[74] The first Melmoths, she reports, arrived in eleventh-century England with William the Conqueror, and the family resided there until the English Civil War, when a son who had served as an officer in Cromwell's army "obtained a grant of lands, the confiscated property of an Irish family attached to the royal cause" (26). That is, he received lands seized from a family affiliated with the Catholic confederacy formed in the 1640s. The elder brother of that family—the titular Melmoth the Wanderer—became a knowledge seeker. He left Ireland to travel in distant countries and especially to seek out alchemists, reportedly to "profit in strange concealments" (29).

In classic Gothic detail, a portrait of and a manuscript about the Wanderer are kept in a locked closet, the key to which John receives as part of his inheritance (21). The portrait is dated 1646, the year Charles I surrendered to Cromwell's army, and the manuscript of "fifteen mouldy and crumbling pages" likewise dates from the seventeenth century, authored by a man named Stanton who records his series of encounters with the Wanderer. Thus Maturin repeatedly highlights this English Revolution period, with its renewed colonization of Ireland under Cromwell, an emphasis that persists all the way to the novel's last interpolated tale of another family's civil war troubles.[75] That night, as John huddles in the closet to read the fragmented manuscript under the portrait's seemingly watchful eyes, he seems to become yet another seeker of translated knowledge amid inter-imperial histories. Noting the "feverish thirst of curiosity that was consuming [John's] inmost soul," the narrator initially compares John to "Michaelis himself, scrutinizing into the pretended autograph of St. Mark at Venice" (32). Foreshadowing later manuscripts, Maturin's wry narrator also mockingly hints at the queer investments of this drive to know, when he remarks, "No antiquarian, . . . hoping to discover . . . some unutterable abomination of Petronius or Martial, . . . or the orgies of the Phallic worshipers, ever pored with more luckless diligence . . . over his task" (65–66).

At the opening of the Stanton manuscript, Maturin immediately locates these frenzied pursuits in an inter-imperial southern Spain. As Stanton travels on a stormy night, he stumbles on the "magnificent remains of two dynasties that had passed away, the ruins of Roman palaces, and of Moorish fortresses," while the narrator makes several references to earlier Catholic-Muslim battles.[76] As the storm intensifies, Stanton sees in the sky "light struggling with darkness," hinting at world-historical struggles between empires. Sexuality then takes its place at center, for when a bolt of lightning shatters the Roman tower, it kills a pair of young illicit lovers who had been trysting there (34–35). As villagers carry away the lightning-charred remains of their bodies, Stanton suddenly hears the "loud, wild, and protracted laugh" of the Wanderer (35)—the laughter that Baudelaire saw as the expression of his suffering and his cynicism—including, we might add, his anguished knowledge of the destruction of love. Hereafter Stanton becomes obsessed with tracking the Wanderer in his own worried version of imperialist identification.

All of Stanton's subsequent encounters with the Wanderer coincide with allusions to the gendered violence of empire, ranging from subsequent sightings of him at a play about Alexander the Great, to the raving mother in the asylum to which the unhinged Stanton is eventually committed (by associates wishing to control his inheritance), and the "mad diplomatic pamphlet" Stanton reads titled "A Modest Proposal" that, in Swiftian fashion, calls for the genocide of Turkish children.[77] The novel thus hints early on that to follow the path of Melmoth the Wanderer is to be possessed by a colonizer's madness and violence, with unmooring effects for all.

Vying Brothers and Queer Bedfellows

As John closes the Stanton manuscript, he hears desperate cries for help on the stormy Irish Sea outside. Enter Alonzo Moncada, a refugee from imperial Spain whose ship has crashed on the Irish shore. John rushes to the seaside with other villagers where he personally rescues the drowning Alonzo. Having set up the troubled inheritance of John, Maturin introduces this disinherited Spanish nobleman fleeing captivity in an Inquisition prison. At the seashore, Maturin immediately initiates the queer subtext that streams through the novel. After John pulls Alonzo ashore, the two faint together on the rocks— "locked in each other's hold, but stiff and senseless" (75). The Wanderer fleetingly appears on the cliff above, laughing his characteristic laugh. Yet the men's life-saving embrace eventually leads to the all-night storytelling session that encompasses the rest of the novel's tales. With these two structuring patterns, of brotherly embrace and Shahrazadian frame, Maturin already hints that a repair of male relations underlies the repair of inter-imperial history.

Alonzo's story begins, like John's, with a tale of two brothers whose alienated relations wreak havoc. Furthermore, his tale directly incriminates agents of the state, who manipulate and corrupt these relations. As he tells it, Alonzo's troubles begin when a priest (referred to only as "the Director") attempts to divert all of Alonzo's inheritance to Alonzo's only brother, Juan, since doing so will also secure the Director's patronage from the prestigious Moncadas, one of "the first" families in Spain. The Director pressures the parents to cooperate by threatening to expose that the mother conceived Alonzo, their firstborn, out of wedlock. Finally, wielding the threat of the empire's Inquisitional powers, the Director convinces Alonzo's mother that, to atone, she must commit Alonzo to a monastery, where he will be forced to take vows and thereby lose all inheritance rights. In the meantime, so as to secure his leverage in the family, the Director has also cultivated the younger brother Juan's loyalty.

The novel devotes several chapters to Alonzo's time in the monastery, casting it as a "theatre" of imperial violence: "There was a coup de theatre to be exhibited," and the monks sought to "play first parts," justifying their sadistic punishments by invoking imperial Roman figures and precedents (105).[78] In this theater of domination, as the monks attempt to manipulate and terrorize Alonzo under pretense of caring for him, they repeatedly address him as "brother," corroding the terms of brotherly relation: "My brother, you are alone"; "But, my brother, you are devoured with ennui"; "Interest yourself, my dear brother, in these questions, and you will not have a moment's ennui to complain of" (113). Alonzo begins to speak with palpable irony of the actions of "the brothers."

In the midst of this hypocrisy, Alonzo receives a letter from his real brother, Juan, that opens "My dearest brother." Alonzo can barely recover from the dissonance ("My God! how I started!"), and even more so when Juan apologizes and reports that he has broken off relations with the Director. Juan anticipates Alonzo's distrust of him with telling reference to his "revolt" ("I see you revolt at the first lines which I address to you"), and he then proceeds to give a burning critique of the maneuvers of "priestly imposition" (131). He has come to see, he says, that "the basis of all ecclesiastical power rests upon fear," and so: "I was taught from my cradle to hate and fear you,—to hate you as an enemy, and fear you as an impostor. This was the Director's plan. He thought the hold he had over my father and mother too slight to gratify his ambition of domestic power, or realize his hopes of professional distinction" (131). And so he hounded their mother "till, in a moment of penitence, my mother, terrified by his constant denunciations if she concealed any secret of her heart or life from him, disclosed the truth" (131).

Juan closes his letter with a plan for Alonzo's escape, for which he has engaged a man to guide Alonzo out of the monastery through its subterranean passages. After Alonzo's first covert meeting with this man in the monastery garden in which he is bedeviled by alternating fits of trust and distrust, he describes his state of anticipation about escape. It epitomizes what I described above as the anticipatory post/colonial consciousness of possible liberation from empire, a sensibility emerging among the colonized and dispossessed in this early nineteenth-century period and registered in Gothic texts. Complete with a telling allusion (one of many in the novel) to "eastern tales," the passage is worth quoting at length. Its disorienting syntax and punctuation serve to capture the anguish of Alonzo's condition.

> The days that followed I have no more power of describing, than of analyzing a dream to its component parts of sanity, delirium, defeated memory, and triumphant imagination. The sultan in the eastern tale who plunged his head in a bason [*sic*] of water, and, before he raised it again, passed through adventures the most vicissitudinous and incredible— was a monarch, a slave, a husband, a widower, a father, childless,—in five minutes, never underwent the changes that of *mind* that I did during that memorable day [*sic*]. I was a prisoner,—free, a happy being, surrounded by smiling infants,—a victim of the Inquisition, writhing amid flames and execrations. I was a maniac, oscillating between hope and despair. I

seemed to myself all that day to be pulling the rope of a bell, whose alternate knell was *heaven—hell*. (208, emphasis in original)[79]

Unfortunately, Alonzo's doubts and his fears of "hell" are proven correct. For like many a dissident, Alonzo and his brother are betrayed by this man, who is actually an agent of the Director and the church authorities.

Maturin's crafting of this sequence allegorizes political and gendered betrayals in several ways. First, although Alonzo repeatedly calls this man the "liberator," he soon learns he is a parricide (as the text later calls him) who has become an undercover agent for the church in exchange for amnesty for the crime of killing his father. Maturin implicitly allegorizes the old inter-imperial tactic of proffering liberation while planning renewed domination. We also learn that, on behalf of the church, the parricide has also killed his sister and her illicit lover, another embedded allegory.

And yet at the same time, before the parricide betrays the brothers, Maturin inserts a series of queer embraces between Alonzo and the parricide, recalling John and Alonzo's embrace after John's seashore rescue of him. The parallel hints that parricide might be unnecessary if brotherly relations could move in another direction, if brothers followed impulses that would pull them away from the machinations of empires. During their underground escape from the monastery, and in a moment of apparent penitence after telling the story of how he killed his sister, the parricide "swoon[s]" into Alonzo's arms. Shortly after, when they reach freedom in the open air, a dizzy Alonzo in his turn "swoon[s]" into the parricide's arms (238). Finally, when the two arrive outside the monastery wall, Alonzo finally greets Juan, cherishing "the embrace of a brother" and holding "close to that of the most generous and affectionate of brothers" (239). It is at this moment that the parricide *qua* liberator stabs and kills Juan, while church guards seize Alonzo and carry him to the Inquisition prison. This betrayal of "generous" brotherhood comes to stand in for the betrayal of persons by states and religious institutions. The triumphant post/colonial vision becomes "defeated memory." But insurrection follows.

Institutions and Insurrections

Most important for my argument here, the parricide's betrayal leads to violent rebellion: such is the logic of the uprising scene that shortly follows. After a fire in the Inquisition prison allows Alonzo and others to escape, church authorities hold a ceremonial procession of the highest clergy to re-establish order and, as Alonzo notes, to awe the population. Problems arise when the gathered crowds see the parricide riding among the clergy, for they recognize him only as a famous murderer, not knowing that he has become an agent of the state. They hiss, throw stones, and begin to obstruct the procession, shouting: "Are the hands that have cut a father's throat fit to support the banner of the cross?" (281). Despite the advice of officers and the parricide's own plea to retreat, the chief inquisitor "bate[s] not a jot of his pride" and leads the procession into the hostile "multitude," which soon "became ungovernable" (282). Enraged at this indifference, the crowd surges forward, pulling the parricide from his horse and mauling him—"as a bull gores the howling mastiff with horns right and left," finally throwing him to the ground, "a mangled lump of flesh" (283). Alonzo watches all of this in terror from his hiding place in the home of a family, which turns out to be that of the covertly Jewish archivist who has him translate the "Tale of the Indians," as I'll discuss shortly.

Maturin first of all inserts his own "archive" into this scene, in the form of a footnote about spontaneous insurrections in Ireland. Although the Irish violence is also depicted as brutal, the comparison implicitly critiques the arrogance and hypocrisy of the imperial authorities—and links Spanish and British imperial rule. The first footnote merely recalls that a similar "circumstance occurred in Ireland in 1797, after the murder of the unfortunate Dr. Hamilton" (284). This historical Hamilton, who had been active in tracking down Irish rebels, was also forcibly seized and gored by a group of Irish men. A second footnote follows on the next page, appended to Alonzo's description of the madness that overcame him as he watched the crowd's murder of the parricide. This longer footnote compares his traumatized response to that of a shoemaker who looked on from his window at a scene of Irish rebellion "in the year 1803, when Emmet's insurrection broke out in Dublin" and "Lord Kilwarden . . . was dragged from his carriage and murdered in the most horrid manner" (285). When Kilwarden is finally "nailed to a door," the witnessing shoemaker becomes unable to move, "as if nailed to" the door himself, and after he becomes "an *idiot for life*" (285, emphasis in original). Although Alonzo is similarly shocked by the violence of the Spanish crowd, the narrative logic places responsibility for the murders on the arrogant Spanish and Irish statesmen. The sequence and footnotes imply that Hamilton and Kilwarden are, like the parricide, criminals deployed and protected by the state. Alonzo's experience of abuse in empire's "theater" of power reinforces this commentary on the criminality of the state. Situating both empires within the long violent history of "brotherly" relations, the text lends moral justification to the "revolution of power" predicted by Emmet.

Maturin also insinuates that racialized reproduction plays a part in this betrayal of relations, especially as it entails coercion of mothers and daughters. He does so by suggesting parallels between Alonzo's and Immalee's family stories. As we saw, in Alonzo's family, the Director blackmails the mother for conceiving a son out of wedlock. In Immalee's case, not only does she herself perish for this "crime," but her mother is similarly coerced by the family confessor, Father Jose. When Immalee's brother ambitiously aims to arrange a profitable and noble marriage for Immalee after her return home, Father Jose quickly rejects the idea, hinting at secrets about the family lineage. At first, the brother dismisses the hint, mocking the lineage claims of the aristocratic Spanish families in distinctly racialized terms when he avers that the "baboon shapes and copper-coloured visages" of these noble families might in fact be improved through a marriage to Immalee. Yet "you forget, son," Father Jose points out, "'The extraordinary circumstances attendant on the early part of your sister's life. There are many of our Catholic nobility who would rather see the black blood of the banished Moors, or the proscribed Jews, flow in the veins of their descendants, than that of one who'—Here a mysterious whisper drew from Donna Clara [the mother] a shudder of distress and consternation" (374–75). The text leaves this matter unclear, yet the sequence seems to suggest illicit, cross-racial relations on the mother's part, which Father Jose hints could manifest in the offspring of Immalee.

Meanwhile, Maturin suggestively affiliates Immalee's family with the (covertly) Jewish family that helps our storyteller Alonzo escape from Spain, by giving the name Don Fernan to both Immalee's brother and the Jewish Adonijah's brother. Maturin puts strong emphasis on the name "Fernan," having the Inquisition officers mention it five times when they come to the Fernans' house in search of Alonzo, where they specifically raise the question of racial lineage; they remind him, "We know that the black blood of Grenada flowed in the tainted veins of your ancestry" (288). It is the brother of *this* Fernan who asks Alonzo to translate Immalee's story, which reveals the extent to which her fate follows from the Catholic "brothers'" efforts to enrich themselves and to reproduce the stratified hegemonic state through women. Through these references—to Al-Andalus, to Jewish scholars, and to Islamicate and earlier empires—Maturin implicitly references the world's long inter-imperial history.[80] Exposing the suppressed Arabic and Jewish pasts of Spanish Empire, the novel also unearths the coercions of women on which those suppressions depend.

In short, Maturin uncovers the sexual matrix of both the repressed inter-imperial, multicultural history of Al-Andalusian Spain and the empire-driven economic histories linking Iberia, Ireland, and India. When we recall that it was a violent uprising that provoked Alonzo's "descent" into this translation of the brotherly and sisterly ruin at the heart of empires, we understand that Maturin himself labored to translate the transhemispheric dialectics that explain his contemporary world's revolutionary violence. It's no coincidence that he positioned a young Anglo-Irishman haunted by recent rebellions as the riveted listener to the Spanish Alonzo's tale.

Through its Shahrazadian structure, Maturin's novel simultaneously asks readers to listen and witness, like Dinarzad in *The Nights*. Listen to Adonijah, listen to Biddy, let their stories inhabit us, just as the "Tale of the Indians" came to inhabit the translator Alonzo, and as all of Alonzo's stories have come to inhabit John. The novel stages this listening across political, religious, class, and cultural boundaries as it enfolds tales not only from Biddy the Irish Sybil but also, for instance, from a Spanish Catholic servant who, at mortal risk, sheltered Anglo-Protestant Stanton and told him stories of the Wanderer. That is, Maturin repeatedly creates tellers or listeners who have been protected by someone who they might normally consider an enemy, all of which is placed against the hypocrisy of supposed liberators who destroy liberty. He also trains readers to continually reorient across multiple tale-tellers and time leaps, as well as to accept uncertain translations, interruptions, and traumatic memories, to pause and notice when Alonzo breaks down in the middle of his account, speechless or sobbing. Readers are called on to avow the violated relations that have constituted us.

In the hands of Shahrazad's creators, of Maturin, and of many authors since, such experimental structures have modeled alternative relational practices *and* alternate historiographic practices, exposing the hollowness of any sovereign narrative of events. In other words, they offer a decolonial phenomenology of history. By embodying the way that events cannot be reconstructed except by historically entangled and perspectivally positioned tellers and listeners, they have also pried historical remembering away from the control of dominators and states. Their Shahrazadian art erodes such hubris, tale by tale. Proliferating the situation of tellers, tales, and listeners, such texts re-create the primal, volatile condition of relationality. This is the political core of their art.

Yet Maturin also acknowledges that to tell these tales and honor this practice can be deadly. Art making is no safety zone. Near the end of the novel he enfolds a parable of the storyteller's precarious position through the fleeting appearance of a writer figure in his novel—a man killed after his attempt to warn Immalee's self-absorbed father about the doom she faces. When this unnamed writer is mysteriously found dead in his room, the Wanderer appears out of thin air, remarking to Immalee's father that this is "the fate of those whose curiosity or presumption breaks on the secrets of that mysterious being, and dares to touch the folds of the veil in which his destiny has been enshrouded by eternity" (488). True to the inter-imperial economy of relations, the innkeeper lavishes attention on Immalee's father because he is "a wealthy merchant," and he pays no mind to the dead man because he is "totally unknown, as being only a writer and a man of no importance" (488).[81]

Likewise, Maturin the cleric served the British Empire, yet as a writer he dared to lift the veil over its Gothic world. His parable quietly anticipates his own demise, for he does indeed die four years later, leaving his family in poverty. Despite Maturin's anguished end, however, his critique anticipated and perhaps encouraged the revolutionary writing of subsequent generations.

Infrastructure, Activism, and Literary Dialectics in the Early Twentieth Century

Leave off looking to men to find out what you are not. . . . As conditions are at present constituted you have a choice between Parasitism, & Prostitution—or Negation. —**MINA LOY**, "Feminist Manifesto" (1914)

We already had communism. We already had surrealist language. . . . Tupi or not Tupi that is the question. —**OSWALD DE ANDRADE**, "Cannibal Manifesto" (1928)

The Modern World is due almost entirely to Anglo-Saxon genius. . . . Machinery, trains, steam-ships, all that distinguishes externally our time. —**WYNDHAM LEWIS**, "BLAST! Manifesto" (1914)

Time and Space died yesterday. We already live in the absolute, because we have created eternal, omnipresent speed.

   We will glorify war—the world's only hygiene—militarism, patriotism, the destructive gesture of freedom-bringers, beautiful ideas worth dying for, and scorn for woman.

   We will destroy the museums, libraries, academies of every kind, will fight moralism, feminism, every opportunistic or utilitarian cowardice. —**FILIPPO TOMMASO MARINETTI**, "Manifesto of Futurism" (1909)

In the long view, the nineteenth century emerges as the dawn of a sharply pitched, globe-encircling battle between empires on the one hand and the world's wealth-producing but exploited denizens on the other, a battle energetically fought through systemic technologies of transport, telegraph, and print. Marx of course pointed in this direction, but he eclipsed some key dynamics. He gave limited attention to the intensifying technologies and to the structuring dimensions of sexuality, gender, and race. When we see that technologies became a central stake in these battles, when we remember that the planet's impoverished persons included most of its women, and when we remember how fundamentally the "sciences" and systems of racial thought were deployed through technology and textbooks to discipline minority men and all women, ordering their labors of reproduction and care, we learn better how to read the structural forces at work. As the epigraphs to this chapter suggest, the dynamics included visions of revolutionary action and visions of violent domination cutting across avant-garde and rear-guard positions. On all sides the struggle included the arts.

By the early twentieth century, in a world shot through with "omnipresent speed," invasions of many kinds were launched. They rolled through the train tracks spanning thousands of miles, through telegraph cables installed under oceans and canals, through airplanes dropping bombs—and through both aggressive "futurist" imaginings like Marinetti's and radical feminist imaginings like Loy's expressed in the manifestos quoted above. Empires' proliferation of violence and domination through distance-spanning technologies ruptured communal histories and, moreover, unsettled communities' *sense* of history. Long-historical memory wobbled like a shrapnel-wounded soldier, only to be forced upright within the lockstep regimen of Greenwich standardizing time, decreed by empires and deployed within nations across the globe. The dizzying (dis)coordinations provoked diverse claims on historicity that, I argue in this and the next two chapters, became contests over temporality itself, over ways of being in time, together.

Scholars in a range of disciplines have discussed the early twentieth century as a time of historical rupture and transformation. Some accounts connect the renewed "scramble" for colonization among Anglo-European empires to the catastrophes of World Wars I and II; some focus on the consolidations and instabilities in the capitalist economy that shaped those events; others analyze breakthroughs in technology and science; and still others foreground revolutionary sociopolitical and artistic movements. Some literary scholars have understood the experimental literatures of this period as critical engagements with both "empire time" and imperial infrastructure.[1] This chapter argues that an inter-imperial, intersectional study of these several dimensions not only clarifies their interlocking coformations but also explains how and why they converged on what I will refer to as techno-infrastructures—telegraphy, railways, steamships, and radio. These material channels of encounter became both bodily and discursive sites of contestation.

In temporal terms, actors on many sides understood that the battles would be fought partly over claims on "the modern" insofar as "modern" and "backward" had emerged as the defining binary terms of history. By the late nineteenth century, evolutionary and eugenic science reinforced Anglo-European narratives of Manifest Destiny and "western" progress, creating "paedomorphic" time lines that assigned "lower maturity" to women and to darker-skinned "races" of the Global South. For some, especially many Anglo-Europeans, the past was no longer celebrated as a reservoir of knowledge and sustaining relation but was instead cast a constraint to shed, in order to lay monopolizing claims on the future. For many others, the past was indeed a resource, including of sustaining practices and collective values, especially crucial for grappling with the shocks of the warring, time-collapsing, and impoverishing present.

As the period's manifestos illustrate and this chapter analyzes, the vying discourses that emerged were variously feminist, masculinist, eugenicist, anti-imperial, antiracist, and civilizationalist. At the same time, due in part to technology, there emerged closer ties between artists and activists as they increasingly worked in tandem through print and art to challenge imperial aggression. Although their efforts, too, sometimes evinced persisting imperial-racial attachments and masculinist subjectivities, many understood the need to avow long-historical legacies of troubled relationality as well as to engage with the material-technological matrices of their present. Writers reconfigured genres to rescue time from total inter-imperial control, both mirroring its destruction and renewing the energies of historical being in their experimental forms.

The brief first section of this chapter gives an initial sense of writers' active attention to the "red planet" of war and their stark or sorrowful appeals to communities around the world. The two next sections then turn to the coforming dynamics of inter-imperial aggression and anti-imperial subversion in the fin-de-siècle period, focusing on the techno-infrastructures deployed by all political sides, especially railways and telegraphy. These inter-imperially generated technologies made the effort to control time more possible, more dangerous, *and* more contested. Because this dialectical unfolding (and time's importance in it) also centrally involved the wars among empires, these sections also consider the proliferating inter-imperial wars of the period. The interlocking dynamics of war, print, telegraphy, transport, and rebellion, epitomized in the Boxer Uprising, the Boer War, and the Russo-Japanese Wars, were crucial to this period's powerful wave of anti-imperial solidarities and discourses.

In this context, the second half of the chapter focuses on print culture as a site of struggle. Again here, timing and travel are implicit elements, insofar as control of these mattered for the organization of political congresses and the dissemination of news, manifestos, and literature. I discuss the transperipheral journalism that, on one hand, fostered transhemispheric anticolonialist solidarity and yet, on the other hand, sometimes expressed masculinist and civilizationalist attachments. Here we glimpse the depth of imperial subjectivization and the challenges of ethical struggle. Finally I offer an interpretive survey of the literary experiments and movements of the period so as to capture the geopolitical unfolding and refolding of ancient and modern poetics, whether in "futurist" and "mechanomorphic" visions or in vernacular, hybridized retoolings of long-historical aesthetic legacies. These, too, sometimes evince a range of attachments and complex inter-imperial maneuverings, yet they nonetheless challenged the warring and coercive inter-imperial order of things. This literary legacy has animated the political consciousness of communities around the world and offered visions that, however invisibly, inform our struggles today.

In other words, this chapter establishes, especially for readers unfamiliar with this period or these literatures, that the coformations of literary culture and geopolitical power continue to transform global struggles. It also explains how the turn into the twentieth century became a key turning point in the consolidation of long-accruing systems *and* the consolidation of *dissent from those systems*. Finally, this chapter lays ground for the book's final pair of chapters in part III, which center on postcolonial fiction writers especially in the Caribbean, who critique long-historical inter-imperiality as part of their project of reimagining the future.

"Sit Down, My Brothers"

Across the global field dominated by multiple warring empires, technologies shaped the projects of both activists and artists. Vladimir Lenin's famous 1917 train journey from Germany to Russia epitomizes the ironies as well as the long-term consequences of these technological matrices. Lenin traveled from Zurich to Saint Petersburg on German-built trains to participate in the class revolution and agitate against Russian participation in World War I, but his mission was backed and the train was literally guarded by a worried German Empire, whose primary agenda was to collapse or at least further destabilize the Russian Empire. In the long term, however, the Russian Revolution succeeded, creating further trouble for the Germans so that, by the end of World War II, their imperial dreams were utterly defeated, dividing Germany itself in half.

So, too, with many dissenting activists, journalists, and writers: they traveled and communicated via the same technologies that empowered domination, never certain of the effects of their labors. Photographers found their way to war fronts and then by telegraph sent out images of the fallen buildings, the destroyed bodies. Political organizers convened congresses and then disseminated their manifestos and political platforms in print. Authors from every corner of the world founded small presses, bookstores, and journals; they told and distributed the untold stories of violence and betrayal, though in some cases their vocabularies and affiliations simultaneously revealed attachments to imperial and other hierarchizing identities, as we will see. Nonetheless, buoyed by the knowledge that others were challenging the imperial and stratified order of things, authors and activists built networks together, all of which began to transform the norms of relationality. Many thematized technology itself, registering its positive, negative, and mixed effects. As they debated which pasts and technologies were usable, all these writers seized the time that was theirs, the present time that their widespread collective activism made theirs, as this chapter details. An international range of writers undertook the revisionary labors of *rememory*, to adapt Toni Morrison's word for the reimagining of lost and violated pasts.

In the hands of authors engaging with technology's time- and space-traversing powers, narrative time and human memory, accordingly, also became sites of redefinition and negotiation, variously deployed against the (dis)remembrance or disavowal of relations past. While Benedict Anderson rightly argues that the imagined communities of nationalism arose in the nineteenth century through "the convergence of capitalism and print technology" together with "the standardization of national calendars, clocks and language," my analysis highlights the other side of the project, casting it within an inter-imperial frame.[2] That is, the homogenizing interpellations achieved through media and clock time also provoked counterimaginings. In her novel *Mrs. Dalloway*, for instance, Virginia Woolf dramatized the force of "standardizing" time through the Westminster Palace clock Big Ben, whose "booming" chimes call the characters' wandering consciousnesses back to order; moving against this "slicing, dividing" call, Woolf's narrator slips in quicksilver fashion through multiple consciousnesses, reconnecting their postwar and queer sexual sorrows.[3] Woolf in effect co-opts technology's electrical movements to render the suppressed relations and critical perspectives of London's inhabitants.[4] The struggle with time appears most pointedly when the traumatized World War I veteran Septimus Warren Smith is told that "it is time" for his appointment with the psychiatric doctor (whose "rest home" plan for Septimus will lead him to suicide). As his wife urges him to be on time, in the mind of the dissociating Septimus, "the word 'time' split its husk" and "poured its riches over him" and his thoughts then attach "themselves to their places in an ode to Time; an immortal ode to Time."[5] Through the ode, Septimus hallucinates that he might recover the intimate comradeship with his dead friend Evans, and there might be "universal love: the meaning of the world," for he feels so acutely that "trees were alive" and that "it was plain enough, this beauty, this exquisite beauty."[6] Woolf traces Septimus's longing for deep-time intimacies and beauties that will stall the system's coercive interpellation through clock time, exposing the empire's reorganization of temporality as a tool of control over relationships to others and to the past.

Authors elsewhere composing in dozens of languages participated in these broodings on temporality, relationality, and aesthetic form. These included the Indian *bhaja* writers experimenting in native languages with new forms of fiction; the exploited Chinese "coolie" laborers using ancient Chinese poetic forms in the protest poems they carved on the wooden walls of their internment cabins on Angel Island off the coast of California; and Afro-Caribbean performers satirizing and reimagining world relations in calypso drama and song. Diverse modernist writers and movements aligned themselves with "the new" and have been understood as such; yet many of them approached this newness, I argue, through engagement with the long troubled but bountiful past. They grappled with the fact that the past's legacies were both killing and sustaining, depending on one's position and identity. Although writers of the period have often been cast as either realist or modernist, bourgeois or communist, I argue that across their differences many undertook the work of sifting through long-accruing sedimented regimes of power. Working in different contexts, authors adopted different modes ranging from a realism documenting histories of labor exploitation, to a magical realism capturing the surreal haunting of the present by the past, and finally to styles at the limits of intelligibility challenging empires' "rational" structuring of time, space, identity, and power.

Poets as well as novelists understood that their struggle was a pitched and dialectical one, as Mina Loy conveyed in a characteristic formulation:

> Pain is no stronger than the resisting force
> Pain calls up in me
> The struggle is equal.[7]

Loy is here speaking of the experience of childbirth, but she links it to "the irresponsibility of the male," which, in its disavowal of relationality, "leaves woman her superior Inferiority." The birthing speaker observes of a neighbor that "he is running upstairs [while] I am climbing a distorted mountain of agony." And yet as a result (like the bondsman in Hegel's scenario), the woman more clearly understands dialectical processes:

> I am knowing
> All about
> Unfolding.

Loy's dialectical assertion captures the ambivalences and ironies of struggle in the period.

Accordingly, many poets registered the presence of other visions, invoking beneficent possibilities. In his poem "Distribution of Poetry," the Brazilian poet Jorge de Lima hails his "brothers" into a different "distribution" of goods. "Listen, my brothers," the poem's speaker begins,

> I took wild honey from the plants.
> I took salt from the waters,
> I took light from the sky.

This receptive "taking" is then contrasted with the world of buying and selling, where "misery goes and returns" as "the ships go and return." In closing, the speaker addresses the Dalit laborers in India and, alluding to one of the oldest regimes of stratified labor, asks what alternative form of state they might imagine:

> O Untouchables, which is the country,
> Which is the country that you desire?[8]

He finally pleads, "Sit down, my brothers." Such poets also bent and expanded time as they faced off against the new "signals" of technology, as Salvador Dali would do in paint. In Loy's portrait of artists in her poem

"Apology of Genius," these "mystic immortelle" poetic seers are formed by "curious disciplines beyond your laws," even as they are "tracked" by the "watchers of the civilized wastes":

Ostracized as we are with God
The watchers of the civilized wastes
reverse their signals on our track

Lepers of the moon
all magically diseased
we come among you
innocent
of our luminous sores . . .

Our wills are formed
by curious disciplines
beyond your laws . . .

While to your eyes
A delicate crop
of criminal mystic immortelles
stands to the censor's scythe.[9]

Understanding their position as social "lepers" facing the blade of censors, these authors embraced their part in world dialectics—consciously "embarking" in Sartre's sense.

To fully appreciate the world conditions in which these writers came to "know all about unfolding," it's necessary first to track the expanding inter-imperial technologies and then to characterize the brutal inter-imperial wars they faced in the fin-de-siècle period.

Switchbacks on the Tracks of Empire

By the later nineteenth century, both state and revolutionary military strategists recognized that battles were to be fought not just with guns, and not just over territory or rights, but over material infrastructures, especially telegraph and railway lines—and with explosives. As I'll highlight here, in this fin-de-siècle period as in so many earlier periods, technologies were generated and extended by inter-imperial mimesis (including neocolonial financing) as well as by anti-imperial rebellions and retoolings. Gesturing toward the inter-imperial dimension, Paul Kramer points out that the "intensify-ing transportation technologies did not simply make possible the aggres-sive military expansion of European and U.S. power in the late nineteenth and early twentieth centuries. They also made the consolidating colonial regimes in Africa and Asia stages for interacting and overlapping empires of commerce and evangelism, which drew 'inter-imperial' communities together around both common and competitive projects."[10] These con-solidations in turn provoked organized resistance, I emphasize. Although, then as now, the pitched battle was tragically uneven, the remarkable fact is that the colonized and the coerced nonetheless persistently fought this battle.

The famous July 1853 arrival of US Commodore Matthew C. Perry in Japan with his impressive fleet perfectly illustrates the mimetic coforma-tions driving these processes. It also marks one historical turning point for the infrastructural and arms races that exploded into World Wars I and II. Acting in the time-honored tradition of empires and under the guise of shar-ing knowledge, Perry presented the emperor with technological "gifts" that exhibited US power: new kinds of weaponry, telegraphic technology, and a steam engine and rails. Tracing the Japanese response, Antoinette Burton and Tony Ballantyne have highlighted its institutional and cultural dimen-sions, including the concerted translation of "barbarian books" by state-employed Japanese scholars:

> Immediately after Perry's visit, a range of bureaucrats, warlords, and scholars based in [Japan's] various political domains explored the pos-sibilities and implications of Perry's "gifts." An important set of plans was drawn up for the establishment of an institution that would guide Japan's exploration of new industrial and military technologies, the Bansho Shi-rabesho (Office for the Investigation of Barbarian Books). This center for learning was directed to assess the military strength, technological devel-opment, and strategic aspirations of Japan's rivals, as well as to translate books on "bombardment," "fortifications," "building warships," "machin-ery" and "products." The establishment of Bansho Shirabesho initiated a substantial reorganization of knowledge production within Japan and of Japan's engagement with the world.[11]

This institution building demonstrates that, as in earlier centuries, trans-lation projects and knowledge production worked in tandem with state for-mation projects. It also reveals that these projects issued from a combination of imperial competition and collusion. In analysis of this and similar technological exchanges, emphasis should be less on what the "the East borrowed from the West" and more on the continual process by which imperial rulers and elites all play the risky game: shrewdly imitating and appropriating the technologies of rivals exactly in order to "defeat" them, even as they also lay claim to autonomous origins for their state and disavow interdependence. In Japan, these projects were consolidated after the Meiji Restoration (1868), so that by 1895 Japan had developed new long-range weaponry and had laid thousands of miles of telegraphic lines and railway tracks. The railways were carefully connected to key ports for, as always, the "routing [was] dictated by strategic concerns," including both commercial and military control, in order to forge the "iron arteries of empire."[12] The state planners also ensured that these arteries were linked to commuter rails, thus connecting scattered populations and channeling them into new social-imperial formations under the sign of Japanese modernity. Just as the translation and dissemination of Chinese Buddhist texts in seventh-century Japan had served to build an island-wide hegemony, so trains in the late nineteenth century provided a basis for national identity that in this case was also harnessed to an imperial identity, as we've seen is so often the case. Thus both materially and ideologically, as one Tokyo journalist observed in 1899, "the means of extending one's own territory without the use of troops . . . is railway policy."[13] Both train and print technologies allowed new control over the conditions and terms of relationality.

Yet by the same token, antagonisms between empires led to ceaseless competition that destabilized their dreams of control. Once built, first of all, these infrastructures attracted the interest of other states. In fighting to gain Manchuria from Russia in the 1904 Russo-Japanese War, as noted earlier, the Japanese well understood that they would benefit from the Russian-built railway and port infrastructures, which would enable transport of the coal required for Japan's manufacturing of weaponry, railways, and other industrial products. Similarly, in its battles with China over Korea, Japan gained control over and then further modernized Russian infrastructures, which fostered the extraction of rice as well as iron ore—not to mention filling the colonial tax coffers for Japan's military and engineering projects.[14]

In all these cases, competitive inter-imperial state formation increasingly centered on infrastructural as well as economic projects. Given this inter-imperial co-constitution of the field, however, those projects and states were also susceptible to combined destabilization, as made evident in the Vienna stock market crash of 1873. The drive toward railway building had been prompted by Germany's rapid defeat of France in the Franco-Prussian War of 1870–71, since Otto von Bismarck's victory was attributed in part to his strategic railway and infrastructure building, which enabled him to mobilize men and long-range arms. His feat was an object lesson to other states. It catalyzed not just an arms race but also an infrastructure race, prompting overinvestment in railways by Europe and the United States. The speculative railway bubble, which burst with the crash of the Vienna stock market in 1873, led to the worldwide Long Depression of 1873–79 and in turn to massive unemployment. This problem provoked labor strikes and riots throughout the latter part of the nineteenth century, as well as racist attacks on nonwhite labor and anti-Semitic scapegoating. Neil Faulkner argues, furthermore, that the collapse of railway companies in Europe and the United States may have encouraged their neocolonial investments while also dramatically increasing states' spending on the military for economic reasons. These conditions pushed Anglo-European empires to "scramble" for new territories and capital in Africa and Asia.[15]

Not surprisingly, anti-imperial resistance targeted the inter-imperially built infrastructures. Inside and outside the metropoles, people understood that trains and telegraph lines were the penetrating mechanisms that reconstellated power relations, suppressed rebellion, and coerced communities into new bodily categories of stratification. In India and Africa, resentment rose as trains and stations became biopolitical instruments for reinforcing race, class, and gender hierarchies via rules about which bodies could ride in which train cars, as Mohandas Gandhi discovered in South Africa.[16] Famously, in *Hind Swaraj* (1910) Gandhi broadly identified the railway as an instrument of Britain's "hold on India," and he rallied a powerful resistance movement around the boycotting of British manufacturers enabled by it. At the same time, like anticolonial nationalist leaders elsewhere, Gandhi eventually advocated a retooling of transport and other systems in the service of an independent India.[17]

This range of effects is clearly visible in the Ottoman Empire, where the building of railway and telegraph lines simultaneously entailed inter-imperial maneuvering and enabled new forms of contestation—vertical, horizontal, and vectored. First, it's worth noting that western European investment in Ottoman infrastructures (as in China and elsewhere) reflected the rise of neocolonial financial strategies. Empires together and separately lent money and technical support to targeted states in order to create indebtedness while also gaining material control over the "iron arteries" of relationality. As an inter-imperial framework highlights, these efforts aimed to forestall the parallel designs of other imperial rivals, who were simultaneously attempting to gain leverage by making counteroffers of capital support. Thus, the French and the British competed to play a role in financing and designing Ottoman techno-infrastructural projects (as they had done with the building of the Suez Canal). As a result, the first Ottoman telegraph and railway lines were routed to facilitate metropole communication not only between the Ottoman metropole and peripheries but also between French and British metropoles and peripheries. By 1860 the Ottoman telegraph network covered fifteen thousand miles of territory. By 1880 the Orient Express train line from Istanbul to Salonica was up and running. And in 1900 the sultan initiated a railway project to connect Damascus to Mecca that would also serve hajj pilgrims, thereby countering Muslim criticism of European-sponsored projects by promoting the sense that these infrastructures served Islam rather than Christian Europe.[18]

Resistance to these projects was widespread: trains and telegraph lines in rural areas were regularly attacked or dismantled—so much so that the central government established a special empire-wide guard to protect the network. Tellingly the Ottoman government offered subsidies to local rulers who created measures to stop the attacks, which suggests that local governors, who themselves were sometimes less than enthusiastic about telegraphy, needed "incentivizing." Some of these regional rulers objected because they considered the technologies a channel for foreign control and cultural westernization, yet some may also have perceived a threat to their provincial autonomy. At the same time, Arab and Kurdish communities in the Ottoman Empire saw railways not only as intrusive westernization but also and perhaps more immediately as a further forced Ottomanization of their territories and, for local leaders, a further threat to Arab suzerainty. Very possibly, they understood the premise of this book: their embattled condition arose from their position between and among competing empires.

The new transport infrastructures also disrupted long-standing labor and trade economies. In the case of the Bedouin, for example, trains exacerbated their economic troubles, already severe since the 1869 opening of the Suez Canal (itself a thoroughly inter-imperial affair),[19] which among other effects flooded the Ottoman and Middle Eastern markets with Anglo-European goods and displaced the Bedouins' artisanal production. In addition, the building of train lines, together with steam transport, deprived many Bedouin of their traditional role of providing protection and camel service to hajj pilgrims traveling to Mecca, for which they had traditionally received government subsidies. The problem partly provoked the Bedouin uprising of 1909.

The convergence of resisting actors prepared the conditions in which techno-infrastructures would become dialectical sites of contestation, as fully illustrated in the "line smashing" of the Ottoman Hejaz railway undertaken during World War I as part of the 1916–18 Arab Revolt. ("Line smashing" referred to the systematic detonation of explosives along miles of track in order to stall transport of troops, weapons, and supplies.) The British directed Arab nationalists to blow up some of the very trains and telegraph lines Britain had helped to fund, aided in this guerrilla tactic by the infamous T. E. Lawrence ("Lawrence of Arabia").[20] Their successes were abetted by the Bedouin, who were motivated to join their cause partly because of the ruinous effects of railways for their economic survival. The combined forces were able to explode twenty-five bridges in May 1918, for instance.[21] This centerpiece of the Arab Revolt's military strategy did indeed cripple the Ottoman Empire's operations, with significant effects, since it ultimately fostered the breakup of the Ottoman Empire and the eventual founding of a British- and US-backed Israeli state in the Middle East. Such are the far-reaching effects in the multivectored field of relations.

In this period, however, railways and telegraphy catalyzed some positive long-term transformations of the relations between subjects and the state, for the new technologies gave openings to women and to remote populations. Interestingly the threat to the Ottoman governors' power arose partly from the creative retooling of the telegraph system by provincial townspeople: locals began using it to express their discontent to the sultan, in effect circumventing local governors and practices by reworking this technology as a new channel for the traditional, legally encoded Islamic practice of petitioning (similar to the maneuvers borderland women seem to have made centuries earlier as Ottoman law gave them new handles for petitioning).[22] Meanwhile, women saw that trains offered new opportunities to enter the public sphere and question customary prohibitions on their visibility there, as noted by Burton and Ballantyne.[23] Early twentieth-century leaders of the anti-veil movement, such as activist Huda Shaarawi, chose to stage a launch of their movement at a train station—where prohibitions on women's visibility could be pointedly challenged. Again we see the multidirectional reconfigurations of dialectical relation created by railways, telegraphy, and other such infrastructures, whose volatility is further explained by the inter-imperial wars of the fin-de-siècle period.

Warring States

English-language historians once characterized the nineteenth century as the era of a global Pax Britannica. Yet recent studies make clear that, on the contrary, battles small and large were the global norm. In the wake of the Napoleonic era and as the United States and European states came into their own as empire builders, scores of land wars, invasions, massacres, and laborer and soldier conscription schemes continued to plague every hemisphere, and they continued to spark rebellion among peasants, slaves, and wage earners. Expansionist states also provoked "land wars" with indigenous peoples in Australasia, Africa, and the Americas, and wars for independence likewise spread among settler, "client," and minority populations. As usual, inter-imperial rivalry fed the flames of rebellion, as each empire armed the insurgents of other empires.

A few numbers establish the pervasiveness of war. In the case of the British Empire, between 1840 and 1900 alone, the British fought more than forty wars, many of them reflecting active resistance to colonization. In addition to the well-known battles, such as the Crimean War (1853–56), the Boxer Uprising (1899–1900), and the two Anglo-Boer Wars (1880–81 and 1899–1902, also called the South African Wars), there were a series of New Zealand land wars; several wars with the Sikh, Xhosa, Zulu, and Ashanti peoples; and ongoing battles with Malay rebels—not to mention the armed conflicts following rebellion in established British colonial territories, such as the Indian Rebellion of 1857 and the Jamaican Morant Bay Rebellion of 1865. Russia likewise continued its intrusions into Ottoman territories while both empires battled to quell peasant uprisings in such places as Hungary, Poland, Arabia, and Greece—or foment them in the other empire's territories.

In the nineteenth century, as the United States expanded its imperial projects under the mantle of Manifest Destiny, it battled steadily, including in two Barbary Wars, the War of 1812, wars with Mexico, the Civil War, and at century's end the "annexation" campaigns in Hawaii, Cuba, and the Philippines. Meanwhile a significant share of the growing US military budget was devoted to the twenty-five or more colonizing land wars carried out against American Indian tribes, including three Seminole wars, the Black Hawk War, and, in the second half of the nineteenth century, an ongoing series of Apache wars and wars with tribes in California. In South America, following the victorious independence struggles against Spain, territorial wars developed, for instance between Argentina and the self-named Empire of Brazil, especially as these two states vied for control of Uruguay and Paraguay. In short, the picture that emerges of the global nineteenth century is one of persistent invasion and persistent uprising against domination.

One way to capture the interlocking and inter-imperial character of these wars, especially as they catalyzed both anticolonial movements and even deadlier world wars, is to juxtapose the 1899–1900 Boxer Uprising in China and the Second Boer War (1899–1902)—and then to notice how these wars prepared the causes and effects of Japan's victory in the Russo-Japanese War (1904–5). Especially on the heels of Ethiopia's 1896 defeat of Italy's invading armies, the Japanese victory against such a massive empire seemed to signal a destabilization of the white European domination of the inter-imperial order. W. E. B. Du Bois said that Japan's victory "marked an epoch," in that "a great white nation has measured arms with a colored nation and has been found wanting," showing that the "awakening of the yellow races is certain" and the "awakening of the brown and black will follow in time."[24] As noted earlier, Japan had purposefully undertaken a mimesis of technologies, which should not be understood as a matter of "catching up" but rather as part of the ongoing historical "double movement" in which, as Hegel described, each strategically imitates the other in order to "supersede this otherness of itself"—as western states had been doing vis-à-vis other hemispheres and continued to do. In addition to noting this multilateral process, it's important to consider the specific prior dynamics among states that created that epochal moment if we are to appreciate the intertwined effects of technology, print culture, and anticolonial and intersectional resistance.

In the last decades of the nineteenth century, China's rivals in the imperial field were circling ever more impatiently. Nineteenth-century Qing China had been destabilized by internal and external battles, including the Opium Wars and the series of large-scale provincial rebellions following the so-called White Lotus Rebellion (1794–1805). At century's end China suffered a further blow with its loss to Japan in the battle over Korea (1894–95). The Treaty of Shimonoseki that sealed this war handed control of Taiwan to the Japanese, saddled the Qing with war debts, and gave foreigners additional rights to trade, to manufacture, and to residency in a wider range of Chinese locations. Staggering under the effects on the local economy, as well as from drought and failed crops, villagers in northern China organized a network of insurgents trained in "boxing" martial arts, galvanized by the belief that the presence of foreigners had upset the ancient harmony of Chinese society. They launched the Boxer Uprising.

The movement targeted foreign influence in trade and education, especially as purveyed through Christian missionary work, and they began to attack foreign missions and Christian churches. As violence escalated and spread to cities, Christians, both foreign and Chinese, barricaded themselves in missions and appealed to external governments for protection. In May 1900 the British moved troops inland and began to occupy forts. At this point the Empress Dowager Cixi declared a state of war. In response, the so-called Eight-Nation Alliance was born. Japan, as one of the eight, provided the largest single contingent of soldiers, joining Italy, Russia, Germany, France, Austria-Hungary, Britain, and the United States. Apparently all saw an opportunity to collapse and finally carve up this tenaciously long-lasting empire.[25]

Given that these eight "nations" were in fact expanding empires, the Boxer Rebellion showcases patterns we saw in the Napoleonic Wars and exemplifies new conditions and results. First, as in the Napoleonic era, interimperially cornered states sometimes gave implicit or explicit license to the embattled civilian populations to undertake guerrilla warfare. At the same time, the rebellion also exemplified new developments, including the increasing centrality of technology-centered resistance, for the Boxers made "railway sabotage . . . crucial to rebellion."[26] Yet by the same token, interimperial wars were becoming ever more deadly and "efficient": the Eight-Nation Alliance defeated the Boxers in a matter of months, leaving Beijing in ruins and tens of thousands of Chinese dead.

The aftereffects of the Boxer Uprising developed in tandem with the Second Boer War. While the eight imperial allies huddled at the treaty table to cripple China, three of these empires—Russia, Britain, and Japan—were simultaneously vying among themselves over other territories. Russia had chosen to support the Boers against the British as part of an effort to hamstring Britain not only in South Africa but also in India, since the South African Cape was a crucial part of the route to India, and Russia continued to harbor designs on northern India. Indeed, already in 1875 Lord Carnarvon argued that a South African confederation was needed precisely to defend England against Russian ambitions (although the discovery of diamonds in South Africa in 1871 also played an important part, as would the discovery of gold in the Transvaal in 1886). Russian leaders were therefore receptive when Boer leaders undertook their inter-imperial maneuvers: when Paul Kruger sent an emissary to request support, Russia agreed, and they seriously considered Jan Smuts's suggestion that Russia foment anti-British dissent in India so as to further strain British resources.

This multisided dynamic shifted again with the British victory over the Boers in 1902, creating new conditions for the competitive relations between the Russian and Japanese Empires. These two states had been vying for control of Korea and Manchuria, and in the Boxer Protocol, Russia had agreed to give Japan the territory of Manchuria with its crucial Port Arthur. But after the failure to contain and weaken Britain in the Second Boer War, Russia violated the protocol agreement by refusing to hand over Manchuria. Japan immediately attacked the Russian fleet. And so began yet another battle—the Russo-Japanese War (1904–5)—followed by Japan's rapid colonization of Manchuria whereby Japan took its place in a long history of imperial torch passing of this "contested borderland," as Prasenjit Duara has traced.[27] Its rapid victory over Russia confirmed Japan's status as a player in the imperial field, while the Russian defeat further fomented the domestic unrest and activism that eventually led to the Russian Revolution. And although Japan was happy to encourage the notion of an Asian solidarity, it fully intended to dominate in that sphere while doing what it needed to secure its stature among warring empires. Writers and journalists took note and entered the fray.

Global Solidarities and Gendered Civilizationalism

Characterizing the Boer Wars as global wars, Pradip Kumar Datta argues that they powerfully changed the "economy of affect" about imperialism; likewise, in *Empires at War*, Robert Gerwarth and Erez Manela document an "anti-imperial contagion" in the period.[28] The exposure of Britain's use of concentration camps and scorched-earth policies in South Africa was one cause of heightened critique, and the wide reach of British colonization was another. Many of the volunteers who came to join the Boers hailed from states that had been either victims of British imperialism or losers in the competition with British hegemony. Thus the foreign volunteers for the Boer side hailed from a remarkable range of nations and regions, as revealed by British prisoner-of-war records: Irish, Hungarian, south Asian, Danish, Greek, Italian, French, German, South American, US American, and Scandinavian.[29] The Catholic Irish went so far as to form their own MacBride's Brigade to fight on the Boer side, whose members could not return to Ireland without facing charges of treason.[30] Animosity toward the British also increased sharply when, after the Second Boer War, the British broke their promises to Gandhi and others by instituting more restrictive and racialized citizenship laws rather than honoring their pledge to increase political participation for Indians in both South Africa and India in exchange for wartime support (a pledge that had motivated Gandhi's organization of an ambulance core for the British). Datta remarks that these betrayals "thinned out imperial loyalism" among members of the educated classes of India who had been leveraging to win rights by showing their bravery and service on behalf of the British Empire.[31] In the face of these betrayals, the incipient nineteenth-century post/colonial consciousness discussed in the last chapter began to come into its own globally.

A striking range of writers stepped forward to offer anti-imperial critiques.[32] They included not only political thinkers such as Lenin, Trotsky, and John A. Hobson, who paid attention to the links between empire building and contemporary capitalism, but also many journalists and creative writers. In 1900, when Mark Twain returned to the United States after living abroad, he immediately announced his stance as "anti-imperialist" in the *New York Herald*, declaring himself a "boxer" and positioning himself against the Eight-Nation Alliance. Eventually assuming the role of vice president of the Anti-Imperialist League, Twain also publicly condemned US intentions in the Philippines: "I have read carefully the treaty of Paris, and I have seen that we do not intend to free, but to subjugate the people of the Philippines. We have gone there to conquer, not to redeem."[33] US women novelists such as Pauline Hopkins, Elizabeth Stuart Phelps, and Louisa May Alcott similarly raised questions about the carving up of the world for the gains of a few. In his novel *Ulysses*, James Joyce featured both the Second Boer War and the Russo-Japanese War as burning topics for his characters, folding them into the novel's epic critique of the "nightmare of history" and its catalog of inter-imperial wars from ancient to contemporary.

Long-distance communication technologies were of course crucial in the growth of these more openly anti-imperial attitudes. Few readers could miss the significance of these wars given the explosion of journalism and activism about them in locales from India to Africa and Ireland.[34] Although radio and the rapid circulation of print and visual forms increased the force of propaganda and military strategizing, these technologies also strengthened transregional solidarity and dissent, as is inherent to material-dialectical processes. The laying of transoceanic and interregional telegraph cables and the beginning of Reuters's news-sharing practices powerfully affected public awareness and sentiment. The circulation of the *London Times* had grown from five thousand printings at the end of the Napoleonic Wars to forty thousand in the early twentieth century, and its influence was further heightened by telegraphy and by placing reporters on the front line, so that they could send their news home within minutes.[35] The widespread awareness of the battles across the world had effects that could not be wholly controlled by the British bias of the reports, especially given that one did not need to be literate to share in this new global awareness: for now the battlefront was being represented not only in print and photographs but also on film and radio, beginning with the Spanish American War of 1898 and the Boxer Uprising. A few decades later, Virginia Woolf described the effects for world consciousness when she observed that a person in one region was "linked to his fellows [in other places] by wires which pass overhead, by waves of sound which pour through the roof and speak aloud to him of battles and murders and strikes and revolutions all over the world."[36] It seems fair to speculate that anyone who glimpsed the photographs or heard the radio would have a sense of widespread world turbulence, of violent invasions and rebellions. Many began to feel, as W. B. Yeats would put it in his poem "The Second Coming" (1919), that "Things fall apart; the centre cannot hold."[37]

Already at the turn of the century, local newspapers in Ireland, India, Africa, and elsewhere tapped into news and pictures sent by telegraph to mount critical commentaries. Armed with up-to-date and detailed information, Indian commentators at the *Maratha*, a Pune newspaper, openly understood the Boxer Uprising as "a patriotic movement incensed by the audacious inroads of foreigners," a sentiment sure to resonate with the paper's Indian readers. Similarly, writers for the *Bengalee* expressed satisfaction when British forces suffered defeat by a mere several thousand "Boer farmers."[38] Writers also seem to have understood the vectored inter-imperial maneuvering that characterized and connected these insurrections, for there was speculation that the Boxer Rebellion was "probably due to Boer instigation."[39]

In Ireland, the *United Irishman*, edited by Arthur Griffith (and precursor to Sinn Féin), was particularly vocal in its support of the Boers and its championing of anti-imperial struggles across the globe. As Elleke Boehmer details, from 1899 forward, the *United Irishman* increasingly reported on independence struggles abroad, especially in its regular "Over the Frontier" column, which gathered news from foreign newspapers to highlight "experiences both of oppression and resistance in countries ranging from Romania to India."[40] Deeming Gandhi's Swadeshi movement the "Sinn Fein policy in India," Griffith suggested that "the Boer and the Russo-Japanese wars have put a new spirit into the Indian people" and that "the patriotic Hindues [*sic*] who had for years been preaching to a people whose spirit was subdued . . . have been transformed, in the people's eyes, from visionaries into statesmen."[41]

The paper regularly reported on the battles fought for the Boers by Mac-Bride's Irish Brigade, while its circulation fostered Maud Gonne's success with the Irish Transvaal Committee (created to collect funds for the Boers) and supported her campaign against recruitment for the British Army, publishing such pieces as "Enlisting for England Is Treason to Ireland" and "England's Difficulty Is Ireland's Opportunity."[42]

At the same time, African Atlantic intellectual activists such as Ida B. Wells, Du Bois, and Marcus Garvey saw a new epoch in the making. They regularly commented on anticolonial and antiracist struggles around the world, as Robin D. G. Kelley has surveyed.[43] Through their work for the World's Congress of Representative Women in 1893 and the first Pan-African Congress in 1900, Black women intellectuals such as Wells and Anna Julia Cooper had been expressing "an international vision—attacking colonial expansion in Africa and Asia and arguing that domestic racist ideology is in part a product of imperialism."[44] In their roles as editors, Du Bois (at the *Crisis*) and Hopkins (at the *Colored American Magazine*) ensured coverage of the expansionism of the United States in Cuba and the Philippines.[45] By the time that journalist Hubert Harrison published such essays as "Our International Consciousness" in his collection *When Africa Awakes* (1920), he was able to urge African Americans to support struggles not just in Africa but in India, Ireland, Egypt, the Philippines, and other oppressed colonies under European domination. As did Du Bois in "The African Roots of War," Harrison argued that World War I was actually a war over "the lands and destinies of the colored majority in Asia, Africa, and the islands of the sea."[46] Accordingly African Atlantic writers (unlike Anglo-European, Irish, and Indian newspapers) addressed the plight of the South African peoples who suffered from these wars, working in solidarity with African journalists such as Solomon Plaatje. Taking a broad antiwar stance and breaking rank with those who saw military service as a path for winning rights, Harrison eschewed participation in war on behalf of any colonial powers.

Amid the complexities, writers were also bedeviled by choices about alliance. This problem is clear, for instance, among Indians navigating the pressures of several empires that sought influence or expansion into India and South Africa. A writer in Hitavadi explains his mixed response to the Boer-British battles: the "oppression of Indians in South Africa has led us to hate the Boers," and yet, he adds, "we praise their bravery [against the British] with a thousand tongues."[47] Other South Asian writers, although critical of the British in the Second Boer War, aligned with the British because of the looming threat of a Russian invasion of India.[48] Additionally some Muslim

Indians hesitated to express sympathy for the Boxers because they knew, through their contacts in Cairo, that the Ottoman Caliphate had given orders to Chinese Muslims to refrain from aligning with the Boxers (partly a measure of inter-imperial pressures facing the Ottoman state). In this complex field of relations, anti-European activists sometimes occupied both sides of the fence. As Burton and Ballantyne note, "those who might sympathize with anticolonial nationalism in one context might be seen as colonizers or colonial sympathizers in another," as in the case of Japanese government men who worked with Indian anticolonial exiles.[49] While Japanese bureaucrats aided the Indians' efforts to build the Indian National Congress, such men were at the same time managing the aggressive colonization of Korea.

Surrounded by the competitive civilizationalist rhetoric of empires, these dissenting journalists and activists also sometimes evinced their own forms of civilizationalism. As this chapter's epigraphs register and as noted by Prasenjit Duara in his study of pan-Asianism, the inter-imperial field of discourse was increasingly characterized by competing forms of civilizationalist and masculinist rhetoric, heard in many corners.[50] As Ballantyne and Burton put it, anti-British dissent among the colonized "could be shot through with competing hierarchies of civilizational value."[51] Some writers in India for instance expressed affiliation with the Japanese as a powerful Asian "civilization," denouncing the Chinese Boxers' murder of a Japanese diplomat because "only Japan has the zeal and power necessary to preserve the ancient civilizations of the east"; other hints of civilizationalist chauvinism peek through in references to the Boxers as religious fanatics who pose a "danger to civilization" and in the proud report about the Indian Sepoy troops deployed by Britain: "as soon as the Indian Army landed in China, the Tartar and Chinese forces retreated."[52] Competitive and worried pronouncements also arose in relation to regional class and religious divisions. C. A. Bayly argues that among some in the wealthier classes of the Kerala region of India, where the ongoing Mappila uprisings among Muslims had targeted upper-class Hindus and Christians, the Boxer violence toward Christians struck a defensive nerve.[53] In another variation of this civilizational ambivalence, Plaatje adopted accommodationist rhetoric about the greatness of European civilization and expressed his loyalty to the British Empire, which undoubtedly appealed to white audiences from whom he wished to raise support for his African land rights movement.[54]

Clearly such positioning among the dispossessed and colonized emerged as part of their effort to confront racism and colonization. They were appropriating and reworking the racialized civilizationalist discourse, which ironically came to serve as a means to combat European racism and to claim status, rights, and alliance. Homi Bhabha's notion of strategic mimicry among colonial populations might be extended into an inter-imperial framework to show that part of what was shrewdly "mimicked" was the discourse of civilizational-imperial competition.[55] Datta proposes that this complex blend of motives explains the celebration by Gandhi and others of the civilizational accomplishments of Hindi or Muslim states as they argued for the rights of Indian populations in Africa and India.[56] Gauri Viswanathan has thoughtfully discussed these patterns in authors such as the Irish poet James Cousins and the Indian poet Rabindranath Tagore.[57] In *Black Empire*, Michelle Stephens reveals similar strains among early twentieth-century Black internationalists, noting that because "empire . . . provided the material conditions for black solidarities to emerge across nation, language, gender, and even class," Black subjectivities and gender formations inevitably also enfolded "imperial discourses and colonial frameworks of consciousness."[58] Therefore some activists "[drew] from discourses of empire in [their] desire for a state."[59] Yet while these discourses provided inter-imperial leverage, they also displayed symptoms of long-historical, gendered, racialized, and otherwise stratified imperial ideologies. The presence of what Datta sees as forms of "imperial subjectivity" in anti-imperial struggles reveals that, at the level of the political unconscious, empires had to some degree succeeded in their strategy of divide and conquer.[60]

These internalizations are especially striking in the case of the Second Boer War. Commenting on British poetry about the war, Malvern van Wyk Smith regrets to report that this body of poetry is "almost completely silent on the experiences and attitudes of South African Blacks."[61] As Smith points out, very few people heeded observations like that of H. M. Hyndman, who remarked that the war was "a struggle between two burglars. . . . The country belongs neither to the Boers nor to the Briton," but rather should and may yet belong "to the black man."[62] Nonetheless, many volunteers who traveled from afar to denounce imperialism and defend Boer "freedom" showed little concern for the indigenous inhabitants of the land. During the Second Boer War, African peoples were once again relocated en masse, moved from the already deracinating, impoverished land reserves to concentration camps, where inadequate medical service and food supplies led to widespread death and where adults were forced into labor for the combatting states. Despite the efforts by figures such as King Khama III of Botswana and journalists like Solomon Plaatje to draw attention to the plight of Africans, many non-African anti-imperialists who flocked to the Boer side saw no grounds for—or perhaps no geopolitical leverage in—claiming solidarity with dispossessed Africans. On the contrary, as Datta notes, Indians in Africa sometimes objected with insulted feelings to new laws that equated them with indigenous African populations. In this and earlier periods, the Irish similarly worried about the contemporary equation of Irish and African, and responded by conjuring a great civilizational history for Ireland that they mistakenly supposed distinguished them from indigenous Africans.

These stratified and incomplete solidarities make clear that the imperialization and gendering of subjectivities reaches deep, shaping anticolonial as well as colonial political imaginations. It also reveals that such subjectivities enter and reenter the inter-imperial field of relations. In each case and over time, they affect the direction of history, helping to determine winners, losers, and future animosities. In this way, even as these activists effected important change, their vestigial attachments inhibited the wider possibilities for collective dissent and transformation.

As World War I soon made fully evident, the persisting investments in gendered imperial subjectivity and the racialized disavowals of relation across the political spectrum ensured the return of global war, although few would have predicted the epic scale of death and destruction. The numbers are worth recalling. On average, each day between 1914 and 1918 more than two thousand humans died on the battlefields. In those four years, 9 million soldiers were killed. The devastation shattered families and lands far and wide, especially since all the warring empires had conscripted troops from their colonized territories.[63] Over the course of the war, Britain mobilized more than 1 million men from India alone. In addition, Britain also deployed 200,000 from Ireland, 100,000 from South Africa, and 15,000 from the West Indies—as well as 500,000 from Canada, 300,000 from Australia, and 100,000 from New Zealand. In 1914, the French army included 90,000 *troupes indigènes* from North Africa, West Africa, Madagascar, and Indochina; by 1918, it had added 500,000 more. In 1917, approximately half of Russia's 11 million troops were of non-Russian ethnic descent, drawn from the 150 ethnic groups of the Russian territories. The Ottoman Empire drew as much as a quarter of its recruits from minority Arabic-speaking provinces, while it also relied heavily on Greek, Assyrian, and Armenian minorities.[64] Further, as Du Bois pointed out and John Morrow has further demonstrated, World War I was fought over "the lands and destinies of the colored majority in Asia, Africa, and the islands of the sea." Lenin made a similar point when he commented that, as an "imperialist war," World War I was "a war for the division and redivision of this kind of booty."[65] As a final blow, a flu pandemic broke out in the wake of the war, killing 21.5 million humans worldwide, with more than half of the casualties in Asia. This worldwide catastrophe only further fueled many of those civilizational and masculine attachments, as World War II soon made manifest.

Here was also born, I propose, a global wave of what Caroline Rooney has named radical distrust, which still animates the conflicts of today.[66] On one hand, it is true that World War I in some ways heightened anticolonial, antiracist, feminist, and anticapitalist activism. Additionally, during the war, the emboldened colonial revolutionaries took advantage of the destabilized inter-imperial field, such as those who planned the Ghader conspiracy aiming at full-scale mutiny in India and likewise the Irish revolutionaries who mounted the 1916 Easter Rising. This maneuvering dramatized the bolder ambitions of revolutionaries and helped to foster visions of later success. Yet many promises were broken after the war, including but not limited to the Treaty of Versailles that divided the "booty" of the war, creating a renewed sense of betrayal among colonized or dominated peoples. I would further speculate that these sentiments resonated with memories of much older inter-imperial defeats and therefore revived energies within the contemporary affective and material fields.

Certainly the treaty made clear that the self-determination principles articulated by Woodrow Wilson in his Fourteen Points speech at the Versailles Peace Conference had no more weight than the paper on which they were written. In 1917, China had agreed to join the entente alliance and supply thousands of laborers for trench and transport work on the condition that, in the event of an entente victory, the German-controlled territories of the Shandong province would be returned. When these were instead apportioned to their bitter Asian rival, the Japanese Empire, and as other Chinese proposals for return of territory were ignored, many Chinese were appalled. Chinese historians see this as a historical turning point, for it catalyzed the May Fourth movement, beginning with student-led protests on May 4, 1919, denouncing the treaty. This movement quickly won support from merchants and universities across the country, leading first to the fall of the Qing dynasty and the rise of a nationalist government and ultimately to the Chinese Communist Revolution, as Mao Zedong himself later suggested.[67] The treaty's betrayal and earlier inter-imperial maneuvers are well remembered in China, undoubtedly feeding the wider population's investment in China's challenges to Anglo-American power today.

Other populations were also tricked into wartime participation. As we saw, because Britain worried over "whether Indian and Irish nationalists would support the war effort," it promised postwar concessions, which were later summarily ignored.[68] The most egregious betrayal, however, concerned the Middle Eastern fighters. With promises to support independent statehood for Arab communities, the British wooed Sharif Hussein ibn Ali, emir of Mecca, and encouraged him to create the pan-Arab army that helped to defeat the Ottoman Empire. All the while, however, the rulers of Britain, France, and Russia were crafting the infamous Sykes-Picot Agreement, in which they carved up the lands of the Middle East for themselves: Russia would control the Kurdish and Armenian lands in the northeast, France would govern Lebanon, Syria, and Cilicia, and Britain would rule in Jordan, Mesopotamia, and Palestine. In 1917, furthermore, Britain decreed that it would create a Jewish "national home" in Palestine, as promised by Foreign Secretary Arthur Balfour to the leader of the Zionist Federation, later known as the Balfour Declaration. When challenged in 1918 about British intentions by a group of Syrian leaders, diplomat Henry McMahon wrote the "Declaration to the Seven," blatantly misrepresenting British plans by stating that Arabs would govern in the region. Here, too, a century later it is clear that the British and Allied betrayal only inspired successively stronger devotion to that original vision and ever bolder seizings of travel technologies to realize that vision, while also keeping alive dreams of past imperial grandeur and preeminence. To paraphrase Mina Loy, this betrayal was no stronger than the resisting force that it called up.

I am suggesting that to position these maneuvers, conscriptions, and betrayals within the longer history of inter-imperial war and domination is to plumb the depths of the attachments that energize the world's political imaginaries today, both consciously and unconsciously. This perspective clarifies why the treachery and disrespect suffered by so many peoples seems to demand—in masculinist terms—a reckoning through further violence. At the same time, the longer perspective calls us to acknowledge the depth of the endurance and commitment to justice that nonetheless has continued to propel alternative actions and visions. As Michelle Stephens describes in the case of Black internationalist writers, although political visions of liberation have "been shaped by empire's international reach and global designs," those visions have also laid ground for future decolonial work.[69] Given the wide range of authors' reparative engagements with these politics over the long twentieth century (as the rest of the book foregrounds), it follows that to read, teach, and study literature and to integrate it into political theorization is one small way to participate in this reparative work within world dialectics.

Literature's Countermotions

To establish this point about the structuring force of literature, in this and the next and final section of this chapter I trace the broad and deep literary activism that emerged as a visible force in the early twentieth century.[70] Its pivotal importance may be measured, first of all, by the fact that Britain, the United States, and the USSR all added special cultural departments for surveillance of artists' and writers' activities, a point to which I'll shortly return. Having shown literature's complex engagements with inter-imperiality over centuries, here I foreground the diverse ways that, engaging with new technologies, twentieth-century writers across hemispheres cultivated dissenting political-aesthetic styles and collective practices.[71]

It needs saying at the outset that the decolonizing turn among authors at the end of the nineteenth century did not, of course, transform aesthetics wholesale. During the military buildup of the late nineteenth century and for many decades to come, literature and the arts continued to feed imperial energies. In the British Empire, statesmen and officers enlisted the work of Lord Tennyson, Rudyard Kipling, and others to stir up nationalist and imperialist sentiment abroad as well as at home—for instance, arranging readings of these authors' texts at missions and forts during the Boxer Uprising. At the same time, as in other empires, a bellicose imaginary flooded into British popular culture in music hall ballads and popular theater as well as through the literary subgenres of boy's adventure fiction and what Patrick Brantlinger calls "imperial gothic."[72]

Furthermore, as the chapter's epigraphs illustrate, some of the period's "futurist" aesthetic movements mimicked and extended their state's masculinist inter-imperial self-fashioning. The vorticists in Britain led by Wyndham Lewis and Ezra Pound wrote their "BLAST! Manifesto" (1914) on the verge of World War I, as German power threatened to eclipse British ascendancy. Their competitive positioning is explicit: affiliating themselves with "Anglo-Saxon genius," they especially championed the Englishman's technological prowess, claiming the "modern" for themselves while denigrating the effeminate French for their "Gallic weakness." These writers also vied directly with the Italian futurists, contrasting their visions with the supposedly effeminate and tame "Futurist Individual of Mr. Marinetti's limited imagination."[73] Meanwhile Italian futurism's most famous spokesperson, Filippo Tommaso Marinetti, went further in his embrace of war, masculinism, and "arsenals," expressing a program to "glorify war—the world's only hygiene—militarism, patriotism, . . . and scorn for woman."[74] His outpourings should be read in light of Italy's diminished secondary place among European empires. In particular, his emphatic nationalist announcement that "it is from Italy that we launch through the world this violently upsetting incendiary manifesto of ours" seems calculated to counter Italy's defeat in the First Italo-Ethiopian War (1895–96).[75] In that war, not only had Italy been successfully outmaneuvered by an African state, but the powerful "European" Russian Empire had allied with Ethiopia instead of Italy, considered a humiliating double insult. In other words, underneath this braggadocio there undoubtedly lurked an anxious geopolitical and gendered uncertainty. The question of which empires would triumph mingled unsettlingly with the question of which men were most manly.

Yet this defensive bellicosity was also provoked by progressive political activism. As the chapter's epigraphs reveal, masculinist-nationalist manifestos arose to challenge the feminist activism and feminist manifestos of this period, including, for instance, the British suffragists' "Votes for Women: New Movement Manifesto" (1906) and Loy's "Feminist Manifesto" (1914). As I will describe at the end of this section, in a wide range of manifestos and other writing, authors with anti-imperial, pacifist, Marxist, feminist-intersectional, indigenous, antiracist, and other such commitments countered these aggressive attitudes, organizing and distributing their work through print and radio technologies.[76] At the same time writers directly engaged with these problems in individual works. With both the Boxer Uprising and the Second Boer War in mind, in 1899 Rabindranath Tagore wrote a poem in Bengali that he later translated into English as "Sunset of the Century" (1918), depicting the fin-de-siècle "carnival of violence" ringing "from weapon to weapon" with "the mad music of death," all "amidst the blood-red clouds of the West and the whirlwind of hatred."[77] Poets writing for the socialist press lamented, "bread should be so dear/ And flesh and blood so cheap."[78] Many seemed to understand that the warring violence fostered evermore deadly violence, as when William Watson critiqued Lord Kitchener's "scorched earth" tactic and Britain's misguided militarism:

> We thought to fire farmsteads: we have lit
> A flame less transient in the hearts of men . . .
> Redder from our red hoof-prints.[79]

Technology was also a dialectical flash point for many writers, artists, and movements. Constructivists from Russia, ultraists such Jorge Luis Borges and Francis Picabia, and Dadaist groups in central and western Europe and the Americas all thematized techno-infrastructures, as in Picabia's "mechanomorphic portraits."[80] Among writers with progressive politics, this emphasis reflected, I suggest, an effort to seize back the world of materiality and technology from the warmongers, whether to expose technology's corrosions of relationality or to retool it for a democratic vision. For instance, the French Dadaists proclaimed in their manifesto (1918) that in the "Dadaist Club," "every man is president and everyone has a vote."[81] They combined their democratic politics with technological imagery, aiming, as they explain, to equalize all levels of "reality" and eschew divisions between "high" and "low" art: "THE BRUITIST POEM describes a tramcar exactly as it is. . . . THE SIMULTANEOUS POEM teaches the interrelationship of things, while Mr. Smith reads his paper, the Balkan express crosses the Nisch Bridge and a pig squeals in the cellar of Mr Bones the butcher."[82] Mina Loy, on the other hand, describes the diminishment of intimacies and sensualities among humans becoming "automatons" in her poem "Human Cylinders":

> The human cylinders
> Revolving in the enervating dusk
> That wraps each closer in the mystery
> Of singularity
> Among the litter of a sunless afternoon
> Having eaten without tasting
> Talked without communion
> And at least two of us
> Loved a very little
> Without seeking
> To know if our two miseries
> In the lucid rush-together of automatons
> Could form one opulent wellbeing[83]

Whether critiquing or embracing technologies, these early twentieth-century poets adapted their aesthetics in order to influence visions of relationality in the geopolitical field. Building on Ruth Jennison's Marxist reading of objectivist poets in this period, we might say that these artists were crafting a conjunctural vision that revealed both intimacies and technologies as elements of an unequal yet interconnected global dialectics.[84]

Living thus on "war's red planet" with its "groaning armies," artists and writers across the world did indeed "sit down," as Jorge de Lima urged, sharing visions and founding movements linking art and politics—often anti-war or anti-imperial, though not strictly so, as we'll see.[85] They convened in villages and rural towns, as well as in metropoles from Seoul, Shanghai, Saint Petersburg, and Bucharest to Kolkata, Cairo, Istanbul, Dublin, and Paris, to Havana, Buenos Aires, and New York. They also "gathered" in print and on radio. Small magazine writers and editors played an important role in these movements, as established by the multivolume *Global Magazines Project* and the AHRC *Modernist Magazines Project*.[86] Just as leaders of independence movements in Ireland, Africa, India, and the West Indies read each other's newspapers, so, too, were editors and authors creating literary magazines that linked writers and political-aesthetic projects across states and hemispheres.

Thus Victoria Ocampo, Argentinian founder and editor of the influential journal *Sur*, published and hosted writers such as the Indian poet Rabindranath Tagore. The US writer Waldo Frank worked with Spanish philosopher José Ortega y Gasset and French writer André Gide to build international literary networks through the journals *Revista de Occidente* and *Nouvelle Revue française*. Authors also connected through radio and often across racial and national lines, for instance, in BBC radio shows such as *Caribbean Voices*, which was developed and produced by the Jamaican writer Una Marson (from 1943 to 1946) and continued until 1958. Such BBC shows were fully embedded in the BBC's mission to maintain a good image of the British Empire; yet they nonetheless hired Marson and others, who broadcast the early work of authors such as George Lamming and fostered a network that included authors from George Orwell and Sylvia Pankhurst to Langston Hughes and James Weldon Johnson.[87]

In the United States, as Carol Batker has shown, authors who were affiliated with pan-Indian, Pan-African, and pan-Jewish activist organizations published in each other's newspapers, and both Batker and Jennifer Wilks point out that journals publishing shorter pieces were especially useful to women writers, who typically had less money, time, and opportunity to write or travel.[88] These literary-political networks also developed the collective consciousness by adding Letters to the Editor sections, creating global dialogues on art and politics, as Eric Bulson notes about the journal *Transition*.[89] Indeed works of art themselves began to splice newspaper print and poetry or painting, most famously in the work of the cubists, while colonial newspapers also spliced poetic forms with news columns, such as in the bilingual *Bechuana Gazette* edited by Plaatje in South Africa.[90] As I'll emphasize again shortly, this splicing encouraged a form of conjunctural reading that joined past and present, straddled languages, and strengthened readers' consciousness of inter-imperially connected histories.

Not surprisingly, then, the political import of these magazines and practices was not missed by state authorities. During the "pink decade" of the 1930s in Britain, some of the most avid British readers of little magazines were officers of the Security Service (MI5).[91] Studying recently available MI5 files, James Smith establishes that MI5 agents tracked magazines ranging from *International Literature* and the *Left Review* to John Lehman's influential literary journal, *New Writing*. They did so as well with the New York–based journal *Orient* (1923–28), edited by Indian nationals Hari Govind Govil and Syud Hossain, activists for home rule in India who had immigrated to New York. *Orient* was distributed in England, France, India, China, and Japan, and it published the likes of Albert Einstein, Gandhi, Kahlil Gibran, Romain Rolland, Tagore, and H. G. Wells. As Sarah Fedirka has shown (based on files released in 1997), *Orient* was closely watched by Britain's Indian Political Intelligence Office (IPIO), which sensed its aim to seize control over relationality, as I would put it. Agents of IPIO described the journal as an effort to "ruin the white man's control in the Orient" and to incite "the actual race war," whereas Govil and Hossain characterized their project as an effort to promote "harmonious" understanding between East and West. The policing of politics in these little magazines also operated from the leftist end of the spectrum, as Michael Rozendal shows in his study of the American modernist journal the *Left: A Quarterly Review of Radical and Experimental Art*. After a negative review of the *Left* in *Literature of the World Revolution: Central Organ of the International Union of Revolutionary Writers*, the editors took a hiatus and then published only two more issues. This emerging bipolar field of the Cold War became one framework for the inter-imperial positioning of authors and artists, a point I revisit later.

Scores of writers and artists around the world explicitly paired their rejection of aggressive, systemic oppression with rejection of entrenched aesthetic conventions, chastising older artists for both their artistic orthodoxies and their timidity about political resistance. Again here manifestos made these platforms explicit, from Loy's Feminist Manifesto to the "London Manifesto" of the Pan-African Congress (1921).[92] In his aesthetic manifesto "The Negro Artist and the Racial Mountain" (1926), Langston Hughes let it be known that "we young Negroes who create now intend to express our individual dark-skinned selves without shame or fear. . . . Let the blare of Negro jazz bands and the bellowing voice of Bessie Smith singing blues penetrate the closed ears of the colored near-intellectuals until they listen."[93] The calm tone of the founding 1936 "Manifesto of the Progressive Writers Association" in India belies the radicalism of the members (who faced censure on many fronts for treating such topics as queer sexuality and caste exploitation): the authors simply explain, "It is the object of our Association to rescue literature from the conservative classes in whose hands they have been degenerating so long to bring arts in the closest touch with the people. . . . While claiming to be the inheritors of the best traditions in India[n] civilization we shall criticize in all its aspects, the spirit of reaction in our country."[94] In his "Cannibal Manifesto" (1928), Brazilian writer Oswald de Andrade writes more provocatively not only "against all the importers of canned conscience" but also explicitly against the import of European worldviews: "Let Levy-Bruhl go study prelogical mentality. . . . We want the Cariba Revolution."[95] He rejects the notion that Europeans created either political or aesthetic modernity: "Without us Europe would not even have had its paltry declaration of the rights of man. . . . We already had communism. We already had surrealist language. . . . Tupi or not tupi that is the question." Ultimately he raises a banner "against all catechisms" and "for the palpable existence of life."

Yet manifestos expressing progressive or radical politics also sometimes evinced attachments to imperial histories. Russian futurism perfectly illustrates this positioning. Their anticapitalist and anti-imperial critiques quietly tap the legacies outlined in chapter 3 that positioned Russia as the vanguard and center. On the one hand, these Russian futurists displayed a less aggressive posturing than the British and Italian futurists, instead affiliating with both Marxist politics and with the new pan-Asian anti-Westernism studied recently by Cemil Aydin.[96] Thus Russian "futurians" such as Velimir Khlebnikov denounced older writers such as Leo Tolstoy and his generation for implicitly colluding with the imperial warmongers, proclaiming that "the youn-n-nger [sic] generation has smashed" their models.[97] They also expressed solidarity with a "united Asia [that] has arisen from the ashes of the Great War" and they offered visions of a more just order: "Until the proletariat seizes power in every state, states can be divided into proletarian states and bourgeois states. The great nations of the Continent of ASSU (China, India, Persia, Russia, Siam, Afghanistan) belong to the list of enslaved states. The islands are the oppressors. . . . The will of Fate has ordained that this union be conceived in Astrakhan, a place that unites three worlds—the Aryan world, the Indian world, the World of the Caspian: the triangle of Christ, Buddha, Mohammed."[98] But at the same time this vision of proletariat solidarity across states, religions, and classes elides the colonizations that had forcibly constructed the "triangle of Christ, Buddha, Mohammed." For Astrakhan was a Muslim khanate until it was conquered by Russia in 1566;

Russia held on to it despite wars over it with Ottoman armies in 1568–70, after which it became the Russian "Gate to the Orient." Thus to call Astrakhan a "place that unites" is to invite forgetfulness about the violence that made it so and to perpetuate the Russian self-image that authorized these colonizations. The apparent call to solidarity actually mystifies this Russian imperial discourse as the "will of Fate."

Yet many other writers undertook deeper-cutting aesthetic departures, especially those embattled on all sides, as I survey in the next and final section.

Shatterzones and Sexualities

Certain world regions have been unrelentingly caught in the crosshairs of multiple empires. It is in these inter-imperial "shatterzones" that we most clearly discern both the stakes and the inventiveness of aesthetic maneuvers. In such places as eastern Europe, the Caribbean, West Africa, the Maghreb, Indonesia, Vietnam, and Korea, where successive empires have wreaked havoc and contemporaneous empires have competed, writers have navigated under especially precarious conditions. In such regions, multiple language traditions and multiple religious, ethnicized, and imperial or national identities have become striated and sedimented, having been installed and dismantled over centuries of invasion, reinvasion, revolution, and counterrevolution as critics have shown.[99] At the same time, political diasporas and technologies propelled disseminations of aesthetic practice among the colonized and dominated. Drawing on both old and new aesthetic forms, writers undertook all kinds of creative splicings and retoolings to intervene in the volatile political field.

In her sample of early twentieth-century Cuban literature, for example, Vicky Unruh conveys the "creole" retoolings of African, Spanish, and Euro-American aesthetic forms by which authors "rehearse a range of strategies to ground shifting perspectives."[100] They scuttle, scatter, and recombine the multiple pressures and technologies surrounding them:

> A 1928 bildungsroman deploys telegraphic vanguard imagery, Afro-Cuban ritual, and naturalist descriptions in a portrait of Cuba's rural proletariat, displaced by U.S.-owned sugar mills, and links this group's activities with the cultural activity of Havana's intellectuals. A 1927 "Afro-Cuban Choreographic Mystery in One Act" . . . stages a contest between

the frenetic labors of a Hollywood businessman filming stereotypic fare about Cuban "natives" and a powerful Afro-Cuban initiation rite. A 1926 poem renders the Cuban zafra (sugar harvest) through eighteen cantos [which reach from] condemnations of nineteenth-century slavery to racialist stereotypes of former slaves, [and from] nostalgic contrasts of colonial sugar plantations with mechanized U.S.-owned mills [to] admonitions to campesinos to work harder. A 1931 poetic ode to a Cuban boxer in New York warns that his pugilistic labors on Broadway nourish the same predator that controls Cuba's cane fields. A 1929 best-selling melodramatic novel about the perils of a free-thinking new woman . . . juxtaposes her tedious office work with the dynamic cultural activity of the male tertulia she joins, a gathering of intellectuals debating Cuban and international art and politics.[101]

Merging ancient rituals with telegraphic forms, in one sense these experiments render the disorientations of colliding histories; in another sense, by forcing conjunctures of then and now, here and there, that culture and this, they reclaim their long-historical, diasporic, and multivectored experience of time and place. In the process, they reconstellate the struggles of labor (campesinos and office workers) and free-thinking women, exposing co-constituted yet incommensurate identities. Their references to Broadway and Hollywood movies, furthermore, operate as self-reflexive gestures, registering the almost unavoidable interweaving of African art forms with these North American entertainment venues. Such aesthetics claim the authority to name the conjunctural and dialectical difficulties of the artists' positions, declining to simplify the contradictory mixture of aesthetics, economies, and political viewpoints.

The Angel Island Chinese poets exemplify a different retooling of ancient forms in order to challenge contemporary inter-imperial exploitation. Forced into trans-Pacific migration from Asia to the Americas by the depredations of several empires, only to find themselves interned off the coast of California by the US government, these mainly Chinese laborers voiced distress by carving poems into the walls of the internment cabins. In doing so, as Yunte Huang shows, they tapped into a centuries-old tradition of Chinese travel writing called *tibishi*, which often lamented the heroic leaders who were exiled under Chinese dynasties and which were traditionally etched into trees, rocks, and walls. Retooling the materiality of the tibishi tradition, they implicitly situated themselves within this long history of empire-induced dislocation.[102] In a further inter-imperial complexity, some of the immigrants held at Angel Island were Koreans who had signed "coolie" contracts so as to flee the coercions of the Japanese Empire. This situation affected the interns' fates, for the ongoing negotiations of the United States with China and Japan sometimes led to preferential treatment for Koreans.[103] The interned Chinese may have envied the Koreans, or felt solidarity, or both, but their similarly coerced conditions would have made clear that they were pawns in an inter-imperial field of maneuvers.

The growing global consciousness among such communities also generated surprising transhemispheric borrowings and gender reconfigurations.[104] Jang Wook Huh brings this point into focus by tracking the figurations of Josephine Baker in early twentieth-century Korean magazines. Working under the triple pressures of Japanese imperialism, western imperial hegemony, and workplace modernization, artists such as the Korean illustrator Kim Gyu-taek tapped the figuration of strong African Atlantic women to empower Korean women. Like Caribbean and other artists, Kim Gyu-taek spliced old and new forms in order to appeal, in his case, to Korean audiences while "importing" dissent from elsewhere. For instance, in his narrative cartoons for the popular magazine *Jogwang* in the 1930s, he rewrote the legendary Korean folktale *Simcheongjeon*, featuring the well-known heroine Gwak-ssi, an obedient daughter who sacrifices her own desires to care for her parents. But in Gyu-taek's rendering, the meek Gwak-ssi has a vision of Josephine Baker—illustrated with "modernist" angularity and in shocking near nudity—holding out birth control medicine, implicitly beckoning the daughter to step outside her traditional role.

Such borrowings were always fraught. As Wook Huh points out, amid Japan's racist denigrations of Koreans as "backward," Gyu-taek's invocation of an African American performer, on one hand, aligns Korean struggles with African Atlantic struggles against racism and colonization. Yet, on the other hand, as Wook Huh also notes, insofar as these images could be seen as caricature, they risked reinscribing racist representations of Blacks. The problem was mirrored in reverse on the other side of the world. African American artists sometimes gestured toward global solidarity with the "yellow races," yet their portrayals sometimes slide toward reductive stereotypes of Asian peoples, as John Gruesser shows.[105] Thus do the circulating energies of anti-imperial intervention cut in several directions. And thus do the arts play an uncontainable, catalyzing part in world dialectics.

I close this chapter with Vietnamese writing in the 1930s, for it epitomizes the intersections of sexual identities and inter-imperial positionalities as they play out in linguistic and aesthetic interventions, as Ben Tran's trenchant analysis reveals.[106] In the 1930s, as French imperialism was forcibly replacing Chinese imperial hegemony, the transition allowed for unexpected coformations of queer, middle-class, and communist positionalities. Tran describes how the language-script policies of successive empires created new conditions for Vietnamese writers in this period. Chinese domination in Vietnam had for centuries been installed through the imposition of a character-based language system for writing and for state exams, establishing a class of "mandarin" intellectuals and artists. In 1910, the colonizing French began to supplant this system and enforce the use of a romanized Vietnamese script (*quốc ngữ*) in schools and official documents.

Ironically, this dethroning of mandarin educational, professional, and language systems opened the door to a new set of Vietnamese intellectuals, creating a wider—yet still fraught—space of negotiation where Vietnamese writers and readers, including women, could sometimes work both sides to create their own transformational middle. That is, the romanized script allowed room for challenges to Confucian political and literary gatekeeping, which, as the Vietnamese well understood, had "served the primary purpose of cultivating a compliant subject in Vietnamese society's hierarchical structures."[107] As Tran explains, the "explosion of quốc ngữ print culture during the late 1920s and 1930s, coupled with mass literacy movements, fostered the development of an unprecedented reading public, which included non-elite classes and women."[108] Writers and intellectuals leveraged the effects of French language policies and retooled the new quốc ngữ print culture for their own ends.[109] In other words, this history exemplifies how imperial transitions create conjunctures—discernible cracks in the uneven system—that colonized subjects must maneuver within but through which they may also gain leverage for decolonization. Literary critics have recently made comparable arguments about other colonized writers.[110]

Furthermore, under these conditions in Vietnam, internationalist labor movements and queer alliances together shaped writers' political-aesthetic choices, leading to reconfigurations of the aesthetic and political binaries that had aligned realism with communism and experimental modernism with capitalism.[111] In the Vietnam case, Tran argues, authors were partly aiming to carve out room for those sexual "individualities" and associate them with communist politics rather than bourgeois capitalism, as indicated by their affiliations with Gide, whose "homosexuality was an open secret" in Vietnam.[112] At the 1935 International Congress for the Defense of Culture, Gide described himself as "a fervent individualist" who was "intensely French" yet equally "strongly internationalist" and "in full agreement with the communist outlook."[113] His combination of communism, individualism, and cultural nationalism appealed to the successively colonized Vietnamese and particularly to those for whom "individuality" seems to have included nonheteronormative sexualities.[114] These latter writers characterized Gide as a man of "restless energy" who aimed to "take off all the yokes: the yokes of the past, of the present, of prejudices, of rules, of ideologies, to have people return to their natural character" and thus tap into "a new world, an infinite amount of resources still untouched by literature."[115] Tran proposes that these writers "sensed the sexual politics behind Gide's communist activism" and that, through quốc ngữ print culture, they undertook an intersectional "doubling back" on imperial pressures.[116] In other words, early twentieth-century Vietnamese authors writing in quốc ngữ occupied one classic kind of inter-imperial positionality, and they leveraged their gendered mediations from that position.

With similar resourcefulness, as I'll discuss in the final two chapters of the book, novelists throughout the long twentieth century have revealed what lies hidden in imperial narratives of the world. They expose the coercive violence of empires and they transform our relations to that violence by recalling and creating other worlds of time, place, and collective being.

PART III PERSISTING TEMPORALITIES

Rape, Revolution, and Queer Male Longing in Carpentier's *The Kingdom of This World*

It could be argued that it actually began thousands of years ago. . . . Before the British took Malabar, before the Dutch Ascendancy, before Vasco de Gama arrived, before the Zamorind's conquest of Calicut. . . . That it really began in the days when the Love Laws were made. The laws that lay down who should be loved, and how. —**ARUNDHATI ROY**, *The God of Small Things*

Persecution . . . all the history of the world is full of it. . . . But it's no use, says he. Force, hatred, history, all that. That's not life for men and women, insult and hatred. And everybody knows that it's the very opposite of that that is really life. —**JAMES JOYCE**, *Ulysses*

. . . the moonfish rose in the air, as the last ruins of the plantation came tumbling down. —**ALEJO CARPENTIER**, *The Kingdom of This World*

In *The God of Small Things*, when the narrator wonders if the violence on a single day in the novel's story "actually began thousands of years ago," Arundhati Roy raises a question shared by many twentieth-century authors, writing in many different languages. Brooding on the bodily violations and intimacies caught in the maelstrom of world politics, they track the persisting force of the "love laws" over centuries. As they follow the sex, so to speak, they also expose the entwining of love laws and labor laws. In Anglophone literature alone, fiction ranging from James Joyce's *Ulysses*, Zora Neale Hurston's *Their Eyes Were Watching God*, Mulk Raj Anand's *Untouchable*, and William Faulkner's *Light in August* to Ayi Kwei Armah's *Two Thousand Seasons* and Roy's *The God of Small Things*, writers have dramatized how the laws defining "who should be loved, and how" serve to conscript laborers for the begetting of wealth and power, and especially for the reproduction of empire. Ultimately these texts rewrite the genre of historical epic as a meditation on the intimate microphysics of the world's dialectical history.

However far afield such literary interventions may seem from the field of struggle, the widespread reading and teaching of these texts in schools, communities, and prisons has implicitly fed, or at least kept alive, a post-independence and post-1960s political consciousness. Here, too, to borrow from Naomi Klein, the Right is right insofar as they perceived that culture was a *structural* battleground (just as, in Klein's assessment, the Right has rightly perceived a structural challenge to capitalism in the movements to stop climate change).[1] That is, cultural engagements are *structural* insofar as they transform the language through which humans live, value, and interact including by deconstructing conscriptive identities. In this way, the arts continue to do their dialectical work.

The last chapter showed how in the early twentieth century some authors pointedly transfigured technosystems in order to pit themselves against the repeating imperial forces in the present. In this chapter, I turn to texts that unfold from a different, more existential angle: they foreground temporality itself as a dimension of dialectical engagement, as theorists of queer temporality have also done (partly by gleaning insight from literature). The reconstructions of being-in-time in these texts at once expose history's determining force and channel the better energies that might feed collectivity—not free from history, certainly not labor-free, but lived side by side with that history and sustained through shared labors. This fiction includes, among many others, the single-day novels of Joyce, Virginia Woolf, and Mulk Raj Anand, and it includes the repeating, looping texts of Gabriel García Márquez, Pramoedya Ananta Toer, Rashid al-Daif, Gayle Jones, Arundhati Roy, Alejo Carpentier, Michelle Cliff, Zakes Mda, and Patricia Powell, to name a few.

In this and the next chapter, I begin by sampling a range of authors so as to establish the project they share; and then I focus on two Caribbean novels so as to trace the distinctiveness and impact of these experimental texts: Alejo

Carpentier's *The Kingdom of This World* (1949) in this chapter and Patricia Powell's *The Pagoda* (1998) in chapter 7. Like other writers, Carpentier and Powell evoke the long-historical, transoceanic economies of vying empires, splicing together old and recent pasts, and they position sexuality as the matrix that reproduces this historical succession. As Carpentier's narrator in *The Kingdom of This World* comments, "There would never be a dearth of workers to carry bricks to the summit of Le Bonnet de l'Évêque . . . as long as there were black women to bear their children."[2] Both this novel and the notion of "the Caribbean Mediterranean" developed by Carpentier implicitly recognize the history of layered and vying imperialisms built on sexual conscription, including those of Rome, Africa, China, Europe, and North America.[3]

Yet on the other hand Carpentier and Powell write specifically from one pivotal "shatterzone" in "the great convergence" of the world's long accruing, inter-imperial legacies.[4] As has been amply documented, together with other parts of the west Atlantic, the Caribbean was first a place in which so-called old and new worlds collided and then became coveted ground for plantations and profits and therefore an arena of especially brutal inter-imperial violence. Yet in turn it also became a place where enslaved communities mounted, as Édouard Glissant put it, "a long succession of . . . countless revolts since the eighteenth century."[5] The history I have told in this book clarifies the degree to which the regularity of revolt in the Caribbean reflected a certain historical dialectic: one in which the concentration of inter-imperial technologies of domination—in transport, agriculture, print, and law—become increasingly retooled for subterfuge, rebellion, and the exposure of betrayal and brutality by activists and artists.[6]

In *The Kingdom of This World* (1949) and *The Pagoda* (1998), Carpentier and Powell, respectively, evince their concern with these historical processes in Atlantic world history by setting their stories in earlier eras of revolution and rebellion, implicitly correlating contemporaneous unrest in the Caribbean with earlier rebellions: in *Kingdom*, the Haitian Revolution, and in *Pagoda*, the late nineteenth-century uprisings that intersected with the arrival of bonded Asian laborers in the Caribbean. The prominence of sexual violence in their novels (as in other Atlantic world novels) likewise registers the widespread practice of rape as a structural feature of the reproduction of labor on Atlantic world plantations, to which we can add the casual practice of rape in the transoceanic slave and coolie trades. Carpentier's and Powell's novels deserve combined study for the different ways they situate the dynamics of labor and rape within these layered inter-imperial histories. Carpentier's equivocal handling of rape offers insight into the complex ways that literature can at once expose and continue the instrumentalizing violation of women's bodies. Furthermore, his hints about the men's queer investments further reveal the imbrications of sexuality and empire. Perhaps unintentionally, Carpentier helps us to understand how these patterns are also inter-imperially generated. Powell's text in turn sheds light on the ambivalent investments and limitations of Carpentier's, while re-creating narration itself as a means to move toward other futures and other forms of relationality.

In linking these elements of *The Kingdom of This World* and *The Pagoda*, these last two chapters build on work by Caribbean feminist scholars such as Donette Francis, who attend to the "multiple imperialisms" shaping contemporary Caribbean women's literature while also highlighting the ways that "state formation" (including both imperial and postcolonial state formation) "unfolds through the micropolitics of intimacy rather than the macropolitics of revolutions."[7] In this chapter I extend these analyses backward to Carpentier as a mid-twentieth-century male novelist partly so as to track his ambivalent, subtextual grappling with these sexual and inter-imperial dimensions. Because the novel stands as a particularly revealing treatment of these politics, I have chosen to treat Carpentier's Spanish-language novel in translation as an exception in this study. I hope native-language readers find my reading of some value despite the limits of this treatment in translation. More broadly, I hope my approach here can prompt dialogue about texts and techniques in other places and languages.[8]

In what follows I first survey a wide range of twentieth-century literary interventions as context for Carpentier's, and I then recall the inter-imperial coordinates of Caribbean history before turning to Carpentier's political activism and his literary-political interventions in *The Kingdom of This World*.

Taking Time

Living through the global wars and activist movements analyzed in chapter 5, and inheriting the longue-durée legacies of empires and revolutions past, mid-twentieth-century authors began to narrate the ordeals of living under successive and vying empires. On the first pages of *Ulysses*, the Irish Catholic protagonist Stephen Dedalus laments his position as a "servant of two masters . . . an English and an Italian," that is, "the imperial British state . . . and the Holy Roman Catholic and apostolic Church."[9] Throughout, Stephen casts the Roman Catholic Church as a vestigial imperial institution that laid ground for and is now complicit with the British Empire. Joyce also saturates his text with wry allusions to imperial battles, from Greek-Persian wars and medieval Danish invasions of Ireland and England (treated as context for Shakespeare's *Hamlet*) to scores of more contemporaneous wars, including the Russo-Japanese, the Anglo-Burmese, and most especially the Boer Wars. Joyce also engages directly with ancient texts, implicitly and self-reflexively commenting on their connections to entanglements of his own. The very title of the novel, *Ulysses* (1922), announces that, like its intertext *The Odyssey*, this book meditates on the long history of imperial violence as it pivots around the political economy of the household, Penelope's suitor-embattled realm. Throughout the novel, Stephen Dedalus broods on what he calls "the brother motive" that drives men's betrayals of other men and domination of women, and the novel ends with the long unpunctuated interior monologue of a woman celebrating eros while deconstructing the men's antagonisms—a section that Joyce himself referred to as the Penelope section.[10]

It's also worth noting that Joyce brooded on dialectics specifically, raising questions about determinism and change that Carpentier and especially Powell also take up as central questions. In the opening chapters Dedalus first of all wonders about the determining power of the warring dialectical past. He asks himself: what if "Pyrrhus [had] not fallen . . . or Julius Caesar not been knifed to death?" Echoing the language of Aristotle's dialectical thought in the *Metaphysics*, he posits that history "must be a movement then, an actuality of the possible of the possible." Yet he also wonders, "or was that only possible what came to pass?"[11] Although declining to resolve the question, Stephen acknowledges the determining force of historical events and their importance for temporal consciousness: for even if these wars and battles might not have happened, they did happen, and so they are "not to be thought away. Time has branded them and fettered they are lodged in the room of the infinite possibilities that they have ousted."[12] Joyce joins many others who make us feel how thoroughly relations are made not born. These authors show that, even as relations and decisions are made and unmade day by day, they have been prepared by a long past, making today's choices both constrained and full of import for tomorrow.

For other writers, the invaders and conditions are different, but the temporal layering of imperialisms and the dynamics of inter-imperial positionality are comparable. In *Untouchable* (1935), Indian author Mulk Raj Anand also positions his protagonist Bakha, a Dalit Indian latrine cleaner, between vying hegemonies. Excluded from Hindu temples and households and indeed the very touch of the Hindu community, while temptingly hailed by the British Empire through decorated army uniforms and fetishized hockey sticks, Bakha feels himself caught between new British colonizers and the long legacy of Hindu oppressors that have positioned his family as hereditary latrine cleaners. Eventually, in Anand's rendering, he perceives "a common quality in the look of hate in the round white face of the Colonel's wife and in the sunken visage of the touched [Hindu] man" who had beaten and humiliated him that morning. By midday he is overcome by a "spirit of resignation," which the narrator tells us derives from "the serfdom of thousands of years" and which Bakha feels "flowing like a wave" through his body.[13]

Encompassing two millennia of African history, in *Two Thousand Seasons* (1973) Ayi Kwei Armah narrates the imperial invasions of Islam and Christianity. His choral narrator insists, "we are not Europeans, we are not Christians, . . . we are not Arabs, we are not Muslims," and then decries the invasions of both "white destroyers" for their "shrieking theologies" and their pursuit of a "predator's" trade in slaves and material wealth.[14] As it cycles through the generations and ordeals of "two thousand seasons" of invasion and resistance, Armah's text retools the oral genre of imperial epic while also implicitly naming the problems of inter-imperial maneuvering in the Cold War period during which he wrote.[15] In *Midnight's Children* (1981), Salman Rushdie rewrites the genre of historical epic in a Shahrazadian storyteller mode, offering a tragicomic tale of two brothers whose competition is shaped by clashing Mughal and British imaginaries. As Armah's text does implicitly, Rushdie's narrator speaks from a "Third World" positionality, foregrounding Kashmir as an age-old, inter-imperial shatterzone, seized by the Mughals in the seventeenth century and now pressured by Cold War contestations and alliances among China, Russia, Britain, and the United States.

Given the logic of imperial reproduction, competing efforts to dominate women's sexuality are often at the center of this fiction, including men's as well as women's texts. In Anand's novel, Bakha's troubled condition comes to crisis with the molestation of his sister by a Hindu priest. In *The God of Small Things* (1997), Arundhati Roy correlates the birth of Ammu's children with inter-imperial wars involving China, Russia, Britain, and the United States, and she links Ammu's father's and husband's domestic violence to their British imperial identifications. As we will see in chapter 7, in Patricia Powell's novel *The Pagoda* (1998), the Chinese Jamaican protagonist, Lowe, escapes from the impoverished Chinese Qing Empire, where she has been sold to pay her father's debts, only to end up in the clutches of a British colonial agent of the coolie trade. She lands in an impoverished Jamaica, where she serves as the store manager and concubine for the white man who has raped her and fathered her daughter. As the novel opens she sits under a pair of "faded portraits on the wall"—one of "Victoria, the old Queen," and the other of "the last Manchu emperor"—attempting to write a letter to her daughter that will explain her hidden life as a raped mother passing as a man.[16]

Some male writers pointedly expose the inflated male self-fashioning and bullying competition bequeathed by inter-imperial history (although others such as Salman Rushdie belie investments in masculinist competition).[17] Armah centers his revisionary epic *Two Thousand Seasons* (1973) on women's position as targeted pawns in men's rivalries and as exploited laborers who in counterpoint model and advocate "reciprocity" in labor and relation. Ngũgĩ wa Thiong'o's *The River Between* (1965) alerts us immediately to the sexual dynamics around which inter-imperiality pivots. Beginning with a description of the two mountain ridges of Kameno and Makuyu, which face each other like "two rivals ready to come to blows for the leadership of the isolated region," the novel quickly comes to its opening crisis over the question of female circumcision following a young woman's postcircumcision death, which splits the community and confounds the male protagonist Waiyaki's effort to bring unity.[18] More recently, Nuruddin Farah's trilogies depict women's in-between positions, as in the novel *Maps* (1986) featuring Somalian Arabic women caught in the long history of intermingled Muslim and Christian legacies in Ethiopian and Somalian states.

To convey the longevity of these problems, all of these texts compress temporality or reconfigure history's "progress." In Armah's text, one set of choral, generational voices merges with the next, as waves of invaders provoke new waves of resistance over two thousand seasons of struggle. Joyce, Woolf, and Anand developed the distinctive subgenre of the "day in the life" novel, which encapsulates the long pasts that stream into one day, one place, and one consciousness in an interpellating, imperial habitus. In another variation, authors such as Roy, Michelle Cliff, and Caryl Phillips have created looping narrative structures to capture the repeating violence of empires, with each loop encompassing a longer or wider backstory. These authors render the ways that characters are burdened by the determining past as they seek to tap other epistemologies. Written under the pressures of deep inter-imperiality and asking about ethical action, their texts both represent and embody temporal convergences: determination by the past, unpredictable contingency in the present, and ethical orientation toward a different future.

Carpentier's *The Kingdom of This World* and Powell's *The Pagoda* share these renarrating projects, yet they also capture distinctively Caribbean histories and waves of resistance. Those histories require attention here before I turn to the novels. In this chapter I focus on Saint-Domingue, Haiti, and Cuba as the islands most relevant for Carpentier's writing, whereas in chapter 7 l focus on Jamaican history as context for Powell's writing.

Inter-imperial Archipelago

In *The Repeating Island* (1992), Antonio Benítez-Rojo highlighted the histories that repeat across Caribbean islands and yet simultaneously divide them. Scholars have since expanded his theorization of the Caribbean as an archipelago.[19] Noting the islands' "struggle to survive among imperialist states," historians such as Mary Renda focus on "the evolution of Haitian politics in the context of global imperial competition of the late nineteenth century," a point that applies equally to the larger Caribbean archipelago in the twentieth century.[20] Others have detailed how the political economy of the Caribbean has been shaped by the linked state-capitalist dynamics that I have argued are inherent to inter-imperial processes.[21] Raphael Dalleo argues that the Caribbean deserves more attention as both a laboratory for neocolonial tactics and a seedbed for decolonial thought.[22] Feminist scholars have analyzed the gendered nature of these Caribbean struggles, as in Carole Boyce Davies and Monica Jardine's discussion of the intertwining of imperial, archipelagic, and gender dynamics.[23] My analysis brings together these elements within a longue-durée framework so as to fathom the depth and dialectics of Carpentier's and Powell's interventions.

As is well known, in their location near the American continents, the Caribbean islands were targeted for colonization by several European empires beginning in the seventeenth century. They were especially crucial for the English, French, and Dutch Empires as "beachheads" (to use Roberto González Echevarría's word), enabling these empires to compete with the Spanish and Portuguese, who already had footholds in the Caribbean and South America.[24] Once the European trade in enslaved Africans and the plantation systems were established, the Caribbean became an epicenter of the world economy, a primary source of the wealth feeding the rise of European and North American empires, especially through the production of sugar, one of the most desired and profitable commodities in the world.

Thus did the Caribbean became an especially intense inter-imperial and anti-imperial battle zone.

Accordingly, the landmark event of the Haitian Revolution not only sparked a spreading anti-imperial consciousness and a corresponding terror among white Europeans, as discussed in chapter 4, but it also recalibrated the balance of power among Atlantic empires. With the plantation system disrupted in Haiti and the polity governed by non-European rulers, the Spanish capitalized on the opportunity to develop Cuba as the main producer of sugar, which also meant that it became the largest importer of enslaved persons in this period (between 200,000 and 350,000 Africans in the next forty years).[25] This labor history would later shape revolutionary Cuba, in which Carpentier would play a part as both activist and writer. When the Spanish abolished slavery in Cuba in 1886, the fates of Cuba and Haiti again converged, for the two Spanish colonies of Cuba and Santo Domingo eventually came to depend on Haitian migrant laborers for their agricultural economic base, mainly the sugar and tobacco plantations. In *The Kingdom of This World*, Carpentier invokes these inter-island dynamics when his protagonist migrates to Cuba during the Haitian Revolution, carried there by his fleeing French master.

By the end of the nineteenth century, vying imperial powers renewed their competitive encroachments, especially as the United States invoked the Monroe Doctrine to justify control of resources and labor in the Caribbean. Over the next several decades, the United States found pretense to invade and occupy all three countries as it worked to fortify its neocolonial hold. The United States wooed many Caribbean governments away from relations with European neocolonizers by promising better loan terms, only to then betray those promises. For instance, in 1893 the United States convinced President Ulises Heureaux of the Dominican Republic to oust the Dutch Westerndorp and Company and to contract instead with the U.S. San Domingo Improvement Company (organized by both capitalists and government officials, such as the secretary of state). Westerndorp had demanded an exorbitant 30 percent of all customhouse revenues from the Dominican Republic, which led Dominican leaders to accept the American terms. But soon the United States far exceeded the exorbitant Dutch terms: by 1896, the "Improvement Company" controlled *all* customs revenues.[26]

As with the Haitian and Dominican struggles, the winning of Cuban independence in 1898 was from the beginning burdened by the designs of surrounding empires, including but not limited to the United States. Having performed the old inter-imperial trick of supporting anticolonial rebels who oust a previous empire, the United States successfully maneuvered to install itself as an occupying power. By the time the United States departed in 1902, it had gotten a strong neocolonial foothold in the Cuban economy. Through the disingenuously named Treaties of Commercial Reciprocity, which regulated trade between the United States and Cuba from 1902 to 1945, the United States held sway over Cuba's economy by limiting Cuba's trade with other countries and creating conditions for trade that strongly favored the United States, to the chagrin of other states. Others nonetheless jostled for an edge, especially Britain, as Servando Valdés Sánchez explains in his analysis of Cuban diplomacy in the 1920s–40s, the years when Carpentier was a young activist, journalist, and eventually a fiction writer moving between Europe and the Caribbean.[27] Later there would be similar inter-imperial jockeying for Jamaica's banana industry, as the United States maneuvered to break the hold of Britain and other European powers. In the case of Cuba, British interest collapsed with the beginning of World War II and even more so after the 1959 Cuban Revolution, as the state nationalized its industry to block inter-imperial intrusion. Thereafter, embargos and subterfuge increased the problems of poverty, repression, and censorship in revolutionary Cuba, encouraging its tighter alliances with the USSR for trade and arms.

In the first half of the twentieth century, Haiti also faced similar neocolonial intrusion, shaped by growing inter-imperial tensions in German-US relations because of the financial influence of Germans in Haiti. With encouragement from their government, Germans had been emigrating and building business connections throughout Latin America and the Caribbean. By the 1910s German businessmen controlled 90 percent of Haiti's internal trade, in addition to Germany's near monopoly of transatlantic shipping through the Hamburg America Line. While German businessmen were embedding themselves in the island's trade and infrastructure building, German agents practiced the inter-imperial tactic of destabilization in this US "sphere of influence" by funding a range of rebel groups who wreaked havoc and who for a brief time helped to put a German-friendly president in office.[28] We might speculate that the United States learned some tactics from them, for certainly it soon followed suit by practicing destabilizing tactics throughout the Caribbean. The German activities allowed US Americans to speak of a "German threat" in the Caribbean, and their rhetoric resonated more effectively after the outbreak of World War I, as the allies lined up against Germany.[29]

US North Americans found exactly the pretense they needed when, in July 1915, the US-backed Haitian president Vilbrun Guillaume Sam was assassinated. At that point, under the guise of "protecting" the country's assets, the United States first seized all financial assets (transferring them to the Bank of New York), and then invaded in 1915—continuing its occupation until 1934 and maintaining its neocolonial influence through the ruthless dictator Rafael Trujillo.[30] In short, hamstrung from the outset by prior inter-imperial histories of extraction, stratification, and divide-and-conquer incitements and faced with explicit "doctrines" such as the Monroe Doctrine proclaiming "spheres of influence" that were violently enforced through puppet governments and financially induced through growing debt, Caribbean postcolonial states struggled for equilibrium.

By mid-century, Caribbean thinkers were analyzing these combined problems. Claudia Jones early detected the danger in Caribbean leaders' efforts to "bargain between the two imperialisms" of Britain and the United States in order to "resolv[e] economic problems," especially since, in what she called the "Anglo American rivalry," the Caribbean archipelago became a pawn (Jones's prescient insights were perhaps enabled by her distance from the masculine investments, as Boyce Davies and Jardine suggest).[31] The Guyanese thinker Walter Rodney extended these insights to argue not just for an anticolonial consciousness but for "an anti-*neo*colonial consciousness" because "we needed to fight the British" but also "we needed to fight the British, the Americans and their indigenous lackeys."[32] His point was echoed in Kwame Nkrumah's *Neo-colonialism: The Last Stage of Imperialism*, which advocated strategies of nonalignment in this geopolitical field.[33] Frank Gerits points out that "Third World" stances of nonalignment (or what Nkrumah also called "positive neutrality") were conceived of as anti-neocolonial foreign policy: they aimed to forestall policies such as the Monroe Doctrine, while also promoting the ethical aspiration to "neutralize" the warring conditions of what Carpentier refers to in *Kingdom* as the "Mighty Powers."[34]

As Benítez-Rojo observed and Carpentier's novel dramatizes, the Caribbean archipelago thus not only suffered repeating waves of invasion and exploitation: it became a dialectical basin for committed resistance. These interventions were encouraged in part by religious and other voluntary associations among the people, which fostered the vernacular dialogues feeding anti-neocolonial attitudes and activist discourses (even though sometimes entangled in colorist hierarchies).[35] Growing out of these legacies, Caribbean fiction makes us feel how a "world-weariness of being" may sometimes be "transformed into the innocence of becoming," as Zita Nunes puts it.[36] All of these conditions and possibilities were on Alejo Carpentier's mind as he wrote his "hymn of terror" about the world's "Mighty Powers" (28, 104).

Positioning Carpentier

In *The Kingdom of This World*, Carpentier imagines the Haitian Revolution mainly from the perspective of one enslaved man, Ti Noël.[37] The novel's four parts track Ti Noël's life on the Saint-Domingue plantation of his first master M. Lenormand de Mézy, his several years in Cuba just after the revolution, and his return to Haiti. Part 1 features Ti Noël's involvement in the attempted revolution led by the slave named Macandal (historically known as "Makandal"); part 2 depicts the later successful revolution and its aftermath, which Ti Noël spends in Cuba, brought there by his fleeing master but soon made the slave of a Cuban master; and part 3 centers on Ti Noël's return to Haiti and his conscription into forced labor under the Haitian king Christophe, including the insurrection that overthrows Christophe. The book's fourth and final section initially shifts to Rome, following Christophe's fleeing family and their slave, the suggestively named Soliman. It then returns to Haiti, where Ti Noël faces another set of "Surveyors" (169). Again the people are conscripted into labor for infrastructure building, this time with "the whip in the hands of Republican mulattos" (170).

Like other figures in twentieth-century fiction, Ti Noël has thus been the servant of many masters, and the novel traces his serial servitude. At the novel's close, we learn that he "began to lose heart at this endless return of chains, this rebirth of shackles, this proliferation of suffering" (171). He feels "countless centuries old," worn down by a "cosmic weariness, as of a planet weighted with stones," and "his shoulders shrunk by so many blows, sweats, revolts" (178). Just as the chanting slaves led by Macandal had earlier echoed "the rending despair of peoples carried into captivity to build pyramids, towers, or endless walls," so again here Carpentier recalls the world's repeating history of domination—and the ever returning need to revolt (41–42).

Scholars have vigorously debated Carpentier's representation of the Haitian Revolution in this novel, comparing the text with the historical evidence, tracing what the text includes and omits, and evaluating whether his treatment of Vodou verges toward primitivization. The underlying question in many of these discussions is whether Carpentier endorses or undercuts revolutionary action.[38] Raphael Dalleo argues that in *Kingdom* Carpentier shows ambivalence about revolution, abandoning the political radicalism of his first noval, *¡Écue-Yamba-Ó!*. Other critics have analyzed the fact that *Kingdom* barely includes the most famous leaders of the revolution, concluding that Carpentier thus elides revolutionary action or deems it hopeless.[39] Some have read Carpentier's narrative against those of other Caribbean authors, most especially those of C. L. R. James, concluding that James more clearly embraces the revolutionary acts of Toussaint Louverture and Jean-Jacques Dessalines. In a close comparison of the gender politics of Caribbean men's literary representations of the Haitian Revolution, and in dialogue with other feminist scholars of the Caribbean, Tanya Shields concludes that although these male writers offer some sympathetic depictions of revolutionary women (especially James), they nonetheless organize their stories around a heroic "imperial manhood."[40]

I agree. Yet I also argue that Carpentier subtextually if ambiguously exposes that masculinism. This subtext comes into clearer view when we take full account of Carpentier's involvement in political activism in Cuba, which is not consistently linked to the politics of *Kingdom* by critics, and when we closely consider the novel's foregrounding of "forced labor" and its connections to sexual violence.[41] I'll turn briefly to Carpentier's political activities before addressing the novel's layered and equivocal representations of these matters.

In the years when he was creating *The Kingdom of This World*, Carpentier was involved in Cuba's movement toward revolution, carrying forward the activism he had practiced since he was a young man, all of which eventually led to his service in Cuba's revolutionary government under Castro. Raised in Cuba from just after his birth in Switzerland in 1904, Carpentier lived inside and outside Cuba throughout his life, often relocating in response to political events. In 1927, at age twenty-three, Carpentier the budding journalist was imprisoned for forty days by the Machado y Morales government for his affiliations with communist groups and his signing of the democratic, anti-imperialist Minorista manifesto. Thereafter he fled to Paris on a false passport, where for a decade he wrote for leftist literary journals of the kind discussed in chapter 5, also founding the journal *Imán* (which reported on events in Cuba under a series of military-backed repressive leaders). He also befriended Cuban dissidents living in exile, including the group Comité de jeune revolutionnaires cubains. Carpentier visited Cuba in 1936 when the Machado regime ended and Fulgencio Batista y Zaldívar took power, a leader who at first seemed a friend of the people, garnering support from Cuban communist and socialist groups. In 1939 Carpentier left Europe to live in Cuba, seemingly drawn back by the promising changes afoot. He may also have been prompted by the Germans' invasion of Poland and their aggressive expansion across Europe. The chaos in Europe seemed to bear out Otto Spengler's thesis in *Decline of the West* and thus confirmed the conviction of Carpentier and other writers that the decadent, violent energies of Europe would give way to positive transformations in the Americas.

During his next six years in Cuba (1939–45), however, Carpentier instead witnessed the increasing impoverishment and repression of the Cuban people under Batista, whose movement away from the political left was pressured by the United States and Britain.[42] Reflections on revolution would also have been encouraged by his 1943 visit to Haiti, where he researched African music and learned more about the role of Vodou rituals in the Haitian Revolution. In Haiti he would likely have heard talk of the 1937 Parsley Massacre carried out by the Dominican dictator Trujillo against Haitians (and to which Carpentier may implicitly allude in *Kingdom*).[43] Carpentier left Cuba in 1945 and moved to Venezuela, where a coup d'état and democratic revolution had just occurred and where he continued his political-literary journalism in support of the new Venezuelan presidency. He also kept in touch with Cubans involved in the returning wave of uprisings and revolutionary movements against Batista-controlled Cuban governments, which struggled to put down the insurgencies. It was during these years that he wrote *The Kingdom of This World* about the Haitian Revolution. I suggest that the novel's foregrounding of repeated betrayals, serial labor coercion, and terrorizing violence reflects Carpentier's experience of the setbacks in Cuba in these years.

Although it postdates the novel, immediately after the success of the Cuban Revolution on January 1, 1959, Carpentier returned to Cuba, having been invited to assume an official leadership role as executive director of the Editorial Nacional, the Cuban state publishing house.[44] This call to government service not only reflects the respect he had garnered as a supporter of the revolution but also indicates that Carpentier was a writer who fully understood the imbrication of culture and geopolitics. In his role as Cuban minister of culture, his knowledge would further deepen. He walked a precarious, inter-imperially pressured line as a publishing author and minister of culture living in the only communist state in the West during the Cold War.[45]

When we bear in mind Carpentier's political life, we better understand the seasoned tenor of his exploration of the Haitian Revolution in *Kingdom*. Carpentier's political consciousness was a revolutionary one attuned to archipelagic, inter-imperial, and—as I'll particularly show—intersectional coordinates. The text directly positions the islands within the vying contests of European empires, as when the narrator remarks that aid for the revolutionaries "would come from the Spanish colonies on the other side of the island, bitter enemies of the French," and also notes again that the revolutionaries "could count on arms offered by the Spaniards" (62, 75). Furthermore, the laborers, far from being primitivized, are keen discerners of the ironies of imperial self-fashioning and the exploiting maneuvers of their masters. In fact, strategically, they are culture makers themselves, retooling African pasts, practices, and narratives as a resource for resistance, as Ti Noël implicitly observes about Macandal's "narrative arts" (13). What Carpentier dramatizes is not so much a cyclical theory of history that makes violent revolution pointless, as some critics have suggested, but rather a dialectical genesis of colonizer/colonized narratives, infused with Carpentier's implicit commentary on the masculinist aesthetics of triumph.[46]

Some readers seem to assume that Carpentier's concern with aesthetics, reflected in his involvement in European surrealism in his early years, distorted or distracted from his politics. I argue on the contrary his attunement to representation and art was part of his political savvy. Indeed, his text foregrounds the co-constitution of politics and art from its opening pages, and throughout it casts aesthetics as a dialectical force. To capture its powers Carpentier develops the narrative mode that he refers to in the novel's prologue as *lo real maravilloso* (the marvelous real)—a mode that he and others considered distinctly American insofar as it newly merged African, Arabic, European, and indigenous traditions on American soil, as scholars have noted.[47] For Carpentier, this mode was especially inspired by a trip to Haiti, where he learned more about African syncretism and where, as he puts it, "I found myself in daily contact with the marvelous in the real."[48] Carpentier creates a "marvelous" compression not only of layered imperial histories but also of layered aesthetics.

Carpentier's transcontinental shaping of aesthetics is particularly important for my analysis because it is one of the two main ways he inserts a critique specifically of gendered violence, though subtextually, equivocally, perhaps even partly unconsciously as I discuss below. His exposure of the aestheticization of empire as a veil for its structural and sexual violence flows together, furthermore, with subtextual currents of queer longing among revolutionary Afro-Caribbean men—a pattern not yet discussed by critics. Perhaps this is so because these critiques and longings in the text lie so well hidden, so unacknowledged, that we might after all say that they are at once expressed and denied. This too may be part of *lo real maravilloso* that constitutes Carpentier's interpositional practice.

Seizing the Tools

As his novel's opening chapter makes evident, Carpentier understood that the practice of violence and the cultivation of beauty have been imperial bedfellows—operating together to instrumentalize bodies for the reproduction of empires. He foregrounds the colonizers' adornment of violence, anticipating the insights of Saidiya Hartman in *Scenes of Subjection* and Simon Gikandi in *Slavery and the Culture of Taste*. Sexuality is at the core of these critiques of empire, yet encoded rather than explicit.

In its first sentences, the text fashions Ti Noël as a man with "a gift for judging" the combined beauties and capacities of reproductive bodies. He has been brought to the port by his French-colonial master, M. Lenormand de Mézy, to select a stallion to expand the horse population on the plantation. Ti Noël's discernment takes center stage, as does his pivotal role in the Atlantic economy.

> Of the twenty stallions brought to Cap Français by the ship's captain, who had a kind of partnership with a breeder in Normandy, Ti Noël had unhesitatingly picked that stud with the four white feet and rounded crupper which promised good service for mares whose colts were coming smaller each year. M. Lenormand de Mézy, who knew the slave's gift for judging horse flesh, had paid the price in ringing louis d'or without questioning his choice. (3)

In this implicit parallel to the trade in human flesh, the novel here alludes to the demands on enslaved women to produce "colts" every year. The skilled Ti Noël has meanwhile been conscripted, like the stallion, into the "good service" of ensuring this reproduction. Over the course of the novel his position will be linked to sexual reproduction in complex ways, as we will see.

Yet on these opening pages, Ti Noël soon uses his visual "gift for judging" to deconstruct the world of the master. While de Mézy visits the barber, Ti Noël sits outside and reflects on the window displays of the barbershop and the adjacent butcher shop. He studies the *representational arts* that serve to reproduce empire.

> While his master was being shaved, Ti Noël could gaze his fill at the four wax heads that adorned the counter by the door. The curls of the wigs, opening on to a pool of ringlets on the red baize, framed expressionless faces. . . . By an amusing coincidence, in the window of the tripe-shop next door there were calves' heads, skinned and each with a sprig of

parsley across the tongue, which possessed the same waxy quality. . . . Only a wooden wall separated the two counters, and it amused Ti Noël to think that alongside the pale calves' heads, heads of white men were served on the same tablecloth. (4–5)

With cunning colonial mimicry, or what the text shortly refers to as his "mental counterpointing" (10),[49] Ti Noël continues to elaborate on stylized butchery in the hands of a "macabre cook":

> Just as fowl for a banquet are adorned with their feathers, so some experienced, macabre cook might have trimmed the heads with their best wigs. All that was lacking was a border of lettuce leaves or radishes cut in the shape of lilies. Moreover, the jars of gum Arabic, the bottles of lavender water, . . . close neighbors to the kettles of tripe and the platters of kidneys, completed . . . that picture of an abominable feast. (5)

In visualizing the heads of white men displayed on a platter together with the calves they eat, Ti Noël's gaze provides "what was lacking" in this "abominable feast." Here Carpentier wryly alludes to Haitian King Christophe, a chef during his enslaved years who eventually helped to serve up white men's heads on a platter.

Ti Noël next turns his gaze to the window of the bookseller and remarks on empire's literary and picture arts, laced with Carpentier's ironic commentary on the enforced illiteracy of slaves:

> The morning was rampant with heads, for next to the tripe-shop the bookseller had hung on a wire with clothespins the latest prints received from Paris. At least four of them displayed the face of the King of France in a border of suns, swords, and laurels. [In other prints] [t]he warriors could be identified by their air of setting out for battle; the judges, by their menacing frowns; the wits, by their smiles, above two crossed pens at the heads of verses that meant nothing to Ti Noël, for the slaves were unable to read. (5)

In the closing comment that "the slaves were unable to read," Carpentier's irony cuts through this taxonomy of empire's agents, for the novel's opening has fully displayed the keen reading skills of the enslaved. This keenness and counterpointing later shape every move of the revolutionaries, and the irony likewise streams through the text, including the inaugural moment of the Haitian Revolution. As the slaves "surrounded the houses of the overseers, seizing the tools," we learn that "the bookkeeper . . . was the first to fall, his throat slit top to bottom by a mason's trowel" (67). This scene will not be the only time that the text associates the slaves' seizure of the tools of infrastructure building with their seizure of the tools of book arts and bookkeepers, as we'll see.

In this opening chapter, Ti Noël's mental counterpointing enters explicitly as a commentary on empires. He is prompted by a picture, which "represented a kind of French admiral or ambassador being received by a Negro framed by feather fans and seated upon a throne adorned with figures of monkeys and lizards" (7). When a bystander tells him that "that is a king of your country," Ti Noël has the following train of thought:

> This confirmation of what he had supposed was hardly necessary, for the young slave recalled those tales Macandal sing-songed in the sugar mill. . . . With deliberately languid tone, the better to secure certain effects, the Mandingue Negro would tell of certain things that had happened in the great kingdoms of Popo, of Arada, of the Nagos, or the Fulah. He spoke of the great migrations of tribes, of age-long wars, of epic battles. . . . He knew the story of Adonhueso, King of Angola, of King Da, the incarnation of the Serpent, which is the eternal beginning, never ending, who took his pleasure mystically with a queen who was the Rainbow, patroness of the Waters and of all Bringing Forth. But, above all, it was with the tale of Kankan Muza that [Macandal] achieved the gift of tongues, the fierce Muza, founder of the invincible empire of the Mandingues, whose horses went adorned with silver coins and embroidered housings. (7)

In attributing an "age-long" political consciousness to Ti Noël and referring to actual historical African states about which Ti Noël has knowledge, Carpentier first of all avoids a "primitivist" representation of Ti Noël as illiterate.[50] The oral telling of this history makes it no less literary or historical (and no less political), for as Bogumil Jewsiewicki and V. Y. Mudimbe long ago pointed out, "oral traditions . . . are also historical discourses. Both a West African griot, for example, and the 'traditionalist' associated with the court of a precolonial state, are . . . even above all, historians in the ordinary sense of the term."[51] As Ti Noël recalls a literary and imperial African past to reposition himself in his colonized condition in the present, readers are called into identification with him.

At the same time, when we read this passage together with the one that directly follows it and together with the novel's stream of references to rape and sexuality, we enter more ambiguous terrain. On the one hand, the text seems to echo racialized stereotypes of sexual prowess, and it may seem to encourage our identification with men "taking their pleasure" with women. On the other hand, Carpentier has put in play a tonal irony that might be heard in the sensationalism of this passage and its clichéd discourse of the "mighty strain of heroes."

The narrative certainly foregrounds the competitive masculinities shaping Ti Noël's perception. After recalling "the invincible empire of the Mandingues," Ti Noël contrasts their "virility" with that of European emperors, for Mandingue rulers were "true kings, and not those sovereigns wigged in false hair who play at cup and ball and were gods only when they strutted on the stage of their court theaters, effeminately pointing a leg in the measures of a rigadoon. . . . In Africa, the king was warrior, hunter, judge, and priest; his precious seed distended hundreds of bellies with a mighty strain of heroes" (8–9). "Hard as anvils," these Mandingue kings have furthermore "ruled the four points of the compass" as "lords of the clouds, of the seed, of bronze, of fire" (7–9).

In short, in the first few pages of *The Kingdom of This World*, Carpentier seems deliberately to have staged a scene of inter-imperial competition centered on a narrative of masculine sexual prowess. Ti Noël himself will eventually scatter the seeds of this imperial imagination and create multiple "distended bellies": he fathers twelve children by the many "wenches" he "takes," and he "passe[s] on the tales of the Mandingue to his children, teaching them little songs he had made up in Macandal's honor" (56–57).

It's possible to read these passages as Carpentier's own romance with imperial subjectivity, and indeed one senses a certain pleasure in the writing of them. Yet in both the final pages of this chapter and the whole of chapter 2 masculine sexuality and colonizing violence are so insistently linked that the text seems to warn against the seductions of this masculinist eros. At the end of chapter 1, as Ti Noël and his master de Mézy leave town, their horses pass "many a quadroon, the light-of-love of some rich official . . . followed by a maid of her own equivocal hue" (9). Sitting "astride the stallion," Ti Noël continues his aesthetic-imperial counterpointing, now explicitly described as such. When they hear the navy's ceremonial shots heralding the arrival of "His Majesty's fleet," and de Mézy begins whistling "a fife march," Ti Noël, "in a kind of mental counterpoint, silently hummed a chanty that was popular among the coopers, heaping ignominy on the King of England" (10).

His counterpointing practice remains entwined with gender as it describes macabre habits among white French women that also, however, expose those conditions leading them to "bury fetuses" in convents: Ti Noël "had little esteem for the King of England, or the King of France, or of Spain, who ruled the other half of the island, and whose wives, according to Macandal, tinted their cheeks with oxblood and buried fetuses in a convent whose cellars were filled with skeletons" (11). Ti Noël muses thus, astride his chosen stallion and holding "the white, chill skull" of the calf's head that de Mézy has bought from the butcher, "thinking how much it probably resembled the bald head of his master hidden beneath his wig" (9). By the end of his opening chapter, Carpentier has already displayed the counterpointing, sexualized aesthetics through which the men will engage as they fight their physical battles.

Titled "The Amputation," chapter 2 repeats this interpellating imperial language, hinting that it leads to Macandal's amputation. The brevity of this two-paragraph chapter reinforces its status as an echo of and commentary on chapter 1. Here as Ti Noël speaks of Macandal's skill at "narrative arts," he also evinces a certain homoerotic attraction, although ultimately the passage hints that these intertwined investments can backfire on the laborers (13). The scene unfolds at the horse-driven circular mill, as Macandal feeds sheaves of cane into the grindstone, and Ti Noël, caretaker of horses, stands by. He soon becomes distracted by the lithe body of Macandal, singer of those epic masculinist visions: "Letting the old horse circle the mill at a pace that habit had made mechanical," Ti Noël first gazes on Macandal's "powerful torso, his incredibly slender waist," and reflects that "the Mandingue exercised a strange fascination" on him. He then turns to musings on African infrastructural achievements, expressing wonder at the way that Macandal's description of the grand "cities of Guinea . . . held the men spellbound" (13).

Again contrasting feminine European and masculine African empires, Ti Noël deems the "belfries," "stone buildings," and indeed the whole town of Cap Français "a trumpery thing compared with the cities of Guinea": "There, cupolas of red clay rose above great fortresses surrounded by battlements," and "the workmen were skilled in working metals, forging swords that cut like razors and weighing no more than a wing" (13–14). The paragraph ends with another hint of homoeroticism as Ti Noël recalls "the holy city of Widah," where "the Cobra was worshipped, the mystical symbol of the eternal wheel, as were the gods who . . . appeared, wet and gleaming, among the canebrakes that muted the banks of the salt lakes" (14).

Yet suddenly at this moment there "came a howl so piercing and prolonged that it reached the neighboring plantations" (14–15). Readers abruptly learn that while Ti Noël has been fantasizing about grandeur and wet male bodies Macandal's arm has been crushed in the iron rollers of the circling millstone. This event makes up the second of the chapter's two paragraphs. The paragraph closes as Ti Noël and others "tie a rope tourniquet under [Macandal's] armpit to stop the bleeding," while "the master called for the whetstone to sharpen the machete to be used in the amputation" (15).

The sequence suggests critique, reinforced by its emphatic title ("The Amputation") hinting at castration. It seems no coincidence that the Guinea imagery of the wheel, the phallic snake, and the gleaming wet canebreak men is interrupted precisely by the crushing wheel of the millstone whose metal rollers mutilate the laboring man. Involved in an attitude "that habit had made mechanical," Ti Noël becomes blind to the "mechanical" labors of horse and man all while being seduced by empire's spellbinding imagery. Crashing through the symbolic wheel there comes a brutally physical one, the "eternal wheel" of empire building. In other words this sequence implies that Ti Noël's imperial and phallic-worshipping subjectivization is a condition for Macandal's "amputation." Following on the arch ironies about the arts of empire in the first chapter, this second chapter creates a more violent "counterpoint" between the mesmerizing pleasures of men's imperial narratives and the howling pain of empires' amputations.

The scene furthermore foreshadows the crushing labors that return after the Haitian Revolution under King Christophe, whose state building likewise yokes the mesmerizing beauties of song and palace to the brutal coercion of labor, as the text's juxtapositions make eminently clear. When Ti Noël returns from Cuba, he first visits de Mézy's plantation and finds that it has "turned into a wasteland" with nothing left of the "indigo works, nor drying sheds, nor barns, nor meat-curing platforms" (106). By contrast he then encounters King Christophe's Sans-Souci Palace, "a rose-colored palace, a fortress with ogival windows, rendered almost ethereal by the high socle of its stone stairway" (107). Next he hears "the sound of a dance orchestra in full rehearsal" and he sees coachmen "polishing a huge, gilded carriage," while priests emerge from a church with white columns and cupola and walk in the elaborately laid-out "terraces, statues, arcades, gardens, pergolas, artificial brooks, and boxwood mazes" (107–8). Ti Noël witnesses a reversal of power on the island particularly as manifested in infrastructures and arts, in effect a realization of the imaginative counterpointing in the first chapter.

Ti Noël is at first delighted that "this marvelous world" is also "a world of Negroes," including "those handsome, firm buttocked ladies circling around a fountain of tritons," a sexualizing comment of a kind that runs throughout the text (108–9.) But as in chapter 2, violence cuts through his gendered reverie. Abruptly, as Ti Noël muses that "the former cook of the Rue des Espagnols . . . now struck off money bearing his initials," both he and readers are yanked out of the reverie when "a heavy blow landed across the old man's back" and "before he cold utter a protest . . . he found himself locked in a cell" (110). He is promptly conscripted to build King Christophe's La Ferrière Citadel, forced to join "the long procession of children, pregnant girls, women, and old men," all laboring "under the vigilance of whip and gun," while in the distance the queen's chaplain reads Plutarch's *Parallel Lives* to the king's son (110, 114, 111). Here, too, Carpentier slips in reference to sexual coercion of reproductive women. Having just noted the "pregnant girls" in the procession of laborers, he also reflects, "As long as there were black women to bear their children—and there always had been and always would be—there would never be a dearth of workers to carry bricks" (117).

Again and again Carpentier returns to the pivotal matter of labor—and to the need to reproduce the endlessly dying laborers. Ti Noël learns that over the last twelve years "the entire population of the North had been drafted" to build the palace and citadel and that "every protest had been silenced in blood" (116). At the same time, laborers regularly fall to their deaths, slipping from the perilous suspension bridges across which they carry bricks and mortar: as soon as one "disappeared into space . . . [a]nother immediately took his place, and nobody gave further thought to the one who had fallen" (114). Here Carpentier may allude to the Panama Canal, also a twelve-year project built by Caribbean laborers that cost many their lives. Blood is mixed into the very cement of the buildings, for, everyday "several bulls had their throats cut so that their blood could be added to the mortar to make the fortress impregnable" (114). In this world of brutal laboring, bodies *become* artful infrastructure.

Yet in his own counterpointing practice, Carpentier suggests that ultimately the king himself meets his death by merging with his empire-imitating infrastructures. In their final uprising, the laborers torch the palace until the flames engulf "the crystal goblets, the crystal of the lamps, glasses, windows, the mother-of-pearl inlay of the console tables" (143–44). Faced with overthrow, King Christophe shoots himself—and then King Christophe's beautiful infrastructures become his stone grave. His loyal servants bury him in concrete so that his body will not be mutilated, whereby, in Carpentier's rendering, "his flesh fused with the very stuff of the fortress, inscribed in its architecture, integrated with its body bristling with flying buttresses. Le Bonnet de l'Evêque, the whole mountain, had become the mausoleum of the first King of Haiti" (150). Like the authors and activists discussed in

chapter 5, Carpentier seems to have perfectly understood that infrastructures have been sites of struggle in the labor-stratified, inter-imperial world.

In another counterpoint, the next and final section of *Kingdom* carries us
to the imperial city of Rome, following the flight of King Christophe's family
after the uprising. Here the text performs both the Mediterranean-Caribbean
connection and the literary connection to English Gothic and Faustian texts
discussed by Carpentier in "The Marvelous Real in America" (83, 85, 88).
The section's first chapter opens in the villa of Christophe's family, in a scene
overflowing with the names, decorations, and arts of empire. Here, "with a
tinkling of bracelets and charms," the two daughters of Christophe perform
"an aria from Rossini's Tancred"—notably, a historical opera about Tancred
the Crusader set during the Normans' twelfth-century taking of Sicily from
Islamicate rulers (152). The sisters perform in a library sporting "the latest
novels, whose covers, after the new fashion, were adorned with woodcuts of
cemeteries at midnight"—a clear reference to those Gothic tropes of "medieval" inter-imperial pasts (which I discussed in chapter 4) (154). The scene
encapsulates the tropes and history of Atlantic world empires, as signaled to
us in the chapter's epigraph from the sixteenth-century Spanish writer Lope
de Vega's *El nuevo Mundo*, with clear commentary on the crimes of colonialism: the Devil asks Providence where he is next sending "Columbus / To
renew my evil deeds?"[52]

These references to the long, dark, and aesthetic underlayers of empire
continue as the text then focalizes through another slave, Soliman, who will
meet his death here in Rome. First, on the streets Soliman sees "beggars
thrust forward stumps of arms, all their gamut of wounds and mutilation,"
and by day's end he finds himself in the mausoleum of Pauline Bonaparte,
whom he had served in Saint-Domingue as a masseur (154). Like King
Christophe's, her body has merged with aestheticized stone, which Soliman
discovers when he drunkenly stumbles on her carved likeness laid out on
top of her casket.[53] Yet to fathom the implications of Soliman's demise in
Rome, we must first consider the sexual subtexts of the novel, including first
the violent and then the queer.

Rape and Masculine Struggle

In Carpentier's hands, the repeating history of empire and resistance includes the perpetual return of sexual violence and aestheticized death. The
repetition reveals women's condition as props in men's mirroring arts and

as tools in their battles for control over labor and over relations. Carpentier admits as much by treating rape as a mundane event in the kingdoms of this world and by positioning it emphatically in the two key moments of resistance: the scene of Macandal's burning at the stake (often taken as a bellwether of Carpentier's view of revolution) and the inaugural moment of the Haitian Revolution. Moreover, as background to these scenes, the novel makes the "taking" of women a regular practice. The text problematically seems to equalize the meanings of violent sexuality for colonizing and colonized men; yet its patterning also helpfully exposes the dialectics of coformation that do shape male practices and imaginaries on both sides.

Given these ambiguities, the text's treatment of rape creates a discomfiting experience for readers. To write about Carpentier's treatment of it in his novel about the Haitian Revolution is to enter difficult and politically fraught terrain. But to look past it is to veil the violence and perhaps misconstrue the import (conscious or unconscious) of Carpentier's text. Moreover, if the history of rape is to be recognized as part of the history of world dialectics, if we wish to take it seriously as part of the Terror in, say, the Vendée during the French Revolution as well as in every other instance of invasion and colonization, then we would do well to notice its handling in literary texts—one of the few records of rape as a recurring practice mostly among men and a common lived experience mostly among women. Carpentier not only pointedly references rape in revolutionary moments, as we'll now see, but he also hints at its world-shaping reverberations through Maman Loi, the conjure woman and teacher of Macandal in Vodou arts.

The "taking" of enslaved women is a steady habit of Ti Noël's master, M. Lenormand de Mézy. His habit is given emphasis by mentions of it at the openings and closing of chapters, often wryly juxtaposed against his series of marriages. Shortly after his first wife has died from the poison distributed by Macandal and shortly before Macandal's burning at the stake, the opening sentence of chapter 7 (part 2) announces: "After reinstating Marinette, the laundress, in his bedchamber for a while, M. Lenormand de Mézy . . . married again, a rich widow, lame and devout" (41). In this same paragraph in chapter 7, however, the narrator depicts the "takings" practiced by enslaved men. Ti Noël and the other slaves are said to welcome the relaxed discipline on the plantation during the Christmas holidays, for it allows them not only to steal a bit of wine or food but also to "slip by night into the quarters of the newly purchased Angola women whom the master was going to mate, with Christian ceremony, after the holidays" (40). Here one could charge Carpentier with falsely equalizing the men's practices and simply indulging in salacious imagining. Then again one could wonder if, even so, enslaved women might have felt themselves positioned between men who, even though their coercions might have different meanings, would nonetheless treat women as theirs to take. And if so, one could credit Carpentier with giving readers a fuller glimpse of enslaved women's predicament.

Carpentier does return to this possibility in two important scenes, prominently casting rape as a counterpointing practice between vying men. The first is the opening scene of the revolt. Unable to sleep and "in a vile humor" about the "Utopian imbeciles in Paris whose hearts bled for the black slaves," de Mézy leaves his white mistress Mlle. Floridor in their bedroom and heads out "to the tobacco shed with the idea of forcing one of the [slave] girls" (65–66). At this moment the slaves break into the overseers' houses, killing the bookkeeper, while de Mézy flees and hides himself in the dry well. Two days later he crawls from his hiding place and ("passing the swollen corpse of the bookkeeper") he enters his bedroom. There he finds "Mlle. Floridor [laid out] on the rug, legs sprawled wide, a sickle buried in her entrails" (69). As the masters have made rape one of their instruments and prerogatives, so too do the enslaved men in their dialectically determined struggles. The insurrectionists express their counterpointing touché by positioning Mlle. Floridor in the style of a painting in the bedroom: "Her dead hand was still clenched around one of the bedposts in a gesture cruelly reminiscent of that sleeping girl in a licentious engraving entitled *The Dream* which adorned the wall" (69–70). In Carpentier's rendering, they purposefully mimic this "adornment" of violence. As the masters have made aestheticization of war, rape, and murder one of their instruments, so too—in Carpentier's rendering—do the enslaved men.

The pattern of references to women's violated bodies as aestheticized weapons in men's battles continues after the revolution when de Mézy and the other French planters flee to Cuba. Again entwined with gendered arts, the first reference is to a French female singer on the boat with de Mézy, "whose only dress was the costume of Dido the Forsaken" (75). Thereafter, the rape of the French planters' daughters is flatly noted: "But the strange thing was that with their fortunes gone, ruined, half their families unaccounted for, and their daughters convalescing from the Negro rapings— which was no small thing—the old colonists seemed to have taken a new lease on life" as they "reveled" in "freedom from obligations" and discovered the "advantages of being single" (76–77). The use of a subordinate clause to mention "daughters convalescing" and the remark about the rapes as "no small thing" seem calculated to draw as much attention to the fathers' brutal callousness as to the raping. In a further juxtaposition, the narrative then mentions the masters' "taking" of Black women: de Mézy, we learn, "began to divide his hours between the card table and prayer. He sold off his slaves one by one to gamble away the money at cardhouses . . . or take home with him Negresses whose beat was the waterfront" (79).

The regularity with which Carpentier enfolds these references to sexual exploitation begs for notice. One might be tempted to speculate about the sources for his acute awareness of sexual violence.[54] At the same time, however, one could ask whether the fathers' indifference to the rapes is also Carpentier's. The novel never enters a raped woman's point of view, and it never narrates her "howls" when violated, as it does when men suffer violence. Furthermore, in his essay, "The Marvelous Real in America," Carpentier stages his own masculinist contest with European men when he not only mocks the French surrealists' interest in depicting (in Lautremont's own words, quoted by Carpentier) "adolescents who find pleasure in raping the fresh cadavers of beautiful dead women," but emphatically disparages them for "not tak[ing] into account that it would be more marvelous to rape them alive"—one sign of "their own impotence."[55] This comment alone certainly suggests that in *Kingdom* Carpentier reenacts sexual violence to gain the admiration and satisfy the pleasure of at least some of his male readers.

Yet, even in this light—or perhaps all the more in this light—the novel's depictions of rape deserve study for their structuring of colonial conflict. Two further moments are particularly telling in this connection. The first moment appears at the climactic close of chapter 7 in which Macandal is burned at the stake. As noted, current scholarly debates about Carpentier's revolutionary commitments often center on this chapter. In my view, by staging discrepant interpretations of Macandal's fate, Carpentier invites readers to become active interpreters—that is, active participants in ongoing dialectical questions and processes. And he has succeeded, as today's lively dialogues about the chapter make clear. Yet perhaps equally telling is the *lack* of discussion about the gendered closure of this scene.

Imprisoned as an instigator of the widespread poisoning of whites and their livestock, the griot and Vodou practitioner Macandal is brought to the town square in chains and tied to the stake for the violent spectacle of a public burning. Here, the spellbinding storyteller Macandal completes his fate as a mythic figure who will himself enter future narratives—"chosen as he was to wipe out the whites and create a great empire of free Negroes in St Domingue" (30). Carpentier has already set up the masculinization of Macandal's return in Ti Noël's comment that once Macandal "had completed the cycle of his metamorphoses" he would return "poised, sinewy and hard, with testicles like rocks" (37).

Yet, as much discussed among critics, Carpentier creates two contradictory perspectives on what happens in this scene—one seemingly "real" and one seemingly "marvelous." In the eyes of the onlooking enslaved community, when the fire engulfs Macandal, "the bonds [fall] off and the body of the Negro [rises] in the air" as the crowd cries, "Macandal saved!" (49). Then "Pandemonium followed," we are told, at which point: "the noise and screaming and uproar were such that very few saw that Macandal, held by ten soldiers, had been thrust head first into the fire, and that a flame fed by his burning hair had drowned his last cry" (46). Carpentier adds emphasis to this mise-en-scène—indeed linking it to the book's title—by recounting that "the slaves returned to their plantations laughing all the way," since "Macandal had kept his word, remaining in the Kingdom of this World." Thus "once more the whites had been outwitted by the Mighty Powers of the Other Shore" (46).

Which is it, escape or death, gendered triumph or gendered defeat? Carpentier refuses to settle who is seeing "correctly" here. For some, the bifurcated rendering of this moment undercuts the value of both revolution and Vodou. These critics conclude that Carpentier is exoticizing the "marvelous" in this scene and implying that the slaves are merely deluded. I see no such certainty. Like Tanya Shields, I believe that something more interactive is in play, whereby Carpentier is challenging readers' ways of framing the "real" in the political field of power.[56]

This challenge extends, however consciously on Carpentier's part, to his closure of the chapter with men's discursive and sexual domination. The final sentence exposes de Mézy as a misreader of the slaves' political consciousness, but then it goes one step further:

> And while M. Lenormand de Mézy in his nightcap commented with his devout wife on the Negroes' lack of feelings at the torture of one of their own—drawing therefrom a number of philosophical considerations on the equality of the human races which he planned to develop in a speech larded with Latin quotations—Ti Noël got one of the kitchen wenches with twins, taking her three times in a manger of the stables." (46–47)

This fleeting juxtaposition of the arrogant master and enslaved revolutionary seems to have escaped most readers' notice, yet it deserves our close attention. As de Mézy performs his masculine European learning before his "devout and lame" wife to justify white men's domination, Ti Noël simultaneously performs his mastery of a Black "wench" to celebrate Black men's revolution (37). The language of the passage—a speech "larded" with Latin and the "taking" of a "wench" in a "manger"—insinuates mockery of both forms of male arrogance, the book-controlling kind and the body-controlling kind. And yet it's important to recall that overall the novel does not assign "book" methods to European men and "body" methods to Black men. As discussed above, de Mézy regularly "takes" women, and Ti Noël regularly offers "counterpoints" to the art and learning of European men. The pairing of their acts in one closing sentence at this climactic moment allows us to see that, in gendered terms, the slave's and the master's epistemologies and practices are not so different. It lets us know that we are witnessing men's pitched battle to "rule the four points of the compass" by displays of "virility" that keep women perpetually "lame" on a deeply uneven inter-imperial playing field.

As Tanya Shields suggests, to read the full implications of mid-twentieth-century men's narratives of the Haitian Revolution, including those of C. L. R. James and Aimé Césaire as well as of Carpentier, we need also to track their texts' gender politics. Shields rightly concludes that although these writers sometimes represent women positively, they are most of all engaged in "a series of exchanges with political and imperial European masculinity."[57] But what if Carpentier nonetheless also enfolds a metacommentary on those exchanges—with whatever investments, motives, and equivocations? And if so, what shall we make of this seeming incommensurability in his representations? I suggest that in such moments we are witnessing a distillation of a long-standing struggle, endemic to imperialized subjectivities and especially to (but not only to) men's imperialized subjectivities: the struggle between the seductive, sometimes profitable interpellation into imperial power and the righteous call to expose and reform the practices of that power. This is the contradictory, agonistic struggle of the Faustian figure epitomized in Gothic texts like Maturin's Melmoth the Wanderer. Maturin and many diversely situated authors choose exposé. Other texts, and I would place Kingdom among them, offer exposé but keep interpellating us into the imperial imaginary, as in the genre of apocalypse movies that decry while feeding us the spectacle of total power and total violence. These creations variously promise release but subtextually practice entrapment.

Doing so, such texts also teach us something, and they often know this too, as I believe is the case with Kingdom of This World. When readers take full stock of these double movements in the art of the world, we find ourselves productively put back on our heels, no longer simply hearing the story told but seeing the author telling it. This effect is salutary. For in revealing the work of texts at a structural level, displaying their structuring force in the world, they can prompt important conversations about our own imperialized subjectivities.

In *Kingdom of This World*, Carpentier may after all register his knowledge of these manifold relational effects in other fleeting yet telling moments. Although, as noted, the book seems never to enter a raped woman's point of view, there is perhaps one exception, one buried hint, in a scene that to my knowledge has not received attention from this angle. Once, and only once, Carpentier lingers in, or at least with, the traumatized point of view of a woman who muses on the pattern of rape and, perhaps, has been raped. Importantly, this woman is Maman Loi, the Vodou teacher who trains Macandal in the herbs with which he eventually poisons the white population, assisted by Ti Noël. In one of their meetings Maman Loi and Macandal talk of "men whom certain spells turned into animals" and of women who "had been raped by huge felines, and at night, substituted roars for words" (19). Immediately hereafter, as Ti Noël observes, "Madam Loi fell strangely silent as she was reaching the climax of a tale" and then suddenly rushes to the kitchen "sinking her arms into a pot full of boiling oil" (19). Yet "her face reflected an unruffled indifference" and afterward "her arms showed no sign of blister or burn" (19–20). Is Carpentier depicting a moment of post-rape dissociation on Maman Loi's part? Is the implication that she has channeled that trauma and self-separation into her Vodou practice?

As with the undecidable scene of Macandal's transformative burning, it may be impossible to draw a conclusion. But it seems that Carpentier's text here registers the deworlding omnipresence of rape while the logic of his text traces its troubled effects. That is, the muffled implication is that the knowledge cultivated by a raped woman has streamed into the apparently male-led revolutionary activity that begins with poisoning the colonizers and their animals. Once again we might recall that sentence in the frame of *The Thousand and One Nights*—that much "lies hidden in the old accounts of bygone peoples and times."[58] In *Kingdom*, this suggestion reverberates back through all other aspects of the text's revolutionary history, including its marvelous dialectical telling of "the real." The undecidability of Macandal's powers should be considered within the undecidability of Maman Loi's powers—and the meaning of her presence in this novel.

And both of these should be considered in relation to the longings that afflict Soliman during his last days in Rome and that accompany Ti Noël's entanglements from beginning to end.

Queer Longings?

Critics have taken little notice of the passing mentions of lesbian sexuality in Carpentier's fiction, for instance the lesbian characters in his 1953 novel, *The Lost Steps*, and the narrator's comment in *Kingdom of This World* that, as the French begin lose control in Saint-Domingue, "many [white] women became tribades, appearing at dances with mulatto girls" (96). Likewise, to my knowledge, no reader has taken notice of the hints of male homoeroticism in *Kingdom*. The lack of comment is unsurprising given the fleeting nature of these elements, especially compared to Carpentier's plotting of heteronormative sexualities. When Soliman travels to the Borghese Palace in Rome and discovers Pauline Bonaparte's tomb with a sculpture of her laid out on top of it, he is at first inconsolable. The scene seems to record Soliman's mourning for Pauline, for whom he was the intimate masseur. But thereafter his yearning desires turn toward the phallic figure of Legba. As he languishes on his deathbed in subsequent weeks, it is Legba he longs for: "Turning his back on all, moaning to the wall papered with yellow flowers on green background, Soliman was seeking a god who had his abode in far-off Dahomey, at some dark crossroad, his red phallus on a crutch he carried for that purpose" (162). He soon perishes, his desire for Dahomey merged with his desire for Legba.

Soliman's sorrow recalls an earlier scene of male longing for an epic phallic figure, for Ti Noël has suffered from a similar desire. When Macandal disappears into the hills after losing his arm (there receiving the herbal tutelage of Maman Loi), Ti Noël becomes "deeply distressed":

> If Macandal had suggested that he run away with him Ti Noël would joyfully have accepted the mission of serving the Mandingue. . . . During the long nights when this idea tormented him, he would get out of the manger where he slept and, weeping, throw his arms around the neck of the Norman stallion, burying his face in the warm, clean-smelling mane. The disappearance of Macandal was also the disappearance of all that world evoked by his tales. . . . Life had lost its savor. (23)

The language seems deliberately suggestive of romantic tales and gestures: the wish to "run away with" Macandal and the "long nights" of torment and weeping, soothed only when he "throw[s] his arms around the neck of the stallion, burying his face in the warm, clean-smelling mane." Equally suggestive is the equation between the loss of Macandal and "all that world evoked by his tales." The return here of the Norman stallion that Ti Noël chose on the novel's first page loops these feelings back through the novel as a whole. These scenes should also be read in light of Ti Noël's dream that after the revolution Macandal would return "poised, sinewy and hard, with testicles like rocks," and in light of Macandal's griot power to "[hold] the men spellbound" by visions of "the gods who ... appeared, wet and gleaming, among the canebrakes" (36, 13). Carpentier hints, in short, that homoerotic desires stream subterraneously through the men's investments in empire, magnetizing the triumphant narratives around which men congregate. Yet after all it may be that, for some, the dream is simply for a male lover in whose mane one could bury one's face.

To see this streaming desire is to see the novel's closing pages as revolutionary in another sense. For Carpentier turns Ti Noël's desire in a distinctly tender direction, queering the norms of aggressive masculinity. In the final chapters, when the weary Ti Noël has returned again to the ruined Lenormand plantation, we learn that he has "decorated" his abode with objects looted from the Sans-Souci Palace. This reclaiming of empire's refuse includes not only "pendulum clocks, chairs, draperies," but also colorful clothes: Ti Noël sports "a coat that had belonged to Henri Christophe, of green silk, with cuffs of salmon-colored lace" (164). Feeling himself "possessed by the spirit of the King of Angola," he "issued orders to the wind" (165). But the orders are "the edicts of a peaceable government," and the government's organizations include "the Order of the Christmas Gift, the Order of the Pacific Ocean, the Order of the Nightshade," and "the most sought after . . . the Order of the Sunflower, which was the most decorative" (166).

In his final, surreal days alone on the plantation, and the last two pages of the novel, Ti Noël sometimes still bursts forth in "declarations of war against the new masters" (179). Yet at the moment of his death, on the novel's last page, Carpentier slips in what may be a further gesture toward queer futurity. He does so, I suggest, through the image of a "moon-fish rising," a buried allusion to an unpublished play by his friend Federico García Lorca, El público—a text that, in Benjamin DeWitt's assessment, "self-consciously dramatizes queer visibility."[59] Lorca wrote this play during his visit to Cuba in the 1930s, where he spent much of his time with Carpentier and other friends and shared some unpublished papers with his Cuban friends, so the odds are that Carpentier at least knew the play. This closing allusion appears when a "great green wind" suddenly sweeps the island, so that "the moon-fish rose in the air, as the last ruins of the plantation came tumbling down."[60] Hereafter, as the final sentence records, "Ti Noël was never seen again, nor his green coat with the salmon lace cuffs" (180). In *El público,* the image of the "moon-fish" appears in a dialogue between two male characters and as a figure marking the homosexual relations between the men that might have been but will not be realized. Possibly then, the rising moonfish at the end of *Kingdom* suggests the same, providing a peroration for Ti Noël's unfulfilled queer longings.

In these last pages Ti Noël is certainly seeking another order of things, a less aggressive masculinist one, where peaceable relations reign and whose emblem is a yellow flower that recalls Soliman's yellow-flowered wallpaper. This kingdom is a place where one can adorn oneself, unharmed, with green silk and salmon-colored lace. Where perhaps sexuality, no longer brutalized, takes whatever peaceable form soothes and pleases. Perhaps it is an archipelagic place of avowed interdependencies and unraped laborers. If so, Carpentier's narrative of kingdoms covertly places sexuality at the heart of revolutionary transformation.

If we do see a hint of queerness in Ti Noël's cuffs of salmon-colored lace and his attraction to the "order of the sunflower" with its wide-open flower face, then we might say that, in *The Pagoda,* Patricia Powell allows this queer life to bloom in her protagonist Lowe. Yet, as in the case of Ti Noël, Lowe's "queer" situation is not simply an expression of freer sexuality. Instead, as Keja Valens argues in relation to *The Pagoda,* and as hinted in the imperial origins of Ti Noël's green silk coat with lacy cuffs, these novels tell the story of an empire-shaped queerness that has been forced and distorted even if ultimately chosen and re-created in new forms.[61] Powell's *Pagoda* plays out a history of repeating empires and repeating rapes more overtly than Carpentier's *Kingdom,* as we will see in the next chapter. Yet both novels carry forward art's dialectical work by immersing us in the difficult project of renarrating and redirecting those pasts that hold our future.

Chapter seven

Inter-imperially Neocolonial

The Queer Returns of Writing in Powell's
The Pagoda

In Michelle Cliff's *No Telephone to Heaven* (1987) we continually approach the moment of revolutionary action. Set during the upheaval of the 1970s in Jamaica, the scene that the novel opens with and continually returns to is that of an old truck lumbering steeply uphill on a muddy, broken road, hauling guns and people in khakis to the site where (although we don't know it yet) they will organize their insurrectionary attack. The novel unfolds in a looping temporal structure, repeatedly returning to this uphill journey before the insurrection and then circling back in time to approach it again from another perspective, each time carrying a new layer of backstory. After the novel's opening moment, we fall back in chapter 1 to the previous years of planning on the farm of Miss Mattie's granddaughter that led to this moment, although we don't know yet who Miss Mattie's granddaughter is. In the next chapter, we begin up the hill again and then fall back to a time just before the plans began in earnest—the night a man named Christopher murders his lighter-skinned employers. In the middle of this same chapter we fall back further, to Christopher's childhood, to the shantytown of the Dungle where he grew up, a world of begging, foraging, disease, and hunger ringed by the contempt of others, and then in the same chapter we move forward to the movements that led him to kill his disrespecting employers.

On this night, we also meet a woman named Clare Savage who, we will eventually learn, is on that truck, along with her transgender friend Harry/Harriet. Clare is Miss Mattie's granddaughter; the farm is her inheritance. In subsequent chapters we loop backward through Clare's earlier life until at novel's end the truck arrives and the attack occurs—tellingly directed at a Hollywood film crew exploitatively making a movie about revolutionary maroons. But the plan has been betrayed. All the revolutionaries are shot dead.

Cliff conveys the overdetermined forces of history, including the media arts of US empire, while also narrating its repeating, uphill complement on this "repeating island": the history of resistance. She shares this temporal technique with a range of recent novels, including Powell's *The Pagoda*, on which I focus here. Cliff's novel is probably the most explicit in its tight interweaving of the dialectics of colonial violence and anticolonial activism, but other texts follow a similar logic, pivoting on a violent event prepared by the raced, gendered, and labor-exploiting economies of empires. These authors write critical-dialectical phenomenologies of this accruing history.

Thus does the protagonist of Rashid al-Daif's novella *Passage to Dusk* (2001) lose his arm from a shrapnel blast during the Lebanese Civil War— he loses it again and again in the text's rendering, as the first-person narrator hovers on the edge of death and endlessly revisits the scene and its aftermath. Ken Seigneurie understands this "iterative" technique as Middle Eastern authors' attempt to capture the state of "ongoing war" in the region. We can also read its iterations as an embodiment of the "ongoing" resistance depicted in many decolonial novels.[1] In Arundhati Roy's *The God of Small Things*, we continually approach the events that break apart all the characters' lives on a single day: the accidental drowning of the Indian English girl Sophie Mol and the police's murder of Velutha, the Dalit Communist activist who is also the lover of the Christian Syrian Ammu. Mentioned early in the novel, the narrative repeatedly moves toward and then circles back from this day of crisis, especially the moment when Ammu's children Rahel and Esthappen are jolted from sleep to witness "history's henchmen" beating Velutha nearly to death.[2] Such techniques immerse us in a history that characters are living as uncertain but whose outcome already haunts the readers. They immerse readers in the overdeterminations of the long past.

Caryl Phillips's *A Distant Shore* (2003) is designed to similar effect: its very first section records the novel's culminating violent event—the murder of Gabriel, an African refugee in England—and subsequent sections circle back in time to reapproach the murder from both his own consciousness and that of the white Englishwoman, Dorothy, his employer and possible friend. William Faulkner's *Light in August* (1932) represents an early instance of this iterative narrative phenomenology, as the story repeatedly circles backward and forward toward the murder of the white Joanna Burden by the biracial Joe Christmas. In a variation on this method, Toni Morrison's *Beloved* (1987) repeatedly alludes to but defers the full telling of Sethe's murder of her daughter. Readers thus must live through a set of experiences that might have ended otherwise, feeling hope for other outcomes and yet girding ourselves for the "inevitable" violence. In other words, through loops and repetitions, readers are made to experience the sense that certain events have "already happened," decreed by material history and ideology. As Roy's narrator remarks about Velutha's death, "There was nothing accidental about what happened that morning. Nothing incidental. It was no stray mugging or personal settling of scores. This was an era imprinting itself on those who lived in it. History in live performance."[3]

And yet, although this looping structure often ends in deadly violence, it simultaneously records resistant or alternative action, in this way leading readers to invest in the potential for alternative histories. Again, in Cliff's text, the struggling uphill movement to which we continually return is an action of resistance to the determinations of imperial history. Her novel dramatizes the fact that this, too—this uphill work of resistance—is a driving world-historical force, undertaken by characters who persistently revive that resistance, though wearily and fearfully, and tinged by the longing for another set of choices. These narratives register a desire to step back from a world in which the violent coercion so unrelentingly demands violent resistance.

Moreover, as the narratives step back from overdetermined crises, they give us an opening in which to imagine ways that these crises might not (have) happen(ed). They create moments when characters begin to see and move toward other possibilities. The texts thus give weight to each move or choice along the way, registering temporal openings toward the possible, a transformed future. Within one such loop, for example, the friendship between the twins and Sophie Mol in *The God of Small Things* develops; against their expectations and despite the grounds for distrust, the narrative lets us see that the children begin to form a bond. Similarly, in *A Distant Shore*, Gabriel and Dorothy sense each other's sorrows, inching toward friendship despite the political and racial gulf dividing them. In the backward temporal lags of *No Telephone to Heaven* Cliff's Clare Savage meets her transsexual friend Harry/Harriet and receives her reeducation about the world, as do the novel's readers, by extension. By foreshadowing the event—the violence—and then whisking us back to a better moment and an alternative current of interactions, these texts gesture toward a path not determined and a future that is neither post- nor colonial, in which the meanings of those words suddenly dissolve within an alternative language, like the one Rahel and Esthappen keep creating together beyond the hearing of adults.

It's worth pausing a moment longer with Roy's *God of Small Things*. The novel comments implicitly on how configurations of time affect action and how reconfigurations allow authors to raise questions about agency. In one striking sentence, Roy exposes the entrapment of "Time" and "Being" in constricting masculinist, heteronormative narratives, anticipating the insights of queer theorists from Eve Kosofsky Sedgwick to Elizabeth Freeman and David Eng. Capitalizing "Time" and "Being," the brother-sister twins Rahel and Estha explain their temporary lack of a surname after their mother's divorce: "For the Time Being they had no surname because Ammu was considering reverting to her maiden name, though she said that choosing between her husband's name and her father's name didn't give a woman much of a choice."[4] The everyday phrase here, "for the time being," marks a brief lag in time created by Ammu, a duration in which she belongs to neither father nor husband. Her choice to reject both alternatives and to linger with the effects of that rejection creates a moment of Time Being, a queerly liminal time.

In turn, Rahel herself harbors an ambition to enter time differently, fantasizing about its unfolding: "Rahel's toy wristwatch had the time painted on it. Ten to two. One of her ambitions was to own a watch on which she could change the time whenever she wanted (which according to her was what Time was meant for in the first place)."[5] In effect, Rahel imagines that, outside imperial time, another "Time Being" might arise. Being might redirect time. If, in this way, the forces of caste, colonization, sexual prohibition, and deadly violence that began "thousands of years ago" could at least temporarily be derailed, then the lived horizon would open more capaciously to "tomorrow," or to "Naaley," the closing words of the novel—a capaciousness Roy embodies by juxtaposing the English and the Malayalam words.

Not merely retrospective, then, these texts undertake the "worlding" work that keeps alive a changing consciousness in the present and for the future. Through their reconstructions of temporality they re-create history's "progress" as history's questions, including about how to act and who to befriend in a pressured, precarious field of relations.[6] Re-creating how it feels to live inside the determinations of history while apprehending suppressed possibilities, they immerse readers in decisions about when and where one enters the dialectic, to paraphrase Paula Giddings.[7]

In Powell's *The Pagoda*, the decisive act to which we continually return is writing itself: the writing of a letter by the novel's protagonist, Lowe, to her daughter. By foregrounding an act of writing as an effort to model the repair of destructive relations, Powell implicitly crafts a metafiction of literature's work in the world, with implications for readers' acts of interpreting and choosing in the world. Lowe's repeated attempts to write the letter are catalyzed by both immediate violence and a long history of violence. The immediate violence stems from an act of collective resistance: a general store in a Jamaican town is burned by the community exploited by the store; the fire also kills the owner, Cecil, who is drunkenly asleep inside. The fire at first triggers a breakdown in Lowe, for as the store's manager she has suffered a life of violation at the hands of Cecil. Yet this event also ultimately leads Lowe to complete her letter, to open her long history to her daughter, refusing further disavowal. As she grapples with the yoked unfolding of force and choice, she approaches the uncertain question of her responsibility.

Meanwhile the text as a whole positions these questions within the interlocking neocolonial and sexual economies of the Caribbean, also connecting Chinese neocolonial debt to Caribbean neocolonial debt. In other words it dramatizes the twentieth-century consolidation of a *neocolonial* inter-imperiality and positions sexual formations as pivotal in this inter-imperial field. My reading here is informed by theorists of queer temporality and the "postcolonial queer," and most especially by approaches grounded first and foremost in specific, historical geopolitics, as modeled in the incisive 2013 special issue of the *International Journal of Middle East Studies*.[8] Similarly my reading of Powell's novel builds on literary scholars who engage with its state, sexual, racial, and colonial politics, while focusing especially on the existential dialectics of resistance, sexuality, and geopolitical economy, including through what I refer to as the novel's anaphoric rendering of temporality.[9] To situate the novel on this terrain requires, first, some further description of Lowe's complex, gender-bending story and its debt-induced origins in China and, second, close attention to the Jamaican context in which Powell wrote the novel and on which it implicitly reflects: the intertwined conditions of debt and labor in 1970s and 1980s Jamaica.

Lowe begins life as a girl raised as a boy in a Chinese port town, and she eventually becomes a woman forced to live as a man in a village in Jamaica. In China, Lowe suffered the fate of an unwanted girl treated by her father as a boy until she reaches puberty, all under the silent gaze of her mother. When Lowe begins to have a woman's body and Lowe's father can no longer sustain the fiction of having a son who will share his sea adventure fantasies, the impoverished father solves two problems at once: erasing his own colonization of Lowe's reality, he also "pays off a debt" to a local man by selling Lowe to him as a wife.[10] Lowe takes action against that patriarchal and debt-burdened betrayal, but her attempt is stalled early on. Although she re-dons her boy's clothes and flees her husband, slips away to the port, and hides as a stowaway on a ship, she soon discovers that its human cargo includes Chinese men coerced or tricked into "coolie" contracts and destined for lives of brutal labor in the Caribbean encumbered by debt. Lowe will share the Chinese and Jamaican men's debt conditions, but her version will be different; this fact emerges starkly after she is discovered in her hiding place by Cecil, who is a broker in this transoceanic trade in Chinese bodies. He imprisons Lowe in his cabin, ties her down, and rapes her throughout the long voyage. After Lowe gives birth to a daughter, Cecil installs her as the "male" shopkeeper of his store in Jamaica, and he "marries" her to a woman, telling her that this role will protect her from abuse by local men even as he continues to visit and rape her.

Lowe's letter attempts to explain her life to her daughter, Elizabeth, now an adult, who does not know she was conceived in rape and who, as far as Lowe and readers know, has thought Lowe was her father and not her mother. With each effort to complete the letter over several years, Lowe struggles to make sense of the histories in which she has been entangled: to sort out the interactions among colonial, racial, and sexual relations, between Chinese and Black Jamaican communities, and between the forces of coercion and the small windows for choice, all while still plagued by local betrayals. Like Carpentier's, this novel's characters move across inter-imperial temporalities and locales, seeking moments of transformation. These movements are dialectical, not merely cyclical, and they take shape within a material habitus. Thus, as Lowe slowly admits her need for avowal, she also gradually embraces her desire to transform her world through the building of a community hall (the titular pagoda). This project is her infrastructural intervention. In contrast to Carpentier's, however, in Powell's text the selling, buying, and raping of women is not the subtext but the excavated matrix of this material and debt economy.

Powell captures the dialectical transformations of Lowe's world in the very grammar and style of her text. She first of all renders Lowe's dizzying memories and identities through the text's pronouns, by having Lowe internalize a male identity and think of herself throughout the text as "he." Indeed for the early sections of the book, readers are not aware that Lowe has a cis-female body. In this third-person narration of Lowe as "he," Powell undertakes an aesthetic deconstructing and remaking of genders, all while re-creating the woman's condition as muffled and bound—like Lowe's breasts—within the men's terms. Readers must thus grapple with the questions that underlie social identity and its grammars, including scholars who must decide which pronouns to use for Lowe. So as to make this gendered predicament continuously felt in this chapter, I will henceforth refer to Lowe as s/he and put [her] and [she] in brackets. In addition to creating pronoun disorientation, Powell captures the dialectics of coercion and transformation at the level of syntax. The text embodies the rhythms of repetition and change not only through looping returns to letter writing, nor only through the start-and-stall progress of pagoda building, but also and most viscerally in the novel's chantlike, anaphoric sentences. More than a mirror of the repetitions of imperial violence, this syntax slowly releases Lowe's critical reflective consciousness about the past. Powell thus reclaims repetition for the rhythms of reparation.

To approach the connection between Powell's aesthetics of repetition and her intersectional critique of neocolonial inter-imperiality, I turn next to the conditions in Jamaica during the 1970s and 1980s, on which the novel implicitly reflects.

Neocolonialism in the Cold War Caribbean

Stephanie Black's 2001 film about Jamaica, *Life and Debt*, highlights the neocolonial economic conditions that Powell explores in *The Pagoda*. Debt is a key term in both the film and the novel, underpinned, I argue, by disavowals and betrayals of interdependence in the world of empires. The very pairing of *life* and *debt* in Black's title signals the foundational force of debt in Caribbean economies. Splicing tourist ads and McDonald's signs together with shots of ruined farms, occupation forces, and shanty houses, the film depicts the structural-representational discrepancies inherent to an inter-imperial political economy built on uneven and combined development. Drawing on Jamaica Kincaid's book *A Small Place* (the film is narrated by Kincaid), Black also enfolds salient critiques by Jamaican farmers, merchants, industrialists, and Rastafarian elders. These spokespersons focus on the debt-inducing, impoverishing effects of the forced replacement of local agricultural industries by transnational corporations owned by foreigners, achieved through the coercive loans of the International Monetary Fund (IMF) and the World Bank. As one Rastafarian analyst says about the loans, "de money come with terms and conditions, terms and conditions"—his own repetition expressing the history of repeated extortions.[11] These terms and conditions are not only extortive; they also entail betrayal of earlier trade deals, as I discuss below. As we will see, *The Pagoda* is likewise concerned with "terms and conditions" whereby debt spawns more debt, in China as in Jamaica, which ultimately defines the connections between them.

After Jamaica won its independence from Britain in 1962, the United States almost immediately began its neocolonial efforts to dominate its economy and labor force. The bipolar inter-imperiality of the Cold War was of course well established by then, and the 1959 Cuban Revolution and movement toward nationalization of industry had intensified the US effort to dominate in the rest of the Caribbean. Again, the dynamics were archipelagic and dialectically interlocking, meaning that whatever happened in Cuba shaped what would happen in Jamaica and vice versa.

Arrangements on the Guantánamo Bay military base in Cuba during the 1960s offer a telling case in point for the archipelagic entanglements of the Caribbean. As Jana K. Lipman traces, these arrangements were provoked not only by the 1962 Cuban Missile Crisis but also the 1964 water crisis. In the latter, Florida's imprisonment of Cuban fishermen said to be illegally fishing in Florida sea zones led Fidel Castro to cut off water supplies to the Guantánamo Bay US military base. The United States promptly laid off approximately fifteen hundred Cuban commuting workers on the base.[12] Thereafter the United States quickly made arrangements with Jamaica's pro-US president to replace the Cubans with Jamaican contract workers. The Jamaican Ministry of Labour's agreement to recruit workers and conduct physical exams and security checks "illustrated Jamaica's dependent position" for, as Lipman points out, Jamaica "did not even have the power to demand an official labor agreement," operating only on the basis of a verbal agreement throughout the 1960s. Thus while the United States "demanded an ideological commitment to anti-communism," it also took advantage of high unemployment and economic distress in both Jamaica and Cuba to force policies that served its own interests—and to pit one island against the other.[13] These export labor arrangements extend into the present, as the Jamaican government not only continues to arrange workers for the Guantánamo base but also places men and women in the hotel and agricultural sectors in the United States and Canada, in what Lipman calls "neocolonial and postmodern labor arrangements."[14] Inter-imperially speaking, old patterns repeat here: the exit of one empire (Britain in Jamaica's case, and Spain in Cuba's) becomes the opening to occupation by another; then, as empires play one island off the others, each island becomes competitively rather than cooperatively tied to the others. The empires' divide-and-conquer strategies thus undermine interisland solidarity—as reflected in the fact that, when some Jamaicans later tried to organize for better conditions on Guantánamo and invoked worker solidarity rhetoric, some Cuban workers labeled them "troublemakers."[15]

These corroding conditions led to a populist pushback in Jamaica and to Michael Manley's landslide victory in the 1972 election for prime minister. As is well known, although hailing from the "high brown" class, Manley moved the People's National Party (PNP) to the left, discomfiting the United States. Embracing both Marxists and Rastafarian leaders (and also marrying a darker-skinned, working-class woman, Beverley Anderson), Manley identified strongly with Pan-African anticolonial movements and new African leaders, especially Julius Nyerere of Tanzania.[16] Remarkably, Manley held power for eight years, although as Paul Ashley documents he struggled mightily under inter-imperial and intra-Caribbean pressures.[17] For instance, Manley worked to secure trade deals for Caribbean bauxite mining and aluminum production with the USSR, Hungary, and Latin American countries, but the deals always carried exorbitant "terms and conditions" and at the same time foundered on interisland jealousies and competition as Manley tried to develop this manufacturing sector in tandem with Guyana and with the Republic of Trinidad and Tobago.

In the 1980s, "East/West tensions played out in all forms" in the bitterly contentious electoral defeat of Manley in 1980 by Edward Seaga, a conservative pro-business Harvard graduate strongly backed by the United States.[18] Amid widespread violence both on the streets and behind the scenes, Seaga ended state control of several industries and built stronger ties with the United States, although like his predecessors he too faced financial coercion, for the IMF and World Bank offered loans only on the condition that Seaga fortify his ties with the United States and other western states.

Probably the single most detrimental turn for Jamaica and other Caribbean islands in these decades issued from the deregulatory "free trade" maneuvers of President Bill Clinton in the so-called Banana Wars (being waged as Powell completed her novel). A downward turning point for Caribbean economies, this battle also typifies the constrained, in-between positionality of states and communities targeted by neocolonial inter-imperial competition. Having received campaign contributions from the large banana marketers Dole and Chiquita (as did the Republicans), Clinton successfully pressured the World Trade Organization (WTO) to end preferential tariffs on banana exports from countries in the African, Caribbean, and Pacific Group of

States, as Heather Russell analyzes. These had been put in place by Britain and other European Union nations as reparations for slavery, but the supposedly socially conscious Clinton simply ignored them—another inter-imperial betrayal. Not only did the WTO decide that the tariffs "violated global trade rules," it also allowed the United States to impose $194.4 million in sanctions.[19] This ruling decimated the banana trade for Caribbean countries, which was a significant proportion of their trade base (in Saint Lucia it had employed a full third of the population), and it dramatically weakened the agricultural sector of most islands, furthering the damage done by the intrusion of US and transnational agricultural industries, as documented in *Life and Debt*.

Men's Debts

It's no coincidence, then, that Powell was attuned to debt as she wrote *The Pagoda* in this period. She places the problem in its global, historical, and gendered context by creating a Chinese Jamaican gender-passing protagonist who embodies not only the inter-imperially exploited laboring subject but also the inter-imperially exploited states from China to the Caribbean. As discussed in earlier chapters, the paracolonial situation of Qing China in the latter half of the nineteenth century included the heavy debts imposed on it by multiple empires through coercive trade and war treaties. These in turn enabled the coercions and success of the "coolie" trade, whereby merchants, inherently or explicitly underwritten by empires, transported bonded labor mainly from China and India to the Caribbean, Africa, and elsewhere. Powell takes the important step of dramatizing two key ways that women served in this economy: for merchants, as sources of profit as well as coerced pleasure and, for impoverished men, as a debt safety net since, if nothing else, they could sell daughters and wives. The novel also encodes the ways that a longer history has generated these conditions.

Lowe's family history is a figure for both China's gendered imperial history and its nineteenth-century inter-imperially squeezed condition. In chapter 1, Powell carefully sets up the inter-imperial mise-en-scène of Lowe's life, immediately marked by allusions to time and empire. In the novel's first sentences, Lowe wakes up at dawn "after the clock's iron music buckled out its final tone . . . [yet] still weary from the torrid dreams," and then heads to a desk, "stopping to wind the pendulum clock" (5). Putting on [her] fake moustache, Lowe sits down under a pair of "faded portraits on the wall":

one of "Victoria, the old Queen" and the other of "the last Manchu emperor" (7). There [she] unearths "the unfinished letter to the daughter . . . from among the . . . ledger accounts, invoices, and IOUs from customers down at his shop" (5). The historical scene has been set.

The first paragraph of the letter—in this first version of the letter readers encounter—explains that in South China "the villages had grown so poor. So destitute. People left China in droves" (8). Lowe and other characters will later elaborate on the point, mentioning that when the Manchu emperor Ch'ien-lung "inherited the country it was reeking with wars and corruption and starvation . . . so many wars, so many invasions" (192). Later in the novel, a recently arrived Chinese laborer alludes to China's inter-imperial troubles, describing the Boxer Rebellion as an expression of "the festering rage that was breaking out against all outsiders," including not only westerners but also "the Japanese, killing and torturing people, taking over" (232). This inter-imperial position explains the "secret societies determined to rid China of all foreign devils," as well as the fact that there are "more and more people rushing to gold-cap mountains in America, more and more Western books pouring in, translated" (232). In one of [her] later letter-writing sessions, Lowe sketches the conditions of Kwangtung, [her] home village, and more emphatically links its poverty to the geopolitics:

> This then is the terrain: mountainous coastlines brimming with butterflies, an arid countryside assaulted by famine, a town swarming with clans and secret societies, an anti-Manchu resistance, . . . a village full of hunger and destitution, a poor and overcrowded village, . . . a China war with Britain, a great war over territory, a war of opium, a China Sea clogged with foreign vessels, . . . the hordes of Chinese leaving, a village bereft of young men, the empire ravaged too by a Hakka sect, a revolution at Taiping, a backdrop of death and destruction, and hunger and debts. (130–31)

It is under these conditions that Lowe's father sells [her] to pay a debt, but long-entrenched gender norms have authorized his action. Lowe later recalls "the old man they gave me to, the cripple, to pay off a debt. That was my value, that was my worth: an old man with no teeth at all in his head, . . . hardly any vision at all, but what a penchant for a young girl, what a penchant for her tough meat, her soft skin" (243–44). The refrain repeats throughout the novel, "a girl betrayed by her father and handed over to an old man . . . he owed a debt to . . . a girl betrayed by her father and turned into a wife overnight[,] a wife who dreams all day at the barred windows of a house" (179). From its outset, Lowe's life and decision-making are conditioned by men's ownership of women's bodies, beginning with "my father who betrayed me, my father without the spine, my father that buckled under tradition" (244). As the repetitions of phrasing convey, Lowe names the repeating sexual-imperial practices in which [her] past and present are caught.

In Jamaica, Lowe slowly learns to listen for subtexts and telling juxta-positions, just as Ti Noël learned to look at his visual world with discern-ment. After the fire that killed Cecil and destroyed the store, Lowe visits with the Chinese communities on the island; [she] begins to analyze the sexual politics of this world as [she] listens to the men's late-night talk. First, "they talked about China and the debts" that led them into "severe losses at gambling," "violent clan fights," and "secret societies," and they talked about "the hunger that drove them to sign contracts" and finally "drove them from China" (43). They go on to describe "the incredible hunger that killed their children and forced them to sell wives" (43). Yet "then their voices would hush" (43). As a daughter who had been sold to pay a debt, Lowe hears something unspoken under the surface of both the talk and the hush.

First [she] notices that the men speak of their economic humiliations in China but not about their humiliating bodily conditions on the ship journey and in Jamaica: "all they talked about was home," dwelling on "the treacher-ousness of the Chinese there . . . those Chinese who sold them per head like rats to barracoon agents, owners of receiving vessels. It was as if that betrayal was greater than any humiliation they had suffered while chained up in those barracoons and beaten daily. . . . It seemed as if nothing could be as bad as that, as bad as being sent into this bondage by your own" (44–45). As [she] listens, Lowe wonders, however, if "the bitterness they carried could only be directed at the crimps, the Chinese who had sold them," because the humili-ations during and after the crossing were worse and less safe to admit. [She] begins to sense that gendered imperial subjectivities are part of what "lies hidden" and part of what's at stake for the men, involving their own bodily vulnerabilities. They don't discuss, for instance, "how they were made to stand naked so the throng of planters could prod their open jaws and hang-ing testicles before buying them, how planters chopped off their glossy im-perial queues and emblazoned, in bold red letters on their skins, the initials of plantations" (45). With testicles exposed and hair queues "chopped off," the men suffer a distinctly sexual humiliation. It turns out that, for the men as well as the women, bodily and economic betrayals go hand in hand. For this gendered sexual exposure is one effect of the economic betrayals by "your own"—that is, by other men of the group. But in disavowing their vulnerability at home, on board, and in Jamaica, these impoverished men also disavow their own betrayals of "their own"—betrayals of the women of their group. They too have sold members of the Chinese community, yet for women this condition includes the violent harm of rape and humiliation by all manner of men. This the men do not discuss; this they hush. Their silence structures their dis(re)membering, to adapt Toni Morrison's word in *Beloved*.[20] And in turn, as Powell shows, that disremembering likewise inhibits any future transformation of the world's inter-imperial economy.

Forced Choices

For Lowe, the men's disavowals explain why none of the Chinese men embraces [her] emerging wish to build a beautiful pagoda and create a benevolent society for the Chinese on the island. For to do so might not only craft an alternative habitus; it might also call the men into a different narrative of relations. After their hushed moments, the men return to the same old stories, which leads them to reinvest in the competitive narratives of getting ahead. Listening to the newest young Chinese arrivals who think they may build a better life in the Caribbean, Lowe thinks silently that they are buying into the very system that betrayed both Chinese and Black Caribbean male laborers, as well as the women: "yes, there were opportunities to be had if they persevered, but only at the expense of other people." After all, Lowe reflects, "They had been brought there only to keep the Negro population in check" and to "keep down wages" (45).

Ultimately, what emerges is a question about the capacity for different choices and the commitment to different narratives. Powell implicitly emphasizes this question about how to act in the face of "choices" defined a priori by owners, empires, and lenders. The men's conversations touch directly if briefly on the matter of coerced choice, bringing into view the pressured interplay of agency and determination. When one of the Chinese men laments his poverty and lack of power, he is asked, "But didn't you come of your own free will?" He retorts, "What is free will? . . . When you don't have one grain of rice, you are not free. When you don't have money, you are not free. . . . Is either immigration or death, no!" (43). Lowe likewise later reflects: "You know how many Chinese die on the ship with me? I didn't know which life was better, the one underneath him whenever he want, [or] the one tie up, shackle underneath the ship" (227). Under these "terms and conditions," they all grapple with the question of how to act in the present amid the traps set by the past.

Exposing this coercion and betrayal as a founding disavowal of relations, *The Pagoda* traces the ways that it spawns many other betrayals, particularly men's disavowals of their (indebted) relations to women. Lowe's whole story centers on coerced choice making. When they arrive in Jamaica, Cecil convinces Lowe that, without his "protection," [she] will soon find [her]self (as a lone Chinese woman in this Caribbean world of bondage) forced into a life of prostitution. As if generously, he proposes that [she] dress as a young man (again) and run his island store—while remaining, in unstated "terms and conditions," his coerced concubine. Lowe has no real option, except between the rapist [she] knows and the rapists [she] doesn't, so Lowe follows the plan. [She] binds [her] breasts, dons a false mustache, and lives the life of Cecil's shop manager, involuntarily exploiting the underpaid local laborers with overpriced goods, and never knowing what the locals know about [her]. "Then he give me the shop. Give me the money, but every time coming back for more of me, wanting to humiliate me" (227). As [she] eventually admits, "During [my] entire life on that island [I] had been indebted to Cecil" (17).

Debt is the principle here, the betraying principle, of neocolonial and gendered relations. As established in the opening scene where the unfinished letter is buried under IOUs from customers, Cecil's Black Jamaican store customers live in debt to his store, just as the coolie laborers live in debt by the terms of their bonded contracts. Powell includes the telling detail that Cecil had originally turned to the coolie trade because he was disowned and disinherited by his wealthy landowning family (it's not clear why), which suggests that this installation of his "concubine" as his capital-extracting agent forms part of his effort to win back a corner of the colonial capital. Cecil is a sort of renegade capitalist, himself in debt, and therefore happy to support or bribe whoever will serve his effort to build his own "empire" of wealth and proxy masters and so regain dominance in his relationships.

Indeed, the household Cecil arranges for Lowe and [her] daughter operates as a microallegory for the practices of capitalists and empire builders who gain leverage—and labor—through forced debts. The coercive operations of this debt economy come to light after Cecil's death. As mentioned, when Lowe became pregnant with a daughter by Cecil, Cecil secured the assistance of a quadroon woman named Miss Sylvie, whom he installs as Lowe's "wife." (As I'll discuss later, Miss Sylvie does genuinely come to love Lowe, including intimately, although Lowe is too plagued by rape flashbacks and memories of betrayals to respond.) Miss Sylvie acts as mother to Elizabeth, winning her love, while the increasingly isolated Lowe runs the shop and lives in denial of these false identities and intimate losses. Yet gradually

Lowe (and readers) also learns that Miss Sylvie's compliance has been extorted, as has that of the two household servants, Omar and Dulcie.

In all three cases, the debt economy has been fully intertwined with the political economy, that is, with the dialectics of domination and resistance. Miss Sylvie, Dulcie, and Omar have all committed violence against the light-skinned and white ruling classes, and Cecil has leveraged their "criminal" vulnerability to his own advantage. Before Lowe arrived in Jamaica, Miss Sylvie was a quadroon passing as white and married to a friend of Cecil's. When her children were born dark skinned, she told her husband they were stillborn, conscripting Dulcie and Omar to create fake coffins and give them away. But when her husband suspected what had happened, he threatened "to kill her for shaming him like that," so Miss Sylvie finds a way to strangle him (146). Eventually Cecil finds out that Sylvie has killed her husband, and so, Sylvie later explains to Lowe, "we made a deal, me and Cecil" (143). While she needed protection from the law, "he wanted a mother for Liz and a way to protect you" (143). Miss Sylvie thus agrees to the fiction of Lowe being man and herself being wife to Lowe. Lowe struggles to understand how Sylvie could accept such a deal, but Sylvie asks, "what women have, Lowe, if it ain't what the father give them, what the husband give them?" (146). Women lack economic options, and their dependence often serves men well, strengthening men's positions when they are disinherited or indebted.

Furthermore, even the rebellions of women and other laborers can be turned into a profit by capitalists and colonizers. Miss Sylvie's rebellious act of murder accrues capital for Cecil insofar as her need of political protection translates into managerial and domestic labor for him. Likewise, Lowe's rebellious flight from [her] Chinese husband yielded capital, labor, and sexual power for Cecil. Furthermore, Lowe and Sylvie are also Cecil's means for accruing surplus. For, although Cecil shares small parts of his land and profits with them, he puts Lowe to work extorting profit in his store and Sylvie to work managing his land, in both cases extracting capital from the locals, especially the Black Jamaicans. This set of relations lays bare the gendered workings of neocolonial capitalism in an inter-imperial system. Eventually Lowe realizes that all of them have been his proxy agents, his "puppet" rulers.

The story of Dulcie and Omar takes this microallegory to the macropolitical level. It dramatizes the coercive political bribery of resistance fighters as part of neocolonial strategy. Before Lowe's arrival in Jamaica, Dulcie had been part of an uprising by Black laborers in her youth. When she was threatened with charges, Cecil paid for her legal aid and offered "protection" to her and her son Omar in return for Dulcie's labors as household servant and Omar's services as labor overseer on Cecil's expanding plantation. This fictional history parallels the historical co-optation of impoverished and the dissenting colonized communities, including in the Caribbean. President Trujillo in Haiti was destitute in his youth, and President Batista in Cuba was a progressive leader. But each of them was bribed and lured into roles as puppets of neocolonial powers, reaping profit and position in return for exploiting and mistreating their own communities. Powell hints as much when she has Lowe witness Omar's mistreatment of the laborers: "He was not at all friendly with the workers, men and women alike who weeded and cleaned and planted and reaped and at whom he barked commands in a fierce and aggressive tone.... One day Omar unbuckled his belt and flogged a man who quarreled with him.... [H]e raised his hand repeatedly to strike the man's head with the buckle of the belt ... The man's knees tottered and he slithered to the ground.... How many strokes?" (121). Lowe is later ashamed that "he just stood there, nailed to the ground, with the fear steep in him. And by not acting, just allowing the spectacle to unfold, it was as though his hands too had been dipped in blood" (121). Meanwhile [she] observes, "It was as if Omar hated [the laborers]. Hated their helplessness. Their false groveling and subservience; he hated their poverty" (121). Thus do history's cycles return in the form of violence against one's own people, driven by both coercion and a sense of shame about being poor, dominated, and entangled in empire's crimes.

In *The Pagoda* as in Caribbean history, furthermore, racist regimes create stratification even among the colonized. While Lowe dutifully runs the store and Dulcie and Omar serve Cecil's household and plantation, Cecil has begun to give the most control to Miss Sylvie, the whitest among them, including ownership of his increasingly large landholdings in Jamaica (eventually 225 acres), while promising Lowe and Sylvie that the land will go to Elizabeth (and clearly not to Dulcie or Omar). Lowe later reflects, "Miss Sylvie had turned the land into an empire, and it came home to him again that she was no fool, that she was indeed a shrewd business-woman, and that compared to her he had nothing at all" (119). Lowe finds that [she] [her]self has been "relegated to the position of Dulcie and Omar, dependent on [Miss Sylvie's] good graces" (119–20).

In short, Powell creates a distilled world history, tracking the inter-imperial dialectics of resistance and domination as they intersect with gendered financial economies. Wielding the threat of violation and betrayal, and sometimes offering material reward, Cecil as the maneuvering neocolonial power creates proxy rulers in Miss Sylvie and Omar. They understand their position as what Omar calls Cecil's "whores": "He turn everybody into whore, sir, man and woman. Young or old. He blackmail everybody.... So he operate.... Plenty Chinese and Indian people and some Negro people he set up in business, if he take a fancy to them. But he was a man with his hands in everything" (226–27).

The character of Lowe meanwhile epitomizes the globally traded laborer, both economic and sexual, in an inter-imperial world. Surviving multiple masters, genders, continents, communities, and temporalities, she embodies the relations among all these elements. She knows well the troubled neocolonial "intimacies of four continents," to borrow Lisa Lowe's apt phrase.[21] Fleeing from one imperial legacy only to be caught in another entangled with the first, Lowe travels forever between them in memory.

Yet as Lowe begins to grasp the structural "terms" of [her] condition, the repetitions of history and memory yield to ever-returning questions and reflections on how to reenter the world while still facing its coerced choices. These processes move Lowe incrementally toward a practice of relational avowal. The accruing repetitions of the novel's structure confirm the insights of diasporic theorists about the ways that the traumas of diasporic subjects can lead to transformed relations and perspectives, exactly because the violent collapse of subjectivity has forced persons and communities to remake themselves from the existential ground up.[22] I wish to take these points further to argue that, through Lowe's critique of the men's betrayals of women and its effects on [her] own life, Powell places the matter of disavowal at the center of existential questions about choice. Lowe eventually comes to see that [she] [her]self has practiced the same kind of humiliated disavowal that [she] observed in the Chinese men. As I argue next, the unspooling of these tightly entangled disavowals and betrayals becomes the underlying action of the text. As Lowe's repeating memories become counterpointing questions about [her] relations to self and others, challenging the self-doubt imposed by sexual-colonial determinations, they also become the vehicle of [her] reentry. Lowe's writing, like Powell's, requires the heavy labor of recalling the past in order to acknowledge it and remake [her]self in the present.

Transforming Repetition

On the dawn that opens the novel, as Lowe attempts again to write to Elizabeth, [she] hears a repeated calling of [her] name, Mister Lowe, Mister Lowe, Mister Lowe, by someone who will tell [her] that the store is on fire with the sleeping drunken Cecil in it. The repeated calling heralds the fact that Lowe [her]self will soon face a calling-out. At first Lowe feels devastated by this event, for not only was the shop to have been [her] daughter's inheritance, but the very scaffolding of Lowe's staged identity has been burned to the ground. Also, being Cecil's proxy Chinese agent, Lowe becomes afraid that retribution could soon be directed toward [her], explicitly recalling the history of anticolonial Black uprisings. At the sounding of a conch shell, [she] "wonder[s] nervously at the power of that shell, how years ago it used to ignite the Negro people to rise up and fight" (19). Powell implicitly establishes that the real catalyst of Lowe's early dawn "awakening" is in effect the accrued Caribbean history of anti-imperial resistance.

At this stage, Lowe is in late middle age but still daily drowning in memories. [She] repeatedly sinks in the abyssal waters of [her] past despite [her] effort to find a calm shore and stable world. Choosing to narrate in close third person, Powell immerses readers in Lowe's dizzying sensate consciousness without pause. Especially in the first several chapters, we, too, must regularly gasp for breath in the capsizing waters of remembered rapes, losses, and betrayal-burdened choices, never quite sure if we are in the present or the past, and not sure who to trust. The looping temporal motions of the first four chapters are structured to dramatize this capsizing motion: after the opening events of the letter writing and the fire, chapter 2 falls back to Lowe's memories of [her] betraying father and preying Chinese husband. Then in chapter 3 we return to the present as Lowe meets with Chinese friends, listens to the men's discontent and disavowal, and visits [her] daughter for the first time in twenty years, although without managing to talk to anyone about the truth of [her] past. This failure sends Lowe back, in chapter 4, into the churning memories of the early years with Elizabeth and Miss Sylvie, which also merge with memories of the father, the husband, and the ship journey with Cecil.

In particular, in chapter 4 it is Miss Sylvie's lovemaking that triggers Lowe's traumatic memories. Miss Sylvie's sexual "straddling" of Lowe merges with Cecil's straddling of Lowe, for the reader as well as for Lowe, as [she] experiences only "spread legs and splayed fingers and darting tongue" and then suddenly also imagines "a square canvas edge of sail" and "haggard breathing. Cecil's!" (113). As Lowe recalls, "so it continued for all those years, Miss Sylvie returning again and again to their room. . . . And Lowe not moving, not rising to her touch or to touch her . . . for each time all [Lowe] could think of was the dark dank of the place" (113). In these moments, [she] also suffers flashbacks of [her] repulsive husband with "a penchant for a young girl," and these return [her] to the misery of "a girl betrayed by her father and handed over to an old man. . . . [A] girl betrayed by her father and turned into a wife overnight[,] a wife who dreams all day at the barred windows of a house" (179). Even though Lowe admits that [she] at times "yearned for [Miss Sylvie's] embrace," [she] feels coerced by her as well, as suggested by the description of Miss Sylvie "returning again and again to their room." Like Cecil, like empire builders, "always [Miss Sylvie] wanted more" (114). Lowe therefore asks [her]self, "who is to say [Miss Sylvie] wouldn't fold up her fantasies into him and turn him further into something he wasn't, as his father had done and then Cecil? And who is to say she wouldn't abandon him once her mission was accomplished. Who is to say?" (114). Readers also endure this repeatedly capsized present, with these confusing pronouns and looping, drowning questions.

Yet as Powell's text also traces, history never simply repeats. Lived in time, the dialectics that carry forward the bullying past also at every moment encounter a new present and new actions—including dissent. Powell includes dissent as a shaping historical force in the burning of the store and in the mention of the protest groups and unrest both in Jamaica and China. Lowe hears news, for instance, of the protests and anger about "the laws that had been passed to deter people from working away from the estates, the high taxes that had been instituted to prevent them from starting their own landholding business, from opening up shops," and likewise about the fact that they have no work although the "government was building more and more schools and hospitals, more almshouses and prisons and lunatic asylums and police stations" (135). Interisland consciousness is also registered, as when they talk of "the death camps in Cuba, where not so long ago Negroes got their freedom" (136). As discussed in chapter 5, a rising anticolonial consciousness characterized this fin-de-siècle period; Powell implicitly makes that historical context a catalyst for Lowe's counterwriting of [her] life.

While this atmosphere partly frightens Lowe, given [her] past as Cecil's pawn, the burning of the store also slowly awakens Lowe to the web of betrayal, secrecy, and layered coercions in which [she] has been living. [She] gradually begins to feel "clean and unburdened" for "somewhere deep in him he knew that [the burning of shop and of Cecil] was handing him the reins to his own life" (33). Lowe begins to see "clearly how they were all thrown in and piled on top of one another and vying for power and trying to carve out niches" (198). [She] further reflects that, as a result, "now here they were killing and killing to cover up more deceptions, more lies. . . .

Here he was fighting Omar for land and property that didn't even belong to them, that was still damp from prior bloodshed. Hadn't they plundered the Arawaks, the Caribs? Yet here they were like hungry dogs, setting upon each other and biting over the one little dry bone Cecil had flung them" (162). Lowe also grasps the divide-and-conquer scheming of the whites as they set up bonded Asian laborers against the Black Jamaican laborers: "How the backra put them between we," as one Black Jamaican puts it, "bringing in the Coolie and the Chinee," so that they can "take advantage of we" (15). Lowe's labors of letter writing in order to repair divisive, broken relations are also Powell's labors of writing this novel for her contemporary audiences.

Increasingly over the course of the novel, Lowe turns this reflective gaze on [her]self. As noted, this movement finds expression in the cantatory style of the novel's prose. To say that the text's repetitive style is *moving* is to speak literally as well as emotionally. From start to finish, Powell sustains an anaphoric prose, repeating a word or phrase at the beginning of successive clauses. The repetitions are slowly transformative, gradually releasing Lowe's insights about determining repetitions, as when Lowe recalls: "Cecil who had brought him here to the island, Cecil who had given him the keys to the shop and the bag of money he was to use as capital, Cecil who had dictated his life up till that very moment" (12–13). Powell thus immerses us not just in another history but in a phenomenology of recovery from history. In effect, in this reparative work, Powell counters the most famous anaphoric pronouncement of all: "I came, I saw, I conquered." Doing so, she also taps into the deeper roots of the term *anaphora*, deriving from the Greek word *anapherein*, meaning "to carry back, to bring up," based on the roots *ana* meaning "back" and *pherein* meaning "to bear" or "to carry." Lowe is indeed going "back" to bring up and bear the weight of a long past. In her text, this grammatical rocking, this forward-backward motion, also gathers energy.

But before the insights accrue, Lowe struggles to work through the repeating violence and betrayals. [She] recalls how, hiding on the ship before Cecil found [her], [she] had learned "how to stifle sneezes and hold back coughs, how to lock the muscles in his rectum and tighten his kidneys, how to squat for long hours" (16). And in another passage [she] remembers how [she] endured "Cecil's face buried in the back of Lowe's head; Cecil's teeth tight on the tip of his earlobe; Cecil's fingers buckling and unbuckling, buckling and unbuckling" (96). Lowe's repeating syntax also captures the plight of laborers, for instance the Chinese laborers who came to the shop: "They came with hands twisted and chewed from water pumps, scarred by deep grooves . . . from cane leaves. . . . They came with spit bubbling with blood, asthmatic and tubercular chests from the dust. They came without flesh, with holes in the skin, half starved from inferior food" (15).

Often, these repeating descriptions are followed by Lowe's effort to understand [her] role in these conditions, for [she] feels embattled and hurt by the possibility that the customers resent [her]. Immediately following the sentence about the workers, [she] thinks: "The shop was there so if they wanted they could come and apprentice with him, till they'd pay off their contracts" (15). This elision of the larger picture, which Lowe has yet to admit and understand, reenacts the repetitions on these "repeating islands" that attempt to keep communities stuck in place. Lowe not only elides [her] role as neocolonial agent but in early chapters remains blind to the effects of [her] long-standing withdrawal from all relations, including the effects for Miss Sylvie, who after all has regularly nursed and cared for Lowe.[23] Thus in the first chapter as the fire subsides, Miss Sylvie stands ready to console Lowe, but "he looked past her clear and grave eyes, he looked past the deep lines around her mouth. He looked past the fragrances of oils and herbs, the harsh wet smell of tobacco. . . . He looked past Miss Sylvie and at the upside-down world turning topsy-turvy at his feet" (18). Yet as the chapter ends, Lowe realizes that "he had to go and see his people. . . . He had to rekindle his spirit. . . . He had to start again" (29).

From here forward these anaphoric repetitions begin to yield delicate shifts, as if we witnessed Lowe thinking and rethinking, gathering the energy that will reconnect [her] to her past and others. Lowe eventually looks at the wider effects of [her] engulfment by trauma and deceit. After an unsatisfactory visit with Elizabeth, Lowe reflects about [her]self, yet again with a male pronoun, "He had never told her stories of his life in that river town. . . . He had never celebrated her birthdays or lunar new years. . . . He had never instilled in her filial piety or ancestor worship. . . . He had never told her of his father's fervid imagination. . . . He had never said a word about his mother. . . . He had never told her any of the stories and poems and songs his father had told him" (76). In short, Lowe sees that [she] had chosen, or at least accepted, the fate of "never." The repetitions then begin to take the form of questions: "He had not been a good parent, and was this now the price? Was this the unfinished business, then, brought over from generation to generation? Was this it, then?" (76).

Most important, Lowe finally begins to imagine life from [her] daughter's perspective, a young Chinese European Jamaican woman now married to a Black Jamaican man. Tellingly, Lowe's movement has been partly prompted by [her] reading of Dulcie's left-behind letters about the planned rebellion, a detail that reinforces critics' interpretations of the novel's inclusion of letters and other historical documents as interruptions of the colonial master narrative.[24] Lowe slowly understands that Elizabeth, too, was "caught up . . . between two estranged worlds" (74). Near novel's end, anticipating Elizabeth's imminent visit, it occurs to Lowe that Elizabeth may have known Lowe's secrets all along and that this knowledge led her to spurn Lowe. The repetitions here convey the increments of widening perspective: "No wonder she had hated him so. No wonder she had clutched so tightly to Miss Sylvie and to her memories of Cecil. No wonder she had kept away all these years, not one word from her. No wonder!" (181). Although the two still do not discuss those secrets when Elizabeth finally arrives, Lowe finally can say, "it felt good to see her again. This daughter that was his own flesh and blood. This daughter that Cecil had forced into him. This daughter he'd not wanted at first" (182). Powell thus refashions anaphoric repetition as a reparative force. While echoing the imperializing syntax of "I came, I saw, I conquered," the text seizes it instead for the refusal and displacement of that choice to conquer. Powell is reclaiming the syntax of arriving for her own reparative forms of encounter.

Powell also makes a further metacritical gesture. The reclaiming of repetition as a form of reknowing and remaking works in tandem with Lowe's rebuilding of [her] Chinese Jamaican habitus and [her] relations with others through art making. Although at novel's end, Miss Sylvie has left Lowe, tired of Lowe's self-involvement, slowly that distance between them enables Lowe to see Miss Sylvie more fully and to "start again" from the ground up. One of Lowe's first actions is to remove the English furniture and the British and Chinese imperial portraits, clearing the domestic economy of the interpellating arts of the past. [She] then begins painting. This activity is rendered through the longest anaphoric sequence in the novel. Thirteen sentences begin: "He painted" (222–23). All the initial paintings are of Miss Sylvie and her surrounds. Next Lowe depicts seascapes and landscapes from both sides of the world—"landscapes ravaged by typhoons, villages made sodden by monsoons, crowded squares packed with jugglers . . . lighted boats afloat on the brim of the water like lighted cities" all "nailed up on the naked walls" (223). Lowe is resituating [her]self in the physical world, remaking the habitus. Accordingly, [she] removes the band covering [her] breasts, loosens [her] hair, and dons silky clothes, seeking out sexual relations with men and women both. Omar and Lowe live in the house together, taking turns cooking, again transforming the domestic economy. In this period, Lowe also begins to tell stories to Elizabeth's older child, to paint with him, to reimagine in watercolor [her] Chinese village, even to tell him a story called "A Father's Betrayal," passing along the knowledge of broken relations—for as [she] knows well, suppression of betrayal only spawns further betrayals and disavowals (191). Powell's incantatory descriptions of these activities represent the building action of Lowe's agency and [her] discovery that some relations had supported [her] and could support [her] in the future. [She] imagines "the possible," and in doing so allows it to push back against the inherited coordinates of "the actual."

Lowe finally completes the pagoda with friends from both communities, the infrastructural and collective centerpiece of [her] reentry into the world. Throughout the novel, that project has faltered, gotten stuck; yet it also repeatedly begins again, especially when Lowe is encouraged by the Black Jamaican carpenter, Jake, who helps Lowe imagine it as "a study in curves"— or, we might say, a study in spiraling yet generative dialectical loops (175). Jake immediately understands that Lowe envisions a "benevolent society kind of thing," drawing from his knowledge of a similar hall built by Black Jamaicans (169). At the same time, as Minjeong Kim points out, Lowe's vision remains Chinese-centered rather than specifically cross-racial, as reflected in the hostility it provokes from Elizabeth's Black Jamaican husband. Kim considers this investment in Chineseness per se one of the unresolved questions at the end of the novel, especially given the increasing economic advantage accruing to the Asian American merchant class on the island, and I would agree.[25] Yet it is worth noting that the pagoda is not yet open at novel's end, and meanwhile it has functioned to prompt Lowe's remembering and rethinking of her past. No grand nation will issue from this infrastructural project, but the building of it enables Lowe to imagine that something could change in the relation between Chinese and Black Jamaicans, and between sexuality and community. In tandem with this aspiration, Lowe anticipates that maybe [she] could embrace Miss Sylvie if she were to return: "Maybe now when Miss Sylvie came to his bed he wouldn't have to run. . . . He had found voice. Now he would put her hand gently to his cheek, kiss the tips of her burning fingers, and try to calm the jumbled images in his mind. . . . 'Wait little,' he would tell her, for he needed to make sure his wrists weren't tied, that that wasn't the heaving hull underneath him but the swaying bed . . . and the harried moans he heard were indeed Miss Sylvie's and not those of some old cripple who had taken him in repayment for a debt" (237). Narratively, Powell has created her own study in curves, temporal curves that carry us back and forth across oceans and temporalities, opening the possibility that one can "wait little" to leave room for the future to take another course.

Powell provides no certain closure. In the end she renders dialectics in the subjunctive, both grammatically and imaginatively. The novel's final chapter is composed solely of Lowe's finished letter to Elizabeth, and its signal word, "maybe," is repeated throughout. Reporting that the pagoda is finished, Lowe hopes "maybe next year we can open it" and "maybe you'll send the grandson and the girl" since "it's for them. Their history. Their past. And yours too, if you want it" (240). And "maybe one day you'll take a ship and you'll show the little boy and the little girl where I was born" (242). Lowe [her]self then travels back in memory to wonder about the lives of [her] father and [her] mother. Unable to remember [her] mother's eyes, [she] thinks, "Maybe she walked around with them closed all the time, refusing to look at the world, or maybe there just wasn't light inside them" (245). After all, "who is to tell? All day long she was out dipping and bending in the fields, with the pole between her stooped shoulders carrying water. . . . So who is to tell?" (245). Yet still, Lowe thinks, addressing [her] mother: "Maybe you're a yearner like me"—a shift of position from Lowe as mother to Lowe as daughter, written in the present tense yet reaching across time as well as diasporic place (244). This elongated present is also the time to enter and to choose: "Maybe it was just time to reach out to you in just this sort of way. Not last week, not next year, but now. And exactly with the words put just so" (245). For the "Time Being" as Arundhati Roy puts it in *The God of Small Things*, Lowe closes the letter, and Powell closes her book.

The repetitions of Powell's cantatory prose restage the repetitions of Shahrazad's nightly tale-telling. Both forms of address refuse empire's constricting "love laws" which create impossible "terms and conditions" for relations and for choice. Both texts imagine the possible in the form of alliances among those whom empires divide. Taking time to listen, witness, and imagine, many such authors have led their listeners back through the repeating betrayals of the past exactly in order to prompt our imagining of another future. In the poet Mina Loy's words, they call us into "knowing all about unfolding."[26]

Conclusion

A River Between

The urgent time of now is densely inhabited by then.

That is, the longue durée persists. Its political presence is not a matter of backward tribalisms rearing their heads to interrupt the forward march of modern systems. Its presence is a matter of prior systems and states enduring in sublated forms that chafe against the very transformations they've provoked. This highly dynamic presence of the past infuses memories, places, arts, and bodies as well as states, economies, and institutions, with volatile effects. These dialectics of past and present constitute world conditions.

I have argued in this book that the concept of inter-imperiality reveals key dimensions of this constitutive past—the structuring, catalyzing past— that are not easily captured by other frameworks. Centered on nations, the field of international relations inherently foreshortens the scope of history and constricts the coordinates of the global political economy, especially through its Eurocentric, androcentric orientation and its limited emphasis on dissent as a structuring force rather than a mere element of "destabilization." Transnational and transperipheral studies, in contrast, do typically foreground the formative power of dissent, and they illuminate the influence of minority formations and intersectional alliances. These formations constitute one aspect of the field of power and the arts of alliance, but, I argue, transnational and transperipheral studies yield even more insight when considered in relation to vectored inter-imperial dynamics. Likewise, postcolonial, Marxist, and materialist studies have fundamentally shaped my treatment of labor and states in the inter-imperial economy. My argument is that these critical approaches are dramatically strengthened by a wider and longer analysis of states and economic systems, especially as these formations co-constitute each other.

Most distinctively, the inter-imperial model anchors its world political analysis in three elements of world history and political economy that typically receive short shrift: intersectional formations; literary formations; and deep-time affective formations. To develop this kind of integrated long-historical model requires, I've learned, full-fledged interdisciplinary collaboration. I could not have written this book without such collaborations, as I note in my acknowledgments. This experience has also taught me that these collaborations require noncompetitive institution building, practiced by scholars and administrators both, in place of the monetizing and ranking of intellectual work bequeathed by empires.

....

At another level, buoyed by these practices, this study of inter-imperiality addresses existential matters. This book is about time and how we live in it. As Henri Bergson observed, because of memory, humans live in time as duration, where the present is the past's vessel into the future. As Pierre Bourdieu later added, memory finds reinforcement in the material world, including in the stratifying habitus. Languages hold both memory and matter, carrying their meanings forward though time, speaking the past across generations. Words that name domination of relation remain in the mouths of communities: boss, master, win, lose, owner, wife, servant, bitch, coolie. Empires count on the persistence of such words to sustain hegemonies, and, when erasing earlier hegemonies, they merely replace one stratifying set of words with another, meanwhile destroying the gathering places where better words were spoken.

But often, too, the temples and the terraced lands, the texts, songs, and turns of phrase carry energies that exceed these hegemonizing forces, energies that persist despite the changing of the guard. Languages retain many words that honor relation, expressions of tending, delighting, listening, and sorrowing together. And words get retooled. Queer, herstory, Dalit, the trans pronoun *they*, and the hashtags #BlackLivesMatter and #MeToo. Each language has its own still-unfolding economy of naming, and as languages interact they reorganize what gets named.

When scholars overlook the deeply embedded pasts entwined in languages, cultures, states, and economies, when we begin our histories with the twentieth century or with "modernity," or when we focus separately on economy, or states, or culture, we mistake a lopped-off limb for the whole living creature. When we speak of premodern and modern, precolonial and colonial, we ignore what we know: both systemic controls and caring sustenance are old. They structure our copresence. Ignoring this history or assuming we already understand it, we risk once more seeing within androcentric, Eurocentric blinders.

Memory militates against the maneuver, however. It keeps alive the pain of conflict, troubles the operations of sublation. Having memory, communities live in friction with the habits of disavowal. They sometimes therefore act to counter those habits. Art sometimes speaks from here. All these crisscrossing streams channel our global dialectical inheritance.

....

In this light, it's worth pausing to reflect a moment longer on states and their institutions, whether the states are empires or small islands. Clearly, states draw the borders, structure the contests, write the laws, broker the trade deals, install the wires, barbed or virtual. States remain the stewards, even if contested, of institutions and infrastructures, of health care, law, education. They bestow or withhold identities in the form of passports, and they craft scripts for "us and them." Doing so, states give themselves leverage points in the global field of relations.

Yet as this book has also shown, the tools of states also sometimes give leverage points to justice-seeking actors. For while states and their cities name, police, and thereby structure relations, the world's inhabitants have renamed and restructured states from within and between. Nonprofits, health care, women's shelters, and homeless shelters: we have these because communities of people have together conceived, demanded, funded, and managed them. The very term *nonprofit* established a new category of institution—a hard-won category. Likewise with other institutions, including schools and universities. Although originally founded as forms of discipline, the dialectics of history show—and indeed ensure—that they are also leverage points, vexed but powerful points of entry. Teachers' unions, affirmative action, family care policies, ethnic studies and gender studies programs: these mark the grounds of engagement; they are evidence of resistant retooling. They have been forged through the difficult work of alliance and action even in a field of relations powerfully defined by centuries of coercion. Arts have dramatized how the narratives and the habits can change, and why they must change. They've shown that words and images are structures, and *these* can change. The labors are ours together. All of us *are* historical dialectics.

....

In his novel *The River Between*, Ngũgĩ wa Thiong'o lays out the terrain of struggle. The story opens with a description of two mountain ranges, Kameno and Makuyu, occupying the horizon, "like sleeping lions."[1] Between them flows the river "called Honia, which meant cure, or bringing-back-to-life." Honia is "the soul of Kameno and Makuyu" and "men, cattle, wild beasts and trees were all united by this life-stream." Yet, "when you stood in the valley, the two ridges ceased to be sleeping lions"; instead they became "antagonists" who "faced each other, like two rivals ready to come to blows in a life and death struggle for the leadership of the isolated region." And so "it began long ago. A man rose in Makuyu."[2] Although at first this struggle might sound simply Hegelian and male centered, Ngũgĩ instead tenderly and critically unveils the gendered order at its heart. The valley community first divides over a girl's death from female circumcision, and the rift opens the doors to Europeans who leverage this division to enable their further incursions.

And so in this valley, too, the young inhabitants must learn the truth that Chang-rae Lee invokes in *Native Speaker*: that "over the mountains there are mountains."[3] *San konno san itta.*

Yet why struggle simply to endure?, we might ask along with Carpentier's Ti Noël in *The Kingdom of This World*.

Because the world of water, wind, sun, earth, and creaturely life that sustains us also calls us into relation. Barely choosing, we respond. Because someone gave birth to each of us, and someone labored to keep us alive, however imperfectly. Because although, as the enslaved Paul D in Toni Morrison's *Beloved* knows, "Mist, doves, sunlight, copper, dirt, moon—everything belonged to the men who had the guns," we nonetheless find ourselves "listening to the doves."[4]

The river runs between the mountains. It calls us back from betrayals and disavowals. It carries care, and cure. It reflects relations. It beckons us to avow and sustain them.

Notes

Theoretical Introduction: Between States

Parts of the introduction appeared in "Inter-Imperiality: Dialectics in a Postcolonial World History," *Interventions: International Journal of Postcolonial Studies* (2013): 1–38; "Dialectics in the Longue Durée: The IIPEC Model of Inter-Imperial Economy and Culture," *Globalizations* 11, no. 5 (2014): 689–709; and in "Inter-imperiality and Literary Study in the Longer Durée," *PMLA* 130, no. 2 (2015): 336–47.

1. Michel Foucault theorizes the "micro-physics of power" in *Discipline and Punish: The Birth of the Prison* (New York: Vintage Books, [1975] 2011), 26–27. "Being-with-and-against" is a variation on Jean-Luc Nancy's notion of "being-with." Jean-Luc Nancy, *Being Singular Plural*, trans. Robert D. Richardson (Stanford, CA: Stanford University Press, 2009). *Forces* is one of Hegel's key terms, as I discuss later in the introduction. See Georg Wilhelm Friedrich Hegel, *The Phenomenology of Spirit*, trans. A. V. Miller (Oxford: Clarendon Press, 1977), 79–103.

2. It's impossible to do justice to the many thinkers who have informed the feminist-intersectional aspects of this project. I cite many of them throughout the book, and in this note I name those who have particularly influenced me. I do so both to honor this work and for the benefit of younger intersectional scholars who are less familiar with this legacy, which in many cases implicitly informs recent intersectional and decolonial thinking.

Mary Louise Pratt's scholarship has been crucial for my thinking, especially her foundational book, *Imperial Eyes: Travel Writing and Transculturation* (New York: Routledge, [1992] 2008). Her naming of the volatilities and dialectics shaping "contact-zone" colonial encounters opened new doors for many of us.

Body-centered philosophical and literary scholarship, especially that of intersectional and postcolonial thinkers, has inspired me for decades, including Gloria Anzaldúa, *Borderlands/La Frontera* (San Francisco: Aunt Lute, 1987); Carole Boyce Davies, *Black Women, Writing and Identity: Migrations of the Subject* (New York: Routledge, 2002); Hélène Cixous, "The Laugh of the Medusa," *Signs* 1, no. 4 (1976): 875–93; Julia Kristeva, "Women's Time," *Signs* 7, no. 1 (1981): 13–35; Paula J. Giddings, *When and Where I Enter: The Impact of Black Women on Race and Sex in America* (New York: William Morrow, 1984); Mae Gwendolyn Henderson, "Speaking in Tongues," in *African American Literary Theory: A Reader*, ed. Winston Napier (New York: New York University Press, 2000), 348–68; Audre Lorde, "The Uses of the Erotic: The Erotic as Power," in *The Lesbian and Gay Studies Reader*, ed. Henry Abelove, Michele Aina Barale, and David M. Halperin (New York: Routledge, 1993), 339–43; Jenny Sharpe, *Allegories of Empire: The Figure of Woman in the Colonial Text* (Minneapolis: University of Minnesota Press, 1993); and Gayatri Chakravorty Spivak, "Woman in Difference: Mahasweta Devi's 'Douloti the Bountiful,'" *Cultural Critique*, no. 14 (1989): 105–28. Also see Ella Shohat's foundational collection featuring "relational multicultural feminisms" in Ella Shohat, ed., *Talking Visions: Multicultural Feminism in a Transnational Age* (Cambridge, MA: MIT Press, [1998] 2001), 11.

Beginning in the 1990s, feminist philosophers of political embodiment writing in English, such as Judith Butler, Seyla Benhabib, Gail Weiss, Drucilla Cornell, Elizabeth Grosz, and Dorothy Olkowski, developed important concepts, although it was not until later that they engaged with thinkers such as Hortense Spillers and Audre Lorde who named the racial and class politics of embodiment. At the same time the theories of Nancy Chodorow and Carol Gilligan began to challenge normative androcentric paradigms of human psychological and ethical development and introduce relational models, while early feminist theorists of democracy such as Iris Marion Young moved political theory away from state-based models toward participatory and dialogical models. My first publications were in dialogue with many of these scholars, while also drawing on the philosophy of Maurice Merleau-Ponty. See Laura Doyle, *Bodies of Resistance: New Phenomenologies of Politics, Agency, and Culture* (Evanston, IL: Northwestern University Press, 2001); Doyle, *Bordering on the Body: The Racial Matrix of Modern Fiction and Culture* (New York: Oxford University Press, 1994); and Doyle, "Toward a Philosophy of Transnationalism," *Journal of Transnational American Studies* 1, no. 1 (2009): n.p.

The scholarship currently interweaving decolonial, sexual, and indigenous studies is exciting for the way it develops the potential of this earlier work by taking it into deeper, often obscured histories.

3. For earlier formulations of the concept of horizonal dialectics, see Doyle, "Toward a Philosophy of Transnationalism"; and Laura Doyle, "Colonial Encounters," in *The Oxford Handbook of Modernisms*, ed. Peter Brooker et al. (New York: Oxford University Press, 2010), 249–66. Although this horizonal and inter-imperial analysis shares an orientation with recent research on political horizon*tality* (focused on activist movements in world history), the framework of this book differs from those discussions in that it tracks the strained, vectored, and manifold *convergences and leveragings* of vertical and horizontal power axes. For a useful account of political horizontality, see Alen Toplisek and Lasse Thomassen, "From Protest to Party: Horizontality and Verticality on the Slovenian Left," *Europe-Asia Studies* 69, no. 9 (2017): 1383–1400.

4. Hegel, *Phenomenology of Spirit*, 111–19.

5. Giorgio Agamben, *Homo Sacer: Sovereign Power and Bare Life* (Stanford, CA: Stanford University Press, 1998).

6. Audra Simpson, *Mohawk Interruptus: Political Life across the Borders of Settler States* (Durham, NC: Duke University Press, 2014).

7. See Simpson, *Mohawk Interruptus*. My project shares a spirit and a method with Simpson's, particularly in its emphasis on the dynamics of denial as they play out in acts of interpretive contestation over "*actual* histories" (22). Both of us draw on Hegelian theory, in Simpson's case to analyze the element of "misrecognition" in these processes. I put more emphasis on the disavowal of relationality per se, as well as on the constitutive processes of interpenetration, coformation, and sublation, because, to my mind, these terms capture the underlying existential substratum of bodily social engagements and in turn they highlight the volatile conditions of life on earth. It's also worth noting that, although Simpson comments that "Hegel's concern is with the *position* of the slave, not the slave himself" (24), Hegel is in fact concerned with the subjectivity of the slave, as I discuss later in the introduction. As he remarks in a key transition: "We have seen what servitude is only in relation to lordship. But it is a self-consciousness, and we have now to consider what as such it is in and for itself" (Hegel, *Phenomenology of Spirit*, 117). He then proceeds to do so (116–19).

8. For instance, for historically oriented conceptualizations of sovereignty and indigeneity, see the essays in Joanne Barker, ed., *Critically Sovereign: Indigenous Gender, Sexuality, and Feminist Studies* (Durham, NC: Duke University Press, 2017). For essays in feminist-decolonial and indigenous theory that focus on agency and the complexities of historically layered relationality, see Priti Ramamurthy and Ashwini Tambe, eds., "Decolonial and Postcolonial Approaches: A Dialogue," special issue, *Feminist Studies* 43, no. 3 (2017). For generative rethinkings of sovereignty not focused mainly on indigeneity, see Michaeline A. Crichlow, Patricia Northover, and Deborah Jenson, eds., "States of Freedom: Freedom of States," special issue, *Global South* 6, no. 1 (2012), including the editors' introduction, "Caribbean Entanglements in Times of Crises," 1–14; Judith Butler, "Thinking Cohabitation and the Dispersion of Sovereignty," in *Sovereignty in Ruins: A Politics of Crisis*, ed. George Edmondson and Klaus Mladek (Durham, NC: Duke University Press, 2017), 220–38; Alexander D. Barder and François Debrix, "Agonal Sovereignty: Rethinking War and Sovereignty with Schmitt, Arendt, and Foucault," *Philosophy and Social Criticism* 37, no. 7 (2011): 775–93; and Ann Laura Stoler, *Duress: Imperial Durabilities in Our Times* (Durham, NC: Duke University Press, 2016), 173–204.

Continuing discernment is required in discussions of sovereignty and agency in part because of their potential to perpetuate what Pradip Kumar Datta calls "imperial subjectivity," which carries residual identifications with empires past and which sometimes informs postcolonial visions. As I analyze in later chapters, old imperial attachments have sometimes shaped liberatory nationalist movements, as groups rally around "their" ancient "civilization," celebrating it as superior and prior to those of the invaders, meanwhile conscripting the (re)productive labors of women and racialized workers, and eliding their "own" "civilization's" histories of both exploitation and coformation with other states. See Pradip Kumar Datta, "The Interlocking Worlds of the Anglo-Boer War in South Africa/India," *South African Historical Journal* 57, no. 1 (2007): 35–59.

9. Édouard Glissant, *Poetics of Relation*, trans. Betsy Wing (Ann Arbor: University of Michigan Press, [1990] 1997).

10. Boyce Davies, *Black Women, Writing and Identity*, 54–58. For recent thought-provoking contributions to discussions of care, see Mayanthi Fernando, "Critique as Care," *Critical Times*

2, no. 1 (2019): 13–22; and María Puig de la Bellacasa, *Matters of Care: Speculative Ethics in More Than Human Worlds* (Minneapolis: University of Minnesota Press, 2017). Also see Laura Briggs, *How All Politics Became Reproductive Politics: From Welfare Reform to Foreclosure to Trump* (Oakland: University of California Press, 2017). More broadly, see scholarship on social reproduction theory, which builds on Marxist critiques of capitalist labor exploitation to analyze the gendered dimensions of labor and care required to sustain and reproduce human communities. For an excellent collection of recent work, see Tithi Bhattacharya, ed., *Social Reproduction Theory: Remapping Class, Recentering Oppression* (London: Pluto Press, 2017).

11. See Maurice Merleau-Ponty, *The Visible and Invisible: Followed by Working Notes*, trans. Alphonso Lingis (Evanston, IL: Northwestern University Press, 1968). For related notions about sociality, see Judith Butler, *Notes toward a Performative Theory of Assembly* (Cambridge, MA: Harvard University Press, 2015); and Judith Butler, "Performativity, Precarity and Sexual Politics," *AIBR* 4, no. 3 (2009): i–xiii. The influence of Merleau-Ponty on Butler's work deserves more notice. For instance, see her early essay, "Performing Acts and Gender Constitution," in *Performing Feminisms: Feminist Critical Theory and Theater*, ed. Sue-Ellen Case (Baltimore: Johns Hopkins University Press, 1990), 270–82; and Judith Butler, "Sexual Difference as a Question of Ethics: Alterities of the Flesh in Irigaray and Merleau-Ponty," in *Bodies of Resistance: New Phenomenologies of Politics, Agency, and Culture*, ed. Laura Doyle (Evanston, IL: Northwestern University Press, 2001), 59–77. Simone de Beauvoir's and Jean-Paul Sartre's (different) articulations of existential "alterity" also deserve mention here: Simone de Beauvoir, *The Second Sex*, trans. H. M. Parshley (New York: Vintage Books, 1953); Simone de Beauvoir, *Ethics of Ambiguity*, trans. Bernard Frechtman (New York: Open Road Media, [1947] 2018); and Jean-Paul Sartre, *Being and Nothingness*, trans. Hazel Barnes (New York: Washington Square Press, 1948).

12. John Hobson and V. I. Lenin understood the field of vying empires as an early twentieth-century phenomenon. See John A. Hobson, *Imperialism: A Study* (London: James Nisbet, 1902); and Vladimir Ilyich Lenin, *Imperialism: The Highest Stage of Capitalism: A Popular Outline* (New York: International Publishers, 1939). Literary critic Fredric Jameson also highlights imperial rivalry in this period as context for his reading of modernist narrative form. See Fredric Jameson, "Modernism and Imperialism," in *Nationalism, Colonialism, and Literature*, by Terry Eagleton, Fredric Jameson, and Edward W. Said (Minneapolis: University of Minnesota Press, 1990), 43–66. More recently, scholars have used the term *inter-imperial* but only in passing and in historical rather than theoretical terms, with reference only to recent history. See Tarak Barkawi, "Empire and Order in International Relations and Security Studies," in *International Studies Encyclopedia*, vol. 3, ed. Robert A. Denmark and Renée Marlin-Bennett (New York: Oxford University Press, 2010), 1360–79; and Anthony G. Hopkins, "Rethinking Decolonization," *Past and Present* 200, no. 1 (2008): 211–47.

13. Hayward R. Alker and Thomas J. Biersteker also aimed to develop an "integrated dialectical theory," although they did not have in mind an intersectional or decolonial theory, nor did they have the benefit of the last four decades of scholarship on these approaches. See Hayward R. Alker and Thomas J. Biersteker, "The Dialectic of World Order: Notes for a Future Archeologist of International Savoir Faire," *International Studies Quarterly* 28, no. 2 (1984): 121–42.

14. Prasenjit Duara, *Decolonization: Perspectives from Now and Then: Rewriting Histories* (London: Routledge, 2004), 20; Ngũgĩ wa Thiong'o, *Decolonising the Mind: The Politics of Language in African Literature* (Nairobi: East African Publishers, 1986); and Linda Tuhiwai Smith, *Decolonizing Methodologies: Research and Indigenous Peoples* (New York: Zed Books, 2013).

15. Donette Francis, *Fictions of Feminine Citizenship: Sexuality and the Nation in Contemporary Caribbean Literature* (New York: Palgrave Macmillan, 2010), 97.

16. See Kiran Asher, "Latin American Decolonial Thought, or Making the Subaltern Speak," *Geography Compass* 7, no. 12 (2013): 832–42. Also see Ramamurthy and Tambe, "Decolonial and Postcolonial Approaches." For the related notion of modernity/coloniality, see Walter Mignolo, *The Idea of Latin America* (Malden, MA: Blackwell, 2005), xiii; and Arturo Escobar, "Worlds and Knowledges Otherwise: The Latin American Modernity/Coloniality Research Program," *Cultural Studies* 21, no. 2 (2007): 179–210.

17. Kuan-Hsing Chen, *Asia as Method: Toward Deimperialization* (Durham, NC: Duke University Press, 2010). For studies that differently explore the lingering effects of empire on postcolonial subjectivities, see Deepika Bahri, *Native Intelligence: Aesthetics, Politics, and Postcolonial Literature* (Minneapolis: University of Minnesota Press, 2003); and Sukanya Banerjee, *Becoming Imperial Citizens: Indians in the Late-Victorian Empire* (Durham, NC: Duke University Press, 2010).

18. For distortions of the legacies of the British Empire and misinformation about the West as the source of "norms of law, order and governance" (xxi) that meanwhile cast nonwestern countries as Orientalized "no man's lands" (144–45), see Niall Ferguson, *Empire: The Rise and Demise of the British World Order and the Lessons for Global Power* (New York: Basic Books, 2004). For comparable forms of Orientalist narratives of world history, see Samuel Huntington, *The Clash of Civilizations and the Remaking of World Order* (New York: Simon and Schuster, 1997); and Robert Kaplan, *Balkan Ghosts: A Journey through History* (New York: St. Martin's Press, 2005).

19. At this late stage of intersectional feminist analysis, for example, it should not need saying that sex and gender practices have long occupied the structural core of the world's political economies, including because control of women and marriages is necessary for racial and labor stratifications. And yet, unfortunately, these established truths do need repeating. Indeed, as Antoinette Burton and others have had to point out, gender structures are still regularly eclipsed in world history and postcolonial analyses of history. See Antoinette Burton, "The Body in/as World History," in *A Companion to World History*, ed. Douglas Northrup (Chichester, UK: Wiley-Blackwell, 2012), 272–84. Also see Louise Yelin's analysis of the erasure of gender and women in studies of globalization in "Globalizing Subjects," *Signs* 29, no. 2 (2004): 439–64, part of a special issue, "Development Cultures: New Environments, New Realities, New Strategies," edited by Françoise Lionnet, Obioma Nnaemeka, Susan H. Perry, and Celeste Schenck.

20. Chinese philosophers such as Laozi and Zhuangzi and Greek philosophers such as Anaximander and Heraclitus sought to describe the elemental strata comprising relationality, in which all living and dying occurs. The Greeks postulated the "indefinite" in which

earth, fire, water, and air interacted, and the Buddhists named *dharma* or *dao* as both source and driving force behind everything that exists.

21. Critiques as well as retoolings emerged in early postcolonial African scholarship, as discussed in B. Jewsiewicki and V. Y. Mudimbe, "Africans' Memories and Contemporary History of Africa," *History and Theory* 32, no. 4 (December 1993): 1–11. Also, Susan Buck-Morss has usefully highlighted the grounds of his thinking in Atlantic world Anglo-European slavery; see Susan Buck-Morss, *Hegel, Haiti, and Universal History* (Pittsburgh, PA: University of Pittsburgh, 2009). Other influential feminist retoolings of the dialectics of alterity include Elizabeth Grosz, *Volatile Bodies* (Bloomington: Indiana University Press, 1994); and Mae Gwendolyn Henderson's "Speaking in Tongues: Dialectics, Dialogics, and the Black Woman Writer's Literary Tradition," in *Speaking in Tongues and Dancing the Diaspora: Black Women Writing and Performing* (New York: Oxford University Press, 2014).

22. See L. H. M. Ling's valuable essay, "Worlds beyond Westphalia: Daoist Dialectics and the 'China Threat,'" *Review of International Studies* 39, no. 3 (2013): 549–68. As I discuss in note 23, there are also some highly problematic appropriations of feminist conceptions of relationality in recent IR theories drawing on Confucian thought.

Concerning the influence of Chinese thought, recent global intellectual histories establish that "western" thought and culture have roots in Global Southeastern philosophies and cultures. German philosophers, most prominently Leibniz, engaged actively with Daoist thought, and Hegel expressed interest in debates about Eastern philosophies. On the latter, see Robert Bernasconi, "With What Must the History of Philosophy Begin? Hegel's Role in the Debate on the Place of India within the History of Philosophy," in *Hegel's History of Philosophy: New Interpretations*, ed. David A. Duquette (Albany, NY: SUNY Press, 2003), 35–50. It's also worth recalling that Hegel's awareness of dialectics in ancient Greek philosophy was likely prepared by earlier Arabic translations. Claims about dialectics as a tradition of thought in western philosophy should be considered in this light.

For broader discussion of these coformations and influences, see J. J. Clarke, *Oriental Enlightenment: The Encounter between Asian and Western Thought* (New York: Routledge, 1997); Donald F. Lach, *Asia in the Making of Europe, Volume I: The Century of Discovery* (Chicago: University of Chicago Press, 1965); Yu Liu, *Seeds of a Different Eden: Chinese Gardening and a New English Aesthetic Ideal* (Columbia: University of South Carolina Press, 2008). For useful sources, but cast within a problematically Eurocentric framework, see Raymond Schwab, *The Oriental Renaissance: Europe's Rediscovery of India and the East, 1680–1880*, trans. Gene Patterson-Black and Victor Reinking (New York: Columbia University Press, 1984). See my discussion of Schwab in chapter 3.

23. See Ling, "Worlds beyond Westphalia." As Ling foregrounds, Daoism suggests that entities change by "dialectically interpenetrating and transforming the other" (568), and Hegel's word *durchdringung* for the relation among entities has been translated as "interpenetration" (in Miller's standard English translation of Hegel). Likewise in Hegel's comments on the "unity" of matter: he remarks that, via dialectical processes, "the universal is in undivided unity with this plurality," distinctly recalling the Daoist notion of oneness or "co-dependent origination" (Hegel, *Phenomenology of Spirit*, 81). Such concepts themselves

manifest the interdependent unfolding of traditions of thought—although until recently the Daoist influence has been elided, or one could say self-servingly sublated, within European traditions, as noted above. For further development of the intersections between Hegel's notions and those of Eastern philosophy, see Douglas Osto, *Power, Wealth, and Women in Indian Mahayana Buddhism: The Gandavyuha-sutra* (New York: Routledge, 2008).

For a telling exposure of what happens when the concept of relationality is developed without attention to the feminist-intersectional or decolonial dimensions of power, see Yaqing Qin, *A Relational Theory of World Politics* (Cambridge: Cambridge University Press, 2018). Aiming to insert concepts of relationality into IR theory, Yaqing Qin on one hand provides useful genealogies of relational concepts in the traditions of Confucian thought, pragmatism, and sociological theory, and he sometimes discusses the challenges of diversity. But the author's lack of feminist-intersectional knowledge shows up in the innocence, or convenient blindnesses in the book's theory of state relations. Deeming relations and "relational management" a key to better power relations, he offers this example: "In dynastic China, marrying daughters of the Han imperial family to rulers of minority nationalities was an important policy for pacifying such groups and maintaining good relations with them"—a striking conflation of pacification and good relations (232). Yet praise for this "landmark" book as the "arrival of a truly global discipline of international relations" comes from eminent IR scholars at Cornell University and the London School of Economics.

24. Kojève reduced the dialectic to a set of ongoing interactions between two opposing forces: in his account, this encounter of opposites transforms into a synthesis or union, which then however encounters another opposing force, so that the binary, cumulative process repeats over time. See Alexandre Kojève, *Introduction to the Reading of Hegel: Lectures on the Phenomenology of Spirit*, ed. Allan Bloom (Ithaca, NY: Cornell University Press, 1980).

25. For this phrase, see Hegel, *Phenomenology of Spirit*, 121. Regarding the binary tendencies, in Marx's case the binaries are expressed in his account of phased class struggle, first between emergent bourgeoisie and aristocracy and then between emergent proletariat and bourgeoisie, a forward procession in which binary, antagonistic forces resolve into a utopian synthesis. Engel's and Lenin's discussions of dialectics similarly continue the binary logic and the problematic vocabulary of evolutionary development and progress. See Lenin, *Imperialism*, 220–21; and also Alker and Biersteker, "Dialectic of World Order," 122, 135.

It's worth noting that although the prefix *dia-* has associations with "two" because of its roots in the Greek word for that number, in Greek *dia* also has the ancient meanings of "across," "through," and "thoroughly"; it functions as a preposition or prefix indicating relation across difference or separateness, as in the word *dialogue*. In the early Greek formulation of dialectical practice by Socrates, it entailed exactly this interacting of plural views.

The retooling of Charles Darwin in the field of evolutionary world politics (EWP) is worth noting given my engagement with the fields of world politics and international relations. As I've discussed elsewhere, in *The Origin of Species* Darwin anticipates Merleau-Ponty's notion of "intercorporeality," by which Merleau-Ponty indicates the orientation of bodies toward each other within a material "habitus" and social "horizon," notions that inform my analyses here as they have my earlier work. Darwin suggestively described the world of organic beings as the result of "beautiful coadaptations . . . of one part of the organization to another part" that occurred "everywhere and in every part of the organic world" (Charles Darwin, *The Origin of Species* [New York: D. Appleton, 1859], 51–52). Ultimately, as does Hegel in *Philosophy of History*, Darwin reduces all relations to the competitive principle of antagonistic struggle and does so within a racist narrative of "higher" and "lower" races (Charles Darwin, *The Descent of Man and Selection in Relation to Sex* [New York: D. Appleton, [1871] 1889], 507–9). For discussion of both Merleau-Ponty and Darwin, see Doyle, *Bordering on the Body*, 64–70.

Unfortunately, traces of Darwin's hierarchical emphasis on competitive struggle circulate in EWP, despite scholars' attempts to emphasize relational and historical models. The shadow of racialized thinking appears (predictably coupled with a turn to population studies as it first was in the "science" of eugenics), for instance when George Modelski considers the explosion of "British stock" around the world between 1600 and 1960 and suggests that "'the quality of British institutions' explain this phenomenal population rise" (16–17). This linking of "stock" and advanced "institutions" has an old racist genealogy. See Laura Doyle, *Freedom's Empire: Race and the Rise of the Novel in Atlantic Modernity, 1640–1940* (Durham, NC: Duke University Press, 2008). Likewise, although Modelski helpfully seeks models outside the nation-state, he continues to think within the model of "stages of historical development," asking whether and why global politics "is less primitive today than it was for instance, one thousand years ago." See George Modelski, "Evolutionary World Politics: Problems of Scope and Method," in *Evolutionary Interpretations of World Politics*, ed. William R. Thompson (New York: Routledge, 2001), 16–17. Whence the model of primitive and advanced? Such strains of thought reveal what lies coiled within the vocabularies of evolution, undercutting EWP efforts to move outside of Eurocentric accounts of state formation.

26. I allude here to Elizabeth Grosz's use of this term in her excellent study of gender and phenomenology, *Volatile Bodies*, cited above.

27. Hegel, *Phenomenology of Spirit*, 60.

28. Hegel, *Phenomenology of Spirit*, 81.

29. Hegel, *Phenomenology of Spirit*, 81.

30. Hegel, *Phenomenology of Spirit*, 60.

31. Buck-Morss, *Hegel, Haiti, and Universal History*.

32. Hegel, *Phenomenology of Spirit*, 111.

33. Hegel, *Phenomenology of Spirit*, 112.

34. See Barbara Fuchs, *Mimesis and Empire: The New World, Islam, and European Identities* (Cambridge: Cambridge University Press, 2001), introduction (1–12) and throughout. See related discussions in Ann Laura Stoler, Carole McGranahan, and Peter C. Perdue, eds., *Imperial Formations* (Santa Fe, NM: School for Advanced Research Press, 2007).

35. For an illuminating analysis of these dynamics as shrewdly captured in the memoirs of those who escaped US slavery, see Nicholas Bromell, *By the Sweat of the Brow: Literature and Labor in Antebellum America* (Chicago: University of Chicago Press, 1993).

36. Hegel, *Phenomenology of Spirit*, 117.

37. Hegel, *Phenomenology of Spirit*, 118.

38. Hegel, *Phenomenology of Spirit*, 118.

39. Hegel, *Phenomenology of Spirit*, 118.

40. Here I am highlighting the labors of women in general but of course minoritized women have also shouldered other women's labor and thereby enabled the standing of bourgeois and elite women, including those who identify as feminist. For close study of these conditions see Pheng Cheah's important analysis in "Biopower and the New International Division of Reproductive Labor," *boundary 2* 34, no. 1 (2007): 79–113; and his book, *Inhuman Conditions: On Cosmopolitanism and Human Rights* (Cambridge, MA: Harvard University Press, 2006). For studies of New International Division of Labor more broadly, see Folker Fröbel, Jürgen Heinrichs, and Otto Kreye, *The New International Division of Labor: Structural Unemployment in Industrialised Countries and Industrialisation in Developing Countries*, trans. Pete Burgess (Cambridge: Cambridge University Press, 1980). Also see essays in Richard Robison, Richard Higgott, and Kevin Hewison, eds., *Southeast Asia in the 1980s: The Politics of Economic Crisis* (Sydney: Allen and Unwin, 1987). More broadly, see the corpus of work by sociologist Saskia Sassen on globalization and migration.

41. Cultural differences deserve further attention here. For instance, Ashis Nandy's classic study, *The Intimate Enemy: Loss and Recovery of Self under Colonialism*, 2nd ed. (Oxford: Oxford University Press, 2009), develops an important analysis of how different family formations in different cultures shape their intersections with colonial politics, including relations between mothers and sons. Yet I cannot agree with recent feminist decolonial theorists, such as Rita Laura Segato, who posit a precolonial "village" life, where gendered realms are separate but equal. In the absence of further details, I am not yet convinced about the equality or reciprocity, especially since Segato's own formulations suggest otherwise. She suggests for instance that, before European colonial invasions, the village was "a world in which the genders occupy two different spaces in social life," yet she goes on to say that in "[this] dual world, both terms are ontologically full and complete, although they can maintain a hierarchical relationship." From whence does this seemingly incidental hierarchy arise? In whose interest and to what end? Her remark that "the dual structure . . . is driven by an ironclad and binding reciprocity" raises further doubts, especially in its "ironclad and binding reciprocity" (616). Why the need for ironclad if all is mutual and voluntary? Recent research on Mesoamerican states indicates, furthermore, that in many Mesoamerican regions, village life had been invaded and restructured long before the arrival of Europeans, as I also describe in chapter 1. The studies by Gayle Rubin and Gerda Lerner cited in note 43 give additional evidence of pre-1500 patriarchy in the villages of the world.

42. Nancy Chodorow, *The Reproduction of Mothering* (Berkeley: University of California Press, 1978).

43. For earlier work, see Gayle Rubin, "The Traffic in Women: Notes on the 'Political Economy' of Sex," in *The Second Wave: A Reader in Feminist Theory*, ed. Linda Nicholson (New York: Routledge, 1997), 27–62; Sheila Rowbotham, *Women's Consciousness, Men's World* (New York: Verso, [1973] 2015); and Gerda Lerner, *The Creation of Patriarchy* (New York: Oxford University Press, 1987). For recent work on social reproduction, see Bhattacharya,

ed., *Social Reproduction Theory*. For two different angles on these economies as enacted in literature, see Doyle, *Bordering on the Body*; and Eve Kosofsky Sedgwick, *Between Men: English Literature and Male Homosocial Desire* (New York: Columbia University Press, 1985).

44. See, for instance, Mwangi wa Gīthīnji, "Erasing Class/(Re)Creating Ethnicity: Politics, Jobs, Accumulation and Identity in Kenya," *Review of Black Political Economy* 42, no. 1 (2015): 87–110.

45. Engels's dependence on Lewis Henry Morgan's stadial and Darwinist conception of human history (supposedly developing from savage to barbarian to civilized) undercuts his analysis from the beginning. The false corollary between monogamy and class society, among other confused claims, likewise cripples Engel's arguments. But he deserves credit for even raising the topic within his materialist critique. See Friedrich Engels, *The Origin of the Family, Private Property, and the State*, trans. Eleanor Burke Leacock (New York: International Publishers, [1940] 1975).

46. Rubin, "Traffic in Women."

47. See Martin Heidegger, *Being and Time*, trans. John Macquarrie and Edward Robinson (Oxford: Blackwell, [1927] 1962), for instance, 219–25, 321–22, and 387.

48. Merleau-Ponty, *Visible and Invisible*, 142–45.

49. Vincent Falger, "Evolutionary World Politics Enriched: The Biological Foundations of International Relations," in *Evolutionary Interpretations of World Politics*, ed. William R. Thompson (New York: Routledge, 2001), 30–51.

50. In this light, we might interpret the fetishization of sovereignty, autonomy, and independence in classic IR theory as convenient fictions that disavow our fraught, difficult interdependence.

51. See Johannes Fabian, *Time and the Other: How Anthropology Makes Its Object* (New York: Columbia University Press, 1983), 31–32. For Hegel's phrases, see Hegel, *Phenomenology of Spirit*, 114.

52. Janet Abu-Lughod, *Before European Hegemony: The World System A.D. 1250–1350* (New York: Oxford University Press, 1989).

53. For the term *shatterzone*, see Omer Bartov and Eric D. Weitz, *Shatterzone of Empires: Coexistence and Violence in the German, Habsburg, Russian, and Ottoman Borderlands* (Bloomington: Indiana University Press, 2013).

54. I am indebted to Bahun's discussion of "interpositionality" in eastern Europe, which helped to shape my concept of inter-imperiality. See Sanja Bahun, "The Balkans Uncovered: Toward *Historie Croisée* of Modernism," in *The Oxford Handbook of Global Modernisms*, ed. Mark Wollaeger and Matt Eatough (New York: Oxford University Press, 2012), 25–47. For work that draws on the long-historical concept of inter-imperiality to discuss language, politics, and literature, see two special issues: Laura Doyle and Sahar Amer, eds., "Reframing Postcolonial and Global Studies in the Longer Durée," special issue, *PMLA* 130, no. 2 (2015): 331–438; and Laura Doyle, ed., "Inter-imperiality," special issue, *Modern Fiction Studies* 64, no. 3 (2018). The latter includes essays on literatures in a range of places including Indonesia,

China, Korea, Eurasia, the Atlantic World, and (by Sanja Bahun) eastern Europe, while the former focuses on underlying methodological questions in literary studies. Robert Kaplan's *Balkan Ghosts* is an infamous example of the many distorted accounts of so-called tribalism in such regions. For exposure of these misrepresentations in the work of recent commentators on the virtues of western empire such as Samuel Huntington, Robert Kaplan, and others, see Catherine Besteman and Hugh Gusterson, eds., *Why America's Top Pundits Are Wrong: Anthropologists Talk Back* (Berkeley: University of California Press, 2005). In this collection, see especially Tona Bringa, "Haunted by the Imaginations of the Past: Robert Kaplan's *Balkan Ghosts*," 60–82.

55. In particular see the following essays in the special PMLA cluster cited above: Annette Lienau Damayanti, "Reframing Vernacular Culture on Arabic Fault Lines: Bamba, Senghor, and Sembene's Translingual Legacies in French West Africa," PMLA 130, no. 2 (2015): 419–29; Lydia Liu, "Scripts in Motion: Writing as Imperial Technology, Past and Present," PMLA 130, no. 2 (2015): 375–83; and Mary Louise Pratt, "Language and the Afterlives of Empire," PMLA 130, no. 2 (2015): 348–57. Also see Nergis Ertürk, *Grammatology and Literary Modernity in Turkey* (New York: Oxford University Press, 2011).

56. Kwame Nkrumah, *Neo-colonialism: The Last Stage of Imperialism* (New York: International Publishers, 1965).

57. Qtd. in David A. Bell, *The First Total War: Napoleon's Europe and the Birth of Warfare as We Know It* (London: Bloomsbury, 2012), 269–70.

58. James Joyce, *Ulysses*, ed. Hans Gabler (New York: Vintage, 1986), 12:1156–58.

59. Stephen Joyce, "Inter-imperial Aesthetics: Korean and Korean Diasporic Literature between Empires," *Modern Fiction Studies* 64, no. 3 (2018): 488–511. The Korean meaning of *han* is linked to the character in Chinese and other languages yet with distinct meaning.

60. Chang-rae Lee, *Native Speaker* (New York: Riverhead, 1995), 333.

61. S. Joyce, "Inter-imperial Aesthetics," 502.

62. S. Joyce, "Inter-imperial Aesthetics," 499.

63. S. Joyce, "Inter-imperial Aesthetics," 499.

64. S. Joyce, "Inter-imperial Aesthetics," 507.

65. Thiong'o, *Decolonising the Mind*.

66. For recent work of this kind, see Jason Frydman, *Sounding the Break: African American and Caribbean Routes of World Literature* (Charlottesville: University of Virginia Press, 2014); Annaliese Hoehling, "Minoritarian 'Marvelous Real': Enfolding Revolution in Alejo Carpentier's *The Kingdom of This World*," *Journal of Postcolonial Writing* 54, no. 2 (2018): 254–67; Heather Wayne, "Gilded Chains: Global Economies and Gendered Arts in U.S. Fiction, 1865–1930" (PhD diss., University of Massachusetts, Amherst, 2019); and the special issues in PMLA and *Modern Fiction Studies* cited in note 54. Also see Walter Cohen, *A History of European Literature: The West and the World from Antiquity to the Present* (Oxford: Oxford University Press, 2017), which provides a wealth of information about literary traditions and genres from ancient to contemporary throughout the world. Cohen also

offers useful attention to the states within which literary histories have formed, but this is not the focus of his project.

67. Critics have especially challenged Pascale Casanova's separation of literary and political "world-systems" in her book, *The World Republic of Letters*, trans. M. B. DeBevoise (Cambridge, MA: Harvard University Press, 2007), while others have critiqued studies that eclipse the politics of translation, as reflected in David Damrosch, *What Is World Literature?* (Princeton, NJ: Princeton University Press, 2003). For critiques, see Emily Apter, *Against World Literature: On the Politics of Untranslatability* (New York: Verso Books, 2013); Sanjay Krishnan, *Reading the Global: Troubling Perspectives on Britain's Empire in Asia* (New York: Columbia University Press, 2007); and Aamir Mufti, *Forget English! Orientalisms and World Literature* (Cambridge, MA: Harvard University Press, 2016). A range of fruitful debates and reconceptualizations have been collected in, for example, David Damrosch, *World Literature in Theory* (Chichester, UK: Wiley Blackwell, 2014); and Christopher Prendergast, ed., *Debating World Literature* (New York: Verso, 2004).

68. See Shu-mei Shih, "Comparison as Relation," in *Comparison: Theories, Approaches, Uses*, ed. Rita Felski and Susan Friedman (Baltimore: Johns Hopkins University Press, 2013), 79–98.

69. Karima Laachir, Sara Marzagora, and Francesca Orsini, "Significant Geographies: In Lieu of World Literature," *Journal of World Literature* 3, no. 3 (2018): 290–310. Also see Alexander Beecroft's flexible way of situating large bodies of literature within both regional and world contexts, as in his book, *An Ecology of World Literature: From Antiquity to the Present Day* (New York: Verso Books, 2015). Although, on one hand, Beecroft's idea of ecologies could be said simply to model historically grounded critical and intertextual practices, the temporal and the geographical reach of his studies, which include Chinese, Greek, and other literatures, performs valuable decentering of Anglo-European literatures.

70. See Revathi Krishnaswamy, "Toward World Literary Knowledges: Theory in the Age of Globalization," *Comparative Literature* 62, no. 4 (2010): 399–419, including for discussion of the bhakti and of early, nonwestern literary theory. Krishnaswamy's work on narrative genres in the longue durée will appear, along with similar studies, in the collection in progress, *Decolonial Reconstellations*, ed. Simon Gikandi, Laura Doyle, and Mwangi wa Gĩthĩnjĩ (working title; not yet under contract). Krishnaswamy's essay for this collection is drawn from her current book project.

71. See for instance the project undertaken by Rebecca Carol Johnson, Richard Maxwell, and Katie Trumpener in "*The Arabian Nights*, Arab-European Literary Influence, and the Lineages of the Novel," *Modern Language Quarterly* 88, no. 2 (2007): 243–78. Although the article tracks specific historical conditions under which the *Nights* and other texts have been readapted, offering suggestive close readings of the transformative powers of literary form, the authors frame their study mainly as evidence of a "complex and cosmopolitan literary history" and testimony to the valuable "discovery of links that make possible the meaningfulness, and the liveliness, of literature" (278). For a more political angle of reading this literary history, see the special issues in *PMLA* and *Modern Fiction Studies* cited in note 54.

72. Both Cheah and I have, for instance, been engaged with the concept of freedom, highlighting the ways that concepts such as freedom have their purchase within the realm of cultural and political economy—the realm where "freedom" as an interpellating word has served contradictory functions, both rallying and equivocating. See Cheah, *Inhuman Conditions*; Doyle, *Freedom's Empire*.

73. See Pheng Cheah, *What Is a World? On Postcolonial Literature as World Literature* (Durham, NC: Duke University Press, 2016), 44.

74. See Cheah, "Biopower," 111.

75. See Cheah, "Biopower," 111.

76. Cheah, *What Is a World?*, 5.

77. Cheah, *What Is a World?*, 74.

78. Cheah, *What Is a World?*, 106.

79. Arendt highlights "natality" as the basis of sociality and in turn politics, but only by referring to the fact that "we are born" and by removing human bodies from the momentous "appearance" or "arrival" of newcomers (qtd. in Cheah, *What Is a World?*, 138). Cheah himself simply notes that "the persistent coming of new others" ensures that "human existence is . . . a dynamic and constantly changing web of relations" (9–10, 103–4), from which however the "primary instance" of relation is excised. Similar problems occur in the thought of Heidegger and most especially Derrida. For a different reading of Arendt, see Rosalyn Diprose and Ewa Plonowska Ziarek, *Arendt, Natality, and Biopolitics:Toward Democratic Plurality and Reproductive Justice* (Edinburgh: Edinburgh University Press, 2018). They implicitly supplement what she leaves out, but give her credit for their own extrapolations.

In the case of Heidegger, Cheah embraces the evocative notion of "the opening that puts all beings into relation" and concludes that "the world is an irreducible openness where *we cannot avoid* being-with-others" (Cheah, *What Is a World?*, 105; emphasis added). The phrase *cannot avoid* may well capture an everyday feeling, but it becomes something more when followed by this unsettling description of Being (*Dasein*) and Being-with (*Mitdasein*): "Even when I do not perceive other-Dasein as *on hand*, they always accompany me as co-Dasein (Mitda-sein) in *my daily absorption* in the world *that is looked after*" (Cheah, *What Is a World?*, 105; emphasis added). Cheah does not identify this habit of not perceiving that the world is looked after even though "they always" accompany us as a problem. He simply lists it as one of "four important traits" that constitute "the irreducible openness" of the world—the first being that the presence of others in this world "is inconspicuous" (Cheah, *What Is a World?*, 105). Here is the problem in the material and mental *habitus*, unintentionally named. For there is of course an unequal gender history that condones, or not, the "daily absorption" that overlooks how and by whom the world is "looked after." A different sense of lived history and a longer, more precise account of economic and colonial history informed by feminist-intersectional research might reframe this political ontology.

In Jacques Derrida's discussion of the "arrivance" of others, the combination of appropriation and erasure is particularly clear. Derrida the master dialectician senses that to minimize these gendered labors while arguing for the irreducibility of sociality is a problem. Thus he must mention—and then sublate—those labors. To make this move, Derrida claims that his theory, and Cheah approvingly quotes, encompasses something more "absolute" than "birth itself": "Birth itself, which is similar to what I'm trying to describe, is perhaps unequal to this absolute 'arrivance' [of others]. Families prepare for a birth; it is scheduled, forenamed, caught up in a symbolic space that dulls the arrivance" (qtd. in Cheah, *What Is a World?*, 172). His caveat appears in the very next sentence—provoked perhaps by his half-conscious apprehension of the resonance of "unequal to" and the bad faith in suggesting that the "symbolic space" "dulls" rather than intensifies those labors. Yet then comes the full erasure of the birthing body and the self-recuperative sublation, through grammatical antics and telling abstractions: "Nevertheless, in spite of these anticipations and prenominations, the uncertainty will not let itself be reduced: the child that arrives remains unpredictable; it speaks of itself as from the origin of another world, or from an-other-origin of this world" (qtd. in Cheah, *What Is a World?*, 172). The birthing person is, by sleights of hand and mind, smoothly replaced with a child, who can then become the arriving author, the widely quoted voice seductively speaking of "an-other-origin of this world." Cheah unfortunately follows suit, only remarking that "the to-come is an openness that promises nothing certain because it does not posit a determinate end of any kind. . . . The other that is to come is simply the absolute *arrivant* . . . that which cannot be determined as a foreigner, a refugee, an immigrant, and so on" (Cheah, *What Is a World?*, 172–73; emphasis in original).

80. This approach limits Cheah's literary readings of women's practices of sociality in literature, most especially his comments on a "feminist-maternal ontopology" in women's fiction. Cheah, *What Is a World?*, 233.

81. See Ngũgĩ wa Thiong'o, *Globalectics: Theory and the Politics of Knowing* (New York: Columbia University Press, 2014).

82. Fredric Jameson, *The Political Unconscious* (Ithaca, NY: Cornell University Press, 1981).

83. Theodor W. Adorno, *Negative Dialectics*, trans. E. B. Ashton (New York: Bloomsbury, 2014).

84. J. Joyce, *Ulysses*, 1:638–44.

85. Husain Haddawy, trans., *The Arabian Nights*, ed. Muhsin Mahdi (New York: Norton, 1990), 11.

86. On colonial intimacy, see Sara Suleri, *The Rhetoric of English India* (Chicago: University of Chicago Press, 1992).

87. See Dipesh Chakrabarty, *Provincializing Europe: Postcolonial Thought and Historical Difference* (Princeton, NJ: Princeton University Press, 2000).

88. Husain Haddawy, trans., *The Arabian Nights*, 15.

89. See, for instance, Adam Barrows, *The Cosmic Time of Empire: Modern Britain and World Literature* (Berkeley: University of California Press, 2011). Also see a prior study on time and modernist literature, thought provoking although not focused on empire: Stephen Kuhn, *The Culture of Time and Space, 1880–1918* (Cambridge, MA: Harvard University Press, [1983] 2003).

Chapter 1: Dialectics in the Longue Durée

Parts of chapter 1 appeared in "Inter-Imperiality: Dialectics in a Postcolonial World History," *Interventions: International Journal of Postcolonial Studies* (2013): 1–38; "Dialectics in the Longue Durée: The IIPEC Model of Inter-Imperial Economy and Culture," *Globalizations* 11, no. 5 (2014): 689–709; and "Inter-imperiality and Literary Study in the Longer Durée," *PMLA* 130, no. 2 (2015): 336–47.

1. See Dariusz Koloziejczyk and Peter F. Bang, eds., *Universal Empire: A Comparative Approach to Imperial Culture and Representation in Eurasian History* (Cambridge: Cambridge University Press, 2012), for a discussion of this pattern of representation. Also see Clifford Ando, "Introduction: States and State Power in Antiquity," in *Ancient States and Infrastructural Power*, ed. Clifford Ando and Seth Richardson (Philadelphia: University of Pennsylvania Press, 2017), 4–7.

2. For a particularly thought-provoking analysis of the European fashioning of Rome as antecedent, see especially Julia Hell, *Conquest of Ruins* (Chicago: University of Chicago Press, 2019). On Roman tropes in medieval European literature, see the first set of essays in Ananya J. Kabir and Deanne Williams, *Postcolonial Approaches to the European Middle Ages: Translating Cultures* (New York: Cambridge University Press, 2005). The notion of a torch-passing, imperial transfer of power, including a supposedly preordained succession of one empire to the next, has its roots in Greco-Roman and Jewish historiography. At times empires have vied over their claim as successors, as when different European empires claimed to be the proper heir of Rome. On the classical, Christian, and Jewish traditions of this idea, see Arnaldo Momigliano, "The Origins of Universal History," in *On Pagans, Jews, and Christians* (Middletown, CT: Wesleyan University Press, 1987), 31–57. Later in this book, especially in chapter 3, I highlight empires' actualization of the twin concept of *translatio studii et imperii* (the translation of learning and power).

3. See Johannes Fabian, *Time and the Other: How Anthropology Makes Its Object* (New York: Columbia University Press, 1983).

4. Fabian, *Time and the Other*.

5. Kathleen Davis, *Periodization and Sovereignty: How Ideas of Feudalism and Secularization Govern the Politics of Time* (Philadelphia: University of Pennsylvania Press, 2008).

6. Niall Ferguson's work most egregiously epitomizes this erasure and distorted myth-making, as noted in the introduction. Yet it sneaks into even some of the more valuable and accurate scholarship, for instance through invocations of one of the most tenacious myths—the notion of a unique Anglo-European adventurousness and boundary-breaking will to change and experimentation. In his valuable revision of US history, for instance, Thomas Bender agrees with other scholars that "Europe's emergence was the result of its interaction with the societies of Africa, Asia, and America" (Blaut and Pomeranz, qtd. in Thomas H. Bender, *A Nation among Nations* [New York: Hill and Wang, 2006], 25), but he correlates the Atlantic crossing with new "cognitive developments," even an "oceanic revolution" in global consciousness (22)—eliding, among other things, the fact that earlier empires crossed the Indian Ocean and the Russians crossed the Pacific.

7. Janet Abu-Lughod, *Before European Hegemony: The World System* A.D. *1250–1350* (New York: Oxford University Press, 1989). For other early scholarship that helped to catalyze recent scholarship, see K. N. Chaudhuri, *Asia before Europe: Economy and Civilization of the Indian Ocean from the Rise of Islam to 1750* (New York: Cambridge University Press, 1990). R. J. Barendse usefully updates and reframes this earlier scholarship in "Trade and State in the Arabian Seas: A Survey from the Fifteenth to the Eighteenth Century," *Journal of World History* 11, no. 2 (2000): 173–225. Barendse also raises a host of useful issues about the historiography of these and earlier periods, including the inadequate attention to Africa and the problem of thinking about the world history only in terms of Europe's impact on other parts of the world. Also see Jane Schneider, "Was There a Pre-capitalist World System?," *Peasant Studies* 6, no. 1 (1978–79): 20–29.

8. Edward W. Said, *Culture and Imperialism* (New York: Knopf, 1993), 188–89.

9. Anthony G. Hopkins, "Back to the Future: From National History to Imperial History," *Past and Present* 164, no. 1 (1999): 203.

10. Drawing on work in archives and archeological sites, a wave of studies has analyzed interconnected empires in periods before western European hegemony and others have traced the dynamics among European and non-European empires in later periods. I will reference many of these studies in the pages to follow, and mention just a few here. For a valuable broad study of early empires, see Jane Burbank and Frederick Cooper, *Empires in World History: Power and the Politics of Difference* (Princeton, NJ: Princeton University Press, 2010). For another broad study, in this case of more recent periods (and which also pays attention to matters of gender and race as well as resistance), see Tony Ballantyne and Antoinette M. Burton, *Empires and the Reach of the Global, 1870–1945* (Cambridge, MA: Harvard University Press, 2014). For an illustrative regional approach, see Stephen Dale, *The Muslim Empires of the Ottomans, Safavids, and Mughals* (Cambridge: Cambridge University Press, 2010). For other calls for long-historical postcolonial and IR scholarship, see B. Buzan and Richard Little, *International Systems in World History: Remaking the Study of International Relations* (New York: Oxford University Press, 2000); Arif Dirlik, "Rethinking Colonialism: Globalization, Postcolonialism, and the Nation," *Interventions: International Journal of Postcolonial Studies* 4, no. 3 (2002): 428–48; Barry K. Gills and William R. Thompson, eds., *Globalization and Global History* (New York: Routledge, 2006); Hannes Lacher, *Beyond Globalization: Capitalism, Territoriality and the International Relations of Modernity* (New York: Routledge, 2006); and R. Palan, "Transnational Theories of Order and Change: Heterodoxy in International Relations Scholarship," *Review of International Studies* 33, no. S1 (2007): 47–69.

11. On the African dimensions, see Barendse, "Trade and State in the Arabian Seas," 178–80. Also see scholars discussed below.

12. Philippe Beaujard, "The Indian Ocean in Eurasian and African World-Systems before the Sixteenth Century," *Journal of World History* 16, no. 4 (2005): 420.

13. See Beaujard, "Indian Ocean," 420–21. On the idea of systemic coordination and pulsations, see essays in Gills and Thompson, *Globalization and Global History*, especially: Christopher K. Chase-Dunn, Daniel Pasciuti, Alexis Alvarez, and Thomas D. Hall, "Growth/

Decline Phases and Semi-Peripheral Development in the Ancient Mesopotamian and Egyptian World-Systems," 114–38; and Ander Gunder Frank and William R. Thompson, "Early Iron Age Economic Expansions and Contraction Revisited," 139–62. For Michael Smith's analysis, see "The Aztec Empire and the Mesoamerican World-System," in *Empires: Perspectives from Archaeology and History*, ed. Susan Alcock, Terence N. D'Altroy, Kathleen D. Morrison, and Carla Sinopoli (Cambridge: Cambridge University Press, 2001), 128–54. Also see Michael Smith and Frances Berdan, eds., *The Postclassic Mesoamerican World* (Salt Lake City: University of Utah Press, 2003).

14. Susan Alcock, Terence N. D'Altroy, Kathleen D. Morrison, and Carla Sinopoli, eds., *Empires: Perspectives from Archaeology and History* (Cambridge: Cambridge University Press, 2001; Andre Gunder Frank and Barry K. Gills, eds., *The World System: Five Hundred Years or Five Thousand?* (New York: Routledge, 1993); Gills and Thompson, *Globalization and Global History*.

15. Marshall Hodgson was among the earliest to do so. See "The Interrelations of Societies," in *Rethinking World History: Essays on Europe, Islam, and World History*, ed. Edmund Burke III (New York: Cambridge University Press, [1963] 1993), 3–28. On the coformations of different and successive Mesoamerican states, see Terence D'Altroy, *The Incas*, 2nd ed. (Malden, MA: Blackwell, 2011); and Darryl Wilkinson, "Infrastructure and Inequality: An Archaeology of the Inka Road through the Amaybamba Cloud Forests," *Journal of Social Archaeology* 19, no. 1 (2019): 27–46. On the contact of American and Afro-Eurasian states, see Sabine MacCormack, *On the Wings of Time: Rome, the Incas, Spain, and Peru* (Princeton, NJ: Princeton University Press, 2009), esp. chapter 7; and Charles C. Mann, *1491: New Revelations of the Americas before Columbus* (New York: Alfred A. Knopf, 2005).

16. J. E. Wills Jr., "Maritime Asia, 1500–1800: The Interactive Emergence of European Domination," *American Historical Review* 98, no. 1 (1993): 83–105.

17. David Christian, "Silk Roads or Steppe Roads? The Silk Roads in World History," *Journal of World History* 11, no. 1 (2000): 25–26. On dialectics, see Arnold Pacey, *Technology in World Civilization* (Cambridge, MA: MIT Press, 1990), viii; and on efflorescences, see Jack Goldstone, "Efflorescences and Economic Growth in World History: Rethinking the 'Rise of the West' and the Industrial Revolution," *Journal of World History* 13, no. 2 (2002): 323–89.

18. Goldstone, "Efflorescences," 375–76.

19. Jerry Brotton, *The Renaissance Bazaar: From the Silk Road to Michelangelo* (New York: Oxford University Press, 2010), 1.

20. Brotton, *Renaissance Bazaar*, 4–5. In *Civilization and Capitalism*, Fernand Braudel sometimes underplays the importance of states in Mediterranean trade networks; he remarks, for example, that in the sixteenth-century Mediterranean trade "ignored the frontiers of empires." Fernand Braudel, *Civilization and Capitalism, 15th-18th Centuries*, vol. 3, *The Perspective of the World*, trans. Siân Reynolds (New York: Harper and Row, [1979] 1984), 22.

21. Recent historical studies vary in the degree to which they offer political interpretations of empire. Most of those listed in this note include such analyses, although not all selections do so. The editors of *Cosmopolitanism and Empire*, for instance, tend to frame the volume in terms of exchange and integration rather than in terms of power. See Alcock,

D'Altroy, Morrison, and Sinopoli, eds., *Empires*; Clifford Ando and Seth Richardson, eds., *Ancient States and Infrastructural Power* (Philadelphia: University of Pennsylvania Press, 2017); Peter Bang and Christopher Bayly, eds., *Tributary Empires in Global History* (New York: Palgrave Macmillan, 2011); Koloziejczyk and Bang, *Universal Empire*; Burbank and Cooper, *Empires in World History*; Miles Lavan, Richard E. Payne, and John Weisweiler, eds., *Cosmopolitanism and Empire: Universal Rulers, Local Elites, and Cultural Integration in the Ancient Near East and Mediterranean* (New York: Oxford University Press, 2016); Ian Morris and Walter Scheidel, eds., *The Dynamics of Ancient Empires: State Power from Assyria to Byzantium* (New York: Oxford University Press, 2008); and Ann Laura Stoler, Carole McGranahan, and Peter C. Perdue, eds., *Imperial Formations* (Santa Fe, NM: School for Advanced Research Press, 2007). Also see Kenneth Pomeranz, "Social History and World History: From Daily Life to Patterns of Change," *Journal of World History* 18, no. 1 (2007): 69–98.

22. On the structures of earlier states, see Michael Mann, *The Sources of Social Power*, vol. 1, *A History of Power from the Beginning to AD 1760* (Cambridge: Cambridge University Press, 1986).

23. Barendse, "Trade and State in the Arabian Seas," 223. Although Barendse focuses on these three centuries he also enfolds a wealth of historical material about earlier periods.

24. Ferdinand Coronil, "After Empire: Reflections on Imperialism from the Américas," in *Imperial Formations*, ed. Ann Laura Stoler, Carole McGranahan, and Peter C. Perdue (Santa Fe, NM: School for Advanced Research Press, 2007), 244.

25. Coronil, "After Empire," 260, 259.

26. See Immanuel Wallerstein, "World System versus World-Systems: A Critique," in *The World System: Five Hundred Years or Five Thousand?*, ed. Andre Gunder Frank and Barry K. Gills (New York: Routledge, 1993), 293–94. For a useful critique and adjustment of world-systems analysis that focuses on the multivectored trade and state histories of the Arabian Seas, see Barendse, "Trade and State in the Arabian Seas."

27. This bias is especially clear in in his dismissal of the role of postcolonial states in international politics. In his closing chapters Wight deems any triangle that would include "third world" states of the twentieth century, as "false triangles"; see Martin Wight, *Systems of States*, ed. Hedley Bull (Leicester: Leicester University Press, 1977), 176.

28. Wight, *Systems of States*, 89.

29. Wight, *Systems of States*, 73–109, 180–81.

30. See Michael Mann, *The Sources of Social Power*, vol. 1, *A History of Power from the Beginning to AD 1760*, 190. Mann's trilogy offers rich material and theorizing about dialectics in the longue durée in its focus on the interactions of state, economic, ideological, and military power. I don't treat military power, though it certainly could be integrated into an inter-imperial framework. For analysis of later periods, see Mann, *The Sources of Social Power*, vol. 2, *The Rise of Classes and Nation-States, 1760–1914* (New York: Cambridge University Press, 1993); and Mann, *The Sources of Social Power*, vol. 3, *Global Empires and Revolution, 1890–1945* (New York: Cambridge University Press, 2012).

31. T. J. Barfield, "The Shadow Empires: Imperial State Formation along the Chinese-Nomad Frontier," in *Empires: Perspectives from Archaeology and History*, ed. Susan Alcock, Terence N. D'Altroy, Kathleen D. Morrison, and Carla Sinopoli (Cambridge: Cambridge University Press, 2001), 10–41; also see Jerry Bentley, "Hemispheric Integration, 500–1500 C.E.," *Journal of World History* 9, no. 2 (1998): 237–54.

32. Chase-Dunn et al., "Growth/Decline Phases"; and Brian Sandberg, "Beyond Encounters: Religion, Ethnicity, and Violence in the Early Modern Atlantic World, 1492–1700," *Journal of World History* 17, no. 1 (2006): 1–25. On the latter point also see Chaudhuri, *Asia before Europe*, 89.

33. See John LeDonne, *The Russian Empire and the World, 1700–1917: The Geopolitics of Expansion and Containment* (New York: Oxford University Press, 1997), 23–37. Although there have sometimes been genuine historical affiliations between a foreign state and its "client" community in another state, such sponsoring relations cannot but be inflected with geopolitical tensions, especially insofar as they provide leverage for influence.

34. This analysis expands on Pieterse's insights into the dialectics of "empire and emancipation" (Jan P. N. Pieterse, *Empire and Emancipation: Power and Liberation on a World Scale* [New York: Praeger, 1989]), and it shares a spirit with James C. Scott's work (*Weapons of the Weak: Everyday Forms of Peasant Resistance* [New Haven, CT: Yale University Press, 1985]; *Domination and the Arts of Resistance* [New Haven, CT: Yale University Press, 1990]; *The Art of Not Being Governed: An Anarchist History of Upland Southeast Asia* [New Haven, CT: Yale University Press, 2009]). Also see William Wertheim, "The State and the Dialectics of Emancipation," *Development and Change* 23, no. 3 (1992): 257–81.

35. See Dušan T. Bataković, "The 1804 Serbian Revolution: A Balkan-Size French Revolution," paper presented at the AAASS, Boston, December 2004. In 1805, Serbian leader Count Tekelija wrote simultaneously to Napoleon I and Emperor Franz of Austria to make a case for this Illyrian state, which, he claimed, would stabilize the region for them. As Dušan T. Bataković points out, in his letter to the French emperor Tekelija named Austria and Russia as threatening rival powers, but in his very similar letter to the Austrian emperor, he mentions only Russia.

36. The coformations of religion, states, and economy deserve more attention than I can give them here. See, for instance, Tansen Sen, *Buddhism, Diplomacy, and Trade: The Realignment of India-China Relations, 600–1400* (Lanham, MD: Rowman and Littlefield, 2016); and for an analysis that also encompasses infrastructure (specifically fort building), see Andrew Peterson, "The Ottoman Ḥajj Route in Jordan: Motivation and Ideology," *Bulletin d'études orientales* 57 (2008): 31–50.

37. For an overview of this history, see Amira K. Bennison, *The Great Caliphs: The Golden Age of the Abbasid Empire* (New Haven, CT: Yale University Press, 2009).

38. See Abu-Lughod, *Before European Hegemony*, 217–24; and Bennison, *Great Caliphs*, chapter 1 (10–53) and throughout the book. The discontent of less elite members of the Persian Empire also played a crucial role, for the Umayyad Caliphate had enforced second-class citizenship for most non-Arabs, even many who had converted, excluding them from

government posts and intermarriage with Arab women. They had also executed many Persian Zoroastrian clergy members and instituted an Arabization program that restricted the use of Persian. Thus, by the early eighth century, a range of populations in conquered Sassanian territories had grown resentful of Umayyad rule and some had attempted to revolt, which then gave leverage to the Abbasids. Apparently the Barmakids' founding of a private militia eventually provoked suspicion, which led the caliph Harun al-Rashid to execute many of the Barmakid family.

39. See James Dickie, "Granada: A Case Study of Arab Urbanism in Muslim Spain," in *The Legacy of Muslim Spain*, ed. Salma Khadra Jayyusi and Manuela Marín (Boston: Brill, 1994), 19.

40. On "differentiated governance," see Burbank and Cooper, *Empires in World History*, 9. For related discussion, see essays in Lavan, Payne, and Weisweiler, *Cosmopolitanism and Empire*. Many empires have followed policies of multicultural "tolerance." Several Chinese dynasties tolerated and occasionally incorporated Buddhist practices; and many Islamicate empires (including the Abbasid and the Ottoman) also favored policies of tolerance of religious and other customs in incorporated territories, although usually with a lower status and limited legal or property rights. Christian empires have typically enforced religious and cultural homogeneity yet there have also been exceptions, as I discuss here in relation to Russia. These cases suggest that Christian forms of empire were not inherently driven by a proselytizing drive but rather that politics, expediency, and location played a role. We might also recall here that Milton pointed to the Ottoman Empire as a model of the "liberal" form of state (Nabil Matar, *Islam in Britain, 1558–1685* [Cambridge: Cambridge University Press, 1998], 87), and Voltaire praised the Chinese Empire as a model of multiconfessional as well as rational structures, critiquing European empire builders for their obsessive commitment to religious conversion (J. J. Clarke, *Oriental Enlightenment: The Encounter between Asian and Western Thought* [New York: Routledge, 1997], 3).

41. Burbank and Cooper, *Empires in World History*, 80–84. These formations created a "multiplicity of 'we's' and 'they's'," as Adeeb Khalid puts it ("The Soviet Union as an Imperial Formation: A View from Central Asia," in *Imperial Formations*, ed. Ann Laura Stoler, Carole McGranahan, and Peter C. Perdue [Santa Fe, NM: School for Advanced Research Press, 2007], 115). Also see Steven L. Hoch "The Serf Economy, the Peasant Family, and the Social Order," in *Imperial Russia: New Histories for the Empire*, ed. Jane Burbank and David Ransel (Bloomington: Indiana University Press, 1998), 199–209; and Willard Sunderland, "An Empire of Peasants: Empire-building, Interethnic Interaction, and Ethnic Stereotyping in the Rural World of the Russian Empire, 1800–1850s," in *Imperial Russia: New Histories for the Empire*, ed. Jane Burbank and David Ransel (Bloomington: Indiana University Press, 1998), 174–98.

42. Jane Burbank, "The Rights of Difference: Law and Citizenship in the Russian Empire," in *Imperial Formations*, ed. Ann Laura Stoler, Carole McGranahan, and Peter C. Perdue (Santa Fe, NM: School for Advanced Research Press, 2007), 80.

43. Khalid, "Soviet Union," 115–16.

44. Burbank, "Rights of Difference," 98.

45. Burbank, "Rights of Difference," 102.

46. See the corpus of work by Ann Laura Stoler, beginning with *Carnal Knowledge and Imperial Power: Race and the Intimate in Colonial Rule* (Berkeley: University of California Press, [2002] 2010). Also see Ida Blom, Karen Hagemann, and Catherine Hall, eds., *Gendered Nations: Nationalisms and Gender Order in the Long Nineteenth Century* (New York: Berg, 2000); and Andrew Parker, Mary Russo, Doris Sommer, and Patricia Yaeger, eds., *Nationalisms and Sexualities* (New York: Routledge, 1992). For a broad range of studies, see Georgina Waylen, Karen Celis, Johanna Kantola, and S. Laurel Weldon, eds. *The Oxford Handbook of Gender and Politics* (New York: Oxford University Press, 2013).

47. See, for instance, Wendy Belcher, *The Life and Struggles of Our Mother Walatta Petros: A Seventeenth-Century African Biography of an Ethiopian Woman* (Princeton, NJ: Princeton University Press, 2015); and her work-in-progress, *The Black Queen of Sheba: A Global History of an African Idea.* On lesbian sexuality in earlier periods and outside of Europe, see for instance Sahar Amer, "Medieval Arab Lesbians and Lesbian-Like Women," *Journal of the History of Sexuality* 18, no. 2 (2009): 215–36.

48. See Leslie Peirce, *Morality Tales: Law and Gender in the Ottoman Court of Aintab* (Berkeley: University of California Press, 2003). Chatterjee's comments appear in the forum on Peirce's book in the *Journal of Women's History* 18, no. 1 (2006): 181–96. See Chatterjee's contribution, "Between West and South: Asianist Women's History and Islam," 192–96. Patricia Skinner's contribution is also valuable: "Morality Tales: A Medieval Inheritance," 186–91. For researchers interested in this line of thought, browsing in this journal, by region or keywords, would be one good first step.

49. See Antoinette Burton, "The Body in/as World History," in *A Companion to World History*, ed. Douglas Northrup (Chichester, UK: Wiley-Blackwell, 2012), 272–84; and Louise Yelin, "Globalizing Subjects," *Signs* 29, no. 2 (2004): 439–64, part of a special issue, "Development Cultures: New Environments, New Realities, New Strategies," edited by Françoise Lionnet, Obioma Nnaemeka, Susan H. Perry, and Celeste Schenck.

50. Lavan, Payne, and Weisweiler, *Cosmopolitanism and Empire*, 10–11. The collection's index includes a single pertinent entry related to any form of dissent—"rebellion"—which refers to one sentence in the editors' introductory essay ("Cosmopolitan Politics: The Assimilation and Subordination," 16). Tamara Chin's essay in the volume ("What Is Imperial Cosmopolitanism? Revisiting *Kosmopolites* and *Mundanus*," 129–52) does, however, address dissent in its focus on the *discourse* of dissent and critique in one philosopher, and Chin accordingly gives close attention to the problems of translation and language both for empires and for scholars studying them.

51. Despite attention to "incorporation" and assimilation of elites and to the preservation of "ethno-elite" classes, none of the essays focuses on the marriage practices that would have been necessary to regulate and direct such stratified forms of strategic incorporation. On mixed marriages, see Christelle Fischer-Bovet's essay, "Toward a Translocal Elite Culture in the Ptolemaic Empire," in *Cosmopolitanism and Empire*, ed. Lavan, Payne, and Weisweiler, 103–28, esp. 125. For brief discussion of masculinity as it is linked to climactic theories

of ethnicity, see John Weisweiler, "From Empire to World State," in *Cosmopolitanism and Empire*, ed. Lavan, Payne, and Weisweiler, 187–208, esp. 201–4.

52. See Yaqing Qin, *A Relational Theory of World Politics* (Cambridge: Cambridge University Press, 2018), 232. The book's top-down, Confucian, managerial approach lacks any substantive attention to dissent and intersectional issues. Although it purports to theorize a "relational" approach to world politics, it mainly dresses the old imperial wolf in sheep's clothing.

53. See blurbs on the back of Yaqing Qin's book; these praiseful assessments were written by Barry Buzan and Amitav Acharya, respectively.

54. Braudel, *Civilization and Capitalism*, 22.

55. Beaujard, "Indian Ocean," 459; Philippe Beaujard, *Les Mondes se l'ocean indien* (Paris: Armand Colin, 2012).

56. Beaujard, "Indian Ocean," 457–58.

57. For these two passages, see, respectively, Abu-Lughod, *Before European Hegemony*, 320; and Bentley, "Hemispheric Integration," 241.

58. See Abu-Lughod, *Before European Hegemony*, 224; and Maya Shatzmiller, "Economic Growth and Economic Performance in the Early Islamic World," *Journal of the Economic and Social History of the Orient* 54 (2011): 132–84. Also see Abraham Udovitch, *Partnership and Profit in Medieval Islam* (Princeton, NJ: Princeton University Press, 1970), 78, 80.

59. On suftaja and commenda as well as on other kinds of capitalist financing, see Abu-Lughod, *Before European Hegemony*, 220–21; and Udovitch, *Partnership and Profit*, 170. On military wages, see Hugh Kennedy, "Military Pay and the Economy of the Early Islamic State," *Historical Research* 75, no. 188 (2002): 155–69.

60. See Abu-Lughod, *Before European Hegemony*, 217–24. For other scholarship on world-system formations in in diverse regions from ancient to modern, see Christopher K. Chase-Dunn and Thomas D. Hall, *Rise and Demise: Comparing World Systems* (Boulder, CO: Westview Press, 1997); Frank and Gills, *World System*; Gills and Thompson, *Globalization and Global History*; and P. Nick Kardulias, ed., *World-Systems Theory in Practice: Leadership, Production, and Exchange* (Lanham, MD: Rowman and Littlefield, 1999).

61. Looking even further back, Michael Mann has shown that ancient imperial states of Mesopotamia "helped create accumulation processes," and he argues that they participated in the "dialectic of development" (Mann, *Sources of Social Power*, 1:148–50, 1:174–76).

62. See D'Altroy, *Incas*, throughout, on these arrangements; and on roads in particular see Wilkinson, "Infrastructure and Inequality."

63. For these phrases, see Edmund Burke III, "Islam at the Center: Technological Complexes and the Roots of Modernity," *Journal of World History* 20, no. 2 (2009): 166–68. Chase-Dunn and Hall have argued that trade of any kind also promotes hierarchical labor and class formations. See Chase-Dunn and Hall, *Rise and Demise*, 13–14. In this they agree with Schneider and disagree with Wallerstein. See their article for references to the latter.

Also see Ando and Richardson, *Ancient States*, esp. chapters 3 and 4, on how some states needed labor more than land.

64. See Shatzmiller, "Economic Growth," 150–53, for slave trade numbers. For discussion of the flood plain *labirs*, see Bennison, *Great Caliphs*, 27, 146.

65. Laura Doyle, ed., "Labor Travels, Art Forms," special issue, *Literature Compass* 13, no. 5 (2016).

66. Abu-Lughod, *Before European Hegemony*, 324.

67. See Beaujard, "Indian Ocean," 449; also see Bentley, "Hemispheric Integration," 241–45; D'Altroy, *Incas*, 5, 315, 363; and Shatzmiller, "Economic Growth," 166. In "Trade and State in the Arabian Seas," Barendse also usefully establishes the importance of agricultural and staples products in early trade (207).

68. Anne F. Broadbridge, *Women and the Making of the Mongol Empire* (Cambridge: Cambridge University Press, 2018).

69. On the extent and varieties of women's capture and enslavement, see Gwyn Campbell, Suzanne Miers, and Joseph C. Millers, *Women and Slavery*, vols. 1 and 2 (Columbus: Ohio University Press, 2007).

70. For a range of studies on infrastructures, see Alcock, D'Altroy, Morrison, and Sinopoli, eds. *Empires*; Burbank and Cooper, *Empires in World History*; Morris and Scheidel, *Dynamics of Ancient Empires*; and Pomeranz, "Social History." Also see Darryl Wilkinson's important theoretical discussion about the different kinds of investment in infrastructure building, ranging from cosmogenic to exploitative: Wilkinson, "Infrastructure and Inequality."

71. On Moche metallurgy, see Heather Lechtman, "Andean Value Systems and the Development of Prehistoric Metallurgy," *Technology and Culture* 25 (1984): 1–36; and for wider discussion of these artisanal histories, see D'Altroy, *Incas*, 51–52.

72. At the same time, as Wilkinson notes, it's important to keep in mind, as in the case of Incan road builders, that the meanings of labor for the laborers can diverge from their meanings for empire builders, including in terms of cosmogenic meanings. See Wilkinson, "Infrastructure and Inequality," 28–31, 37–41.

73. See Bryce Beemer, "Bangkok, Creole City: War Slaves, Refugees, and the Transformation of Culture in Urban Southeast Asia," *Literature Compass* 13, no. 5 (2016): 266–76.

74. See Burke, "Islam at the Center," 165, 175; and Hobson, "Is Critical Theory," 109. Also see John M. Hobson, "Provincializing Westphalia: The Eastern Origins of Sovereignty," *International Politics* 46 (2009): 671–90.

75. Burke, "Islam at the Center," 170. Burke focuses on Mesopotamian and Middle Eastern regions, yet archeologists have also studied the Americas, as discussed below, and other regions. See the important work of Vernon L. Scarborough on the link between ancient water systems and centralized societies in his important book, *The Flow of Power: Ancient Water Systems and Landscapes* (Santa Fe, NM: School of American Research Press, 2003); and his thoughtful discussion of Liangzhu culture (3300–4300 BP) in "The Hydraulic Lift

of Early States Societies," *Proceedings of the National Academy of Sciences of the United States of America* 114, no. 52 (2017): 13600–1.

76. Burke, "Islam at the Center," 169–73.

77. Andrew Watson, *Agricultural Innovation in the Early Islamic World* (Cambridge: Cambridge University Press, 1983).

78. For revision of Watson, see Michael Decker, "Plants and Progress: Rethinking the Islamic Agricultural Revolution," *Journal of World History* 20, no. 2 (2009): 187–206. See Burke, "Islam at the Center," 174, for modified assessment of the effects.

79. Burke, "Islam at the Center," 175.

80. Brian Bauer, *The Development of the Inca State* (Austin: University of Texas Press, 1992); D'Altroy, *Incas*; and MacCormack, *On the Wings of Time*. Also see studies that highlight the European colonization of the Americas as pivotal in world history and political economy, for example, Aníbal Quijano and Immanuel Maurice Wallerstein, "Americanity as a Concept; or, The Americas in the Modern World-System," *International Social Science Journal* 134 (1992): 549–57.

81. Kenneth Pomeranz, *The Great Divergence: China, Europe, and the Making of the Modern World Economy* (Princeton, NJ: Princeton University Press, 2000).

82. Some have productively postulated multiple modernities or alternative modernities; see Dilip Parameshwar Gaonkar, ed., *Alternative Modernities* (Durham, NC: Duke University Press, 2001); and Masoud Kamali, *Multiple Modernities, Civil Society, and Islam: The Case of Iran and Turkey* (Liverpool: University of Liverpool Press, 2006). But I am increasingly inclined to think in terms of connected, intensifying processes of "modernization" that ramify distinctively in each site.

83. See Scarborough, "The Hydraulic Lift," 13601. Also see Scarborough, *The Flow of Power*.

84. Here I supplement Mann's point about ancient states, which he says displayed "a dialectic between centralizing and decentralizing forces, powerful imperial states and private-property classes" (Mann, *Sources of Social Power*, 1:175–76).

85. The body of work on African syncretism in the Americas is too vast to cite here, but one key seminal text is Lawrence Levine, *Black Culture and Black Consciousness: Afro-American Folk Thought from Slavery to Freedom* (New York: Oxford University Press, 1977). For a later overview and extension of this work see Babacar M'Baye, *The Trickster Comes West: Pan African Influence in Early Black Diasporan Narratives* (Jackson: University of Mississippi Press, 2009). On Thailand and the tradition of *yikay sipsong phasa*, see Beemer, "Bangkok, Creole City."

86. Braudel, *Civilization and Capitalism*, 71.

87. In commenting on trade in the fifteenth- and sixteenth-century Mediterranean world, Fernand Braudel observed, for instance, that when "merchant vessels sailed across [the Mediterranean] everyday" they "ignored the frontiers of empires" (*Civilization and Capital-*

ism, 22). It seems more likely, however, that no one could ignore the frontiers of empire, whether trader or laborer, man or woman. In the sixteenth-century Mediterranean world, monitoring states would have included the rapidly expanding Ottoman Empire as well as Spanish, Italian, Middle Eastern, and North African states. In this setting, we might imagine, traders would have carefully abided by or eluded imperial codes for port residency, and enslaved women would have eagerly sought out information about which imperial port they had entered, or which courts or ports to avoid, if possible. In other words, the analyses of both Braudel and Wallerstein can be enriched by direct attention to the structuring and multidimensional forces of *interacting and plural* imperial economies and their inhabitants, including both before and after the entry of western European states.

Giancarlo Casale reinforces this point in *The Ottoman Age of Exploration*: the Ottomans carefully built and administered their land-and-sea empire in this period, avidly commissioning both merchant and military vessels for its development, importing and transporting lumber across great distances to the shipbuilding ports, and actively defending and expanding its territory along the Red Sea and East African coast as well as the Mediterranean. Regardless of whether one agrees with Casale's implication that the Ottomans imagined their projects as grand schemes of "exploration," certainly that empire exercised its dominance in the Mediterranean world through financial and port rules, officially exacting taxes and forms of tribute from other empires, states, and agents doing business within its sphere of influence. Giancarlo Casale, *The Ottoman Age of Exploration* (New York: Oxford University Press, 2012).

88. Chaudhuri, *Asia before Europe*, 82.

89. See Mark E. Lewis, *Writing and Authority in Early China* (Albany, NY: SUNY Press, 1999); see pp 63–83 on the relation between scholar, state, and economy. Also see Denis Twitchett, *Printing and Publishing in Medieval China* (New York: Frederic C. Beil, 1983.)

90. See Thomas H. C. Lee, "Academies: Official Sponsorship and Suppression," in *Imperial Rulership and Cultural Change in Traditional China*, ed. Frederick P. Brandauer and Chun-Chieh Huang (Seattle: University of Washington Press, 1994), 117–43; and George Makdisi, *The Rise of Humanism in Classical Islam and the West* (Edinburgh: Edinburgh University Press, 1990). Also see the scholarship on viziers in chapter 2.

91. Amir Said Arjomand, "Law, Agency, and Policy in Medieval Islamic Society: Development of the Institutions of Learning from the Tenth to the Fifteenth Century," *Comparative Studies in Society and History* 41, no. 2 (1999): 285–86.

92. See Jonathan M. Bloom, *Paper before Print: The History and Impact of Paper in the Islamic World* (New Haven, CT: Yale University Press, 2001), esp. 117–19.

93. Bloom, *Paper before Print*, 117.

94. See Richard E. Payne, "Iranian Cosmopolitanism: World Religions at the Sasanian Court," in *Cosmopolitanism and Empire: Universal Rulers, Local Elites, and Cultural integration in the Ancient Near East and Mediterranean*, ed. Miles Lavan, Richard E. Payne, and John Weisweiler (New York: Oxford University Press, 2016), 209–30, esp. 215–16. It was under Husraw I for instance that *Panchatantra* was translated from Sanskrit into Middle

Persian, and his patronage also supported translations from Latin, Greek, and other Asian languages, including astronomy and other scientific texts.

95. On Japan, see Joan R. Piggott, *The Emergence of Japanese Kingship* (Stanford, CA: Stanford University Press, 1997).

96. Bloom, *Paper before Print*, 118–22.

97. Gerald MacLean, *Looking East: English Writing and the Ottoman Empire before 1800* (New York: Palgrave, 2007), 20–23.

98. See Mercedes García-Arenal and Fernando Rodríguez Mediano, "Sacred History, Sacred Languages: The Question of Arabic in Early Modern Spain," in *The Teaching and Learning of Arabic in Early Modern Europe*, ed. Jan Loop, Alastair Hamilton, Charles Burnett (Leiden: Brill, 2017), 133–62; see 136.

99. See D'Altroy, *Incas*, 22.

100. Burke, "Islam at the Center," 183–84.

101. Although Europeans make much of Gutenberg's invention of the printing press, it must be noted that, as with many scientific inventions, the ground had been laid by others, including the Chinese and Koreans. On the rise of early woodblock printing and the development of movable type (including Johannes Gutenberg's exposure to this technology before 1456), see Joseph Needham, *Science and Civilization in China*, vol. 5, part 1 (New York: Cambridge University Press, 1985); and Tsien Tsuen-Hsuin, *Paper and Printing* (Cambridge: Cambridge University Press, 1985), 201–22, 313–19.

102. On the ubiquity of the IR Westphalian narrative, see Hobson, "Provincializing Westphalia." As Hobson also argues elsewhere, this Eurocentric narrative not only frames institutional, classical, and neorealist IR but also circulates residually in the work of Marxist, feminist, transnational, and other scholars in Critical International Relations Theory (CIRT). See Hobson, "Is Critical Theory Always for the White West and for Western Imperialism? Beyond Westphilian towards a Post-Racist Critical IR," *Review of International Studies* 33, S1 (2007): 91–116. Implicitly this reigning narrative perpetuates blind spots and anti-African perspectives even among some pioneering scholars, as Jan Nederveen Pieterse points out in his review of Jack Goody, *Renaissances: The One or the Many?* (Cambridge: Cambridge University Press, 2010). See Pieterse, "Many Renaissances, Many Modernities?," *Theory, Culture and Society* 28, no. 3 (2011): 149–60. For Pieterse's discussion of Goody, see 150–51.

103. John B. Thompson, *The Media and Modernity: A Social Theory of the Media* (Stanford, CA: Stanford University Press, 1995), 57.

104. See Thompson, *Media and Modernity*, 57, on Martin Luther and translation, and 63–71, for discussion of newspapers and pamphlets in the English revolution against the Stuarts. Also see Laura Doyle, *Freedom's Empire: Race and the Rise of the Novel in Atlantic Modernity, 1640–1940* (Durham, NC: Duke University Press, 2008), esp. chapter 1.

105. Sean Foley, "Muslims and Social Change in the Atlantic Basin," *Journal of World History* 20, no. 3 (2009): 377–98.

106. See Foley, "Muslims and Social Change," 385. On capitalism, see Kerem Nisancioglu, "The Ottoman Origins of Capitalism: Uneven and Combined Development and Eurocentrism," *Review of International Studies* 40, no. 2 (2014): 325–47. More generally one might argue that if the Dutch and English mercantile states were central to the rise of capitalism, and capitalism was formative in modern "Westphalian" states, then Ottoman and African states played specific geopolitical roles in the world's "modern" history. Foley elaborates his point as follows: "when[ever] Ottoman armies appeared to threaten Europe—Protestant states in Germany refused to contribute soldiers or discuss funding wars against the Ottomans with Catholic Hapsburg officials before all internal religious issues had been resolved" (Foley, "Muslims and Social Change," 386). More directly, the Dutch victory against the Hapsburgs in 1609 depended in significant part on Ottoman alliance and military support (as when the Ottomans declined to honor the Spanish embargo). As Nabil Matar and Linda Colley have also traced, Queen Elizabeth undertook calculated inter-imperial maneuvering, balancing relations with the Ottoman regencies of Libya, Tunisia, and Algeria on the one hand and the powerful independent kingdom of Morocco on the other hand. See Nabil Matar, *Britain and Barbary, 1589–1689* (Gainesville: University of Florida Press, 2005); and Linda Colley, *Captives: Britain, Empire, and the World, 1600–1850* (New York: Anchor Books, 2002).

107. Quoted in Matar, *Islam in Britain*, 87. On this point, also see MacLean, *Looking East*; and Gerald MacLean, "Milton, Islam and the Ottomans," in *Milton and Toleration*, ed. Sharon Achinstein and Elizabeth Sauer (Oxford: Oxford University Press, 2007), 299–304.

108. See Glynn Anderson, "Sovereignty and the Materiality of Caliphal Encounters," PMLA 130, no. 2 (2015): 393–401, for discussion of the inscriptions of sovereignty as a concept in early Islamicate states. On European methods of diplomacy as formed in interactions with the Ottoman Empire, see Daniel Goffman, "Negotiating with the Renaissance State: The Ottoman Empire and the New Diplomacy," in *The Early Modern Ottomans: Remapping the Empire*, ed. Virginia H. Aksan and Daniel Goffman (Cambridge: Cambridge University Press, 2007), 61–74. On coffeehouses, see Gerald MacLean (*Looking East*, 58), who makes this point with respect to Jürgen Habermas's argument in *The Structural Transformation of the Public Sphere: An Inquiry into a Category of Bourgeois Society*, trans. Thomas Burger (Cambridge, MA: MIT Press, [1962] 1989), 32–43. For additional recontextualizations of the "modern" values typically thought to originate wholly from Anglo-European traditions or character, see Clarke, *Oriental Enlightenment*; and Yu Liu, *Seeds of a Different Eden: Chinese Gardening and a New English Aesthetic Ideal* (Columbia: University of South Carolina Press, 2008). On other Muslim influences on Anglo-Atlantic political thought, see Foley, "Muslims and Social Change," 390–91; and on Mediterranean contests that catalyzed discourses of rights and freedom, see Gillian Weiss, "Barbary Captivity and the French Idea of Freedom," *French Historical Studies* 28, no. 2 (2005): 231–64.

109. See, respectively, Paul A. Kramer, "Empires, Exceptions, and Anglo-Saxons: Race and Rule between the British and United States Empires, 1880–1910," *Journal of American History* 88, no. 4 (2002): 1315; and Stoler, McGranahan, and Perdue, *Imperial Formations*, 14.

110. See Suzanne Conklin Akbari and Karla Mallette, eds., *A Sea of Languages: Rethinking the Arabic Role in Medieval Literary History* (Toronto: University of Toronto Press, 2013).

Akbari and Mallette are among the scholars detailing the political field in which literary formations emerged, and my arguments here draw on their work.

111. Below I cite specific studies. More generally, see Geraldine Heng, *Empire of Magic: Medieval Romance and the Politics of Cultural Fantasy* (New York: Columbia University Press, 2003) and *The Invention of Race in the European Middle Ages* (New York: Cambridge University Press, 2018); and Candace Barrington and Jonathan Hsy, "Editors' Introduction: Chaucer's Global Orbits and Global Communities," *Literature Compass* 15, no. 6 (2018): 1–12. Also see the discussion and notes in chapter 3 on the influence of *The Thousand and One Nights*.

112. For earlier studies of these exchanges and influences, see Américo Castro, *The Structure of Spanish History*, trans. Edmund L. King (Princeton, NJ: Princeton University Press, 1954); Dorothee Metlitzki, *The Matter of Araby in Medieval England* (New Haven, CT: Yale University Press, 1977); Maria Rosa Menocal, *The Arabic Role in Medieval Literary History* (Philadelphia: University of Pennsylvania Press, 1987); and Alois Richard Nykl, *Hispano-Arabic Poetry and Its Relations with the Old Provençal Troubadours* (Baltimore: Literary Licensing, 1946). Also see Makdisi, *Rise of Humanism*. On earlier denials and debates over what was sometimes called the "arabist theory" of Eastern influences on medieval European literature, see Roger Boase, *The Origin and Meaning of Courtly Love* (Manchester: Manchester University Press, 1977). For two quite different recent examples of the coforming relations between Arabic-Islamicate and European-Christian literary-political cultures, see Gregory B. Stone, *Dante's Pluralism and the Islamic Philosophy of Religion* (New York: Macmillan Palgrave, 2006); and Sahar Amer, *Crossing Borders: Love between Women in Medieval French and Arabic Literatures* (Philadelphia: University of Pennsylvania Press, 2008).

See notes below for a wide range of scholarship on the Afro-Eurasian influences on western Europe since the twelfth century, including public-sphere and court culture as well as philosophy, science, art, and literature. For an overview of this scholarship, see Laura Doyle, "Notes toward a Dialectical Method: Modernities, Modernisms, and the Crossings of Empire," *Literature Compass* 7, no. 3 (2010): 201–6. In addition to the scholars I name below, Goody points to diverse locations and sources of a "renaissance" in the middle of the second millennium, but his account is in some ways still inflected by Eurocentrism and it misrepresents African cultural formations; Goody, *Renaissances*. See review by Jan Nederveen Pieterse, "Many Renaissances, Many Modernities?," *Theory, Culture and Society* 28, no. 3 (2011): 149–60; and specifically for Pieterse's discussion of Goody, see 150–51.

113. John Harvey, "Corony Flowers and Their 'Arabick' Background," in *The "Arabick" Interests of the Natural Philosophers in Seventeenth-Century England*, ed. Gul A. Russell, (Leiden: Brill, 1994), 297.

114. For discussion of these men and others, see Harvey, "Corony Flowers and Their 'Arabick' Background," 297–303. For the quote from Daniel Morley, see Charles Burnett, *The Introduction of Arabic Learning into England* (London: British Library, 1997), 60–61. His study originated as the 1996 Panizzi Lectures.

115. See Stone, *Dante's Pluralism and the Islamic Philosophy of Religion*, 15–53.

116. For an account of both Chaucer and the field of literary of interactions in this period, see the introduction to the 2018 special issue of *Literature Compass* on Chaucer (Barrington and Hsy, eds., "Chaucer's Global Orbits and Global Communities"). On Chaucer in Italy, see David Wallace, *Chaucerian Polity: Absolutist Lineages and Associational Forms in England and Italy* (Stanford, CA: Stanford University Press, 1997). For an early, rich analysis of the influence of Arabic-language thought as well as literary forms on Chaucer and others, see Katharine Slater Gittes, "*The Canterbury Tales* and the Arabic Frame Tradition," PMLA 98, no. 2 (1983): 237–51. For a full study of Eastern sources in Chaucer, see Carol Heffernan, *The Orient in Chaucer and the Medieval Romance* (Rochester, NY: D. S. Brewer, 2003). For broader analysis of languages and genres as influenced by Mediterranean and other cross-cultural encounters, see for instance Akbari and Mallette, *Sea of Languages*; and John M. Ganim and Shayne Aaron Legassie, eds., *Cosmopolitanism and the Middle Ages* (New York: Palgrave Macmillan, 2013).

117. For extensive discussion of Dante's *Comedy*, see Stone, *Dante's Pluralism and the Islamic Philosophy of Religion*. For a multiauthor study that includes Dante, see Menocal, *Arabic Role*. For other multiauthor studies, see the following: Metlitzki, *Matter of Araby*; Amer, *Crossing Borders*; Sahar Amer, *Ésope au féminin: Marie de France et la politique de l'interculturalité* (Amsterdam: Rodopi, 1999); Sahar Amer, "Reading Medieval French Literature from a Global Perspective," PMLA 130, no. 2 (2015): 367–74; Maria Bullon-Fernandez, ed., *England and Iberia in the Middle Ages, 12th–15th Century: Cultural, Literary, and Political Exchanges* (New York: Palgrave Macmillan, 2007); Peter Caracciolo, ed., *The Arabian Nights in English* (New York: St. Martin's Press, 1988); Geraldine Heng, *Empire of Magic: Medieval Romance and the Politics of Cultural Fantasy* (New York: Columbia University Press, 2003); Karla Mallette, *European Modernity and the Arab Mediterranean: Toward a New Philology and a Counter-Orientalism* (Philadelphia: University of Pennsylvania Press, 2010); and Cynthia Robinson, *In Praise of Song: The Making of Courtly Culture in al-Andalus and Provence, 1005–1134 A.D.* (Boston: Brill, 2002).

118. For Ezra Pound on the troubadours, see *The Spirit of Romance* (Norfolk, CT: New Directions, [1910] 1932). For Pascale's arguments, see Pascale Casanova, *The World Republic of Letters*, trans. M. B. DeBevoise (Cambridge, MA: Harvard University Press, 2007). In sharp contrast to Pound, Geraldine Heng has recently argued that the genre of romance arose from the European need to mediate and justify the Crusades. Her approach exemplifies the very different, more politically grounded literary criticism of recent years. See Heng, *Empire of Magic*.

119. See Walter Cohen, "The Rise of the Written Vernacular: Europe and Eurasia," PMLA 126 (2011): 719–29.

120. Maria Menocal proposes that the muwashshahât influenced the rise of European vernaculars (Menocal, *Arabic Role*, 24–29). Yet literary historians of this period agree that evidence of direct influence is hard to gather, especially since differences in alphabetic script between European and Arabic make the task more challenging, and there is little manuscript evidence of direct translations of Arabic literature into European languages. Yet as Sahar Amer has argued, there are ways to track and analyze these encounters other than

through a model of direct influence or translation. She proposes that scholars focus less on wholesale translations and borrowings than on piecemeal and quiet formal influences, as she has done in tracing the presence of individual episodes from *The Thousand and One Nights* in French medieval literature. See Amer Sahar, *Ésope au féminin: Marie de France et la politique de l'interculturalité* (Amsterdam: Rodopi Press, 1999). For other rich studies of literary coformations and their political contexts, see Lutz Richter-Bernburg, "Linguistic Shu'ūbīya and Early Neo-Persian Prose," *Journal of the American Oriental Society* 94, no. 1 (1974): 55–64; Luce López-Baralt, "The Secret Literature of the Last Muslims of Spain," *Islamic Studies* 36, no. 1 (1997): 21–38; Robert W. Felkel, "The Theme of Love in the 'Mozarabic Jarchas' and in 'Cante Flamenco,'" *Confluencia* 4, no. 1 (1988): 23–40; Eleazar Birnbaum, "The Ottomans and Chagatay Literature: An Early 16th Century Manuscript of Navā'ī's Dīvān in Ottoman Orthography," *Central Asiatic Journal* 20, no. 3 (1976): 157–90; Linda T. Darling, "Political Literature and the Development of an Ottoman Imperial Culture in the Fifteenth Century," *Journal of the Ottoman and Turkish Studies Association* 1, nos. 1–2 (2014): 57–69; Timothy J. Fitzgerald, "Reaching the Flocks: Literacy and the Mass Reception of Ottoman Law in the Sixteenth-Century Arab World," *Journal of the Ottoman and Turkish Studies Association* 2, no. 1 (2015): 5–20; Mecdut Mansuroğlu, "The Rise and Development of Written Turkish in Anatolia," *Oriens* 7, no. 2 (1954): 250–64. I thank Professor Hayrettin Yücesoy for bringing these articles to my attention.

121. Cynthia Robinson establishes this point in *In Praise of Song*, 8. Also performed to musical accompaniment, these poetries are typically set in court gardens and they address a cruel or betraying lover, who is sometimes implicitly or explicitly the prince and patron, in tones that mix the political and the homoerotic. Robinson establishes that these poetries laid ground for the troubadour lyric poetry of Christian French Mediterranean courts, which likewise merged romantic and political registers.

122. See Lola Badia, Joan Santanach, and Albert Soler, *Ramon Llull as a Vernacular Writer: Communicating a New Kind of Knowledge* (Woodbridge, UK: Tamesis, 2016). Llull's hostile discourse about Muslim infidels may also have served to reassure the popes and monarchs that he was no infidel himself, despite his intimacy with Arabic-language learning. I thank my UMass colleague Professor Albert Lloret for bringing Llull to my attention.

123. Hayrettin Yücesoy, "Language of Empire: Politics of Arabic and Persian in the Abbasid World," *PMLA* 130, no. 2 (2015): 384–92. For other studies of the ways that languages and literatures have been entangled with imperial projects and cultural coformations, see Birnbaum, Darling, and Fitzgerald. For studies of how this history has affected more recent literatures, see Annette Damayanti Lienau, "Reframing Vernacular Culture on Arabic Fault Lines: Bamba, Senghor, and Sembene's Translingual Legacies in French West Africa," *PMLA* 130, no. 2 (2015): 419–29; Lydia H. Liu, "Scripts in Motion: Writing as Imperial Technology, Past and Present," *PMLA* 130, no. 2 (2015): 375–83; Ben Tran, *Post-Mandarin: Masculinity and Aesthetic Modernity in Colonial Vietnam* (New York: Fordham University Press, 2017); Jason Frydman, *Sounding the Break: African American and Caribbean Routes of World Literature* (Charlottesville: University of Virginia Press, 2014); and Laura Doyle, ed. "Interimperiality," special issue, *Modern Fiction Studies* 64, no. 3 (2018).

124. Karla Mallette, *The Kingdom of Sicily, 1100–1250* (Philadelphia: University of Pennsylvania Press, 2005); see 4–7, as well as later discussion.

125. For discussion of comparable moves elsewhere, see Yücesoy, "Language of Empire." Also see Ben Tran's analysis in *Post-Mandarin* of the unexpected opportunities opened to Vietnamese writers when the French took power, demoted Mandarin, abolished the exclusionary examination system, and installed French as the language of state and learning, which allowed a wider range of Vietnamese, including women, to become educated authors.

126. See Paul Oppenheimer, *The Birth of the Modern Mind: Self, Consciousness, and the Invention of the Sonnet* (New York: Oxford University Press, 1989). Some critics of this argument about the "modern mind" have also suggested that the sonnet borrowed from popular Arabic forms, although again direct influence is hard to establish, as Mallette notes in *Kingdom of Sicily*, 75–78.

127. Natalie Zemon Davis, *Trickster Travels: A Sixteenth-Century Muslim between Worlds* (New York: Hill and Wang, 2006).

128. See essays in Laura Doyle, ed., "Labor Travels, Art Forms," special issues, *Literature Compass* 13, no. 5 (2016); and *Literature Compass* 17, no. 1 (2020).

Chapter 2: Refusing Labor's (Re)production in
The Thousand and One Nights

Parts of chapter 2 appeared in "Shahrazad's 1001 Mediations: Translation in the Interimperial Economy," in the special issue, "Translating Medieval Culture: A Global Gaze," *Parergon* 35, no. 2 (2018): 7–28.

1. I follow Haddawy's usage in spelling the names of the imperial husband and wife in the frame as "Shahrayar" and "Shahrazad," and likewise I follow him in referring to the "Sassanid Empire" rather than adopting the now-standard usage "Sassanian Empire."

2. This is Fernand Braudel's phrase, discussed in chapter 1. See Fernand Braudel, *Civilization and Capitalism, 15th–18th Centuries*, vol. 3, *The Perspective of the World*, trans. Siân Reynolds (New York: Harper and Row, [1979] 1984), 22.

3. The following list offers entry points into the immense range of work on this text. This chapter later cites from many of these works more specifically. I also wish to thank Professors Sahar Amer, Mazen Naous, and Johan Mathew for advising me about Arabic-language nuances in the text and sharing scholarly resources.

For historical work, see especially Muhsin J. al-Musawi, *The Islamic Context of "The Thousand and One Nights"* (New York: Columbia University Press, 2009); and Richard Hovannisian and George Sabagh, eds., *"The Thousand and One Nights" in Arabic Literature and Society* (New York: Cambridge University Press, 1997). Also see Hasan El-Shamy, *A Motif Index of "The Thousand and One Nights"* (Bloomington: Indiana University Press, 2006). For an early seminal literary history of the text's influence on English literature, see Muhsin Jassam Ali, *Scheherezade in England: A Study of Nineteenth-Century English Criticism of the "Arabian Nights"* (Washington, DC: Three Continents Press, 1979).

For important book-length studies situating the text across traditions and also address-ing its gender themes, see Sahar Amer, *Esope au féminin: Marie de France et la politique de l'interculturalité* (Amsterdam: Rodopi, 1999); Ros Ballaster, *Fabulous Orients: Fictions of the East in England, 1662–1785* (Oxford: Oxford University Press, 2005); Ferial J. Ghazoul, *Noc-turnal Poetics: "The Arabian Nights" in Comparative Context* (Cairo: American University in Cairo Press, 1996); and Bridget Orr, *Empire on the English Stage* (Cambridge: Cambridge University Press, 2001).

And for a range of recent critical perspectives, including both feminist and postcolonial, see the following collections: Peter Caracciolo, ed., *"The Arabian Nights" in English Litera-ture* (New York: St. Martin's Press, 1988); Susan Muaddi Darraj, ed., *Scheherazade's Legacy: Arab and Arab American Women on Writing* (London: Praeger, 2004); Saree Makdisi and Felicity Nussbaum, eds., *"The Arabian Nights" in Historical Context: Between East and West* (Oxford: Oxford University Press, 2009); Ulrich Marzolph, ed., *"The Arabian Nights" in Transnational Perspective* (Detroit: Wayne State University Press, 2007); and Yurkiko Ya-manka and Tetsuo Nishio, *"Arabian Nights" and Orientalism: Perspectives from East and West* (London: I. B. Tauris, 2006).

4. As parodied by James Joyce in *Ulysses*, ed. Hans Gabler (New York: Vintage, 1986), 2.390–94.

5. For details on transmission and textual history of *The Nights*, see the preface in Muhsin Mahdi, ed., *The Thousand and One Nights*, 3 vols. (Leiden: Brill, 1984–94). Professor Mahdi located a Syrian edition of the text in Baghdad, which he dated to the fourteenth century; and he unearthed references to *The Nights* by both a tenth-century Arabic-language his-torian and a tenth-century Baghdadi bookseller. He also confirmed that this was the ver-sion that Antoine Galland learned about from his Syrian acquaintance, Hanna Diab. Some scholars debate whether this manuscript dates to the fourteenth or fifteenth century. For arguments in favor of a fifteenth-century dating, see Heinz Grotzfeld, "The Age of the Galland Manuscript of *The Nights*: Numismatic Evidence for Dating a Manuscript?," in *The Arabian Nights Reader*, ed. Ulrich Marzolph (Detroit: Wayne State University Press, 2006), 105–21. For other discussions of textual history, see Madeline Dobie, "Translation in the Contact Zone: Antoine Galland's *Mille et une Nuits*: contes arabes," in *"The Arabian Nights" in Historical Context: Between East and West*, ed. Saree Makdisi and Felicity Nuss-baum (New York: Oxford University Press, 2009), 25–49; and Ulrich Marzolph, "The Per-sian *Nights*: Links between *Arabian Nights* and Iranian Culture," in *"The Arabian Nights" in Transnational Perspective* (Detroit: Wayne State University Press, 2007), 221–44.

6. The choice of title has sometimes gotten caught up in debates about the text's lineage, especially Persian versus Arabic. Galland titled his translation *Les mille et une nuits*, but by the end of the nineteenth century, many Europeans referred to the text as *Arabian Nights*. In the later twentieth century, Mahdi retained the fourteenth-century, Persian-associated title for his translation (*The Thousand and One Nights*), yet Husain Haddawy chose *Arabian Nights* for his now standard English translation. For some readers, these titles carry politi-cal resonance insofar as they seem to favor either Persian or Arabic affiliations. As I note later, these debates sometimes also carry traces of the inter-imperial competition I examine

here. In recent criticism, we may see this competition in what Ulrich Marzolph calls "ethnical" accounts of the Persian or the Arabic elements (and also of possible Indian or Greek influences). See Marzolph, "Persian *Nights*," 222–29. Also see Dobie, "Translation in the Contact Zone."

7. For helpful discussion of the complex cultural streams flowing into the text, see both Dobie, "Translation in the Contact Zone"; and Marzolph, "Persian *Nights*." For an intriguing deconstructive approach to the text's authorship, see Ibrahim Muhawi, "'Arabian Nights' and the Question of Authorship," *Journal of Arabic Literature* 36, no. 3 (2005): 323–37. In *Sheherazade through the Looking Glass* (New York: Routledge, 1999), Eva Sallis also pointed in this direction, with an emphasis on European translations.

8. Husain Haddawy, trans., *The Arabian Nights*, ed. Muhsin Mahdi (New York: Norton, 1990), 11; hereafter cited parenthetically in the text. One note about terminology in my discussion. The translation uses the word *king* as a translation for Shahrazad's husband Shahrayar, which has quaint connotations for many English-language readers. But in the Persian Empire the prefix *shah* typically indicated the emperor, or blood-related princes of the empire. It seems clear that this shah who rules over Persia in what the text specifically refers to as the era of the Sassanid dynasty and whose "power reached the remotest corners of the land and its people" is in fact an emperor, as is Harun al-Rashid, the Abbasid caliph who appears in many of the tales. We should therefore read the word *king* in these contexts as we would in the cases of, for example, King Louis XIV of France or Queen Victoria of England—that is, kings and queens who are emperors. I use the word *emperor* to keep this dimension in view.

9. The opening frame remains the same in all extant versions, beginning with the Arabic text, found in Baghdad and traced to Syria yet apparently extant in some form in tenth-century Abbasid Baghdad. See note 5 on the textual history. A few scholars have noted the text's anachronistic feature but usually only in passing. For one suggestive analysis of what he reads as simultaneous temporality, see Srinivas Aravamudan, "The Adventure Chronotope and the Oriental Xenotrope: Galland, Sheridan, and Joyce Domesticate *The Arabian Nights*," in *"The Arabian Nights" in Historical Context: Between East and West*, ed. Saree Makdisi and Felicity Nussbaum (Oxford: Oxford University Press, 2009), 235–63, esp. 240–45.

10. See al-Musawi, *Islamic Context*, 3, 23–25, 33–34.

11. See notes 5 and 6 regarding questions about the Persian and Arabic lineages of the texts.

12. In a neat indication of the intertwining of business, learning, sexuality, and empire in this period, this affair begins in the "shop" of the pharmacist Abu al-Hasan of Baghdad, himself of a man of "wealth and high status" who is "patronized by the sons of princes and notable men" (296).

13. Hayrettin Yücesoy, "Language of Empire: Politics of Arabic and Persian in the Abbasid World," *PMLA* 130, no. 2 (2015): 384–92.

14. I thank my colleague Professor Mazen Naous for pointing out these etymologies and ironies. Personal correspondence with the author, July 2015.

15. Although in an Arabic translation from about 750 CE the *Panchatantra* is attributed to a man called Bidpai, others have considered evidence that women contributed significantly—including perhaps the sister of the Persian emperor Darius. See Marzolph, "Persian *Nights*," 223.

16. Samuel Butler, *The Authoress of the Odyssey* (New York: AMS Press, [1897] 1968).

17. Tales about brothers have been catalogued by Hasan El-Shamy, "Siblings in Alf laylah wa-laylah," in *"The Arabian Nights" in Transnational Perspective*, ed. Ulrich Marzolph (Detroit: Wayne State University Press, 2007), 473–74.

18. In fact, perhaps influenced by the brother and sister pairs in *The Nights*, Anglophone novels have brooded on brother/sister trouble since their inception. See Juliet Flower McCannell's study, *The Regime of the Brother* (New York: Routledge, 1991), which analyzes eighteenth-century Anglo-European political discourses showing the entanglement of this vocabulary with the political philosophies. Also see my discussion in Laura Doyle, *Freedom's Empire* (Durham, NC: Duke University Press, 2008), chapter 5; and Joyce, *Ulysses*, 9.956.

19. The Sassanid Empire did not extend this far, suggesting that this statement stakes a claim more than it states a fact.

20. See Tamara T. Chin, "Defamiliarizing the Foreigner: Sima Qina's Ethnography and Han-Xiongnu Marriage Diplomacy," *Harvard Journal of Asiatic Studies* 70, no. 2 (2010): 311–54; and Amanda Podany, *The Brotherhood of Kings: How International Relations Shaped the Ancient Near East* (New York: Oxford University Press, 2010). Chin likewise shows that the Xiongnu introduced a new form of nontributary imperial relations wherein the *heqin* agreement used an egalitarian language of "brotherly" relations. She suggests that this discourse influentially served to rationalize imperial ambitions under Emperor Wu 武帝 (r. 141–87 BCE).

21. Qtd. in Podany, *Brotherhood of Kings*, 265.

22. Podany, *Brotherhood of Kings*, 264–68.

23. The historiographic debate has mainly to do with whether al-Rashid in effect divided the empire and granted al-Ma'mun the powers of autonomous rule, an interpretation that historian Tayeb el-Hibri has challenged. See Tayeb El-Hibri, "Harun al-Rashid and the Mecca Protocol of 802: A Plan for Division or Succession?" *International Journal of Middle East Studies* 24, no. 3 (1992): 461–80.

24. See Tayeb El-Hibri, *Parable and Politics in Early Islamic History: The Rashidun Caliphs* (New York: Columbia University Press, 2010), 7–8. He points to commentators such as el-Tabari who invoke these precedents in their interpretations of the Prophet's choice.

25. My thanks to Professor Johan Mathew for these observations. Personal correspondence with the author, May–June 2017.

26. The racialization of slaves in the text deserves further study. Although, as Gerry Heng has discussed, various forms of racism did circulate in the "medieval" period, in this text slavery is not equated with blackness, as in the mention of both white and black slaves, likely referring to the capture of people from eastern Europe ("Slavs" being one origin of the English word *slaves*). Most important for my reading is the fact that the text implicitly sympathizes with

the subterfuges of wives. See Geraldine Heng, *The Invention of Race in the European Middle Ages* (Cambridge: Cambridge University Press, 2018).

27. The word has political associations dating to this period because it is used in conjunction with other nouns such as *Beit ul-mal* (the treasury, or House of Wealth), *Beit ul-hikma* (the name of the famous Abbasid House of Wisdom), and more recently, *Beit al-Ummah*, meaning House of Parliament, as pointed out by Professor Mazen Naous and Professor Johan Mathew in correspondence (in July 2015 and June 2017, respectively).

28. al-Musawi, *The Islamic Context of "The Thousand and One Nights"*, 140–45.

29. Said Amir Arjomand, "Law, Agency and Policy in Medieval Islamic Society: Development of the Institutions of Learning from the Tenth to the Fifteenth Century," *Comparative Studies in Society and History* 41, no. 2 (1999): 265.

30. I thank Professor Esther Klein, University of Sydney, for this connection. For a full translation of *The Great Learning* and other texts, with commentary, see Daniel K. Gardner, *Chu Hsi and the Ta-hsueh: Neo-Confucian Reflection on the Confucian Canon* (Cambridge, MA: Harvard University Press, 1986). A very simple public domain translation of *The Great Learning* was available but is not currently available here: https://ebooks.adelaide.edu.au /c/confucius/c748g/. Some selections may now be available here: http://curriculit.com /wordpress/0295-confucius/. Please note that in some versions there is a typo in the name of the translator, which should be James Legge, not Legg.

31. See Confucius, *The Analects*, trans. D. C. Lau (Hong Kong: Chinese University Press, 1983), 181, 17.25. This is a bilingual reprint of the 1979 Penguin edition of *The Analects*. "Small men" is typically understood to refer to servants.

32. Arjomand, "Law, Agency and Policy," 271.

33. Arjomand, "Law, Agency and Policy," 267–73.

34. Arjomand, "Law, Agency and Policy," 281.

35. Arjomand, "Law, Agency and Policy," 281.

36. Arjomand, "Law, Agency and Policy," 282.

37. Qtd. in Arjomand, "Law, Agency and Policy," 283.

38. Qtd. in Arjomand, "Law, Agency and Policy," 283.

39. Arjomand, "Law, Agency and Policy," 285.

40. Arjomand, "Law, Agency and Policy," 286.

41. Arjomand, "Law, Agency and Policy," 283.

42. Arjomand, "Law, Agency and Policy," 285.

43. Arjomand, "Law, Agency and Policy," 285–86.

44. Arjomand, "Law, Agency and Policy," 270.

45. Haddawy, *Arabian Nights*, 295. Several tales end with emperors, tellers, or listeners calling to have them recorded. Perhaps Shahrazad's own tales, told to an emperor, have

also been recorded under such circumstances? For variations of this demand that tales be recorded, see Haddawy, *Arabian Nights*, 150, 153, 206, 213–14, and 281. This textual self-reflexiveness is also implied in the many stories of viziers: see, for example, "King Yunan and the Sage Duban," 39–41; "The Husband and the Parrot," 41–42; and "The First Dervish's Tale," 86–92.

Chapter 3: Remapping Orientalism among Eurasian Empires

1. Edward W. Said, *Orientalism* (New York: Vintage, 1979), 25.

2. See Amit Chaudhuri, "East as a Career," *New Left Review* 40 (2006): 117. For related discussions, see Aamir Mufti, "Orientalism and the Institution of World literatures," *Critical Inquiry* 36, no. 3 (2010): 466; Kamran Rastegar, *Literary Modernity between the Middle East and Europe: Textual Transactions in Nineteenth-Century Arabic, English, and Persian Literatures* (New York: Routledge, 2007); and Mohamad Tavakoli-Targhi, "Orientalism's Genesis Amnesia," in *Antinomies of Modernity: Essays on Race, Orient, Nation*, ed. Vasant Kaiwar and Sucheta Mazumdar (Durham, NC: Duke University Press, 2003), 98–125.

3. Said makes this point of course, and many other individual studies have addressed it. Influential studies include for instance Joseph Boone, *Libidinal Currents* (Chicago: University of Chicago Press, 1998); Reina Lewis, *Rethinking Orientalism* (New Brunswick, NJ: Rutgers University Press, 2004); and Diane Long Hoeveler and Jeffrey Cass, eds., *Interrogating Orientalism* (Columbus: Ohio State University Press, 2006). For more recent work which also lends itself to an inter-imperial approach, see Alessia Bell and Anna Loretoni, eds., "Gender, Identity, and Belonging: New Citizenships Beyond Orientalism," special issue, *Journal of Balkan and Near Eastern Studies* 19, no. 5 (2017); and Öktem Öz, "Re-Orienting Gender and Islamic Alterity in Early Modern English Drama," *English Studies* 100, no. 2 (2019): 133–48.

4. Below I cite several studies that help to correct this distortion. On the importance of Russia in particular, see R. J. Barendse, "Trade and State in the Arabian Seas: A Survey from the Fifteenth to the Eighteenth Century," *Journal of World History* 11, no. 2 (2000): 173–225; see 180–81. Also see Nicholas Dew, *Orientalism in Louis XIV's France* (New York: Oxford University Press, 2009). Dew similarly emphasizes that, during the emergence of Orientalist studies, European states were not yet in a position of dominance relative to these other empires, and he valuably tracks the many circulating scholars, texts, and ideas that influenced the emergence of Enlightenment thought in France. Dew also characterizes his book as a study of the "two-way relationship between power and the production of knowledge" (5), yet he gives limited attention to the specific wars and geopolitical maneuvers shaping these productions.

5. See Rastegar, *Literary Modernity*, 43, 72; and Sunil Sharma, "Redrawing the Boundaries of *Ajam* in Early Modern Persian Literary Histories," in *Iran Facing Others: Identity Boundaries in Historical Perspective*, ed. Abbas Amanat and Farzin Vejdani (New York: Palgrave Macmillan, 2012), 52. "Self-indigenizing" is Mufti's term; see "Orientalism and the Institution," 477–79.

6. Orr, *Empire on the English Stage*, 6.

7. For histories of both the state and economic dimensions of these relations, see Stephen Dale, *The Muslim Empires of the Ottomans, Safavids, and Mughals* (Cambridge: Cambridge University Press, 2010); and Barendse, "Trade and State in the Arabian Seas." Also see Sanjay Subrahmanyam, *Explorations in Connected History: Mughals and Franks* (New York: Oxford University Press, 2005).

8. See Peter C. Perdue, "Boundaries and Trade in the Early Modern World: Negotiations at Nerchinsk and Beijing," *Eighteenth-Century Studies* 43, no. 3 (2010): 341–56, 342, 343–47.

9. Perdue, "Boundaries and Trade," 342.

10. As mentioned earlier, in the eighteenth century, China's manufacturing sectors were the most productive in the world and the standards of living for the general population were the highest; Britain became competitive only in the nineteenth century. See Kenneth Pomeranz, *The Great Divergence: Europe, China, and the Making of the Modern World* (Princeton, NJ: Princeton University Press, 2000).

On the effects of border peoples, see T. J. Barfield, "The Shadow Empires: Imperial State Formation along the Chinese-Nomad Frontier," in *Empires: Perspectives from Archaeology and History*, ed. Susan Alcock, Terence N. D'Altroy, Kathleen D. Morrison, and Carla Sinopoli (Cambridge: Cambridge University Press, 2001), 10–41; and Jerry Bentley, "Hemispheric Integration, 500–1500 C.E.," *Journal of World History* 9, no. 2 (1998): 237–54. Also see Christopher K. Chase-Dunn, Daniel Pasciuti, Alexis Alvarez, and Thomas D. Hall, "Growth/Decline Phases and Semi-peripheral Development in the Ancient Mesopotamian and Egyptian World-Systems," in *Globalization and Global History*, ed. Barry K. Gills and William R. Thompson (New York: Routledge, 2006), 114–38.

11. See John Archer, *Old Worlds: Egypt, Southwest Asia, India, and Russia in Early Modern English Writing* (Stanford, CA: Stanford University Press, 2002), 112. The well-known Richard Hakluyt drew support for his travels and writings from the Worshipful Company of Skinners and Worshipful Company of Clothmakers. In his study of this early writing, Archer does not use the term *inter-imperial*, but his materials regularly display its applicability. Also see Barendse, "Trade and State in the Arabian Seas," for a parallel reassessment of the Europeans' position relative to the Russian, Mughal, and Safavid Empires, as well as in relation to African states.

12. Qtd. in Archer, *Old Worlds*, 112.

13. Archer, *Old Worlds*, 116.

14. Tellingly, given the role of print, translation, and the vernacular in inter-imperial history, the severe unrest among his people led to Henry VIII's reversal of the Protestant principle of access to the Bible. English-language Bibles were removed from parishes and Henry decreed that only Protestants of noble birth had the right to read the Bible. In this classic dialectical dynamic, vernacular Bibles became sites of contestation, destabilizing the very hegemonies that the Bible had been made to serve (as it would do in other contexts, for example among diasporic African Atlantic communities in the Americas).

15. Protestant Queen Elizabeth also dealt harshly with perceived traitors and dissenters, and her bold entry into the inter-imperial field also fed concern about domestic tyranny, as I discuss shortly. Instability again emerged under Elizabeth's successor, the Catholic-leaning, absolutist, and overspending Stuart king, Charles I. Charles made excessive demands for funds; he increasingly excluded Parliament from decision-making; and he censored and imprisoned both Protestant legal scholars championing "Anglo-Saxon rights" and radical religious dissenters. His absolutism culminated with his eleven-year dissolution of Parliament throughout the 1630s, provoking the English Civil War. Although Charles lost the war and was publicly beheaded in 1649, these events quickly led to the Cromwellian Interregnum of the 1640s and 1650s, which entailed the renewed persecution of Catholics throughout Ireland, Scotland, Wales, and England, and the suppression of Diggers, Levellers, and other dissenting groups. Also important for the argument of this book, Cromwell undertook the closing of theaters and further censorship of the press.

16. On diplomacy, see Daniel Goffman, "Negotiating with the Renaissance State: The Ottoman Empire and the New Diplomacy," in *The Early Modern Ottomans: Remapping the Empire*, eds. Virginia Aksan and Daniel Goffman (New York: Cambridge University Press, 2007), 61–74. On belatedness in trade, see Archer, *Old Worlds*, 42.

17. Nabil Matar, *Britain and Barbary, 1589–1689* (Gainesville: University of Florida Press, 2005); Nabil Matar, *Islam in Britain, 1558–1685* (Cambridge: Cambridge University Press, 1998).

18. See recent work by literary scholars such as Nabil Matar, John Archer, Jane Degenhardt, Bridget Orr, and others. In addition to the work I cite throughout this chapter, see earlier postcolonial scholarship on links between the "old" and "new" worlds in these periods: Stephen Greenblatt, ed., *New World Encounters* (Berkeley: University of California Press, 1993); Stephen Greenblatt, *Renaissance Self-Fashioning: From More to Shakespeare* (Chicago: University of Chicago Press, 1980); Roland Greene, *Unrequited Conquests: Love and Empire in the Colonial Americas* (Chicago: University of Chicago Press, 1999); Jeffrey Knapp, *An Empire Nowhere* (Berkeley: University of California Press, 1992); Ania Loomba, *Shakespeare, Race, and Colonialism* (New York: Oxford University Press, 2002); Ania Loomba and Martin Orkin, eds., *Postcolonial Shakespeares* (New York: Routledge, 1998); Mary Louise Pratt, *Imperial Eyes: Travel Writing and Transculturation* (New York: Routledge, [1992] 2008); and Roberto Fernández Retamar, *Caliban and Other Essays*, trans. Edward Baker (Minneapolis: University of Minnesota Press, 1989).

19. On Shakespeare, see Peter Linebaugh and Marcus Rediker, *The Many-Headed Hydra: Sailors, Slaves, Commoners, and the Hidden History of the Revolutionary Atlantic* (Boston: Beacon Press, 2000), 16–22, 30–32.

20. See Jane Degenhardt, *Fortune's Empire: Opportunity, Risk, and Value in Early Modern English Drama and Culture* (forthcoming Oxford University Press, 2021); this quotation is from the manuscript; for this point, see the introduction in the published version. For further specifics, see Kathleen E. McLuskie and Felicity Dunsworth, "Patronage and the Economics of Theater," in *A New History of Early English Drama*, ed. John D. Cox and David Scott Kastan (New York: Columbia University Press, 1997), 423–40; Lucy

Munro, "'As It Was Played in the Blackfriars': Jonson, Marston, and the Business of Playmaking," *English Literary Renaissance* 50, no. 2 (2020): 256–95; and Rebecca Rogers and Kathleen McLuskie, "Who Invested in the Early-Modern Theatre?," *Research Opportunities in Renaissance Drama* 41 (2001): 29–61. My thanks to Professor Degenhardt for these sources.

21. Giles Fletcher, *Of the Russe Commonwealth* (Cambridge, MA: Harvard University Press, 1966), 116.

22. Archer, *Old Worlds*, 41–42, 47–62.

23. When we read these English authors, we are already witnessing an inter-imperial reading situation, since many of them were reading Latin-language translations of Arabic-language translations of ancient Greek and later Roman ethnographies and imperial histories, as discussed in chapter 1. Our own situation as English-language yet empire-critical scholars constitutes a further dialectical unfolding of these reading histories.

24. Archer, *Old Worlds*, 72.

25. Archer, *Old Worlds*, 72. In this debate, Herodotus had favored Egypt but Diodorus Siculus claimed that Ethiopia had fostered wider literacy and a shared language between commoners and elites.

26. Qtd. in Archer, *Old Worlds*, 32.

27. Qtd. in Archer, *Old Worlds*, 73–74.

28. See Jane Degenhardt, "The Reformation, Inter-imperial World History, and Marlowe's *Doctor Faustus*," PMLA 130, no. 2 (2015): 402–11.

29. Christopher Marlowe, *Doctor Faustus*, ed. David S. Kaston (New York: W. W. Norton, [1604/1616] 2005), 1.1.84–5, 1.1.133–4. See Degenhardt, "Reformation," 403–8, for discussion of these details.

30. Marlowe, *Doctor Faustus*, 1.3.106.

31. Writers have repeatedly "spoken back" to Shakespeare's colonialist, racist portrait of Caliban and his mother Sycorax, beginning with Aime Césaire in *Une tempête* (Paris: Editions du Seuil, 1969). In the world of scholarship, the groundbreaking study was that of Roberto Fernández Retamar, *Caliban and Other Essays* (Minneapolis: University of Minnesota Press, 1989; trans. Edward Baker). The vast body of subsequent postcolonial and feminist scholarship on Caliban and Sycorax is too large to cite here. I will only note two aspects of Shakespeare's play that repeats inter-imperial patterns. First, the situation in Shakespeare's play originates in the violent legacies of vying brothers, for Prospero has been banished by his usurping brother Antonio, and he has turned to colonization as his solution, for which he needs to enslave laborers. Second, women play instrumental roles: Prospero has carried his infant daughter to the island, for she represents his promise of reproduction, either in the colony or (as it happens) when he returns to Milan; and Caliban's mother has brought him to this island as a result of her own banishment; her powers of sorcery operate as one key resource for Caliban. Two of the novels I discuss in later chapters, *Melmoth the Wanderer* (chapter 4) and *The Kingdom of This World* (chapter 6), may implicitly evoke these

legacies, respectively in the vying brothers and the shipwrecked Spanish daughter Immalee (*Melmoth*) and in Madame Loi (*Kingdom*).

32. See Laura Doyle, *Freedom's Empire: Race and the Rise of the Novel in Atlantic Modernity, 1640–1940* (Durham, NC: Duke University Press, 2008), which traces the racialization of the freedom narrative in the coformed narratives of the novel and the "Whig" English historiography. In resistance to the censorship and tyrannies in their own state, English Parliament members and merchants began to articulate what they deemed their "rights and privileges" as "freeborn Anglo-Saxons" with a Germanic heritage. But eventually the idea underwrote the ideology of Manifest Destiny, whereby Anglo-Americans fashioned themselves as the next imperial torchbearers, founding what Thomas Jefferson shrewdly called an "empire of liberty," a phrase he used on multiple occasions, as when he predicted that "we shall add to the Empire of liberty an extensive and fertile Country" in a letter to George Rogers Clark, December 25, 1780. See Julian T. Boyd, Lyman H. Butterfield, and Mina R. Bryan, eds., *The Papers of Thomas Jefferson* (Princeton, NJ: Princeton University Press, 1950), 4:237–38. Reginald Horsman has also shown that this racialized discourse of freeborn Anglo-Saxons against enslaving "Norman" invaders traveled across the Atlantic with the Puritan colonizers, where it became a founding racial narrative for the "manifest destiny" of colonization, while also feeding into racist discourses against Africans and others, deemed incapable of freedom. See Reginald Horsman, *Race and Manifest Destiny* (Cambridge, MA: Harvard University Press, 1981).

33. Archer, *Old Worlds*, 112.

34. Archer, *Old Worlds*, 114.

35. Qtd. in Archer, *Old Worlds*, 11.

36. Qtd. in Archer, *Old Worlds*, 112.

37. See Robert Ralston Cawley, *Milton and the Literature of Travel* (Princeton, NJ: Princeton University Press, 1951). Cawley establishes that Heylyn's book was a popular compendium of travel and antiquarian writing, with six editions issued between 1652 and 1670 (9). See also Archer, *Old Worlds*, 77.

38. Qtd. in Archer, *Old Worlds*, 78. As Archer also discusses (98), in book 12 of *Paradise Lost* Milton associates Charles II with the figure of Nimrod, who wrongly usurps the "Dominion absolute" that rightly belongs to God. John Milton, *Paradise Lost*, ed. William Kerrigan, John Rumrich, and Stephen M. Fallon (New York: Modern Library, [1667] 2008), 12.63–71.

39. For discussion of this connection, see Doyle, *Freedom's Empire*, esp. the introduction and chapters 1 and 2. Archer rightly takes issue with scholars who distinguish this early writing from Orientalism proper and who understand this literature as *mere* discourse, with little effect on policy or practice. When we follow the overlap of theatrical with diplomatic writing, and notice these authors' literal investment in England's entry into the old-world inter-imperial system, we see the opposite.

40. Orr, *Empire on the English Stage*, 108, 104, 47.

41. Qtd. in Orr, *Empire on the English Stage*, 2. Orr also comments on the "double-edged nature" of the plays, which "allowed for both critique of current political affairs in England and for the depiction of fascinating, threatening, and opulent Oriental empires with which the English were engaged in trade and sometimes war" (105). As discussed later in this chapter, Barbara Fuchs analyzed such strategic uses of performance in *Mimesis and Empire: The New World, Islam, and European Identities* (Cambridge: Cambridge University Press, 2001).

42. Qtd. in Orr, *Empire on the English Stage*, 6.

43. Orr, *Empire on the English Stage*, 6.

44. Orr, *Empire on the English Stage*, 6.

45. The process is perfectly illustrated, Fuchs shows, in the 1570 ceremonial welcome of the Viceroy Francis Toledo to the city of Cuzco, Peru. The "Moorish castle" constructed for the main pageant was strategically built at the traditional site of Incan imperial festivals in the town center. Here the Spanish arranged the performance of a gendered plot of captivity and rescue in which women flee Moors who are played by indigenous *conversos* and rescued by the Spanish. The vignette allegorized the replacement of one state by another at this once-Incan site—perhaps especially felt as such by the indigenous actors made to perform Moorish roles, and by women of all identities who stood witness to the pageant. Amid the instabilities of Mediterranean and Atlantic geopolitics, the drama of rescue and control offers a symbolic, stabilizing, proleptic substitute.

Fuchs points to a comparable staging in Bristol, England, in 1613 during Queen Anne's visit. This Bristol ceremony included mock combat between a Christian ship and two Turkish ships. After a lively mock battle, as Fuchs's eyewitness source observed, the "Turks" are "brought as prisoners before the Queen, who laughingly observes that they are 'not only like Turks by their apparell, but by their countenances [sic].'" See Fuchs, *Mimesis and Empire*, 1.

46. Orr, *Empire on the English Stage*, 41.

47. Greenblatt, *Renaissance Self-Fashioning*.

48. See Yu Liu, *Seeds of a Different Eden: Chinese Gardening and a New English Aesthetic Ideal* (Columbia: University of South Carolina Press, 2008).

49. See Wendy Belcher, *Abyssinia's Samuel Johnson: Ethiopian Thought in the Making of an English Author* (New York: Oxford University Press, 2012); Abdulla Al-Dabbagh, *Shakespeare, the Orient, and the Critics* (New York: Peter Lang, 2010); and Arjun Appadurai, *Modernity at Large: Cultural Dimensions of Globalization* (Minneapolis: University of Minnesota Press, 1996).

50. Raymond Schwab, *The Oriental Renaissance: Europe's Rediscovery of India and the East, 1680–1880*, trans. Gene Patterson-Black and Victor Reinking (New York: Columbia University Press, 1984). Said suggested that Schwab's method paved the way for the likes of Michel Foucault, including because Schwab had avoided the most reductive "dualities, opposition, polarities—as between Orient and Occident" and instead studied "lines that criss-cross" (Said, *Orientalism*, ix). Nonetheless, Schwab takes Europe as the gold standard for intellectual achievement, as expressed, for example, in his comment that "in that progressive

era [the eighteenth century], the West perceived that it was not the sole possessor of an admirable intellectual past . . . that there had been other Europes" (Schwab, *Oriental Renaissance*, xxiii).

51. I refer to this recent scholarship throughout this discussion. See below and see note 2 for complete citations.

52. Tavakoli-Targhi, "Orientalism's Genesis Amnesia," 104.

53. Rastegar, *Literary Modernity*, 106–7.

54. Chaudhuri, "East as a Career," 117.

55. Mufti, "Orientalism," 477–79, 466.

56. See Hayrettin Yücesoy, "Language of Empire: Politics of Arabic and Persian in the Abbasid World," *PMLA* 130, no. 2 (2015): 384–92.

57. Sharma, "Redrawing the Boundaries."

58. Sharma, "Redrawing the Boundaries," 51–52.

59. Sharma, "Redrawing the Boundaries," 51.

60. See Rastegar, *Literary Modernity*, 43, 72; and Sharma, "Redrawing the Boundaries," 52.

61. David Schimmelpenninck van der Oye, *Russian Orientalism: Asia in the Russian Mind from Peter the Great to the Emigration* (New Haven, CT: Yale University Press, 2010); on the Russian interest in Persian manuscripts, see page 60.

62. Schimmelpenninck van der Oye, *Russian Orientalism*, 38.

63. Jennifer Milam, "Toying with China: Cosmopolitanism and Chinoiserie in Russian Garden Design and Building Projects under Catherine the Great," *Eighteenth-Century Fiction* 25, no. 1 (2012): 115–38, esp. 116.

64. Schimmelpenninck van der Oye, *Russian Orientalism*, 45.

65. Schimmelpenninck van der Oye, *Russian Orientalism*, 45–46.

66. Kerstin S. Jobst, "Where the Orient Ends? Orientalism and Its Function for Imperial Rule in the Russian Empire," in *Deploying Orientalism: From Germany to Central and Eastern Europe*, ed. James Hodkinson, John Walker, Shaswati Mazumdar, and Johannes Feichtinger (New York: Camden House, 2013), 190–208. See page 202.

67. Qtd. in Orr, *Empire on the English Stage*, 6.

68. Mufti, "Orientalism," 465–66.

69. Madeline Dobie, "Translation in the Contact Zone: Antoine Galland's *Mille et Une Nuits*: Contes Arabes," in *"The Arabian Nights" in Historical Context: Between East and West*, ed. Saree Makdisi and Felicity Nussbaum (New York: Oxford University Press, 2009), 29–35.

70. See Rastegar, *Literary Modernity*, 59–73. Note that one commentator in the journal puzzles over the Persian frame.

71. Mufti, "Orientalism," 465–66; Said, *Orientalism*, 25.

72. Schimmelpenninck van der Oye, *Russian Orientalism*, 59–66.

73. Qtd. in Schimmelpenninck van der Oye, *Russian Orientalism*, 46.

74. This comment is from Victor Hugo, preface to *Les Orientales*, as cited in Nasser Al-Tace, "*The Arabian Nights* and the Contemporary Arabic Novel," in "*The Arabian Nights" in Historical Context: Between East and West*, ed. Saree Makdisi and Felicity Nussbaum (New York: Oxford University Press, 2009), 269.

75. See Belcher, *Samuel Johnson's Abyssinia*.

76. Muhsin Jassim Ali, *Scheherezade in England: A Study of Nineteenth-Century English Criticism of the Arabian Nights* (Washington, DC: Three Continents Press, 1979), 11. Also see Dwight Reynolds, "*A Thousand and One Nights*: A History of the Text and Its Reception," in *The Cambridge History of Arabic Literature*, vol. 6, edited by Roger Allen and D. S. Richards (Cambridge: Cambridge University Press, 2006), 270–91.

77. Peter Caracciolo, ed. "*The Arabian Nights" in English Literature* (New York: St. Martin's Press, 1988).

78. William Wordsworth and Samuel Taylor Coleridge, *Lyrical Ballads*, ed. Fiona Stafford (Oxford: Oxford University Press, [1798] 2013), 96.

79. Qtd. in Caracciolo, "*Arabian Nights" in English Literature*, 8.

80. Wordsworth and Coleridge, *Lyrical Ballads*, 96–97.

81. Qtd. in Ali, *Scheherezade in England*, 18.

82. Qtd. in Rastegar, *Literary Modernity*, 3.

83. Qtd. in Ali, *Scheherezade in England*, 9.

84. Similarly, in the *History of Fiction* (1841) John Dunlop noted the role of merchants and bourgeois life. Both Sismondi and Dunlop are cited in Ali, *Scheherezade in England*, 72.

85. Ali, *Scheherezade in England*, 21; Caracciolo, "*Arabian Nights" in English Literature*, 2.

86. Ros Ballaster, *Fabulous Orients: Fictions of the East in England, 1662–1785* (Oxford: Oxford University Press, 2005), 58.

87. Qtd. in Ali, *Scheherezade in England*, 38.

88. Qtd. in Ali, *Scheherezade in England*, 37.

89. Martha Pike Conant, *The Oriental Tale in England in the Eighteenth Century* (New York: Routledge, [1908] 2013), 243.

90. Qtd. in Caracciolo, "*Arabian Nights" in English Literature*, 47.

91. Saree Makdisi, *Making England Western: Occidentalism, Race, and Imperial Culture* (Chicago: University of Chicago Press, 2013). As Makdisi explains, "The world of cultural difference that [Orientalist] Jones proposed to explore thus both enabled and required a firmer sense of the identity from which it marked a departure; it helped inaugurate the process I am calling Occidentalism. . . . [T]his investment in Occidental self-definition entailed the emergence of an altogether new, modern sense of imperial and national subjectivity, a sense

of self that could be defined against the Asiatic others who were subjected to the empire" (12). Makdisi pinpoints an important aspect of the dialectical exchanges by which states are co-constituted and states subjects undergo "imperialization."

92. See Ussama Makdisi on the Ottoman Empire's instrumentalization of Orientalism in "Ottoman Orientalism," *American Historical Review* 117, no. 3 (2008): 768–96; and Manuela Boatcă on Eastern European Orientalisms in "The Quasi Europes: World Regions in Light of the Imperial Difference," in *Global Crises and the Challenges of the 21st Century Antisystemic Movements and the Transformation of the World-System*, ed. Tom Reifer (London: Paradigm Publishers, 2012), 132–53. Also see essays in Francois Puillion and Jean-Claude Vatin, eds., *After Orientalism: Critical Perspectives on Western Agency and Eastern Re-appropriations* (Leiden: Brill, 2014).

93. On Orientalist medievalizing of Latin America, see Nadia R. Altschul, *Politics of Temporalization: Medievalism and Orientalism in Nineteenth-Century South America* (Philadelphia: University of Pennsylvania Press, 2020). On the later complexities of Orientalizing discourses in South America, see Chisu Teresa Ko, "Self-Orientalism and Inter-imperiality in Anna Kazumi Stahl's *Flores de un solodía*," *Latin American and Caribbean Ethnic Studies* 14, no. 1 (2018): 1–20.

94. For studies on Orientalism as it shaped discourses in both in North and South America, see Rebecca Cole Heinowitz, *Spanish America and British Romanticism, 1777–1826: Rewriting Conquest* (Edinburgh: University of Edinburgh Press, 2010); and Eric Wertheimer, *Imagined Empires: Inca, Aztecs, and the New World of American Literature, 1771–1876* (New York: Columbia University Press, 1999). For specifically Latin American studies, see Julia Kushigian, *Orientalism in the Hispanic Tradition: In Dialogue with Borges, Paz, and Sarduy* (Albuquerque: University of New Mexico Press, 1991); and Ko, "Self-Orientalism and Inter-imperiality." For Orientalisms in US literature and culture, see Malini Johar Schueller, *US Orientalisms: Race, Nation, and Gender in Literature, 1790–1890* (Ann Arbor: University of Michigan Press, 1998); and Mari Yoshihara, *Embracing the East: White Women and American Orientalism* (New York: Oxford, 2003).

95. See Bridget Orr, "Galland, Georgian Theatre, and the Creation of Popular Orientalism," in *"The Arabian Nights" in Historical Context: Between East and West*, ed. Saree Makdisi and Felicity Nussbaum (New York: Oxford University Press, 2009), 129.

96. Orr, "Galland, Georgian Theatre," 129.

97. See Ko, "Self-Orientalism and Inter-imperiality."

98. Joseph Lennon, *Irish Orientalism: A Literary and Intellectual History* (Syracuse, NY: Syracuse University Press, 2008).

99. Lennon, *Irish Orientalism*, 73.

100. Lennon, *Irish Orientalism*, xxviii. As we will see in chapter 5, by the twentieth century, this doubling comes to characterize a range of writers and activists. On this point, also see Gauri Viswanathan, "Ireland, India, and the Poetics of Internationalism," *Journal of World History* 15, no. 1 (2004): 7–30. Irish identifications would take yet further turns when carried to the US, where the Irish "became white." See Noel Ignatiev, *How the Irish Became White*

(London: Routledge, 1995); and David Roediger, *The Wages of Whiteness* (New York: Verso Books, 1991). As these authors describe, in the face of job and housing discrimination and equations of Irish- and African-descended peoples, Irish immigrants in the United States began to identify as white. That legacy of racism also found expression in the Irish American coterie of President Trump, and so this dialectical history continues.

Chapter 4: Global Revolts and Gothic Interventions

Parts of this chapter previously appeared in Laura Doyle, "At World's Edge: Post/Coloniality, Charles Maturin, and the Gothic Wanderer," *Nineteenth-Century Literature* 65, no. 4 (2011): 513–47.

1. Qtd. in David A. Bell, *The First Total War: Napoleon's Europe and the Birth of Warfare as We Know It* (London: Bloomsbury, 2012), 269–70.

2. Bell, *First Total War*, 263. Also see Christopher Tozzi, *Nationalizing France's Army: Foreigners, Jews, and Blacks in the French Military, 1715–1831* (Charlottesville: University of Virginia Press, 2016). Although the numbers of Haitian troops were not large, their presence is noteworthy.

3. In their essay collection *The Age of Revolutions in Global Context*, David Armitage, Sanjay Subrahmanyam, and contributors frame this period as a global age of revolutions—not just an age of Anglo-European revolutions in the Atlantic world. See David Armitage and Sanjay Subrahmanyam, eds., *The Age of Revolutions in Global Context, c. 1760–1840* (New York: Palgrave, 2009). Also see the discussion in in Jane Burbank and Frederick Cooper, *Empires in World History: Power and the Politics of Difference* (Princeton, NJ: Princeton University Press, 2010), esp. chapter 8, "Empire, Nation, and Citizenship in a Revolutionary Age."

4. Bell, *First Total War*, 263.

5. "Nervous conditions" is a phrase used by Jean-Paul Sartre in his preface to Frantz Fanon's *The Wretched of the Earth*, trans. Constance Farrington (New York: Grove Press, 1963), 20; and echoed by Zimbabwean author Tsitsi Dangarembga in her novel *Nervous Conditions* (Seattle: Seal Press, [1988] 2001).

6. See A. P. Maingot, "Haiti and the Terrified Consciousness of the Caribbean," in *Ethnicity in the Caribbean*, ed. Gert Ootindie (London: Macmillan, 1996), 53–80. See note 33 for a fuller list of sources on this topic. My discussion in this chapter builds on several decades of scholarship about the ripple effects of the Haitian Revolution, beginning with Robin Blackburn's *The Overthrow of Colonial Slavery, 1776–1848* (New York: Verso Books, 1988). For further documentation and analysis, see Doris L. Garraway, ed., *Tree of Liberty: Cultural Legacies of the Haitian Revolution in the Atlantic World* (Charlottesville: University of Virginia Press, 2008); and David Geggus, ed., *The Impact of the Haitian Revolution in the Atlantic World* (Columbia: University of South Carolina Press, 2001), including Ifeoma C. K. Nwankwo's discussion of "white fear" in her essay, "'Charged with Sympathy for Haiti': Harnessing the Power of Blackness and Cosmopolitanism in the Wake of the Haitian Revolution," in

Garraway, *Tree of Liberty*, 91. Also see P. J. N. Tuck, *Warfare, Expansion, and Resistance* (London: Routledge, 2002), esp. 212. For another important analysis of Atlantic-world resistance, see Peter Linebaugh and Marcus Rediker, *The Many-Headed Hydra: Sailors, Slaves, Commoners, and the Hidden History of the Revolutionary Atlantic* (Boston: Beacon Press, 2000). Also, see Saree Makdisi, *Romantic Imperialism: Universal Empire and the Culture of Modernity* (New York: Cambridge University Press, 1998). For an earlier formulation of my thesis here about Atlantic-world narratives, see Laura Doyle, "At World's Edge: Post/Coloniality, Charles Maturin, and the Gothic Wanderer," *Nineteenth-Century Literature* 65, no. 4 (2011): 513–47.

7. In addition to the scholarship cited in this note, also see note 37, especially regarding Irish anticolonialism and the Gothic. Beginning with Terry Eagleton, several critics have considered the Gothic as expressing a kind of colonial political unconscious, which I suggest could be further understood as an inter-imperial unconscious. See Terry Eagleton, *Heathcliff and the Great Hunger: Studies in Irish Culture* (New York: Verso Books, 1995), esp. 187; Margot Gayle Backus, *The Gothic Family Romance: Heterosexuality, Child Sacrifice, and the Anglo-Irish Colonial Order* (Durham, NC: Duke University Press, 1999); Julian Moynihan, "The Politics of Anglo-Irish Gothic: Maturin, Le Fanu, and 'the Return of the Repressed,'" in *Studies in Anglo-Irish Literature*, ed. Heinz Kosok (Bonn: Bouvier Verlag Herbert Grundmann, 1982), 43–54; and Katie Trumpener, *Bardic Nationalism: The Romantic Novel and the British Empire* (Princeton, NJ: Princeton University Press, 1997). Backus tracks the "self-protective projection" of colonialism's crimes on to others (109); Julian Moynihan discusses the "return of the repressed" of colonial politics among Anglo-Irish writers generally and includes brief remarks on Melmoth (48–49); and Trumpener interprets Gothic narrative form as a "historical and political repetition compulsion" (152). On the Gothic and colonialism more broadly, see Andrew Smith, ed., *Empire and the Gothic: The Politics of Genre* (New York: Palgrave, 2003).

For critics who specifically discuss *Melmoth the Wanderer*, see Massimiliano Demata, "Discovering Eastern Horrors: Beckford, Maturin, and the Discourse of Travel," in *Empire and the Gothic: The Politics of Genre*, ed. Andrew Smith (New York: Palgrave, 2003), 13–34; Luke Gibbons, *Gaelic Gothic: Race, Colonization, and Irish Culture* (Galway: Arlen House, 2004); Murray Pittock, *Scottish and Irish Romanticism* (New York: Oxford University Press, 2008); David Punter, "Scottish and Irish Gothic," in *The Cambridge Companion to Gothic Fiction*, ed. Jerrold E. Hogle (Cambridge: Cambridge University Press, 2002), 112–25; and Julia M. Wright, "Devouring the Disinherited: Familial Cannibalism in Maturin's *Melmoth the Wanderer*," in *Eating Their Words: Cannibalism and the Boundaries of Cultural Identity*, ed. Kristen Guest (New York: SUNY Press, 2001), 79–105. More generally, the following give attention to Gothic texts' investment in discourses of race and nationalism: H. L. Malchow, *Gothic Images of Race in Nineteenth-Century Britain* (Stanford, CA: Stanford University Press, 1996); and Cannon Schmitt, *Alien Nation: Nineteenth-Century Gothic Fictions and English Nationality* (Philadelphia: University of Pennsylvania Press, 1997).

For studies of the United States and the wider Atlantic, see Jesse Alemán, "The Other Country: Mexico, the United States, and the Gothic History of Conquest," in *Hemispheric American Studies*, ed. Caroline F. Levander and Robert S. Levine (New Brunswick, NJ: Rutgers University Press, 2008), 75–95; Doyle, *Freedom's Empire*; Teresa A. Goddu, *Gothic*

America: Narrative, History, and Nation (New York: Columbia University Press, 1997); Jennifer Rae Greeson, "The 'Mysteries and Miseries' of North Carolina: New York City, Urban Gothic Fiction, and *Incidents in the Life of a Slave Girl*," *American Literature* 73, no. 2 (2001): 277–309; Saidiya V. Hartman, *Scenes of Subjection: Terror, Slavery, and Self-Making in Nineteenth-Century America* (New York: Oxford University Press, 1997); and Kari J. Winter, *Subjects of Slavery, Agents of Change: Women and Power in Gothic Novels and Slave Narratives, 1790–1865* (Athens: University of Georgia Press, 1992). Recent work on "haunting," especially in American studies, also touches on this connection. See Renée L. Bergland, *The National Uncanny: Indian Ghosts and American Subjects* (Hanover, NH: University Press of New England, 2000); Kathleen Brogan, *Cultural Haunting: Ghosts and Ethnicity in Recent American Literature* (Charlottesville: University of Virginia Press, 1998); Lizabeth Paravisini-Gebert, "Colonial and Postcolonial Gothic: The Caribbean," in *The Cambridge Companion to Gothic Fiction*, ed. Jerrold E. Hogle (Cambridge: Cambridge University Press, 2002), 229–57; and Hershini Bhana Young, *Haunting Capital: Memory, Text, and the Black Diasporic Body* (Hanover: University Press of New England, 2006). Patrick Brantlinger, *Rule of Darkness: British Literature and Imperialism 1830–1914* (Ithaca, NY: Cornell University Press, 1988), extends this discussion into the later nineteenth century in his treatment of the British "late-imperial gothic" (see chapter 8, 227–54).

8. See Stephen Shapiro, "Transvaal, Transylvania: Dracula's World-System and Gothic Periodicity," *Gothic Studies* 10, no. 1 (2008): 29–47.

9. See Vijay Mishra, *The Gothic Sublime* (Albany, NY: SUNY Press, 1994), 246, for his discussion of "mediatization" in this fiction—that is, literary mediation of politics.

10. See Victor Sage, introduction to *Melmoth the Wanderer*, by Charles Maturin (New York: Penguin Books, 2000), xiii–xiv.

11. Dostoevsky reported that he "learned a great deal about the depiction of anxiety" from Gothic novels, particularly Maturin's *Melmoth the Wanderer*. See Robin Feuer Miller, *Dostoevsky's Unfinished Journey* (New Haven, CT: Yale University Press, 2007), xvi. Miller also remarks that "moments that we tend to think of [as] 'pure Dostoevsky' [vibrate] with a strong resonance of Maturin's [novel]" (xvi). In the preface to his sequel, Balzac explained that he set his story in the world of the Paris stock exchange in order to show that in nineteenth-century Paris the Faustian protagonist Melmoth would easily have found "a thousand persons to one" who would have accepted his Faustian offers. Qtd. in Sage, introduction to *Melmoth the Wanderer*, xiii. Honoré de Balzac, *Melmoth Reconciled*, trans. Ellen Marriage (Auckland: Floating Press, [1835] 2014).

12. Recent work on the Haitian Revolution has particularly made this point. See Blackburn, *Overthrow of Colonial Slavery*; Garraway, *Tree of Liberty*; and Geggus, *Impact of the Haitian Revolution*. On the interconnections among Atlantic-world revolutions in this period, also see Janet Polasky, *Revolutions without Borders: The Call to Liberty in the Atlantic World* (New Haven, CT: Yale University Press, 2015).

13. On the increase in troops and the turn toward conscription, see Bell, *First Total War*, 296–97 and chapter 8 more broadly.

14. See Eve Kosofsky Sedgwick, *Epistemology of the Closet* (Berkeley: University of California Press, 1990). Also see her published dissertation for her early suggestions about gay sexuality in the Gothic, *The Coherence of the Gothic* (New York: Arno Press, 1980). On the racial aspect, see Doyle, *Freedom's Empire*, 201–11.

15. On Russian taxes and budgets in this period, see Lindsey Hughes, *Russia in the Age of Peter the Great* (New Haven, CT: Yale University Press, 2000); on military budgets, see Nicholas Riasanovsky, *A History of Russia* (New York: Oxford University Press, [1937] 1984), 284.

16. On the waves of revolts, see Yuri Bosin, "Pugachev's Rebellion," in *International Encyclopedia on Revolution and Protest* (New York: Wiley, 2009), 2775–76.

17. See Bosin, "Pugachev's Rebellion," 2775–76.

18. See Rebecca C. Heinowitz, *Spanish America and British Romanticism, 1777–1826: Rewriting Conquest* (Edinburgh: University of Edinburgh Press, 2010); and Eric Wertheimer, *Imagined Empires: Incas, Aztecs, and the New World of American Literature, 1771–1876* (New York: Columbia University Press, 1999).

19. See Peter C. Perdue, "Erasing the Empire, Re-racing the Nation: Racialism and Culturalism in Imperial China," in *Imperial Formations*, ed. Ann Laura Stoler, Carole McGranahan, and Peter C. Perdue (Santa Fe, NM: School for Advanced Research Press, 2007), 141–69. For discussion of discontent with the Qing dynasty and the desire to return to the Ming dynasty, see Elizabeth Weber, "Reimagining Coolie Trajectories: The Triumphant Return as Political Statement in Late Qing 'Coolie' Fiction," *Literature Compass* 13, no. 5 (2016): 300–10.

20. See Dušan T. Bataković, "The 1804 Serbian Revolution: A Balkan-size French Revolution" (paper presented at the AAASS, Boston, December 2004). In 1805, Serbian leader Count Tekelija wrote simultaneously to Napoleon I and Emperor Franz of Austria to make a case for this Illyrian state, which, he claimed, would stabilize the region for them. As Dušan T. Bataković points out, in his letter to the French emperor Tekelija named Austria and Russia as threatening rival powers, but in his very similar letter to the Austrian emperor, he mentions only Russia.

21. See Thomas Clarkson, "The True State of the Case, respecting the Insurrection at St. Domingo" (1792), reprinted in *Slave Revolution in the Caribbean, 1789–1804: A Brief History with Documents*, ed. Laurent Dubois and John D. Garrigus (New York: Palgrave Macmillan, 2006), 113–15.

22. Qtd. in Bell, *First Total War*, 240–41.

23. Shelley's untitled poem was published in his pamphlet "Poetical Essay on the Existing State of Things," as cited by Bell, *First Total War*, 263.

24. For this quote and these details, see Bell, *First Total War*, 155–57.

25. There are very few studies of pre-twentieth-century periods, although there is a growing field of study of conflict-related sexual violence (CRSV). See for instance, Elizabeth Heineman, ed., *Sexual Violence in Conflict Zones* (Philadelphia: University of Pennsylvania Press,

2011); Tuba Inal, *Looting and Rape in Wartime: Law and Change in International Relations* (Philadelphia: University of Pennsylvania Press, 2013); Sabrina Ramet, ed., *Gender Politics in the Western Balkans* (University Park: Pennsylvania State University Press, 1999), especially the chapter on rape; and Mary Louise Roberts, *What Soldiers Do: Sex and the American GI in World War II France* (Chicago: University of Chicago Press, 2013).

26. Bell, *First Total War*, 7.

27. Bell, *First Total War*, 254.

28. Bell, *First Total War*, 263.

29. Bell, *First Total War*, 267.

30. Bell, *First Total War*, 269.

31. Bell, *First Total War*, 266.

32. See Amitav Ghosh, "Mutinies: India, Ireland and Imperialism," in *Ireland and Postcolonial Theory*, eds. Claire Carroll and Patricia King (Cork, Ireland: Cork University Press, 2003), 122–28. For further documentation and analyses of the impact of the Haitian Revolution in particular, see the essays in Geggus, *Impact of the Haitian Revolution*; and also in Garraway, *Tree of Liberty*—especially, in the latter, Nwankwo's discussion of "white fear" ("'Charged with Sympathy for Haiti,'" 91). Also see Tuck, *Warfare, Expansion, and Resistance*, 212. For other important, wide-ranging histories of resistance see Blackburn, *Overthrow of Colonial Slavery*; Linebaugh and Rediker, *Many-Headed Hydra*; and Ifeoma C. K. Nwankwo, *Black Cosmopolitanism: Racial Consciousness and Transnational Identity in the Nineteenth-Century Americas* (Philadelphia: University of Pennsylvania Press, 2014).

33. See Robin Blackburn, *The Overthrow of Colonial Slavery, 1776–1848* (London: Verso, 1988), 257. Also see Maingot, "Haiti and the Terrified Consciousness." Blackburn notices the anticolonial energies unleashed as well, commenting that "Black rebels in Cuba in 1812, in the United States in 1820, in Jamaica and Brazil in the 1920's, found inspiration in Haiti" (257). For further discussion of both the "white fear" and the Black solidarity, see Ifeoma C. K. Nwankwo, "'Charged with Sympathy for Haiti': Harnessing the Power of Blackness and Cosmopolitanism in the Wake of the Haitian Revolution," in Doris L. Garraway, ed., *Tree of Liberty: Cultural Legacies of the Haitian Revolution in the Atlantic World* (Charlottesville: University of Virginia Press, 2008), 91–112; and Blackburn, *The Overthrow of Colonial Slavery, 1776–1848* (New York: Verso Books, 1988). For further documentation and analysis, see the other essays in Garraway, ed., *Tree of Liberty*; David Geggus, ed., *The Impact of the Haitian Revolution in the Atlantic World* (Columbia: University of South Carolina Press, 2001); and P. J. N. Tuck, *Warfare, Expansion, and Resistance* (London: Routledge, 2002), esp. 212. For analysis of earlier periods of Atlantic-world resistance, see Peter Linebaugh and Marcus Rediker, *The Many-Headed Hydra: Sailors, Slaves, Commoners, and the Hidden History of the Revolutionary Atlantic* (Boston: Beacon Press, 2000).

34. See Maingot, "Haiti and the Terrified Consciousness." That is, as the colonial French ruling and plantation-owning classes fled Saint-Domingue they influenced attitudes and policies in their new locales and sometimes also encountered suspicion. See essays in

Garraway, *Tree of Liberty*; Geggus, *Impact of the Haitian Revolution*; Polasky, *Revolutions without Borders*; and Blackburn, *Overthrow of Colonial Slavery*.

35. See Tim Watson, *Caribbean Culture and British Fiction in the Atlantic World, 1780–1870* (Cambridge: Cambridge University Press, 2008); and Tim Watson, "Working the Edges of the Nineteenth-Century British Empire," *Literature Compass* 13, no. 5 (2016): 288–99.

36. Nwankwo, *Black Cosmopolitanism*; Ellen Malenas Ledoux, *Social Reform in Gothic Writing: Fantastic Forms of Change, 1764–1834* (New York: Palgrave Macmillan, 2013).

37. Amy E. Martin, "Gothic Internationalism: Irish Nationalist Critiques of Empire as a System of Violence and Trauma," in *Traumatic Tales: British Nationhood and National Trauma in Nineteenth-Century Literature*, ed. Lisa Kasmer (Routledge: New York, 2017), 97–117; Partha Chatterjee, *The Nation and Its Fragments: Colonial and Postcolonial Histories* (Princeton, NJ: Princeton University Press, 1993). Martin defines Gothic Internationalism "as a mode of the Gothic that operates as a form of radical anticolonial critique" and which "seeks to shift the reader's experience away from the traumatic experience of those subject to insurgent violence and to relocate it in an understanding of colonialism itself as a kind of sustained violence and trauma from which such insurgency emerges" (103, 100). For related scholarship on the Gothic and anticolonial Irish politics, see the following (in addition to works cited in note 7): Jim Hansen, *Terror and Irish Modernism: The Gothic Tradition from Burke to Beckett* (Albany, NY: SUNY Press, 2010); Siobhan Kilfeather, "Terrific Register: The Gothicization of Atrocity in Irish Literature," *boundary 2* 31, no. 1 (2004): 49–71; Jarlath Killeen, *The Emergence of Irish Gothic Fiction* (Edinburgh: Edinburgh University Press, 2014); and Jarlath Killeen, *Gothic Ireland: Horror and the Irish Anglican Imagination in the Long Eighteenth Century* (Dublin: Four Courts Press, 2005). For broader literary-political analysis of nineteenth-century genres, see Julia Wright, *Ireland, India, and Nationalism in Nineteenth Century Literature* (Cambridge: Cambridge University Press, 2007).

38. See Carlyle's infamous pamphlet, *Occasional Discourse on the Nigger Question* (London: Thomas Bosworth, 1853).

39. See Doyle, *Freedom's Empire*.

40. For an earlier formulation of my thesis here, see Doyle, "At World's Edge." As I argue in this earlier article, the slash I have inserted in "post/colonial" also may be understood to align with the slash in what Walter Mignolo and Arturo Escobar have deemed the "modern/colonial" structure of the world, by which they name the interdependent unfolding of modernizing and colonizing processes, a structurally determinate combination that enriches some while impoverishing others. See Walter Mignolo, *The Idea of Latin America* (Malden, MA: Blackwell, 2005), xiii; and Arturo Escobar, "Worlds and Knowledges Otherwise: The Latin American Modernity/Coloniality Research Program," *Cultural Studies* 21, no. 2 (2007): 179–210.

41. See Nelson Maldonado-Torres, "On the Coloniality of Being: Contributions to the Development of a Concept," *Cultural Studies* 21, nos. 2/3 (2007): 240–70, 243. On the concept of coloniality, also see Aníbal Quijano's earlier formulation in "Coloniality of Power, Eurocentrism, and Latin America," *Nepantla: Views from the South* 1, no. 3 (2000): 533–80.

My analysis supplements earlier discussions of the Gothic, including Franco Moretti's Marxist argument that the Gothic's literature is "born precisely out of the terror of a split society" (Franco Moretti, "The Dialectic of Fear," *New Left Review* 136, no. 1 [1982]: 67–85, 83). It may also be useful to link this split to David Punter's discussion of the landscape of fissures in Gothic fiction ("Scottish and Irish Gothic," esp. 111–13); and Andrea Cabajsky's description of picturesque and sublime landscape in Ann Radcliffe's and Charles De Guise's fiction. For the latter, see Andrea Cabajsky, "Catholic Gothic: Atavism, Orientalism, and Generic Change in Charles De Guise's *Le Cap au Diable*," in *Unsettled Remains: Canadian Literature and the Postcolonial Gothic*, ed. Cynthia Sugars and Gerry Turcotte (Waterlook: Wilfrid Laurier University Press, 2009), 1–17, esp. 2–3.

42. Robert Emmet, "The Speech from the Dock," accessed August 2009, www.robertemmet .org/speech.htm, 1–3, esp. 3.

43. In "Colonial Encounters," I discuss this post/coloniality as an element that also later underlies the experiments of modernism, and creates the common historical ground for postcolonial and modernist fiction. Laura Doyle, "Colonial Encounters," in *The Oxford Handbook of Modernisms*, ed. Peter Brooker, Andrzej Gasiorek, Deborah Parsons, and Andrew Thacker (New York: Oxford University Press, 2010), 249–66.

44. For the notion of "colonial intimacy," see Sara Suleri, *The Rhetoric of English India* (Chicago: University of Chicago Press, 1992).

45. Matthew G. Lewis, *The Monk* (New York: Grove Press, 1952), 93. See discussion of *The Monk* and *Wieland* along these lines in Doyle, *Freedom's Empire*, 220–23 and 228–35. The difference between *Melmoth* and *The Monk* might be measured by their footnoted allusions to the colonial: in *The Monk* there is merely a footnote indicating that the cientipedro spider that stings Ambrosio is from Cuba (Lewis, *The Monk*, 93), while in Maturin's text two footnotes refer directly to Irish rebellions, and indicate shared Spanish and British culpability. See Maturin, *Melmoth*, 284 and 285.

46. See John Berryman's introduction to *The Monk*, 19–20.

47. Berryman, introduction to *The Monk*, 25–26.

48. In this era of Orientalism, Walpole became a devoted antiquarian of European materials, building a faux Gothic castle outside of London and referring to the English Parliament as the Witenagemot—understood as the medieval source of Britain's "Anglo-Saxon" tradition of representative and "free" rather than tyrannical government. That is, in inter-imperial terms, when Walpole turns to "ancient" materials he enters the competitive discursive field aiming to fashion "native" European lineages that would undergird British claims to superiority over Eastern aesthetics, as I've discussed elsewhere. See Doyle, *Freedom's Empire*, esp. chapter 8; and Laura Doyle, "The Racial Sublime," in *Romanticism, Race, and Imperial Culture, 1780–1834*, ed. Alan Richardson and Sonia Hofkosh (Bloomington: Indiana University Press, 1996), 15–39.

49. Muhsin Jassam Ali, *Scheherazade in England: A Study of Nineteenth-Century English Criticism of the "Arabian Nights"* (Washington, DC: Three Continents Press, 1979), 31.

50. Horace Walpole, *The Castle of Otranto* (New York: Oxford University Press, 1996), in his preface to the first edition, 5.

51. Karla Mallette, *The Kingdom of Sicily, 1100–1250* (Philadelphia: University of Pennsylvania Press, 2005), 4–7.

52. In this way Walpole also lays down what will become yet another Gothic pattern: mediation of the discourses of tyranny and liberty and their attendant plots of captivity, as discussed in Doyle, *Freedom's Empire*, chapters 1, 2, and 8. Also see chapter 3 of the present study for discussion of these discourses in relation to Russia.

53. Walpole, *The Castle of Otranto*, 112.

54. Napoleon also tried his hand at philosophical discourse and historical fiction, submitting his "Discourse on Happiness" to the essay contest founded by Raynal. See Martin, *Napoleon the Novelist*, 15–33.

55. For rich discussion of this early writing, see Martin, *Napoleon the Novelist*. Also see the first two chapters of David Bell's *The First Total War* for mention of Napoleon's literary writing as part of Bell's analysis of the shift in Europe's military culture from an aristocracy of literate gentlemen to a massive force encompassing a wide range of civilian populations (25–27).

56. Napoleon, "Napoleon's Addresses: The Italian Campaigns," ed. Tom Holberg, Napoleon Series website, accessed April 29, 2019, https://www.napoleon-series.org/research/napoleon/speeches/c_speeches1.html.

57. Bell, *First Total War*, 198.

58. The novel *She* is the story of a sorceress queen who has lived for two millennia and threatens to bring madness upon the white men who visit her ancient African kingdom. See Patrick Brantlinger's discussion in *Rule of Darkness* (chapter 8, 227–54).

59. See Lizabeth Paravisini-Gebert, "Colonial and Postcolonial Gothic"; Goddu, *Gothic America*; Winter, *Subjects of Slavery*; Greeson, "'Mysteries and Miseries'"; Alemán, "Other Country"; and Doyle, *Freedom's Empire*.

60. Critics often mention the complicated structure of the novel, ranging from disparaging references to its "creaky" and "preposterously convoluted" form to more appreciative analyses (Chris Baldick, introduction to *Melmoth the Wanderer*, by Charles Maturin [New York: Oxford University Press, 1992], x–xi). Here I expand on Vijay Mishra's comments on this structural "mediatization" (Vijay Mishra, *Gothic Sublime*, 246), and Victor Sage's notice of the "witness-narrators" of the novel (Sage, introduction to *Melmoth the Wanderer*, xvii). Sage also comments on the historical allusions to Spanish, Moorish, and European history, which I link to its witness-narrators. Also of interest is Murray Pittock's discussion of Moncada and young John Melmoth as "doubles" (*Scottish and Irish Romanticism*, 228).

61. Qtd. in Sage, introduction to *Melmoth the Wanderer*, xiv. Baudelaire's comment on the laugh calls to mind a description of dying French soldiers on the retreat from Moscow, given by one of Napoleon's officers, Jean-Michel Chevalier: they no longer looked

like soldiers but rather like "phantoms covered in rags" including one "wretch" whose "blood came out of the nose" and who laughed "a satanic and convulsive laugh," then "spun about like a drunk, and fell, laughing an infernal laugh" (qtd. in Bell, *First Total War*, 260).

62. For the concept of modernity/coloniality see Escobar, "Worlds and Knowledges Otherwise"; and Mignolo, *The Idea of Latin America*. For discussion of Maturin's text in relation to his poverty, see Chris Baldick's introduction to the Oxford edition of *Melmoth the Wanderer*, xviii-xix. For related comments on Melmoth as a figure embodying the fraught and ambivalent position of the Anglo-Irish, see Backus, *Gothic Family Romance*, 113; Demata, "Discovering Eastern Horrors," 27–29; Eagleton, *Heathcliff and the Great Hunger*, 190–93; Moynihan, "Politics of Anglo-Irish Gothic," 44–47; Pittock, *Scottish and Irish Romanticism*, 212–15; and Trumpener, *Bardic Nationalism*, 146. For the standard biography of Maturin, see Nilo Idman, *Charles Robert Maturin: His Life and Works* (London: Constable, 1923); and see Robert E. Lougy, *Charles Robert Maturin* (Lewisburg, PA: Bucknell University Press, 1975), for a shorter, more recent account.

63. Thomas Bartlett, Kevin Dawson, and Dáire Keough, *The 1798 Rebellion* (Niwot, CO: Roberts Rinehart, 1998), 148–49; emphasis in original.

64. Emmet, "Speech from the Dock," 3.

65. Emmet, "Speech from the Dock," 2.

66. Emmet "Speech from the Dock," 1. See Nigel Leask, "Irish Republicans and Gothic Eleutherarchs: Pacific Utopias in the Work of Theobald Wolfe Tone and Charles Brockden Brown," *Huntington Library Quarterly* 63, no. 3 (2000): 247–67.

67. Charles Maturin, *Melmoth the Wanderer* (New York: Penguin Books, 2000), 334. Subsequent citations appear in the text in parentheses.

68. I discuss this point below. For valuable readings of the gender and identity politics of Immalee's role in the novel, see Backus, *Gothic Family Romance*, 121–26; and Joseph W. Lew, "'Unprepared for Sudden Transformations': Identity and Politics in *Melmoth the Wanderer*," *Studies in the Novel* 26, no. 2 (1994): 173–95, esp. 189 and 191–93. The connection of her fate to imperialist capitalism is also indicated in the account of the shipwreck: "There was . . . a certain Spanish merchant, who set out prosperously in business; but, after a few years, finding his affairs assume an unfavourable aspect, and being tempted by an offer of partnership with a relative who was settled in the East Indies, had embarked for those countries with his wife and son, leaving behind him an infant daughter in Spain. . . . Two years of successful occupation restored him to opulence, and to the hope of vast and future accumulation. Thus encouraged, our Spanish merchant entertained ideas of settling in the East Indies, and sent over for his young daughter with her nurse, who embarked for the East Indies with the first opportunity. . . . [A] storm . . . wrecked the vessel . . . [but] the child survived, and grew up a wild and beautiful daughter of nature" (561–62).

69. For instance, in earlier fiction such as *The Milesian Chief*, explicitly concerned with the 1798 rebellion, Maturin attempts to distance both himself and his brave, well-intentioned Irish protagonist from the chaotic violence of "savage" Irish vengeance and rebellion.

Yet these novels' exposure of power politics and religious hypocrisy (further influenced, perhaps, by his own Huguenot lineage), along with the espousal of "universal love" in *Melmoth*, suggest that he stood at a critical distance from sectarian loyalty and simple religious or national chauvinism. At the same time, the "Chinese-box" structure of this narrative also sometimes makes it unclear which sentiments are endorsed or mocked by Maturin.

70. For discussions of the Gothic with reference to Marx's own Gothic rhetoric, see Franco Moretti, *Signs Taken for Wonders: Essays in the Sociology of Literary Forms* (New York: Verso Books, 1988); Paulson, *Representations of Revolution*; and the special issue of *Gothic Studies* on "Material Gothic," edited by Stephen Shapiro, including his own essay treating the Gothic in relation to capitalist cycles: Stephen Shapiro, "Transvaal, Transylvania: Dracula's World-System and Gothic Periodicity," *Gothic Studies* 10, no. 1 (2008): 29–47. On the discourse of cannibalism in relation to both capitalism and colonialism, including attention to Marx's Gothic rhetoric, see especially Francis Barker, Peter Hulme, and Margaret Iverson, eds., *Cannibalism and the Colonial World* (Cambridge: Cambridge University Press, 1998); and Wright, "Devouring the Disinherited."

71. The biblical citation "gold and silver, and the souls of men" is from Revelation 13:12–13, as cited in this Penguin edition of the novel, 639.

72. Emmet, "Speech from the Dock," 2.

73. See Backus, *Gothic Family Romance*, 113; Moynihan, "Politics of Anglo-Irish Gothic," 44–47; Trumpener, *Bardic Nationalism*, 146; and especially Eagleton, *Heathcliff and the Great Hunger*, 190–93, for related comments on Melmoth as a figure embodying the fraught and ambivalent position of the Anglo-Irish.

74. See discussion of John and "Irishisms" in Backus, *Gothic Family Romance*, 113; and Pittock, *Scottish and Irish Romanticism*, 226.

75. This final tale set during the renewed colonization under Cromwell involves the Royalist Mortimer family, whose daughter joins the Puritans and creates a split in the family that ultimately issues in a grandson's madness.

76. See for instance Maturin, *Melmoth the Wanderer*, 36–37, in addition to the fortress passage, 33.

77. For the Turkish reference, see Maturin, *Melmoth the Wanderer*, 52. In the Alexander passage, Maturin implicitly mocks the aesthetics of empire—with which his own rendering starkly contrasts. For instance, in the play, as his narrator comments, "there were absurdities enough to offend a classical, or even a rational spectator. There were Grecian heroes with roses in their shoes, feathers in their hats, and wigs down to their waists; and Persian princesses in stiff stays and powdered hair" (48). At the same time, more serious insinuations appear in the jail scenes. Stanton finds himself housed in a cell between a Royalist and a Puritan, the latter of whom was "driven mad by a single sermon from the celebrated Hugh Peters" (58–59). That is, Stanton finds himself thrown back into his own nation's stormy history as it takes its turn toward empire. The two inmates, representing England's opposing parties, are now both of them raving maniacs who every night shout at each other from

their cells, volleying curses and accusations across the cell of Stanton. Stanton occupies the place between these parties of the period, suggesting his troubled position—not unlike Maturin's—on its ideological and political fault lines. He is imprisoned at the conjuncture, and driven insane by this condition.

78. The Superior summons Alonzo to his office and recalls for him, with cruel irony, the speech of Volumnia to her son Coriolanus (as imagined by Shakespeare in his play *Coriolanus*) in an attempt to persuade Coriolanus to leave Rome unharmed and peacefully. The Superior presents this story to Alonzo as follows: "You remember a remarkable story of the Roman general, who spurned from the steps of his tribune, people, senators, and priests, —trampled on all law, —outraged all religion, —but was at last moved by nature, for, when his mother prostrated herself before him, and exclaimed, 'My son, before you tread the streets of Rome, you must first tread on the body of her who bore you!' he relented.' 'I remember all, but to what does this tend?' 'To this,' and [the Superior] threw open the door; 'now, prove yourself, if you can, more obdurate than a heathen.' As the door opened, across the threshold lay my mother, prostrate on her face. She said in a stifled voice, 'Advance, —break your vows, —but you must rush to perjury over the body of your mother.' I attempted to raise her, but she clung to the ground, repeating the same words; and her magnificent dress, that overspread the floor of stone with gems and velvet, frightfully contrasted her posture of humiliation, and the despair that burned in her eyes, as she raised them to me for a moment" (110). At this, Moncada agrees to finalize his vows, and thereafter becomes an "automaton."

79. The tale he refers to is "The History of Chec Chahabeddin" by Chec Zade, translated into English in 1708 and reprised in the *Spectator* on June 18, 1711, which is likely Maturin's source.

80. Maturin's description of Alonzo's encounter with this past deserves more attention than I give it here, but some details are worth mention. After the riot, as police pound on the door, Don Fernan guides Alonzo to a trapdoor and a secret labyrinthine passage. Alonzo had already seen the family secretly practicing a Jewish ritual, and now he encounters the deeper layers of Spain's imperial racialized history through the scholar Adonijah, Fernan's brother, who has lived underground for decades. Although initially the text seems to make an anti-Semitic comedy of Alonzo's first encounter with the Fernan family, it is telling that Maturin creates a change in Alonzo's attitudes as he becomes better acquainted with the family's history. After witnessing Adonijah's grief when he narrates his loss of his mother and daughter, Alonzo explains that the experience "subdued my prejudices—it had certainly softened my heart—and at this moment I half-believed that a Jew might find entrance and adoption amid the family and fold of the blessed" (298). It is during this encounter in this underground archival space—an image of sedimented, suppressed histories—that Adonijah presents Alonzo with the "Tale of the Indians" manuscript, offering to help Alonzo escape Spain if he will translate it.

81. We might read this scene as Maturin's distillation of the "Hunchback's Tale" in *The Nights*—itself a parable of the artist riskily, precariously positioned within inter-imperial and economic fields of power, as I suggest in chapter 2.

Chapter 5: Infrastructure, Activism, and Literary Dialectics in the Early Twentieth Century

1. Adam Barrows, *The Cosmic Time of Empire: Modern Britain and World Literature* (Berkeley: University of California Press, 2011). See also Stephen Kern, *The Culture of Time and Space, 1880–1918* (Cambridge, MA: Harvard University Press, [1983] 2003); Michael Rubenstein, *Public Works: Infrastructure, Irish Modernism, and the Postcolonial* (Notre Dame, IN: University of Notre Dame Press, 2010); and Michael Rubenstein, Bruce Robbins, and Sophia Beal, eds., "Infrastructuralism," special issue, *Modern Fiction Studies* 61, no. 4 (2015).

2. Benedict Anderson, *Imagined Communities: Reflections on the Origin and Spread of Nationalism* (New York: Verso, [1983] 2006), 46.

3. Virginia Woolf, *Mrs. Dalloway* (New York: Harcourt, [1925] 1953).

4. Woolf's Anglocentrism, however, meant that she never registered the diversity of that citizenry, as Sarah Blair discusses in "Local Modernity, Global Modernism: Bloomsbury and the Places of the Literary," *ELH* 71, no. 3 (2004): 813–38; see esp. 821–30. For excellent analysis of Woolf's mixture of anti-imperial, feminist politics with chauvinist or racist assumptions, see Urmila Seshagiri, *Race and the Modernist Imagination* (Ithaca, NY: Cornell University Press, 2010).

5. Woolf, *Mrs. Dalloway*, 69–70.

6. Woolf, *Mrs. Dalloway*, 148, 21–22.

7. These lines are from her poem "Parturition"; see Mina Loy, "Parturition," in *The Lost Lunar Baedeker*, ed. Roger L. Conover (New York: Farrar, Straus and Giroux, [1914] 1996), 67–71.

8. Jorge de Lima, "Distribution of Poetry," in *Modern Brazilian Poetry: An Anthology*, trans. John Nist and Yolande Leite (Bloomington: Indiana University Press, 1962).

9. Mina Loy, "Apology of Genius," in *The Lost Lunar Baedeker*, ed. Roger L. Conover (New York: Farrar, Straus and Giroux, [1914] 1996), 4–5.

10. See Paul Kramer, "Empires, Exceptions, and Anglo-Saxons: Race and Rule between the British and United States Empires, 1880–1910," *Journal of American History* 88, no. 4 (2002): 1316.

11. Tony Ballantyne and Antoinette Burton, *Empires and the Reach of the Global, 1870–1945* (Cambridge, MA: Harvard University Press, 2014), 102.

12. Ballantyne and Burton, *Empires and the Reach*, 112, 94.

13. Qtd. in Ballantyne and Burton, *Empires and the Reach*, 101.

14. For these details, see Ballantyne and Burton, *Empires and the Reach*, 104–7. As they point out, for instance, the extraction of resources became central to the Japanese economy: by 1910 Japan imported seventeen thousand tons of rice from Korea, and the coercion of the Korean laborers only increased, so that by the mid-1930s Korea produced 1.5 million tons of rice for Japan (106).

15. Neil Faulkner further suggests that "the Long Depression was ended, like the Great Depression, by military expenditure," pointing to the fact that British military spending more than doubled (from £32 million in 1887 to £77 million in 1914), and German naval spending more than quadrupled from the mid-1890s to 1914 (rising from 90 million marks to 400 million). Such floods of spending stimulated the growth of large corporations in the arms industry and their control over states. See Neil Faulkner, "The Long Depression, 1873–1896," in *A Marxist History of the World: From Neanderthals to Neoliberals*, ed. Neil Faulkner (London: Pluto Press, 2013), 165–68.

16. See Laura Bear, *Lines of the Nation: Indian Railway Workers, Bureaucracy, and the Intimate Historical Self* (New York: Columbia University Press, 2007); and Laura Gbah Bear, "Miscegenations of Modernity: Constructing European Respectability and Race in the Indian Railway, 1857–1931," *Women's History Review* 3 (1994): 531–48. Also see Ballantyne and Burton, *Empires and the Reach*, 120–24.

17. Ballantyne and Burton, *Empires and the Reach*, 124–27.

18. Ballantyne and Burton, *Empires and the Reach*, 110–12.

19. The building of the Suez Canal differently displays the dialectics of inter-imperial coformation, anti-imperial intervention, and labor solidarity forged exactly at the site of infrastructure building. First, the conception and engineering of the canal was a thoroughly inter-imperial affair—one in which imperial collaboration and competition combined. Having received a concession from the Ottoman governor of Egypt, in 1854, the former French diplomat Ferdinand de Lesseps secured the services of the Austrian engineer Alois Negrelli, and eventually the British government purchased Egypt's share. The canal project also included a telegraph line laid alongside the waterway, allowing messages to cross seas, oceans, and continents in minutes. As such it served trade and military purposes, assuring the "safety of the empire" (Ballantyne and Burton, *Empires and the Reach*, 87). Yet the project was a catastrophe for many of the 1.5 million workers who participated in the eleven-year construction of it: approximately 120,000 workers died, and most of the laborers were forcibly transported to the site from North Africa and the Middle East. Yet for these very reasons, as Joel Beinin and Zachary Lockman point out in *Workers on the Nile: Nationalism, Communism, Islam, and the Egyptian Working Class, 1882–1954* (Cairo: American University in Cairo Press, 1998), 106–9, the building of the Suez Canal spawned a laborers' movement in the region.

20. On the use of European weaponry, also see O'Brien Browne, "Creating Chaos," MHQ: *The Quarterly Journal of Military History* 23, no. 1 (2010): 14–26. In his unconventional memoir, *Seven Pillars of Wisdom* (London: Wordsworth, [1926] 1997), Lawrence practices a singular bad faith, paraded as existentialist confession. Lawrence details his tactical decision-making as an adventurous leader of the army's train-blasting exploits, describing his inter-imperial maneuvering in the Arab Revolt, all while evasively registering his ongoing betrayals of Arab soldiers and leaders. At the same time he dwells on the bodily yearning and bonding among the men, as well as the pain and loss inflicted by inter-imperial contests. In his case, experimental form serves to obfuscate political betrayal. For suggestive discussion of the book, see Sean Francis Ward, "*Seven Pillars of Wisdom*, the Queer Times of Revolt, and Modernist Form," *Modernism/Modernity* 23, no. 2 (2016): 297–318.

21. Ballantyne and Burton, *Empires and the Reach*, 125–26.

22. See Leslie Peirce, *Morality Tales: Law and Gender in the Ottoman Court of Aintab* (Berkeley: University of California Press, 2003). Also see the forum on this book by Patricia Skinner, Indrani Chatterjee, and Julie Hardwick in the *Journal of Women's History* 18, no. 1 (2006): 181–96. Chatterjee's comments are particularly pertinent for an inter-imperial analysis.

23. Ballantyne and Burton, *Empires and the Reach*, 113.

24. Du Bois's comment is quoted in John Cullen Gruesser, *The Empire Abroad and the Empire at Home: African American Literature and the Era of Overseas Expansion* (Athens: University of Georgia Press, 2012), 110. It appeared originally in W. E. B. Du Bois, "The Color Line Belts the World," *Collier's Weekly*, October 20, 1906. Du Bois also observed that the "older idea that the whites would eventually displace the native races" has been "rudely shaken in the increase of American Negroes, the experience of the English in Africa, India, and the West Indies, and the development of South America." Also see Bill V. Mullen and Cathryn Watson, eds. *W. E. B. Du Bois on Asia: Crossing the World Color Line* (Jackson: University Press of Mississippi, 2005), 33–35.

25. For fuller discussion, see Robert Bickers and R. G. Tiedemann, eds., *The Boxers, China, and the World* (Lanham, MD: Rowman and Littlefield, 2007).

26. Ballantyne and Burton, *Empires and the Reach*, 105.

27. See Prasenjit Duara, "The Imperialism of 'Free Nations': Japan, Manchukuo, and the History of the Present," in *Imperial Formations*, ed. Anne Stoler, Carole McGranahan, and Peter C. Perdue (Santa Fe, NM: School for Advanced Research Press, 2007), 219–20. Also see Ballantyne and Burton, *Empires and the Reach*, 105–7.

28. Pradip Kumar Datta, "The Interlocking Worlds of the Anglo-Boer War in South Africa/India," *South African Historical Journal* 57, no. 1 (2007): 55–56; Robert Gerwarth and Erez Manela, *Empires at War: 1911–1923* (New York: Oxford University Press, 2014), 16.

29. Gerwarth and Manela, *Empires at War*, 16.

30. Donal P. McCracken, *MacBride's Brigade: Irish Commandos in the Anglo-Boer War* (Dublin: Four Courts Press, 1999).

31. Datta, "Interlocking Worlds," 52, 40–41; Gerwarth and Manela, *Empires at War*, 10, 167–76; and Ballantyne and Burton, *Empires and the Reach*, 147–70.

32. See Ballantyne and Burton, *Empires and the Reach*, 158–60; Elleke Boehmer, *Empire, the National, and the Postcolonial, 1890–1920: Resistance in Interaction* (Oxford: Oxford University Press, 2002); Pradip Kumar Datta, "Interlocking Worlds," 55–56; and Malvern van Wyk Smith, *Drummer Hodge: The Poetry of the Anglo-Boer War, 1899–1902* (Oxford: Oxford University Press, 1978), 257.

33. See Selina Lai-Henderson, *Mark Twain in China* (Stanford, CA: Stanford University Press, 2015). She remarks that to this day "Twain is seen in China as a courageous anti-imperialist" (2–3). For Alcott, see Heather Wayne, "Gilded Chains: Global Economies and Gendered Arts in U.S. Fiction, 1865–1930" (PhD diss., University of Massachusetts, Amherst, 2019).

34. See Apollon Davidson and Irina Filatova, *The Russians and the Anglo-Boer War: 1899–1902* (Cape Town: Human and Rousseau, 1998). Also see Richard B. Mulanax, *The Boer War in American Politics and Diplomacy* (Lanham, MD: University Press of America, 1994); and Keith Wilson, ed., *The International Impact of the Boer War* (Chesham, UK: Acumen, 2001).

35. van Wyk Smith, *Drummer Hodge*, 11; also see Ballantyne and Burton, *Empires and the Reach*, chapter 2.

36. Virginia Woolf, "Narrow Bridge of Art," in *Collected Essays of Virginia Woolf*, ed. Leonard Woolf (Boston: Harcourt, 1966), 2:218–29; see 2:222.

37. Yeats published the poem first in *The Dial* in 1919 and then in *Michael Robartes and the Dancer* (Dublin: Cuala Press, 1921).

38. Qtd. in C. A. Bayly, "The Boxer Uprising and India: Globalizing Myths," in *The Boxers, China, and the World*, ed. Robert Bickers and R. G. Tiedemann (Lanham, MD: Rowman and Littlefield, 2007), 147–56, esp. 150, 148, and 153. In this collection, also see Anand Yang, "(A) Subaltern('s) Boxers: An Indian Soldier's Account of China and the World in 1900–1901," 43–64. For discussions of communications, see Ballantyne and Burton, *Empires and the Reach*, esp. chapter 2, including in relation to the Boxer Uprising (105).

39. Bayly, "Boxer Uprising," 150.

40. Boehmer, *Empire*, 31.

41. Qtd. in Boehmer, *Empire*, 31.

42. Boehmer, *Empire*, 26.

43. See Robin D. G. Kelley's groundbreaking essay, "But a Local Phase of a World Problem: Black History's Global Vision, 1883–1950," *Journal of American History* 86, no. 3 (1999): 1045–77, 1057.

44. Kelley, "But a Local Phase," 1053.

45. Gruesser, *Empire Abroad*, 113.

46. Qtd. in Kelley, "But a Local Phase," 1057.

47. Qtd. in Datta, "Interlocking Worlds," 55. Also see Datta's discussion of civilizationalism, including its implications for African peoples, 46–49, 57–58.

48. See discussions in Bayly, "Boxer Uprising"; Ballantyne and Burton, *Empires and the Reach*; and Datta, "Interlocking Worlds."

49. Ballantyne and Burton, *Empires and the Reach*, 177–78.

50. See Duara, "Imperialism of 'Free Nations,'" 214. Also see Duara's full discussion for important information and analysis.

51. Ballantyne and Burton, *Empires and the Reach*, 178. Also see van Wyk Smith, *Drummer Hodge*, 254–55, including his point that US Americans supporting the Boers invoked the racialist Anglo-Saxon myth.

52. Qtd. in Bayly, "Boxer Uprising," 150.

53. Bayly, "Boxer Uprising," 150–51.

54. Elleke Boehmer, "Peripheral Avant-gardes: Mafeking and Calcutta on or around 1910" (paper presented at Modernist Communities conference, Institute du Monde Anglophone, Université Nouvelle Sorbonne, Paris, April 24–26, 2014).

55. Homi Bhabha, *The Location of Culture* (New York: Routledge, 1994).

56. Datta, "Interlocking Worlds," 39–44, 48–49, 53–56.

57. See Gauri Viswanathan, "Ireland, India, and the Poetics of Internationalism," *Journal of World History* 15, no. 1 (2004): 7–30. Viswanathan takes Cousins and Tagore as her case studies for exploring these difficulties.

58. Michelle Stephens, *Black Empire: The Masculine Global Imaginary of Caribbean Intellectuals in the United States, 1914–1962* (Durham, NC: Duke University Press, 2005), 5–6.

59. Stephens, *Black Empire*, 13.

60. See both Kuan-Hsing Chen, *Asia as Method: Toward Deimperialization* (Durham, NC: Duke University Press, 2010); and Datta, "Interlocking Worlds."

61. van Wyk Smith, *Drummer Hodge*, xii.

62. H. M. Hyndman, *Justice*, July 20, 1901, qtd. in van Wyk Smith, *Drummer Hodge*, 135.

63. For statistics on numbers killed, see the introduction to Gerwarth and Manela, *Empires at War*; and John Morrow, *The Great War: An Imperial History* (New York: Vintage, 2004), esp. 283–85.

64. See Gerwarth and Manela, *Empires at War*, 6.

65. For Du Bois's remark, see Kelley "But a Local Phase," 1057. For Lenin, see his preface to the first edition of "State and Revolution," in *V. I. Lenin Collected Works*, vol. 25, *June–September 1917* (Moscow: Progress, 1964), 1. Lenin argued that "the so-called Great Powers have long been exploiting and enslaving a whole number of small and weak nations. And the imperialist war is a war for the division and redivision of this kind of booty."

66. See the Kent Research Group led by Caroline Rooney, "Radical Distrust: A Cultural Analysis of the Emotional, Psychological and Linguistic Formations of Religious and Political Extremism," UK Research and Innovation, accessed March 20, 2020, http://gtr.rcuk .ac.uk/projects?ref=ES%2FG034362%2F1. Also see Caroline Rooney, "The Disappointed of the Earth," *Psychoanalysis and History* 11, no. 2 (2009): 159–74.

67. See Guoqi Xu, *China and the Great War: China's Pursuit of a New National Identity and Internationalization* (New York: Cambridge University Press, 2001); also see "100 Years Legacies: The Lasting Impact of World War I," *Wall Street Journal*, July 10, 2014, http:// online.wsj.com/ww1/chinese-communism.

68. Gerwarth and Manela, *Empires at War*, 157.

69. Stephens, *Black Empire*, 13.

70. The term *literary activism* has recently been used to describe the actions in the last decade of the Underground Literary Alliance. I am referring to a much earlier and wider

phenomenon, one which, in effect, created the aesthetic-political field of relations in which more recent forms operate.

71. African-Atlantic artist-activists played key parts. See Kate Baldwin, *Beyond the Color Line and the Iron Curtain: Reading Encounters between Black and Red, 1922–1963* (Durham, NC: Duke University Press, 2002); Brent Edwards, *Practice of Diaspora: Literature, Translation, and the Rise of Black Internationalism* (Cambridge, MA: Harvard University Press, 2009); Fred Ho and Bill V. Mullen, *Afro-Asia: Revolutionary Political and Cultural Connections between African Americans and Asian Americans* (Durham, NC: Duke University Press, 2008); and Jahan Ramazani, *A Transnational Poetics* (Chicago: University of Chicago Press, 2009). For discussion of other arts in the period, see Stephen Ross and Allana C. Lindgren, eds., *The Modernist World* (New York: Routledge, 2015)—although because their discussions are divided by region, they give limited space to the interconnections among movements.

72. Patrick Brantlinger, *Rule of Darkness: British Literature and Imperialism 1830–1914* (Ithaca, NY: Cornell University Press, 1988), esp. chapter 8. For further study of the bellicosity of this period as it entered literature, see Cecil Degrotte Eby, *The Road to Armageddon: The Martial Spirit in English Popular Literature, 1870–1914* (Durham, NC: Duke University Press, 1987).

73. Lewis, "BLAST! Manifesto."

74. Filippo Tommaso Marinetti, "The Founding and the Manifesto of Futurism," in *Let's Murder the Moonshine: Selected Writings*, ed. and trans. R. W. Flint (Los Angeles: Sun and Moon Classics, [1909] 1991), 47–52.

75. Marinetti, "Founding and the Manifesto of Futurism." Marinetti (1876–1944) was a young man living in Egypt during the First Italo-Ethiopian War, and his manifesto suggests that he was determined to overcome the sense of defeat. His investment in recovering Italian pride is further suggested by the fact that he volunteered at the ripe age of sixty to serve in the Second Italo-Ethiopian War of 1935–36, which was equally disastrous for Italy. In this light, we might also wonder if Friedrich Nietzsche, whose writings inspired many futurists, might himself have been writing under the pressure of this inter-imperial nervousness and ressentiment, as suggested in his correspondence with Georg Brandes, where the two share their chagrin at the censorship or dismissal of their books in the German and Russian Empires. See George Brandes, *Friedrich Nietzsche* (London: William Heinemann, 1914), 91.

76. On manifestos of the period, see especially Janet Lyon, *Provocations: Manifestoes of the Modern* (Ithaca, NY: Cornell University Press, 1999); and Laura Winkiel, *Modernism, Race, and Manifestoes* (New York: Cambridge University Press, 2011).

77. In *The English Writings of Rabindranath Tagore*, ed. Sisir Kumar Das (New Delhi: Sahitya Akademi, 1994), 2:466. This version of the poem draws together phrases from several of Tagore's Bengali poems; it bears the most resemblance to "Satabdir Surya Aji" ("Today Is the Centenary's Sun"). I thank my colleague at the University of Massachusetts-Amherst, Professor Malcolm Sen, for this information.

78. van Wyk Smith, *Drummer Hodge*, 137.

79. van Wyk Smith, *Drummer Hodge*, 134.

80. See Catherine Walworth, *Soviet Salvage: Imperial Debris, Revolutionary Reuse, and Russian Constructivism* (University Park: Pennsylvania State University Press, 2017).

81. Tristan Tzara, "Dada Manifesto" (1918), accessed April 29, 2019, http://writing.upenn.edu/library/Tzara_Dada-Manifesto_1918.pdf.

82. Tzara, "Dada Manifesto" (1918).

83. Loy, "Human Cylinders," in *The Lost Lunar Baedeker*, ed. Roger L. Conover (New York: Farrar, Straus and Giroux, [1914] 1996), 12–13, 12.

84. See Ruth Jennison, *The Zukofsky Era: Modernity, Margins, and the Avant-Garde* (Baltimore: Johns Hopkins University Press, 2012). Also see Warwick Research Collective, *Combined and Uneven Development: Towards a New Theory of World-Literature* (Liverpool: Liverpool University Press, 2015).

85. The lines about "war's red planet" are from Laurence Binyon's poem, "Europe, MDCCCI—to Napoleon," qtd. in van Wyk Smith, *Drummer Hodge*, from 33. Also see van Wyk Smith for poems reflecting on the power of new weaponry to create mass death, e.g., Stephen Phillips's "Midnight—The 31st of December, 1900," which remarks that "a man shall set his hand to a handle and wither/ Invisible armies and fleets" (qtd. in van Wyck Smith, *Drummer Hodge*, 33).

86. See Peter Brooker, Sascha Bru, Andrew Thacker, and Christian Weikop, eds., *The Oxford Critical and Cultural History of Modernist Magazines*, vol. 3, *Europe, 1880–1940* (New York: Oxford University Press, 2013); Peter Brooker and Andrew Thacker, eds., *The Oxford Critical and Cultural History of Modernist Magazines*, vol. 1, *Britain and Ireland, 1880–1955* (New York: Oxford University Press, 2009); Peter Brooker and Andrew Thacker, eds., *The Oxford Critical and Cultural History of Modernist Magazines*, vol. 2, *North America, 1894–1960* (New York: Oxford University Press, 2012); Eric Bulson, *Little Magazine, World Form* (New York: Columbia University Press, 2016); and the *Modernist Journals Project*, accessed May 31, 2019, http://modjourn.org/index.html.

87. See Alison Donnell, "Heard but Not Seen: Women's Short Stories and the BBC's *Caribbean Voices* Programme," in *The Caribbean Short Story: Critical Perspectives*, ed. L. Evans, M. McWatt, and E. Smith (Leeds, UK: Peepal Tree Press, 2011), 29–43.

88. See Carol Batker, *Reforming Fictions: Native, African, and Jewish American Women's Literature and Journalism in the Progressive Era* (New York: Columbia University Press, 2000); and Jennifer Wilks, "Print Diasporas: Genre and the Circulation of Black Women's Modernist Texts" (paper presented at Modernist Communities conference, Institute du Monde Anglophone, Université Nouvelle Sorbonne, Paris, April 24–26, 2014). Also see Donnell, "Heard but Not Seen."

89. Eric Bulson, "Little Magazine, World Form," in *The Oxford Handbook of Global Modernisms*, ed. Mark Wollaeger and Matt Eatough (New York: Oxford University Press, 2012), 267–77.

90. Elleke Boehmer discussed this pastiche in her paper "Peripheral Avant-gardes." Also see her discussion in "The View from Empire: The Turn-of-the-Century Globalizing World,"

in *Late Victorian into Modern*, ed. Laura Marcus, Michèle Mendelssohn, Kirsten Shepherd-Barr (Oxford: Oxford University Press, 2016), 305–18.

91. James Smith, "The Radical Literary Magazine of the 1930s and British Government Surveillance: The Case of Storm Magazine," *Literature and History* 19, no. 2 (2017): 69–86.

92. See Loy, "Feminist Manifesto," in *The Lost Lunar Baedeker*, ed. Roger L. Conover (New York: Farrar, Straus and Giroux, [1914] 1996), 269–71; and *A Pan-African Manifesto*, August 30, 1921, W. E. B. Du Bois Papers (MS 312), Special Collections and University Archives, University of Massachusetts Amherst Libraries. On modernist manifestos, see especially Lyon, *Provocations*; and Winkiel, *Modernism*.

93. Langston Hughes, "The Negro Artist and the Racial Mountain," in *Double-Take*, ed. Venetria K. Patton and Maureen Honey (New Brunswick, NJ: Rutgers University Press, 2001), 40. Hughes's manifesto was first published in the *Nation*, June 1926.

94. Progressive Writers Association, "Manifesto of the Progressive Writers Association" (1936), SAPF Online, accessed April 29, 2019, http://pwa75.sapfonline.org/gpage4.html.

95. de Andrade, "Cannibal Manifesto."

96. See discussion in Cemil Aydin, *The Politics of Anti-Westernism in Asia: Visions of World Order in Pan-Islamic and Pan-Asian Thought* (New York: Columbia University Press, 2007). Aydin also notes that Pan-Asianism is not simply anti-imperial, for it took inspiration from the rise of Japan and also found expression in Russian imperial self-fashioning as a union of East and West, as discussed above. Also see Harsha Ram's discussion of Italian and Russian futurisms, particularly his observation that both groups "displayed a hypertrophied awareness of the competitive and hierarchical nature of the international literary system," in "Futurist Geographies: Uneven Modernities and the Struggle for Aesthetic Autonomy: Paris, Italy, Russia, 1909–14," in *The Oxford Handbook of Global Modernisms*, ed. Mark Wollaeger and Matt Eatough (New York: Oxford University Press, 2012), 330.

97. See Velimir Khlebnikov, "*Futurian!*" (1918), in *Collected Works of Velimir Khlebnikov*, vol. 1, *Letters and Theoretical Writings* (Cambridge, MA: Harvard University Press, 1987), 260–62.

98. Velimir Khlebnikov, "An Indo-Russian Union," in *Collected Works of Velimir Khlebnikov*.

99. See essays in Laura Doyle, ed., "Inter-imperiality," special issue, MFS: *Modern Fiction Studies* 64, no. 3 (2018), especially Jacqulyn Gaik Ing Teoh, "Shadow Plays with Imperial Pasts: Writing Wayang in Pramoedya Ananta Toer's *The Fugitive*," 403–30; S. Bahun, "Gaps, or the Dialectics of Inter-imperial Art: The Case of the Belgrade Surrealist Circle," 458–87; Stephen Joyce, "Inter-imperial Aesthetics: Korean and Korean Diasporic Literature between Empires," 488–511; Lynda Ng, "Xinjiang's Indelible Footprint: Reading the New Imperialism of Neoliberalism in *English* and *Waiting for the Barbarians*," 512–36; and Nayoung Aimee Kwon, "Japanophone Literature? A Transpacific Query on Absence," 537–58. On modernist literature specifically, see Sanja Bahun, "The Balkans Uncovered: Toward Historie Croisée of Modernism," in *The Oxford Handbook of Global Modernisms*, ed. Mark Wollaeger and Matt Eatough (New York: Oxford University Press, 2012), 25–47; and Vicky Unruh, "Modernity's Labors in Latin America: The Cultural Work of Cuba's

Avant-Gardes," in *The Oxford Handbook of Global Modernisms*, ed. Mark Wollaeger and Matt Eatough (New York: Oxford University Press, 2012), 341–66. Also see Annette Damayanti Lienau, "Re-Framing Vernacular Culture on Arabic Fault Lines: Bamba, Senghor, and Sembene's Translingual Legacies in French West Africa," *PMLA* 130, no. 2 (2015): 419–29.

100. Unruh, "Modernity's Labors in Latin America," 342.

101. Unruh, "Modernity's Labors in Latin America," 341.

102. See Yunte Huang, *Transpacific Imaginations: History, Literature, Counterpoetics* (Cambridge, MA: Harvard University Press, 2008). As Yunte Huang points out, many tibishi works made coded political reflections, signaled by references to legendary figures exiled or oppressed by imperial Chinese dynasties; and the inscription sites were often politically freighted, for instance near the gates of a palace or temple. Huang therefore describes the tibishi tradition as an ancient form of counterhistory, blossoming outside the strict control of official dynastic histories. The *Angel Island* writers also strike notes of longing for China to return to its past grandeur as an empire, as when one poet laments: "We Chinese of a weak nation" (Erika Lee and Judy Yung, *Angel Island: Immigrant Gateway to America* [New York: Oxford University Press, 2010], 63). In this way their stance may be compared with some Chinese writers who back home were writing "coolie" fiction, as studied by Elizabeth Weber, "Reimagining Coolie Trajectories: The Triumphant Return as Political Statement in Late Qing 'Coolie' Fiction," *Literature Compass* 13, no. 5 (2016): 300–10. While such writers decried Western exploitation and mistreatment of Chinese labor, some of them also imagined a "utopian" return of the Ming empire while implicitly marking the Qing dynasty as itself a foreign, Chinese-betraying imposition. For another suggestive instance, see Mu Shiying, "The Shanghai Foxtrot (a Fragment)," introduced by Sean Macdonald, *Modernism/Modernity* 11, no. 4 (2004): 797–807. These examples all indicate how layered imperial histories often underlie the shape of dissenting texts.

103. See Lee and Yung, *Angel Island*.

104. See, for instance, Baldwin, *Beyond the Color Line*; Edwards, *Practice of Diaspora*; and Ho and Mullen, *Afro-Asia*. Elleke Boehmer uses the term *interdiscursive* to characterize the traveling practices and ideas, in *Empire, the National, and the Postcolonial*, esp. 8–12. For a longer-historical perspective on the role of laborers in the travels of aesthetic formations, see Laura Doyle, ed., "Labor Travels, Art Forms," special issues, *Literature Compass* 13, no. 5 (2016); and *Literature Compass* 17, no. 1 (2020).

105. Gruesser discusses, for instance, James Weldon Johnson and his brother J. Rosamund Johnson who were writers of musical comedies. In some of their work they aimed to parody the US discourse of the "yellow peril" but their representations could be interpreted as negatively stereotyping Asian characters. As Gruesser suggests, it is sometimes difficult to distinguish between internalized racism and strategic parodies of such racism; and it is in any case impossible to control the potential reinforcement of racism among audiences. See Gruesser, *Empire Abroad*, chapter 4.

106. Citations here are from Ben Tran, "Queer Internationalism and Modern Vietnamese Aesthetics," in *Oxford Handbook of Global Modernisms*, ed. Mark Wollaeger and Matt

Eatough (New York: Oxford University Press, 2012), 367–84. Also see Ben Tran's later book on these topics: *Post-Mandarin: Masculinity and Aesthetic Modernity in Colonial Vietnam* (New York: Fordham University Press, 2017).

107. Tran, "Queer Internationalism," 372.

108. Tran, "Queer Internationalism," 372.

109. Tran suggests that this period laid seeds for the later cultivation of Vietnamese national literature, although those seeds would be forced to lie fallow for decades, first because of World War II, when Germany (briefly) occupied the country; and then, after the war, because the country suffered partition and complex imperial domination by France and the United States as well as China. See Tran, "Queer Internationalism," 372.

110. See Laura Doyle, ed., "Inter-imperiality," special issue, MFS: *Modern Fiction Studies* 64, no. 3 (2018); and Laura Doyle and Sahar Amer, eds., "Reframing Postcolonial and Global Studies in the Longer Durée," special issue, PMLA 130, no. 2 (2015). In the PMLA cluster, see especially essays by Annette Damayanti Lienau, "Reframing Vernacular Culture on Arabic Fault Lines," 419–29; Lydia H. Liu, "Scripts in Motion: Writing as Imperial Technology, Past and Present," 375–83; Mary Louise Pratt, "Language and the Afterlives of Empire," 348–57; and Hayrettin Yücesoy, "Language of Empire: Politics of Arabic and Persian in the Abbasid World," 384–92.

111. For some comparable dynamics in India, see Priyamvada Gopal, *Literary Radicalism in India: Gender, Nation and the Transition to Independence* (New York: Routledge, 2005).

112. See Tran, "Queer Internationalism," 376. Mark Hussey points in a similar direction in his account of the queer sexual politics of the Bloomsbury Group in Britain; see Mark Hussey, "Mrs. Thatcher and Mrs. Woolf," MFS: *Modern Fiction Studies* 50, no. 1 (2004): 8–30.

113. Qtd. in Tran, "Queer Internationalism," 370.

114. As Tran notes, both Gide and many Vietnamese saw that "fascism's agenda of national supremacy, imperial aggression, and aesthetic censorship" was a serious threat ("Queer Internationalism," 370).

115. Qtd. in Tran, "Queer Internationalism," 377.

116. Tran, "Queer Internationalism," 377, 372.

Chapter 6: Rape, Revolution, and Queer Male Longing in Carpentier's *The Kingdom of This World*

1. Naomi Klein, *This Changes Everything: Capitalism vs. the Climate* (New York: Simon and Schuster, 2014).

2. Carpentier, *The Kingdom of This World*, trans. Harriet de Onís (New York: Farrar, Straus and Giroux, 1957; renewed by Alfred A. Knopf, 1985), 117.

3. For his notion of the links between the Caribbean and the Mediterranean, see Alejo Carpentier, "On the Marvelous Real in America," trans. Tanya Huntington and Lois Parkinson

Zamora, in *Magical Realism: Theory, History, Community*, edited by Lois Parkinson Zamora and Wendy B. Faris (Durham, NC: Duke University Press, 1995), 75–88; see 83. I will return to this text later for its comments on rape and sexuality.

Also see Susan Gillman's comments on Carpentier's notion in relation to C. L. R. James and *The Black Jacobins* and, more broadly, to the Caribbean intellectuals' ways of brooding on old world and new world relations. I place more emphasis on structural co-formations, and indeed it would be valuable to look more closely at these two regions together. One might not only compare systemic and inter-imperial transformations in the tenth- to the fifteenth-century Mediterranean to those of the fifteenth- to the twentieth-century Caribbean but also consider their linked historical and dialectical unfolding. See Gillman, "Black Jacobins and New World Mediterraneans," in *Surveying the American Tropics: A Literary Geography from New York to Rio*, ed. Maria Cristina Fumagalli, Peter Hulme, Owen Robinson, and Lesley Wylie (Liverpool: Liverpool University Press, 2013), 159–82. It's also noteworthy, as I've discussed elsewhere, that Hegel thought about the Americas in relation to the Mediterranean. See Laura Doyle, *Freedom's Empire: Race and the Rise of the Novel, 1640–1940* (Durham, NC: Duke University Press, 2008), 338–40.

4. I allude here to the title of Kenneth Pomeranz's book, *The Great Divergence*, echoing my point in chapter 1 that his valuable account of the growing imbalance of power (the "divergence") between south/eastern and north/western economies in the early nineteenth century also represented a "convergence" of systems and economies. The word *shatterzone* alludes to the book by Omer Bartov and Eric D. Weitz, *Shatterzone of Empire: Coexistence and Violence in the German, Habsburg, Russian, and Ottoman Borderlands* (Bloomington: Indiana University Press, 2013).

5. Édouard Glissant, *Caribbean Discourse: Selected Essays*, trans. J. Michael Dash (Charlottesville: University of Virginia Press, 1989), 5.

6. On the importance of technology to neoimperialism in the Caribbean, see Hilbourne A. Watson, "The Political Economy of U.S.-Caribbean Relations," *Black Scholar* 11, no. 3 (1980): 30–41, esp. 32–36.

7. Donette Francis, *Fictions of Feminine Citizenship: Sexuality and the Nation in Contemporary Caribbean Literature* (New York: Palgrave Macmillan, 2010), 3, 97. The body of scholarship on gender, literature, and masculinity politics in the Caribbean is capacious. See for example Belinda Edmondson, *Making Men: Gender, Literary Authority, and Women's Writing in Caribbean Narrative* (Durham, NC: Duke University Press, 1998); Belinda Edmondson, ed., *Caribbean Romances: The Politics of Regional Representation* (Charlottesville: University of Virginia Press, 1999); Curdella Forbes, *From Nation to Diaspora: Samuel Selvon, George Lamming, and the Cultural Performance of Gender* (Kingston, Jamaica: University of the West Indies Press, 2005); R. Reddock, ed., *Interrogating Caribbean Masculinities: Theoretical and Empirical Analyses* (Kingston, Jamaica: University of West Indies Press, 2004); P. Mohammed, ed., *Gendered Realities: Essays in Feminist Caribbean Thought* (Kingston, Jamaica: University of West Indies Press, 2002); Carol Bailey, *A Poetics of Performance: The Oral-Scribal Aesthetics in Anglophone Caribbean Fiction* (Kingston, Jamaica: University of West Indies Press, 2014); Maurice Hall, "Negotiating Jamaican Masculinities," in *Global Masculinities and Manhood*,

ed. Ronald L. Jackson and Murali Balaji (Urbana: University of Illinois Press, 2011), 31–51; and Faith Smith, ed., *Sex and the Citizen: Interrogating the Caribbean* (Charlottesville: University of Virginia Press, 2011).

8. For recent discussion of texts in other languages, see the special issue on "Interimperiality" in *MFS: Modern Fiction Studies* 64, no. 3 (2018), with essays on Indonesian, Turkish, Yugoslav, and Korean literatures, as well as on English literature in relation to China and the Atlantic world. Also see Chisu Teresa Ko, "Self-Orientalism and Interimperiality in Anna Kazumi Stahl's *Flores de un solodía*," *Latin American and Caribbean Ethnic Studies* 14, no. 1 (2018): 1–20.

9. Joyce, *Ulysses*, 1.638–44.

10. Joyce, *Ulysses*, 9.956. The body of criticism on this novel, including interpretative debates about the sexual politics of Molly Bloom's monologue, is too vast to document here. Suffice it to say that Joyce provoked a world of thought on these matters.

11. Joyce, *Ulysses*, 2.49–52, 2.67, 2.49–51.

12. Joyce, *Ulysses*, 2.49–53. Stephen's reflections on the "actual" and the "possible" draw on Aristotle's discussion in the *Metaphysics*. For discussion of Aristotle's ideas, see the entry on actuality and potentiality in the *Stanford Encyclopedia of Philosophy*, October 8, 2000 (updated June 15, 2016), https://plato.stanford.edu/entries/aristotle-metaphysics/#ActuPote.

13. Anand also raises questions about empire, civilization, and longue-durée history in relation to a speech by Gandhi that Bakha hears. Although sensing Gandhi's own condescension toward the Dalit community, Bakha is inspired by a debate among some listeners about the prospects for India's independent path toward modernization, tellingly staged between a Muslim barrister and a Hindu poet. Both men celebrate "ancient India's" infrastructure building (the canals installed "four thousand years before Christ") even as their historical divisions and civilizational chauvinisms affect their disagreements about India's long-historical inheritances. Mulk Raj Anand, *Untouchable* (London: Penguin Books, [1935] 2014), 140. Also see Banu Subramaniam, *Holy Science: The Biopolitics of Hindu Nationalism* (Seattle: University of Washington Press, 2019) for an analysis of the persisting imbrication of empire, science, and competitive claims to "archaic modernities" in India.

14. Ayi Kwei Armah, *Two Thousand Seasons* (Popenguine, Senegal: Per Ankh, [1973] 2000), 24.

15. Armah's work deserves more attention and appreciation from this angle. I've written a chapter that could not be included here but may make it into print elsewhere.

16. Patricia Powell, *The Pagoda* (New York: Knopf, 1998), 7.

17. In *Midnight's Children*, for example, Rushdie's story mocks the rivalry between Saleem and Shiva but ultimately blames women for the state legacies of violence.

18. Ngũgĩ wa Thiong'o, *The River Between* (London: Heinemann, 1965), 1.

19. Antonio Benítez-Rojo, *The Repeating Island: The Caribbean and the Postmodern Perspective*, trans. James E. Maraniss (Durham, NC: Duke University Press, 1997). In Benítez-Rojo's account of the archipelago, the clustered presence of multiple islands in the Caribbean, whose borders are at once distinct and fluidly interconnected, means that while each

island is easily colonized it is also unsettlingly close to those of rival colonizers, from the various European colonizers' perspectives, while for inhabitants this proximity has both fostered and hampered interisland solidarities. For later scholarship, see Brian R. Roberts and Michelle A. Stephens, eds., *American Archipelagic Studies* (Durham, NC: Duke University Press, 2017). My approach has also been shaped by the thought of Elizabeth M. DeLoughery, *Routes and Roots: Navigating Caribbean and Pacific Island Literatures* (Honolulu: University of Hawai'i Press, 2007); Maria Cristina Fumagalli, *On the Edge: Writing the Border between Haiti and the Dominican Republic* (Liverpool: Liverpool University Press, 2015); Christopher P. Iannini, *Fatal Revolutions: Natural History, West Indian Slavery and the Routes of American Literature* (Chapel Hill: University of North Carolina Press, 2012); and Nelson Maldonado-Torres, *Against War: Views from the Underside of Modernity* (Durham, NC: Duke University Press, 2008). Also see my discussion of Maldonado-Torres's work in chapter 4.

20. See the roundtable forum featuring Patrick Bellegarde-Smith, Alex Dupuy, Robert Fatton Jr., Mary Renda, Ermitte St. Jacques, and Jeffrey Sommers, "Haiti and Its Occupation by the United States in 1915: Antecedents and Outcomes," *Journal of Haitian Studies* 21, no. 2 (2015): 10–43; for Renda's comments, see 15. Also see Mary A. Renda, *Taking Haiti: Military Occupation and the Culture of U.S. Imperialism: 1915–1940* (Chapel Hill: University of North Carolina Press, 2001); and Brenda Gayle Plummer, "The Metropolitan Connection: Foreign and Semiforeign Elites in Haiti, 1900–1915," *Latin American Research Review* 19, no. 2 (1984): 119–42.

21. In "The Metropolitan Connection," Plummer remarks that imperial maneuvers in early twentieth-century Haiti particularly revealed "the manner in which commerce, rather than plantation enterprise or extensive capital investment, could foster socio-economic decline"; and Hilbourne Watson observes that capitalists and imperialists have worked together to "counteract and contain the dialectic of the national liberation revolution." See Plummer, "Metropolitan Connection," 119; and Hilbourne A. Watson, "The Political Economy of U.S.-Caribbean Relations," *Black Scholar* 11, no. 3 (1980): 31.

22. See Raphael Dalleo, *American Imperialism's Undead: The Occupation of Haiti and the Rise of Caribbean Anticolonialism* (Charlottesville: University of Virginia Press, 2016).

23. See Carole Boyce Davies and Monica Jardine, "Imperial Geographies and Caribbean Nationalism: At the Border between 'A Dying Colonialism' and U.S. Hegemony," CR: *The New Centennial Review* 3, no. 3 (2003): 151–74. Also see the feminist criticism cited in note 7.

24. See Roberto González Echevarría, *Alejo Carpentier: The Pilgrim at Home* (Ithaca, NY: Cornell University Press, 1977), 25.

25. Dalleo, *American Imperialism's Undead*, 126.

26. Also see Frank Moya Pons, *The Dominican Republic: A National History*, 3rd ed. (Princeton, NJ: Markus Weiner Press, 2010).

27. Valdés Sánchez points out that although the United States and Britain were "political allies in the Cold War"—and they both backed the dictators who served their interests in Cuba—"they were commercial rivals when it came to trade." Yet Cuban diplomats also maneuvered shrewdly around the United States to maintain bilateral trade, for instance arrang-

ing the import of British-manufactured buses and the British building of electric plants, although the United States frowned upon it. See Servando Valdés Sánchez, "Anglo-Cuban Diplomacy: Economic and Political Links with Britain (1945–60)," *International Journal of Cuban Studies* 8, no. 1 (2016): 57.

28. Melvin Small, "The United States and the German 'Threat' to the Hemisphere, 1905–1914," *Americas* 28, no. 3 (1972): 252–70. Written from the perspective of US "interests" in the region, Small's 1972 article is far from leftist, but it includes valuable information.

29. Another inter-imperial story is in play here involving the Ottoman Empire and Lebanese Christians. The United States wedged its way into Haitian internal trade partly via the so-called Syrian community (as called by Haitians), which was actually mostly Lebanese Christians who had fled poverty and oppression under the Ottoman Empire. Throughout the occupation, the United States worked with mixed success to enlist the Lebanese merchants as a US "protected" client community. See Brenda Gayle Plummer, "Race, Nationality, and Trade in the Caribbean: The Syrians in Haiti, 1903–1934," *International History Review* 3, no. 4 (1981): 517–39.

30. The US support for Trujillo was a bumpy ride, in part because Trujillo's extreme violence sometimes endangered US labor and trade interests on the island. For instance, Trujillo's racist-inflected massacre of Haitians along the Haitian–Dominican Republic border in the 1937 Parsley Massacre (estimates of the Haitian deaths range from twelve thousand to thirty-five thousand) caused widespread destabilization and renewed resistance in the region among both Haitians and Dominicans. The United States had helped to foster the programs for the migration of seasonal bracero laborers here and throughout the Caribbean, by which underpaid laborers increased the profits of both local elites and US capitalists and state actors, but it hesitated to expose or restrain Trujillo since his brutally repressive government otherwise enabled US neocolonialism. As Fumagalli discusses in *On the Edge*, the later literature of these countries explores the complex animosities and struggles spawned by Haiti's and the Dominican Republic's interlocking histories, reaching from the 1822 annexation of the newly independent Dominican Republic (for twenty years) and beyond the 1937 Parsley Massacre to Trujillo's assassination in 1961.

31. Qtd. in Boyce Davies and Jardine, "Imperial Geographies," 162–63.

32. Qtd. in Monique Bedasse, *Jah Kingdom: Rastafarians, Tanzania, and Pan-Africanism in the Age of Decolonization* (Chapel Hill: University of North Carolina Press, 2017), 83; emphasis added.

33. See Kwame Nkrumah, *Neo-colonialism: The Last Stage of Imperialism* (London: International Publishers, 1965). For valuable discussion of Nkrumah and nonalignment as a carefully calibrated policy of international relations, see Frank Gerits, "'When the Bull Elephants Fight': Kwame Nkrumah, Non-Alignment, and Pan-Africanism as an Interventionist Ideology in the Global Cold War, 1957–66," *International History Review* 37, no. 5 (2015): 951–69. Interestingly these decolonial thinkers also write about the longer histories of learning and scholarship, as in Nkrumah's article, "Africa Had Scholars before Europe," *Evening News*, September 4, 1963.

34. Gerits, "'When the Bull Elephants Fight,'" 954; Carpentier, *The Kingdom of This World,* hereafter cited parenthetically by page number.

35. On these associations, see Lara Putnam, "Nothing Matters but Color: Transnational Circuits, the Interwar Caribbean, and the Black International," in *From Toussaint to Tupac: The Black International since the Age of Revolution,* ed. Michael O. West, William G. Martin, and Fanon Che Wilkins (Chapel Hill: University of North Carolina Press, 2009), 107–29; and Dave Gosse, "Examining the Promulgation and Impact of the Great Commission in the Caribbean, 1492–1970: A Historical Analysis," in *Teaching All Nations: Interrogating the Matthean Great Commission,* ed. Mitzi J. Smith and Jayachitra Lalitha (Minneapolis: Fortress Press, 2014), 33–56.

36. Nunes is reflecting on the work of Wilson Harris but her comments apply more broadly. See Zita Nunes, *Cannibal Democracy: Race and Representation in the Literature of the Americas* (Minneapolis: University of Minnesota Press, 2008), 174.

37. Paul Miller, Annaliese Hoehling, and Amaryll Chanady give attention to this focalization through Ti Noël, arguing for different degrees of distancing or closeness between readers and Ti Noël. Echevarría on the other hand characterizes Ti Noël as a passive onlooker, and Phillip Kaisary refers to Ti Noël's interiority but oddly suggests that he "lacks emancipatory vision." See Miller, *Elusive Origins,* 38, 42–43; Hoehling, "Minoritarian 'Marvelous Real'"; Amaryll Chanady, "La Focalización como Espejo de Contradicciones en el Reino de Este Mundo," *Revista Canadiense de Estudios Hispánicos* 12 no. 3 (1988): 446–58 (see 452–53); Echevarría, *Alejo Carpentier,* 157; and Phillip Kaisary, *The Haitian Revolution in the Literary Imagination: Radical Horizons, Conservative Constraints* (Charlottesville: University of Virginia Press, 2014), 122.

38. Many critics discuss the novel in relation to revolution. Early discussions of his attention to revolution include Selwyn R. Cudjoe, *Resistance and Caribbean Literature* (Athens: Ohio University Press, 1980); Echevarría, *Alejo Carpentier;* Simon Gikandi, *Writing in Limbo: Modernism and Caribbean Literature* (Ithaca, NY: Cornell University Press, 1992). For critics who aim specifically to assess Carpentier's stance on revolution, see notes 39 and 46. On Carpentier's representation of Vodou and Africans in the Haitian Revolution, see Victor Figueroa, "The Kingdom of Black Jacobins: CLR James and Alejo Carpentier on the Haitian Revolution," *Afro-Hispanic Review* 25, no. 2 (2006): 55–71; Rafael Ocasio, "The Revolution of Santería and Hispanic Hagiography in Cuba," *Journal of the Fantastic in the Arts* 8, no. 2 (1997): 235–43; José Piedra, "A Return to Africa with a Carpentier Tale," *MLN* 97, no. 2 (1982): 401–10; and Kristin L. Squint, "Vodou and Revolt in Literature of the Haitian Revolution," *CLA Journal* 51, no. 2 (2007): 170–85. Some of these readers emphasize the problematic primitivism in his rhetoric; others align the syncretism of Vodou traditions (e.g., including Catholic and non-monotheistic African religions) with the syncretism of Carpentier's baroque aesthetics as they mix Arabic, African, southern European, and new world genres specifically as signaled in his notion of the marvelous real (*lo real maravilloso*). For a wonderfully full-fledged tracing of these traditions in Carpentier and others, see Jason Frydman, *Sounding the Break: African American and Caribbean Routes of World Literature* (Charlottesville: University of Virginia Press, 2014). In "Different Substance, Different

Form," Aristedes Dimitriou also notices the inter-imperial context for the novel and he offers a balanced assessment of both the primitivist and the more productive handling of syncretism in the novel, although with no attention to the problematical masculinism in these materials. See Aristides Dimitriou, "Different Substance, Different Form: Alejo Carpentier's Hemispheric American Modernism," *College Literature* 46, no. 1 (2019): 96–126.

39. See Dalleo, *American Imperialism's Undead*, chapter 5; and for full discussion of what Carpentier elides, see Lizabeth Paravasini-Gebert, "The Haitian Revolution in Interstices and Shadows: A Re-reading of Alejo Carpentier's 'The Kingdom of This World'," *Research in African Literatures* 35, no. 2 (2004): 114–27.

40. See Tanya L. Shields, *Their Bones Would Reject Yours: Feminist Rehearsal and Imagining Caribbean Belonging* (Charlottesville: University of Virginia Press, 2014), 60. For related discussions see, for instance, Belinda Edmondson, *Making Men*; and Michelle A. Stephens, *Black Empire: The Masculine Global Imaginary of Caribbean Intellectuals in the United States, 1914–1962* (Durham, NC: Duke University Press, 2005).

41. In his literary biography of Carpentier, *Alejo Carpentier: The Pilgrim at Home*, Echevarría provides a general outline of Carpentier's activism but not as support for a reading of Carpentier's revolutionary investments.

42. On the British dimension, see Servando Valdés Sánchez, "Anglo-Cuban Diplomacy."

43. See, for instance, his mention of parsley in the novel's opening scene (4). I thank Professor Donette Francis for pointing out this detail.

44. Echevarría, *Alejo Carpentier*, 216–17.

45. Carpentier played a complicated double role, as Marike Janzen describes, since on one hand he supported state propaganda and implicitly condoned censorship while on the other hand he himself wrote works that had an unclear relation to the cultural politics of the state. As a result, he published several works outside of Cuba, and sometimes found himself entangled in Cold War politics or cast by contemporaries as a Yankee puppet. Janzen's essay offers a thoughtful account of his precarious in-between position in her study of what she calls "messengers writers" who occupy official state positions and are forced to balance domestic and foreign pressures—or what I would call their inter-imperial positionality. See Marike Janzen, "Messenger Writers: Anna Seghers and Alejo Carpentier in the Cold War," *Comparative Literature* 62, no. 3 (2010): 283–301. On the politics of his publications in the United States, see Deborah Cohn, "Retracing *The Lost Steps*: The Cuban Revolution, the Cold War, and Publishing Alejo Carpentier in the United States," CR: *The New Centennial Review* 3, no. 1 (2003): 81–108.

46. For critics who argue that Carpentier sidesteps full embrace of violent revolution, see Dalleo, *American Imperialism's Undead*; Sharae Deckard, "The Political Ecology of Storms in Caribbean Literature," in *The Caribbean: Aesthetics, World-Ecology, Politics*, ed. Chris Campbell and Michael Niblett (Liverpool: Liverpool University Press, 2016), 25–45; Phillip Kaisary, *The Haitian Revolution in the Literary Imagination*; Natalie M. Leger "Faithless Sight: Haiti in the Kingdom of the World," *Research in African Literatures* 45, no. 1 (2014): 85–106; Lizabeth Paravasini-Gebert, "The Haitian Revolution in Interstices and Shadows:

A Re-reading of Alejo Carpentier's 'The Kingdom of This World,'" *Research in African Literatures* 35, no. 2 (2004): 114–27; and Paul Miller, *Elusive Origins: The Enlightenment in the Modern Caribbean Historical Imagination* (Charlottesville: University of Virginia, 2010). Although not discussing revolution per se, Maurice Hall stresses that the narratives in the Caribbean are declensions of the heroism narrative and, following Curdella Forbes, notes that they are often narratives of exile. Hall emphasizes that "the tenor" of these narratives "is existential rather than heroic," a description that I think also applies to *Kingdom*. See Hall, "Negotiating Jamaican Masculinities," 41; and Curdella Forbes, *From Nation to Diaspora: Samuel Selvon, George Lamming, and the Cultural Performance of Gender* (Kingston, Jamaica: University of the West Indies Press, 2005).

47. For useful analysis of *lo real maravilloso* and summary of critical debates about it, see Annaliese Hoehling, "Minoritarian 'Marvelous Real': Enfolding Revolution in Alejo Carpentier's *The Kingdom of This World*," *Journal of Postcolonial Writing* 54, no. 2 (2018): 254–67. Hoehling links this notion and Carpentier's novel to the baroque aesthetic. In *Sounding the Break* Frydman does so as well and he furthermore establishes that the baroque was fed by several aesthetic streams including Arabic, Greek, and Germanic (for instance see 78–79).

48. Carpentier later expanded this prologue into an essay. See Alejo Carpentier, "On the Marvelous Real in America," trans. Tanya Huntington and Lois Parkinson Zamora, in *Magical Realism: Theory, History, Community*, edited by Lois Parkinson Zamora and Wendy B. Faris (Durham, NC: Duke University Press, 1995), 75–88. Carpentier's formulation of *lo real maravilloso* accorded with the theorization among Latin American artists and intellectuals sometimes characterized as *mundonovismo* (New Worldism).

49. With the phrase *mental counterpoint*, Carpentier very likely alludes to Fernando Ortiz's book, *Cuban Counterpoint: Tobacco and Sugar* (Durham, NC: Duke University Press, [1940] 1995).

50. In *Sounding the Break*, Jason Frydman also stresses this implication; see 73–79.

51. See Bogumil Jewsiewicki and V. Y. Mudimbe, "Africans' Memories and Contemporary History of Africa," *History and Theory* 32, no. 4 (1993): 1–11, 3.

52. Lope de Vega, *El nuevo Mundo, descubierto por Cristobol Colon* (New York: Peter Lang, [1614] 2001).

53. Carpentier refers to the "Venus Victrox," an actual nude statue of Pauline Bonaparte created by the famous Roman sculptor of this era, Antonio Canova.

54. Critics have rarely dwelled on the break in Carpentier's family, whereby his father abruptly abandoned the family, leaving them without financial support, which forced the teenage Carpentier to drop out of school and work to support himself and his mother. Antonio Benítez-Rojo offers a psychoanalytic reading, yet without discussion of the causes of this sudden split. Could Carpentier's critical view of men have some source in this family rupture and his alienation from his father? As far as I know, no biographer has addressed this question. See Antonio Benítez-Rojo, "Alejo Carpentier: Between Here and Over There," *Caribbean Studies* 27, nos. 3–4 (1994): 183–95.

55. Carpentier "The Marvelous Real," 85.

56. I also agree with Tanya Shields that death at a purely bodily level "does not limit the power to lead and inspire" (Shields, *Their Bones Would Reject Yours*, 83–84). After all, like Macandal, historical figures such as Malcolm X and Harriet Tubman have lived on powerfully in the practices and memories of Black activists.

57. Shields, *Their Bones Would Reject Yours,* 85.

58. Husain Haddawy, trans., *The Arabian Nights*, ed. Muhsin Mahdi (New York: Norton, 1990), 3.

59. See Ben De Witte, "Dramatizing Queer Visibility in *El público*: Federico García Lorca in Search of a Modern Theatre," *Modern Drama* 60, no. 1 (2017): 25–45, 27. I have found no direct evidence that Carpentier himself was queer or gay, but he needn't have been to appreciate the problems of heterosexuality and to point in this direction. James J. Pancrazio does however cast Carpentier as sexually transgressive, pointing for example to the "Jacqueline texts," a series of articles apparently authored by Carpentier under the pseudonym Jacqueline Carpentier for Havana's society magazine *Social* in the 1920s. See Pancrazio, *The Logic of Fetishism: Alejo Carpentier and the Cuban Tradition* (Lewisburg, PA: Bucknell University Press, 2004), chapter 3.

60. For suggestive analysis of the link between storms and revolution in this novel and others, see Sharae Deckard, "The Political Ecology of Storms in Caribbean Literature," 25–45.

61. Keja Valens, "Excruciating Improbability and the Transgender Jamaican," in *Trans Studies: The Challenge to Hetero/Homo Normativities*, ed. Yolanda Martinez-San Miguel and Sarah Tobias (New Brunswick, NJ: Rutgers University Press, 2016), 65–82.

Chapter 7: Inter-imperially Neocolonial

1. Ken Seigneurie, "Ongoing War and Arab Humanism," in *Geomodernisms: Race, Modernism, Modernity*, ed. Laura Doyle and Laura Winkiel (Bloomington: Indiana University Press, 2004), esp. 102–3.

2. Arundhati Roy, *The God of Small Things* (New York: Harper Perennial, 1997), 292.

3. Roy, *God of Small Things*, 293.

4. Roy, *God of Small Things*, 36–37.

5. Roy, *God of Small Things*, 37.

6. Also see Donette Francis's "temporal reading" of contemporary novels and specifically her emphasis on the way that *The Pagoda* "reconfigures narratives of Atlantic and specifically Caribbean modernity to encompass eastern as well as western continents" (24). As noted in chapter 6, my analyses in these last two chapters build on Donette Francis's close tracing of the co-formation of sexuality and states, both imperial and postcolonial. See Donette Francis, *Fictions of Feminine Citizenship: Sexuality and the Nation in Contemporary Caribbean Literature* (New York: Palgrave Macmillan, 2010).

7. See Paula Giddings, *When and Where I Enter: The Impact of Black Women on Race and Sex in America* (Harper Collins-Perennial, [1984] 2001).

8. See both sections of this issue of *International Journal of Middle East Studies*: both the set of full essays on "Queer Affects," which encompass the realms of literature as well as politics, Hanadi Al-Samman and Tarek El-Ariss, eds., *International Journal of Middle East Studies* 45, no. 2 (2013): 205–329; and the roundtable on "Queer Theory and Middle East Studies," in which all contributions highlight the co-constitution of states, economies, geopolitics, and sexualities, Paul Amar and Omnia El Shakry, eds., *International Journal of Middle East Studies* 45, no. 2 (2013): 331–52.

More broadly also see, Sandeep Bakshi, Suhraiya Jivraj, and Silvia Posocco, eds., *Decolonizing Sexualities: Transnational Perspectives, Critical Interventions* (Oxford: Counterpress, 2016); Sarah Hunt and Cindy Holmes, "Everyday Decolonization: Living a Decolonizing Queer Politics," *Journal of Lesbian Studies* 19, no. 2 (2015): 154–72; and John C. Hawley and Dennis Altman, *Postcolonial, Queer: Theoretical Intersections* (Albany: SUNY Press, 2001).

Scholarship on "queer temporality" has exploded since Judith Halberstam coined the term in *In a Queer Time and Place: Transgender Bodies, Subcultural Lives* (New York: NYU Press, 2005). I cannot do justice this growing body of work, but to gain a sense of some of the most influential scholars in the field, see the discussion hosted by Elizabeth Freeman with Carolyn Dinshaw, Lee Edelman, Roderick A. Ferguson, Carla Freccero, Judith Halberstam, Annamarie Jagose, Christopher S. Nealon, and Tan Hoang Nguyen: "Theorizing Queer Temporalities: A Roundtable Discussion," in *GLQ: A Journal of Lesbian and Gay Studies* 13, no. 2 (2007): 177–95. Also see Elizabeth Freeman, *Queer Temporalities, Queer Histories* (Durham, NC: Duke University Press, 2010) for an excellent, wide-ranging development of the conceptual work in this field.

9. For readings that strongly link the sexual and the colonial or geopolitical dimensions of novel, see Donette Francis, *Fictions of Feminine Citizenship*, 23–48; Minjeong Kim, "Globetrotting Queerness: Patricia Powell's *The Pagoda*," *Wagadu* 12, no. 14 (2014): 125–47; and Jason Frydman, "Jamaican Nationalism, Queer Intimacies, and the Disjunctures of the Chinese Diaspora: Patricia Powell's *The Pagoda*," *Small Axe* 15, no. 1 (2011): 95–109. Francis's and Kim's studies also contain useful historical sources and analyses of both the trade in Asian indentured labors and Caribbean history. Other studies touch on the geopolitical but focus mainly on sexuality or race and ethnicity. See Timothy Chin, "The Novels of Patricia Powell: Negotiating Gender and Sexuality across the Disjunctures of the Caribbean Diaspora," *Callaloo* 30, no. 2 (2007): 533–45; Keja Valens, "Excruciating Improbability and the Transgender Jamaican," in *Trans Studies: The Challenge to Hetero/Homo Normativities*, ed. Yolanda Martinez-San Miguel and Sarah Tobias (New Brunswick, NJ: Rutgers University Press, 2016), 65–82; and Lisa Li-Shen Yun, "An Afro-Chinese Caribbean: Cultural Cartographies of Contrariness in the Work of Antonio Chuffat Latour, Margaret Cezair-Thompson, and Patricia Powell," *Caribbean Quarterly* 50, no. 2 (2004): 26–43.

Critics model different approaches to the protagonist Lowe's cross-dressing, queer sexuality in the novel. As Francis points out, Yun's account of the protagonist's sexual identity as lesbian overlooks the complexity of this character's "transgenderedness," in Francis's words (31), and Francis is among those who treat sexuality as utterly intertwined with colonial, nationalist, and citizenship formations. Valens, Frydman, and Kim further emphasize that, as Frydman puts it, Powell's creation of Lowe does not represent "merely the 'presence and affirmation' of individual queer subjects absent from colonial and nationalist historiography. *The Pagoda* does not set queer subjects against straight subjects but charts the thoroughly queer operations of colonial society" (103). Frydman goes on to argue that "the novel appropriates this queer terrain, furthermore, to ground the utopian possibility of an anticolonial Jamaican nationalism" (103). Although agreeing with Frydman, Kim points out, that this queering of Jamaican nationalism sits uneasily, as the novel acknowledges, with Lowe's wish for a specifically Chinese nationalist gathering place through the building of a pagoda on the island. See my own analysis later in this chapter.

Most studies give limited attention to the experimental form of the novel beyond commentary on to its letters. I look closely at the novel's challenging form, yet the recent formulations of queer and decolonial temporalities could undoubtedly shed further light. For analyses of the letters, see Donette Francis, *Fictions of Feminine Citizenship*, 45–47; and Wendy Walters, "Archives of the Black Atlantic: Postcolonial Citation in *The Pagoda*," *Novel* 43, no. 1 (2010): 163–68; and in passing, Kim, "Globetrotting Queerness," 127–28.

10. Patricia Powell, *The Pagoda* (New York: Knopf, 1998), 242; hereafter cited parenthetically in the text by page number.

11. Qtd. in Heather D. Russell, "Post-Blackness and All of the Black Americas," in *The Trouble with Post-Blackness*, ed. Houston A. Baker and K. Merinda Simmons (New York: Columbia University Press, 2015), 110–43, 119.

12. Jana K. Lipman, *Guantánamo: A Working-Class History between Empire and Revolution* (Berkeley: University of California Press, 2008), 181–86.

13. Lipman, *Guantánamo*, 195.

14. Lipman, *Guantánamo*, 198.

15. Lipman, *Guantánamo*, 192.

16. See Monique Bedasse, *Jah Kingdom: Rastafarians, Tanzania, and Pan-Africanism in the Age of Decolonization* (Chapel Hill: University of North Carolina Press, 2017), for a recent book-length account of Manley's politics.

17. See Paul Ashley, "Natural Resource Diplomacy: Non-alignment versus Regional Cooperation," *Boletín de estudios latinoamericanos y del Caribe* 33 (1982): 144–51.

18. This remark was made retrospectively by Winston Davidson, a contemporary of Manley's and fellow member of the Worker's Party of Jamaica. See "The Bloody General Election that Changed Jamaica," *Jamaican Observer*, October 30, 2012, http://www.jamaicaobserver.com/news/The-bloody-general-election-that-changed-Jamaica.

19. Mimi Sheller, *Consuming the Caribbean* (New York: Routledge, 2003), 201. For further analysis, see Russell, "Post-Blackness," esp. 113–14. Also see Belal Ahmed, "The Impact of Globalization on the Caribbean Sugar and Banana Industries," in *The Society for Caribbean Studies Annual Conference Papers*, vol. 2, edited by Sandra Courtman (2001), accessed March 2020, http://community-languages.org.uk/SCS-Papers/olv2p1.pdf; and Hilary

Beckles, *Britain's Black Debt: Reparations for Caribbean Slavery and Native Genocide* (Kingston, Jamaica: University of the West Indies Press, 2013).

20. Famously, in *Beloved*, Sethe speaks of her remembering processes as "rememory." See Toni Morrison, *Beloved* (New York: Alfred A. Knopf, 1987), 36.

21. See Lisa Lowe's transhemispheric study of empires and bodily history, with an emphasis on colonial archives, in *The Intimacies of Four Continents* (Durham, NC: Duke University Press, 2015). Also see Peter Hudson, *Bankers and Empires: How Wall Street Colonized the Caribbean* (Chicago: University of Chicago Press, 2017).

22. While this point has been made by many critics, among Caribbean intellectuals, Édouard Glissant is one of the most seminal, and Carole Boyce Davies has been one of the most groundbreaking especially for her emphasis on the forms of relationality affected by this legacy. See Édouard Glissant, *Poetics of Relation*, trans. Betsy Wing (Ann Arbor: University of Michigan Press, [1990] 1997); and Carol Boyce Davies, *Black Women, Writing and Identity: Migrations of the Subject* (New York: Routledge, 2002). Timothy Chin explores this point specifically in relation to Powell's fiction. See Chin, "Novels of Patricia Powell," 534.

23. As Powell herself notes in an interview, Cecil is not only a "violator" and "Lowe is not simply a victim." See Patricia Powell, "The Dynamics of Power and Desire in *The Pagoda*," in *Winds of Change: The Transforming Voices of Caribbean Women Writers and Scholars*, ed. Adele S. Newson and Linda Strong-Leek (New York: Peter Lang, 1998), 189–94, 191. For discussion of Powell's other commentary on and participation in LGBT issues in the Caribbean, see Chin, "Novels of Patricia Powell," 533–34.

24. See Wendy Walters, "Archives of the Black Atlantic," 163–68; and Donette Francis, *Fictions of Feminine Citizenship*, 45–47.

25. Kim, "Globetrotting Queerness," 142–43.

26. See Mina Loy's poem "Parturition," in *The Lost Lunar Baedeker*, ed. Roger L. Conover (New York: Farrar, Straus and Giroux, [1914] 1996), 67–71. See chapter 5 for discussion of Loy and this poem.

Conclusion: A River Between

1. Ngũgĩ wa Thiong'o, *The River Between* (Johannesburg: Heinemann, 1965), 1.

2. Thiong'o, *River Between*, 1.

3. Chang-rae Lee, *Native Speaker* (New York: Riverhead, 1995), 333.

4. Toni Morrison, *Beloved* (New York: Alfred A. Knopf, 1987), 162.

Bibliography

Abu-Lughod, Janet. *Before European Hegemony: The World System* A.D. *1250–1350*. New York: Oxford University Press, 1989.

Adorno, Theodor W. *Negative Dialectics*. Translated by E. B. Ashton. London: Bloomsbury Academic, 2014.

Agamben, Giorgio. *Homo Sacer: Sovereign Power and Bare Life*. Translated by Daniel Heller-Roazen. Stanford, CA: Stanford University Press, 1998.

Ahmed, Belal. "The Impact of Globalization on the Caribbean Sugar and Banana Industries." In *The Society for Caribbean Studies Annual Conference Papers*, vol. 2, edited by Sandra Courtman (2001). http://community-languages.org.uk/SCS-Papers/olv2p1.pdf.

Akbari, Suzanne Conklin, and Karla Mallette, eds. *A Sea of Languages: Rethinking the Arabic Role in Medieval Literary History*. Toronto: University of Toronto Press, 2013.

Aksan, Virginia, and Daniel Goffman, eds. *The Early Modern Ottomans: Remapping the Empire*. Cambridge: Cambridge University Press, 2007.

Alcock, Susan, Terence N. D'Altroy, Kathleen D. Morrison, and Carla Sinopoli, eds. *Empires: Perspectives from Archaeology and History*. Cambridge: Cambridge University Press, 2001.

Al-Dabbagh, Abdulla. *Shakespeare, the Orient, and the Critics*. New York: Peter Lang, 2010.

Alemán, Jesse. "The Other Country: Mexico, the United States, and the Gothic History of Conquest." In *Hemispheric American Studies*, edited by Caroline F. Levander and Robert S. Levine, 75–95. New Brunswick, NJ: Rutgers University Press, 2008.

Alker, Hayward R., and Thomas J. Biersteker. "The Dialectics of World Order: Notes for a Future Archeologist of International Savoir Faire." *International Studies Quarterly* 28, no. 2 (1984): 121–42.

al-Musawi, Muhsin J. *The Islamic Context of "The Thousand and One Nights"*. New York: Columbia University Press, 2009.

Al-Samman, Hanadi, and Tarek El-Ariss, eds. "Queer Affects." Special issue, *International Journal of Middle East Studies* 45, no. 2 (2013).

Al-Taee, Nasser. "*The Arabian Nights* and the Contemporary Arabic Novel." In *"The Arabian Nights" in Historical Context: Between East and West*, edited by Saree Makdisi and Felicity Nussbaum, 265–96. New York: Oxford University Press, 2009.

Altschul, Nadia R. *Politics of Temporalization: Medievalism and Orientalism in Nineteenth-Century South America*. Philadelphia: University of Pennsylvania Press, 2020.

Amar, Paul, and Omnia El Shakry, eds. "Queer Theory and Middle East Studies" (roundtable). *International Journal of Middle East Studies* 45, no. 2 (2013): 331–52.

Amer, Sahar. *Crossing Borders: Love between Women in Medieval French and Arabic Literatures*. Philadelphia: University of Pennsylvania Press, 2008.

Amer, Sahar. *Ésope au féminin: Marie de France et la politique de l'interculturalité*. Amsterdam: Rodopi, 1999.

Amer, Sahar. "Medieval Arab Lesbians and Lesbian-Like Women." *Journal of the History of Sexuality* 18, no. 2 (2009): 215–36.

Amer, Sahar. "Reading Medieval French Literature from a Global Perspective." PMLA 130, no. 2 (2015): 367–74.

Anand, Mulk Raj. *Untouchable*. London: Penguin Books, (1935) 2014.

Anderson, Benedict. *Imagined Communities: Reflections on the Origin and Spread of Nationalism*. London: Verso, (1983) 2006.

Anderson, Glynn. "Sovereignty and the Materiality of Caliphal Encounters." PMLA 130, no. 2 (2015): 393–401.

Ando, Clifford. "Introduction: States and State Power in Inquiry." In *Ancient States and Infrastructural Power*, edited by Clifford Ando and Seth Richardson, 4–7. Philadelphia: University of Pennsylvania Press, 2017.

Ando, Clifford, and Seth Richardson, eds. *Ancient States and Infrastructural Power*. Philadelphia: University of Pennsylvania Press, 2017.

Andrade, Oswald de. "Cannibal Manifesto." Translated by Mary Ann Caws and Claudia Caliman. *Exquisite Corpse Cyber* 11 ([1928] 2002). http://college.cengage.com/history /world/keen/latin_america/8e/assets/students/sources/pdfs/64_oswald_andrade _cannibal_manifesto.pdf.

Anzaldúa, Gloria. *Borderlands/La Frontera*. Vol. 3, *The New Mestiza*. San Francisco: Aunt Lute, 1987.

Appadurai, Arjun. *Modernity at Large: Cultural Dimensions of Globalization*. Minneapolis: University of Minnesota Press, 1996.

Apter, Emily. *Against World Literature: On the Politics of Untranslatability*. New York: Verso Books, 2013.

Aravamudan, Srinivas. "The Adventure Chronotope and the Oriental Xenotrope: Galland, Sheridan, and Joyce Domesticate *The Arabian Nights*." In *"The Arabian Nights" in Historical Context: Between East and West*, edited by Saree Makdisi and Felicity Nussbaum, 235–63. Oxford: Oxford University Press, 2009.

Archer, John. *Old Worlds: Egypt, Southwest Asia, India, and Russia in Early Modern English Writing*. Stanford, CA: Stanford University Press, 2002.

Arjomand, Said Amir. "Law, Agency, and Policy in Medieval Islamic Society: Development of the Institutions of Learning from the Tenth to the Fifteenth Century." *Comparative Studies in Society and History* 41, no. 2 (1999): 263–93.

Armah, Ayi Kwei. *Two Thousand Seasons*. Popenguine, Senegal: Per Ankh, (1973) 2000.

Armitage, David, and Sanjay Subrahmanyam. *The Age of Revolutions in Global Context, c. 1760–1840*. New York: Palgrave, 2009.

Asher, Kiran. "Latin American Decolonial Thought, or Making the Subaltern Speak." *Geography Compass* 7, no. 12 (2013): 832–42.

Ashley, Paul. "Natural Resource Diplomacy: Non-Alignment versus Regional Co-operation." *Boletín de estudios latinoamericanos y del Caribe* 33 (1982): 139–54.

Aydin, Cemil. *The Politics of Anti-Westernism in Asia: Visions of World Order in Pan-Islamic and Pan-Asian Thought.* New York: Columbia University Press, 2007.

Backus, Margot Gayle. *The Gothic Family Romance: Heterosexuality, Child Sacrifice, and the Anglo-Irish Colonial Order.* Durham, NC: Duke University Press, 1999.

Badia, Lola, Joan Santanach, and Albert Soler. *Ramon Llull as a Vernacular Writer: Communicating a New Kind of Knowledge.* Woodbridge, UK: Tamesis, 2016.

Bahri, Deepika. *Native Intelligence: Aesthetics, Politics, and Postcolonial Literature.* Minneapolis: University of Minnesota Press, 2003.

Bahun, Sanja. "The Balkans Uncovered: Toward Historie Croisée of Modernism." In *The Oxford Handbook of Global Modernisms*, edited by Mark Wollaeger and Matt Eatough, 25–47. Oxford: Oxford University Press, 2012.

Bahun, Sanja. "Gaps, or the Dialectics of Inter-imperial Art: The Case of the Belgrade Surrealist Circle." *MFS: Modern Fiction Studies* 64, no. 3 (2018): 458–87.

Baldick, Chris. Introduction to *Melmoth the Wanderer*, by Charles Maturin, vii–xxix. New York: Oxford University Press, 1992.

Baldwin, Kate. *Beyond the Color Line and the Iron Curtain: Reading Encounters between Black and Red, 1922–1963.* Durham, NC: Duke University Press, 2002.

Ballantyne, Tony, and Antoinette M. Burton. *Empires and the Reach of the Global, 1870–1945.* Cambridge, MA: Harvard University Press, 2014.

Ballaster, Ros. *Fabulous Orients: Fictions of the East in England, 1662–1785.* Oxford: Oxford University Press, 2005.

Balzac, Honoré de. *Melmoth Reconciled.* Translated by Ellen Marriage. Auckland: Floating Press, (1835) 2014.

Banerjee, Sukanya. *Becoming Imperial Citizens: Indians in the Late-Victorian Empire.* Durham, NC: Duke University Press, 2010.

Bang, Peter, and Christopher Bayly, eds. *Tributary Empires in Global History.* New York: Palgrave Macmillan, 2011.

Barder, Alexander D., and François Debrix. "Agonal Sovereignty: Rethinking War and Politics with Schmitt, Arendt, and Foucault." *Philosophy and Social Criticism* 37, no. 7 (2011): 775–93.

Barendse, R. J. "Trade and State in the Arabian Seas: A Survey from the Fifteenth to the Eighteenth Century." *Journal of World History* 11, no. 2 (2000): 173–225.

Barfield, T. J. "The Shadow Empires: Imperial State Formation along the Chinese-Nomad Frontier." In *Empires: Perspectives from Archaeology and History*, edited by Susan Alcock, Terence N. D'Altroy, Kathleen D. Morrison, and Carla Sinopoli, 10–41. Cambridge: Cambridge University Press, 2001.

Barkawi, Tarak. "Empire and Order in International Relations and Security Studies." In *The International Studies Encyclopedia*, vol. 3, edited by Robert A. Denmark and Renée Marlin-Bennett, 1360–79. New York: Oxford University Press, 2010.

Barkawi, Tarak, and Mark Laffey. "Retrieving the Imperial: Empire and International Relations." *Millennium* 31, no. 1 (2002): 109–27.

Barker, Francis, Peter Hulme, and Margaret Iverson, eds. *Cannibalism and the Colonial World*. Cambridge: Cambridge University Press, 1998.

Barker, Joanne, ed. *Critically Sovereign: Indigenous Gender, Sexuality, and Feminist Studies*. Durham, NC: Duke University Press, 2017.

Barrington, Candace, and Jonathan Hsy. "Editors' Introduction: Chaucer's Global Orbits and Global Communities." *Literature Compass* 15, no. 6 (2018): 1–12.

Barrows, Adam. *The Cosmic Time of Empire: Modern Britain and World Literature*. Berkeley: University of California Press, 2011.

Bartlett, Thomas, Kevin Dawson, and Dáire Keough. *The 1798 Rebellion*. Niwot, CO: Roberts Rinehart, 1998.

Bartov, Omer, and Eric D. Weitz. *Shatterzone of Empires: Coexistence and Violence in the German, Habsburg, Russian, and Ottoman Borderlands*. Bloomington: Indiana University Press, 2013.

Bataković, Dušan T. "The 1804 Serbian Revolution: A Balkan-Size French Revolution." Paper presented at the AAASS, Boston, December 2004.

Batker, Carol. *Reforming Fictions: Native, African, and Jewish American Women's Literature and Journalism in the Progressive Era*. New York: Columbia University Press, 2000.

Bauer, Brian. *The Development of the Inca State*. Austin: University of Texas Press, 1992.

Bayly, C. A. "The Boxer Uprising and India: Globalizing Myths." In *The Boxers, China, and the World*, edited by Robert Bickers and R. G. Tiedemann, 147–56. Lanham, MD: Rowman and Littlefield, 2007.

Bear, Laura. *Lines of the Nation: Indian Railway Workers, Bureaucracy, and the Intimate Historical Self*. New York: Columbia University Press, 2007.

Bear, Laura Gbah. "Miscegenations of Modernity: Constructing European Respectability and Race in the Indian Railway Colony, 1857–1931." *Women's History Review* 3, no. 4 (1994): 531–48.

Beaujard, Philippe. "The Indian Ocean in Eurasian and African World-Systems before the Sixteenth Century." *Journal of World History* 16, no. 4 (2005): 411–65.

Beaujard, Philippe. *Les mondes se l'ocean indien*. Paris: Armand Colin, 2012.

Beauvoir, Simone de. *Ethics of Ambiguity*. Translated by Bernard Frechtman. New York: Open Road Media, (1947) 2018.

Beauvoir, Simone de. *The Second Sex*. Translated by H. M. Parshley. New York: Vintage Books, 1952.

Beckles, Hilary. *Britain's Black Debt: Reparations for Caribbean Slavery and Native Genocide*. Kingston, Jamaica: University of the West Indies Press, 2013.

Bedasse, Monique. *Jah Kingdom: Rastafarians, Tanzania, and Pan-Africanism in the Age of Decolonization*. Chapel Hill: University of North Carolina Press, 2017.

Beecroft, Alexander. *An Ecology of World Literature: From Antiquity to the Present Day*. London: Verso, 2015.

Beemer, Bryce. "Bangkok, Creole City: War Slaves, Refugees, and the Transformation of Culture in Urban Southeast Asia." *Literature Compass* 13, no. 5 (2016): 266–76.

Beinin, Joel, and Zachary Lockman. *Workers on the Nile: Nationalism, Communism, Islam, and the Egyptian Working Class, 1882–1954*. Cairo: American University in Cairo Press, 1998.

Belcher, Wendy. *Abyssinia's Samuel Johnson: Ethiopian Thought in the Making of an English Author*. New York: Oxford University Press, 2012.

Belcher, Wendy. *The Life and Struggles of Our Mother Walatta Petros: A Seventeenth-Century African Biography of an Ethiopian Woman*. Princeton, NJ: Princeton University Press, 2015.

Bell, Alessia, and Anna Loretoni, eds. "Gender, Identity, and Belonging: New Citizenships beyond Orientalism." Special issue, *Journal of Balkan and Near Eastern Studies* 19, no. 5 (2017).

Bell, David A. *The First Total War: Napoleon's Europe and the Birth of Warfare as We Know It*. London: Bloomsbury, 2012.

Bender, Thomas H. *A Nation Among Nations: America's Place in World History*. New York: Hill and Wang, 2006.

Benítez-Rojo, Antonio. *The Repeating Island: The Caribbean and the Postmodern Perspective*. Translated by James E. Maraniss. Durham, NC: Duke University Press, 1997.

Bennison, Amira K. *The Great Caliphs: The Golden Age of the Abbasid Empire*. New Haven, CT: Yale University Press, 2009.

Bentley, Jerry. "Hemispheric Integration, 500–1500 C.E." *Journal of World History* 9, no. 2 (1998): 237–54.

Bergland, Renée L. *The National Uncanny: Indian Ghosts and American Subjects*. Hanover, NH: University Press of New England, 2000.

Bernasconi, Robert. "With What Must the History of Philosophy Begin? Hegel's Role in the Debate on the Place of India within the History of Philosophy." In *Hegel's History of Philosophy: New Interpretations*, edited by David A. Duquette, 35–50. Albany, NY: SUNY Press, 2003.

Berryman, John. Introduction to *The Monk*, by Matthew G. Lewis, 11–28. New York: Grove Press, 1952.

Besteman, Catherine, and Hugh Gusterson, eds. *Why America's Top Pundits Are Wrong: Anthropologists Talk Back*. Berkeley: University of California Press, 2005.

Bhattacharya, Tithi, ed. *Social Reproduction Theory: Remapping Class, Recentering Oppression*. London: Pluto Press, 2017.

Bickers, Robert, and R. G. Tiedemann, eds. *The Boxers, China, and the World*. Lanham, MD: Rowman and Littlefield, 2007.

Birnbaum, Eleazar. "The Ottomans and Chagatay Literature: An Early 16th Century Manuscript of Navā'i's *Dīvān* in Ottoman Orthography." *Central Asiatic Journal* 20, no. 3 (1976): 157–90.

Blackburn, Robin. *The Overthrow of Colonial Slavery, 1776–1848*. London: Verso, 1988.

Blair, Sarah. "Local Modernity, Global Modernism: Bloomsbury and the Places of the Literary." *ELH* 71, no. 3 (2004): 813–38.

Blom, Ida, Karen Hagemann, and Catherine Hall, eds. *Gendered Nations: Nationalisms and Gender Order in the Long Nineteenth Century*. New York: Berg, 2000.

Bloom, Jonathan M. *Paper before Print: The History and Impact of Paper in the Islamic World*. New Haven, CT: Yale University Press, 2001.

Boase, Roger. *The Origin and Meaning of Courtly Love*. Manchester: Manchester University Press, 1977.

Boatcă, Manuela. "The Quasi Europes: World Regions in Light of the Imperial Difference." In *Global Crises and the Challenges of the 21st Century: Antisystemic Movements and the Transformation of the World-System*, edited by Tom Reifer, 132–53. London: Paradigm, 2012.

Boehmer, Elleke. *Empire, the National, and the Postcolonial, 1890–1920: Resistance in Interaction*. Oxford: Oxford University Press, 2002.

Boehmer, Elleke. "Peripheral Avant-Gardes: Mafeking and Calcutta on or around 1910." Paper presented at Modernist Communities conference, Institute du Monde Anglophone, Université Nouvelle Sorbonne, Paris, April 24–26, 2014.

Boehmer, Elleke. "The View from Empire: The Turn-of-the-Century Globalizing World." In *Late Victorian into Modern*, edited by Laura Marcus, Michèle Mendelssohn, and Kirsten E. Shepherd-Barr, 305–18. Oxford: Oxford University Press, 2016.

Boone, Joseph. *Libidinal Current: Sexuality and the Shaping of Modernism*. Chicago: University of Chicago Press, 1998.

Bosin, Yuri. "Pugachev's Rebellion." In *The International Encyclopedia on Revolution and Protest*, edited by Immanuel Ness, 2775–76. New York: Wiley, 2009.

Boyce Davies, Carole. *Black Women, Writing and Identity: Migrations of the Subject*. New York: Routledge, 2002.

Boyce Davies, Carole, and Monica Jardine. "Imperial Geographies and Caribbean Nationalism: At the Border between 'A Dying Colonialism' and U.S. Hegemony." *CR: The New Centennial Review* 3, no. 3 (2003): 151–74.

Boyd, Julian T., Lyman H. Butterfield, and Mina R. Bryan, eds. *The Papers of Thomas Jefferson*. Princeton, NJ: Princeton University Press, 1950.

Brandes, George. *Friedrich Nietzsche*. London: William Heinemann, 1914.

Brantlinger, Patrick. *Rule of Darkness: British Literature and Imperialism 1830–1914*. Ithaca, NY: Cornell University Press, 1988.

Braudel, Fernand. *Civilization and Capitalism, 15th–18th Centuries*. Vol. 3, *The Perspective of the World*. Translated by Siân Reynolds. New York: Harper and Row, (1979) 1984.

Briggs, Laura. *How All Politics Became Reproductive Politics: From Welfare Reform to Foreclosure to Trump*. Berkeley: University of California Press, 2017.

Bringa, Tona. "Haunted by the Imaginations of the Past: Robert Kaplan's *Balkan Ghosts*." In *Why America's Top Pundits Are Wrong: Anthropologists Talk Back*, edited by Catherine Besteman and Hugh Gusterson, 60–82. Berkeley: University of California Press, 2005.

Broadbridge, Anne F. *Women and the Making of the Mongol Empire*. Cambridge: Cambridge University Press, 2018.

Brogan, Kathleen. *Cultural Haunting: Ghosts and Ethnicity in Recent American Literature*. Charlottesville: University of Virginia Press, 1998.

Bromell, Nicholas. *By the Sweat of the Brow: Literature and Labor in Antebellum America*. Chicago: University of Chicago Press, 1993.

Brooker, Peter, and Andrew Thacker, eds. *The Oxford Critical and Cultural History of Modernist Magazines*. Vol. 1, *Britain and Ireland, 1880–1955*. New York: Oxford University Press, 2009.

Brooker, Peter, and Andrew Thacker, eds. *The Oxford Critical and Cultural History of Modernist Magazines*. Vol. 2, *North America, 1894–1960*. New York: Oxford University Press, 2012.

Brooker, Peter, Sascha Bru, Andrew Thacker, and Christian Weikop, eds. *The Oxford Critical and Cultural History of Modernist Magazines*. Vol. 3, *Europe, 1880–1940*. New York: Oxford University Press, 2013.

Brotton, Jerry. *The Renaissance Bazaar: From the Silk Road to Michelangelo*. New York: Oxford University Press, 2010.

Browne, O'Brien. "Creating Chaos." MHQ: *The Quarterly Journal of Military History* 23, no. 1 (2010): 14–26.

Buck-Morss, Susan. *Hegel, Haiti, and Universal History*. Pittsburgh, PA: University of Pittsburgh Press, 2009.

Bullon-Fernandez, Maria, ed. *England and Iberia in the Middle Ages, 12th–15th Century: Cultural, Literary, and Political Exchanges*. New York: Palgrave Macmillan, 2007.

Bulson, Eric. *Little Magazine, World Form*. New York: Columbia University Press, 2016.

Bulson, Eric. "Little Magazine, World Form." In *The Oxford Handbook of Global Modernisms*, ed. Mark Wollaeger and Matt Eatough, 267–87. New York: Oxford University Press, 2012.

Burbank, Jane. "The Rights of Difference: Law and Citizenship in the Russian Empire." In *Imperial Formations*, edited by Ann Laura Stoler, Carole McGranahan, and Peter C. Perdue, 77–112. Santa Fe, NM: School of Advanced Research Press, 2007.

Burbank, Jane, and Frederick Cooper. *Empires in World History: Power and the Politics of Difference*. Princeton, NJ: Princeton University Press, 2010.

Burke, Edmund, III. "Islam at the Center: Technological Complexes and the Roots of Modernity." *Journal of World History* 20, no. 2 (2009): 166–68.

Burnett, Charles. *The Introduction of Arabic Learning into England*. London: British Library, 1997.

Burton, Antoinette. "The Body in/as World History." In *A Companion to World History*, edited by Douglas Northrup, 272–84. Chichester, UK: Wiley-Blackwell, 2012.

Butler, Judith. "Arendt: Thinking Cohabitation and the Dispersion of Sovereignty." In *Sovereignty in Ruins: A Politics of Crisis*, edited by George Edmondson and Klaus Mladek, 220–38. Durham, NC: Duke University Press, 2017.

Butler, Judith. *Notes toward a Performative Theory of Assembly*. Cambridge, MA: Harvard University Press, 2015.

Butler, Judith. "Performativity, Precarity and Sexual Politics." AIBR 4, no. 3 (2009): i–xiii.

Butler, Judith. "Performing Acts and Gender Constitution." In *Performing Feminisms: Feminist Critical Theory and Theater*, edited by Sue-Ellen Case, 270–82. Baltimore: Johns Hopkins University Press, 1990.

Butler, Judith. "Sexual Difference as a Question of Ethics: Alterities of the Flesh in Irigaray and Merleau-Ponty." In *Bodies of Resistance: New Phenomenologies of Politics, Agency, and Culture*, edited by Laura Doyle, 59–77. Evanston, IL: Northwestern University Press, 2001.

Butler, Samuel. *The Authoress of the Odyssey*. New York: AMS Press, (1897) 1968.

Buzan, Barry, and Richard Little. *International Systems in World History: Remaking the Study of International Relations*. New York: Oxford University Press, 2000.

Cabajsky, Andrea. "Catholic Gothic: Atavism, Orientalism, and Generic Change in Charles De Guise's *Le Cap au Diable*." In *Unsettled Remains: Canadian Literature and the Postcolonial Gothic*, edited by Cynthia Sugars and Gerry Turcotte, 1–17. Waterloo, ON: Wilfrid Laurier University Press, 2009.

Campbell, Gwyn, Suzanne Miers, and Joseph C. Millers, eds. *Women and Slavery*. Vol. 1, *Africa, the Indian Ocean World, and the Medieval North Atlantic*, and vol. 2, *The Modern Atlantic*. Columbus: Ohio State University Press, 2007.

Caracciolo, Peter, ed. *"The Arabian Nights" in English Literature*. New York: St. Martin's Press, 1988.

Carlyle, Thomas. *Occasional Discourse on the Nigger Question*. London: Thomas Bosworth, 1853.

Carpentier, Alejo. *The Kingdom of This World*. Translated by Harriet de Onís. New York: Farrar, Straus and Giroux, 1957; renewed by Alfred A. Knopf, 1985.

Carpentier, Alejo. "On the Marvelous Real in America." Translated by Tanya Huntington and Lois Parkinson Zamora. In *Magical Realism: Theory, History, Community*, edited by Lois Parkinson Zamora and Wendy B. Faris, 75–88. Durham, NC: Duke University Press, 1995.

Casale, Giancarlo. *The Ottoman Age of Exploration*. New York: Oxford University Press, 2012.

Casanova, Pascale. *The World Republic of Letters*. Translated by M. B. DeBevoise. Cambridge, MA: Harvard University Press, 2007.

Castro, Américo. *The Structure of Spanish History*. Translated by Edmund L. King. Princeton, NJ: Princeton University Press, 1954.

Cawley, Robert Ralston. *Milton and the Literature of Travel*. Princeton, NJ: Princeton University Press, 1951.

Césaire, Aime. *Une tempête*. Paris: Editions du Seuil, 1969.

Chakrabarty, Dipesh. *Provincializing Europe: Postcolonial Thought and Historical Difference*. Princeton, NJ: Princeton University Press, 2000.

Chanady, Amaryll. "La Focalización como Espejo de Contradicciones en el Reino de Este Mundo." *Revista Canadiense de Estudios Hispánicos* 12, no. 3 (1988): 446–58.

Chase-Dunn, Christopher K., and Thomas D. Hall. *Rise and Demise: Comparing World Systems*. Boulder, CO: Westview, 1997.

Chase-Dunn, Christopher K., Daniel Pasciuti, Alexis Alvarez, and Thomas D. Hall. "Growth/Decline Phases and Semi-peripheral Development in the Ancient Mesopotamian and Egyptian World-Systems." In *Globalization and Global History*, edited by Barry K. Gills and William R. Thompson, 114–38. New York: Routledge, 2006.

Chatterjee, Indrani. "Between West and South: Asianist Women's History and Islam." *Journal of Women's History* 18, no. 1 (2006): 192–96.

Chatterjee, Partha. *The Nation and Its Fragments: Colonial and Postcolonial Histories*. Princeton, NJ: Princeton University Press, 1993.

Chaudhuri, Amit. "East as a Career." *New Left Review* 40 (2006): 111–26.

Chaudhuri, K. N. *Asia before Europe: Economy and Civilization of the Indian Ocean from the Rise of Islam to 1750*. New York: Cambridge University Press, 1990.

Cheah, Pheng. "Biopower and the New International Division of Reproductive Labor." *boundary 2* 34, no. 1 (2007): 90–113.

Cheah, Pheng. *Inhuman Conditions: On Cosmopolitanism and Human Rights.* Cambridge, MA: Harvard University Press, 2006.

Cheah, Pheng. *What Is a World? On Postcolonial Literature as World Literature.* Durham, NC: Duke University Press, 2016.

Chen, Kuan-Hsing. *Asia as Method: Toward Deimperialization.* Durham, NC: Duke University Press, 2010.

Chin, Tamara T. "Defamiliarizing the Foreigner: Sima Qina's Ethnography and Han-Xiongnu Marriage Diplomacy." *Harvard Journal of Asiatic Studies* 70, no. 2 (2010): 311–54.

Chin, Tamara. "What Is Imperial Cosmopolitanism? Revisiting *Kosmopolitēs* and *Mundanus.*" In *Cosmopolitanism and Empire: Universal Rulers, Local Elites, and Cultural Integration in the Ancient Near East and Mediterranean,* edited by Miles Lavan, Richard E. Payne, and John Weisweiler, 129–52. New York: Oxford University Press, 2016.

Chin, Timothy. "The Novels of Patricia Powell: Negotiating Gender and Sexuality across the Disjunctures of the Caribbean Diaspora." *Callaloo* 30, no. 2 (2007): 533–545.

Chodorow, Nancy. *The Reproduction of Mothering.* Berkeley: University of California Press, 1978.

Christian, David. "Silk Roads or Steppe Roads? The Silk Roads in World History." *Journal of World History* 11, no. 1 (2000): 25–26.

Cixous, Hélène. "The Laugh of the Medusa." *Signs: Journal of Women in Culture and Society* 1, no. 4 (1976): 875–93.

Clarke, J. J. *Oriental Enlightenment: The Encounter between Asian and Western Thought.* New York: Routledge, 1997.

Clarkson, Thomas. "The True State of the Case, respecting the Insurrection at St. Domingo" (1792). Reprinted in *Slave Revolution in the Caribbean, 1789–1804: A Brief History with Documents,* edited by Laurent Dubois and John D. Garrigus, 113–15. New York: Palgrave Macmillan, 2006.

Cohen, Walter. *A History of European Literature: The West and the World from Antiquity to the Present.* Oxford: Oxford University Press, 2017.

Cohen, Walter. "The Rise of the Written Vernacular: Europe and Eurasia." *PMLA* 126, no. 3 (2011): 719–29.

Cohn, Deborah. "Retracing *The Lost Steps*: The Cuban Revolution, the Cold War, and Publishing Alejo Carpentier in the United States." *CR: The New Centennial Review* 3, no. 1 (2003): 81–108.

Colley, Linda. *Captives: Britain, Empire, and the World, 1600–1850.* New York: Anchor Books, 2002.

Confucius. *The Analects.* Translated by D. C. Lau. Hong Kong: Chinese University Press, 1983.

Coronil, Ferdinand. "After Empire: Reflections on Imperialism from the Américas." In *Imperial Formations,* edited by Ann Laura Stoler, Carole McGranahan, and Peter C. Perdue, 241–74. Santa Fe, NM: School for Advanced Research Press, 2007.

Crichlow, Michaeline A., Patricia Northover, and Deborah Jenson. "Caribbean Entanglements in Times of Crises." *Global South* 6, no. 1 (2012): 1–14.

Crichlow, Michaeline A., Patricia Northover, and Deborah Jenson, eds. "States of Freedom: Freedom of States." Special issue, *Global South* 6, no. 1 (2012), including the editors' introduction, "Caribbean Entanglements in Times of Crises," 1–14.

Cudjoe, Selwyn R. *Resistance and Caribbean Literature*. Athens: Ohio University Press, 1980.

Dale, Stephen. *The Muslim Empires of the Ottomans, Safavids, and Mughals*. Cambridge: Cambridge University Press, 2010.

Dalleo, Raphael. *American Imperialism's Undead: The Occupation of Haiti and the Rise of Caribbean Anticolonialism*. Charlottesville: University of Virginia Press, 2016.

D'Altroy, Terence. *The Incas*. 2nd ed. Malden, MA: Blackwell, 2011.

Damayanti Lienau, Annette. "Reframing Vernacular Culture on Arabic Fault Lines: Bamba, Senghor, and Sembene's Translingual Legacies in French West Africa." PMLA 130, no. 2 (2015): 419–29.

Damrosch, David. *What Is World Literature?* Princeton, NJ: Princeton University Press, 2003.

Damrosch, David. *World Literature in Theory*. Chichester, UK: Wiley Blackwell, 2014.

Dangarembga, Tsitsi. *Nervous Conditions*. Seattle: Seal Press, 2001.

Darling, Linda T. "Political Literature and the Development of an Ottoman Imperial Culture in the Fifteenth Century." *Journal of the Ottoman and Turkish Studies Association* 1, nos. 1–2 (2014): 57–69.

Darraj, Susan Muaddi, ed. *Scheherazade's Legacy: Arab and Arab American Women on Writing*. London: Praeger, 2004.

Darwin, Charles. *The Descent of Man and Selection in Relation to Sex*. New York: D. Appleton, (1871) 1889.

Darwin, Charles. *The Origin of Species*. New York: D. Appleton, 1859.

Datta, Pradip Kumar. "The Interlocking Worlds of the Anglo-Boer War in South Africa/ India." *South African Historical Journal* 57, no. 1 (2007): 35–59.

Davidson, Apollon, and Irina Filatova. *The Russians and the Anglo-Boer War: 1899–1902*. Cape Town: Human and Rousseau, 1998.

Davis, Kathleen. *Periodization and Sovereignty: How Ideas of Feudalism and Secularization Govern the Politics of Time*. Philadelphia: University of Pennsylvania Press, 2008.

Davis, Natalie Zemon. *Trickster Travels: A Sixteenth-Century Muslim between Worlds*. New York: Hill and Wang, 2006.

Deckard, Sharae. "The Political Ecology of Storms in Caribbean Literature." In *The Caribbean: Aesthetics, World-Ecology, Politics*, edited by Chris Campbell and Michael Niblett, 25–45. Liverpool: Liverpool University Press, 2016.

Decker, Michael. "Plants and Progress: Rethinking the Islamic Agricultural Revolution." *Journal of World History* 20, no. 2 (2009): 187–206.

Degenhardt, Jane. *Fortune's Empire: Opportunity, Risk, and Value in Early Modern English Drama and Culture*. New York: Oxford University Press, forthcoming.

Degenhardt, Jane. "The Reformation, Inter-imperial World History, and Marlowe's *Doctor Faustus*." PMLA 130, no. 2 (2015): 402–11.

de Lima, Jorge. "Distribution of Poetry." In *Modern Brazilian Poetry: An Anthology*, translated by John Nist and Yolanda Leite. Bloomington: Indiana University Press, 1962.

DeLoughery, Elizabeth M. *Routes and Roots: Navigating Caribbean and Pacific Island Literatures.* Honolulu: University of Hawai'i Press, 2007.

Demata, Massimiliano. "Discovering Eastern Horrors: Beckford, Maturin, and the Discourse of Travel." In *Empire and the Gothic: The Politics of Genre,* edited by Andrew Smith, 13–34. New York: Palgrave, 2003.

de Vega, Lope. *El nuevo Mundo, descubierto por Cristobol Colon / The New World by Christopher Columbus.* Edited and translated by Robert M. Shannon. New York: Peter Lang, (1614) 2001.

Dew, Nicholas. *Orientalism in Louis XIV's France.* New York: Oxford University Press, 2009.

De Witte, Ben. "Dramatizing Queer Visibility in *El público*: Federico García Lorca in Search of a Modern Theatre." *Modern Drama* 60, no. 1 (2017): 25–45.

Dickie, James. "Granada: A Case Study of Arab Urbanism in Muslim Spain." In *The Legacy of Muslim Spain,* edited by Salma Khadra Jayyusi and Manuela Marín, 88–111. Boston: Brill, 1994.

Dimitriou, Aristides. "Different Substance, Different Form: Alejo Carpentier's Hemispheric American Modernism." *College Literature* 46, no. 1 (2019): 96–126.

Dimock, Wai Chee. *Through Other Continents: American Literature across Deep Time.* Princeton, NJ: Princeton University Press, 2006.

Dinshaw, Carolyn, Lee Edelman, Roderick A. Ferguson, Carla Freccero, Elizabeth Freeman, Judith Halberstam, Annamarie Jagose, Christopher S. Nealon, and Tan Hoang Nguyen. "Theorizing Queer Temporalities: A Roundtable Discussion." GLQ: *A Journal of Lesbian and Gay Studies* 13, no. 2 (2007): 177–95.

Diprose, Rosalyn, and Ewa Plonowska Ziarek. *Arendt, Natality, and Biopolitics: Toward Democratic Plurality and Reproductive Justice.* Edinburgh: Edinburgh University Press, 2017.

Dirlik, Arif. "Rethinking Colonialism: Globalization, Postcolonialism, and the Nation." *Interventions: International Journal of Postcolonial Studies* 4, no. 3 (2002): 428–48.

Dobie, Madeline. "Translation in the Contact Zone: Antoine Galland's *Mille et Une Nuits: Contes Arabes.*" In *"The Arabian Nights" in Historical Context: Between East and West,* edited by Saree Makdisi and Felicity Nussbaum, 25–49. New York: Oxford University Press, 2009.

Donnell, Alison. "Heard but Not Seen: Women's Short Stories and the BBC's Caribbean Voices Programme." In *The Caribbean Short Story: Critical Perspectives,* edited by L. Evans, M. McWatt, and E. Smith, 29–43. Leeds, UK: Peepal Tree Press, 2011.

Doyle, Laura. "At World's Edge: Post/Coloniality, Charles Maturin, and the Gothic Wanderer." *Nineteenth-Century Literature* 65, no. 4 (2011): 513–47.

Doyle, Laura, ed. *Bodies of Resistance: New Phenomenologies of Politics, Agency, and Culture.* Evanston, IL: Northwestern University Press, 2001.

Doyle, Laura. *Bordering on the Body: The Racial Matrix of Modern Fiction and Culture.* New York: Oxford University Press, 1994.

Doyle, Laura. "Colonial Encounters." In *The Oxford Handbook of Modernisms,* edited by Peter Brooker, Andrzej Gasiorek, Deborah Parsons, and Andrew Thacker, 249–66. New York: Oxford University Press, 2010.

Doyle, Laura. *Freedom's Empire: Race and the Rise of the Novel in Atlantic Modernity,*
1640–1940. Durham, NC: Duke University Press, 2008.

Doyle, Laura, ed. "Inter-imperiality." Special issue, MFS: *Modern Fiction Studies* 64, no. 3
(2018).

Doyle, Laura, ed. "Labor Travels, Art Forms." Special issues, *Literature Compass* 13, no. 5
(2016); and *Literature Compass* 17, no. 1 (2020).

Doyle, Laura. "Notes toward a Dialectical Method: Modernities, Modernisms, and the
Crossings of Empire." *Literature Compass* 7, no. 3 (2010): 201–6.

Doyle, Laura. "The Racial Sublime." In *Romanticism, Race, and Imperial Culture, 1780–1834,*
edited by Alan Richardson and Sonia Hofkosh, 15–39. Bloomington: Indiana University
Press, 1996.

Doyle, Laura. "Toward a Philosophy of Transnationalism." *Journal of Transnational American*
Studies 1, no. 1 (2009): n.p.

Doyle, Laura, and Sahar Amer. "Reframing Postcolonial and Global Studies in the Longer
Durée." PMLA 130, no. 2 (2015): 331–438.

Doyle, Laura, and Laura Winkiel, eds. *Geomodernisms: Race, Modernism, Modernity.*
Bloomington: Indiana University Press, 2004.

Duara, Prasenjit. *Decolonization: Perspectives from Now and Then: Rewriting Histories.*
London: Routledge, 2004.

Duara, Prasenjit. "The Imperialism of 'Free Nations': Japan, Manchukuo, and the History of
the Present." In *Imperial Formations,* edited by Anne Stoler, Carole McGranahan, and
Peter C. Perdue, 211–40. Santa Fe, NM: School for Advanced Research Press, 2007.

Du Bois, W. E. B. "The Color Line Belts the World." *Collier's Weekly,* October 20, 1906.

Du Bois, W. E. B. *A Pan-African Manifesto.* August 30, 1921. W. E. B. Du Bois Papers (MS 312).
Special Collections and University Archives, University of Massachusetts Amherst
Libraries.

Eagleton, Terry. *Heathcliff and the Great Hunger: Studies in Irish Culture.* New York: Verso
Books, 1995.

Eby, Cecil Degrotte. *The Road to Armageddon: The Martial Spirit in English Popular Literature,*
1870–1914. Durham, NC: Duke University Press, 1987.

Echevarría, Roberto González. *Alejo Carpentier: The Pilgrim at Home.* Ithaca, NY: Cornell
University Press, 1977.

Edmondson, Belinda, ed. *Caribbean Romances: The Politics of Regional Representation.*
Charlottesville: University of Virginia Press, 1999.

Edmondson, Belinda. *Making Men: Gender, Literary Authority, and Women's Writing in*
Caribbean Narrative. Durham, NC: Duke University Press, 1998.

Edwards, Brent. *Practice of Diaspora: Literature, Translation, and the Rise of Black*
Internationalism. Cambridge, MA: Harvard University Press, 2009.

El-Hibri, Tayeb. "Harun Al-Rashid and the Mecca Protocol of 802: A Plan for Division or
Succession?" *International Journal of Middle East Studies* 24, no. 3 (1992): 461–80.

El-Hibri, Tayeb. *Parable and Politics in Early Islamic History: The Rashidun Caliphs.*
New York: Columbia University Press, 2010.

El-Shamy, Hasan. *A Motif Index of "The Thousand and One Nights".* Bloomington: Indiana
University Press, 2006.

El-Shamy, Hasan. "Siblings in Alf laylah wa-laylah." In *The Arabian Nights" in Transnational Perspective*, edited by Ulrich Marzolph, 83–102. Detroit: Wayne State University Press, 2007.

Emmet, Robert. "The Speech from the Dock." Accessed August 2009. www.robertemmet .org/speech.htm.

Engels, Friedrich. *The Origin of the Family, Private Property, and the State*. Translated by Eleanor Burke Leacock. London: International Publishers, (1940) 1975.

Ertürk, Nergis. *Grammatology and Literary Modernity in Turkey*. New York: Oxford University Press, 2011.

Escobar, Arturo. "Worlds and Knowledges Otherwise: The Latin American Modernity/ Coloniality Research Program." *Cultural Studies* 21, no. 2 (2007): 179–210.

Fabian, Johannes. *Time and the Other: How Anthropology Makes Its Object*. New York: Columbia University Press, 1983.

Falger, Vincent. "Evolutionary World Politics Enriched: The Biological Foundations of International Relations." In *Evolutionary World Politics Enriched in World Politics: Evolutionary Interpretations*, edited by William R. Thompson, 30–51. New York: Routledge, 2001.

Fanon, Frantz. *The Wretched of the Earth*. Translated by Constance Farrington. New York: Grove Press, 1963.

Faulkner, Neil. "The Long Depression, 1873–1896." In *A Marxist History of the World: From Neanderthals to Neoliberals*, edited by Neil Faulkner, 165–68. London: Pluto Press, 2013.

Felkel, Robert W. "The Theme of Love in the 'Mozarabic Jarchas' and in 'Cante Flamenco.'" *Confluencia* 4, no. 1 (1988): 23–40.

Ferguson, Niall. *Empire: The Rise and Demise of the British World Order and the Lessons for Global Power*. New York: Basic Books, 2004.

Fernández Retamar, Roberto. *Caliban and Other Essays*. Translated by Edward Baker. Minneapolis: University of Minnesota Press, 1989.

Fernando, Mayanthi. "Critique as Care." *Critical Times* 2, no. 1 (2019): 13–22.

Figueroa, Víctor. "The Kingdom of Black Jacobins: C. L. R. James and Alejo Carpentier on the Haitian Revolution." *Afro-Hispanic Review* 25, no. 2 (2006): 55–71.

Fischer-Bovet, Christelle. "Toward a Translocal Elite Culture in the Ptolemaic Empire." In *Cosmopolitanism and Empire: Universal Rulers, Local Elites, and Cultural Integration in the Ancient Near East and Mediterranean*, edited by Miles Lavan, Richard E. Payne, and John Weisweiler, 103–28. New York: Oxford University Press, 2016.

Fitzgerald, Timothy J. "Reaching the Flocks: Literacy and the Mass Reception of Ottoman Law in the Sixteenth-Century Arab World." *Journal of the Ottoman and Turkish Studies Association* 2, no. 1 (2015): 5–20.

Fletcher, Giles. *Of the Russe Commonwealth*. Cambridge, MA: Harvard University Press, 1966.

Foley, Sean. "Muslims and Social Change in the Atlantic Basin." *Journal of World History* 20, no. 3 (2009): 377–98.

Forbes, Curdella. *From Nation to Diaspora: Samuel Selvon, George Lamming, and the Cultural Performance of Gender*. Kingston, Jamaica: University of the West Indies Press, 2005.

Foucault, Michel. *Discipline and Punish: The Birth of the Prison.* Translated by Alan Sheridan. New York: Vintage Books, (1975) 2011.

Francis, Donette. *Fictions of Feminine Citizenship: Sexuality and the Nation in Contemporary Caribbean Literature.* New York: Palgrave Macmillan, 2010.

Frank, Andre Gunder, and Barry K. Gills, eds. *The World System: Five Hundred Years or Five Thousand?* New York: Routledge, 1993.

Frank, Andre Gunder, and William R. Thompson. "Early Iron Age Expansion and Contraction Revisited." In *Globalization and Global History*, edited by Barry K. Gills and William R. Thompson, 139–62. New York: Routledge, 2006.

Freeman, Elizabeth. *Time Binds: Queer Temporalities, Queer Histories.* Durham, NC: Duke University Press, 2010.

Fröbel, Folker, Jürgen Heinrichs, and Otto Kreye. *The New International Division of Labor: Structural Unemployment in Industrialised Countries and Industrialisation in Developing Countries.* Translated by Pete Burgess. Cambridge: Cambridge University Press, 1980.

Frydman, Jason. "Jamaican Nationalism, Queer Intimacies, and the Disjunctures of the Chinese Diaspora: Patricia Powell's *The Pagoda.*" *Small Axe* 15, no. 1 (2011): 95–109.

Frydman, Jason. *Sounding the Break: African American and Caribbean Routes of World Literature.* Charlottesville: University of Virginia Press, 2014.

Fuchs, Barbara. *Mimesis and Empire: The New World, Islam, and European Identities.* Cambridge: Cambridge University Press, 2001.

Fumagalli, Maria Cristina. *On the Edge: Writing the Border between Haiti and the Dominican Republic.* Liverpool: Liverpool University Press, 2015.

Ganim, John M., and Shayne Aaron Legassie, eds. *Cosmopolitanism and the Middle Ages.* New York: Palgrave Macmillan, 2013.

Gaonkar, Dilip Parameshwar, ed. *Alternative Modernities.* Durham, NC: Duke University Press, 2001.

García-Arenal, Mercedes, and Fernando Rodríguez Mediano. "Sacred History, Sacred Languages: The Question of Arabic in Early Modern Spain." In *The Teaching and Learning of Arabic in Early Modern Europe*, edited by Jan Loop, Alastair Hamilton, and Charles Burnett, 133–62. Leiden: Brill, 2017.

Gardner, Daniel K. *Chu Hsi and the Ta-hsueh: Neo-Confucian Reflection on the Confucian Canon.* Cambridge, MA: Harvard University Press, 1986.

Garraway, Doris L., ed. *Tree of Liberty: Cultural Legacies of the Haitian Revolution in the Atlantic World.* Charlottesville: University of Virginia Press, 2008.

Geggus, David P., ed. *The Impact of the Haitian Revolution in the Atlantic World.* Columbia: University of South Carolina Press, 2001.

Gerits, Frank. "'When the Bull Elephants Fight': Kwame Nkrumah, Non-alignment, and Pan-Africanism as an Interventionist Ideology in the Global Cold War, 1957–66." *International History Review* 37, no. 5 (2015): 951–69.

Gerwarth, Robert, and Erez Manela, eds. *Empires at War: 1911–1923.* New York: Oxford University Press, 2014.

Ghazoul, Ferial J. *Nocturnal Poetics: "The Arabian Nights" in Comparative Context.* Cairo: American University in Cairo Press, 1996.

Ghosh, Amitav. "Mutinies: India, Ireland and Imperialism." In *Ireland and Postcolonial Theory*, edited by Claire Carroll and Patricia King, 122–28. Cork: Cork University Press, 2003.

Gibbons, Luke. *Gaelic Gothic: Race, Colonization, and Irish Culture*. Galway: Arlen House, 2004.

Giddings, Paula J. *When and Where I Enter: The Impact of Black Women on Race and Sex in America*. New York: William Morrow, 1984.

Gikandi, Simon. *Slavery and the Culture of Taste*. Princeton, NJ: Princeton University Press, 2011.

Gikandi, Simon. *Writing in Limbo: Modernism and Caribbean Literature*. Ithaca, NY: Cornell University Press, 1992.

Gillman, Susan. "Black Jacobins and New World Mediterraneans." In *Surveying the American Tropics: A Literary Geography from New York to Rio*, edited by Lesley Wylie, Peter Hulme, and Owen Robinson, 159–82. Liverpool: Liverpool University Press, 2013.

Gills, Barry K., and William R. Thompson, eds. *Globalization and Global History*. New York: Routledge, 2006.

Gĩthĩnji, Mwangi wa. "Erasing Class/(Re)Creating Ethnicity: Politics, Jobs, Accumulation and Identity in Kenya." *Review of Black Political Economy* 42, no. 1 (2015): 87–110.

Gittes, Katharine Slater. "*The Canterbury Tales* and the Arabic Frame Tradition." *PMLA* 98, no. 2 (1983): 237–51.

Glissant, Édouard. *Poetics of Relation*. Translated by Betsy Wing. Ann Arbor: University of Michigan Press, (1990) 1997.

Glissant, Édouard. "The Quarrel with History." In *Caribbean Discourse*, translated by J. Michael Dash, 61–66. Charlottesville: University of Virginia Press, 1989.

Goddu, Teresa A. *Gothic America: Narrative, History, and Nation*. New York: Columbia University Press, 1997.

Goffman, Daniel. "Negotiating with the Renaissance State: The Ottoman Empire and the New Diplomacy." In *The Early Modern Ottomans: Remapping the Empire*, edited by Virginia H. Askan and Daniel Goffman, 61–74. New York: Cambridge University Press, 2007.

Goldstone, Jack. "Efflorescences and Economic Growth in World History: Rethinking the 'Rise of the West' and the Industrial Revolution." *Journal of World History* 13, no. 2 (2002): 323–89.

Goody, Jack. *Renaissances: The One or the Many?* Cambridge: Cambridge University Press, 2010.

Gopal, Priyamvada. *Literary Radicalism in India: Gender, Nation, and the Transition to Independence*. New York: Routledge, 2005.

Gosse, Dave. "Examining the Promulgation and Impact of the Great Commission in the Caribbean, 1492–1970: A Historical Analysis." In *Teaching All Nations: Interrogating the Matthean Great Commission*, edited by Mitzi J. Smith and Jayachitra Lalitha, 33–56. Minneapolis: Fortress Press, 2014.

Greenblatt, Stephen, ed. *New World Encounters*. Berkeley: University of California Press, 1993.

Greenblatt, Stephen. *Renaissance Self-Fashioning: From More to Shakespeare*. Chicago: University of Chicago Press, 1980.

Greene, Roland. *Unrequited Conquests: Love and Empire in the Colonial Americas.* Chicago: University of Chicago Press, 1999.

Greeson, Jennifer Rae. "The 'Mysteries and Miseries' of North Carolina: New York City, Urban Gothic Fiction, and *Incidents in the Life of a Slave Girl.*" *American Literature* 73, no. 2 (2001): 277–309.

Grosz, Elizabeth A. *Volatile Bodies: Toward a Corporeal Feminism.* Bloomington: Indiana University Press, 1994.

Grotzfeld, Heinz. "The Age of the Galland Manuscript of *The Nights*: Numismatic Evidence for Dating a Manuscript?" In *The Arabian Nights Reader,* edited by Ulrich Marzolph, 105–21. Detroit: Wayne State University Press, 2006.

Gruesser, John Cullen. *The Empire Abroad and the Empire at Home: African American Literature and the Era of Overseas Expansion.* Athens: University of Georgia Press, 2012.

Habermas, Jürgen. *The Structural Transformation of the Public Sphere: An Inquiry into a Category of Bourgeois Society.* Translated by Thomas Burger. Cambridge, MA: MIT Press, (1962) 1989.

Haddawy, Husain, trans. *The Arabian Nights.* Edited by Muhsin Mahdi. New York: Norton, 1990.

Halberstam, Judith. *In a Queer Time and Place: Transgender Bodies, Subcultural Lives.* New York: New York University Press, 2005.

Hall, Maurice. "Negotiating Jamaican Masculinities." In *Global Masculinities and Manhood,* edited by Ronald L. Jackson and Murali Balaji, 31–51. Urbana: University of Illinois Press, 2011.

Hansen, Jim. *Terror and Irish Modernism: The Gothic Tradition from Burke to Beckett.* Albany, NY: SUNY Press, 2010.

Hansen, Valerie. *The Silk Road: A New History.* New York: Oxford University Press, 2015.

Hardt, Michael, and Antonio Negri. *Empire.* Cambridge, MA: Harvard University Press, 2001.

Hartman, Saidiya V. *Scenes of Subjection: Terror, Slavery, and Self-Making in Nineteenth-Century America.* New York: Oxford University Press, 1997.

Harvey, John. "Corony Flowers and Their 'Arabick' Background." In *The "Arabick" Interests of the Natural Philosophers in Seventeenth-Century England,* edited by Gul A. Russell, 297–303. Leiden: Brill, 1994.

Heffernan, Carol. *The Orient in Chaucer and the Medieval Romance.* Rochester, NY: D. S. Brewer, 2003.

Hegel, Georg Wilhelm Friedrich. *The Phenomenology of Spirit.* Translated by A. V. Miller. Oxford: Clarendon Press, 1977.

Heidegger, Martin. *Being and Time.* Translated by John Macquarrie and Edward Robinson. Oxford: Blackwell, (1927) 1962.

Heineman, Elizabeth, ed. *Sexual Violence in Conflict Zones.* Philadelphia: University of Pennsylvania Press, 2011.

Heinowitz, Rebecca Cole. *Spanish America and British Romanticism, 1777–1826: Rewriting Conquest.* Edinburgh: University of Edinburgh Press, 2010.

Hell, Julia. *The Conquest of Ruins: The Third Reich and the Fall of Rome.* Chicago: University of Chicago Press, 2019.

Henderson, Mae Gwendolyn. "Speaking in Tongues." In *African American Literary Theory: A Reader*, edited by Winston Napier, 348–68. New York: New York University Press, 2000.

Heng, Geraldine. *Empire of Magic: Medieval Romance and the Politics of Cultural Fantasy.* New York: Columbia University Press, 2003.

Heng, Geraldine. *The Invention of Race in the European Middle Ages.* Cambridge: Cambridge University Press, 2018.

Ho, Fred, and Bill V. Mullen, eds. *Afro-Asia: Revolutionary Political and Cultural Connections between African Americans and Asian Americans.* Durham, NC: Duke University Press, 2008.

Hobson, John A. *Imperialism: A Study.* London: James Nisbet, 1902.

Hobson, John M. "Is Critical Theory Always for the White West and for Western Imperialism? Beyond Westphilian towards a Post-racist Critical IR." *Review of International Studies* 33, no. S1 (2007): 91–116.

Hobson, John M. "Provincializing Westphalia: The Eastern Origins of Sovereignty." *International Politics* 46, no. 6 (2009): 671–90.

Hoch, Steven L. "The Serf Economy, the Peasant Family, and the Social Order." In *Imperial Russia: New Histories for the Empire*, edited by Jane Burbank and David Ransel, 199–209. Bloomington: Indiana University Press, 1998.

Hodgson, Marshall. "The Interrelations of Societies." In *Rethinking World History: Essays on Europe, Islam, and World History*, edited by Edmund Burke III, 3–28. New York: Cambridge University Press, (1963) 1993.

Hoehling, Annaliese. "Minoritarian 'Marvelous Real': Enfolding Revolution in Alejo Carpentier's *The Kingdom of This World.*" *Journal of Postcolonial Writing* 54, no. 2 (2018): 254–67.

Hopkins, Anthony G. "Back to the Future: From National History to Imperial History." *Past and Present* 164 (1999): 198–243.

Hopkins, Anthony G. "Rethinking Decolonization." *Past and Present* 200, no. 1 (2008): 211–47.

Horsman, Reginald. *Race and Manifest Destiny.* Cambridge, MA: Harvard University Press, 1981.

Hovannisian, Richard, and George Sabagh, eds. *"The Thousand and One Nights" in Arabic Literature and Society.* New York: Cambridge University Press, 1997.

Huang, Yunte. *Transpacific Imaginations: History, Literature, Counterpoetics.* Cambridge, MA: Harvard University Press, 2008.

Hudson, Peter. *Bankers and Empires: How Wall Street Colonized the Caribbean.* Chicago: University of Chicago Press, 2017.

Hughes, Langston. "The Negro Artist and the Racial Mountain." In *Double-Take: A Revisionist Harlem Renaissance Anthology*, edited by Venetria K. Patton and Maureen Honey, 40–44. New Brunswick, NJ: Rutgers University Press, 2001.

Hughes, Lindsey. *Russia in the Age of Peter the Great.* New Haven, CT: Yale University Press, 2000.

Huntington, Samuel. *The Clash of Civilizations and the Remaking of World Order.* New York: Simon and Schuster, 1997.

Hussey, Mark. "Mrs. Thatcher and Mrs. Woolf." *MFS: Modern Fiction Studies* 50, no. 1 (2004): 8–30.

Iannini, Christopher P. *Fatal Revolutions: Natural History, West Indian Slavery, and the Routes of American Literature*. Chapel Hill: University of North Carolina Press, 2012.

Idman, Nilo. *Charles Robert Maturin: His Life and Works*. London: Constable, 1923.

Ignatiev, Noel. *How the Irish Became White*. London: Routledge, 1995.

Inal, Tuba. *Looting and Rape in Wartime: Law and Change in International Relations*. Philadelphia: University of Pennsylvania Press, 2013.

Jameson, Fredric. "Modernism and Imperialism." In *Nationalism, Colonialism, and Literature*, by Terry Eagleton, Fredric Jameson, and Edward W. Said, 43–66. Minneapolis: University of Minnesota Press, 1990.

Jameson, Fredric. *The Political Unconscious*. Ithaca, NY: Cornell University Press, 1981.

Janzen, Marike. "Messenger Writers: Anna Seghers and Alejo Carpentier in the Cold War." *Comparative Literature* 62, no. 3 (2010): 283–301.

Jassam Ali, Muhsin. *Scheherezade in England: A Study of Nineteenth-Century English Criticism of the "Arabian Nights"*. Washington, DC: Three Continents Press, 1979.

Jennison, Ruth. *The Zukofsky Era: Modernity, Margins, and the Avant-Garde*. Baltimore: John Hopkins University Press, 2012.

Jewsiewicki, B., and V. Y. Mudimbe. "Africans' Memories and Contemporary History of Africa." *History and Theory* 32, no. 4 (1993): 1–11.

Jobst, Kerstin S. "Where the Orient Ends? Orientalism and Its Function for Imperial Rule in the Russian Empire." In *Deploying Orientalism: From Germany to Central and Eastern Europe*, edited by James Hodkinson, John Walker, Shaswati Mazumdar, and Johannes Feichtinger, 190–208. New York: Camden House, 2013.

Johnson, Rebecca Carol, Richard Maxwell, and Katie Trumpener. "*The Arabian Nights*, Arab-European Literary Influence, and the Lineages of the Novel." *Modern Language Quarterly* 88, no. 2 (2007): 243–78.

Joyce, James. *Ulysses*. Edited by Hans Gabler. New York: Vintage, 1986.

Joyce, Stephen. "Inter-imperial Aesthetics: Korean and Korean Diasporic Literature between Empires." *MFS: Modern Fiction Studies* 64, no. 3 (2018): 488–511.

Kabir, Ananya J., and Deanne Williams. *Postcolonial Approaches to the European Middle Ages: Translating Cultures*. New York: Cambridge University Press, 2005.

Kaisary, Phillip. *The Haitian Revolution in the Literary Imagination: Radical Horizons, Conservative Constraints*. Charlottesville: University of Virginia Press, 2014.

Kamali, Masoud. *Multiple Modernities, Civil Society, and Islam: The Case of Iran and Turkey*. Liverpool: Liverpool University Press, 2006.

Kaplan, Robert. *Balkan Ghosts: A Journey through History*. New York: St. Martin's, 2005.

Kardulias, P. Nick, ed. *World-Systems Theory in Practice: Leadership, Production, and Exchange*. Lanham, MD: Rowman and Littlefield, 1999.

Kelley, Robin D. G. "But a Local Phase of a World Problem: Black History's Global Vision, 1883–1950." *Journal of American History* 86, no. 3 (1999): 1045–77.

Kelly, Louis G. *The True Interpreter: A History of Translation Theory and Practice in the West*. New York: St. Martin's Press, 1979.

Kennedy, Hugh. "Military Pay and the Economy of the Early Islamic State." *Historical Research* 75, no. 188 (2002): 155–69.

Kent Research Group. "Radical Distrust: A Cultural Analysis of the Emotional, Psychological and Linguistic Formations of Religious and Political Extremism." UK Research and Innovation. Accessed March 21, 2020. http://gtr.rcuk.ac.uk/projects?ref =ES%2FG034362%2F1.

Kern, Stephen. *The Culture of Time and Space, 1880–1918*. Cambridge, MA: Harvard University Press, (1983) 2003.

Khalid, Adeeb. "The Soviet Union as an Imperial Formation: A View from Central Asia." In *Imperial Formations*, edited by Ann Laura Stoler, Carole McGranahan, and Peter C. Perdue, 113–40. Santa Fe, NM: School for Advanced Research Press, 2007.

Khlebnikov, Velimir. "An Indo-Russian Union." In *Collected Works of Velimir Khlebnikov*. Vol. 1, *Letters and Theoretical Writings*. Cambridge, MA: Harvard University Press, 1987.

Kilfeather, Siobhan. "Terrific Register: The Gothicization of Atrocity in Irish Literature." *boundary 2* 31, no. 1 (2004): 49–71.

Killeen, Jarlath. *The Emergence of Irish Gothic Fiction*. Edinburgh: Edinburgh University Press, 2014.

Killeen, Jarlath. *Gothic Ireland: Horror and the Irish Anglican Imagination in the Long Eighteenth Century*. Dublin: Four Courts Press, 2005.

Knapp, Jeffrey. *An Empire Nowhere*. Berkeley: University of California Press, 1992.

Ko, Chisu Teresa. "Self-Orientalism and Inter-imperiality in Anna Kazumi Stahl's *Flores de un solodía*." *Latin American and Caribbean Ethnic Studies* 14, no. 1 (2018): 1–20.

Kojève, Alexandre. *Introduction to the Reading of Hegel: Lectures on the "Phenomenology of Spirit"*. Edited by Allan Bloom. Ithaca, NY: Cornell University Press, 1980.

Koloziejczyk, Dariusz, and Peter F. Bang, eds. *Universal Empire: A Comparative Approach to Imperial Culture and Representation in Eurasian History*. Cambridge: Cambridge University Press, 2012.

Kramer, Paul A. "Empires, Exceptions, and Anglo-Saxons: Race and Rule between the British and United States Empires, 1880–1910." *Journal of American History* 88, no. 4 (2002): 1315–53.

Krishnan, Sanjay. *Reading the Global: Troubling Perspectives on Britain's Empire in Asia*. New York: Columbia University Press, 2007.

Krishnaswamy, Revathi. *Effeminism: The Economy of Colonial Desire*. Ann Arbor: University of Michigan Press, 1998.

Krishnaswamy, Revathi. "Toward Literary Knowledge: Theory in the Age of Globalization." *Comparative Literature* 62, no. 4 (2010): 399–419.

Kristeva, Julia. "Women's Time." Translated by Alice Jardine and Harry Blake. *Signs: Journal of Women in Culture and Society* 7, no. 1 (1981): 13–35.

Kuhn, Stephen. *The Culture of Time and Space, 1880–1918*. Cambridge, MA: Harvard University Press, (1983) 2003.

Kushigian, Julia. *Orientalism in the Hispanic Tradition: In Dialogue with Borges, Paz, and Sarduy*. Albuquerque: University of New Mexico Press, 1991.

Kwon, Nayoung Aimee. "Japanophone Literature? A Transpacific Query on Absence." *MFS: Modern Fiction Studies* 64, no. 3 (2018): 537–58.

Laachir, Karima, Sara Marzagora, and Francesca Orsini. "Significant Geographies: In Lieu of World Literature." *Journal of World Literature* 3, no. 3 (2018): 290–310.

Lach, Donald F. *Asia in the Making of Europe*. 2 vols. Chicago: University of Chicago Press, 1965.

Lach, Donald F., and Edwin J. Van Kley. *Asia in the Making of Europe*. Vol 3. Chicago: University of Chicago Press, 1993.

Lacher, Hannes. *Beyond Globalization: Capitalism, Territoriality and the International Relations of Modernity*. New York: Routledge, 2006.

Lacher, Hannes. "Putting the State in Its Place: The Critique of State-Centrism and Its Limits." *Review of International Studies* 29, no. 4 (2003): 521–41.

Lai-Henderson, Selina. *Mark Twain in China*. Stanford, CA: Stanford University Press, 2015.

Lavan, Miles, Richard E. Payne, and John Weisweiler, eds. *Cosmopolitanism and Empire: Universal Rulers, Local Elites, and Cultural Integration in the Ancient Near East and Mediterranean*. New York: Oxford University Press, 2016.

Lawrence, T. E. *Seven Pillars of Wisdom*. London: Wordsworth, (1926) 1997.

Leask, Nigel. "Irish Republicans and Gothic Eleutherarchs: Pacific Utopias in the Work of Theobald Wolfe Tone and Charles Brockden Brown." *Huntington Library Quarterly* 63, no. 3 (2000): 247–67.

Lechtman, Heather. "Andean Value Systems and the Development of Prehistoric Metallurgy." *Technology and Culture* 25, no. 1 (1984): 1–36.

LeDonne, John P. *The Russian Empire and the World, 1700–1917: The Geopolitics of Expansion and Containment*. New York: Oxford University Press, 1997.

Ledoux, Ellen Malenas. *Social Reform in Gothic Writing: Fantastic Forms of Change, 1764–1834*. New York: Palgrave Macmillan, 2013.

Lee, Chang-rae. *Native Speaker*. New York: Riverhead, 1995.

Lee, Erika, and Judy Yung. *Angel Island: Immigrant Gateway to America*. New York: Oxford University Press, 2010.

Lee, Thomas H. C. "Academies: Official Sponsorship and Suppression." In *Imperial Rulership and Cultural Change in Traditional China*, edited by Frederick P. Brandauer and Chun-Chieh Huang, 117–43. Seattle: University of Washington Press, 1994.

Leger, Natalie M. "Faithless Sight: Haiti in the Kingdom of the World." *Research in African Literatures* 45, no. 1 (2014): 85–106.

Lenin, Vladimir Il'ich. *Imperialism: The Highest Stage of Capitalism: A Popular Outline*. New York: International Publishers, 1939.

Lenin, Vladimir Il'ich. "State and Revolution." In *V. I. Lenin Collected Works, vol. 25: June–September 1917*, edited by Stepan Apresyan and Jim Riordan, 385–496. Moscow: Progress, 1964.

Lennon, Joseph. *Irish Orientalism: A Literary and Intellectual History*. Syracuse, NY: Syracuse University Press, 2008.

Lerner, Gerda. *The Creation of Patriarchy*. New York: Oxford University Press, 1987.

Levine, Lawrence. *Black Culture and Black Consciousness: Afro-American Folk Thought from Slavery to Freedom*. New York: Oxford University Press, 1977.

Lew, Joseph W. "'Unprepared for Sudden Transformations': Identity and Politics in *Melmoth the Wanderer*". *Studies in the Novel* 26, no. 2 (1994): 173–95.

Lewis, Mark E. *Writing and Authority in Early China*. Albany, NY: SUNY Press, 1999.

Lewis, Matthew G. *The Monk*. New York: Grove Press, 1952.

Lewis, Reina. *Rethinking Orientalism*. New Brunswick, NJ: Rutgers University Press, 2004.

Lewis, Wyndham. "BLAST! Manifesto" (1914). University of Pennsylvania website. Accessed April 29, 2019. http://writing.upenn.edu/library/Blast/Blast1-1_Manifesto.pdf.

Linebaugh, Peter, and Marcus Rediker. *The Many-Headed Hydra: Sailors, Slaves, Commoners, and the Hidden History of the Revolutionary Atlantic*. Boston: Beacon Press, 2000.

Ling, L. H. M. *Postcolonial International Relations: Conquest and Desire between Asia and the West*. New York: Palgrave Macmillan, 2002.

Ling, L. H. M. "Worlds beyond Westphalia: Daoist Dialectics and the 'China Threat.'" *Review of International Studies* 39, no. 3 (2013): 549–68.

Lipman, Jan. *Guantanamo: A Working-Class History between Empire and Revolution*. Oakland: University of California Press, 2008.

Liu, Lydia H. "Scripts in Motion: Writing as Imperial Technology, Past and Present." *PMLA* 130, no. 2 (2015): 375–83.

Liu, Yu. *Seeds of a Different Eden: Chinese Gardening and a New English Aesthetic Ideal*. Columbia: University of South Carolina Press, 2008.

Long Hoeveler, Diane, and Jeffrey Cass, eds. *Interrogating Orientalism*. Columbus: Ohio State University Press, 2006.

Loomba, Ania. *Shakespeare, Race, and Colonialism*. New York: Oxford University Press, 2002.

Loomba, Ania, and Martin Orkin, eds. *Postcolonial Shakespeares*. New York: Routledge, 1998.

López-Baralt, Luce. "The Secret Literature of the Last Muslims Of Spain." *Islamic Studies* 36, no. 1 (1997): 21–38.

Lorde, Audre. "The Uses of the Erotic: The Erotic as Power." In *The Lesbian and Gay Studies Reader*, edited by Henry Abelove, Michèle Aina Barale, and David M. Halperin, 339–43. New York: Routledge, 1993.

Lougy, Robert E. *Charles Robert Maturin*. Lewisburg, PA: Bucknell University Press, 1975.

Lowe, Lisa. *The Intimacies of Four Continents*. Durham, NC: Duke University Press, 2015.

Loy, Mina. *The Lost Lunar Baedeker*. Edited by Roger L. Conover. New York: Farrar, Straus and Giroux, (1914) 1996.

Lyon, Janet. *Provocations: Manifestoes of the Modern*. Ithaca, NY: Cornell University Press, 1999.

MacCormack, Sabine. *On the Wings of Time: Rome, the Incas, Spain, and Peru*. Princeton, NJ: Princeton University Press, 2009.

Macdonald, Sean. "Introduction." *Modernism/Modernity* 11, no. 4 (November 2004): 797–807.

MacLean, Gerald. *Looking East: English Writing and the Ottoman Empire before 1800*. New York: Palgrave, 2007.

MacLean, Gerald. "Milton, Islam and the Ottomans." In *Milton and Toleration*, edited by Sharon Achinstein and Elizabeth Sauer, 299–304. Oxford: Oxford University Press, 2007.

Mahdi, Muhsin S., ed. *The Thousand and One Nights*. 3 vols. Leiden: Brill, 1984–94.

Maingot, A. P. "Haiti and the Terrified Consciousness of the Caribbean." In *Ethnicity in the Caribbean*, edited by Gert Ootindie, 53–80. London: Macmillan, 1996.

Makdisi, George. *The Rise of Humanism in Classical Islam and the West*. Edinburgh: Edinburgh University Press, 1990.

Makdisi, Saree. *Making England Western: Occidentalism, Race, and Imperial Culture*. Chicago: University of Chicago Press, 2013.

Makdisi, Saree. *Romantic Imperialism: Universal Empire and the Culture of Modernity*. New York: Cambridge University Press, 1998.

Makdisi, Saree, and Felicity Nussbaum, eds. *"The Arabian Nights" in Historical Context: Between East and West*. Oxford: Oxford University Press, 2009.

Makdisi, Ussama. "Ottoman Orientalism." *American Historical Review* 107, no. 3 (2008): 768–96.

Malchow, H. L. *Gothic Images of Race in Nineteenth-Century Britain*. Stanford, CA: Stanford University Press, 1996.

Maldonado-Torres, Nelson. *Against War: Views from the Underside of Modernity*. Durham, NC: Duke University Press, 2008.

Maldonado-Torres, Nelson. "On the Coloniality of Being: Contributions to the Development of a Concept." *Cultural Studies* 21, nos. 2–3 (2007): 240–70.

Mallette, Karla. *European Modernity and the Arab Mediterranean: Toward a New Philology and a Counter-Orientalism*. Philadelphia: University of Pennsylvania Press, 2010.

Mallette, Karla. *The Kingdom of Sicily, 1100–1250*. Philadelphia: University of Pennsylvania Press, 2005.

Mann, Charles C. *1491: New Revelations of the Americas before Columbus*. New York: Alfred A. Knopf, 2005.

Mann, Michael. *The Sources of Social Power*. Vol 1, *A History of Power from the Beginning to AD 1760*. Cambridge: Cambridge University Press, 1986.

Mann, Michael. *The Sources of Social Power*. Vol. 2, *The Rise of Classes and Nation-States, 1760–1914*. New York: Cambridge University Press, 1993.

Mann, Michael. *The Sources of Social Power*. Vol. 3, *Global Empires and Revolution, 1890–1945*. New York: Cambridge University Press, 2012.

Manning, Patrick. *Migrations in World History*. 2nd ed. New York: Routledge, 2012.

Manning, Patrick. *World History: Local and Global Interactions*. Princeton, NJ: Markus Weiner, 2006.

Mansuroğlu, Mecdut. "The Rise and Development of Written Turkish in Anatolia." *Oriens* 7, no. 2 (1954): 250–64.

Marinetti, Filippo Tommaso. "The Founding and the Manifesto of Futurism." In *Let's Murder the Moonshine: Selected Writings*, edited and translated by R. W. Flint, 47–52. Los Angeles: Sun and Moon Classics, (1909) 1991.

Marlowe, Christopher. *Doctor Faustus*. Edited by David S. Kaston. New York: Norton, (1604/1616) 2005.

Martin, Amy E. "Gothic Internationalism: Irish Nationalist Critiques of Empire as a System of Violence and Trauma." In *Traumatic Tales: British Nationhood and National Trauma in Nineteenth-Century Literature*, edited by Lisa Kasmer, 97–117. New York: Routledge, 2017.

Martin, Andy. *Napoleon the Novelist*. Cambridge: Polity Press, 2000.

Martínez-San Miguel, Yolanda. *Coloniality of Diasporas: Rethinking Intra-Colonial Migrations in a Pan-Caribbean Context*. New York: Palgrave, 2014.

Marzolph, Ulrich, ed. *"The Arabian Nights" in Transnational Perspective*. Detroit: Wayne State University Press, 2007.

Marzolph, Ulrich. "The Persian *Nights*: Links between *Arabian Nights* and Iranian Culture." In The Arabian Nights *in Transnational Perspective*, edited by Ulrich Marzolph, 221–44. Detroit: Wayne State University Press, 2007.

Matar, Nabil. *Britain and Barbary, 1589–1689*. Gainesville: University of Florida Press, 2005.

Matar, Nabil. *Islam in Britain, 1558–1685*. Cambridge: Cambridge University Press, 1998.

Maturin, Charles. *Melmoth the Wanderer*. New York: Penguin Books, (1820) 2000.

M'Baye, Babacar. *The Trickster Comes West: Pan-African Influence in Early Black Diasporan Narratives*. Jackson: University Press of Mississippi, 2009.

McCannell, Juliet Flower. *The Regime of the Brother*. New York: Routledge, 1991.

McCracken, Donal P. *MacBridge's Brigade: Irish Commandos in the Anglo-Boer War*. Dublin: Four Courts Press, 1999.

McLuskie, Kathleen E., and Felicity Dunsworth. "Patronage and the Economics of Theater." In *A New History of Early English Drama*, edited by John D. Cox and David Scott Kastan, 423–40. New York: Columbia University Press, 1997.

Menocal, Maria Rosa. *The Arabic Role in Medieval Literary History*. Philadelphia: University of Pennsylvania Press, 1987.

Merleau-Ponty, Maurice. *The Visible and Invisible: Followed by Working Notes*. Translated by Alphonso Lingis. Evanston, IL: Northwestern University Press, 1968.

Metlitzki, Dorothee. *The Matter of Araby in Medieval England*. New Haven, CT: Yale University Press, 1977.

Mignolo, Walter. *The Idea of Latin America*. Malden, MA: Blackwell, 2005.

Milam, Jennifer. "Toying with China: Cosmopolitanism and Chinoiserie in Russian Garden Design and Building Projects under Catherine the Great." *Eighteenth-Century Fiction* 25, no. 1 (2012): 115–38.

Miller, Paul. *Elusive Origins: The Enlightenment in the Modern Caribbean Historical Imagination*. Charlottesville: University of Virginia Press, 2010.

Miller, Robin Feuer. *Dostoevsky's Unfinished Journey*. New Haven, CT: Yale University Press, 2007.

Milton, John. *Paradise Lost*. Edited by William Kerrigan, John Rumrich, and Stephen M. Fallon. New York: Modern Library, (1667) 2008.

Mishra, Vijay. *The Gothic Sublime*. Albany, NY: SUNY Press, 1994.

Modelski, George. "Evolutionary World Politics: Problems of Scope and Method." In *Evolutionary Interpretations of World Politics*, edited by William R. Thompson, 16–29. New York: Routledge, 2001.

Modernist Journals Project. Accessed May 31, 2019. http://modjourn.org/index.html.

Momigliano, Arnaldo. "The Origins of Universal History." In *On Pagans, Jews, and Christians*, 31–57. Middletown, CT: Wesleyan University Press, 1987.

Moretti, Franco. "The Dialectic of Fear." *New Left Review* 136, no. 1 (1982): 67–85.

Moretti, Franco. *Signs Taken for Wonders: Essays in the Sociology of Literary Forms*. London: Verso, 1988.

Morris, Ian, and Walter Scheidel, eds. *The Dynamics of Ancient Empires: State Power from Assyria to Byzantium*. New York: Oxford University Press, 2008.

Morrison, Toni. *Beloved*. New York: Alfred A. Knopf, 1987.

Morrow, John. *The Great War: An Imperial History*. New York: Vintage, 2004.

Moynihan, Julian. "The Politics of Anglo-Irish Gothic: Maturin, Le Fanu, and 'the Return of the Repressed.'" In *Studies in Anglo-Irish Literature*, edited by Heinz Kosok, 43–54. Bonn: Bouvier Verlag Herbert Grundmann, 1982.

Mufti, Aamir. *Forget English! Orientalisms and World Literature*. Cambridge, MA: Harvard University Press, 2016.

Mufti, Aamir. "Orientalism and the Institution of World Literatures." *Critical Inquiry* 36, no. 3 (2010): 458–93.

Muhawi, Ibrahim. "'Arabian Nights' and the Question of Authorship." *Journal of Arabic Literature* 36, no. 3 (2005): 323–37.

Mulanax, Richard B. *The Boer War in American Politics and Diplomacy*. Lanham, MD: University Press of America, 1994.

Mullen, Bill V., and Cathryn Watson, eds. *W. E. B. Du Bois on Asia: Crossing the World Color Line*. Jackson: University Press of Mississippi, 2005.

Munro, Lucy. "'As It Was Played in the Blackfriars': Jonson, Marston, and the Business of Playmaking." *English Literary Renaissance* 50, no. 2 (2020): 256–95.

Nancy, Jean-Luc. *Being Singular Plural*. Translated by Robert D. Richardson. Stanford, CA: Stanford University Press, 2009.

Nandy, Ashis. *The Intimate Enemy: Loss and Recovery of Self under Colonialism*. 2nd ed. Oxford: Oxford University Press, 2009.

Napoleon. "Napoleon's Addresses: The Italian Campaigns." Edited by Tom Holberg. Napoleon Series website. Accessed April 29, 2019. https://www.napoleon-series.org /research/napoleon/speeches/c_speeches1.html.

Needham, Joseph. *Science and Civilization in China*. Vol. 5, part 1. New York: Cambridge University Press, 1985.

Ng, Lynda. "Xinjiang's Indelible Footprint: Reading the New Imperialism of Neoliberalism in *English* and *Waiting for the Barbarians*." MFS: *Modern Fiction Studies* 64, no. 3 (2018): 512–36.

Nisancioglu, Kerem. "The Ottoman Origins of Capitalism: Uneven and Combined Development and Eurocentrism." *Review of International Studies* 40 (2014): 325–47.

Nkrumah, Kwame. *Neo-colonialism: The Last Stage of Imperialism*. New York: International Publishers, 1965.

Nunes, Zita. *Cannibal Democracy: Race and Representation in the Literature of the Americas*. Minneapolis: University of Minnesota Press, 2008.

Nwankwo, Ifeoma C. K. *Black Cosmopolitanism: Racial Consciousness and Transnational Identity in the Nineteenth-Century Americas*. Philadelphia: University of Pennsylvania Press, 2014.

Nwankwo, Ifeoma C. K. "'Charged with Sympathy for Haiti': Harnessing the Power of Blackness and Cosmopolitanism in the Wake of the Haitian Revolution." In *Tree of Liberty: Cultural Legacies of the Haitian Revolution in the Atlantic World*, edited by Doris L. Garraway, 91–133. Charlottesville: University of Virginia Press, 2008.

Nykl, Alois Richard. *Hispano-Arabic Poetry and Its Relations with the Old Provençal Troubadours*. Baltimore: Literary Licensing, 1946.

Ocasio, Rafael. "The Revolution of Santería and Hispanic Hagiography in Cuba." *Journal of the Fantastic in the Arts* 8, no. 2 (1997): 235–43.

Oppenheimer, Paul. *The Birth of the Modern Mind: Self, Consciousness, and the Invention of the Sonnet*. New York: Oxford University Press, 1989.

Orr, Bridget. *Empire on the English Stage*. Cambridge: Cambridge University Press, 2001.

Orr, Bridget. "Galland, Georgian Theatre, and the Creation of Popular Orientalism." In *"The Arabian Nights" in Historical Context: Between East and West*, edited by Saree Makdisi and Felicity Nussbaum, 103–30. New York: Oxford University Press, 2009.

Ortiz, Fernando. *Cuban Counterpoint: Tobacco and Sugar*. Durham, NC: Duke University Press, (1940) 1995.

Osto, Douglas. *Power, Wealth and Women in Indian Mahayana Buddhism: The Gandavyuha-sutra*. New York: Routledge, 2008.

Öz, Öktem. "Re-Orienting Gender and Islamic Alterity in Early Modern English Drama." *English Studies* 100, no. 2 (2019): 133–48.

Pacey, Arnold. *Technology in World Civilization*. Cambridge, MA: MIT Press, 1990.

Palan, R. "Transnational Theories of Order and Change: Heterodoxy in International Relations Scholarship." *Review of International Studies* 33, no. S1 (2007): 47–69.

Pancrazio, James J. *The Logic of Fetishism: Alejo Carpentier and the Cuban Tradition*. Lewisburg, PA: Bucknell University Press, 2004.

Paravisini-Gebert, Lizabeth. "Colonial and Postcolonial Gothic: The Caribbean." In *The Cambridge Companion to Gothic Fiction*, edited by Jerrold E. Hogle, 229–57. Cambridge: Cambridge University Press, 2002.

Paravasini-Gebert, Lizabeth. "The Haitian Revolution in Interstices and Shadows: A Re-reading of Alejo Carpetier's 'The Kingdom of This World.'" *Research in African Literatures* 35, no. 2 (2004): 114–27.

Parker, Andrew, Mary Russo, Doris Sommer, and Patricia Yaeger, eds. *Nationalisms and Sexualities*. New York: Routledge, 1992.

Paulson, Ronald. *Representations of Revolution, 1789–1820*. New Haven, CT: Yale University Press, 1983.

Payne, Richard E. "Iranian Cosmopolitanism: World Religions at the Sasanian Court." In *Cosmopolitanism and Empire: Universal Rulers, Local Elites, and Cultural Integration in the Ancient Near East and Mediterranean*, edited by Miles Lavan, Richard E. Payne, and John Weisweiler, 209–30. New York: Oxford University Press, 2016.

Peirce, Leslie. *Morality Tales: Law and Gender in the Ottoman Court of Aintab*. Berkeley: University of California Press, 2003.

Perdue, Peter C. "Boundaries and Trade in the Early Modern World: Negotiations at Nerchinsk and Beijing." *Eighteenth-Century Studies* 43, no. 3 (2010): 341–56.

Perdue, Peter C. "Erasing the Empire, Re-racing the Nation: Racialism and Cultural-ism in Imperial China." In *Imperial Formations*, edited by Ann Laura Stoler, Carole McGranahan, and Peter C. Perdue, 141–69. Santa Fe, NM: School for Advanced Research Press, 2007.

Peterson, Andrew. "The Ottoman Ḥajj Route in Jordan: Motivation and Ideology." *Bulletin d'études orientales* 57 (2008): 31–50.

Piedra, José. "A Return to Africa with a Carpentier Tale." MLN 97, no. 2 (1982): 401–10.

Pieterse, Jan P. Nederveen. *Empire and Emancipation: Power and Liberation on a World Scale*. New York: Praeger, 1989.

Pieterse, Jan Nederveen. "Many Renaissances, Many Modernities?" *Theory, Culture and Society* 28, no. 3 (2011): 149–60.

Piggott, Joan R. *The Emergence of Japanese Kingship*. Stanford, CA: Stanford University Press, 1997.

Pike Conant, Martha. *The Oriental Tale in England in the Eighteenth Century*. New York: Routledge, (1908) 2013.

Pittock, Murray. *Scottish and Irish Romanticism*. New York: Oxford University Press, 2008.

Plummer, Brenda Gayle. "The Metropolitan Connection: Foreign and Semiforeign Elites in Haiti, 1900–1915." *Latin American Research Review* 19, no. 2 (1984): 119–42.

Plummer, Brenda Gayle. "Race, Nationality, and Trade in the Caribbean: The Syrians in Haiti, 1903–1934." *International History Review* 3, no. 4 (1981): 517–39.

Podany, Amanda. *The Brotherhood of Kings: How International Relations Shaped the Ancient Near East*. New York: Oxford University Press, 2010.

Polasky, Janet. *Revolutions without Borders: The Call to Liberty in the Atlantic World*. New Haven, CT: Yale University Press, 2015.

Pomeranz, Kenneth. *The Great Divergence: Europe, China, and the Making of the Modern World*. Princeton, NJ: Princeton University Press, 2000.

Pomeranz, Kenneth. "Social History and World History: From Daily Life to Patterns of Change." *Journal of World History* 18, no. 1 (2007): 69–98.

Pons, Frank Moya. *The Dominican Republic: A National History*. 3rd ed. Princeton, NJ: Markus Weiner Press, 2010.

Pound, Ezra. *The Spirit of Romance*. Norfolk, CT: New Directions, (1910) 1932.

Powell, Patricia. *The Pagoda*. New York: Knopf, 1998.

Pratt, Mary Louise. *Imperial Eyes: Travel Writing and Transculturation*. New York: Routledge, (1992) 2008.

Pratt, Mary Louise. "Language and the Afterlives of Empire." PMLA 130, no. 2 (2015): 348–57.

Prendergast, Christopher, ed. *Debating World Literature*. New York: Verso, 2004.

Progressive Writers Association. "Manifesto of the Progressive Writers Association" (1936). SAPF Online. Accessed April 29, 2019. http://pwa75.sapfonline.org/gpage4.html.

Puig de la Bellacasa, María. *Matters of Care: Speculative Ethics in More than Human Worlds*. Minneapolis: University of Minnesota Press, 2017.

Puillion, Francois, and Jean-Claude Vatin, eds. *After Orientalism: Critical Perspectives on Western Agency and Eastern Re-appropriations*. Leiden: Brill, 2014.

Punter, David. "Scottish and Irish Gothic." In *The Cambridge Companion to Gothic Fiction*, edited by Jerrold E. Hogle, 112–25. Cambridge: Cambridge University Press, 2002.

Putnam, Lara. "Nothing Matters but Color: Transnational Circuits, the Interwar Caribbean, and the Black International." In *From Toussaint to Tupac: The Black International since the Age of Revolution*, edited by Michael O. West, William G. Martin, and Fanon Che Wilkins, 107–29. Chapel Hill: University of North Carolina Press, 2009.

Qin, Yaqing. *A Relational Theory of World Politics*. Cambridge: Cambridge University Press, 2018.

Quijano, Aníbal. "Coloniality of Power, Eurocentrism, and Latin America." *Nepantla: Views from the South* 1, no. 3 (2000): 533–80.

Quijano, Aníbal, and Immanuel Maurice Wallerstein. "Americanity as a Concept; or, The Americas in the Modern World-System." *International Social Science Journal* 44, no. 4 (1992): 549–57.

Ram, Harsha. "Futurist Geographies: Uneven Modernities and the Struggle for Aesthetic Autonomy: Paris, Italy, Russia, 1909–14." In *The Oxford Handbook of Global Modernisms*, edited by Mark Wollaeger and Matt Eatough, 313–40. New York: Oxford University Press, 2012.

Ramamurthy, Priti, and Ashwini Tambe, eds. "Decolonial and Postcolonial Approaches: A Dialogue." Special issue, *Feminist Studies* 43, no. 3 (2017).

Ramazani, Jahan. *A Transnational Poetics*. Chicago: University of Chicago Press, 2009.

Ramet, Sabrina, ed. *Gender Politics in the Western Balkans*. University Park: Pennsylvania State University Press, 1999.

Rastegar, Kamran. *Literary Modernity between the Middle East and Europe: Textual Transactions in Nineteenth-Century Arabic, English, and Persian Literatures*. New York: Routledge, 2007.

Renda, Mary A. *Taking Haiti: Military Occupation and the Culture of U.S. Imperialism: 1915–1940*. Chapel Hill: University of North Carolina Press, 2001.

Reynolds, Dwight. "*A Thousand and One Nights*: A History of the Text and Its Reception." In *The Cambridge History of Arabic Literature*, vol. 6, edited by Roger Allen and D. S. Richards, 270–91. Cambridge: Cambridge University Press, 2006.

Riasanovsky, Nicholas. *A History of Russia*. New York: Oxford University Press, (1937) 1984.

Richter-Bernburg, Lutz. "Linguistic Shuʿūbīya and Early Neo-Persian Prose," *Journal of the American Oriental Society* 94, no. 1 (1974): 55–64.

Roberts, Brian R., and Michelle A. Stephens, eds. *American Archipelagic Studies*. Durham, NC: Duke University Press, 2017.

Roberts, Mary Louise. *What Soldiers Do: Sex and the American GI in World War II France*. Chicago: University of Chicago Press, 2013.

Robinson, Cynthia. *In Praise of Song: The Making of Courtly Culture in al-Andalus and Provence, 1005–1134 A.D.* Boston: Brill, 2002.

Robison, Richard, Richard Higgott, and Kevin Hewison, eds. *Southeast Asia in the 1980s: The Politics of Economic Crisis*. Sydney: Allen and Unwin, 1987.

Roediger, David. *The Wages of Whiteness*. London: Verso, 1991.

Rogers, Rebecca, and Kathleen McLuskie. "Who Invested in the Early-Modern Theatre?" *Research Opportunities in Renaissance Drama* 41 (2001): 29–61.

Rooney, Caroline. "The Disappointed of the Earth." *Psychoanalysis and History* 11, no. 2 (2009): 159–74.

Ross, Stephen, and Allana C. Lindgren, eds. *The Modernist World.* New York: Routledge, 2015.

Rowbotham, Sheila. *Women's Consciousness, Men's World.* New York: Verso, (1973) 2015.

Roy, Arundhati. *The God of Small Things.* New York: Harper Perennial, 1997.

Rubenstein, Michael. *Public Works: Infrastructure, Irish Modernism, and the Postcolonial.* Notre Dame, IN: University of Notre Dame Press, 2010.

Rubenstein, Michael, Bruce Robbins, and Sophia Beal, eds. "Infrastructuralism." Special issue, MFS: *Modern Fiction Studies* 61, no. 4 (2015).

Rubin, Gayle. "The Traffic in Women: Notes on the 'Political Economy' of Sex." In *The Second Wave: A Reader in Feminist Theory,* edited by Linda Nicholson, 27–62. New York: Routledge, 1997.

Ruskola, Teemu. "Canton Is Not Boston: The Invention of American Imperial Sovereignty." *American Quarterly* 57, no. 3 (2005): 859–84.

Russell, Heather D. "Post-Blackness and All of the Black Americas." In *The Trouble with Post-Blackness,* edited by Houston A. Baker and K. Merinda Simmons, 110–43. New York: Columbia University Press, 2015.

Sade, Marquis de. "An Essay on Novels." Preface to *The Crimes of Love,* translated by David Coward, 3–20. New York: Oxford University Press, 2005.

Sage, Victor. Introduction to *Melmoth the Wanderer,* by Charles Maturin, vii–xxix. New York: Penguin Books, 2000.

Said, Edward W. *Culture and Imperialism.* New York: Knopf, 1993.

Said, Edward W. *Orientalism.* New York: Vintage, 1979.

Sallis, Eva. *Sheherazade through the Looking Glass: The Metamorphosis of the "Thousand and One Nights".* New York: Routledge, 1999.

Sánchez, Servando Valdés. "Anglo-Cuban Diplomacy: Economic and Political Links with Britain (1945–60)." *International Journal of Cuban Studies* 8, no. 1 (2016): 56–73.

Sandberg, Brian. "Beyond Encounters: Religion, Ethnicity, and Violence in the Early Modern Atlantic World, 1492–1700." *Journal of World History* 17, no. 1 (2006): 1–25.

Sartre, Jean-Paul. *Being and Nothingness.* Translated by Hazel Barnes. New York: Washington Square Press, 1948.

Sartre, Jean-Paul. Preface to *The Wretched of the Earth,* by Frantz Fanon, translated by Constance Farrington, xliii–xli. New York: Grove Press, 1963.

Scarborough, Vernon L. "The Hydraulic Lift of Early States Societies." *Proceedings of the National Academy of Sciences of the United States of America* 114, no. 52 (2017): 13600–13601.

Scarborough, Vernon L. *The Flow of Power: Ancient Water Systems and Landscapes.* Santa Fe, NM: School of American Research Press, 2003.

Schimmelpenninck van der Oye, David. *Russian Orientalism: Asia in the Russian Mind from Peter the Great to the Emigration.* New Haven, CT: Yale University Press, 2010.

Schmitt, Cannon. *Alien Nation: Nineteenth-Century Gothic Fictions and English Nationality.* Philadelphia: University of Pennsylvania Press, 1997.

Schneider, Jane. "Was There a Pre-capitalist World System?" *Journal of Peasant Studies* 6, no. 1 (1978–79): 20–29.

Schueller, Malini Johar. *US Orientalisms: Race, Nation, and Gender in Literature, 1790–1890.* Ann Arbor: University of Michigan Press, 1998.

Schwab, Raymond. *The Oriental Renaissance: Europe's Rediscovery of India and the East, 1680–1880.* Translated by Gene Patterson-Black and Victor Reinking. New York: Columbia University Press, 1984.

Scott, James C. *The Art of Not Being Governed: An Anarchist History of Upland Southeast Asia.* New Haven, CT: Yale University Press, 2009.

Scott, James C. *Domination and the Arts of Resistance.* New Haven, CT: Yale University Press, 1990.

Scott, James C. *Weapons of the Weak: Everyday Forms of Peasant Resistance.* New Haven, CT: Yale University Press, 1985.

Sedgwick, Eve Kosofsky. *Between Men: English Literature and Male Homosocial Desire.* New York: Columbia University Press, 1985.

Sedgwick, Eve Kosofsky. *The Coherence of the Gothic.* New York: Arno Press, 1980.

Sedgwick, Eve Kosofsky. *Epistemology of the Closet.* Berkeley: University of California Press, 1990.

Seigneurie, Ken. "Ongoing War and Arab Humanism." In *Geomodernisms: Race, Modernism, Modernity,* edited by Laura Doyle and Laura Winkiel, 96–113. Bloomington: Indiana University Press, 2004.

Sen, Tansen. *Buddhism, Diplomacy, and Trade: The Realignment of India-China Relations, 600–1400.* Lanham, MD: Rowman and Littlefield, 2016.

Seshagiri, Urmila. *Race and the Modernist Imagination.* Ithaca, NY: Cornell University Press, 2010.

Shapiro, Stephen. "Transvaal, Transylvania: Dracula's World-System and Gothic Periodicity." *Gothic Studies* 10, no. 1 (2008): 29–47.

Sharma, Sunil. "Redrawing the Boundaries of *Ajam* in Early Modern Persian Literary Histories." In *Iran Facing Others: Identity Boundaries in Historical Perspective,* edited by Abbas Amanat and Farzin Vejdani, 49–62. New York: Palgrave Macmillan, 2012.

Sharpe, Jenny. *Allegories of Empire: The Figure of Woman in the Colonial Text.* Minneapolis: University of Minnesota Press, 1993.

Shatzmiller, Maya. "Economic Performance and Economic Growth in the Early Islamic World." *Journal of the Economic and Social History of the Orient* 54 (2011): 132–84.

Sheller, Mimi. *Consuming the Caribbean.* New York: Routledge, 2003.

Shields, Tanya L. *Their Bones Would Reject Yours: Feminist Rehearsal and Imagining Caribbean Belonging.* Charlottesville: University of Virginia Press, 2014.

Shih, Shu-mei. "Comparison as Relation." In *Comparison: Theories, Approaches, Uses,* edited by Rita Felski and Susan Friedman, 79–98. Baltimore: Johns Hopkins University Press, 2013.

Shiying, Mu. "The Shanghai Foxtrot (a Fragment)." Introduced by Sean Macdonald. *Modernism/Modernity* 11, no. 4 (November 2004): 797–807.

Shohat, Ella, ed. *Talking Visions: Multicultural Feminism in a Transnational Age*. Cambridge, MA: MIT Press, (1998) 2001.

Simpson, Audra. *Mohawk Interruptus: Political Life across the Borders of Settler States*. Durham, NC: Duke University Press, 2014.

Skinner, Patricia. "Morality Tales: A Medieval Inheritance." *Journal of Women's History* 18, no. 1 (2006): 186–91.

Skocpol, Theda. *States and Social Revolutions*. New York: Cambridge University Press, 1979.

Small, Melvin. "The United States and the German 'Threat' to the Hemisphere, 1905–1914." *Americas* 28, no. 3 (1972): 252–70.

Smith, Faith, ed. *Sex and the Citizen: Interrogating the Caribbean*. Charlottesville: University of Virginia Press, 2011.

Smith, James. "The Radical Literary Magazine of the 1930s and British Government Surveillance: The Case of *Storm* Magazine." *Literature and History* 19, no. 2 (2017): 69–86.

Smith, Linda Tuhiwai. *Decolonizing Methodologies: Research and Indigenous Peoples*. London: Zed Books, 2013.

Smith, Michael. "The Aztec Empire and the Mesoamerican World-System." In *Empires: Perspectives from Archaeology and History*, edited by Susan Alcock, Terence N. D'Altroy, Kathleen D. Morrison, and Carla Sinopoli, 128–54. Cambridge: Cambridge University Press, 2001.

Smith, Michael, and Frances Berdan, eds. *The Postclassic Mesoamerican World*. Salt Lake City: University of Utah Press, 2003.

Spivak, Gayatri Chakravorty. "Woman in Difference: Mahasweta Devi's 'Douloti the Bountiful.'" *Cultural Critique* 14 (1989): 105–28.

Squint, Kristin L. "Vodou and Revolt in Literature of the Haitian Revolution." CLA *Journal* 51, no. 2 (2007): 170–85.

Stephens, Michelle. *Black Empire: The Masculine Global Imaginary of Caribbean Intellectuals in the United States, 1914–1962*. Durham, NC: Duke University Press, 2005.

Stoler, Ann Laura. *Carnal Knowledge and Imperial Power: Race and the Intimate in Colonial Rule*. Berkeley: University of California Press, (2002) 2010.

Stoler, Ann Laura. *Duress: Imperial Durabilities in Our Times*. Durham, NC: Duke University Press, 2016.

Stoler, Ann Laura, Carole McGranahan, and Peter C. Perdue, eds. *Imperial Formations*. Santa Fe, NM: School for Advanced Research Press, 2007.

Stone, Gregory B. *Dante's Pluralism and the Islamic Philosophy of Religion*. New York: Macmillan Palgrave, 2006.

Subrahmanyam, Sanjay. *Explorations in Connected History: Mughals and Franks*. New York: Oxford University Press, 2005.

Subramaniam, Banu. *Holy Science: The Biopolitics of Hindu Nationalism*. Seattle: University of Washington Press, 2019.

Suleri, Sara. *The Rhetoric of English India*. Chicago: University of Chicago Press, 1992.

Sunderland, Willard. "An Empire of Peasants: Empire-building, Interethnic Interaction, and Ethnic Stereotyping in the Rural World of the Russian Empire, 1800–1850s." In *Imperial Russia: New Histories for the Empire*, edited by Jane Burbank and David Ransel, 174–98. Bloomington: Indiana University Press, 1998.

Tavakoli-Targhi, Mohamad. "Orientalism's Genesis Amnesia." In *Antinomies of Modernity: Essays on Race, Orient, Nation,* edited by Vasant Kaiwar and Sucheta Mazumdar, 98–125. Durham, NC: Duke University Press, 2003.

Teoh, Jacqulyn Gaik Ing. "Shadow Plays with Imperial Pasts: Writing Wayang in Pramoedya Ananta Toer's *The Fugitive.*" MFS: *Modern Fiction Studies* 64, no. 3 (2018): 403–30.

Thiong'o, Ngũgĩ wa. *Decolonising the Mind: The Politics of Language in African Literature.* Portsmouth, NH: Heinemann Educational, 1986.

Thiong'o, Ngũgĩ wa. *Globalectics: Theory and the Politics of Knowing.* New York: Columbia University Press, 2014.

Thiong'o, Ngũgĩ wa. *The River Between.* London: Heinemann, 1965.

Thompson, John B. *The Media and Modernity: A Social Theory of the Media.* Stanford, CA: Stanford University Press, 1995.

Thompson, William. *World Politics: Evolutionary Interpretations.* New York: Routledge, 2001.

Tilly Charles. *Coercion, Capital, and European States, AD 990–1992.* Malden, MA: Blackwell, 1992.

Tozzi, Christopher. *Nationalizing France's Army: Foreigners, Jews, and Blacks in the French Military, 1715–1831.* Charlottesville: University of Virginia Press, 2016.

Tran, Ben. *Post-Mandarin: Masculinity and Aesthetic Modernity in Colonial Vietnam.* New York: Fordham University Press, 2017.

Tran, Ben. "Queer Internationalism and Modern Vietnamese Aesthetics." In *The Oxford Handbook of Global Modernisms,* edited by Mark Wollaeger and Matt Eatough, 367–84. New York: Oxford University Press, 2012.

Trumpener, Katie. *Bardic Nationalism: The Romantic Novel and the British Empire.* Princeton, NJ: Princeton University Press, 1997.

Tsuen-Hsuin, Tsien. *Paper and Printing.* Cambridge: Cambridge University Press, 1985.

Tuck, P. J. N. *Warfare, Expansion, and Resistance.* London: Routledge, 2002.

Twitchett, Denis. *Printing and Publishing in Medieval China.* New York: Frederic C. Beil, 1983.

Tzara, Tristan. "Dada Manifesto" (1918). Accessed April 29, 2019. http://writing.upenn.edu/library/Tzara_Dada-Manifesto_1918.pdf.

Udovitch, Abraham. *Partnership and Profit in Medieval Islam.* Princeton, NJ: Princeton University Press, 1970.

Umberto I, King of Italy. Opening address to delegates of the XII International Congress of Orientalists (1899). Archived in the International Dunhuang Project. Accessed March 22, 2020. http://idp.bl.uk/4DCGI/education/orientalists/index.a4d.

Unruh, Vicky. "Modernity's Labors in Latin America: The Cultural Work of Cuba's Avant-Gardes." In *The Oxford Handbook of Global Modernisms,* edited by Mark Wollaeger and Matt Eatough, 341–66. New York: Oxford University Press, 2012.

Valens, Keja. "Excruciating Improbability and the Transgender Jamaican." In *Trans Studies: The Challenge to Hetero/Homo Normativities,* edited by Yolanda Martinez-San Miguel and Sarah Tobias, 65–82. New Brunswick, NJ: Rutgers University Press, 2016.

van Wyk Smith, Malvern. *Drummer Hodge: The Poetry of the Anglo-Boer War, 1899–1902.* Oxford: Oxford University Press, 1978.

Viswanathan, Gauri. "Ireland, India, and the Poetics of Internationalism." *Journal of World History* 15, no. 1 (2004): 7–30.

von Tunzelmann, Alex. *Red Heat: Conspiracy, Murder, and the Cold War in the Caribbean.* New York: Henry Holt, 2011.

Wallace, David. *Chaucerian Polity: Absolutist Lineages and Associational Forms in England and Italy.* Stanford, CA: Stanford University Press, 1997.

Wallerstein, Immanuel. "World System versus World-Systems: A Critique." In *The World System: Five Hundred Years or Five Thousand?*, edited by Andre Gunder Frank and Barry K. Gills, 293–94. New York: Routledge, 1993.

Walpole, Horace. *The Castle of Otranto.* New York: Oxford University Press, 1996.

Walt, Stephen. *Revolution and War.* Ithaca, NY: Cornell University Press, 1996.

Walters, Wendy. "Archives of the Black Atlantic: Postcolonial Citation in *The Pagoda.*" *Novel* 43, no. 1 (2010): 163–68.

Walworth, Catherine. *Soviet Salvage: Imperial Debris, Revolutionary Reuse, and Russian Constructivism.* University Park: Pennsylvania State University Press, 2017.

Ward, Sean Francis. "*Seven Pillars of Wisdom*, the Queer Times of Revolt, and Modernist Form." *Modernism/Modernity* 23, no. 2 (2016): 297–318.

Warwick Research Collective. *Combined and Uneven Development: Towards a New Theory of World-Literature.* Liverpool: Liverpool University Press, 2015.

Watson, Andrew. *Agricultural Innovation in the Early Islamic World.* Cambridge: Cambridge University Press, 1983.

Watson, Hilbourne A. "The Political Economy of U.S.-Caribbean Relations." *Black Scholar* 11, no. 3 (1980): 30–41.

Watson, Tim. *Caribbean Culture and British Fiction in the Atlantic World, 1780–1870.* Cambridge: Cambridge University Press, 2008.

Watson, Tim. "Working the Edges of the Nineteenth-Century British Empire." *Literature Compass* 13, no. 5 (2016): 288–99.

Waylen, Georgina, Karen Celis, Johanna Kantola, and S. Laurel Weldon, eds. *The Oxford Handbook of Gender and Politics.* New York: Oxford University Press, 2013.

Wayne, Heather. "Gilded Chains: Global Economies and Gendered Arts in U.S. Fiction, 1865–1930." PhD diss., University of Massachusetts, Amherst, 2019.

Weber, Elizabeth. "Reimagining Coolie Trajectories: The Triumphant Return as Political Statement in Late Qing 'Coolie' Fiction." *Literature Compass* 13, no. 5 (2016): 300–10.

Weiss, Gillian. "Barbary Captivity and the French Idea of Freedom." *French Historical Studies* 28, no. 2 (2005): 231–64.

Weisweiler, John. "From Empire to World State." In *Cosmopolitanism and Empire: Universal Rulers, Local Elites, and Cultural Integration in the Ancient Near East and Mediterranean,* edited by Miles Lavan, Richard E. Payne, and John Weisweiler, 187–208. New York: Oxford University Press, 2016.

Wertheim, William. "The State and the Dialectics of Emancipation." *Development and Change* 23, no. 3 (1992): 257–81.

Wertheimer, Eric. *Imagined Empires: Incas, Aztecs, and the New World of American Literature, 1771–1876.* New York: Columbia University Press, 1999.

Wight, Martin. *Systems of States*. Edited by Hedley Bull. Leicester: Leicester University Press, 1977.

Wilkinson, Darryl. "Infrastructure and Inequality: An Archaeology of the Inkan Road through the Amaybamba Cloud Forests." *Journal of Social Archaeology* 19, no. 1 (2019): 27–46.

Wilks, Jennifer. "Print Diasporas: Genre and the Circulation of Black Women's Modernist Texts." Paper presented at Modernist Communities conference, Institute du Monde Anglophone, Université Nouvelle Sorbonne, Paris 3, April 24–26, 2014.

Wills, J. E., Jr. "Review: 'Maritime Asia, 1500–1800: The Interactive Emergence of European Domination.'" *American Historical Review* 98, no. 1 (1993): 83–105.

Wilson, Keith, ed. *The International Impact of the Boer War*. Chesham, UK: Acumen, 2001.

Winkiel, Laura. *Modernism, Race, and Manifestoes*. New York: Cambridge University Press, 2011.

Winter, Kari J. *Subjects of Slavery, Agents of Change: Women and Power in Gothic Novels and Slave Narratives, 1790–1865*. Athens: University of Georgia Press, 1992.

Wollaeger, Mark, and Matt Eatough, eds. *The Oxford Handbook of Global Modernisms*. New York: Oxford University Press, 2012.

Wood, Ellen Meiksins. *Empire of Capital*. New York: Verso Books, 2003.

Woolf, Virginia. *Mrs. Dalloway*. New York: Harcourt, (1925) 1953..

Woolf, Virginia. "Narrow Bridge of Art." In *Collected Essays of Virginia Woolf*, edited by Leonard Woolf, 2:218–29. Boston: Harcourt, (1925) 1966.

Wordsworth, William, and Samuel Taylor Coleridge. *Lyrical Ballads*. Edited by Fiona Stafford. Oxford: Oxford University Press, (1798) 2013.

Wright, Julia M. "Devouring the Disinherited: Familial Cannibalism in Maturin's *Melmoth the Wanderer*." In *Eating their Words: Cannibalism and the Boundaries of Cultural Identity*, edited by Kristen Guest, 79–105. Albany: SUNY Press, 2001.

Wright, Julia. *Ireland, India, and Nationalism in Nineteenth-Century Literature*. Cambridge: Cambridge University Press, 2007.

Xu, Guoqi. *China and the Great War: China's Pursuit of a New National Identity and Internationalization*. New York: Cambridge University Press, 2001.

Yamanka, Yurkiko, and Tetsuo Nishio. *"Arabian Nights" and Orientalism: Perspectives from East and West*. London: I. B. Tauris, 2006.

Yang, Anand. "(A) Subaltern('s) Boxers: An Indian Soldier's Account of China and the World in 1900–1901." In *The Boxers, China, and the World*, ed. Robert Bickers and R. G. Tiedemann, 43–64. Lanham, MD: Rowman and Littlefield, 2007.

Yeats, William Butler. *Michael Robartes and the Dancer*. Dublin: Cuala Press, 1921.

Yelin, Louise. "Globalizing Subjects." *Signs* 29, no. 2 (2004): 439–64.

Yoshihara, Mari. *Embracing the East: White Women and American Orientalism*. New York: Oxford University Press, 2003.

Young, Hershini Bhana. *Haunting Capital: Memory, Text, and the Black Diasporic Body*. Hanover, NH: University Press of New England, 2006.

Yücesoy, Hayrettin. "Language of Empire: Politics of Arabic and Persian in the Abbasid World." *PMLA* 130, no. 2 (2015): 384–92.

Index

Abbasid Empire: and Arabic language, 44, 64–65; and capitalist instruments, 50; and the Chinese Tang dynasty, 57; engineering projects of, 53–54; and Harun al-Rashid, 72, 74, 77–78, 89, 273n38, 287n8, 288n23; institutions and knowledge of, 57–58; inter-imperial emergence of, 44; overthrow of Umayyad by, 44, 50, 273n38; and paper, 57; and the Persian Sassanid Empire, 72–73; and labor, 51; and state-merchant coformation, 49–51; translation projects in, 58, 279n94; viziers of, 83–84; wage systems of, 50

Abu-Lughod, Janet, 15, 20, 37, 39, 41

activism, 28, 132, 158–60. *See also* arts and activism; dissent; literary activism

Adelard of Bath, 62, 66

Adorno, Theodor, 25

Agamben, Giorgio, 2

agency, 3, 239, 249, 257n8; and ethics, 230–31

age of revolution: and the American Revolution, 126; and Chinese uprisings, 127–28; and elite-labor alliances, 122; and the French Revolution, 122, 128–29; global scope of in nineteenth century, 21–22; guerrilla warfare in, 127–28, 130, 181; impressment and conscription in, 124; and Indian rebellions, 125; inter-imperial competition as catalyst in, 126–27; literature in, 122–23, 132–55; Napoleon's role in, 121–22; origins of, 121–26; post/

colonial consciousness in, 122; rape in, 129–30; and Russian uprisings, 125; and the Serbian Revolution, 127–28, 302n20; and South American rebellions, 126–27; taxation as catalyst of, 124–26. *See also* dissent; rebellion; revolutions

Al-Andalus, 58, 61–64, 283n120

Alcott, Louisa May, 173

Ali, Muhsin Jassam, 121, 136

Amer, Sahar, 275n47, 283n120, 285n3, 319n110

Anand, Mulk Raj, 199–201

anarchy, 14

Anderson, Benedict, 160

Andrade, Oswald de, 156, 186

anti-imperialism, 173–76, 181, 312n33. *See also* inter-imperial analysis

Appadurai, Arjun, 109

Arabic language, 61–65, 69, 110–11

Archer, John, 100–101, 103, 106, 294n39

Arendt, Hannah, 267n79

Aristotelian model of state: gender in, 83–84; and *The Nights*, 83–84

Arjomand, Said Amir, 57, 84–85

Armah, Ayi Kwei, 200–201

arts and activism, 157–60, 181–86, 195–98, 206–9; and capitalist inter-imperiality, 101–3, 105; and literature, 182–87, 190–91, 314n70, 317n96; and newspapers, 184; and performance, 295n45; and time, 160–61, 310n4. *See also* literary activism; Orientalism

Astrakhan, 186–87
Asymmetrical parenting, 12, 263n41
Aydin, Cemil, 186, 317n96

Bacon, Roger, 62
Bahun, Sanja, 16, 264n54
Ballantyne, Tony, 176
Balzac, Honoré de, 123, 301n11
Barendse, R. J., 40–41, 270n7, 272n26
Barfield, T. J., 42
Barmakids, 44, 49–50, 273n38
Batker, Carol, 184
Bayly, C. A., 176
Beaujard, Philippe, 39, 49
Bedouins, 167–68
Beecroft, Alexander, 266n69
Belcher, Wendy, 109, 116
Bell, David, 122, 128, 138
Beloved, 229, 254
Bender, Thomas, 269n6
Benítez-Rojo, Antonio, 202, 321n19, 326n54
Bergson, Henri, 252
betrayal: banana tariffs and, 236; of the
    Caribbean by the US, 203, 234; and
    China in World War I, 179; of creole
    rebels by the Spanish, 126; and dialectical
    history, 77, 180; gendered, 38–40, 70, 123,
    238–40; in Gothic literature, 123, 151, 153;
    of India by the British, 172–73; in *Mel-
    moth the Wanderer*, 151, 153; in *The Nights*,
    70–71, 75, 78–80; in *The Pagoda*, 238–40;
    in World War I, 179–80
Bhabha, Homi, 177
Bismarck, Otto von, 166
Black, Stephanie, 233
Blackburn, Robin, 131–32, 303n33
Black internationalist writers, 175, 177, 180
"BLAST! Manifesto," 156, 181
Boehmer, Elleke, 174, 318n104
Boer Wars, 171–72, 174–78. See also South
    African wars
Bosin, Yuri, 125
Bourdieu, Pierre, 54–55, 252
Boxer Uprising, 170–72, 174, 176, 236
Brantlinger, Patrick, 181

Braudel, Fernand, 55, 272n22, 278n87
bribery, neocolonial, 242
British Empire: and Boer War dissent,
    171–76; and the Boxer Uprising, 171;
    and Cuba, 204, 322n27; and the French
    Empire, 43, 96, 140; and the Haitian
    Revolution, 131–32; Indian Political Intel-
    ligence Office of, 185; and inter-imperial
    maneuvering, 107–9, 137–40, 167–69,
    171–72, 181, 185, 204–5, 281n106; and Irish
    revolutionaries, 140–41; and Japanese
    Empire, 43; and Ottoman infrastructure,
    167; and Pax Britannica myth, 169; and
    the Russian Empire, 96–97, 100–103,
    106–7; wars fought, nineteenth century,
    169; and World War I, 178, 180. See also
    the Boer Wars; Orientalism
British Empire and literary interventions:
    102–9, 115–18, 132–39, 154–55, 157–63, 181, 199
Broadbridge, Anne F., 51
brothers in inter-imperial history,
    76–78, 137, 149–51. See also *Melmoth the
    Wanderer*; *The Thousand and One Nights*
Brotton, Jerry, 40
bubonic plague, 41
Buck-Morss, Susan, 10
Burbank, Jane, 46
Burke, Edmund, III, 54
Burmese labor resettlement, 53
Burton, Antoinette, 164, 176, 250n10
Butler, Judith, 3, 257n8

Canada, 3
Canterbury Tales, The, 62–63
capitalism, 23, 41, 60, 240–41, 281n106
Caracciolo, Peter, 116
care, labors of, 1–3, 12–13, 15
Caribbean: and Anglo-American rivalry,
    203–5, 323n30; anti-colonial thought
    in, 197, 202–5; as archipelago, 202, 238,
    321n19; and the Banana Wars, 235–36;
    and the Dominican Republic, 203;
    feminist analyses of, 202; German inter-
    est in, 204; Gothic internationalism and,
    132; inter-imperial contests and, 15–16,

42, 187; inter-island entanglements and 234–35; and Jamaica, 135, 233–36; political economy of, 202–5, 233–37, 322n21; resistance and revolts in, 128, 131–32, 197, 205; and Saint Domingue, 131; writers, 31, 184. *See also* "coolie" laborers and trade; Cuba; Haiti; the Haitian Revolution; *The Kingdom of this World*; *The Pagoda*

Caribbean Mediterranean, 197, 319n3

Carlyle, J. Dacre, 116–17

Carlyle, Thomas, 132

Carpentier, Alejo: activism of, 207–9; aesthetics of, 209; and African syncretism, 209; biography of, 207–8, 326n54; government service of, 208, 325n45; in Haiti, 208–9; and "The Marvellous Real in America," 220; sexuality of, 327n59. See also *The Kingdom of this World*

Cartwright, John, 103–5

Casale, Giancarlo, 278n87

Casanova, Pascale, 63

Castle of Otranto, The, 135–38

Catherine the Great, 112–13, 116, 125

Chancellor, Richard, 103

chapter overviews, 28–32

Chatterjee, Indrani, 47

Chatterjee, Partha, 132

Chaucer, Geoffrey, 62

Chaudhuri, Amit, 110, 113

Cheah, Pheng, 22–24, 267n79, 268n80

Chen, Kuan-Hsing, 6

Chin, Tamara T., 288n20

China: Communist Revolution origins in, 179; expansion of, 98; household-state models in, 84; and inter-imperial Eurasian relations, 98; and labor relocation, 51; and literacy-centered state building, 57; manufacturing sectors in, 51, 291n10; and the May Fourth movement, 179; and Mongolia, 98; paper's impact in, 56–57; and the Russian Empire, 98–99; Tang dynasty of, 57; and Korea, 165, 170

China, Qing: and the Boxer Uprising, 170–72, 174, 176, 236; and debt, 236; and expansion, 98; inter-imperial destabi-

lization of, 170; and the White Lotus Rebellion, 127–28

Chinese philosophy, 8, 84, 260n22

Chodorow, Nancy, 12

Christian, David, 39–40

Christian empires, homogeneity in, 274n40

civilizationalist rhetoric, 176–77

Clarkson, Thomas, 128

Cliff, Michelle, 227

Clinton, Bill, and Caribbean, 235–36

clothing, inter-imperial uses of, 108, 295n45

Cohen, Walter, 63

Colbert, Jean-Baptiste, 114

Colley, Linda, 281n106

colonialism *versus* coloniality, 133

colonized communities and inter-imperial rivalries, 42–44, 125–28

commenda agreements, 50

Conant, Martha Pike, 118

Confucius, 84

conquered peoples and imperial governance, 45–46, 274n40

conscription, 124

Constantinople, 114

"coolie" laborers and trade: overview of, 236; at Angel Island, 189; in *The Pagoda*, 200, 232, 240, 246; and protest poems, 161; and rape, 197

Cooper, Anna Julia, 175

Coronil, Ferdinand, 41

Cosmographie in Four Books, 105–6, 294n37

Cossacks, 112, 125

Cuba: Batista government and, 208, 242; Guantánamo Bay military base in, 234; Haiti, economic ties to, 203; literature of, 187–88; revolution and, 204–05; slavery in, 203; and the United States, 203–4, 234, 322n27. See also *The Kingdom of This World*

culture as structural battleground, 196

Dabbagh, Abdullah al-, 109

Dadaism, 182–83

Daif, Rashid, al-, 228

Dalleo, Raphael, 206

Dante, 62–63, 66

Daoism, 8, 260n23

Darwin, Charles, 261n25

Datta, Pradip Kumar, 172–73, 177–78

Davies, Carole Boyce, 3, 202

Davis, Kathleen, 36

Davis, Natalie Zemon, 67

debt, 144, 166, 204–5, 233–34, 236. See also
 The Pagoda, debt in

decimal system, and capitalism, 59

decoloniality, 5–7

decolonizing the mind, 5

Degenhardt, Jane, 102–3, 105

Delacroix, Eugène, 123

Dennis, John, 108

Derrida, Jacques, 267n79

Dew, Nicholas, 290n4

DeWitt, Benjamin, 225

Diab, Hanna, 97, 115

dialectical history, 15–20, 77, 108–9,
 199, 251

dialectical theory: overview of, 1–4, 8;
 and Alexander Kojève, 8, 261n24;
 Buddhist sources of, 259n20; and
 Chinese philosophy, 8, 259n20, 260n23;
 gendered elisions in, 13; and Greek
 philosophy, 8, 259n20; and Hegel, 8–11,
 14–15; and Marx, 8–9

disavowal, 2, 3, 13, 18, 25, 28, 37, 38, 70, 92,
 133, 160, 162, 178, 231, 233, 239–40, 243–44,
 249, 253, 254, 257n7

dissent: overview of, 42; and centralizing
 systems, 55; and institutions, 253–54;
 and inter-imperial maneuvering, 43; in
 inter-imperial theory, 6, 17, 19, 25, 28;
 and print, 59–60; scholarly neglect of,
 275n50, 278n52

dissent, in historical dialectics: 38, 42–48,
 66–67, 74–75,118–19,123–30,157–60,
 167–68, 171, 173, 176, 178, 181, 251–52

Distant Shore, A, 228–29

Doctor Faustus, 105–6

Dominican Republic, 203

Dostoevsky, Fyodor, 123, 301n11

Du Bois, W. E. B., 170, 175, 178, 312n24

Hibri, Tayeb, el-, 78

Emmet, Robert, 133, 141, 143, 146, 152–53

empires: overview of, 6–7; dialectics of,
 in world history, 1–2, 4–5, 10, 15–17;
 differences between, 6–7; disavowals
 of dependence, 35–37; and language,
 4, 13, 44, 64, 189–90, 252. *See also* inter-
 imperial analysis

Engels, Friedrich, 14, 264n45

England, fourteenth to seventeenth centuries: Arabic-Islamicate shaping of, 58–67,
 116–17; and Charles I, 101, 292n15; clothing
 and imperial ambition in, 108, 295n45; dramas of state in, 107, 295n41; and Elizabeth
 I, 101–2, 292n15; Eurasia, interest in, 96;
 and Henry VIII, 101, 291n14; inter-imperial
 maneuvering of, 101–5, 107–11; and inter-
 imperial mimesis, 10, 107–08; and Ireland,
 101; and Oliver Cromwell, 101, 292n15; and
 Orientalist discourses, 106–7, 118–19; Ottoman Empire's influence on, 60–71; poetry
 and inter-state rivalry in, 108; religion and
 inter-imperiality in, 101, 291n14, 292n15;
 and Russia, 97, 100–103, 106; tyranny and
 liberty discourses in, 106–7, 118–19; the
 vernacular in, 63–64,104. *See also* the British Empire; the British Empire and literary
 interventions

Enlightenment, 60, 109

enslaved peoples and state building, 51

Escobar, Arturo, 304n40

Ethiopia, 6–7, 109, 170, 182

Eurasian inter-imperiality, 98–100

Eurocentrism, 36, 39

Europe: eastern, 16, 264n54; and the
 Enlightenment and foreign sources, 60,
 109; and Eurocentric historiography,
 ideologies of, 61–62; and imperial envy
 and libraries, 58; medieval, 61–65; the
 Mughal Empire's influence on, 110;
 The Nights in, 97–98, 115–18; and non-
 European systems, 54; the Ottoman
 Empire's influence on, 59–61; and Protes-
 tant Revolution, 59–60; western, 98, 100.
 See also *individual states and empires*

Evelyn, John, 108
evolutionary world politics, theories of, 261n25

Fabian, Johannes, 15, 36
Fanon, Frantz, 8
Farah, Nuruddin, 201
Fatimid Empire, 45
Faulkner, Neil, 166, 311n15
Faulkner, William, 229
Fedirka, Sarah, 185
feminist empire studies, 47
feminist intersectional and decolonial theory, 1–3, 5–6, 12–13, 47, 123, 198
feminist manifestos, 156–57, 182, 185
Ferguson, Niall, 7, 269n6
financial strategies, neocolonial, 166–67
Fletcher, Giles, 103, 106
Foley, Sean, 60, 281n106
Ford, Ford Madox, 118
Foucault, Michel, 86
framed tales, 69. See also *The Thousand and One Nights*
Francis, Donette, 5, 198, 327n6
Franco-Prussian war, 166
Frederick II, 65–66, 136
freedom discourses, 106–7, 294n32
French Empire: and Victor Hugo, 116; *The Nights* in, 116; and the Ottoman Empire, 114, 167; and Vietnam, 190; World War I in, 178, 180. See also age of revolution; Napoleon; French Revolution; Antoine Galland
French Revolution, 122, 128–29
Fuchs, Barbara, 10, 107–8, 295n45
futurists, 181–82, 186–87, 317n96

Galland, Antoine: in Constantinople, 97, 114; and Hanna Diab, 97, 115; and French national library, 114; and *The Nights* translation, 70, 97, 115, 286nn5–6; translation work of 114–15
Gandhi, Mohandas, 166
Garvey, Marcus, 175
gender: and betrayal, 38–40, 70, 123, 238–40; and class and race stratification, 12–14,

264n45; and dialectical theory, 2, 12–13; and labor, 2, 267n79; scholarly neglect of, 47–48; and state formation, 12–14, 47; world politics, impact on, 45, 196. *See also* disavowal; feminist intersectional and decolonial theory; inter-imperial analysis; labor; sexuality; state formation; and individual texts: *The Kingdom of this World; Melmoth the Wanderer; The Pagoda; The Thousand and One Nights*
Gerits, Frank, 205
Germany, 160
Gibbon, Edward, 117
Gide, André, 184, 190–91
Glissant, Édouard, 3, 197
The God of Small Things, 195, 200, 228–30
Goody, Jack, 282n112
Gothic Internationalism, 132, 304n37
Gothic literature: and African Atlantic tradition, 139; and Anglo-American tradition, 138; and *The Castle of Otranto*, 135–38; freedom-slavery tropes in, 137, 306n52; gendered betrayal plots in, 123; historical medieval figures in, 136–37; and inter-imperial unconscious, 300n7; and *The Kingdom of This World*, 135; manuscript tropes in, 135; and Mediterranean tropes, 135–36; and *The Monk*, 134–35, 305n45; Napoleon and, 137–38; and *The Nights*, 135, 137; Orientalism, links to, 135–36; post/colonial consciousness in, 122, 133–34, 138; rape in, 129, 134–35; readings of, 123; rebellion in, 122–23; and *She*, 138, 306n58; socio-political contexts of, 122–23; and world-system instabilities, 123. See also *Melmoth the Wanderer*
Govil, Hari Govind, 185
Griffith, Arthur, 174
Gruesser, John, 189, 318n105

Haddawy, Husain, 69, 285n1, 285n6
Haiti: Cuba, economic ties to, 203; independence struggles, 43; neocolonial intrusions, 204; Ottoman connections, 322n29; Trujillo dictatorship, 205, 242, 323n30; and the US, 204–5, 323nn29–30

Haitian Revolution: and the British Empire, 131–32; colonial elites fleeing, 132, 303n34; economic impact of, 203; and Gothic literature, 122; inter-imperial dynamics and, 131; in *The Kingdom of this World*, 203, 206–7, 215–16, 218; literary representations of, 206–7, 222; men's narratives of, 222; and Napoleon's army, 121–22; post/colonial influences of, 131–33; and white fear, 131–32

Hakluyt, Richard, 101, 291n11

han, 19–20

Harrison, Hubert, 175

Harvey, John, 62

Hegel, G. W. F.: and Chinese philosophy, 8, 260n23; dialectical philosophy, 8–11, 14–15; human encounters as struggles, 10–11; on labor, 2, 10–11, 13; Marx, influence on, 11; racism of, 8

Heidegger, Martin, 267n79

Henderson, Mae, 8

Heng, Geraldine, 283n118

Heylyn, Peter, 106–7

Hole, Richard, 117

Hopkins, Anthony G., 37–38

Hopkins, Pauline, 173

horizonal dialectics, 1–2, 256n3

Hossain, Syud, 185

household models of state, 83–84

Huang, Yunte, 188, 318n102

Hughes, Langston, 184, 185

Hugo, Victor, 116

hydraulic engineering projects, 53–54

identity, as structure of political economy, 13, 28, 52, 120, 298n100

imagined communities, 160

imperial mimesis, 107

imperial subjectivity, 257n8

impressment, 124

the Incan Empire: and Chimor infrastructure, 52; labor conscription, 50–51; reascendence myths, 126–27; record keeping, 56; road builders, 277n72; the Spanish Empire and, 41

India: Boer Wars, perspectives on, 175–76; British betrayals of, 172–73; civilizationalism in, 176; and inter-imperial maneuvering, 17; newspapers in, 174; Progressive Writers' Association, 17; tax rebellions, 125; uprisings in, 125

infrastructure: and anti-imperialism, 173–74; and competitive state formation, 60, 165; expansion of, 52; and the Incas, 52, 277n72; and inequality and oppression, 54–55, 166; in *The Kingdom of this World*, 215–17; as long-historical force, 55; merchant dependence on, 49; of the Ottoman Empire, 167; in *The Pagoda*, 232, 249; railways as, 163–68; and resettlement, 52; in the Russo-Japanese War, 18, 52, 165; as sites of contest, 18, 52, 60, 165–66; and state formation, 60; sublation and dissemination of, 53; and the Suez Canal, 167, 311n19; and the telegraph, 160–68, 173; in war, 163–64

institutions, 253–54. *See also* knowledge; translation

instrumentality, 23

interdependence, denials of, 35, 66. *See also* disavowal

inter-imperial analysis: overview of, 4–5, 24–25; art at center of, 96; authors and, 25–26; and the constitutive past, 251; and dialectical relationality, 6, 37, 42–43; ethics and relationality and, 26; and genre, 27; and Hegelian dialectics, 10; and historical sublations, 18–19; and infrastructure, 55, 60; interdisciplinarity of, 252; inter-imperial positionality and, 25; and literary histories, 26–27; the local in, 37; and negative dialectics, 25–26; and political unconscious, 25; and resistance, 16–17; and revolution, 45. *See also* disavowal; dissent; gender; infrastructure; revolution; temporality

international relations, 8, 48, 251, 260n23, 264n50. *See also* Westphalian narrative of modern state

Ireland: Boers, anti-British support for, 172; civilizational rhetoric in, 178; eastern genealogies and, 120; Easter Rising of 1916, 179; French alliance with, 140; independence struggles of, 43; newspapers in, 132; post/colonial consciousness in, 133; revolutionary history of, 43, 139–41, 146, 152

Irish identities, 120, 298n100

Islamicate states: and Afro-Eurasian systems, 41; bureaucracies of, 57; libraries in, 58; literacy and state-building in, 57–58, 85–86; and *The Nights*, 71; and paper, 57; relations between, 99; religious tolerance and, 274n40; state-merchant relations in, 57; translation projects and, 58, 279n94. *See also* the Abbasid Empire; Umayyad Caliphate

Italy, 170, 181–82, 317n96

I'tisam al-din, Mirza, 110

Jamaica, 135, 233–36

James, C. L. R., 207

Japan: and the Boxer Uprising, 171; China, inter-imperial conflicts with, 18, 52, 165; as empire, 6–7; and Indian anticolonialists, 176; institution and infrastructure building in, 164–65, 170; and Korea, 165, 170, 172, 310n14; literacy and state-building in, 58; and the Russo-Japanese War, 18, 52, 165, 170, 172, 312n24

Jardine, Monica, 202

Jenkinson, Anthony, 103, 106

Jennison, Ruth, 183

Jewsiewicki, Bogumil, 212

Jobst, Kirsten, 113

Johnson, Rebecca Carol, 266n71

Johnson, Samuel, 109

Jones, Claudia, 205

Jones, William, 110

Johnson, James Weldon, 184

Joyce, James, 25, 76, 173, 195, 198–99. See also *Ulysses*

Joyce, Stephen, 19–20

Kaplan, Robert, 264n54

Kashmir, and inter-imperiality, 15–16

Kelley, Robin D.G., 175

Kelly, Louise G., 95

Khalid, Adeeb, 46

khans of Mongolia, 98–99

Kim, Minjeong, 249

Kim Guy-taek, 189

Kincaid, Jamaica, 233

Kingdom of this World, The: overview of, 206

Kingdom of this World, The, aesthetics and inter-imperiality: the bookkeeper as trope in, 211–12; counterpointing aesthetics in, 211–14, 219, 326n49; commentary on imperial aesthetics in, 210–13, 215, 225–26; Gothic literature tropes in, 217; imperial aestheticization of violence in; 209–11, 217, 219; infrastructures and imperial aesthetics of, 215–17; and inter-imperial economies, 197, 202–05, 209; interpretation, intentionally ambiguous of, 220, 222–23, 226; and the marvelous real, 209, 324n38; and *The Pagoda*, 226; and representation of revolution, 208–9; in Rome scenes, 217, 224; Soliman and, 217, 223–24; and Ti Noël as aesthetic focalizer, 197, 210–213, 217; Ti Noël and queer aesthetics in, 214, 223–26

Kingdom of this World, The, gender/sexuality: aestheticized violation of women in, 219; ambiguities regarding, 212–13; and inter-imperial competition, 213, 221–22; and imperial reproduction, 197, 210, 213, 216; and labor, 209, 215–216; and lesbian representation, 224; Maman Loi and rape in, 223; narration of women's point of view in, 220, 223; and queer masculinity, 198, 209, 214, 224–25, 262; rape, 197–98, 218–20, 223; and state formation, 198, 210, 213, 216; and revolution, 221–22, 226; symbolic castration in, 214–215; Ti Noël and masculinist narrative in, 213–14; and violence, 213–14, 217–23. *See also* gender; queer

Kingdom of this World, The, history and revolution: destabilizing representation

Kingdom of this World (continued)
of, 220, 222–23, 226; Haitian Revolution
in, 206–7, 215–16, 218; historical contexts
of, 203–5, 208; imperial subjectivization
and, 213–15, 225; King Christophe and,
211, 215–17; labor and, 209–10, 215–216;
infrastructure, art, and empire in, 215–17;
Macandal and burning at the stake in,
218, 220–21, 223; Maman Loi as revolutionary actor in, 223
Klein, Naomi, 196
knowledge, inter-imperial construction of,
58–59
Ko, Teresa, 120
Kojève, Alexander, 8, 261n24
Korea: *han* philosophy in, 19–20; imperial
conflicts over, 165, 170, 172; inter-imperial
maneuvering and, 189; as shatterzone,
187, 189
Kramer, Paul, 164
Krishnaswamy, Revathi, 22, 35, 266n70

Laachir, Karima, 21
labor: of care, 1–3, 12–13, 15; control of,
12–13; gendered, 2, 12–13, 267n79; and
Hegel's lord and bondsman, 2, 10–11;
histories of, 7; and identity stratification,
13; and interdependency, 11; meanings of,
277n72; migration of, 55; and relocations and resettlement, 51, 52–53, 55; and
slaves, 51; in state-building, 50–51; wars
over, 52–53; women's, 11–13, 263n40
Lamming, George, 184
language: and empires, 4, 13, 44, 64, 189–
190, 252; and inter-imperial maneuvering, 64–66, 285n125; and inter-imperial
politics, 110–11; and memory, 252; and
naming, 252–53; vernacular, 63–64, 104,
283n120. *See also* translation
Lawrence, T. E., 168, 311n20
Ledoux, Ellen Malenas, 132
Lee, Chang-rae, 19
Lenin, Vladimir, 159–60, 314n65
Lennon, Joseph, 120
Leo X, Pope, 66–67
Lewis, Matthew Gregory, 134–35

Lewis, Wyndham, 156, 181
libraries, 58, 111, 114
Light in August, A, 229
Lima, Jorge de, 162, 183
Ling, L. H. M., 8, 260n23
Lipman, Jana K., 234
literary activism, 182–87, 190–91, 314n70,
317n96. *See also* activism; arts and activism; shatterzones
literary history, medieval Mediterranean,
61–66, 283n120, 284n121
literary studies, 21–23, 266n67, 266n71.
See also inter-imperial analysis
literature: and activism, 132; Cuban, 187–88;
and education systems, 132; experimental, 157–58; and inter-imperiality, 4–6, 19,
68; and ideological mediation 102–03,115,
120, 191; nationalist, 181; relationality of,
26, 68–69; and the state, 132; statecraft,
83; temporality of, 23–24. *See also*
activism; arts and activism;
Llull, Ramon, 64, 284n122
the Long Depression, 166, 311n15
Lorca, Federico García, 225
Louis-Philippe, comte de Ségur, 116
Loy, Mina: Feminist Manifesto, 156–57, 182;
mentioned, 250; poetry of, 162–63, 183
Luther, Martin, and inter-imperial maneuvering, 59–60

madrasas, 85–86
Maingot, Anthony, 122
Makdisi, Saree, 118, 297n91
Maldonado-Torres, Nelson, 133
Mallette, Karla, 64–65
manifestos, 156–57, 181–82, 185
Mann, Michael, 40, 42, 55, 276n61, 278n84
Maps, 201
Marinetti, Filippo Tommaso, 156–57,
181–82, 315n75
Marlowe, Christopher, 105–6
Marquis de Sade, 121
Martin, Amy, 132, 304n37
Marx, Karl, 8–9, 11, 143, 157, 261n5
Marzagora, Sara, 21
Matar, Nabil, 281n106

mathematical systems and world dialectics, 58–59

Mathew, Johan, 285n3, 288n25, 289n27

Maturin, Charles, 139, 141, 143, 145, 155, 307n69. See also *Melmoth the Wanderer*

Maxwell, Richard, 266n71

Mayan Empire, 59

mediation, 102–03,115, 120, 191

Mediterranean world, 61–63. *See also* literary history; medieval Mediterranean

Melmoth the Wanderer: overview of, 123

Melmoth the Wanderer, aesthetics and inter-imperiality: and Alonzo Moncada as inter-imperial storyteller, 141–42; conditions of production encoded in, 143, 154; influence on Balzac, 123, 130; influence on Dostoevsky, 123, 130; inter-imperiality represented in, 148, 153–55; language and translation in, 142; listening and witnessing in, 154; Jewish scholar Adonijah and translation of, 153, 309n80; manuscripts in, 142, 147–48, 309n80; Orientalism in, 139, 142, 145–47, 309n81; phenomenology of history in, 154; and rebellion, footnoting of, 152; and *The Nights* and frame structure of, 139–41, 154, 306n60; and "Tale of the Indians," 142; writer figure and negative dialectics of, 154–55

Melmoth the Wanderer, gender and sexuality: brothers and competitive political economy in, 149–151; coercion of mothers and daughters in, 137, 142, 144, 149–50, 153; and Imalee, 142, 144–45, 153, 155, 307n68; queer sexuality in 140, 148–49, 151; and racial lineages, 153

Melmoth the Wanderer, historical and political: betrayal in, 151, 153; and the Catholic Church, critiques of, 149–51; colonial allusions in, 305n45; and complicity represented in Wanderer, 142; and complicity represented in the parricide, 151; and County Wicklow, 146; Cromwell and colonization in, 147–48, 308n75; and empire, critiques of, 142–45, 148, 152–53, 308n77; historical contexts of, 139–41; Islamic and "Moor" in, 148;

Marxist structural critique and, 143; Maturin's self-reflexivity in, 145–46; merchants in, 155, 308n67; moral-sexual and economic-political crises in, 134; post/colonial consciousness in, 147, 150; on poverty and inequality, 143–45; on extractivist colonialism, 145; rebellion in, 146, 151, 152, 154; Spanish and British inter-imperiality in, 139–40, 141–43, 149; on war, 144

Menocal, Maria, 283n120

merchants, 47–50, 57, 87–89, 276n61, 278n87

Merleau-Ponty, Maurice, 4, 14, 261n25

Mesopotamia, 53

Midnight's Children, 200, 321n17

Mignolo, Walter, 304n40

Milam, Jennifer, 112

Milton, John, 60, 103, 107

Moche civilization, 52

Modelski, George, 261n25

modernism, and history, 161; and politics of communist and capitalist,161, 190

modernity, 36–37, 39, 278n82

Mongolia, 49, 98–99

Monk, The 134–35, 305n45

Morley, Daniel, 62

Morrison, Toni, 160, 229

Mudimbe, V. Y., 212

Mufti, Aamir, 96, 110, 113

Mughal Empire: Europe, influence on, 110; expansion of, 99; inter-imperial Eurasian relations and, 98–99; and Persian language, 111; and the Russian Empire, 111, 113; and the Safavid Empire, 99, 111; self-indigenizing discourses and, 97, 113; Orientalism and translation projects and, 111, 113

multiconfessional states, 45

Murk, Nazim al-, 85–86

Musawi, Mushin al-, 72

Naous, Mazen, 74–75, 285n3, 287n14, 289n27

Napoleon, 17, 121–22, 137–38, 306n54

Napoleonic Wars, 130–31, 138, 171

Neorealist political theory, 14, 280n102

Nerchinsk Treaty, 98–99
newspapers, 173–75, 184
Nietzsche, Friedrich, 315n75
Nkrumah, Kwame, 17, 205
No Telephone to Heaven, 227–28, 227–29
Nunes, Zita, 205
Nwankwo, Ifeoma, 132

Ocampo, Victoria, 184
Orientalism: class, race, and disciplinary
   functions and, 118–19; and inter-
   imperiality, 96–98, 100, 107–20; and
   Mughal and Safavid scholars, 111; and *The
   Nights*, 95–98, 114–18; and racism, 119–20;
   Russian, 97, 111–13; and Safavid libraries,
   111–14; structural uses of, 96, 118–19
Orient (magazine), 185
Orr, Bridget, 95, 107, 119, 295n41
Orsini, Francesca, 21
Ortega y Gasset, José, 184
Orwell, George, 184
Ottoman Empire: and the Arab Revolt,
   168; and the Boxer Uprising, 176; and
   capitalism, 60, 281n106; dissent in, 43,
   168; and French Empire, 114, 167; Haitian
   connections to, 322n29; influence on
   early European state formation, 59–60;
   and inter-imperial Eurasian relations,
   98; petitioning laws in, 168; and the
   Protestant Revolution, 60, 281n106;
   railway infrastructure in, 166–68; and the
   Safavid Empire, 99; Serbian inter-imperial
   maneuvering and, 43, 273n35; women in,
   dissenting in, 168; and World War I, 168

Pagoda, The, overview: 231–33
Pagoda, The, aesthetics and inter-
   imperiality: anaphoric syntax and
   transformation in, 246–48; documents
   in, 248; gender and language in, 232–33;
   male pronoun use in, 232–33; neocolonial allegories and, 240–41; and *The
   Nights*, 250; pagoda project and, 239, 249;
   painting of, 248–49; repetition and temporal looping in, 231–33, 243–44, 246–49

Pagoda, The, gender and sexuality: betrayal
   and disavowal and, 233, 239–40, 243;
   gender and language and, 232–33;
   daughter-selling in, 232, 237–38, 245;
   inter-imperial position of women in,
   236–37, 248; inter-imperial position
   of men in, 238–40, 242; rape in, 197,
   200–201, 232, 244–45; sexuality in, 197,
   200–1, 231–32, 244; and women in, 236,
   238–42, 244–45, 247–49
Pagoda, The, historical and political:
   agency and ethics in, 239, 249; betrayal
   in, 238–40; and the coolie trade, 238–40;
   debt in, 232–33, 236–38, 240–41; disavowal
   and, 233, 239–40, 243; dissent in, 245–46;
   infrastructure in, 232, 249; inter-island
   consciousness and, 245; Jamaican historical contexts in, 231–32, 233–36, 240,
   245; and *The Kingdom of This World*, 226;
   workers and, 216, 242, 246–27; rebellion
   in, 241; resistance fighter bribery and,
   241–42; inter-imperial economies in, 197,
   231–236; and world history, 236, 242–43
Palestine, creation of, 180
Pankhurst, Sylvia, 184
paper, 56–57, 59
Paradise Lost, 107, 294n38
Park Kyong-ni, 20
Passage to Dusk, 228
Perdue, Peter, 98–99
periodization, 36, 41, 253
Perry, Matthew C., 164
Persian language, 64–65, 110–11. *See also*
   Arabic language
Persian Sassanid Empire, 53, 58, 71–73
Peter the Great, 111–12
Phelps, Elizabeth Stuart, 173
Phillips, Caryl, 228
Pierce, Leslie, 47
Pieterse, Jan P. N. 273n34, 280n102
Podany, Amanda, 77
poetry: on the Boer Wars, 177; "coolie"
   protest, 161; ekphrastic, 68–69; and
   inter-state rivalry, 108; of Jorge de Lima,
   162; lyric, 63–64, 283n120; of Mina Loy,

162–63, 183; troubadour, 63. *See also* vernacular

political unconscious, inter-imperial, 25

polities as co-constituted, 2

Pomeranz, Kenneth, 54, 320n4

Portugal, 54, 108

post/colonial consciousness: overview of, 122; and the age of revolution, 122; and coloniality's afterlives, 132–33; emergence of, 173; in Gothic literature, 122, 133–34, 138; in Ireland, 133; literature channeling, 132; and the Napoleonic Wars, 130

postcolonial and decolonial studies, 5

Pound, Ezra, 63, 181

Powell, Patricia, 330n23. See also *The Pagoda*

Pratt, Mary Louise, 108

Preacher's Travels, The, 103–5

print, 59–60, 157–59, 280n101

Protestant Revolution, 59–60

Pushkin, Alexander, 115

Qin, Yaqing, 48, 260n23

Queer: alliance,190; futurity, 225; longing, 209, 223–26, sexuality, narration of, 32, 124, 135,149–51; temporality, 230–31; theorization of, 230–31; visibility, 225

racism, 105, 119–20, 176–77, 189, 288n26, 298n100, 318n105

radical distrust, 179

radical relationality *versus* radical freedom, 3

rape: and "coolie" trade, 197; wartime estimates of, 129; during the French Revolution, 129; in Gothic literature, 129, 134–35; in *The Kingdom of this World*, 197–98, 218–20, 223; in literature, importance of, 218; in *The Pagoda*, 197, 200–1, 232, 244–45; structural effects of, 129; and world dialectics, 218

Rashid, Harun al-, 72, 74, 77–78, 89, 273n38, 287n8, 288n23

rebellion: the Boxer Uprising, 170–72, 174, 176, 236; and dialectics of state forma-tion, 128; fear of, 128; in India, 125; in *Melmoth the Wanderer*, 151–52, 154; in *The Pagoda*, 241; in Qing China, 127–28; in the Russian Empire, 125; in South America, 126–27; and Túpac Amaru II, 126–27

relational conflict and resource re-distribution, 14

relationality, 2–4, 12, 14, 260n23. *See also* dialectical theory

Renda, Mary, 202

resettlement of laborers, 52–53, 55

resistance, 16–17, 166, 205, 228–29. *See also* dissent; rebellion; revolutions

revolutions: Abbasid 44–45, 273n38; Chinese Communist, 179; Cuban, 204; dialectical effects of, 45; French, 122, 128–29; and historical legacies, 44; and infrastructure, 60; in Ireland, 139–41; in Russia, 46; Russian, 159–60, 172. *See also* the age of revolution

River Between, The, 201, 254

Robert of Ketton, 62

Robinson, Cynthia, 63–64, 284n121

Rodney, Walter, 205

Romantic-era English literature: influence of Arabic-language genres on, 116–17

Rooney, Caroline, 179

Roy, Arundhati, 76, 195, 228

Rozendal, Michael, 185

Rushdie, Salman, 76, 200

Russian Empire: and American revolution-aries, 126; and the Boxer Uprising, 171; and the British Empire, 96–97, 100–103, 106–7; and Catherine the Great, 112–13, 116, 125; and China, 98–99; conquered peoples in, 46, 274n41; and Crimean colonization, 112; and cultural invasion, 111–13; and Ethiopia, 182; and Eurasian inter-imperiality, 98–99, 103, 111; expan-sion of, 96–98; and Japan, 18, 52, 165, 170, 172, 312n24; and Mongolia, 98; and the Mughal Empire, 111, 113; *The Nights* in, 115; Orientalist projects of, 97, 111–13; and peasant uprisings, 125; peripheral peoples in, 46; and Peter the

Russian Empire (continued)
Great, 111–12; Pugachev's Rebellion and, 125; and Alexander Pushkin, 115; and the Safavid Empire, 97, 99, 111; and the Second Boer War, 171–72; tax unrest in, 125; and Tsarskoye Selo, 112; wars fought by, nineteenth century, 169, 171–72; and western Europe, 98; World War I and, 178, 180

Russian futurism, 186

Russian Revolution, 159–60, 172

Russo-Japanese War, 18, 52, 165, 170, 172, 312n24

Safavid Empire, 97–100, 111

Said, Edward, 37, 96, 109–10, 115, 295n50

Scarborough, Vernon, 55

Schimmelpenninck van der Oye, David, 111–13

Schwab, Raymond, 109–10, 295n50

Scott, James, 273n34

Seigneurie, Ken, 228

Serbian Revolution, 127–28, 302n20

sexuality: and state formation, 12–14, 47, 264n45. *See also* gender; queer; and literary texts: *Melmoth the Wanderer; The Kingdom of this World; The Pagoda; The Thousand and One Nights*

shadow empires, 42

Shakespeare, William, 102, 105

Sharma, Sunil, 111

shatterzones: and aesthetic experiments, 187–88; and Angel Island, 188–89, 318n102; and the Caribbean, 197; and Cuba, 187–88; examples of, 15–16, 187; global connections to, 189; as inter-imperial zones, 15–16; legal histories of, 16; linguistic histories of, 16

She, 138, 306n58

Shelley, Percy Byshe, 129

Shields, Tanya, 207, 221–22, 327n56

Shih, Shu-mei, 21

Sicily, and inter-imperiality, 64–66

Simpson, Audra, 3, 8, 257n7

Sismondi, John, 117

slave memoirs, 139

Smith, James, 185

Smith, Michael, 39

sonnets and Eurocentrism, 66, 285n126

South African wars, 171–72, 174–78

South America: the Incas and, 50–52, 277n72; Orientalizing discourses and, 119; Rebellion of Túpac Amaru II in, 126–27; tax unrest in, 125–26; uprisings in, 126; wars and, nineteenth century, 169–70

Southey, Robert, 116–17

sovereignty, 2–3, 88, 154, 257n8

Spain and the Spanish Empire: and Al-Andalus, 58, 61–64, 283n120; and American revolutionaries, 126; Arabic book confiscation and, 58; the Bourbon government and, 125–26; and imperial performance, 108, 295n45; and Mesoamerican empires, 41; and South American resources, 54; and the Spanish-American War, 174; tax rebellion and, 125–26

state building, 48–58. *See also* dialectics; inter-imperiality

state building, Westphalian account of, 59–60, 280n102

state-merchant relations, 47–50, 57, 276n61, 278n87

states and decolonial leveraging, 253

Stephens, Michelle, 177, 180

strategic mimicry, 177

sublation, 18–19, 53, 55, 108–9

Suez Canal, 167, 311n19

Suleri, Sara, 26

Sydney, Philip, 103

systemization, processes of, 54

Tagore, Rabindranath, 182, 184, 315n77

Tavakoli-Targhi, Mohamad, 110

technology: agricultural, 53; dialectical appropriation and circulation of, 52–55,165; and inequality, 55, 157; generation and extension of, 163–64; and labor resettlement, 52–53; and literary activism, 182–83; as site of contestation, 18, 165, 168; and Japan, 164–165; print, 280n101; record-keeping, 56; and revolution, 60; and state formation, 60; sublations of, 53; water management, 53–54. *See also* infrastructure

Tempest, The, 105, 293n31

temporality, day in the life novels, 201; and ethical agency, 230–31, 239, 249; and *The God of Small Things,* 200, 230; looping narratives and, 201; and *Maps,* 201; and *Midnight's Children,* 200, 321n17; and *The River Between,* 201, 254; and *Two Thousand Seasons,* 200–1; and *Ulysses,* 198–99; and *Untouchable,* 199–200, 321n13; women's interventions in, 200–201, 230, 321n17. See also *The Kingdom of This World; The Pagoda; The Thousand and One Nights*

temporality, queer, 196

temporal looping in twentieth-century fiction, 227–30; *Beloved,* 229; *A Distant Shore,* 228–29; *The God of Small Things,* 228–30; *Light in August,* 229; *No Telephone to Heaven,* 227–29; *Passage to Dusk,* 228. See also *The Pagoda,* repetition and temporal looping

Thailand, 53, 55

Thousand and One Nights, The: overview of, 71; allusions to, 76, 139, 142, 146–47, 309n81

Thousand and One Nights, The, aesthetics and inter-imperiality: art and political economy and, 69, 83–86; authorship of, 75; "The Barber's Tale" and temporality and, 91; decolonial phenomenology in, 154; and Dinarzad, 69, 83–84, 89; emperors' demand for tales in, 91–92, 289n45; in Europe, 97–98, 114–18; fantastic and realist elements of, 69–70; figure of the artist and Hunchback tale in, 90–92; Galland's translation of, 70, 97, 115, 286nn5–6; inter-imperial temporality and anachronism in, 71–72, 75, 89, 91–92; inter-imperiality of frame story of, 69–74, 287n9; negative dialectics of, 90–92; Persian-Sassanid politics and, 73–

75; textual history of, 70, 286n5, 286n6, 287n9; translation, alliance, and betrayal in "The Tale of the Ox and Donkey" and, 87–88; vizier and tales of state in, 83–84, 86–89

Thousand and One Nights, The, gender/sexuality: brothers and state control, 70–71, 75–83; Dinarzad, witnessing, and alternative relationality in, 69, 83–84, 89; feminist readings of, 69, 75–76; and gendered Aristotelian model of household and state, 83–84, 87–89; gendered betrayal in, 70, 75–82; and labor and subterfuge, 78–80, 87–89; and *The Pagoda,* 250; racialized sexual relations in, 79–80; sexual crisis and reproduction of the state in, 70–71, 75–76; 78–80, 86–89

Thousand and One Nights, The, history and political economy: Aristotelian model of state, 83–84, 87–89; art and political economy, 83–86, 90–92; betrayal and brothers in, 70–71, 75, 78–80; merchants in, 87–89; and Persian-Sassanid Empire, 73–75; history, phenomenology of, 154; inter-imperiality in, 26, 72–77, 82, 91–92; laborers in, 70, 79, 87–88; negative dialectics of, 90–92; Qur'an allusions, 81–82; racialized sexual relations, 79–80; Harun al-Rashid, 89; translation and state control of labor, 86–89; viziers and Islamicate political economy, 83–89

Thiong'o, Ngũgĩ wa, 24, 201, 254

tibishi writing, 188, 318n102

time, homogenization of, 158, 160–61, 310n4

Tone, Wolfe, 140

Toussaint Louverture, François-Dominique, 16, 131, 140, 207

trade, 2, 47–48, 51

Tran, Ben, 189–91, 319n109

translatio imperii, 35, 65, 102, 107–8, 139

translation in literature, 87–89, 142

translation projects: Abbasid, 58, 279n94; and dissent, 59–60; impact of, 60–61; Islamicate state, 58, 279n94; Mughal Empire, 113; and state formation, 66–67, 164 translations: and English authors, 103, 293n23; medieval, from Arabic, 61–62, 64; of *The Nights*, 70, 97, 115, 286nn5–6

translatio studii, 62, 65, 107–8

transnational studies, 251–52

transperipheral studies, 251–52

trauma, diasporic, 243

Trotsky, Leon, 143, 145

Trumpener, Katie, 266n71

Túpac Amaru II (José Gabriel Condorcanqui), 126–27

Tushratta, king of Syria, 77

Twain, Mark, 173, 312n33

Two Thousand Seasons, 200–201

Ulysses, 25, 76, 173, 195, 198–99

Umayyad Caliphate: in Al-Andalus, 44–45; Arabization programs, 110; and hydraulic engineering, 53; influence on European scholasticism and state formation of, 45, 61–62; and the Persian Sassanid empire, 72–73; revolutionary overthrow of, 44–45, 50, 273n38

Umberto I, 95

uneven and combined development, 143, 233, 281n106

United States: and the Caribbean, 203–4, 323n30; and Cuba, 203–4, 234, 322n27; and Haiti, 204–5; and Jamaica, 234–35; and Manifest Destiny, 169, 294n32; and Orientalizing discourses, 119; and the Revolutionary War, 126, 140; wars fought by, nineteenth century, 169

Unruh, Vicky, 187–88

Untouchable, 199–200, 321n13

Valdés Sánchez, Servando, 204, 322n27

van Wyk, Smith Malvern, 177

vernacular language and states, 63–64, 104, 283n120

Vietnam, 189–91, 319n109

Viswanathan, Gauri, 177

viziers, 84–86

vorticists, 181

Wallerstein, Immanuel, 20, 39

Walpole, Horace, 135–38, 305n48

wars, nineteenth century: and the Boer Wars, 171–72, 174–78; and the Boxer Uprising, 170–72, 174, 176, 236; interimperial character of, 170; media coverage of, 173–74; pervasiveness of, 169–70; Russo-Japanese, 18, 52, 165, 170, 172, 312n24. *See also* age of revolution

water management technologies, 53–54

Watson, Andrew, 53

Watson, William, 182

Wazzan, al-Hasan al- (Leo Africanus), 66–67

Wells, Ida B., 175

western progress narratives, 158

Westphalian narrative of modern state, 59–60, 280n102, 281n106

Wight, Martin, 41–42, 272n27

Wilks, Jennifer, 184

women: and dialectics, 2–3, 45; and Hegel's lord-and-bondsman, 2, 10–12; historical blame of, 19, 70; impoverishment of, 157; in the Mongol dynasty, 49; and *The Odyssey*, 75; in the Ottoman Empire, 168; and the *Panchatantra*, 75, 288n15; in vizier families, 86. *See also* disavowal; gender; inter-imperial analysis; labor; sexuality; and individual literary texts: *The Kingdom of this World*; *Melmoth the Wanderer*; *The Pagoda*; *The Thousand and One Nights*

Wook Huh, Jang, 189

Woolf, Virginia, 160–61, 174, 310n4

Wordsworth, William, 116–17, 128

world economy studies, 55–56

world literature, 21–22, 266n67

world-systems, 20, 37, 39–41

world-systems, literary studies, 20–21, 23, 266n67

World War I, 178–80, 314n65

Yeats, W. B., 174

Yücesoy, Hayrettin, 64–65, 110–11, 113